Luminos is the Open Access monograph publishing program from UC Press. Luminos provides a framework for preserving and reinvigorating monograph publishing for the future and increases the reach and visibility of important scholarly work. Titles published in the UC Press Luminos model are published with the same high standards for selection, peer review, production, and marketing as those in our traditional program. www.luminosoa.org

The Importance of Being Gorgeous

TRANSFORMATION OF THE CLASSICAL HERITAGE
Peter Brown, General Editor

The Importance of Being Gorgeous

Gender and Christian Imperial Rule in Late Antiquity

Susanna Elm

UNIVERSITY OF CALIFORNIA PRESS

University of California Press
Oakland, California

Suggested citation: Elm, S. *The Importance of Being Gorgeous: Gender and Christian Imperial Rule in Late Antiquity*. Oakland: University of California Press, 2026. DOI: https://doi.org/10.1525/luminos.251

Library of Congress Cataloging-in-Publication Data

Names: Elm, Susanna, author.
Title: The importance of being gorgeous : gender and Christian imperial rule in late antiquity / Susanna Elm.
Other titles: Transformation of the classical heritage ; 66.
Description: Oakland, California : University of California Press, [2026] | Series: Transformation of the classical heritage ; LXVI | Includes bibliographical references and index.
Identifiers: LCCN 2025011016 (print) | LCCN 2025011017 (ebook) | ISBN 9780520425675 (cloth) | ISBN 9780520413344 (paperback) | ISBN 9780520413351 (ebook)
Subjects: LCSH: Masculinity—Religious aspects—Christianity—History—To 1500. | Emperors—Rome—Religious aspects—Christianity. | Masculinity—Political aspects. | Rome—History—Theodosians, 379–455.
Classification: LCC BV4597.565 .E555 2026 (print) | LCC BV4597.565 (ebook)

LC record available at https://lccn.loc.gov/2025011016
LC ebook record available at https://lccn.loc.gov/2025011017

GPSR Authorized Representative: Easy Access System Europe, Mustamäe tee 50, 10621 Tallinn, Estonia, gpsr.requests@easproject.com

34 33 32 31 30 29 28 27 26 25
10 9 8 7 6 5 4 3 2 1

Clara Cecilia Elm Nettesheim (November 17, 2005–)

In memoriam *Kaspar Elm (September 23, 1929, Xanten–February 5, 2019, Berlin)*

CONTENTS

I wrote the first draft of this book in Tübingen between the summers of 2020 and 2021 during a sabbatical leave made possible by generous grants from the American Council of Learned Societies and the Loeb Classical Library Foundation. It was not the book I had planned to write, nor were the circumstances anything like what I had anticipated when applying: I wanted to write about Augustine and enslavement, in Berkeley so that our daughter would not be faced with relocations and disruptions during her last years at Berkeley High School. Over the course of the summer of 2020 it became evident that we would not be returning to California for a while. And as I was looking over essays about new Romans and late antique male fashion I wanted to publish as a collection (before turning to Augustine) it occurred to me that I had enough for a short book about the consul and eunuch Eutropius. As so often, the sources instead had a far more interesting story to tell: that of *the importance of being gorgeous*.

Not that the story of Eutropius is not already very interesting, especially for persons observing the global political landscape of the early twenty-first century with its recurrent competitions between contrasting images of masculinity and the fashion the protagonists use to represent themselves. My first close encounter with the poet Claudian's portrayal of Eutropius came during the fall of 2016, when I taught the text in a graduate seminar because I was already interested in the many ways late antique authors spoke about sumptuous male dress, even when one does not expect them to do so, and because I thought the moment called for it (my students agreed). Since then, I have had occasion to present my evolving ideas about Eutropius, what late antique bishops wore to synods, how to dress Moses, and what to make of Gothic pelts, jewel-encrusted riding boots, and imperial manliness to a variety of audiences. I am immensely grateful to my host in the Department of Theology as 2017 Hedi-Fritz-Niggli Diversity Professor at the University of Zürich, Silke-Petra Bergjan, as well as Jörg Frey, Beat Näf, Christoph Riedweg, and Andreas Victor Walser. I owe a very special debt of gratitude to Samuel, who knows more about the *Life of Heliogabalus* than anyone. Volker Henning Drecoll and Irmgard Männlein invited me to participate as guest researcher in their Sonderforschungsbereich "Bedrohte Ordnung" in the summer of 2018—a wonderful opportunity and another milestone in a friendship and collaboration that began many years earlier. I also owe a debt of gratitude to Sebastian Schmidt-Hofner, and to Martin Kovacs who saved me from many (but certainly not all) egregious mistakes. Johannes Brachtendorf's continuing hospitality in the Tübinger Augustinus-Zentrum has been an incredible gift. Wolfgang Graf Vitzthum gave me Philip von Rummel's *Habitus Barbarus* as a present, and I cannot thank both enough! Barbara Vinken's *Angezogen* has, of course, been influential, but the references to that work in what follows do not do justice to our decades of conversations; she knows how much I owe her and her appreciation of beauty in all its forms.

I am incredibly grateful to the external reviewers for UC Press, Caroline Humfress, Christopher Kelly, and Mark Masterson. Their comments and suggestions were absolutely fantastic, and I am deeply moved by their collegiality and the time and effort they invested. The same is true for the help and support I received from friends and colleagues who read earlier versions of the manuscript: Diliana Angelova, whose counsel in all things visual was essential, as well as Mary Beard, C. Michael Chin, Carla Hesse, Thomas Laqueur, Rebecca Lyman, Michael Maas, Duncan MacRae, Ellen Muehlberger, Kristina Sessa, Ethan Shagan, Jonathan Sheehan, and Edward Watts. I am truly grateful to Emily Albu, Beth Digeser, Hal Drake, Michele Salzman, and Ed Watts, my California late antiquity gang, and to Brian Delay, Erich Gruen, Emily Mackil, Maureen Miller, and Carlos Noreña. Audiences at the University of Pennsylvania's Hyde Lecture and at St. Andrews, Duke, Liverpool, London, Minneapolis, Naples, Oxford, Rome, Santa Barbara, and Berkeley, especially at the Feldman Lecture, gave much valuable feedback.

It is a great privilege to be able to thank so many friends and family who have inspired and sustained me, in addition to those I already mentioned: Jamie Bigelow, Kathy Brady, Andrew Bridges, Kate Lyman Bridges, Thomas Lyman Bridges, Clara's friends, Catherine Conybeare, Giuseppe D'Andrea, Cynthia De Nardi, Dorothee Elm von der Osten, Eva Elm, Veit Elm, Ken Haas, Brian Haber, Todd Kuebler, Anja Lilie, Catherine Lorenz, Neil McLynn, the Mermaids, Phoebe Moser, Christoph Nettesheim, Peter Nettesheim, Ruth Nettesheim, Karen Newton, Sylvia Ronchey, Claudia Tavolieri, Cynthia Verges, Mark Vessey, Hennning von der Osten, Todd Wexman, and Felicitas Winzek. I very much miss Tom Brady, Liz Clark, Bobb Gregg, Robert Knapp, Hans Moser, and Ross Thomas.

This book is an homage to my Doktorvater, John Matthews. I hope that his guiding spirit will be visible throughout. I am very grateful that Peter Brown accepted it for his series Transformations of the Classical Heritage at the University of California Press, where I thank Eric Schmidt for this book, my previous book, and for our many years of collaboration in between. I also thank Jyoti Arvey for their fantastic work. Juliana Froggatt brought her magic to my English and transformed the book. Catherine Osborne's copyediting was essential, and I am truly grateful to Jeff Anderson and Chloe Wong. Joshua Benjamins, Lily Callendar, Samuel Stubblefield, and in particular Flavio Santini (who also compiled the index) were of immense help throughout: they made all the difference.

Martin Nettesheim fills my life with light. I dedicate this book to our greatest joy, our daughter Clara Cecilia Elm Nettesheim. I also dedicate it to the memory of my father, Kaspar Elm, who told me once how beauty saved his life, and who always encouraged me to look and try to understand, the beautiful as well as the ugly.

ABBREVIATIONS

CCSG	*Corpus Christianorum Series Graecae.* Turnhout, 1977–.
CCSL	*Corpus Christianorum Series Latina.* Turnhout, 1953–.
CIL	*Corpus Inscriptionum Latinarum.* Berlin, 1863–.
CSEL	*Corpus Scriptorum Ecclesiasticorum Latinorum.* Vienna, 1866–.
FC	*Fontes Christiani.* Turnhout, 2002–.
GCS	*Die griechischen christlichen Schriftsteller der ersten Jahrhunderte.* Leipzig and Berlin, 1897–.
ICUR	*Inscriptiones Christianae Urbis Romae septimo saeculo antiquiores.* Ed. G. B. de Rossi. Rome, 1861.
I Ephesos	*Die Inschriften von Ephesos.* 8 vols. Ed. H. Wankel. Bonn, 1979–84.
IG	*Inscriptiones Graecae.* Berlin, 1860–.
ILS	*Inscriptiones Latinae selectae.* Ed. H. Dessau. Berlin, 1892–1916.
LCL	*Loeb Classical Library.* London—Cambridge, MA, 1912–.
OLD	*Oxford Latin Dictionary.* Ed. P. G. W. Glare. Oxford, 2012.
PG	*Patrologiae cursus completus, Series Graeca.* Ed. J. P. Migne et al. Paris, 1857–66.
PGL	*A Patristic Greek Lexicon.* Ed. G. W. H. Lampe. Oxford, 1961.
PL	*Patrologiae cursus completus, Series Latina.* Ed. J. P. Migne et al. Paris, 1857–66.
PLRE	*The Prosopography of the Later Roman Empire.* 3 vols. Ed. A. H. M. Jones, J. R. Martindale, and J. Morris. Cambridge, 1971–92.
RIC	*The Roman Imperial Coinage.* London, 1923–.
SC	*Sources chrétiennes.* Paris, 1941–.
TLG	*Thesaurus lingua Graeca.* Irvine, CA, 1972–.

Introduction

I gave him military toys: a tank, tin soldiers, a sniper rifle. . . . He was a boy, he needed to become a warrior. . . . I remember how surprised I was when one of the teachers at school told me that in Sweden I think it was, they'd outlawed war-related toys. How are you supposed to raise a man? A defender?[1]

When many bishops, from different regions of the earth, had assembled around the emperor Maximus, a man of fierce character, further elated by victory in the civil wars, and a mood of shameful adulation toward the ruler on everyone's part became notable, and the episcopal dignity with degenerate inconsistency had submitted to the king's patronage, in Martin alone apostolic authority continued.[2]

I sing of arms and men. . . .
   Remember, Roman, your own arts, to rule the peoples with law, impose your customs on peace, grant the conquered clemency, and crush the proud in war.[3]

I have loved a man [dilexi]. *. . . Yes, I have loved, I admit it, and for that reason my grief has pained me to the core of my being.*[4]

1. Alexievich, *Secondhand Time*, 144. I have been deeply influenced by Alexievich's assembling of individual voices into a powerful choir.

2. Sulp., *Vit. Mart.* 20.1.425–430 ("Cum ad imperatorem Maximum, ferocis ingenii virum et bellorum civilium victoria elatum, plures ei diversis orbis partibus episcopi convenissent et foeda circa principem omnium adulatio notaretur seque degenere inconstantia regiae clientelae sacerdotalis dignitas subdidisset, in solo Martino apostolica auctoritas permanebat"). See also Burton, *Sulpicius*, 116–17. In what follows, I use Latin forms of proper names. All translations in the book modify those listed in the bibliography or are my own.

3. Virg., *Aen.* 1.1 ("Arma virumque cano"), 6.851–853 ("Tu regere imperio populos, Romane, memento; / hae tibi erunt artes: pacisque imponere morem / parcere subiectis, et debellare superbos"). See also Bartsch, *Aeneid*, 3, 148.

4. Ambr., *De ob. Theod.* 34, 37.

The mosaics decorating the Rotunda in Thessalonica, now the Church of Saint George, are among the most splendid to have survived from the later Roman and early Byzantine period.[5] Originally erected as part of the palace complex of the emperor Galerius, who ruled between 293 and 311 and made Thessalonica his residence, the Rotunda was transformed into a church at the end of the fourth or in the early fifth century, when it also received its magnificent mosaics. At its center rises a dome nearly twenty-eight meters high, which is covered in gold and silver, as are the vaults and window openings below. At the dome's apex, one can faintly detect a majestic figure: Christ in midstride on a silver shield.[6] For the initiated—including the late Roman viewers who saw the mosaics in full splendor, undiminished by time—the image recalls the "shield of virtue," or *clipeus virtutis*, that Augustus received in 27 BCE from the Roman Senate and people, which in turn evoked the shields of Achilles and Aeneas as described by Homer and Virgil respectively.[7] The one at the Rotunda's apex is held aloft by four enormous angels, whose wings span nearly five meters. In the east, they are accompanied by a phoenix, and in the north, rays of light forming a cross remain barely visible.[8] Below these four (arch)angels one can make out the sandaled feet and the edges of the robes of twenty-eight figures (probably also angels) in motion. The zone beneath them is dominated by twenty monumental front-facing male figures, each about 2.5 meters high; one of them, a soldier and martyr called Onesiphorus, has golden locks in the style of Alexander the Great.[9] Fifteen are preserved nearly intact, positioned in front of elaborate jewel-encrusted gold-on-gold architectural elements adorned with peacocks, wreaths, and lamps, glittering as they reflect the light.

According to the inscriptions accompanying them, these extant figures represent seven martyred soldiers, two bishops, two physicians, a priest, a saint, a flute player, and a servant. The civilians are beautifully clad in silvery white or purple paenula cloaks. The soldiers are particularly magnificent. Dressed in shimmering, colorful tunics and white or purple chlamyses, or mantles, that are adorned with

---

5. Torp, *Rotonde palatine*, 1:13–34 (relevance and preservation of the mosaics); Kiilerich and Torp, *Rotunda in Thessaloniki*, 6 (restoration by 2015 after the 1978 earthquake), 46–52 (medallion with supporting angels), 53 (mosaics originally covered 900 square meters); Bakirtzis and Kourkoutidou-Nikolaidu, *Mosaics of Thessaloniki*, 48–127.

6. Torp, "*Christus Verus Sol*," 179 (current state of the Christ figure and the shield, preserved in preliminary sketches on the cupola's brickwork). See also Torp, "Chronology," 41–42.

7. *RGDA* 34.2 (Senate and people honor Augustus's *virtus*, *clementia*, *iustitia*, and *pietas* with a golden shield); Hom., *Il.* 18.478–480; Virg., *Aen.* 8.626–728. A 26 BCE copy of the *clipeus/clupeus* is in Arles (Musee de l'Arles antique, inv. 51–195): see Feldherr, "Viewing Myth," 281–318; S. J. Harrison, "Survival and Supremacy," 70–76; Welch, "Shields of Virtue(s)," 282–304 (287–92 for other presentations).

8. Torp, "*Christus Verus Sol*," 179–87; Torp, *Rotonde palantine*, 1:353–83; Nasrallah, "Empire," 484–86.

9. Kiilerich, "Color, Light," 54; Kiilerich and Torp, *Rotunda in Thessaloniki*, 36. Nasrallah, "Empire," 488, wonders "why only men," given that Thessalonica had several early fourth-century female martyrs.

FIGURE 1. Overview of the Rotunda, 4/5th c. CE, Thessalonica. (After Hjalmar Torp.) Courtesy of Bente Knold Kiilerich.

decorative medallions (*segmenta*) and gathered by elaborate fibulae, they are spectacular examples of the military look.[10] Each soldier is rendered as a unique person, but they are all sparkling and youthful, with full hair and smooth, rosy faces; the youngest, Priscus, is hardly more than an adolescent.[11] In short, they are very much worth looking at.[12]

After Galerius, the emperor Theodosius I also resided in Thessalonica, first between 378 and 380 and then briefly together with Valentinian II in the late 380s.[13] The original Rotunda, linked by a colonnaded stoa to Galerius's triumphal arch, remained incomplete when Galerius died in 311. It was enlarged and decorated with light-reflecting marble sheets and the ornate, costly mosaics when it was converted into the church.[14] When this conversion occurred and who sponsored the mosaics

10. Von Rummel, *Habitus barbarus*, 90–92 (paenula), 210–31 (chlamys as military look).

11. Priscus, panel 6 (north): see Kiilerich, "Picturing Ideal Beauty," 324, fig. 4; Torp, *Rotonde palatine*, 1:204–5; see also chapter 7, fig. 19.

12. Kiilerich, "Picturing Ideal Beauty," 322–28, 335–36; Kiilerich, "Optical Colour Blending," 165–73; Torp, *Christus Verus Sol*," 178.

13. Nasrallah, "Empire," 472–84; Mentzos, "Reflections," 76.

14. Torp, *Rotonde palatine*, 1:35–68. For the integration into Galerius's ensemble see also L'Orange, *Roman Empire*, 177–78 and plates 89–94.

and their iconographic program remain fiercely debated. I am sympathetic to those who argue for Theodosius I as the impetus (though my argument here does not depend on that dating).[15] Scholars are unanimous in highlighting the imperial character of this church, seen in its expensive decoration, massive proportions, technically demanding and highly sophisticated mosaics, and a sumptuous color scheme of rainbow, silver, and gold, with a preponderance of purple and other imperial hues.[16] That theme culminates in the figure of Christ at the summit of the golden dome. This was Christ triumphant. Though only partially preserved, the Christus Imperator or Christus Victor, surrounded, supported, and enhanced by his celestial court, crowns "a rhetoric of elite male power . . . a kind of peaceful force and authority. . . . These men are depicted as a Christian imperial elite [and] a new senatorial class."[17]

The Rotunda at Thessalonica is a spectacular example of the Theodosian emperors' representational program expressed in monumental buildings. Scholars differ in their interpretation of specific aspects of its iconography, debating, for example, whether the mosaics are meant to evoke the heavenly realm of the apocalypse or a second coming of Christ, visualized as the imperial court, or whether the soldiers were donors rather than martyrs, but no one doubts the majestic impact of the integrated whole.[18] Each tier presents a proliferation of youthful, sparkling exemplars of male beauty to form a light-filled, harmonious, united ensemble.[19] Every figure, each in its own capacity, contributes to the glory of the supreme divine being; each reflects and augments the majesty of the "present God" at the Rotunda's apex.[20] The architectural structure and the sumptuous mosaics together point to the

15. The "Scandinavian school," represented by Torp and Kiilerich, dates the start of the conversion to Theodosius's residence between 379 and 380 and holds that it was later completed under his patronage; see Torp, "Chronology," 32–49; Kiilerich, "Picturing Ideal Beauty," 321–22; Theocharidou, "Rotunda," 57–76. Nasrallah, "Empire," 474, places the mosaics' installation in the late fourth or early fifth century; Mentzos, "Reflections," 59–74, attributes it to Galla Placidia, c. 425; Brenk, "Mosaics of Thessaloniki," 21–31, leans toward the late fifth or early sixth century; Cormack, "Exploring Thessaloniki," 321–23, has a mid-fifth-century date. Bakirtzis and Mastora, "Mosaics," 33–45, believe the church to be a Constantinian mausoleum; see also Mastora, "Virtual Lighting," 217. The majority date the mosaics to between the late fourth and the mid-fifth century.

16. Iliadis, "Natural Lighting," 13–24 (choice of colors, their significance, lighting effects); Kiilerich, "Optical Colour Blending," 163–92.

17. Nasrallah, "Empire," 490. See also Mentzos, "Reflections," 73–79.

18. See, e.g., Nasrallah, "Empire," 475–83 (imperial structures from Diocletian to Galerius), 489 (donors versus soldier martyrs), 491 (representation of Christian wealth and power), 493–504 (theological interpretations with reference to Revelation or to a second coming [*parousia*]); James, *Mosaics in the Medieval World*, 174–80 (summary of the interpretations).

19. Onesiphorus, panel 2 (south): see, e.g., Kiilerich, "Color, Light," 54, fig. 22; Torp, *Rotonde palatine*, 1:201–2.

20. Veg., *Mil.* 2.5. Vegetius's *Epitoma* was most likely dedicated to Theodosius I: see Milner, *Vegetius*, xxxvii–xliii.

FIGURE 2. Onesiphorus, 4/5th c. CE, mosaic, panel 2 (S), Rotunda, Thessalonica. (Hjalmar Torp.) Courtesy of Bente Knold Kiilerich.

summit and thereby refract the unifying power of the divine being at its center, who embodies and represents on earth the heavenly realm without end.[21]

No one I am aware of suggests that the iconography of the Rotunda depicts Christ at the apex as out of touch, enclosed in solitary splendor. Nor do scholars claim that being so high up, so remote, lessens (infantilizes even) the supreme divine being's power, making it largely ceremonial, while strong men and warlords like the archangels supporting the shield actually govern the heavenly (and terrestrial) realm. No one questions the power of this divine being, because, of course, the ensemble praises the omnipotent majesty of Christus Victor or Christus Imperator.[22] Therefore, the iconography as a whole can be read only as celebrating the eternal, omnipotent divine sovereign and the magnificent unity of the celestial realm, where everyone, all the people (*cunctos populos*, or *panta ta ethne*), serve as a choir to praise God in harmony.[23]

The Rotunda's splendid men in their shimmering ambience might help us to picture an event that took place on January 10, 402 CE, in Constantinople. On that day, the eastern Roman emperor Arcadius elevated his son, Theodosius II, as augustus.[24] Shortly before, Arcadius had walked "with a cheerful face that was shining more brightly than the purple he was wearing" from the Great Church (Hagia Sophia) to the imperial palace through streets decorated with garlands and silk banners, surrounded by his senators and other eminent dignitaries in elaborate dress glittering with gold and jewels.[25] The titles denoting the ranks of these senators matched the splendor of their garments: in descending order, utterly "illuminated man" (*illustris vir, illoustrios*); "man well worth looking at" (*spectabilis vir, spektabilios* or *peribleptos*); and "shiniest man" (*clarissimus vir, lamprotatos*). Other members of the elites were titled "most perfect men" (*perfectissimi viri*).[26] Their combined sparkle enhanced the majestic glitter of the purple-clad emperor at the center of the procession. The occasion was indeed festive: the proud father Arcadius was celebrating the baptism of his son, the same Theodosius II whom he

21. Mastora, "Virtual Lighting," 218 (the apex as a mirror gathering and reflecting the external and internal light); Torp, *Rotonde palatine*, 1:221–69 (iconography), 319–52 (heavenly imperial palace).

22. Kleinbauer ("Original Name," 59, quoted by Nasrallah, "Empire," 493) suggested that the church was originally called Christos Theou Dynamis (To Christ, the Power of God).

23. *Cunctos populos* are the first two words of an edict issued by Theodosius I from Thessalonica in 380 that later became known by this phrase (CTh 16.1.2; CJ 1.1). *Panta ta ethne* refers to the resurrected Christ's mandate to disperse the word: see Mt 28:19; Lk 24:47.

24. *Cons. Const.*, a. 402; Marc., *Chron.*, a. 402. The elevation took place at the Hebdomon, a military training ground outside Constantinople. See Cameron and Long, *Barbarians*, 170–71; Falcasantos, *Constantinople*, 8–19, 46–53.

25. Marc. Diac. 47. See also Rapp, "Mark the Deacon," 53–56. The original Hagia Sophia burned down in 402: see Bauer, "Urban Space," 46–47; Bauer, *Stadt*, 151–53; Dagron, *Naissance*, 92–97, 100–2.

26. Masterson, *Man to Man*, 10 (translations of the titles); Jones, *Later Roman Empire*, 2:528–30; Lizzi Testa, *Christian Emperors*, 52–79 (importance of the Roman Senate); Dillon, "Inflation of Rank," 53–64; Salzman, *Falls*, 91; Schlinkert, *Ordo senatorius*, 85–94; Ch. Kelly, *Ruling*, 18–26 (dress and court ceremonial).

then made a fully fledged coemperor a few days later, at the ripe old age of eight months.[27] Theodosius II became the sole eastern emperor at barely seven when his father died on May 1, 408, and he governed without challenges until his death in a riding accident in 450 CE.[28] Arcadius himself was five or six when he became the first child to be elevated to eastern augustus, in 383; his younger brother Honorius followed suit aged nine. In 395, at ten, Honorius rose to the position of sole western ruler, and like his nephew Theodosius II he enjoyed a long reign, until he died of an illness in 423.[29]

Three years before elevating his infant son, Arcadius had honored one of these glittering senators with the highest civilian office. This *illustris vir* deserved the new rank. He had helped Arcadius stabilize his regime after Theodosius I's death in 395 and had successfully campaigned against Hunnic federations in 397 and 398, which had garnered him the honorific *patricius*. Many considered him "father of the ruler."[30] Now, in recognition of all that this sparkling man had done, Arcadius made him the eastern consul for the year 399, granting him a position surpassed only by that of the emperor whom he represented (even embodied) when the latter was absent. This consul, who would give his name to the year, was called Eutropius. He was a formerly enslaved eunuch, who had been castrated at birth.[31]

An assembly of beautiful, glittering soldier martyrs enhancing a victorious Christ carried on his shield of virtue, an infant augustus who proceeded to sole rule at seven without causing a ripple, and a castrated former slave as a consul each tell their own story. Once combined into one choir, however, they offer a

27. Theodosius II was born in April 401. The baptism is attested only by Mark the Deacon, who misdates Theodosius II's birth to January 401. Holum, *Theodosian Empresses*, 55n31, dates the baptism to January 6, 402, and is followed by van Nuffelen, "Playing the Ritual Game," 192, and Ch. Kelly, "Rethinking Theodosius," 3n1, meaning it would have preceded the elevation by four days.

28. Pfeilschifter, *Kaiser und Konstantinopel*, 56 (Theodosius II's peaceful reign), 147 (Theodosius II's death). The *imperator*, or augustus, was a full ruler, so the concept of a regent ruling in his place is misleading: if the child emperor was without a father, he required a *tutor* (or *curator* if puberty had been reached), *epitropos* in Greek—that is, a guardian. See McEvoy, *Child Emperor Rule*, 4–5 (role of coaugustus), 10–12 (guardian). Dynastic interests increased after Constantine, though succession never became hereditary by law: see, e.g., Severy, *Augustus and the Family*, 68–77; Hekster, *Emperors and Ancestors*, 2–21; Börm, "Born to Be Emperor," 243–59.

29. McEvoy, *Child Emperor Rule*, 137–38 (Arcadius's elevation), 137n8 (Honorius's brief elevation to caesar before augustus in 389), 135–37 (Honorius's long reign and death). The Theodosian dynasty in the west ended in 455 with the assassination of Valentinian III, who became augustus as a six-year-old: McEvoy, *Child Emperor Rule*, 223–34 (accession), 300–1 (assassination). For the rarity of Roman emperors dying as peacefully as the other Theodosians, see Retief and Cilliers, "Causes of Death," 89–106.

30. Claud., *Eutr.* 2 praef. 2.50 ("principis esse pater"); Philost., *HE* 11.4. See also Long, *Claudian's "In Eutropium,"* 9–13; and see chapter 6.

31. Castration was outlawed in the Roman Empire and this prohibition enforced by civil penalties, so many eunuchs were (allegedly) imported from regions to the east. Because they were high-value slaves, however, the practice never ceased, including in the empire. See, e.g., Kuefler, *Manly Eunuch*, 32; Messis, *Les eunuques*, 45–51.

new reading of Roman imperial power under the Theodosians. They demonstrate that the dynasty's founder, Theodosius I, and his two sons, Arcadius and Honorius, gradually and then decisively created a novel, layered, and capaciously gendered imperial manliness to make visible their interpretation of Christianity. This imperial manliness, or *virtus*, was both hard and soft, well defined and fluid, mature and youthful. At all times, it was important that the Theodosian emperors be gorgeous. Because they were divine—gods one could see—their beauty was also divine. Their virtuous manliness, or, as I prefer to call it, their *vir*-ness, was the face and body of God. The emperors' splendid clothing and sparkling regalia, reflecting and conveying how they wished their bodies to be seen by their elite subjects—some of whom authored the texts on which my analysis is based—were as important as laws, taxes, and armies, because imperial beauty subdued enemies, transformed civil war rivals into allies, and bound together the elites. In devising their divinely beautiful *vir*-ness, the emperors strategically deployed male same-sex erotic desire to enhance the unity of the realm in times of increasing tensions between the western and eastern parts—that is, between the Old and the New Rome (Constantinople). They consciously incorporated the signifying potency of child emperors to increase that desire and the cohesion it created. And they succeeded in shaping a flexible yet stable model of Christian sovereignty that was to last for centuries.

. . .

This is the story of my book. It is not how the story of the early Theodosians has been told so far. One version of that story is well known and eloquently captured by the painter Jean-Paul Laurens, who in 1880 portrayed the young emperor Honorius as a bored teenager slouching on the imperial throne.[32] Laurens brilliantly conveyed a nineteenth-century vision of Rome's decadent decline, brought about by inadequate imperial heirs idling away their time while enclosed in the palace, dwarfed by the insignia of rule, and controlled by their mothers, wives, barbarian generalissimos, and court eunuchs.[33] Recent scholarship is more charitable, at least regarding Theodosius I and II. Scholars agree that the dynasty's founder, praised only a decade after his death as "the best of the gods" (*optimus ille divorum*) and

---

32. For Laurens as a history painter, see M. Eberle, *Spiegel der Geschichte*, 326–39; Des Cars, "Jean-Paul Laurens," 23–34, 101–3; Doyle, *Honorius*, 2–4.

33. Kulikowski, *Rome's Gothic Wars*, 2, indicates the tenor of this narrative: Honorius "was a weakling and an incompetent, rumoured to be a half-wit even by those who wished him well. Holed up in the coastal town of Ravenna, safe behind marshes and causeways and readily supplied by sea, he was unreachable and the workings of his court inscrutable." Bleckmann, "Honorius," 561–64, and Börm, "End of the Roman Empire," 191–95, offer a succinct overview of the (immense) scholarship on (Honorius's contribution to) the fall of the empire in the fifth century; see also Doyle, *Honorius*, 4–5. Goffart, *Barbarian Tides*, 194, considered these general(issimo)s to be murderers.

FIGURE 3. Jean-Paul Laurens (1838–1921). *The Late Empire: Honorius*, 1880, oil on canvas, 60½ × 42½ in. (153.7 × 108 cm). Chrysler Museum of Art, gift of Walter P. Chrysler Jr., 71.671.

today still known as "the Great," ushered in a profound change in Roman imperial rule with lasting consequences.[34]

Fortified by military expertise and strategic use of venerated conceptions and representations of imperial rule that reached back to Augustus and Rome's Republic, Theodosius I announced a rejuvenated empire and advanced a clear vision of his Christian faith. He was a true Roman emperor (or at least as true as it was possible to be in the *late* Roman Empire), who "struggled with [his] problems manfully and heroically," actively (if not always successfully) shaping how he governed rather than merely reacting to what he faced.[35] In the east, he initiated a civic emperorship with predominantly ceremonial function, beginning the imperial practice of permanent residence in Constantinople and tight linkage to the city's elites and populace, which made the eastern emperors less dependent on military support.[36] By focusing on its liturgical aspects, Theodosius II significantly expanded and consolidated that role into *the* model of the civilian, ceremonial Christian Roman emperor—legitimized by his piety—which would last for centuries.[37] Consequently, even though military victory remained central to imperial prestige, Theodosius I's successors no longer went into the field and indeed hardly ever left the capital—until the seventh century, when Heraclius, much to the consternation of his contemporaries, resumed campaigning.[38]

In the west, Theodosius I's rule marked a turning point because he and his eastern army twice defeated western strongmen who tried to usurp the throne (the means by which he too may have gotten his start), a clear indication that Constantinople was on the rise.[39] Moreover, he decided to implement child

34. Quote in Claud., *VI Cons. Hon.* 55–56; here and elsewhere Weiß and Wiener translate *divorum* as "divinized emperors" ("vergöttlichte Kaiser"). For Icks, "Inadequate Heirs," 73, Theodosius I "fundamentally redefined [the emperor's role], but old expectations were still very much alive." Leppin, *Theodosius*, 231–39, considers him (239) "kein[en] Gestalter der Geschichte . . . nichts Brilliantes haftet ihm an; was er tat, hätten andere ebenso vollbringen können." See also Williams and Friell, *Theodosius*, 159–71; Hebblewhite, *Theodosius*, 2–5 (modern assessments).

35. Williams and Friell, *Theodosius*, 171. Schmidt-Hofner, *Reagieren*, remains fundamental for the late Roman emperor's reactive versus proactive role.

36. Maier, *Palastrevolution*, 11–15; Pfeilschifter, *Kaiser und Konstantinopel*, 21–24, 41–75, 211–51; Heather, *Goths and Romans*, 165–77; Croke, "Reinventing Constantinople," 242–43; Diefenbach, "Zwischen Liturgie," 21–27; Diefenbach, "Frömmigkeit," 42–45. See also chapter 5.

37. Ch. Kelly, "Rethinking Theodosius," 10–18, 42–49, 64; Diefenbach, "Zwischen Liturgie," 21–46; Diefenbach, "Frömmigkeit," 47–48, 63 (relic transfers as enhancement of piety); van Nuffelen, "Playing the Ritual Game," 186–93 (emphasizing the emperor's skill in managing unpredictable ceremonial expectations); Pfeilschifter, *Kaiser und Konstantinopel*, 56–57, 76–119; Stewart, *Soldier's Life*, 168–73 (Sozomen's praise of Theodosius II as a military and pious ruler).

38. For detailed analysis of the emperors' movements prior to Heraclius, see McCormick, *Eternal Victory*, 210–20; Pfeilschifter, *Kaiser und Konstantinopel*, 58–74. In 590 or 592, Mauricius assumed command of a military campaign which ended without engaging the enemy, so Heraclius's campaigns were indeed the first since Theodosius I; see Pfeilschifter, *Kaiser und Konstantinopel*, 64–68; also 597–611.

39. McEvoy, *Child Emperor Rule*, 71–80; Szidat, "Gaul and the Roman Emperors," 119–34; Omissi, *Emperors*, 255–90 (Theodosius as usurper); Sivan, "Was Theodosius I a Usurper?"

emperor rule in the east despite witnessing some of the difficulties this novel practice caused when it began in 367 with Valentinian I's elevation of his eight-year-old son Gratian to coaugustus: it privileged dynastic concerns over merit (though Theodosius himself had ascended for the opposite reason), which in turn invited better-prepared adult men to compete for power and hence increased the risk of civil war.[40]

Long neglected as a curiosity, the "unexpected phenomenon" of child emperor rule, "entirely without precedent in Roman imperial history," has begun to receive the attention it deserves.[41] It brings us back to Honorius and Arcadius. As Meghan McEvoy has shown, Honorius consolidated the (boy) emperor's ceremonial role in the west. In close partnership with his general Stilicho, the young emperor transitioned successfully into adulthood and ruled for thirty years, while his general handled most matters of state, led armies, and provided the prestige of military victories.[42] However, even though McEvoy has elucidated the undeniable success of the collaboration between the emperor and his all-powerful manager, which "truly changed the political culture of the Roman west," she has not been able to rehabilitate Honorius entirely: he remains an inadequate heir, whose passive ceremonial rule magnified intra-elite competition and enabled (future) fierce (barbarian) generalissimos and warlords to cause destabilizing civil wars that accelerated the fall of the western empire.[43] Indeed, even McEvoy's persuasive argument that Honorius's inactivity was due not "to dimness or lethargy" but rather to his insight that in this arrangement his duty was to remain passive because the new ceremonial role meant, "in effect, the infantilization of the imperial office," cannot quite hide a sense of nostalgic regret for the loss of the valiant, battle-hardened, active emperor of old (or as old as Theodosius I).[44]

Arcadius too is no longer considered, in Alan Cameron's words, "notoriously and beyond any possibility of confutation a spineless booby."[45] Scholars now grant that he consolidated his father's initiatives, though in ways that departed from Theodosius's precedent: like Honorius, Arcadius "abandoned the ideal of the emperor as a victorious general, replacing it with a 'palace emperorship' that broke with

40. Amm. Marc. 26.6.4 (Gratian); Börm, "Born to Be Emperor," 257–59.

41. McEvoy, *Child Emperor Rule*, 2.

42. McEvoy, *Child Emperor Rule*, 136–52, 308–11; see also Pfeilschifter, *Kaiser und Konstantinopel*, 125–33.

43. McEvoy, *Child Emperor Rule*, 308, also 310 ("active, all-powerful manager"); Icks, "Inadequate Heirs," 81–83; Börm, "End of the Roman Empire," 195–200 (importance of civil wars and warlords in the west); Janssen, *Stilicho*, 70–103; Salzman, *Falls*, 97–98, 104–6; Wijnendaele, "Sarus the Goth," 469–73; Wijnendaele, "*Generalissimos* and Warlords," 432–43.

44. McEvoy, *Child Emperor Rule*, 318, 324. See also Doyle, *Honorius*, 9–10 (Honorius's sense of realpolitik); Icks, "Inadequate Heirs," 70 (regret).

45. Cameron, *Claudian*, 422. See also Pfeilschifter, *Kaiser und Konstantinopel*, 477n56, for an overview of the predominantly negative modern scholarship.

centuries of imperial tradition."[46] It is clear that Arcadius deserves attention and rehabilitation as an emperor who (actively) managed a major transition in the nature of imperial governance.[47] His rule was stable enough to allow him to declare augustus the youngest child ever by a considerable margin—an infant—without any discernable reaction (including by scholars), thus inaugurating Theodosius II's long reign.

The Theodosians, in sum, have garnered mixed reviews. Theodosius I and his grandson Theodosius II have received the lion's share of scholarly attention, the first because he was an active, indeed victorious, Roman emperor, and the second because even though he was palace-bound, his reign was "astonishingly" stable thanks to his piety, learning, and skill in generating acceptance by the Constantinopolitan elites, which made him one of the most successful premodern emperors.[48] Honorius and Arcadius, though no longer considered mere "nominal" rulers under the "regency" of strong men, have had a much harder time clawing back some scholarly respect, because they institutionalized the ceremonial emperorship, which was durable but, if not outright infantilized, certainly passive.[49] With its emphasis on ceremony, faith, negotiation, diplomacy, and the mobilization of cultural resources, that form of imperial rule ceased to privilege hard in favor of soft power, and the problem with soft power, to quote Joseph Nye, is that "it's, well, soft."[50] The story, if no longer a linear one of decline, is then one of a transition from the ideal warrior emperor to the Christian (child) emperor who rules from the palace rather than the battlefield, with all the attendant risks that courtly politics invite.

Indeed, that *is* the story of Theodosian imperial rule. However, the Thessalonica Rotunda, infant emperors, and a eunuch as consul can present that story in an as yet untold way: as that of late Roman imperial manliness, or masculinity, and the importance of being gorgeous as a means of both incarnating and exercising power. This book proposes that the Rotunda's sparkling men enhancing Christ's majesty encapsulate a practice that began slowly with Gratian, continued in earnest with Theodosius I, and was consolidated by Honorius and Arcadius. Here male beauty acted as a unifying force emphasizing that everyone—at the imperial court, from general to eunuch, and in the entire realm—together formed an ensemble designed to enhance the glory of the divine Christian emperor at the apex and center.[51]

46. Icks, "Inadequate Heirs," 71. See also Pfeilschifter, *Kaiser und Konstantinopel*, 95; Maier, *Palastrevolution*, 8–9 (gradual progression toward palace emperorship with intensification under Theodosius I), 442–62.

47. McEvoy, "Imperial Jellyfish," 182–83, 194 (Arcadius was "surely no less important in his own time than his father or his son").

48. Maier, *Palastrevolution*, 12, 15, 459 ("erstaunlich stabil"); Pfeilschifter, *Kaiser und Konstantinopel*, 57 ("Theodosius II. war einer der erfolgreichsten Herrscher der Antike").

49. Jones, *Later Roman Empire*, 1:95 (nominal rule), 177 (quasi-regency).

50. Nye, "Soft Power: Evolution," 205. See also 200–1; Nye, "Soft Power," 153–71.

51. Leon, panel 1 (southeast): Torp, *Rotonde palatine*, 1:206; see also Kiilerich, "Picturing Ideal Beauty," 323–28, 333–36; Hatzaki, "Peacocks," 68–69 (descriptions of male beauty by Libanius, Menander Rhetor, and Ps. John Chrysostom).

FIGURE 4. Leon, 4/5th c. CE, mosaic, panel 1 (SE), Rotunda,
Thessalonica. Photo: Bente Knold Kiilerich, 2009.

Being gorgeous was not simply a way of representing imperial power. It was a mode of governance, a means of getting people to do and not do things. These emperors, the reader will discover in the pages that follow, used a highly capacious, fluid, flexible male gender performance to exercise sovereignty. This is political history that focuses on the centrality of imperial beauty, in all its sparkle, for establishing Theodosius and his sons as arbiters of elite manliness. It shows how they manifested and deployed male same-sex desire, indeed queerness, at the center of power to declare their unifying force as the most sacred and divine rulers, tasked with guaranteeing the eternity of the realm. That is, this is a history not of gender as such but of gender as integral to the exercise of political power.

But before delving into the methodological and historical contingencies on which this argument is predicated, I want to return briefly to the third vignette: Arcadius's elevation of Eutropius as consul in 399. Eutropius was the first and last eunuch to become a consul, which has garnered him quite a bit of attention, overwhelmingly focused on his physical condition.[52] Following the assessment of ancient historians who wrote after he fell from grace, scholars still consider him the power behind the throne who dominated a weak emperor.[53] Putting eunuchs in influential offices was, however, not unusual; every late Roman emperor, including

52. Long, *Claudian's "In Eutropium,"* 1–3; Sidéris, "Rise and Fall," 71–79; Schlinkert, *Ordo senatorius,* 266–70 (Eutropius as paradigmatic for weak emperor/strong eunuch), 277–81 (Eutropius's elevation as symptomatic of the loss of senatorial power). See also Tougher, *Roman Castrati,* 89–97; Ch. Kelly, *Ruling,* 166–68; Kuefler, *Manly Eunuch,* 65–67, 98; Guyot, *Eunuchen,* 167–70; Messis, *Les eunuques,* 82–84 (Eutropius as a model "bad eunuch" in later receptions because of his powerful position).

53. Pfeilschifter, *Kaiser und Konstantinopel,* 487–90; Cameron and Long, *Barbarians,* 4–8; Liebeschuetz, *Barbarians and Bishops,* 93–103.

those who actively campaigned, did so.[54] On the assumption that Arcadius, who was twenty-one at the time, knew what he was doing, the question that puzzled me was why the emperor chose to make Eutropius *consul*. This was the highest civilian office, and a consul not only represented but in fact embodied the emperor when the latter was absent. What changes to notions of imperial power made it possible for Arcadius to consider it self-understood that a eunuch, illuminated *vir* and successful military leader though he was, could, indeed should, be consul?[55] What did that say about the relation between physical condition and office?[56] The reactions of Arcadius's contemporaries—authors in the west and the east of the empire, all members of the elite, highly sensitive observers of imperial power and its representations—offered answers. Each author reacted differently to Eutropius, his rise, and his eventual fall. But what at first seems a chorus of disparate individual voices, once read together, becomes a choir that makes imperial beauty legible as a governing strategy.

IMPERIAL VIRTUE AND *VIR*-NESS

The Rotunda's sparkling soldiers, the child emperors, the castrated consul, and elite reactions to the latter demonstrate that competing concepts of manliness were central to late Roman imperial rule. However, none of the recent, superb studies of late Roman, and more specifically Theodosian, imperial rule use the emperor's masculinity as an analytic category.[57] This lacuna may in part be explained by the significance of the structural approach to the functioning of the Roman monarchy known as *Kaiserakzeptanz*. Introduced by Egon Flaig's 1992 study of the principate and the early empire, this approach focuses on the emperor's interaction with three groups—the Senate, the military, and the populace—whose acceptance (rather than dynastic succession) determined his legitimacy.[58] Recent scholarship

54. See, e.g., Sidéris, "Rise and Fall," 63–64; Tougher, "In or Out?," 143–59; Ringrose, *Perfect Servant*, 166–76 (later evolutions of these positions).

55. Daube, "Self-Understood," 124–38.

56. Gardner's observation is interesting in the context of child emperor rule ("Sexing a Roman," 137): jurists debated whether eunuchs, who were legally men—that is, could marry and adopt—were adults, since they could not have children. Kuefler, *Manly Eunuch*, 19–36, views their legal status as contradictory.

57. With few exceptions: see Masterson, *Man to Man*, 41–89 (Julian), 138–69 (Ammianus Marcellinus's emperors); Stewart, *Soldier's Life*, 97–112 (Julian), 180–85 (Theodosius II). Stewart, *Masculinity*, addresses Justinian and Procopius. Most studies on Roman masculinity focus on the Republic and the early empire: see, e.g., Racette-Campbell, *Crisis*, 47–80 (*virtus* under the principate); Pope, *Lucretius*, 147–93 (Lucretius's de- and reconstructed men), with bibliography. Scholarship on the topic in the Middle Ages is intense: see, e.g., La Rocca, "Masculinity," though often focused on the clergy. See also Conway, "Masculinity Studies," 77–93.

58. Flaig, *Den Kaiser herausfordern*, 11–195 (shift from a legal-constitutional framing of Roman imperial rule to a structural one, based on anthropological-political methods), 174–207 (acceptance group versus dynastic concerns). Flaig (14–18, 347, 462) calls his approach "praxeological," which grants less analytic value to the texts of ancient authors.

has added nuance and extended the scope of investigation forward to the later Roman Empire, expanding the acceptance groups to include the administrative elites, the Senate in Constantinople, and the bishops and other high-ranking clergy.[59] The emperors' interactions with these groups are also fundamental to my book. However, masculinity, or gender more broadly speaking, offers a more direct means to focus on the emperors when analyzing the construction of late Roman imperial power.[60] When discussing the emperors' active versus passive behavior, the dilemma caused by their decreasing room to maneuver militarily while being expected to win, or the relevance of regalia, the recent, structural studies of late Roman rule do, in fact, address manliness.[61] However, they never do so up front, only obliquely, and therefore consider aspects such as the emperor's sumptuous clothing to be symptomatic rather than constitutive of imperial rule.

At the same time, scholars who engage late Roman masculinities have explored the topic largely in the context of a Christian (and comparative) religious framework, focusing on ascetics, monks, bishops, saints, and eunuchs.[62] To the extent that emperors, who after all were also Christian, enter the discussions, their role in generating norms and possibilities for late Roman masculine expression has been peripheral. This emphasis on the religious sphere, as Michael Stewart has observed, has led to a somewhat skewed assessment of the enduring relevance of traditional manly ideals—especially victoriousness in battle, or military excellence—in favor of "Christian" ones.[63] In Virginia Burrus's words, "Receding is the venerable figure of the civic leader and familial patriarch; approaching is a man marked as a spiritual father, by virtue of his place in the . . . apostolic succession, and also as the leader of a new citizenry, fighting heroically in a contest of truth in which . . . the weapon of choice is the 'sword of the word.'"[64] This turns us to the question of sources.

Emperors lose out in battles fought with words, because (apart from Marcus Aurelius and Julian) they did not write. Reconstructing imperial intent is therefore difficult, since it can be assembled only from a complex set of interlocking communications (on which more below) that do not take the form of lengthy

59. For the later empire, see, e.g., Pfeilschifter, *Kaiser und Konstantinopel*, 1–37; Maier, *Palastrevolution*, 11–15, 37–67 (late Roman acceptance groups). For complementary analyses of the earlier empire, see, e.g., Ando, *Imperial Ideology*, 336–405; Noreña, *Imperial Ideals*, 1–26.

60. See Meister, *Körper*, 11–19, for a comparable approach to mine, focused on the early principate.

61. Wienand, *Der Kaiser als Sieger*, 13–86; Ch. Kelly, *Ruling*, 232–45; Rollinger, "Importance," 36–72; Alföldi, *Monarchische Repräsentation*, 25–118.

62. Burrus, *Begotten, Not Made*, and Kuefler, *Manly Eunuch*, remain foundational. See also Stewart, *Soldier's Life*, 147–65 (Antony and others); Masterson, *Man to Man*, 90–137 (Antony); Kuefler, "Between Bishops," 37–62 (late Roman imperial masculinity in tension with bishops and barbarians); Jacobs, *Christ Circumcised*, 15–40; Strassfeld, *Trans Talmud*, 33–54, 183–201.

63. Stewart, *Soldier's Life*, 8–9 (skewed view because of the privileging of Christian genres), 163–64 (critique of Kuefler, *Manly Eunuch*, 287, 296: Christian ascetic ideals as repudiation of and substitute for declining military values).

64. Burrus, *Begotten, Not Made*, 4–5, quoting Gr. Nyss., *Eun.* 1.87.9; see also 103–7.

treatises. Among the most important of these imperial communications is each emperor's selection and publication of appropriate virtues. Imperial virtues, consequently, have attracted a great deal of attention, especially as they transformed from traditional or classic into Christian.[65]

Virtus and "virtue" derive from the Latin term *vir. Vir* denotes a man. But being a *vir* required more than being, and presenting as, male (*mas, homo*).[66] The word indicated someone who lived by the codes that defined elite male gender comportment: "For it is from the word *vir* that the word *virtue* is derived."[67] *Virtus*, like the Greek *andreia*, from *aner*, "adult man," is often translated as "courage," "valor," or "excellence," but it always also means manliness, because strong, brave, courageous conduct made a person into a *vir*.[68] These associations explain the oscillation of *virtus* between agonistically acquired manliness—winning and ruling (*imperare*)—and ethical and moral behavior, or virtue, in Greek *arete*, frequently a synonym for *andreia*.[69] The Gallic author Sulpicius Severus demonstrates that oscillation in his *Life of Martin*, composed between 397 and 400.[70] Here, Sulpicius describes contests between his hero Martin and opponents in three different arenas: the battlefield, the ecclesiastic sphere, and the imperial court. Each one proves the superior manliness of the former military tribune and new saint. He faces down barbarian enemies to win without shedding blood, shames degenerate (*degenere*) bishops by speaking truth to power, impresses the "ferocious" civil war victor Magnus Maximus, and unmasks a splendidly robed emperor as the devil, all because his *virtus*, or manly courage, derived its power from "apostolic authority."[71]

Virtue and being a *vir* were also codeterminate with being Roman, or, at a minimum, not barbarian.[72] By the later Roman Empire, being Roman (having

65. Noreña, "Ethics of Autocracy," 267–79; Noreña, *Imperial Ideals*, 37–100; Balmaceda, *Virtus Romana*, 14–47; Chambers, *Augustine*, 45–118.

66. *Homo* means "human being" (e.g., CTh 5.7.2. pr.) but usually denotes a man or male-presenting person who lacked the status of *vir*: see Gradenwitz, *Heidelberger Index*, 277–78. See also, e.g., Pope, *Lucretius*, 16–17.

67. Cic., *Tusc.* 2.13.34 ("apellata est enim ex viro virtus"). As the references throughout this book show, the scholarship on this topic is immense.

68. Women and others, such as eunuchs, could also act virtuously—that is, achieve *vir*-like status while remaining women (or eunuchs). In Gleason's succinct formulation (*Making Men*, 59), "Masculinity in the ancient world was an achieved state, radically undetermined by anatomical sex." See also, e.g., McInerney, "Plutarch's Manly Women," 319–44; Stefaniw, "Becoming Men," 341–55. For the difficulty in translating *vir, virtus,* and *andreia,* see also Williams, *Roman Homosexuality*, 132–35; McDonnell, *Roman Manliness*, 3.

69. Cic., *Tusc.* 2.53.4 ("ut tibi imperes"). See McDonnell, "Roman Men and Greek Virtue," 235–61, on the nexus of *andreia, arete,* and *virtus*.

70. Stancliffe, *Saint Martin*, 9 (date of the *Life*); Burton, *Sulpicius*, 2–4.

71. Sulp., *Vit. Mart.* 4.1.88–108 (victory over barbarians), 20.1.425–8.456 (bishops, Magnus Maximus), 24.4.542–7.556 (devil as emperor). See also Sághy, "*Veste Regia Indutus*," 50; Dinshaw, *Getting Medieval*, 1.

72. Ingleheart, "Romosexuality," 1–36; Williams, *Roman Homosexuality*, 135. Aspects of Connell and Messerschmidt's "Hegemonic Masculinity," 829–59, echo the connection between being a Roman *vir* and *imperium*. See also Dench, *Romulus' Asylum*, 37–92.

Romanitas, or Romanness), together with being a *vir*—or having, as I will call it in what follows, *vir*-ness—was less a physical or ethnic identity than a status-driven and malleable position.[73] Acting courageously with appropriate strength signaled virtue, which granted ethical and moral authority because it demonstrated that one was a bona fide member of the Roman elite.[74] Anything else resulted automatically in "less-than-*vir*-ness" and hence "less-than-Romanness," with the corresponding decrease of moral authority revealed by degenerate conduct.[75] Manliness—that is, *vir*-ness—was situational and therefore offered members of the elite a prime means to think with and write about power. Becoming and being a *vir* (achieving *vir*-ness) was a relational and thus dynamic process, signaled through what Carlos Noreña has described as panoramas of virtues (and vices).[76] Even though a core set of virtues remained remarkably stable over the centuries, their assembly allowed for flexibility and made historically contingent what virtuous conduct—and thus being a *vir*—looked like and how that was projected.[77] The elite authors whose texts I analyze in what follows were highly sensitive to these contingencies: they were seismographs of the power to which they all sought privileged access.[78]

THE AESTHETICS OF AUTOCRACY

At the apex of Roman elite manliness, or *vir*-ness, stood the most sacred, divine emperor, or *sacratissimus divinus imperator*.[79] He embodied (or was supposed to embody, if he was a good—that is, legitimate—ruler) a "kaleidoscope" of essential

73. Though I consider my book a contribution to the study of masculinities, I am not using that term, because I want to emphasize the historically specific, premodern, status-based notion of being a *vir*, in its matrix of ethnic identity, age, dress, and sexual behavior. See Racette-Campbell and Mc-Master, "Toxic Masculinity," 1–7; see also Bonnell Freidin, "Gender in the Roman Empire"; Gunderson, *Staging Masculinity*, 192; Kamen and Levin-Richardson, "Revisiting Roman Sexuality," 449–60. For gender as a continuum, see Gilhuly, *Feminine Matrix*, 1–11, 19–24.

74. Woolf, *Becoming Roman*, 48–76. *Romanitas* was also available to the Greek-speaking Roman elite, who shared the same imperial notion that eternal triumph over foreign enemies was a Roman's birthright and ancestral privilege: see Stewart, *Soldier's Life*, 3, quoting Agathias, *Hist.* 2.12.2. See also Millar, *Greek Roman Empire*, 41–42; Jacobs, *Christ Circumcised*, 7–10.

75. Sulp., *Vit. Mart.* 20.1.429.

76. Noreña, "Ethics of Autocracy," 268.

77. Noreña, "Ethics of Autocracy," 272–79; Börm, "Antimonarchic Discourse," 15–20.

78. Ch. Kelly, *Ruling*, 114–37 (access).

79. The title of this section alludes to Noreña, "Ethics of Autocracy." See also Noreña, *Imperial Ideals*, 101–11. As far as I am aware, there is no systematic discussion of late Roman imperial aesthetics—at least not with an emphasis on manliness—comparable to what McCall offers for the Renaissance (*Brilliant Bodies*, 1–16), Hatzaki for medieval Byzantium (*Beauty*, 1–32, 49–65), or Sernagiotto for the early Middle Ages ("Importance of Being Lothar," 127–59). See also Bildhauer, *Medieval Things*, 19–58 (on shine). Neri, *La bellezza*, 109–51, and Masterson, *Man to Man*, 41–62, 108–10, 138–69, are the most sustained analyses of late Roman imperial beauty. Konstan, *Beauty*, 128–34, 148–56, focuses on the ancient and Hellenistic Greek contribution to (modern) aesthetics, as does Nehamas, *Promise*.

virtues, including justice, piety, modest restraint or self-control, clemency, benevolence, fortitude, and courage, or *virtus*.[80] Beauty was a central means by which the emperor communicated the virtues he chose to signal as the characteristics of his rule—and by which the elites received and commented upon them. They noted his beauty, his *pulchritudo, forma* (shape), *decus* and *decor* (attractiveness), *venustas* (loveliness), and in Greek his being *kalos*, "beautiful"/"noble," and also *kallos*, "beautiful"/"sexually desirable."[81] Late Roman emperors, including Theodosius, his sons, and his grandson, were divine, gods who were present and whom one could see, and they expected to be received among the (other) gods by senatorial decree after their death.[82] Consequently, (good) emperors were divinely beautiful, with heavenly faces, and they had no problem recognizing themselves in the gods whom they considered the most beautiful in the whole world (*toto orbe pulcherrimum*).[83]

The splendid vestments and costly insignia of the emperor—crowned by a diadem of pearls in double or triple strands with pearl and gem pendants (evoking Alexander the Great), draped in a purple cloak fastened with jewel-encrusted fibulae over bejeweled and gold-embroidered garments, and shod in richly decorated purple boots—made his divinity manifest for all to see.[84] Initiated by the tetrarchic rulers and expanded by Constantine and his successors, elaborate ornateness became integral to imperial rule.[85] In John Chrysostom's pithy formulation, "The imperial mantle (*himation basilikon*) is the ruler's body (*soma despotikon*)."—an

80. In Greek, following Plato, these virtues were *dikaiosyne* (justice), *sophia/phronesis* (foresight or wisdom), *sophrosyne* (restraint or temperance), and *andreia* (courage/manliness): see Noreña, "Ethics of Autocracy," 268, 272–76; the expression "kaleidoscope of virtues and vices" is his (272).

81. See *Pan. lat.* (6)7.17.2 ("virtus pulchritudini coniuncta"); also Neri, *La bellezza*, 133–35; Masterson, *Man to Man*, 42–44 (*kalos/kallos*), 141 (*venustas*); Konstan, *Beauty*, 148–61; Gunderson, *Staging Masculinity*, 192–93 (*decus*), 203–4 (*pulcher*), 127–28 (*venustas*).

82. According to Plin., *Pan.* 4.4, the emperor was "equal to the immortal gods." For Theodosius as *deus*, see, e.g., Veg., *Mil.* 2.5 ("deus praesens"); *Pan. lat.* (2)12.4.5 ("deum . . . quem videmus"). Whether *Christian* Roman emperors were divine or gods has been hotly debated, but Theodosius II's law of 425 restricting veneration to his *numen*, his divinity (CTh 5.4.1), supports that they were divine although distinct from the One God: see, e.g., Bardill, *Constantine*, 63–125, 341–58; Cracco Ruggini, "Apoteosi," 432–39; Clauss, *Kaiser und Gott*, 533–35; Diefenbach, "Frömmigkeit," 40; S. Elm, "Emperor Julian on Statues"; Kahlos, "Emperor's New Images."

83. *Pan. lat.* (6)7.21.3. See also *Pan. lat.* (7)6.3.3 ("celestes . . . vultus"), (6)7.17.4 ("Itaque te cum ingredientem milites vident . . . deo se obsequi putant, cuius tam pulchra forma est quam certa divinitas"), (6)7.21.5 ("Vidisti teque in illius specie recognovisti"; here Apollo); Neri, *La bellezza*, 140; Ch. Kelly, "Emperors as Gods"; Tantillo, "L'impero." For earlier divinely beautiful emperors, see, e.g., Vout, *Power and Eroticism*, 27–34.

84. Eus., *Vit. Const.* 3.10.3: Constantine as a "heavenly messenger of God, clothed in raiment which glittered as it were with rays of light, reflecting the glowing radiance of a purple robe, and adorned with the brilliant splendor of gold and precious stones." For the divine made material, see, e.g., Markschies, *Gottes Körper*, 38–40, 57–85 (philosophical schools), 113–43 (on statues); Cox Miller, *Corporeal Imagination*, 9–11, 79; Betancourt, "Why Sight Is Not Touch," 1–24.

85. Alföldi, *Monarchische Repräsentation*, 161–86; Bardill, *Constantine*, 11–19; Kovacs, "*Praeclara in veste*," 380–89.

FIGURE 5. Solidus of Constantine, obverse, 335 CE, gold, die-axis: 6 o'clock, weight: 4.560 g, Nicomedia, British Museum, 1844, 1015.310. © The Trustees of the British Museum.

analogy between the sovereign and the incarnate divine that lasted until Marie Antoinette ripped it apart at its seams.[86]

As the Rotunda so brilliantly illustrates, the emperor did not stage his sacrality alone.[87] Arrayed around him were his bodyguards, in figure-hugging garments, tight pants, high boots, and long hair; his eunuchs, clad in white; the consul in his gold-encrusted vestment, the *trabea*; and the glittering senators and military leaders, all dressed in the military look that Philip von Rummel has so splendidly analyzed. Together they composed a living, multihued picture that expressed divine beauty every time the emperor "appear[ed] in the midst of his followers like an angel of God descended from heaven."[88] In other words, the language of sumptuous *male* fashion—on which the vast majority of the late Roman sources lavish their attention—was a language of power that compelled obedience, amply demonstrated by the analogy between the imperial court and the heavenly realm: each imagined in the other.[89]

86. J. Chrys., *De sanct. mart.* 3 (PG 50.654) (ἱμάτιόν ἐστι βασιλικὸν τὸ σῶμα τὸ δεσποτικόν); Delmaire, "Le vêtement, symbole de richesse"; Weber, *Queen of Fashion*, 3–9, 13–74, 85–87, 151–63, 239–44, 289–92; Vinken, *Angezogen*, 48–69.

87. Ch. Kelly, *Ruling*, 18–26; Ivanovici, "Iconic Presences," 130; Rollinger, "Importance"; R. R. R. Smith, "Public Image of Licinius."

88. Von Rummel, *Habitus barbarus*, 386–94, 401–6; see also MacMullen, "Some Pictures in Ammianus Marcellinus," 435–55 (the military look as elite male fashion); Harlow, "'Clothes Maketh the Man,'" 68–69; Olson, *Masculinity*, 5–11. Quote in J. Chrys., *De Macc.* 1.1. See also Ambr., *Exp. ps.* 118.8.19 ("Procedit imperator . . . concurrunt omnes et in tanta multitudine illum solum aspicere gestiunt et de fulgore purpurae plus quiddam esse in vultu imperatoris existimant"); August., *Serm.* 373.2; Zos., *HN*, 4.28.2; Amm. Marc. 16.10.7–8; Coripp., *In laud. Iust.* 4.233–245; Roberts, "Light, Color, and Visual Illusion."

89. These sources are in stark contrast to modern scholars, who instead focus on female dress and that of male ascetics, comparable to the emphases in masculinities: see, e.g., Upson-Saia, *Early Christian Dress*, with bibliography. For the literary creation of fashion, see Barthes, *Language of Fashion*, 3–19; see also Barthes, *The Fashion System*. Vinken, *Angezogen*, 8–99, addresses the richness of male dress prior

Splendid clothes were, however, not the only method by which late Roman emperors revealed their beauty. The emperor's body, his physical characteristics, also mattered. As we have already seen, members of the elite who wrote about the emperors discussed their faces and bodies. Among the most prolific means by which emperors disseminated their vision of their beauty and the virtues it conveyed were coins and statues, both of which depicted their faces and bodies.[90] So what did (early Theodosian) physical imperial beauty look like? We must start with *imperator*, which originally meant "commander in battle": victories remained foundational to imperial rule. Thus, it is not surprising that Theodosius and his precursors, but also his son Honorius, were praised for their military excellence, their strength (*duritia, robur, fortitudo*), their height (*longitudo, vastitas*), the piercing splendor of their eyes (*fulgor oculorum*), and the serene tranquility of their faces (unperturbed by the demands of war and rule).[91] But the emperor was the most beautiful (*pulcherrimus*) not only by being valorous but also by being youthful (*iuvenis*)—that is, by projecting the immense desirability of "a young man whose beard is just coming out, one whose youth is at its most attractive," who fills those who behold him with pangs of erotic passion (*erota*).[92] Such beauty was smooth, soft, and subtle.[93] Because it was also divine and imperial, smooth softness gradually developed into a language of power, beginning with Gratian, evolving under Theodosius I, and operating decisively by the time of Honorius and Arcadius.[94]

---

to the French Revolution and particularly the advent of the suit. She also highlights the glitter in the military and its reflection in fashion (162). For male sparkle, see also McCall, *Brilliant Bodies*, 17–80, 119–64 (as power expression); M. Miller, "Material Culture," 1–17; M. Miller, *Clothing the Clergy*, 1–50. For the analogy between the celestial and (Christian) imperial courts, see, e.g., Torp, "*Christus Verus Sol*," 180–84; Pazdernik, "Paying Attention," 64–70; Masterson, *Man to Man*, 84–89. *Pace* Mathews, *Clash*, 14–22, I see continuity between Roman imperial and Christian representations.

90. Because of the reuse of statues, whose bodies they represent has to be determined case by case, though tendencies can be identified, and (colossal) size is a good indicator. See Kovacs, *Kaiser, Senatoren*, 47–99; Guidetti, "Between Expressionism and Classicism," 155–71; R.R.R. Smith, "Statue Practice," 15–19; Gehn, *Ehrenstatuen*, 34–75; Bodnaruk, "Politics of Memory," 9–32.

91. Amm. Marc. 22.14.3, 25.4.22 ("venustate oculorum"), 30.9.6; *HA, Hadr.* 26.1–2; *HA, Max.* 3.6 ("Longitudine autem corporis et vastitate et forma atque oculorum magnitudine et candore inter omnes excelleret"); *Epit. de Caes.* 45.5 ("vultu decens"); *Pan. lat.* (6)7.17.1, (12)9.19.6 ("fulgor oculorum"), (2)12.9.4–7, (2)12.20.4–6. See also Neri, *La bellezza*, 138–39; R. R. R. Smith, "Public Image of Licinius," 181–87; see also chapters 1 and 4.

92. Them., *Or.* 13.164c, 13.165a (Gratian), quoting Hom., *Il.* 24.348. See also *Pan. lat.* 6.(7)21.6 (Constantine) ("iuvenis et laetus et salutifer et pulcherrimus"). For the desirability of youth, see, e.g., Konstan, *Beauty*, 62–80; Hatzaki, "Peacocks," 64–70; Vout, *Power and Eroticism*, 22–23. In other words, the Theodosians combined what had been rival images with long traditions into a new one: see, e.g., Zanker, *Power of Images*, 33–78.

93. In this book I use variations of "soft," "subtle," and "smooth" to render the Latin *mollis* (noun *mollitia*). I avoid the usual translation, "effeminate" or "effete," because I want to emphasize that the term also conveys elegance, urbanity, splendor, and similar variations of male beauty. For further discussion, see below, n. 102. See also Meister, *Körper*, 63–85; C. Edwards, *Politics of Immorality*, 63–75.

94. The erotics of *late antique* imperial power (and the sex lives of the emperors) has rarely been addressed: see, e.g., Masterson, *Man to Man*, 34–40 (review of scholarship). Similar to Vout, *Power and*

One significant component of this soft-power language was the use of male same-sex desire.[95] This impulse was part of a range of social bonds and interactions among elite men, cumulatively described as homosocial, that included friendship, cooperation, rivalry, competition, hostility, and sexual relations with those of lower and similar status.[96] In the later Roman Empire, many of these interactions were expressed through metaphors of love, longing, and sexual or erotic yearning, frequently cast as reciprocal. Here, it is important to keep in mind that declarations of longing and pleasure are not the same as sexual acts (though the latter are not excluded). Terms of affection, attraction, love, and mutual desire consolidated peers. Offered by or attributed to the emperor, tender, desiring words and gestures bridged the gap separating the divine ruler from even his loftiest subjects and bound the latter closer to the former.[97]

Same-sex erotic desire could be aroused by the emperor's battle-hardened, robust body, as illustrated by the tetrarchs Diocletian and Maximian.[98] But young, gorgeously smooth (imperial) men radiated a more potent attractiveness—to the extent that the desire they incited had to be carefully modulated. Theodosius, his two sons, and those who acted on their behalf, as we shall see, used the aesthetics of both hard and smooth bodies.[99] Through trial and error, they carefully layered, paired, assembled, and magnified both to create a new, expansive form of imperial manliness, or beauty, that transcended monogendered expressions in ways that I call queer. This exuberant, almost unbound *vir*-ness was designed to signal a capacious unity that embraced all the people in their realm, across hierarchies, with a novel, deeper reach.[100]

Eroticism, 7, I focus "on stories and images of the emperor desiring and being desired by his subjects," which were intended to promote feelings of identification—an erotics of *imperium* (8).

95. Ernst Kantorowicz, a member of the George-Kreis (or literary circle), was perfectly aware of the political power of such attraction, I imagine, but had to cordon it off in *The King's Two Bodies*, ix–xxii: see Schmidt-Hofner, "Epiphanien," 239–68.

96. The term *homosocial* was coined by Sedgwick, *Between Men*, 1. See, e.g., Gunderson, *Staging Masculinity*, 4–15, for the importance of homosocial concepts in analyzing ancient manliness.

97. Masterson, *Man to Man*, 11–12, shows that status-based honor/shame models aligned with penetrating and being penetrated and claimed for the empire's earlier days (by, e.g., Williams, *Roman Homosexuality*, 17–19, 156–70, 230–31) must be modified for its later period. See also Masterson, *Between Byzantine Men*, 4–23; Krueger, "Between Monks," 28–61; Rapp, *Brother-Making*, 6–57.

98. See Şare Ağtürk, *Painted Tetrarchic Reliefs*, 54–59 (cat. nr. 16, fig. 3.8.c). According to Şare Ağtürk, "the 'imperial embrace' is a uniquely Tetrachic motif reflecting the ideals of concord and harmony between the co-ruling emperors. . . . Never before had Roman emperors been shown in such physically intimate contact, even with their family members. . . . Once established, the 'Tetrarchic embrace' seems to have become a popular imperial pattern" (56). See also 47–50; Şare Ağtürk, "Embracing Emperors."

99. As many scholars have shown for the principate and early empire, the boundaries of the (military excellence) norms of *virtus* were always porous and often undercut by (positive) descriptions of soft elite men: as resistance and critique, but also playfully. See, e.g., C. Edwards, *Politics of Immorality*, 36–97; Nappa, *Making Men Ridiculous*, 167–95 (satires of paternity); Pope, *Lucretius*, 22, 45–56 (Lucretius reversed the criticism of Epicureans as effeminate to argue that all men are soft); Gleason, *Making Men*, xxvi–xxix, 55–76.

100. Art historians consider the youthful visual language to be a Theodosian Renaissance: see, e.g., Kovacs, *Kaiser, Senatoren*, 91–96; Guidetti, "Between Expressionism and Classicism," 155–64, 169–71: Kiilerich, *Late Fourth Century Classicism*, 12–18, 196–219. See also chapter 5.

FIGURE 6. Nicomedia Frieze, ca. 290 CE, height: 104 cm, length: 217 cm, thickness of the block: 30 cm, depth of relief: 13 cm, height of plinth: 14 cm. Detail of the tetrarchs embracing. Mus. Inv. No. CKBG 2009/21, Exc. Inv. No. CKBG 2009/42. Credit: © Nicomedia-Çukurbağ Archaeological Project (TÜBİTAK 115K242) / Kocaeli Archaeology Museum.

Here I understand queerness not as identity but as Eve Kosofsky Sedgwick has described it: an "open mesh of possibilities, gaps, overlaps, dissonances and resonances, lapses and excesses of meaning when the constituent elements of anyone's gender, of anyone's sexuality aren't made (or *can't be* made) to signify monolithically."[101] In settling on my terminology—"*vir*-ness" and "less-than-*vir*-ness"—I hope to have found ways to describe such an exuberance, which remains firmly located on the continuum of "male" but broadens it to include eunuchs, infants, father figures, men as women, and imperial women as men, based on concepts of *vir* shaped in relation to and by tensions between elite men.[102] It is this capacious, expansive (imperial) *vir*-ness that Eutropius made visible, manifest, and legible for everyone.[103] It is a manliness as unencumbered by the strictures of gender (binaries) as the divine it represented and embodied, with one exception: like God, the emperor had to be able to become a father.[104]

WHAT DID IMPERIAL BEAUTY HAVE TO ACCOMPLISH?

Theodosius, Honorius, Arcadius, and their courts chose particular virtues and developed their imperial images in response to external and internal challenges and in order to communicate specific goals they wished to achieve. In January 379,

101. Sedgwick, *Tendencies*, 8 (emphasis hers). See also LaFleur, "Against Consensus," 366–68 (noting that Sedgwick does maintain gendered binaries); LaFleur, Raskolnikov, and Kłosowska, "Introduction," 1–24; Franco, "Byzantine Lives," 561–70; see also chapter 4. Throughout this book I identify what I consider queering moves.

102. Rather than as opposed to what, equally fluidly, was considered being a woman. I largely avoid "nonbinary" for the same reason that I don't use "masculinities": these terms convey the premodern sources inadequately (see LaFleur, "Against Consensus," 370–75). I also (see n. 93) translate only (the rarely used) *effeminatus* and its Greek equivalent as "effeminate," and not (as most translators do) terms such as *mollis* (soft, fluid, or delicate). Though I appreciate that *effeminate* characterizes masculinities because such traits matter only when displayed by male-presenting persons (Connell, *Masculinities*, 55–6, 76–81, 89–181), precise translations strengthen Burrus's observation that "the scholarly consensus [holds] that gender in antiquity was mapped not as a binary of two fixed and 'opposite' sexes . . . but rather as a dynamic spectrum or gradient of relative masculinities" ("Mapping as Metamorphosis," 4). Eder, *How the Clinic Made Gender*, 1–54, 195–230 (creation of modern notions of gender), has been enormously helpful, as have trans* studies, e.g., Keegan, "Transgender Studies," 66–87; Betancourt, *Byzantine Intersectionality*, 89–120; Moore, "Queer Theory;" Burger and Kruger, "Introduction," xi–xxiv.

103. This book considers eunuchs as part of investigating gender as it relates to late Roman imperial power, and not per se. I hope to contribute to the (aesthetic) reassessments of eunuchs in the late Roman Empire en route to their Byzantine career as angels and saints: see Tougher, "Aesthetics of Castration," 48–72; Hatzaki, *Beauty*, 86–115; Vout, *Power and Eroticism*, 136–212 (on Nero and Domitian's imperial eunuch). See Davis, *Queer Beauty*, 23–50, for a formal aesthetic approach to what one might want to call queer beauty.

104. For the ungendered divine, see, e.g., Carlà-Uhink, "'Between the Human," 3–37; Marchal, *Appalling Bodies*, 32–50 (primordial androgyny in Paul's letters); Varner, "Transcending Gender," 189–93, 196–202. See also chapter 6.

the western emperors and half-brothers Gratian and Valentinian II proclaimed Theodosius, a general without any connection to the ruling dynasty, augustus of the eastern empire. About five months earlier their uncle, the eastern emperor Valens, had perished, together with two-thirds of his army, in a catastrophic defeat by a coalition of Goths, Alans, and Huns near Adrianople (modern-day Edirne).[105] This was the second loss of an eastern emperor in sixteen years; in 363, the emperor Julian had died in battle against Persia. The disaster sent shock waves through the realm, and although scholars no longer consider it the beginning of Rome's end, this was the moment when the empire started to feel the effects of the barbarian migrations in earnest.[106]

Theodosius, at thirty-three, was the junior emperor by rank to the senior emperors Gratian (nineteen) and Valentinian II (eight). His elevation—which may well have been the western emperors' grudging legitimization of a usurpation on his part—demonstrated that merit and necessity now overrode the dynastic considerations that had led Valentinian I to elevate the young Gratian. The new eastern emperor moved to the imperial residence in Thessalonica, not Constantinople, where he remained until late 380 because of its easier access to the regions where the hostile Gothic, Alan, and Hunnic federations were located. For his campaigns against them, he had to assemble a fighting force in addition to and independent of Gratian's western army. Theodosius accomplished this—barely—over the next several years through recruitment drives. He also incorporated conquered Gothic, Alan, and Hunnic contingents into the eastern army by awarding their leaders high-ranking military positions—and corresponding incomes.[107] The restoration of the eastern army became even more urgent when the Persian ruler increased the pressure on Rome's eastern frontier. By 383, Theodosius had managed to negotiate agreements with both the Gothic contingents and the Persians, granting the former, who remained undefeated, unprecedented autonomy. This resulted in the inclusion of more Gothic commanders and troops in the eastern Roman army than ever before.[108]

Managing foreign enemies was not Theodosius's only challenge. Civil wars, provoked by usurpation within the empire in the late fourth century, resulted in massive losses of military manpower.[109] In the summer of 383 Magnus Maximus, like Theodosius also a general from Spain, declared himself augustus, moved against Gratian (whom he fatally defeated near Lyon), and took up residence in the

---

105. Amm. Marc. 13.13.18. See also Batty, *Rome and the Nomads*, 11–52, 77–150; Lenski, *Failure of Empire*, 308–19.

106. Lenski, *"Initium mali,"* 129–68; Lenski, *Failure of Empire*, 320–67; Omissi, *Emperors*, 255–90; Hebblewhite, *Theodosius*, 18–25.

107. Zos., *HN* 4.25.2–4, 4.31.2–4; Lee, *War in Late Antiquity*, 81–85; Heather, *Goths and Romans*, 150–55; Kulikowski, *Rome's Gothic Wars*, 149–52; Williams and Friell, *Theodosius*, 28–35.

108. Hebblewhite, *Theodosius*, 30–39; Williams and Friell, *Theodosius*, 41; see also chapter 5.

109. Omissi, *Emperors*, 72.

imperial palace in Trier.[110] In January of that year, Theodosius had made his five- or six-year-old son Arcadius augustus. With this action, he resumed the proclamation of children as emperors, which he need not have continued. This was also the practice's first use in the east. At the same time, he made his consort an augusta, resurrecting a title not used since Constantine.[111] Magnus Maximus followed suit by elevating his own young son as augustus in 383. Initially Theodosius, focused on establishing his dynasty in Constantinople and on managing further conflicts with Persia, tacitly accepted Magnus Maximus's rule.[112] However, in 387 the latter invaded Italy, the area under Valentinian II's control, a move that was a serious provocation to Theodosius, who now had to decide how much association with the ruling Valentinians counted for him. He opted for Valentinian II. Theodosius moved from Constantinople, where he had been living since 380, to Thessalonica to join Valentinian II, who had already arrived there from his residence in Milan, married the western emperor's sister Galla, and marched against Maximus. In the summer of 388 he defeated the usurper and executed him together with his son.[113] In 389, the eastern emperor decided to celebrate that civil war victory with his own son Honorius by conducting a triumphal entry into Rome.[114] After that celebration they returned to Milan, where they remained until 391, when they moved back to Constantinople. In 392, Valentinian II died under unclear circumstances. Within a few months, his general Arbogast elevated a certain Eugenius as the western emperor. This time Theodosius reacted more promptly. In January 393, he declared Honorius augustus in Constantinople, thus rejecting the new contender, and returned west to wage another civil war that ended after a costly battle, defeating Eugenius in 394.[115] Honorius traveled to Milan, expecting to join his father for another triumphal entry, but before that could happen, Theodosius fell ill and then died, on January 17, 395.

To succeed as emperor, Theodosius relied on his beauty—an expression of his imperial rule—to accomplish four interrelated goals. First, after the death of two successive emperors in battle, he had to convey that he was a Roman *imperator* who was reliably victorious and could manage the sudden influx of unprecedented numbers of (Gothic) foreigners into the empire.[116] Second, the representation of his power had to appeal to a geographically and culturally diverse group of military leaders with different agendas. These included westerners, some with

110. McEvoy, *Child Emperor Rule*, 83–95; Lunn-Rockliffe, "Commemorating," 319–23; Ch. Kelly, "Pliny and Pacatus," 215–16.

111. Heather and Moncur, *Politics*, 214; Holum, *Theodosian Empresses*, 31.

112. *Epit. de Caes.* 48.6; Soz., *HE* 7.13; Zos., *HN* 4.37.3, 4.71; Matthews, *Western Aristocracies*, 178–79; Omissi, *Emperors*, 263–69; Vera, "Rapporti," 267–301; Szidat, *Usurpator*, 112–13, 222–32, 282–86.

113. Soz., *HE* 7.13; Zos., *HN* 4.53; *CIL* 8.22076; Omissi, *Emperors*, 266–69; McEvoy, *Child Emperor Rule*, 87–92.

114. Claud., *IV Cons. Hon.* 169–70.

115. At the Frigidus: see Cameron, *Last Pagans*, 91–135; Heather, *Empires and Barbarians*, 190–200.

116. Roman emperors rarely died in battle: see Retief and Cilliers, "Causes of Death," 103–6.

Frankish backgrounds; key Greek eastern generals; and Vandal, Persian, and Gothic commanders, new Romans whose loyalty to himself and his sons he had to ensure.[117] Third, Theodosius had to signal that his new dynasty legitimately continued the Valentinians' while reintegrating those members of the elite who had cast their lot with those rulers' challengers. In other words, as the reader will learn in greater detail, his imperial image had to radiate both severity (to ward off further attempts at usurpation) *and* reconciliation after two civil wars.[118]

Theodosius achieved these three aims by projecting military excellence and drawing on Republican and Augustan themes of renewal, which he expressed by radiating eternal youthfulness.[119] The attractiveness of that youth was enhanced (and softened) by his (actually) young coaugusti, a pairing that strengthened the unifying force of this male beauty. Indeed, it is possible that harnessing the full powers of youth contributed to Theodosius's decision to make his sons augusti; the practice remains difficult to explain, because dynastic considerations could have been satisfied by elevating successors as caesars.[120] The emperor further excelled through his outstanding clemency and (not yet manly) mercy (*misericordia*). Loss in civil war instantly reduced former exemplary Roman *viri* to very much less-than-manly, "foreign," enslaved persons, but the emperor's *clementia* could, equally instantly, restore the losers (who had survived) back to Roman *vir*-ness: elite manliness was fragile, and Theodosius, harsh yet mild, was its arbiter.

The pairing of military hardness with progressively more pronounced youthfulness may also have allowed Theodosius to resolve a fourth important difficulty of his rule: how to visually project the form of Christianity that he, according to his divine mandate, thought his subjects ought to embrace. A year after his acclamation and while he was still in Thessalonica, the emperor sent an edict to Constantinople, where he had never been, to clarify his religious preferences in response to inquiries from clergy and lay elites there. Formulated with the help of Thessalonica's bishop, it conveyed his desire that "all the peoples" (*cunctos populos*) in Constantinople and throughout his realm should dwell in the form of Christianity that he considered universal (*catholicos*): this interpretation, defined by the bishops of Rome and Alexandria, proclaimed one deity under equal majesty (*unam deitatem sub pari maiestate*) and in the form of a pious Trinity.[121] Specifically, the emperor indicated that for him (and thus for his subjects), following the council of Nicaea in 325, God the Father was the same in essence as the Son (and the Holy Spirit); this was the message that the resurrected Christ had tasked his

117. Hebblewhite, *Theodosius*, 46.

118. Tantillo, "Emperors and Tyrants," 39.

119. Hekster, *Caesar Rules*, 111–18 (victory); Hekster, *Emperors and Ancestors*, 162–76 (longevity of the Augustan model).

120. Dench, *Romulus' Asylum*, 276–92 (dynastic impetus).

121. CTh 16.1.2; McLynn, "Moments of Truth."

apostles to spread to all the peoples, *panta ta ethne*.[122] The edict indicated that the most sacred, divine emperor and present god intended to do just that. But how could he convey to all the peoples that they were united through a universal majesty in which divine father(s) and son(s) were from the beginning in essence equal?[123] This book suggests that he accomplished this by elaborating versions of imperial beauty that creatively layered and merged mature and youthful in ways that softened and even transcended the boundaries between Romans and non-Romans, men and women, maybe even enslaved and free.[124]

Though I consider the potential theological implications of the new forms of Theodosius's, Honorius's, and Arcadius's *vir*-ness tremendously important, they function more like a *basso sostenuto* in this book—that is, I will not address them systematically. Honorius and Arcadius (and their courts) faced different challenges than their father and adjusted the imperial image accordingly. Their version of Christian doctrine remained unchanged from his, but its implementation required continuing effort tailored to local requirements.[125] Each imperial son needed to develop his own visual language of power, a task made urgent by the steadily increasing tensions between the western and eastern courts. Honorius was ten when he became the sole augustus, after a civil war: he, his court, and his most important general, Stilicho, immediately needed to consolidate an army whose members had just fought against each other, and Stilicho's claim that the deceased Theodosius had entrusted him with the military control of the entire empire was, naturally, rejected by Constantinople.[126]

As I will show in chapter 4, Honorius and Stilicho created an imperial image that expanded Theodosius's combination of hardness and softness by pairing a battle-hardened father with a son whom he was preparing for battle. That father was no longer Theodosius but now Stilicho, while the son, Honorius, embodied a youthful subtleness including that of a young woman, just as the young Achilles had done by wearing women's clothes. Marriage and actual fatherhood further anchored that new composite picture of imperial beauty: Stilicho and Honorius together represented the Old Rome's eternal youth and stability, manifested by the (anticipated) birth of many future augusti and augustae.

Arcadius was nineteen when he assumed sole rule. Though firmly ensconced in Constantinople, he too was affected by the aftermath of Eugenius's defeat. Gothic federations threatened his city and its surroundings even after the parts of the eastern army that had been in the west returned, and Hunnic and other antagonistic Gothic contingents were destabilizing the east and causing friction

122. Matthew 28:19; Luke 24:47.

123. McLynn, "'*Genere Hispanus*,'" 79–88 (Nicene background); Hunt, "Imperial Law," 57–62. See Humfress, "Ordering Divine Knowledge," 168–72, for Theodosius II's use of the *Cunctos populos* law.

124. Galatians 3:28.

125. Berzon, "Strategies of Containment," 124–49; Escribano Paño, "Social Exclusion," 42–57.

126. Börm, *Westrom*, 42–43.

with the west.[127] Still, Arcadius had already gained administrative experience by ruling the east while his father was campaigning. He used his first years of sole rule to rearrange his personnel, replacing some of Theodosius's elite supporters and promoting others, get married, father daughters, and complete many of the building projects that left a Theodosian-Arcadian mark on Constantinople. Indeed, Constantinople's increasing importance as the New Rome contributed to steadily mounting tensions with Honorius and his court, who claimed to represent the one and only *caput mundi*.[128] However, these tensions did not mean that Arcadius and Honorius no longer considered themselves together the sacred rulers of Rome, the empire.[129] On the contrary, despite their rivalries, their unity remained a cardinal tenet.

THE SEISMOGRAPHS OF POWER AND THEIR PERFORMATIVE TEXTS

Arcadius was an imperial father and secure ruler, whose eastern army had twice defeated western challengers, when he decided to make the eunuch Eutropius a consul in 399. This was as majestic a demonstration of his transformative power as arbiter of *vir*-ness as was his elevation of Theodosius II: if the emperor declared a eunuch to be a consul and *illustris vir* and an infant in diapers to be an augustus, that is what they were. But what else did Arcadius's choice of Eutropius as consul signal about imperial beauty and the manly virtues that the emperor wished to express? And how would we know? In what follows I focus on the roughly two decades leading up to the year 399 because I want to capture the moment as unencumbered by hindsight as possible. The heart of my book is a series of engaged performative texts, selected to achieve temporal and generational cohesion, what Denis Hollier (or Aristotle) calls the "unity of subject or of action."[130]

Composed by contemporary members of the elite—Pacatus, the author of the *Historia Augusta*, Claudian, Ambrose of Milan, Themistius, Synesius, and John Chrysostom—these texts reflected and reacted to imperial power, but they also allowed their writers to help create that power and influence how it operated.[131] These authors were part of the groups on whose acceptance the emperor's legitimacy depended, with which he had to negotiate. Moreover, through these texts, including how they handled manliness, these authors also negotiated and

---

127. Heather, *Goths and Romans*, 150–55; Kulikowski, *Rome's Gothic Wars*, 149–52.

128. Hekster, *Caesar Rules*, 276–85.

129. Börm, *Westrom*, 43–44.

130. Hollier, *Absent*, 2. I understand "performative" as, in Hollier's words, "a speech act that that does not leave the world within which it is produced intact. Every page of a . . . text must have the force of *actualité*, of active currency: it must weigh upon its era, engrave itself upon time, leave an indelible trace" (21).

131. Hollier, *Absent*, 22–23.

established their own standing vis-à-vis their peers: each of them wrote on behalf of himself as well as on behalf of his audience. That audience was multifaceted. It encompassed the emperor, the author's well-defined circles—the Senate, leading officials, the clergy, other empire-wide elites—and, last but not least, the entire realm, Christendom, and posterity.

Part 1 traces the period (pre-Theodosius, Theodosius, Honorius) leading up to 399, with the principal focus on the west. Here, the first performative text (discussed in chapter 1) is Pacatus's panegyric celebrating Theodosius's triumphant entry into Rome after the civil war against Magnus Maximus. Pacatus delivered this speech in the presence of Theodosius in the Senate—that is, also in the presence of senators who had supported the defeated. Modeled on Pliny's praise of Trajan, Pacatus's panegyric adds a new twist: for the first time, half is devoted to the loser, thus presenting in one text two competing models of *virtus*—Theodosius the manly versus Magnus Maximus the less-than-manly homegrown slave and monstrous eastern tyrant.[132] Chapter 2 uses a series of sources, including Themistius's *On Royal Beauty*, to talk about child consuls and boy emperors. First in chapter 1, and here again, I introduce laws regulating adult male same-sex encounters and the wearing of boots and trousers. I consider these to be, based on Sebastian Schmidt-Hofner's important article, "ostentatious legislation."[133] According to Schmidt-Hofner, such laws, though enforceable, were not primarily legislative but rather "part of a deliberate strategy . . . to use legislation as a medium of propaganda in order to consolidate and promote [the emperors'] rule at a moment of political crisis."[134] Like coins, statues, silver donatives, mosaics, and monumental buildings, they allowed emperors to communicate directly with their subjects, both as a collective and in specific groups.[135]

Chapter 3 focuses on the *Historia Augusta*'s *Life of Heliogabalus*. This *Life* crystallizes—in no uncertain terms—elite resistance to the (boy) emperor's soft beauty, and thus the challenges facing those who formulated the representation of imperial adolescents and their transitions into adulthood. Chapter 4 considers Claudian's panegyrics for Honorius as consul and, in 400, for Stilicho's consulate, which represented the countermeasures undertaken by the court in Milan to address these challenges. It culminates in Claudian's celebration of Honorius's marriage to Stilicho's daughter Maria, making the latter into the young emperor's father in addition to brother-in-law (Stilicho was married to Honorius's sister):

---

132. A perfect case of orientalism *avant la lettre*. See Osterhammel, *Die Entzauberung*, 297: "Anyone speaking of Oriental despotism around 1750 was thinking of Europe, while anyone speaking of Oriental despotism around 1800 was thinking of Asia." See also Boone, *Homoerotics*, 23–109, 362–68.

133. Schmidt-Hofner, "Ostentatious Legislation," coined the term to describe a flurry of legislation issued by Valentinian and Valens in 364 and 365, a period of high instability after the death of Julian.

134. Schmidt-Hofner, "Ostentatious Legislation," 68.

135. Lemcke, *Bridging Center*, 4–13, 87–132, 174–78 (imperial communication and empire-wide responses).

a poetic crescendo in praise of Rome's eternity thanks to Stilicho and Honorius as fathers. Chapter 5 pivots to Theodosius in Constantinople. Themistius's three orations praising the new eastern ruler demonstrate how he and Theodosius transformed the emperor's most important virtue, clemency—in its Greek iteration philanthropy, or love of (hu)mankind—into a weapon of war (that is, soft power or diplomacy). This transformation occurred at the same time as Theodosius's promulgation of another example of ostentatious legislation, the edict *Cunctos populos*. And it was accompanied by the elevation of both Arcadius and Aelia Flaccilla, Theodosius's consort, as augusti: the empress too wore the regalia of the emperor. Together, the triad of Theodosius, Arcadius, and Aelia Flaccilla, all three augusti, thus signified and embodied an increasingly capacious, fluid, subtle imperial beauty. Chapter 5 concludes back west in Milan with Ambrose's lament for the deceased Theodosius as divine emperor who loved and was loved—*dilexi*.

Part 2 is dedicated to Eutropius as consul. Unlike Theodosius and Honorius, Arcadius did not have a Pacatus or Claudian—that is, an author who cooperated with the court in formulating the emperor's praise—or at least, no evidence of such has been preserved. However, we have the reactions of members of the elites, both in Milan and in Constantinople, to Eutropius's appointments to powerful offices, culminating in the consulship. Their texts create one western and two eastern images of Eutropius, through which the authors comment on and refract Arcadius's rule. Chapter 6 features Claudian's two invectives against Eutropius. Here, the poet created this eunuch as an icon of ugliness, diametrically opposed to everything that made an emperor beautiful. This is Eutropius as seen from the western court, a monstrous threat to the empire's eternal dominance: proof that Constantinople could never aspire to equal Rome, the *caput mundi*. Claudian's brilliantly achieved "Eutropius" also shaped, in his reception, the eastern ruler who "created" him, "Arcadius" the degenerate, though the poet himself carefully preserved the sacrality of Honorius's imperial brother.

In chapter 7, Synesius's *On Kingship* offers a Constantinopolitan assessment of Eutropius, which focuses more on his office than on his condition. This eastern "Eutropius" also served to shape "Arcadius"—this time as a Platonic Christian ruler. But this ideal Arcadius was currently absent because he had concentrated too much power in the hands of a single person, Eutropius, who in turn had shared it, because of their essential kinship as eunuchlike Scythians, with one other: the Gothic general Alaric. These two, but especially Eutropius, had made Arcadius too much like themselves, too soft and jellyfishy. But as soon as Arcadius tempered that softness through new, hard, Roman advisers (namely, Synesius's friends), the real emperor would come to the fore like a new Achilles and a new Cyrus and use these two "Scythians" as they should be used: as perfect servants. The eastern Eutropius makes his final appearance in chapter 8, in the Hagia Sophia, where he begged for asylum when he fell from grace. John Chrysostom's Eutropius was *the* powerful rich man whose misuse of wealth for worldly ambition caused his downfall. In the hands of Constantinople's bishop, Eutropius became the central actor in a didactic theater. As an adornment of the altar, he showcased the power of the weapon newly wielded by the emperor and always by the bishop, as father and mother: that of philanthropy. Here, John transformed and expanded (imperial) philanthropy into affectionate love and merciful compassion. John's Eutropius thus embodied a new virtue and *vir*-ness, which encompassed everyone, the emperor included, as scarred human beings in need of the mercy and loving compassion of the one who truly granted Rome *imperium* without end: the Christian God.[136]

---

136. Virg., *Aen.* 1.279 ("imperium sine fine dedi").

PART I

Forever Young

Theodosius and Honorius in the 380s and 390s

1

Civil War Triumphs and Delicate Men

Pacatus's Panegyric *for Theodosius*

For we are not writing Histories, *but* Lives, *and in the most conspicuous deeds there is not always an example of virtue or vice. Instead, a small thing like a phrase or a joke often provides a reflection of character more than battles that kill thousands.*[1]

Moribus antiquis res stat Romana virisque.
The Roman state is built on ancient mores and on men.[2]

Early in summer 390, the Roman emperors Theodosius I, forty-three; Valentinian II, nineteen; and Arcadius, twelve, signed an imperial letter with the force of law addressed to Orientius, the deputy prefect, or *vicarius*, of the city of Rome.[3] They wished to impress upon their "most dear and delightful Orientius" that they would no longer endure

> the city of Rome, the mother of all [manly] virtues [*virtutes*], to be defiled . . . by the contamination of effeminized shame in men and that rustic strength [inherited] from the ancient founders [of the city], which has been diminished by the unmanly softening of the people, to cast disapproval on the centuries of the founders or the emperors. . . . Your praiseworthy skill will therefore seize, as the enormity of their outrage demands, all those whose habitual crime is to use their manly body in a womanly manner and to condemn it to the passive role of the sex that is not theirs [*alienus*], drag them out of (we are ashamed to use the words) brothels of men, and expiate [their crime] by means of the flames of vengeance with the people watching, so that all may understand that the lodging place of a man's soul must be sacrosanct

1. Plut., *Alex.* 1.1.2–3.
2. Cic., *Rep.* 5.1, quoting Enn., *Ann.* 156.
3. For the position of *vicarius Urbis Romae*, vicar or deputy prefect, see Sinnigen, "*Vicarius Urbis Romae*," 97–112; Ch. Kelly, *Ruling*, 72.

35

to everyone and that he who has foully thrown away his own sex and sought to be the alien [*alienus*] one will not remain without the highest penalty. Posted on the day before the Ides [14] of May at Rome in the atrium of Minerva.[4]

The imperial message was clear. The emperors, of whom Valentinian II was the most senior by rank although far younger than Theodosius, had lost patience with a custom of long standing in the city of Rome: men of very low status (*infami*) and enslaved men offering sexual service in specialized "brothels of men." To halt these practices, the rulers decreed that such persons should be subjected to the harsh penalties considered appropriate for their humble lot.[5]

Normally, however, Roman emperors did not expend a great deal of thought on the sex lives of the enslaved or others of inferior status. This was an unusual intervention, and closer reading reveals a broader scope. The emperors were reacting to the current state of Rome, "the mother of all virtues [*virtutes*]," or manly excellences, which was apparently threatened with defilement. Virtue and its preservation did not concern enslaved or other low-status male persons but were instead the responsibility of Rome's *viri*, its elite men. In other words, those who were at that moment defiling Rome's rustic strength were male members of the elite, and it was their behavior that called for the emperors' intervention. Though ostensibly targeting slaves and *infami*, therefore, the letter was addressing elite men in the city of Rome because something was so amiss among them that it required legislative attention.[6]

4. The letter is preserved in *Coll. Mos.* 5.3.1–2. I am using the edition (with modifications) of Frakes, *Compiling the Collatio*, 170 (text), 213 (translation) ("IMPP[P] Valentinianus Theodosius et Arcadius Augg[g]. ad Orientium vicarium urbis Romae: Non patimur urbem Romam virtutum omnium matrem diutius effeminati in viris pudoris contaminatione foedari et agreste illud a priscis conditoribus robur fracta molliter plebe tenuatum convicium saeculis vel conditorum inrogare vel principum, Orienti k[arissime] ac iuc[undissime] nobis. 2. Laudanda igitur experientia tua omnes, quibus flagitiosus luxus est virile corpus muliebriter constitutum alieni sexus damnare patientia nihilque discretum habere cum feminis occupatos, ut flagitii poscit inmanitas, atque omnibus eductos, pudet dicere, virorum lupanaribus spectante populo flammis vindicibus expiabit, ut universi intellegant sacrosantum cunctis esse debere hospitium virilis animae nec sine summo supplicio alienum expetisse sexum qui suum turpiter perdidisset. Prop. pr(idie). id. Maias Romae in atrio Minervae.") For further discussion see pp. 265–67. This translation (with modifications) is by Barnes, "Leviticus," 54–55; see also Harries, *Law and Empire*, 21; Masterson, *Man to Man*, 20.

5. Mathiesen, "*Provinciales, Gentiles,* and Marriages," 144–45, cautions that capital punishment was more often threatened—as a deterrent—than actually enforced.

6. For the much-discussed nexus of virtue and elite manliness, see, e.g., Masterson, *Man to Man*, 28; Gunderson, *Staging Masculinity*, 7–57, 65–67, 70–86 (beauty, dress, and manliness), 132–42 (Quintillian's comments on Terence's *The Eunuch*), 187–222 (*decus*, beauty, and love), 191 ("preservation and reproducing of a ruling class"), 195 (*vir bonus dicendi peritus*); Nappa, *Making Men Ridiculous*, 100–4, 121–26, 179–90; Kuefler, *Manly Eunuch*, 19; Humphries, "Body Politic"; Richlin, "Not Before Homosexuality"; Späth, *Männlichkeit und Weiblichkeit*, 58–120; Williams, *Roman Homosexuality*; C. Edwards, *Politics of Immorality*, 11–17, 20–22. On *vir* and *homo*, see Walters, "Invading the Roman Body," 32, but see Williams's review in *BMCR*; further bibliography in what follows.

The imperial letter's broader scope is signaled by its distinct rhetorical flourishes. It is replete with allusions to republican virtues celebrated in Virgil's *Aeneid* and cherished by Sallust and Cicero, harking back to the time before Rome's strength had been weakened by the (Greek) luxuries of the empire's success.[7] Thus, the letter or constitution contrasts the rustic strength (*agreste robur*) of the ancient founders (*prisci conditores*) with the fractured softness of people currently inhabiting the city (*fracta molliter plebe*), which inevitably led men to endure the sexual roles of women (*viri muliebria pati*). Further, as Mark Masterson has shown, the term that the writers used to signal the end of the emperors' forbearance, "non patimur," derives from *patior*, or *pati*, and the related noun *patientia*, all three of which indicated the passive sexual position proper to the other sex, "alieni sexus . . . patientia." In short, the emperors and those who drafted this letter were in the know, speaking to their peers about practices of which all of them were aware.[8]

Such literary allusions are rare in imperial laws. This has led scholars to conclude that the drafter of the law and therefore the person speaking on behalf of the emperors was a certain Virius Nicomachus Flavianus the Elder. This prominent pagan aristocrat was the *quaestor sacri palatii*, the emperor's spokesperson, with a decisive role in drafting legislation. Holding that role from 388 to 390, when he was promoted to praetorian prefect, Nicomachus was also a highly regarded historian. The emperor for whom he spoke was not Valentinian II, who was nominally in charge of Rome, but the eastern emperor Theodosius I, then residing in Milan, to whom Nicomachus soon dedicated his now lost major historical work, the *Annales*.[9] What, then, was going on in Rome

7. E.g., Virg., *Aen.* 2.472, 2.531, 9.603, 9.607; Sall., *Cat.* 11.3, 13. 3; see also Eigler, *Lectiones vetustatis*, 24, 158–64, for the significance of such Republican affinity in the shaping and cohesion of late antique Latin-speaking elites. Discussions of *mollitia* are numerous: for Republican political implications, see, e.g., C. Edwards, *Politics of Immorality*, 63–97; Lowrie and Vinken, "Married to Civil War," 263–91; the still foundational Dalla, *Ubi Venus*.

8. The term *patientia* is unusual in the context of legislation: CTh 9.7.6 (390) has it, but that law is an abbreviated version of *Coll. Mos.* 5.3.1; see also Masterson, *Man to Man*, 20–23, 25–29.

9. Tony Honoré's suggestion that Nicomachus was the author, in *Law in the Crisis of Empire*, 14, 57–58, 135, 194, has found widespread acceptance, most recently by Vitiello, "Theodosius." This law was posted—that is, potentially enforced—in Rome in May 390; it could have been signed earlier, but probably not by much because Valentinian II and Theodosius were in Milan in 390: see Seeck, *Regesten*, 277; Matthews, *Laying Down the Law*, 277–79. CIL 6.1738, an inscription mentioning Nicomachus Flavianus's history and its dedicatee, is the subject of Hedrick, *History and Silence*. For Nicomachus Flavianus's career see *PLRE* 1:348. This constitution is part of six extant laws formulated by Nicomachus Flavianus Senior as *quaestor sacri palatii*; Harries, "Roman Imperial *Quaestor*," 150–52, emphasizes that the voice of the *quaestor* merged into that of the emperor, but see the critical remarks of de Bonfils, "Considerazione sui *quaestores*," 289–314. For Nicomachus Flavianus's *Annales*, dedicated to Theodosius between 390 and 392, see Cameron, *Last Pagans*, 627–90. Interesting too are Ratti, *Antiquus error*, 140–49; Matthews, *Western Aristocracies*, 238–40; Corcoran, *Empire of the Tetrarchs*, 11.

in 390 to call for imperial intervention in Nicomachus Flavianus's exquisite legislative prose?

THEODOSIUS'S *ADVENTUS*, OR HOW TO CELEBRATE ROMAN VIRTUE AFTER A CIVIL WAR TRIUMPH

The answer is fairly straightforward. In the summer of 387, the de facto ruler of the west, Magnus Maximus, crossed a line that, in hindsight, he should not have: he invaded Italy and thus the territory nominally controlled by Valentinian II, which included Africa and therefore Rome's grain supply. Valentinian II fled from Milan to Thessalonica, then under the control of Theodosius. In response, Theodosius decided to cast his lot with the Valentinian dynasty and moved west from Constantinople to Thessalonica, where he married Valentinian II's sister Galla and prepared for battle, thus ending his low-key toleration of Magnus Maximus as the western ruler.[10] In 388, Theodosius defeated Maximus near Poetovio (today's Ptuj in Slovenia). Maximus then fled to Aquileia, where he was executed, as was his young son Flavius Victor, whom he had made coaugustus in 383 or 384, shortly after Theodosius had made his own six-year-old son Arcadius coaugustus.[11] In the summer of 389 Theodosius, accompanied by his five-year-old son Honorius, celebrated his victory with a triumphal celebration in Rome.[12] One year later, the imperial constitution targeting "brothels of men," formulated by his quaestor, was posted in the city.

Scholars frequently discuss this imperial constitution in the context of the establishment of Christian sexual norms. A common interpretation posits that this law, ostensibly banning same-sex intercourse and issued by Theodosius, an avowed Nicene Catholic, represents a milestone in the late Roman Empire's inexorable march toward a Christianized understanding of sexuality, which culminated in Justinian's repression of behaviors he considered deviant.[13] Other scholars assume that it expressed Theodosius's "appalled, violent, and temporary reaction

10. *Epit. de Caes.* 48.6; Soz., *HE* 7.13; Zos., *HN* 4.37.3, 4.71. The extent to which Theodosius recognized Maximus as legitimate remains subject to debate: see Omissi, *Emperors*, 263–69, esp. 267 for low-key acceptance; McEvoy, *Child Emperor Rule*, 103; Vera, "I rapporti"; Lunn-Rockliffe, "Commemorating," 320–23; Szidat, *Usurpatur*, 112–13, 222–32, 282–86; for theoretical conceptualizations, especially the notion of *Kaiserakzeptanz*, see Flaig, *Den Kaiser herausfordern*, 174–207.

11. Soz., *HE* 7.13; Zos., *HN* 4.53; *CIL* 8.22076; Omissi, *Emperors*, 266–69; McEvoy, *Child Emperor Rule*, 87–92.

12. According to McCormick, *Eternal Victory*, 85, Theodosius's Roman visit included "victory observances." Scholars debate whether these should be called triumphs, but as Beard, *Roman Triumph*, 289, 314–28, has convincingly argued, Roman triumphs adapted and changed over time, thus eliding categorical distinctions between them and victory observances. See also Hölscher, "Transformation of Victory," 28–40.

13. Most recently proposed by Harper, *Shame*, 141–43, 153–55; for critical views see Masterson, *Man to Man*, 27n62, and Dunning, "John Chrysostom and Same-Sex Eros," 638–69; Dalla, *Ubi Venus*, 170–73, discusses the potential imprint of Ambrose on this particular law, first posited by Seeck, *Geschichte des Untergangs*, 299, which Dalla considers unlikely.

to what he was discovering about *la dolce vita* during his stay in Rome."[14] This view might be supported by two of Ammianus Marcellinus's famous digressions in his history, or *Res gestae,* where the pagan Antiochene historian derides just such a *dolce vita.* According to Ammianus, Rome had indeed once been "the home of all virtue" (virtutum omnium domicilium Roma), but now visitors encountered a city teeming with indolent senators wrapped in extravagant silks and surrounded by dancing girls, bands of slaves, and armies of eunuchs.[15] It is easy to see why scholars think that Theodosius, also a visitor to Rome from the east, might have felt similarly and reacted with this constitution.

However, Theodosius's triumphal celebration a year earlier is far more central to this constitution and what it wished to regulate. In summer 389, Theodosius and his coemperor Honorius had celebrated a victory in a city under the control of Valentinian II without any evidence of his presence. More important, Theodosius's victory had been won in a civil war that pitted two legitimate Roman emperors against each other. As a consequence of his loss in battle, one of them was henceforth branded a usurper.[16] Among those watching the triumphal procession in the eternal *urbs Roma* were members of the elite who had supported the vanquished Maximus and were thus themselves the foe over whom Theodosius and Honorius now gloried. Granted, in 389, triumphal celebrations of bloody civil war victories were no longer a novelty in Rome. They had been introduced by the emperor Constantine after his victory over another emperor right outside the city's boundary at the Milvian Bridge in 312.[17] But they remained rare: Theodosius's was only the third such celebration. Moreover, they were a risky, fraught undertaking, as Ammianus makes clear in describing the second one, for a victory by Constantius II in 357:

> As if the temple of Janus had been closed and all his enemies overthrown, Constantius was eager to visit Rome and after the death of Magnentius to celebrate, without a title, a triumph over Roman blood [*ex sanguine Romano*]. For neither in person did he vanquish any nation that made war upon him, nor learn of any conquered by the valor of his generals; nor did he add anything to his empire . . . but he desired to display an inordinately long procession, banners stiff with goldwork, and the splendor of his retinue, to a populace living in perfect peace and neither expecting nor desiring to see this or anything like it.[18]

14. Barnes, "Leviticus," 57.

15. Amm. Marc. 14.6.21; see also 16.10.13 ("imperii virtutumque omnium larem"); the digressions are at 14.6, 28.4. See also Ross, "Ammianus;" Lizzi Testa, *Senatori, popolo,* 35–42, 48–49.

16. Whether the accession of Theodosius himself was a usurpation has long been debated. Omissi, *Emperors,* 255–90, has most recently and convincingly argued for usurpation; see also McEvoy, *Child Emperor Rule,* 71–80; Szidat, "Gaul and the Roman Emperors"; Sivan, "Was Theodosius I a Usurper?"

17. Humphries, "Emperors, Usurpers," 158–60.

18. Amm. Marc. 16.10. Cf. the less critical Them., *Or.* 3.43a–c; see also Claud., *VI Cons. Hon.* 392–396; Proba, *Cento* 1–8; Tantillo, "Emperors and Tyrants," esp. 39.

Ammianus expressed his grave misgivings while writing in Rome in the early 390s, soon after Theodosius's triumph.[19] Evidently, he did not think that the slaughter of fellow Romans deserved to be celebrated as if external enemies had been vanquished, and his opinion was shared by others who had just been present at such an occasion—Theodosius's procession—without "desiring to see this or anything like it."

One man fully cognizant of the tension that Theodosius's civil war triumph generated in Rome's elite—its male members, *viri*, above all—was a certain Latinius Pacatus Drepanius. Pacatus, a noted orator connected to the school of Bordeaux and a Christian, had traveled from Gaul to Rome in summer 389 because he had been granted the immense honor of praising the victor with a panegyric delivered on behalf of the Senate in Theodosius's presence.[20] It was a career-defining moment. If Pacatus succeeded, he could expect a meteoric rise at Theodosius's court (and succeed he did), but failure was undoubtedly an unpleasant possibility.[21] After all, he had to address the emperor on his own behalf, as a member of the Gallic elites who had supported Maximus, and on behalf of the Roman senators, many of whom had likewise supported the defeated. However, Pacatus was also entrusted with conveying the victorious Theodosius's message, so he was effectively mediating among three constituencies, not counting considerations of personal advancement.[22]

Pacatus modeled his speech on earlier panegyrics, most directly the famous one in which Pliny the Younger praised the emperor Trajan under similar circumstances: he too had supported a disgraced ruler.[23] However, Pacatus introduced a striking new feature. He was the first panegyrist to mention by name

19. That is, while writing about Constantius he would have been aware of the statues celebrating Theodosius, Valentinian II, and Arcadius as eradicators of tyrants—e.g., *CIL* 6.31413, 6.31414, 6.36959; see also Lejdegård, *Honorius*, 31–38.

20. *Pan. lat.* (2)12. Rees, *Commentary*, 112–89. See also Wienand, *Der Kaiser als Sieger*, 26–43; Omissi, *Emperors*, 269–90; Omissi and Ross, "Imperial Panegyric"; Rees, "Authorizing Freedom of Speech." On Pacatus, see Turcan-Verkerk, *Poète latin chrétien*, 71–130, 139–41 for his possible conversion from Priscillianism to Nicene orthodoxy; Rees, *Commentary*, 7–8, points out that he might have converted after 389.

21. Pacatus became the proconsul of Africa in 390, followed by a position at Theodosius's eastern court: see Rees, *Commentary*, 2–5; Matthews, *Western Aristocracies*, 86; Turcan-Verkerk, *Poète latin chrétien*, 10–12, 149–52. For brief discussions of Ammianus and Pacatus, see Lunn-Rockliffe, "Commemorating," 332–36; G. Kelly, "Sphragis," 230–31.

22. Rees, *Commentary*, 20–22.

23. Who edited the *Panegyrici Latini*, which was most likely published in late 389, remains subject to scholarly debate, though Pichon's suggestion, in "Origins of the *Panegyrici Latini*," that it was Pacatus himself, who juxtaposed his own panegyric to Pliny's, has been widely accepted. For judicious summaries of the scholarship, see Rees, *Commentary*, 45–56; Rees, *Layers of Loyalty*, 12–17; Rees, "Pacatus the Poet," 241–59; Rees, "Bright Lights, Big City," 203–22; Nixon and Rodgers, *Latin Panegyrics*, 437–47; Jussen, "Collection and Its Collective," 874n10, 879; Ch. Kelly, "Pliny and Pacatus," 215–16; Lippold, "Ideal of the Ruler."

a defeated civil war opponent whose memory had been condemned.[24] Indeed he devoted nearly half of his panegyric to characterizing Magnus Maximus as a less-than-manly foe. In short, when Pacatus celebrated Theodosius's civil war victory in summer 389, he did so by contrasting two images of elite and imperial manliness. One represented the apex of divine, imperial *vir*-ness by combining Roman Republican virtues with the sublime beauty of the *sacratissimus imperator*, while the other was a paradigm of soft, fractured less-than-*vir*-ness: a most negligent little homegrown slave (*neglegentissimus vernula*) and monstrous tyrant.

PACATUS'S PANEGYRIC

Pacatus began his speech by exalting the majesty of the Senate, of the Eternal City, and above all of the man to whom Rome owed the "liberty [he had just] protected bearing arms and . . . the dignity [he had] increased wearing the toga" (cuius et libertatem armatus adservisti et auxisti dignitatem togatus).[25] Theodosius truly was a "god we can see" (deum . . . quem videmus).[26] He "surely . . . would be elected by everyone" as the most sacred emperor because "his homeland was blessed, his house famous, his physical beauty divine, his age mature, his experience [that] of military and civilian affairs" (cui felix patria cui domus clara cui forma divina cui aetas integra cui militarium civiliumque rerum usus contigisset).[27] Pacatus's words painted a picture of a sovereign who was the best of all rulers because he combined true Roman Republican *virtus* with imperial splendor—just like Trajan, the other ideal ruler, or *optimus princeps*, who likewise had come from Spain. Following the rules of the genre, Pacatus addressed Theodosius's early years by praising both the region of his birth and his father, himself a divine gift and unique human because he excelled by combining all the virtues that were considered praiseworthy when encountered individually.[28] In short, the ruling emperor was blessed with an illustrious ancestry, whose brilliance he exceeded through his own merit: "O nobility worthy of an emperor, the leader to be the son of the man who ought to have been the leader . . . [because of] his bravery and wisdom but also . . . his bodily grace [*decore*] and dignity!—just as this your venerable beauty [*forma venerabilis*] so matches its fortune, so graces the empire, conspicuous far and wide,

24. Lunn-Rockliffe, "Commemorating," 319–28; for the complex, specifically Roman practice of memory sanctions, see E. Elm, *Damnatio memoriae*, 133–56.

25. *Pan. lat.* (2)12.1.2. See also (2)12.2.2–4, for free speech, *securitas loquendo*; Vitiello, "Theodosius' Liberty."

26. *Pan. lat.* (2)12.4.5. See also Rodgers, "Divine Insinuations," 91–96.

27. *Pan. lat.* (2)12.3.6–8. See also (2)12.7.2, (2)12.8.3, (2)12.47.2–3.

28. *Pan. lat.* (2)12.5.4 ("Dixisse sufficiat unum illum divinitus exstitisse, in quo virtutes simul omnes vigerent quae singulae in omnibus praedicantur"). See also Pernot, "What Is a 'Panegyric'?," 29–33.

that it is clearly in doubt whether your virtue more puts you in our minds or your face in our eyes!"[29]

Theodosius's beauty and virtue had been shaped in military camps, "[in] winters spent under animal skins, [in] summers sweated in between campaigns, [in] days and nights taken up fighting or standing guard, [in] most serious fights fought on land and sea."[30] However, he tempered the rough strength of his military body and the "battle-honed glory" (*bellicae rei gloria*) it had garnered with periods of civil life spent in cities and in the countryside.[31] There the future emperor "always rubbed off the rust of insidious leisure with [hard farm]work [*labor*]," rusticating like the Curii, Coruncani, and Fabricii of old who had exchanged the consular robe, or *trabea*, for the farmer's cloak once they were done fighting and ruling.[32] As emperor, Theodosius preserved these manly virtues, living as a true *princeps civilis*, civil ruler, "in public and private with the hardness of old [*priscorum duritia*]."[33] As any conscientious sovereign should, Theodosius wished to rule by example and to extend his virtues to those he governed. Thus, though he made sure that reforms began with himself, "living sparingly and with restraint," "when [he] first offered [himself] to the empire, not content to have moved far away from vices [himself, he] added [his] concern to correct the vices of others."[34]

As it happened, correcting the vices of others was a tall order. Prompted by extended exposure to the habits of the east (*Orientis usu*) and encouraged by the laxity (*remissio*) of his precursors, some elite Romans had become so "infected by their luxurious living [*quosdam luxus infecerat*]" that their habits of self-indulgence (*adulta consuetudo lasciviae*) were very nearly beyond remedy.[35] These "delicate and fluid [or lax] men [*delicati illi ac fluentes*] . . . considered themselves insufficiently chic unless their luxury had turned the year back to front, unless winter roses had swum in wine bowls, unless Falernian [wines] had broken summer ice in voluminous crystals [and unless they reckoned, as] in the case of a certain past emperor,

---

29. *Pan. lat.* (2)12.6.2–3 ("O digna imperatore nobilitas, eius esse filium principem qui princeps esse debuerit . . . non solum fortitudine atque sapientia sed decore etiam corporis et dignitate potuerit aequare!—velut tua haec forma venerabilis quam fortunae suae par est, quam longe laeteque conspicua commendat imperium, ut plane in ambiguo sit utrumne te magis nostris mentibus virtus an obtutibus vultus insinuet!").

30. *Pan. lat.* (2)12.8.3–4 ("Castrense collegium, actas sub pellibus hiemes, aestates inter bella sudatas, dies noctesque proeliando aut vigilando consumptas, gravissimas pugnas terra marique pugnatas"). On *forma, decus, durus* and *duritia*, and manliness and dignity, see Gunderson, *Staging Masculinity*, 133, 179, 192–213; for the implication of such manliness or virtue for dominion over feminized "foreigners" in Republican and early imperial authors, see Williams, *Roman Homosexuality*, 132–42.

31. *Pan. lat.* (2)12.8.2–3.

32. *Pan. lat.* (2)12.9.4–7.

33. *Pan. lat.* (2)12.20.4–6.

34. *Pan. lat.* (2)12.13.2, 3 ("parce contenteque viventem"), 1–2 ("quin ubi primum te imperio praestitisti, non contentus ipse ultra vitia recessisse, aliorum vitiis corrigendis curam adiecisti").

35. *Pan. lat.* (2)12.13.2.

FIGURE 7. Solidus of Theodosius I, obverse, Trier, 379–395 CE, gold, weight: 4.5 g, Springhead hoard, British Museum, 1965, 1203.3. © The Trustees of the British Museum.

often not a meal but a course at 100,000 sesterces."[36] Obviously only a dignified, virtuous, manly emperor such as Theodosius, harder (*duriorem*) and more frugal (*frugalitas*) than a Spartan, whose valor and very name struck terror in any barbarian, could correct such vices and liberate Rome from the grip of these delicate, fluid, lax, self-indulgent, less-than-manly men.[37]

Indeed, Theodosius's liberating and corrective intervention became urgently necessary when all of a sudden—while the sovereign battled said barbarians and cared for the well-being of the east—like a Spartacus redux the leader of a band of gladiators (*mirmilionum agmen*), pirates, and fugitive slaves (*fugitives*) rose up in the west. From small beginnings, he erupted like a pestilence to take on the imperial robes and became nothing short of a tyrant: none other than Magnus Maximus.[38] Gaul was his first target. There the raging beast (*belua furens*) drank the blood of innocents and impoverished all through his insatiable avarice. Before long, however, insanity derailed this purple-clad butcher or executioner (*carnifex*). In his demented fury he invaded Italy.[39] This prompted Theodosius to intervene. As soon as the raging beast and purple-clad butcher encountered the true ruler on the battlefield, he revealed himself to be a coward. He and his gang acted just like Herodotus's famous band of rebellious Scythian slaves had done when they

36. *Pan. lat.* (2)12.14.1–4. *Fluens* and *fluere* have positive connotations—e.g., when indicating blood flow that proves *virtus*—in addition to the negative ones of unmanly behavior: see Sen., *Prov.* 1.6, 4.4. See also Rees, *Commentary*, 273, 275 (the past emperor might have been Vitellius).

37. *Pan. lat.* (2)12.13.4, (2)12.22.1–2 ("Virtutis tuae fulmen exceperint, nominis terrore percussi"). See also Stone, "Inviting the Enemy In."

38. *Pan. lat.* (2)12.23.

39. *Pan. lat.* (2)12.24.1–6, (2)12.30.1–2.

turned their backs in flight as soon as they were threatened by whips in a fight against their master.[40]

Indeed, Magnus Maximus's men, his army, resembled their leader just as Theodosius's army was molded by him. In Pacatus's vivid presentation, Magnus Maximus's army acted like that troop of Egyptians whom Cleopatra had led against Octavian during Rome's civil wars. Sent forth by the "warm Pharus," the "soft [*mollis*] Canopes," and the Nile, "nurturer of lightweight peoples," these soldiers were shimmering in diaphanous robes and shielded themselves from harsh sunlight with light linen, advancing like "a band of dancers" to the rhythm of their rattles. Men like these soft, dancing Egyptians led by their queen now confronted Theodosius's army. These mighty soldiers had come from the Caucasus, the Taurus, and the Danube, "the hardener of huge bodies." They, like their commander, were battle-formed, "weighed down with breastplates and encased in iron," and advanced to the sound of trumpets and bugles.[41] Faced with the onslaught of these hardened bodies, Maximus's army crumbled. Tepid and soft as he was, Maximus turned his back, and "like a madman, he was flying off stunned." To further emphasize his less-than-manly, womanlike behavior, Pacatus inserted a piece of "in-character speech," or prosopopoeia, in which Maximus frantically deliberates in the manner of a tragic heroine about whether he should kill himself.[42] Of course, he is unable to muster the manly courage required to embrace such a dignified death, the best response to imminent capture.[43] Instead, this embodiment of "impiousness, lust, cruelty, and a collection of all crimes and extreme vices" dithers until being caught, after which he is despoiled of his imperial ornaments, bound, stripped naked, and decapitated.[44]

Civil war was nothing new to the Roman Empire. Everyone listening to Pacatus in the Senate on that hot summer day was familiar with the outcome of the battle of Actium, which had pitted Marc Antony and Cleopatra against Octavian, better known as Augustus.[45] But comparing Magnus Maximus to Cleopatra and Marc Antony and thus Theodosius to Augustus also highlighted an explanatory challenge that Pacatus had to overcome. By depicting Maximus and his soldiers as "Egyptian"—that is, eastern and Greek-speaking—he aligned them with the delicate, fluid softness associated with the "habits of the east" (*Orientis usu*), which Octavian then and Theodosius now had so triumphantly overcome with the true hardness of the

---

40. *Pan. lat.* (2)12.30.4–5; Hdt. 4.1–4. See also Claud., *Eutr.* 1.507–513.

41. *Pan. lat.* (2)12.33.2–5.

42. *Pan. lat.* (2)12.38.1–5; quote in Rees, *Commentary*, 391.

43. Sen., *Prov.* 1.6; Cic., *Fin.* 3; Cic., *Off.* 1.107–125; August., *De civ. D.* 1.23; and many others praised self-killing by sword as the appropriate response, as modeled by exemplars such as Cato the Younger: see Rees, *Commentary*, 393–94; Rees, "(Not) Making Faces," 56–59; S. Elm, "'Law of War.'"

44. *Pan. lat.* (2)12.31.3 ("Impietatem libidinem crudelitatem et omnium scelerum postremorumque vitiorum stare collegium?"); (2)12.43.2–4. As Hurley, *Suetonius*, 281, points out, "For the Romans, the manner of dying weighed heavily in the assessment of a life."

45. *Pan. lat.* (2)12.33.3 (Marc Antony); see also Lowrie, "Egyptian Within," 13–28.

western Roman *vir*. In short, Pacatus appeared to adhere to the dictum, eloquently elaborated by Cicero, Sallust, Lucan, and others, that those who suffered defeat in a civil war were essentially non-Roman.[46] According to this logic, a civil war in the empire could be legitimately resolved solely if the Romans who had suffered defeat had been Romans in name only: lesser men devoid of *humanitas*, led by a gladiator, pirate, or brigand.[47] Such a leader from the margins did not know how to act with virtue and thus, by definition, could not be a true Roman *vir*. Because leaders without virtue lacked restraint, they became filled with arrogance (*superbia*) and uncontrolled desire (*libido*), which led to excessive avarice and indulgence in exuberant luxuries that made men soft, tepid, and fluid or lax. These traits also shaped those who followed such a leader, so that they too were lightweight, delicate "foreigners" rather than real, hard, Roman men: *delicati illi ac fluentes*.[48] In contrast, every victor in a civil war was, per the logic of the argument, the opposite: a Roman *vir* of exceptional *virtus*, or elite manliness.[49] Such a leader's battle-hardened *forma*, or beauty, exuded austere self-control, honed through fasts and vigils and displayed through restrained simplicity, and those who followed him shared those traits. They too were quintessentially Roman *viri*, elite men.

However, all knew, first, that in this war (as in the one that pitted Antony against Octavian), Roman fighting men had battled other Roman fighting men—and it is worth highlighting that the most massive losses suffered by Roman armies in the fourth century CE were against each other rather than against external enemies.[50] Moreover, all also knew that Theodosius was the eastern emperor and had vanquished a western ruler, in a clear reversal of the traditional "ethnic" arrangement. This time, battle-hardened troops from Greek Constantinople had decimated the soft dancers of the western ruler.

Until his loss, moreover, that western emperor had resembled the eastern one to a significant extent. Indeed, the threat that the increasingly powerful Magnus Maximus represented to Theodosius's dynastic interests may well have prompted the latter to act against him after five years of considering him essentially a legitimate ruler. Like Theodosius, Maximus was a seasoned military commander originally from Spain and a Christian of the Catholic or Nicene variety;[51] moreover,

---

46. The literature on Republican and early imperial civil war rhetoric is immense: see, e.g., Gildenhard, *Creative Eloquence*, 197–218, 300–326, 334, 338–41; for a detailed analysis of early Augustan civil war rhetoric using Antony and Cleopatra, see Oliensis, *Rhetoric of Authority*, 138–43.

47. *Pan. lat.* (2)12.46.6; see also Lowrie, "Egyptian Within," 15–23; Lowrie and Vinken, "Married to Civil War," 263–91; Bartsch, *Ideology in Cold Blood*, 15–19 (dismembered bodies); Charles and Anagnostou-Laoutides, "Unmanning an Emperor"; Omissi, "Civil War" (does not mention Republican or early imperial precursors).

48. Lunn-Rockliffe, "Commemorating," 324–29.

49. Neri, "Usurpatore come tiranno;" Lizzi Testa, *Senatori, popolo*, 40–41.

50. Omissi, *Emperors*, 72.

51. In 386 Maximus promised in a letter, *Coll. Av.* 40, to Bishop Siricius of Rome—that is, in the territory of the Homoian or Arian Valentinian II—that he would further Nicene orthodoxy once in

just as Maximus seized power illegitimately in 383 by defeating the ruling western emperor Gratian, Theodosius, scholars have persuasively argued, acceded to the throne in 379 as the result of usurpation.[52] Theodosius had recognized Maximus's choice of consul for 386 and paired him with the two-year-old Honorius; statues of Maximus were displayed in Alexandria and thus throughout the east; and the imperial mint in Constantinople issued coins bearing Maximus's name.[53] Finally, as both Pacatus and his audience were well aware, the two Roman armies that had just battled each other consisted to a significant degree of non-Roman auxiliary troops—specifically Gothic, Alan, and Hunnic.[54] In Pacatus's rhetoric, defeat turned Maximus's soldiers, whether Roman, Goth, Alan, or Hun, into soft and fluid men. Like their leader, they had become less-than-manly "Egyptians" and slavelike "Scythians," who fled when faced with the whip, the quintessential instrument of a slave's torture. Conversely, Theodosius's men had all acted as and thus become true "Romans." "Goth and Hun and Alan responded to his name-call, and took his turn on watch, and feared to be noticed absent without leave. No outcry, no confusion, no pillaging—as was customary from a barbarian. . . . He demanded this alone instead of every prize and every payment—that he be called yours."[55]

Pacatus's panegyric, to reiterate, reflected his own interests as someone from Gaul—where Magnus Maximus had first exercised power and whose inhabitants might thus be accused of insufficient resistance—but also those of the Senate, on whose behalf he spoke, as well as those of the victorious emperor whom he praised.[56] His novel move, contrasting the defeated Maximus as a raging beast, purple-clad butcher, and less-than-manly, queenlike Egyptian with the apex of imperial Roman manliness and virtue, thus signaled the reception of and conveyed a message that Theodosius wanted to be clearly understood: what determined the *vir*-ness, or true Roman manliness, of a *vir*, whether emperor or member of the elite, was victory, especially in a civil war. It confirmed that the winner was divinely sanctioned and made manifest that he and those who supported him, both his soldiers and members of the ruling elite, were true Roman *viri*. Moreover, in this case it proved that Theodosius had always been a legitimate emperor and a most sacred and divine *numen*, as those who had observed his splendid, battle-hardened beauty had (or should have) known all along. Theodosius, the perfect Roman *vir* and divine ruler, battle-hardened, dignified, civil, the son of an equally

charge in Italy. Sulp., *Vit. Mart.* 20.2–3, describes Maximus's reign as following *nutus divinus*; see also Günther, *Epistulae imperatorum pontificium aliorum*, 1.88–90; Escribano Paño, "Maximus's Letters," 66–74, with further bibliography.

52. Scholars have pointed out, for example, that Gratian took five months before officially declaring Theodosius an augustus: see Omissi, *Emperors*, 255–64; McEvoy, *Child Emperor Rule*, 83–95.

53. Omissi, *Emperors*, 263–69; Vera, "I rapporti"; Lunn-Rockliffe, "Commemorating," 320–23.

54. *Pan. lat.* (2)12.32.4–5.

55. *Pan. lat.* (2)12.32.5. See also Maas, *Conqueror's Gift*, 53–57, 86–90.

56. Rees, "From Alterity to Unity." For the distinct element of self-fashioning on the part of a panegyrist, here in relation to Trajan, see Noreña, "Self-Fashioning in the *Panegyricus*," 29–44.

FIGURE 8. Solidus of Magnus Maximus, obverse, 383–388 CE, gold, weight: 4.53 g, British Museum, 1964, 1203.163. © The Trustees of the British Museum.

distinguished father, had liberated Rome and was now celebrating his victory in the city.

But this liberation also meant that Rome had been enslaved. The one who had enslaved it—and the elites there who had supported him—was, of course, Magnus Maximus, now revealed by his loss to have been nothing more than a "most negligent little homeborn slave," *neglegentissimus vernula.*[57] *Vernula* is the diminutive of *verna*, a generic term for a homeborn or homegrown slave, here further designated as male through the rare adjective *neglegentissimus.*[58] Because a *verna* or *vernula* was a homegrown slave, the term evokes the sexual role of all household slaves: namely, to be available at all times to their masters in the passive position, *pati* or *pati muliebria.*[59]

By utterly denigrating Maximus as a *vernula* and his troops as slavelike Scythians and Egyptians, Pacatus emphasized two points. However powerful Maximus had once been, he had always been a slave, because he had been born as such. Therefore, he could, by definition, never have become a true Roman *vir* and legitimate ruler. The power he had amassed had thus been only that of a raging, "foreign" brute of ambiguous gender, and his closest supporters, his *factio* or clique, shared these characteristics.[60] Yet most of the Roman elite men who had supported Maximus, now revealed as less-than-manly because enslaved by him,

57. *Pan. lat.* (2)12.31.1.

58. Rees, *Commentary*, 352–53, suggests that *vernula* also derided Maximus's claim to be related to Theodosius.

59. In Harper's apt words, in *Slavery*, 442, "The Roman slave system was a sex racket established by and for men of the higher classes"; see also Masterson, *Man to Man*, 29; Corbeill, *Sexing the World*, 5–11.

60. For the depiction of the civil war opponent's followers as a *factio*, see Sall., *Iug.* 31.15; *RGDA* 1; Leppin, "Coping."

had once been true Roman *viri*. Consequently, once liberated from their enslavement, they could be restored to their former status.

The outcome of a civil war was, thus, transformative. It made the commanders and their supporters into either true, battle-hardened Roman *viri* or less-than-manly *delicati, fluentes* non-Romans afflicted by "Oriental customs," regardless of the actual ethnic affiliations or earlier battle experiences of those concerned. It also offered the possibility of restoration. Still, Pacatus's celebratory words left little doubt—not that any of those listening had much doubt to begin with—that every Roman *vir* could turn into a less-than-manly, slavelike, lascivious villain in an instant. All he had to do was back the wrong leader. In short, in 389 and 390, elite *vir*-ness in the city of Rome was a fraught and fragile affair.

CIVIL WAR TRIUMPHS: THE USURPER AS TYRANT

You know that Romans must march against the barbarians in all cases but when Roman fights Roman the goal must be the correction of mistakes. When it is possible to cure an ailing body part by using medicine but the healer elects to cut it off, he doesn't cure the whole organism but weakens it for what is left. In the same way the entire Roman Empire is one like a city: harm affects us all alike.[61]

Pacatus's innovative decision to devote nearly half of his panegyric to shaping the loser Magnus Maximus into a less-than-manly *vernula* allowed him to emphasize with great intensity the transformative power of victory and the enormous costs of loss in civil war. Nothing could make the latter more vivid than the contrast between the victorious Theodosius, the epitome of imperial divine beauty and hence virtue, and Magnus Maximus figured as a house slave. However, Pacatus, who spoke for Rome's Senate as well as for Theodosius and his court, was well aware of the problematics of praising a civil war victory, of publicly highlighting that (elite) Roman men, *viri*, had defeated other (equally elite) Roman men, that Roman emperors had beaten other Roman emperors—in short, that Roman imperial and elite *vir*-ness could be so speedily and profoundly transformed.[62] Pacatus had come well prepared. He had in all probability edited the *Latin Panegyrics* and was at any rate familiar with the earlier panegyrics in that collection.[63] Two of

61. Them., *Or.* 7.16.94c-d (καὶ ὅτι βαρβάρων μὲν Ῥωμαίους ἄχρι παντὸς ἐπεξιέναι προσήκει, Ῥωμαίοις δὲ μέτρον ἐπικεῖσθαι κατὰ Ῥωμαίων, τὴν τοῦ πταίσματος ἐπανόρθωσιν. καὶ ὥσπερ σώματος ἑνὸς τὸ μέρος τὸ ἀρρωστῆσαν ὁ θεραπεύειν ἐνὸν φαρμάκοις ἀποκόπτειν προαιρούμενος οὐκ ἰᾶται τὸ σύμπαν, ἀλλ᾽ ἀσθενέστερον ποιεῖ τῷ ἐλλείποντι, οὕτω καὶ τῆς ἀρχῆς μιᾶς οὔσης τῆς ὅλης Ῥωμαίων ὥσπερ πόλεως, ἀκριβῶς ἅπαν γίνεται βλάβος).

62. As Amm. Marc. 16.10.1–2, criticizing Constantius II's triumph, confirms; see also Humphries, "Emperors, Usurpers."

63. Jussen, "Collection and Its Collective," 871–74; Ch. Kelly, "Pliny and Pacatus," 224–26; Lunn-Rockliffe, "Commemorating," 324–32; McCormick, *Eternal Victory*, 40–46.

these, one by an anonymous author speaking in Trier in 313 and the other delivered by Nazarius in Rome in 321, were the first to praise a civil war triumph. They presented the new imperial message with remarkable consistency.[64]

Maxentius, Constantine's brother-in-law and his opponent at the battle of the Milvian Bridge, had been declared augustus in Rome in 306. He was supported by many aristocrats, including a significant part of the Roman Senate. After Maxentius's loss, Constantine and his court crafted the triumphal procession to carry their message unambiguously, inviting these men to celebrate their own defeat.[65] For example, while the authors of earlier panegyrics had focused on detailed descriptions of foreign campaigns to highlight the military prowess of their subjects, studiously avoiding descriptions of brutal battles against other Romans, the anonymous panegyrist and Nazarius portrayed Constantine's engagement in this civil war as hands-on: he was present during the fiercest melees.[66] The bloodier the battle, the greater Constantine's divine virtue. He was a divine presence (*praesens numen*), storming into the densest fray to emerge with "heaving breast, and bloodied hands. . . . [He was] most savage in battle and most gentle when safety [had] been procured."[67] Such direct involvement was necessary because Constantine's opponents, according to the panegyrists, were not those "little Greeks" (*Graeculi*) known from earlier civil wars.[68] Rather than "weak Medes, unwarlike Syrians, the Parthians' flighty arms, and Asians desirous of a change of enslavement, [Constantine] had to conquer soldiers [who were]—for shame!—Roman shortly before, armed with every weapon in the manner of the first rank and, because of their consciousness of wrongdoing, prepared never to yield except in death."[69] Constantine had vanquished battle-hardened Roman

64. Both authors were conscious of the novelty of their argument: see Wienand, *Der Kaiser als Sieger*, 200–5, 210–15; Omissi, *Emperors*, 123–24.

65. *Pan. lat.* (12)9.18.3 (*ioci triumphales*); (4)10.30.5, (4)10.32.1: (*triumphus*). The representational challenge was significant regardless of whether Constantine's entry into the city in 312 was an actual triumph or a triumphant *adventus*; Wienand, "*O tandem felix*," argues for a triumph, while Diefenbach, *Römische Erinnerungsräume*, 126, is more cautious; see also Rees, *Commentary*, 16; n. 12 above. For processions in the context of elite representation, see Borg and Witschel, "Veränderungen im Repräsentationsverhalten," 104–5; for a summary of the abundant scholarship on the battle of the Milvian Bridge and its antecedents, Omissi, *Emperors*, 117–44.

66. Wienand, *Der Kaiser als Sieger*, 98–127, 139–46 (a panegyrist's need to adjust to rapidly changing circumstances), 152–65 (earlier rhetorical strategies to temper cruelty toward a civil war opponent), 199–225, with further bibliography.

67. *Pan. lat.* (12)9.9.4–5 ("Densissimis hostium globis miscuisti . . . in media hostium tela deveneris et, nisi uiam tibi caedibus aperuisses"); (12)9.10.3–5 ("Anhelum pectus, cruentas manus et quidquid de sanguine profundae caedis emerserat . . . in proeliis ferocissimus et parta securitate mitissimus"); trans. Nixon and Rodgers. See also *Pan. lat.* (4)10.26.1–5.

68. *Pan. lat.* (12)9.6.1–2, (12)9.24.1–2.

69. *Pan. lat.* (12)9.5.3 ("Contra leves Medos et imbelles Syros et Parthorum arma volatica et Asiaticos optantes mutare servitium rem gesit proelii unius eventu: tibi vincendi erant milites (pro nefas!) paulo ante Romani, armis omnibus more primae classis armati et pro facinorum conscientia numquam nisi morte cessuri"). See also *Pan. lat.* (4)10.14.3–5, (4)10.17.3–18.6, (4)10.22.3–4, (4)10.24.1–7.

contingents, *Subalpini*, which had forced him to shed so much blood "that victory itself became almost distasteful" (*paene displicuit ipsa victoria*).[70] These were real confrontations on savage battlefields rather than vehicles for the panegyrist to highlight the emperor's subsequent acts of clemency.[71]

In the hands of these two panegyrists, Constantine's battle-hardened *Roman* opponents served to enhance his extraordinary military *virtus* and therefore the undeniable magnitude of his divine *vir*-ness. Like Pacatus after them, these panegyrists also stressed the emperor's power to mold his men and enhance their manliness and, conversely, the destructive power of Maxentius to lessen that of his followers. Here they introduced a novel argument. Because Constantine had defeated true Roman soldiers, "armed with every weapon in the manner of the first rank," rather than mere pirates, bandits, or foreigners, his opponents' willful abandonment of their true Roman virtues required explanation. According to Constantine's panegyrists, this wrongdoing was possible only because these men had been under the sway of a Roman leader who was extraordinary in his negative power: in short, they had been seduced by a tyrant.

The two panegyrics in praise of Constantine mark the beginning of the late Roman custom of conflating usurper and tyrant.[72] No adversary of a reigning emperor had ever been designated as a *tyrannus*, certainly not in official documents or inscriptions, when Constantine introduced this use of the term after his victory over Maxentius in 312.[73] Maxentius was the antithesis of a good ruler: he may have been a legitimate emperor, recognized by the Senate and residing in Rome, but he was very, very bad, even more debauched than if he had been a robber, bandit, or foreigner.[74] As a tyrant, he also became an internal enemy as an emblem of absolute illegitimacy, a vile leader supported by a small coterie of equally vile followers. The (allegedly) illegitimate son of the emperor Maximian (*Maximiani suppositus*), Maxentius was a hideous, deformed prodigy (*turpissime, deforme prodigium*), "contemptibly small in stature, twisted and slack of limb," an abomination, a disgrace (*dedecus*), a monster (*monstrum*).[75] Victory over this vile *monstrum* cravenly squatting in the city required exceptional brutality because Rome's liberty (*libertas*) had been at stake, as Constantine's triumphal procession made vividly clear.[76]

70. *Pan. lat.* (12)9.5.5, (12)9.7.3, (4)10.7–8.

71. Wienand, *Der Kaiser als Sieger*, 211–14. See also Grünewald, *Constantinus Maximus Augustus*, 63–77.

72. Barnes, "Oppressor, Persecutor, Usurper," 60–62; Neri, "Usurpatore come tiranno," 73–86.

73. Constantine promulgated three laws, two in 312 and one in 313, abolishing acts of the *tyrannus* (CTh 15.14.3–4, 5.8.1), and a day celebrating the eviction of the tyrant was added to the Roman calendar, probably after the victory over Maxentius: see Tantillo, "Emperors and Tyrants," 28–29.

74. Tantillo, "Emperors and Tyrants," 36–37.

75. *Pan. lat.* (12)9.4.3–4, (12)9.7.1, (12)9.17.2, (12)9.17.3.5, (12)9.17.3.4. For a recent discussion of the monstrous in Horace and Ovid, inter alia, see Emmrich, *Ästhetische Monsterpolitiken*, 11–18, 31–86. For descriptions of Constantine's corresponding sublime beauty, see, e.g., *Pan. lat.* (4)10.14.3–5.

76. *Pan. lat.* (12)9.14.2–3, (4)10.29.5–30.3.

"After the body [of Maxentius, drowned in the Tiber] had been found and hacked up, the entire populace of Rome broke out in vengeful rejoicing, and throughout the whole city where it was carried affixed to a spear that sinful head did not cease to suffer disfiguration, and meanwhile, in the customary jests of a triumph [*ioci triumphales*], it was mocked."[77] Constantine's triumphal *adventus* was "the first time in Roman history [that] the head of a toppled emperor was paraded through the city . . . to the jubilation of the masses," a fate previously reserved for the subdued whom the Senate declared *hostis publicus*, or public enemy.[78] As Nazarius emphasized, the emperor was a victorious warrior splattered with the blood of Roman soldiers rather than that of "timid creatures unfit for war, such as the pleasant regions of Greece and the charms of Asia produce, who can barely tolerate a light cloak and silken garments."[79] A dismembered corpse was all that was left of the monstrous tyrant who had enslaved the city, denigrated as *vernula purpuratus*, a "little homeborn slave draped in imperial purple"—the same term that Pacatus later used in defaming Maximus as a *vernula neglegentissimus*.[80] Consequently, Constantine was now celebrating a powerful victory, more significant than the crushing of barbarian foes or the defeat of a bandit-like usurper. He had vanquished a tyrant—and that meant someone who had been a *princeps*, however *malus*—and thus liberated a Rome that this tyrant had enslaved.[81] The Senate did not hesitate to express its gratitude, as evidenced by its members' commissioning of the Arch of Constantine. Here they not only represented Romans fighting Romans, an absolute rarity, but also memorialized Constantine as the avenger of the Senate and the Republic by divine inspiration: "cum exercito suo tam de tyranno quam de omni eius factione uno tempore [i]ustis rem publicam ultus est armis."[82] Constantius II followed Constantine's precedent, celebrating a triumphal *adventus* in Rome in 357, five years after his victory over Magnentius, at which he

77. *Pan. lat.* (12)9.17.2–3. See also (4)10.31.4–5; Wienand, *Der Kaiser als Sieger*, 217.

78. Wienand, "*O tandem felix*," 183–87, quote at 177; Kristensen, "Maxentius' Head," 323–39; McCormick, *Eternal Victory*, 40–46; Östenberg, *Staging the World*, 189–99, 225–30, 248–51 (for the placement of captives and spoils during triumphs). Claud., *Bell. Gild.* 427 proves that declaring someone a *hostis publicus* remained a senatorial prerogative, even if the emperors usually took the initiative.

79. *Pan. lat.* (12)9.24.1–2.

80. *Pan. lat.* (12)9.16.3. See also Humphries, "Emperors, Usurpers," 157–58; Wienand, *Der Kaiser als Sieger*, 240–43.

81. Omissi, *Emperors*, 21–40.

82. *CIL* 6.1139 ("To the emperor Flavius Constantine the great, pious, and fortunate, because he avenged the republic on both the tyrant and all his faction by divine inspiration [*instinctu divinitatis*] and his own greatness of spirit [*mentis magnitudine*] with his army at once in rightful battle, the Senate and People of Rome dedicated this arch as a mark of triumph"). See also Wienand, *Der Kaiser als Sieger*, 211–22. Constantine's building program underscored the message in a lasting manner: see Diefenbach, *Römische Erinnerungsräume*, 122–33; Curran, *Pagan City and Christian Capital*, 219–36; Angelova, "'By Divine Inspiration.'"

too was hailed as the restorer of the city of Rome and extinguisher of a pestiferous tyranny (*extinctor pestiferae tyrannidis*).[83]

MAKING MEN MANLY AGAIN

> *The fact is that if—as the argument so far suggests—you are the mind of the state and the state is your body, you see, I think, how essential clementia is: you are showing mercy to yourself when you seem to be showing it to someone else. So you should show mercy even to citizens who deserve condemnation just as you would to ailing limbs. And if there is ever a need to let blood, you should restrain the blade to stop it cutting more deeply than is necessary.*[84]

Constantine's (and later Constantius's) presentation of civil war victory as Rome's liberation from the tyrannical rule of a monstrous erstwhile coemperor made a further move possible. As a tyrant, Maxentius had enslaved Rome's men, its *viri*. According to traditional norms, tyrants, even more than foreigners and bandits, lacked all self-control and were thus themselves enslaved to their unfettered desires, which made them into less-than-manly persons of ambiguous gender. Maxentius's tyranny had made all Roman elite *viri*, especially those who supported him, less-than-manly too. However, Constantine's victory and their resulting liberation offered the potential for those who had supported the "stupid and worthless animal" (*stultum et nequam animal*) to return to their former status as Roman *viri*. One signal aspect of civil war that earlier authors had particularly stressed was the demand that the victorious party show clemency. Once subdued, foreign barbarians could and indeed ought to be crushed and only sparingly extended clemency. This was not the case for the opponents in a civil war. Rather, the greater the civil war victory, the more clemency should be extended. Thus, after he had defeated the tyrant Maxentius, Constantine showed his merciful clemency by returning to Rome, as Romans, "all those private individuals whom that monstrous plague [*illa monstrosa labes*] made exiles from their own homes," thereby uniting all the people of the liberated *res publica* under his virtuous rule.[85]

In praising Theodosius's triumphal procession through Rome, Pacatus took these notions one step further. Though the procession did not feature Magnus Maximus's severed head on a stake (it had already been carried through the provinces and may have been the worse for wear), Pacatus, as Sophie Lunn-Rockliffe has

---

83. *CIL* 6.1158; see also 6.1163. Tantillo, "Emperors and Tyrants," 16–34, highlights the concentration of such representation in Rome and Constantinople.

84. Sen., *Clem.* 1.5.1 ("Nam si, quod adhuc colligitur, tu animus rei publicae [tuae] es, illa corpus tuum, uides, ut puto, quam necessaria sit clementia; tibi enim parcis cum uideris alteri parcere. parcendum itaque est etiam improbandis civibus non aliter quam membris languentibus, et, si quando misso sanguine opus est, sustinenda est <acies> ne ultra quam necesse sit incidat"). See also 2.2.1.

85. *Pan. lat.* (12)9.14.3. See also (4)10.33.6–7.

shown, created vivid word pictures of the decapitated "tyrant" that made it easy for those listening to envision Maximus's naked dismembered body.[86]

> Immediately, the bravest generals ready themselves to set up the triumph, the diadem is shaken from his head, his clothing is snatched off his shoulders, the ornaments torn from his feet; finally the whole man is fitted for his deserts. The public despoiler is publicly stripped, the rapacious hands are bound, the fugitive's legs are laid bare; finally he is brought before your eyes such as befits a captive to be brought before his victor, a slave before his master, a tyrant before his emperor.[87]

It is a haunting picture of emasculated humiliation, designed to ensure that no one, neither those present nor anyone else in the realm, would forget the lesson anytime soon: "It is relevant to the security of all ages that what is done is seen, so that if anybody has ever conceived of wicked ambitions, having reviewed the monuments of our era, he should drink in innocence through his eyes. Whenever anybody thinks to clothe his shoulders in regal purple, let Maximus, stripped, occur to him. Whoever desires gold and jewels for his non-imperial feet, let Maximus appear to him with his bare soles. Whoever considers placing a crown on his head, let him see Maximus's head torn from his shoulders and the torso without a name."[88]

But then Pacatus contrasted this powerful picture with another one. "With the exception of a few of the enemy Moors, whom like some hellish battle line [Maximus] had shut in with himself when going to die, and two or three of the furious gladiator's trainers slaughtered in atonement for the war, an enfolding pardon surrounded all the rest, as if in a maternal embrace"—the maternal embrace of Rome, the mother of all virtues, including those of the mild and clement ruler.[89] Even on the battlefield, Theodosius had hesitated to torture the loser, while others had deliberated how to despoil Maximus's corpse even further. The emperor had "lowered [his] eyes and reddened [his] face with a blush and [was] beginning to speak with pity," with a mother's *misericordia*.[90] Indeed, "nobody's goods were confiscated, nobody's freedom punished, nobody's previous rank diminished. Nobody was branded with a stigma. . . . All were restored to their own homes, all to their

86. Lunn-Rockliffe, "Commemorating," 324–32. See also Brilliant, "'Let the Trumpets Roar!,'" 222–28; Ch. Kelly, "Pliny and Pacatus," 224–26; McCormick, *Eternal Victory*, 40–46.

87. *Pan. lat.* (2)12.43.2–4 ("Actutum fortissimi duces instruendo accinguntur triumpho, capiti diadema decutitur, humeris vestis aufertur, pedibus ornatus evellitur, totus denique homo aptatur ad meritum. Publice publicus spoliator exuitur, nectuntur manus rapaces, nudantur crura fugitivo, talis denique tuis offertur oculis qualem offerri decebat victori captum, domino servum, imperatori tyrannum"). See also *Pan. lat.* (2)12.31.1–2.

88. *Pan. lat.* (2)12.45.1–3. Cf. Virg., *Aen.* 2.557–558, on the death of Priam; see also Lunn-Rockliffe, "Commemorating," 329–30.

89. *Pan. lat.* (2)12.45.5–7. Pacatus was probably referring here to Maximus's generals, including Andragathius, who drowned himself: see Leppin, "Coping," 207–9.

90. *Pan. lat.* (2)12.44.2.

wives and children, finally all to innocence (which is sweeter). See, emperor, what you achieved by this clemency: you made it that with you as conqueror, to himself nobody seems conquered."[91] The city that had witnessed so many civil wars finally saw one "finished by . . . the peace of the soldiers, the recovery of Italy, your own freedom; you [Rome] saw finished, I say, a civil war for which you could decree a triumph."[92]

As a consequence of his immense, divine clemency, Theodosius's civil war victory granted victory even to the vanquished. Because his imperial beauty, *vir*-ness, and sacrality were so powerful, they could transform those whom the deformed *monstrum*, purple-clad butcher, and little *verna* had made into a coterie of soft, less-than-manly men, *delicati illi ac fluentes*, back into victorious and thus proper Roman senators and elite *viri* in an instant—as if they had never lost their Roman manliness. Granted, a few henchmen (*satellites*) suffered swift sanctions, but all it took to restore most of Maximus's erstwhile delicate supporters to unity, innocence, Roman virtue, and manly dignity was Theodosius's imperial fiat through his merciful clemency.[93]

This was what Pacatus wanted to highlight in his capacity as the speaker on behalf of the Senate. Through him, the assembled senators, all *clarissimi, spectabiles*, and *illustris viri*, signaled to Theodosius that they understood the lesson the panegyrist was so eloquently elaborating. After all, already in 388 (just after Maximus's bloody defeat), Rome's urban prefect had erected three statues in front of the Senate house, or *curia*, where Theodosius had certainly stopped during his *adventus* to address the people prior to entering. These statues honored Theodosius, Valentinian II, and Arcadius as *extinctori tyrannorum*.[94] As Pacatus forcefully suggested, Theodosius could now afford to be extravagant in granting his transformative clemency to all present. Moreover, the panegyric reflects a consensus that Theodosius as the conquering victor became the arbiter of both manliness and Romanness, at least as far as members of the ruling elites—some of whom needed his clemency to have these qualities restored—were concerned.

Among the significant number of elite Roman men who had supported Magnus Maximus was the senator Quintus Aurelius Symmachus.[95] In 387, he had traveled

91. *Pan. lat.* (2)12.45.6–7.

92. *Pan. lat.* (2)12.46.4.

93. *Pan. lat.* (2)12.29.3 ("satellites"). Pacatus repeatedly exhorted Theodosius's clemency: see, e.g., *Pan. lat.* (2)12.24.2–3, (2)12.36.3–4, (2)12.45.5–7, (2)12.46.4; Ambrose concurred: see *De ob. Theod.* 1, 12–13; also Raspanti, "*Clementissimus imperator*," 45–56.

94. *Pan. lat.* (2)12.47.3 ("Qualem te Urbi dies primus invexerit; quis in curia fueris, quis in rostris"). The statues are no longer extant, but see *CIL* 6.1154, 6.36959, 6.3791a–b. After Constantine, emperors shortened the triumphal parcour, no longer ascending to the Campidoglio but instead ending at the Forum, where they addressed the people from the *rostra* and then the Senate in the *curia*: see Liverani, "Roma tardoantica come spazio," 494–98, 591–93.

95. Symm., *Ep.* 2.32; Matthews, *Western Aristocracies*, 229–31; McLynn, *Ambrose*, 311–12; Sogno, *Q. Aurelius Symmachus*, 76; Machado, *Urban Space*, 63–83, 111–16.

to Milan to deliver a now lost panegyric in praise of Magnus Maximus. In a letter he sent in 389 to his good friend Nicomachus Flavianus the Elder, he voiced his deep fear that this choice might mean he could never return to his status as a distinguished senator and *illustris vir*, or utterly illuminated man. However, in the fall of that year, Theodosius pardoned and rehabilitated him, awarding him the consulship for 390: *illustris vir redux*.[96] In short, as Sextus Aurelius Victor, the urban prefect for 388 and 389, stated in the inscription on the base of a new statue honoring the emperor in the Forum of Trajan, while in Rome, Theodosius "exceeded the clemency, uprightness, and generosity of the emperors of old." As a distinguished historian of emperors, Aurelius Victor knew whereof he spoke.[97]

SACROSANCT *VIR*-NESS

This, then, was the immediate context of the imperial letter regulating soft and fractured Roman men who voluntarily assumed the sexual role of women, formulated by Nicomachus Flavianus and posted in the same Forum of Trajan in the summer of 390. Evocations of the hardness of Rome's rustic founders and the frugal austerity of its Republican heroes and condemnations of the delicate softness of the present-day elites, enslaved by luxurious desires (*libido*) and derailed by the blind arrogance (*superbia*) of unfit rulers, had little to do with an unusual spell of *la dolce vita* in Rome during the 390s or the inexorable forward march of Christian sexual ethics.[98] Rather, elite authors such as Ammianus, Pacatus, and Nicomachus Flavianus—the latter two speaking for Theodosius and his court—were grappling with thoroughly contemporary concerns: how to deal with usurpation, civil war, and their aftermath.[99] In addressing and seeking to influence, through their writing, urgent matters of the day, they used expansive degrees of elite masculinity to think and, as spokesmen of the imperial court, to legislate with: what should elite *vir*-ness look like under the intense pressure of potential and actual usurpation and thus the specter of civil war?

The full text of the imperial constitution cited at the beginning of this chapter has been preserved in the so-called *Collatio legum mosaicarum et romanarum*,

---

96. Symm., *Ep.* 2.13, 2.30–31; Sogno, *Q. Aurelius Symmachus*, 68–79.

97. *CIL* 6.1186. On the statue, see Chenault, "Statues of Senators," 122–24; Ch. Kelly, "Pliny and Pacatus," 219. On Aurelius Victor's career and his *De Caesaribus*, see Bird, *"Liber De Caesaribus,"* vii–xii. See also Lizzi Testa, *Senatori, popolo*, 35–40.

98. For further Republican *exempla*, see Vitiello, "Theodosius' Liberty," 573–98.

99. Lunn-Rockliffe, "Commemorating"; Ch. Kelly, "Pliny and Pacatus," 217–38. Ammianus's digressions have been read as autobiographical asides through which his intended and actual readership can be identified. Beginning with G. Kelly, *Ammianus Marcellinus*, 72 (use of first-person narrative), 104–58, recent research argues for the late Roman elites in general rather than a particular subset of that elite (such as the Senate) as the audience: see Rohrbacher, "Ammianus's Roman Digressions"; Frakes, "Ammianus Marcellinus"; Sánchez Vendramini, "Audience of Ammianus Marcellinus"; Ross, "Ammianus," 357–58; Sogno, "Persius," 370–77.

assembled shortly after 390 in or near Rome, in all probability by a Christian or Jewish jurist who wished to demonstrate to fellow jurists and members of the imperial administration that Roman and Mosaic law were compatible.[100] Unlike Nicomachus Flavianus, its anonymous compiler did not belong to the upper echelons of the elite, but he too was concerned with proper male behavior.[101] Three of his sixteen topic sections, or "Titles," address illicit sexual relations (*stuprum*), and one of those three is devoted to men having intercourse with other men.[102] To demonstrate the extent to which the Mosaic law prohibiting such intercourse (Lev. 20:13) corresponded to the recent imperial legislation, the compiler copied the official text from the tablets posted in the atrium of the Temple of Minerva soon after they were put up. Perhaps because this constitution was so recent, the compiler did not note the consular year, which we can derive, however, from the much shorter excerpt that survives in the Theodosian Code, copied from tablets posted in the Forum of Trajan.[103] In accordance with their conventions, the editors of the Theodosian Code reduced the constitution to what they considered essential: "All those who are in the shameful habit of treating the male body as if it were a woman's and condemn it by enduring what is appropriate to the other sex . . . shall expiate a crime of this sort, as the enormity of their disgrace demands, [by being burned] with avenging flames in full view of the people."[104] Gone from the later version are all the specifics of the original, because in the 430s the important thing was that passive partners during intercourse between men deserved to be punished.[105]

100. *Coll. Mos.* 5.3; Frakes, *Compiling the Collatio*, 140–51. Barnes, "Leviticus," 46–62, argues that the compiler was Jewish and merely altered an existing collation after 390. Both conjectures are part of a long scholarly discussion of the text and its compiler, as the bibliographies make clear: for an overview of recent scholarship and an argument for a competent jurist as the author, see Pilipow, "Jeweled Jurist"; Ratti, *Polémiques*, 156–60, posits Jerome as the compiler; Letteney, *Christianization of Knowledge*, 247, points to a debate over whether Ambrosiaster was the author.

101. Dalla, *Ubi Venus*, 165–74.

102. Namely, Titles 4–6: see Frakes, *Compiling the Collatio*, 99–101, 257–73 (illicit sexual relations).

103. CTh 9.7.6 ("Idem AAA. Orientio vicario urbis Romae: Omnes, quibus flagitii usus est virile corpus muliebriter constitutum alieni sexus damnare patientia, nihil enim discretum videntur habere cum feminis, huiusmodi scelus spectante populo flammae vindicibus expiabunt. Pp. in foro Traiani VIII id. Aug. Valentiniano A. III et Neoterio conss"). See also Barnes, "Leviticus," 57–58; Vitiello, "Theodosius," 320; Frakes, *Compiling the Collatio*, 81; Dalla, *Ubi Venus*, 183–84.

104. The Theodosian Code typically contains only highly adapted, shortened, or excerpted versions of the earlier laws, edicts, and decrees: see Matthews, *Laying Down the Law*, 279; Barnes, "Leviticus," 56. Chastagnol, "Trois études," 89n29, thinks that this text is an excerpt.

105. It is tempting to read Ambrose's *Ep.* 15 (*Maur.* 69), in which he addresses the rarely discussed prohibition of Deut. 22:5 against men dressing as women, in the context of *Coll. Mos.* 5.3, but the letter, included in the collection he published between 395 and 397, cannot be securely dated. In it, in traditional Roman Republican terms of virtue/manliness, Ambrose chastises men who dressed as women as slaves of *luxuria*, influenced by foreign habits. For the dating, see Liebeschuetz, "Letters of Ambrose of Milan," 100–2; Doerfler, "Coming Apart at the Seams," 39–47.

However, that was not the driving force of the original. As discussed above, this letter, which reflected the imperial intent, ordered the punishment of *infami*. Yet befitting "ostentatious legislation," its aim was far broader.[106] Just like Pacatus's republican-inspired praise of Theodosius as a *civilis princeps* intent on correcting delicate men, the letter emphasized terms such as *vir, virilitas,* and *virtutes,* evoking Rome's illustrious Republican past through reference to the virtues of its rustic founders.[107] Moreover, it concluded with a forceful explication of the constitution's pedagogical aim: to ensure, through the *summum supplicium* of the *infami,* "that all may understand that the lodging place of a man's soul [*hospitium virilis animae*] ought to be sacrosanct for everyone."

As Mark Masterson has convincingly argued, the rhetorical tenor of the constitution suggests that these *infami* were adult men.[108] This is an important observation. Prostitution by adult males who assumed the passive sexual position was nothing new in Rome (or elsewhere), but targeting them in such a way was unusual. So was Nicomachus Flavianus's use of the term *vir* and its cognates to characterize these persons and their workplace: *virorum lupanariae, in viris pudor, virile corpus, virilis animae hospitium.* Normally, those who assumed the passive role in male sexual intercourse and at times looked like women were low-status or enslaved prepubescent boys or eunuchs. If they were past puberty or adults, earlier sources called them *cinaedi* or *ex(s)oleti.*[109] What they were decidedly not were *viri,* (actively penetrating) men of elite status whose lives were governed by *virtutes,* the codes of elite male behavior. According to Masterson, "The result is that the appearance of the word *vir* attributes a desire for men to men," which the drafter of the law seems to have acknowledged, because he did not use the technical vocabulary that would have relegated the object of these desires to the status of non-men—that is, men who behaved as women. Masterson continues, "If the deployment of *vir* in the *Collatio* 5.3 is read against expectations for its meaning recoverable from other sources . . . late-ancient disagreement about the meaning of *vir* becomes visible."[110] I could not agree more: indeed, once placed firmly into the context of 389, this disagreement assumes far greater historic specificity and sharpness.

---

106. Schmidt-Hofner, "Ostentatious Legislation."

107. *Pan. lat.* (2)12.20.4–6.

108. Masterson, *Man to Man,* 25–29; similarly, Dalla, *Ubi Venus,* 165–84, esp. 173–75.

109. Late antique sources rarely use the term *cinaedi*; an in-depth analysis of late Latin homoerotic vocabulary remains a desideratum. See Zinsli, *Kommentar,* 197–99, 500–1; Masterson, *Man to Man,* 26–28; Masterson, "*Kinaidos,*" 274–76; Dunning, "Same-Sex Relations," 575; de Wet, "John Chrysostom on Homoeroticism," 198; Richlin, "Not Before Homosexuality," 531; Gunderson, *Staging Masculinity,* 149–86; Williams, *Roman Homosexuality,* 83–84.

110. Masterson, *Man to Man,* 28.

Theodosius, through Nicomachus Flavianus and the imperial administration, used the threat of harsh punishment for adult male prostitutes to teach *all* Roman men a lesson about the state of elite manliness at Rome, the mother of *all* virtues, *mater omnium virtutum*, because Rome's virtues were threatened by the unmanly comportment of some men. Their comportment affected everyone because every man was responsible for the corporate manliness of the mother of all virtues. Every male body—and particularly every elite male body—that failed to "preserve the sanctity of the abode of the *virilis anima*" (ut universi intellegant sacrosantum cunctis esse debere hospitium virilis animae) contaminated the (maternal) body politic. Moreover, men in the *urbs aeterna* who failed to preserve their sacrosanct body's full *vir*-ness threatened the sanctity of the most visible embodiment of Rome's sacred manliness: the *divina forma* of the *sacratissimus imperator*. Hence the emperors, at the end of their patient endurance (*pati, patientia*), wanted to be certain that *all* comprehended (*universi intellegant*) that the lodging place of the manly soul—the manly body—always had to be sacrosanct and that the preservation of that sanctity was the duty of all *viri*.[111]

Presumably, if they were actually imposed, the supreme punishments would affect only low-status male prostitutes. But just their threat ostentatiously signaled the intensity of the imperial message addressed to Rome's elite men, who knew whereof the emperors spoke: barely a year prior, some of them had voluntarily made themselves into *delicati illi ac fluentes* as supporters of Magnus Maximus. The law addressed to the "most dear and delightful" Orientius put all men who mattered on notice to examine their desires carefully. Desiring a strong man other than Theodosius could have dire consequences: it could lead a *vir* to submit himself to a man who might be revealed to be a debauched (*turpis*) tyrant. The letter offered fair warning, posted in Rome while Theodosius acted as the arbiter of true *vir*-ness through his imperial clemency, which could instantly restore men who had voluntarily accepted the passive sexual role of an *exoletus* to the sacrosanct innocence of true *virtus* and *Romanitas*.[112]

It was good advice to examine one's desires carefully, but Nicomachus Flavianus himself failed to heed it. Theodosius returned to Constantinople in 391. In 392, Valentinian II, then twenty-one years old, died, probably by suicide. His leading adviser, the military commander Arbogast, declared a certain Eugenius as augustus. Eugenius was recognized as emperor in Rome in 393. Nicomachus Flavianus supported him.[113] As it turned out, however, Eugenius and the strongman Arbogast were also too soft and delicate for Theodosius. In 394, he defeated them in a battle near the river Frigidus in the Julian Alps. Once again, Romans had spilled

111. On the philosophical background of this notion, see Vitiello, "Theodosius," 332–33.

112. Symm., *Ep.* 2.13, 2.30–31; Matthews, *Western Aristocracies*, 229–31; McLynn, *Ambrose*, 311–12; Sogno, *Q. Aurelius Symmachus*, 68–79.

113. Salzman, "Ambrose."

the blood of Romans (with the help of Gothic, Alan, and Hunnic contingents), at enormous cost to the western and eastern armies. In yet another triumphal celebration of civil war victory, Eugenius's severed head was paraded around Italy.[114] Nicomachus Flavianus and Arbogast killed themselves as real men were supposed to, but, to quote Masterson once more, "disagreement about the meaning of *vir*" was by no means resolved.[115]

114. Matthews, *Western Aristocracies*, 238–47.
115. Masterson, *Man to Man*, 28.

2

The Importance of Being Splendid

Beauty, Desire, and Child-Emperor Rule

Pacatus's panegyric and Nicomachus Flavianus's ostentatious law demanding that members of the Roman (senatorial) elite probe their desires for (strong) men carefully expose the deep, personal link between the emperor's manliness and that of members of the senatorial aristocracy, as well as the threat that usurpers represented to all concerned. As John Weisweiler has emphasized, the steep rise in the number of senators after Constantine assumed power reshaped the self-definition of the senatorial aristocracy and of the elites in general in significant ways. Increasingly, membership in the Senate was less a consequence of birth and instead rewarded service. It had become an appointment that often depended on imperial favor.[1] In Weisweiler's words, "The senate [had transformed] from a Republican aristocracy, in which rank was decided by the traditional magistracies of the Roman city-state, into an explicitly monarchical elite, in which the worth of an aristocrat depended on his imagined closeness to a divine emperor."[2] The result was a growing asymmetry between the ruler and his senators. The imperial person became ever more distant and divine, out of reach for ordinary mortals, senators included. The emperor's remote divinity, his sacrality, was made manifest and visible in his ornamentation: the diadem, introduced by Constantine, heavy with pearls and jewels; large fibulae; jewel-encrusted purple boots, *campagi regia*; gold-embroidered and bejeweled vestments.[3]

I take my title from Rollinger's chapter of the same name.

    1. Weisweiler, "Domesticating the Senatorial Elite," 17–41; see also Schmidt-Hofner, "Ehrensachen," 209–43.

    2. Weisweiler, "Domesticating the Senatorial Elite," 26. See also Weisweiler, "From Equality to Asymmetry," 319–50; Jones, *Later Roman Empire*, 2:529; Tantillo, "I ceremoniali di corte," 543–84.

    3. According to *Epit. de Caes.* 39.3, Diocletian introduced jewel-encrusted shoes as part of the imperial regalia; cf. Eutr., *Brev.* 9.26; see also Alföldi, *Monarchische Repräsentation*, 161–86; Hekster, *Caesar Rules*, 69–105.

FIGURE 9. Male figurative bust, late 4th/early 5th c. CE, marble, height: 72 cm, head: 27 cm. Findspot: Kopanos, near Veria, MTH 1061. © Archaeological Museum of Thessaloniki, Hellenic Ministry of Culture—Hellenic Organization of Cultural Resources Development.

Men who wanted to become *clarissimi* (most shiny or bright), *spectabiles* (well worth looking at), or *illustres* (utterly illuminated)—in ascending order the highest ranks within the Senate—increasingly fashioned themselves in relation to the divine emperor, on whose favor their appointment depended.[4] For the senatorial aristocracy and the empire-wide elites, the emperor was the reference point. In their self-representation, these elites strove to be illuminated by the emperor's

4. Masterson, *Man to Man*, 10; Kuhoff, "Die Bedeutung der Ämter"; Kuhoff, *Studien zur zivilen senatorischen Laufbahn*, 228–55; Schlinkert, *Ordo senatorius*, 234–36; Ch. Kelly, "Bureaucracy and Government"; McEvoy, "Rome"; Cameron, *Last Pagans*, 11–13; foundational is Näf, *Senatorisches Standesbewusstsein*, 28–82.

divine beauty (*forma*) and virtue to enhance their own standing. However, as the individualized, rugged features of Roman senatorial portraits demonstrate, they were fully conscious that their splendor, however glittering, could and indeed should never imitate the divine beauty of the ruler.[5] The emperor's *forma* and *decus*, his manly splendor, were meant to be unattainable: only he was the god one can see.[6] However, this was a reciprocal relationship. While the elites sought to enhance their status through their relation to the emperor—the closer the better—and reflected it in their gold-embroidered robes, the *sacratissimus imperator* had every incentive to hold the virtues of his leading men, the *clarissimi, spectabiles*, and *illustres*, to the highest standards. Or, as the letter of the *Collatio* put it, all should remember to preserve the sanctity of their *vir*-ness.[7] Elite *viri* should glitter and sparkle to their hearts' content, but their glitter had to enhance the emperor's divine splendor: they had to sparkle the right way.

This reciprocal though asymmetric relationship of divine and elite manliness, manifested in bejeweled robes and sparkling ornaments, is well illustrated by the proliferation of honorific gilded statues in public spaces in Rome beginning in the later fourth century.[8] Originally, gilded statues were reserved for the imperial family. However, the vast majority of those from fourth- and fifth-century Rome honored senators, military leaders, and the highest public officials. Significantly, though, all who confidently presented themselves as glittering, utterly illuminated, and well worth looking at took great care to point out in inscriptions at the bases of these statues that they were covered in gold "on the order of our lords the emperors."[9] These splendid men had claimed the golden eternity these statues promised not unilaterally but by imperial invitation: they and their sparkling representations reflected and enhanced the emperors' most sacred splendor.[10] Persons thus honored successfully maintained the complex balance between distinction manifest through glittering gold and too much glitter that might bring an *illustris vir* perilously close to the unattainable, divine beauty of the emperor.

5. See Figure 9. For the increasing distance between imperial and senatorial representation post-Constantine, see Kovacs, *Kaiser, Senatoren*, 47–90, 87 and Kat. B 149 (image); Kovacs, "*Praeclara in veste,*" 375–89; Dillon, "Inflation of Rank," 53–64.

6. Kovacs, "*Praeclara in veste,*" 380; Chastagnol, *Le Sénat romain*, 293–324.

7. *Coll. Mos.* 5.3 ("Ut universi intellegant sacrosanctum cunctis esse debere hospitium virilis animae").

8. Gilded statues from the 360s and 370s: *CIL* 6.1698 (*PLRE* I Symmachus 3); *CIL* 6.1721 (*PLRE* I Eugenius 5); *CIL* 6.1736 (*PLRE* I Hymetius); *CIL* 6.1764 (*PLRE* I Secundus 3); *CIL* 6.41336 (*PLRE* I Taurus 3). Fifth-century gilded statues: *CIL* 6.1725 (*PLRE* II Draucus); *CIL* 6.1727 (*PLRE* II Saturninus 7). The editors later added *auro* to *CIL* 6.41347 and 6.41398; *CIL* 6.40804 may belong to a gilded statue of Galla Placidia. See Kovacs, *Kaiser, Senatoren*, 86–88; Niquet, *Monumenta virtutum titulique*, 63–69, 151–72, 229–33.

9. Weisweiler, "From Equality to Asymmetry," 324–39 (quote at 326); Chenault, "Statues," 114.

10. Amm. Marc. 14.6.8 criticizes those who erected such statues as "thinking that they can be recommended to eternity by means of statues, strongly desire them as though they would gain more benefits from bronze images that lack all feeling than from the knowledge of deeds done honestly and correctly."

It was a high-wire act. All members of the elite were—or should have been—aware of their responsibility to keep their *virtus* sacrosanct because it refracted that of the emperors. They were likewise required to present it properly, with the right amount of sparkle—signified, for example, by the senatorial titles. This duty, especially in the *urbs Roma,* was a challenge to all who were considered *viri,* whether Christian, pagan, "barbarian," or "Roman." They had to shimmer, but just the right measure of rustic hardness needed to temper that brilliance so that they would not be perceived as too delicate and fluid—a dangerous outcome, as those who had supported Magnus Maximus and Eugenius could easily attest.

BOOTS AND TROUSERS

Emperor Theodosius died on January 17, 395, within five months of his victory over Eugenius. Arcadius, at eighteen, became the sole augustus of the east and Honorius, at ten, the sole emperor of the west. In 397, these young emperors issued a law addressed to the people of Rome, which was displayed in the Forum of Trajan and reiterated in 399 during the consulship of Manlius Theodorus, when it was addressed to the *praefectus urbi* Virius Nicomachus Flavianus, the son of the author of the constitution of 390.[11] The law's two versions are preserved only in the Theodosian Code, which omits further specifics. However, this law illuminates yet another facet of the challenges facing those thinking with—and legislating—the appropriate display of *vir*-ness in late fourth-century Rome. The content of both versions is largely the same, but the reissued edict stipulates harsher penalties.[12] Initially, perpetrators would suffer "merely" confiscation of their property and perpetual exile. Two years later, those who obstinately persisted in the forbidden behavior faced punishment in accordance with their status and expulsion from the sacred city. These were the issues at stake: "Within the venerable City no person should be allowed to appropriate for himself [*usurpare*] the use of the *tzangae* [boots] or the *bracae* [trousers]."

Tzangae, or *tzancae,* were over-the-knee leather boots that were popular with the cavalry and other members of the army by the early fourth century. They came in a plain version and a deluxe one, richly decorated with jewels and pearls. As

11. Nicomachus Flavianus the Younger was Symmachus's son-in-law and had only recently been rehabilitated by Stilicho: see Matthews, *Western Aristocracies,* 238–47, 266–67; Hedrick, *History and Silence,* 20–22.

12. CTh 14.10.2 ("Impp. Arcadius et Honorius aa. ad populum. Usum tzangarum adque bracarum intra urbem venerabilem nemini liceat usurpare. Si quis autem contra hanc sanctionem venire temptaverit, sententia viri illustris praefecti spoliatum eum omnibus facultatibus tradi in perpetuum exilium praecipimus. Et cetera. Dat. proposita Romae in foro divi Traiani Caesario et Attico conss" [397 apr.?]); 14.10.3 ("Honorius and Arcadius Idem aa. Flaviano praefecto Urbi. Intra urbem Romam nemo vel bracis vel tzangis utatur. Quod si quisquam post praeceptum nostrae clementiae in hac contumacia perduraverit, prout condicio siverit, cohercitus sacra urbe pelletur. Et cetera. Dat. VIII id. iun. Brixiae. Theodoro v. c. cons. [399 iun. 6]").

items of conspicuous luxury so often were said to have done, *tzangae* were supposed to have come from Persia. *Bracae*, in Greek *anaxyrides*, were tight pants or trousers, also originally part of military dress and likewise associated with Persia.[13] By the end of the fourth century, as Ramsay MacMullen and Philip von Rummel have shown, both items of clothing had become part of elite male fashion, while still being worn by soldiers: together with brooches and colorful, elaborately designed cloaks, they conveyed the military look, which preserved aspects of soldiers' ethnic origins in certain dress forms.[14] This adoption of *tzangae* and *bracae* was thus the opposite of a trend observed by a contemporary author—namely, that "the poor Roman imitates the Goth, while the rich Goth imitates the Roman."[15]

Why two consecutive laws targeted these boots and trousers in 397 and 399 has been a matter of lively debate. Scholars agree that proper elite male comportment, or at least display, was at stake.[16] Emperors seeking to regulate the dress of their elites, senators above all, was not new. In 382 and 386, for instance, Gratian, Valentinian II, and Theodosius—primarily the latter—demanded that Constantinopolitan senators bring their dress in line with the standards to which Roman senators adhered, by wearing the uncomfortable and decidedly old-fashioned toga (except in the morning, when they should wear a "peaceful" paenula cloak) rather than the popular chlamys, a shorter robe originally used only by members of the military and then, in the third century, predominantly worn by those administrators whose positions had evolved from military ones, such as the *praefecti praetorii*.[17] The chlamys became the dress of civilian officeholders in part because it could easily be embellished (for example with brooches), and many in Constantinople sported it regardless of their rank.[18] In addition, the emperors decreed that Constantinopolitan senators should use their official carriages when in the city and that all administrative functionaries should always wear their clothes draped to reveal the belt (*cingulum*) signifying their position. In sum, these were laws intended, first, to clarify who was what kind of imperial officeholder in Constantinople and to

---

13. Arce, "Dress Control," 33–44; Harlow, "'Clothes Maketh the Man'"; Harlow, "Female Dress." For material representations of such shoes and pants, see, e.g., the ivory diptych of Probianus: Delbrück, *Die Consulardyptichen*, 252; Volbach, *Elfenbeinarbeiten der Spätantike*, plate 34 nr. 62. For general background, see F. Morgan, *Dress and Personal Appearance*, 14–28, esp. 17–19; for the *bracae*, M. Pausch, *Die römische Tunika*, 46–47.

14. MacMullen, "Some Pictures in Ammianus Marcellinus"; von Rummel, *Habitus barbarus*, 156–61, and for further material representations 200–7, 226, 228, 232–36, 246; see also Matthews, *Western Aristocracies*, 264–67.

15. Anonymus Valesianus 12.61 ("Romanus miser imitatur Gothum, et utilis Gothus imitatur Romanum").

16. See von Rummel, *Habitus barbarus*, 156–58, for a summary of the scholarship.

17. CTh 14.10.1, 14.12.1; Arce, "Dress Control," 38–40; Kovacs, "*Praeclara in veste*," 402–18; Schlinkert, *Ordo senatorius*, 147–53.

18. For a detailed analysis of the relationship between the *togati* and the *chlamydati* in late antiquity, see Gehn, *Ehrenstatuen*, 17–34.

make the men in question instantly recognizable; second, to highlight the civilian character of the imperial administration and hence imperial rule; and finally, to emphasize the equivalence of the Constantinopolitan and Roman Senates.[19]

Though likewise reflecting concerns regarding appropriate forms of dress and display among male elites, the boot and trouser laws of 397 and 399 were different. First, they addressed men in the *urbs aeterna* itself. Second, they again couched demands placed on elite men in Rome, the principal target, in universal terms: all men—*ad populum, nemini*—were called upon to forgo these items of luxurious foot- and legwear, because in the Eternal City all men were bound to comport themselves properly. This is an important point, as it weakens earlier scholarly interpretations according to which these laws sought to curtail the presence of "barbarian" soldiers in the city.[20] *All viri* had to dress and adorn themselves appropriately when in Rome, although those who belonged to the higher military ranks, the imperial administration, the Roman aristocracy, and the Senate carried particular obligations when displaying their manly virtue.[21] They were perfectly entitled to play with fashion, to express their luxurious tastes as much as their coffers permitted—until the sparkler-in-chief decided otherwise, perhaps because his legitimacy was under particular threat.

In 397 and again in 399, a style of bejeweled boots and a certain cut of trousers were evidently not imperially sanctioned ways to showcase wealth, status, and manliness as a proper *vir*.[22] Why were these specific clothes off limits? The Persian, "barbarian" connotation of the usurped *tzangae* and *bracae* and the age-old associations of luxury, the east, and delicate, soft, or subtle men they evoked appear to have contributed to their disfavor. Such evocations took on a more menacing flavor when considered in relation to the so-called *calcatio colli*, a ritual wherein the emperor placed his imperial boot on the neck of a defeated "barbarian" (or usurper) in an unmistakable gesture of dominance and humiliation. Such scenes were frequently depicted on fourth-century coins and might well have hovered in the representational background.[23]

But why were these laws issued at this moment? After all, by the late 390s, neither military fashion with "barbarian" connotations, "barbarian" military commanders, nor imperial boots on barbarian necks were novel.[24] Nor was the

19. Von Rummel, *Habitus barbarus*, 161.

20. See e.g. Delmaire, "Le vêtement, symbole de richesse," 87–88, with bibliography.

21. Arce, "Dress Control," 41–44; von Rummel, *Habitus barbarus*, 156–66, convincingly argues that these laws sought to limit the presence of military persons in general in Rome to protect the Senate; for positive connotations of "barbarian" dress elements, see Kovacs, *Kaiser, Senatoren*, 189–92.

22. Ammianus was also highly attuned to footwear, as his allusion to the boots worn by tragic actors (*cothurnus, kothornoi*) in a slight against Constantius demonstrates: see Amm. Marc. 21.16.1, 27.11.2. For an illustration of these platform shoes see, e.g., Şare Ağtürk, *Painted Tetrarchic Reliefs*, plate 33, 143–44.

23. Malone, "Violence on Roman Imperial Coinage," 59–69.

24. Lee, "Emperors and Generals," 100–18; Kuefler, *Manly Eunuch*, 55–61.

threat of usurpers new—although the court in Milan might have felt it particularly acutely in 397 and 399. In 397, Honorius had been the sole western ruler for more than two years after his father won yet another civil-war victory and died not long after. Honorius was twelve years old and stood under the guardianship, or *commendatio*, of the *magister militum* Flavius Stilicho, the husband of his sister Serena, Theodosius's niece and adopted daughter.[25] In 397, Stilicho had engaged rebellious Gothic troops under the leadership of a certain Alaric with rather mixed results. At the same time, a North African military leader named Gildo threatened to redirect its grain supply from Rome and the western empire to Constantinople. In other words, relations between the courts of Honorius and Arcadius were tense and the balance of power was shifting in favor of the east.[26]

Given these circumstances, the boot and trouser laws addressed to the *urbs aeterna* assume further relevance. After Theodosius moved to Constantinople in 380, he became the first Roman emperor to spend the majority of his time in the New (or Second) Rome. As will be addressed in chapters 5 and 6, his continued presence in the new capital signaled its rise in importance at the expense of the Eternal City, a (potential) loss of prestige that many people, mostly but not only in the west, noted with resentment.[27] Still, as Theodosius's triumphal *adventus* in 389 demonstrated, Rome retained its tremendous symbolic power as the "head of the world," *caput mundi*.[28] Rome and its aristocrats, particularly the senators, remained the (self-declared) custodians and arbiters of that symbolic power, which included appropriate display, as the dress regulations discussed above confirm.[29] By issuing an edict regulating military-style boots and trousers with "eastern" connotations at a moment of tension with the eastern court, Honorius and his court in Milan may well have wished to signal to those in Rome (and, through them, to all in the realm) that they, not the eastern court, represented the "true" Rome, the *caput mundi* (and its empire), and that the same was true for all (elite) men in the *urbs*, which was also the mother of all virtues. Therefore, elite Roman comportment was again under heightened imperial scrutiny, this time with special attention paid to boots and trousers with "eastern," luxurious, delicate, and fluid implications.

At the same time, Honorius and his court made clear that they were fully conscious of the legitimating and stabilizing power of the Eternal City's elites; they

25. Serena grew up in Theodosius's household after her father died, but Cameron, "Status of Serena," doubts whether Theodosius legally adopted her, as implied by Claud., *Laus Ser.*, 104. See also McEvoy, *Child Emperor Rule*, 9–13.

26. McEvoy, *Child Emperor Rule*, 141–59; Heather, *Goths and Romans*, 193; as McLynn, *Ambrose*, 366, points out, in the early years Honorius, his court, and the Roman Senate collaborated rather well.

27. Grig and Kelly, *Two Romes*, 18; Long, "Claudian and the City," 3–15.

28. Humphries, "Emperors, Usurpers," 160–68; Schmidt-Hofner, "Ostentatious Legislation," 85–89; Gillett, "Rome, Ravenna"; Lejdegård, *Honorius*, 45–59.

29. The enlarging of existing aristocratic houses and the building of more splendid ones in late fourth-century Rome indicate its continuing significance: see Machado, *Urban Space*, 58–61, 63–83, 204–30.

FIGURE 10. Head of Emperor Honorius as a child, late 4th c. CE, marble, overall: 4 × 3¼ × 3¾ in. (10.2 × 8.3 × 9.5 cm). Detroit Institute of Arts, gift of Dr. Wilhelm R. Valentiner, 37.157.

were aware that it was a good idea for new(ish) Roman emperors, even with the best dynastic credentials, to earn the latter's support.[30] An emperor who was ten at the time of accession may well have faced a steeper challenge in persuading everyone that he was the apex of most sacred, divine, imperial virtue. However, beginning with Constantius, emperors signed their laws with "Mea Aeternitas" (My Eternity), claiming that they acted with perennial force.[31] Young Honorius therefore embodied the Roman Empire's eternity just as much as the eternal *urbs* itself, regardless of what anyone might have thought. Nevertheless, in 397 and 399, his sole rule was still tenuous, which might well have prompted his court to remind the Eternal City's elites that it was incumbent on them to safeguard Rome's eternity through their own comportment as *viri*, for example by refraining from excessive displays of eastern, "Persian," and thus less-than-manly affinities—in this case represented by their boots and trousers.

30. Börm, "Born to Be Emperor," 257–59.

31. Constantius's inscription of 357 discussed above (see chapter 1) ends with "victor, triumphator, perennial [*semper*] augustus" (*CIL* 6.1158); see also CTh 4.22.2, 6.4.30 (probably from 396; "aeterni principis"), 6.24.6, 8.4.23, 10.10.22, 10.20.11, 12.1.160 ("mea aeternitas"), 13.3.14, 14.4.4, 14.5.1, 16.2.47, 16.10.20.

ELITE ROMAN BEAUTY AND CHILD EMPERORS

As Honorius, Arcadius, and even Magnus Maximus's son Flavius Victor demonstrate, by 397 children and teens as emperors, coemperors, and consuls had become an imperial reality that the west could no longer ignore.[32] Valentinian I's elevation of his eight-year-old son Gratian to coaugustus in 367 had started the trend, a risky and contentious move that set a precedent.[33] Though earlier Roman emperors had been as young as thirteen, Gratian was the first prepubescent boy to be elevated directly to full-fledged coruler rather than just young prince in training.[34] Valentinian I was secure enough to carry this off. Quite possibly his military background and that of his close advisers helped. After all, as Neil McLynn has pointed out, by the time of the Valentinians, "the whole army had become a family business."[35] In the late Roman army, young children accompanied their fathers, especially those in the officer corps, as a matter of course and were automatically placed on the payroll (a practice that Valentinian tried to end).[36] From that perspective, making a son who had been acculturated in the army by accompanying his father from posting to posting into an equal (emperor) even at a very young age might have been a "natural" step, though it was not accepted imperial practice. Valentinian's experiment was promising enough for his brother Valens, the eastern emperor, to make his son a consul at age three, adding the title *nobilissimus puer*, and to tolerate the elevation of Gratian's half-brother, the four-year-old Valentinian II, as the coemperor of the west when Valentinian I died unexpectedly in 375.[37] Significantly, the western elites also eventually accepted this elevation. Indeed, when Maximus came to power in 383, he too elevated his young son, as we have seen, and Theodosius's elevation of his six-year-old son Arcadius as coaugustus that same year marked the introduction of the practice to the eastern court, by an emperor steeped in the same military traditions as Valentinian I.[38]

Nevertheless, children as emperors remained contested and fraught. In the early 390s, Ammianus criticized Valentinian—and by implication Theodosius—for having "overstepped the traditional order" when elevating his young son.[39] Gratian managed to flourish until he was fatally defeated at twenty-four, but in 392 Valentinian II either committed suicide or was killed at twenty-one, which

---

32. McEvoy, *Child Emperor Rule*, 1–2, 136–51.

33. By 397, the west had witnessed the elevation of four children under ten as coaugusti (Gratian, Valentinian II, Maximus's son Victor, Honorius): see McEvoy, *Child Emperor Rule*, 48–131; Cameron, *Last Pagans*, 39–131, though with a different focus; Börm, *Westrom*, 28–53; Errington, *Roman Imperial Policy*, 200–16, with further bibliography; Sivan, "Was Theodosius I a Usurper?"

34. Lenski, *Failure of Empire*, 89–92; Jussen, "Enduring the Dust," 253–55.

35. McLynn, "'Genere Hispanus,'" 102, see also 91–93.

36. CTh 7.1.11.

37. The child consul, Valens's son Valentinian Galates, died around 372: see Lenski, *Failure of Empire*, 91. See G. Kelly, "Political Crisis," 358–73, for the fraught nature of Valentinian II's elevation.

38. Lenski, *Failure of Empire*, 137–38; McEvoy, *Child Emperor Rule*, 52–60; Omissi, *Emperors*, 247–53.

39. Amm. Marc. 27.6.16 ("Valentinianus morem institutum antiquitus supergressus").

indicates just how much could go wrong.[40] The challenges facing a boy emperor and his court while he transitioned into adulthood cannot be overstated. Honorius's nearly thirty-year rule, which began when Theodosius made him a caesar at about four years old in 389 (before elevating him to coaugustus at eight in 393), is a testament to the skill with which his court managed the representational aspects.[41] Should the central virtues associated with the Roman emperor—military prowess, victory on the battlefield, clemency, evenhanded administration of justice, dignified erudition, dazzling divine beauty (*forma*)—be adjusted to fit a growing boy? And if so, how? When Honorius became the sole emperor, it was far from certain whether those in power would support another divine imperial child. No blueprint prescribed how a child emperor should be represented so that his transition into an adult sovereign would be favorably received.[42] In short, the concept of *vir*—specifically, the imperial *vir* and *sacratissimus imperator*—had to stretch to accommodate boys and young men barely past puberty.

THE BEAUTY OF IMPERIAL BOYS

Casting a child as the embodiment of Roman imperial virtue required the accomplishment of at least three distinct goals. First, the boy in question had to be established as a divinely beautiful *sacratissimus imperator*, which demanded, second, his representation as a victorious leader. This, as will become apparent, was difficult but not impossible. The third task—how to shape the boy's advancement through and past puberty—was more complex. As long as his father was alive, military valor could be achieved through association: the imperial boy could be portrayed as accompanying his fearsome warrior father on his victorious campaigns like any other high-ranking soldier's offspring and thus participate in his glory. However, when senior commanders took over after the death of the imperial fathers (Valentinian and Theodosius), different representational moves became necessary. To be sure, loyal commanders had always fought on behalf of their emperors, just as Merobaudes, Richomeres, Bauto, Arbogast, and Stilicho did for Gratian, Valentinian II, and Honorius, and their victories were those of the emperor regardless of his age or physical distance from the battlefield.

Indeed, this was the solution to the representational conundrum that Ambrose, the bishop of Milan, faced upon the death of Theodosius.[43] Preaching a sermon in Milan's central church in the presence of Honorius, who stood facing his father's

40. McEvoy, *Child Emperor Rule*, 137.

41. By praising Theodosius's mature manhood at *Pan. lat.* (2)12.7.5–6, Pacatus also gestured toward the age composition of the imperial triad, but he never mentioned the senior augustus, Valentinian II, who was of course younger than Theodosius.

42. Noreña, "Ethics of Autocracy," 266–79; Icks, Jussen, and Manders, "Generaals."

43. Biermann, *Die Leichenreden*, 13; Groß-Albenhausen, *Imperator christianissimus*, 125–33 (critical of Ambrose's claim to have been a mentor to Theodosius); Zimmerl-Panagl, "Zu Überlieferung und Textgeschichte."

casket before its journey to Constantinople, Ambrose emphasized that Theodosius, "an emperor of such greatness, then, has withdrawn from us. But he has not wholly withdrawn; for he has left us his children, in whom we can both see and embrace him. Their age should not trouble us! The loyal support [*fides*] of his soldiers makes the emperor's age fully grown [*perfecta*]. For age is fully grown [*perfecta*] when strength/manliness [*virtus*] is. This is reciprocal. For the faith/loyalty [*fides*] of the emperor is the strength [*virtus*] of his soldiers."[44] An emperor was as old and hence strong/brave/manly as his soldiers, and the soldiers as strong/brave/manly as their leader: echoes of Pacatus. Whether those who might have required persuasion in 395—for example, Theodosius's and now Honorius's military leaders, also present in that church—concurred that the *fides* of the soldiers strengthened the *virtus* of a child emperor and vice versa was an open question.[45] In the event, Stilicho remained loyal, but this should not distract us for a moment from remembering that in 395 and even 397 the jury was still out.[46]

Moreover, the very military prowess, longevity, and loyalty of a senior commander fighting on behalf of an imperial boy could create a formidable representational challenge, especially in connection with the emperor's splendid, sublime beauty. Portraying a young boy as exquisitely beautiful was not difficult, nor was it per se problematic to represent a beautiful prepubescent boy accompanied and even guided by an older man who was not his father. But representing a divinely beautiful young man as the embodiment of Roman *vir*-ness if he was past puberty and still guided by the same older man was something else entirely. As the following chapter discusses, what was essential while the emperor was a child could prove fatal once he grew up. No wonder that even accomplished orators feared this representational conundrum. As Augustine wrote, "How miserable I was . . . on that day when I was preparing to recite praises to the emperor [Valentinian II], in which I falsely said many things, and I, who was lying, enjoyed the favor of those who knew [that I was lying]."[47] To

44. Ambr., *De ob. Theod.* 6 ("Ergo tantus imperator recessit a nobis, sed non totus recessit; reliquit enim nobis liberos suos, in quibus eum debemus agnoscere, et in quibus eum et cernimus et tenemus. Nec moveat aetas: fides militum imperatoris perfecta est aetas; est enim perfecta aetas, ubi perfecta est virtus. Reciproca haec, quia et fides imperatoris militum virtus est"); see also Liebeschuetz, *Ambrose of Milan*, 180.

45. Ambrose's *De ob. Theod.* is a ring composition centered on the concept of *fides*; T. Morgan, *Roman Faith*, offers a nuanced overview of the word field for *fides*, including *loyalty* and *trust* (5–26), and its relation to the divine in the early imperial period (77–120, 129–37). See also McLynn, *Ambrose*, 358; McEvoy, *Child Emperor Rule*, 145–46.

46. Most of the senior commanders remained loyal to the young princes, thanks to generous financial rewards, elevated status, and the threat of swift sanctions: see Amm. Marc. 31.7–12; Zos., *HN* 4.35.2–3, 4.22.4, 4.33.1, 4.34.1, 4.53.1–4; Eunap., *Hist.* 9.58.2; J. Antioch, frag. 187; Matthews, *Western Aristocracies*, 38–67; McLynn, *Ambrose*, 159–65; Lee, "Emperors and Generals," 102–18; Sivan, *Ausonius*, 120–25.

47. August., *Conf.* 6.6.9 ("Quam ergo miser eram . . . die illo, quo cum pararem recitare imperatori laudes, quibus plura mentirer, et mentienti faveretur ab scientibus").

extoll a boy emperor's manly excellence in front of an audience in the know required skill and fortitude.[48]

LOVING/DESIRING THE VALIANT EMPEROR

Panegyrists (including Augustine, one presumes) were up to the task, in particular when celebrating a young emperor's beauty. In 376 or 377, the Constantinopolitan senator and philosopher Themistius, who had come west to convey Valens's views on the emerging Gothic crisis along the Danube and to conciliate Rome, praised Gratian, then sixteen or seventeen, in the Roman Senate in a speech titled *A Discourse on Love [or Desire], or Concerning the Emperor's Beauty.*[49] The young emperor was not present, which allowed Themistius to express his deep longing even more lavishly, in language that evoked Plato and Homer. Gratian's desirable beauty (*kallos*) had stunned Themistius into giving this speech: "Suffering the pain of that love which philosophy had written in me, for the beauty of a beautiful and lovable young man, who combines the beauty of the soul with that of the body, gleaming with friendliness and steadiness in manly luxury [ἐν ἀνδρείᾳ ἡδυπαθείας]—'a young man whose beard is just coming out, one whose youth is at its most attractive'[50]—suffering the pain of being in love with such beauty . . . is like [nothing else] on earth or on the sea."[51]

Significantly, Themistius juxtaposed his praise of Gratian's youthful beauty and utter desirability directly to that of his military vigor, linking the emperor and his "soldier's belt," or *cingulum / zone.*[52] Rather than conquer solely with his sword, Gratian, whom the philosopher addressed as his boy lover (*ta paidika*), transformed his foes into lovers through the force of his "beauty and cultured soul." Indeed, to support his claim that "not only do philosophers love the splendor of Gratian, it seems, but the barbarians do as well," Themistius declared twice that "our emperor is blessed in that [he renders] the barbarians obedient not through the sword but

48. Masterson, *Man to Man,* 41–89, 138–69; see Rapp, *Brother-Making,* 13–47, 88–132, for a monastic context.

49. Them., *Or.* 13 ("Erotikos [logos] e peri kallous basilikou"). Themistius probably delivered the first part of the speech in Trier with Gratian present, and added the ending, designed to woo the Roman Senate, for his delivery there a few months later (without Gratian); G. Kelly, "Political Crisis," 383–85, 393–97; Konstan, "Themistius' *On Royal Beauty,*" 179–88; Konstan, *Beauty,* 128–34; Jussen, "Enduring the Dust," 262–65 (adds Symmachus's panegyric, together with those of Themistius and of Ausonius; these are the first panegyrics addressed to a child emperor); Swain, *Themistius,* 305–15; Vanderspoel, *Themistius and the Imperial Court,* 179–84; Heather and Moncur, *Politics,* 201–3.

50. Hom., *Il.* 24.348, *Od.* 10.279, referring to Hermes.

51. Them., *Or.* 13.164c–165a, trans. Masterson, *Man to Man,* 171, with modifications.

52. Them., *Or.* 13.177c: "I am the praiser and lover [*erastes*] of both the soldier's belt and emperors" (trans. Masterson, *Man to Man,* 174). At *Or.* 13. 162c-d Themistius characterized Eros's beauty as both soft and hard in military terms.

through his beauty."[53] Gratian "makes the barbarian beautiful, the Goth gentle, the Persian tame, the Armenian already Roman, the Iberian Greek, the nomad a householder: each changing his former shame to the opposing beauty."[54]

As Mark Masterson has pointed out, Themistius portrayed Gratian as a young man "at the upper age limit to be a beloved boy" yet always in full possession of a soldier's and warrior's commanding authority.[55] As emperor, Gratian conquered through military might, and he wielded the immense desire that his stunning beauty generated as a unifying force. This, as Themistius made clear, applied to the many barbarians whose belligerence his beauty tamed, as well as to the senators whom Themistius addressed. Indeed, Themistius's greatest wish was for "[the gods to] grant my beloved boy [*paidika*] that he love [*eran*] Rome and that be loved by Rome in return [*anterasthai*]."[56] The emperor's remote yet present beauty, although physically out of reach for both those near the center of Rome's power and those at its margins, created a desire that united these groups. Moreover, the emperor's loving desire for all of his subjects, senators as much as barbarians, offered a reciprocal bond that bridged the gulf separating the god we can see from those in his care. Such metaphorical language did not change the social status of either the appeased "barbarians" or the exalted Roman senators, but as a reflection of imperial affection it lessened the harshness of the distinction between them and invited those who witnessed it most closely—here the Roman senators—to return that affection in kind.[57]

Two years later, Decimius Magnus Ausonius, the consul of 379, addressed a speech of thanks (*Gratiarum actio*) to Gratian at Trier soon after the military disaster of Adrianople, about which he said very little.[58] Like Themistius, Ausonius, who may have spoken without Gratian present, juxtaposed beauty and military bearing. After a lengthy preamble that caused impatient murmurs (*prope murmure*), he highlighted Gratian's extraordinary erudition and noted that it was matched only by the emperor's striking and noble entrances in both civilian and military dress, his subtle movements, and his facility on horseback.[59] Ausonius's

53. Them., *Or.* 13.176b-c, trans. Masterson, *Man to Man*, 172. Themistius praised Gratian's sway over these barbarians as Rome struggled with Gothic migrations into Thrace, leading to setbacks at Marcianople and later Ad Salices; Lenski, *Failure of Empire*, 328–30.

54. Them., *Or.* 13.166c-d, trans. Masterson, *Man to Man*, 174; here Valens prefigures Gratian's pacifying beauty.

55. Them., *Or.* 13. 169b; Masterson, *Man to Man*, 173.

56. Them., *Or.* 13.180a–b.

57. Masterson, *Man to Man*, 30–40.

58. Aus., *Grat. act.* The speech's date and emperor's presence are matters of debate. Sivan, *Ausonius*, 199, assumes that it was delivered January 1, when Gratian would have been absent. Matthews, *Roman Empire*, 69–87, argues for later in the year and in his presence. Coşkun, *Die gens Ausoniana*, 82–87, posits oral and written versions; see also Dewar, "Spinning the *Trabea*."

59. Aus., *Grat. act.* 13.62. In addition to saying little about Adrianople, Ausonius omitted mention of Theodosius: see Omissi, *Emperors*, 258–61.

Gratian also conquered barbarians through force and forgiveness.[60] Throughout, the consul praised the young emperor's Republican virtues, such as regular military training, frugal habits, sincerity, restraint, and exemplary chastity.[61] The emphasis on modesty and chastity might signal Christian-inflected nuances of imperial virtue. However, it is important to remember that desire does not mean consummation—rather, it is heightened by untouchability. Good emperors, young ones in particular, were utterly beautiful but always (modestly) out of reach.

Ammianus's slightly ambivalent praise underscores this point. While extolling the "fiery gleam of [Gratian's] eyes, the delightful charm of his face and his whole body, and the noble nature of his heart," he inserted (with the hindsight of Gratian's eventual defeat) a note of caution: the emperor might have grown into an exemplar of ancient virtue and proper Roman manly excellence had not the depraved acts of his intimates cast a shadow over his still unstable *vir*-ness.[62] The stunning beauty of utterly desirable imperial youths had to be approached with circumspection, as Ausonius also suggested when praising Gratian's sober restraint, especially because of the force of (reciprocal) male erotic desire.

Ambrose's evocation of the young Valentinian II in a lament preached in his church in Milan shortly after the latter's death, probably by his own hand, after a violent altercation with his general Arbogast, displays such desire in full force. Though addressing Valentinian's soul, Ambrose made vivid the full physicality of the deceased beloved. Throughout, he evoked Valentinian as the young lover of the

60. Aus., *Grat. act.* 2.7–8, echoing Themistius: "I may call you Germanicus, because of the surrender of that people to you, Alamannicus, because you carried over their captives, Sarmaticus, because you conquered and forgave them." See also Icks, Jussen, and Manders, "Generaals," 548–49; Jussen, "Enduring the Dust," 266–68.

61. Aus., *Grat. act.* 14.63–65: "Nullum tu umquam diem ab adulescentia tua nisi adorato dei numine et reus voti et ilico absolutus egisti, lautis manibus, mente pura, inmaculabili conscientia et, quod in paucis est, cogitatione sincera. cuius autem umquam egressus auspicatior fuit aut incessus modestior aut habitudo cohibitior aut familiaris habitus condecentior aut militaris accinctior? in exercendo corpore quis cursum tam perniciter incitavit? quis palaestram tam lubricus expedivit? quis saltum in tam sublime collegit? nemo adductius iacula contorsit, nemo spicula crebrius iecit aut certius destinata percussit" (From your boyhood you have never let a single day pass without worshipping God, without discharging your vows the moment that they became due, with clean hands and a pure heart, a stainless conscience, and—a rare quality—with undivided thoughts. Was there ever a prince whose going forth was attended with better auguries, whose progress was less ostentatious, whose state was less extravagant, whose attire in private life was more approriate or in the field more severe? In athletic pursuits who ever matched your speed at running, who was as supple in disengaging at wrestling, who cleared so great a height in leaping? No one ever launched a javelin with a more forceful swing, no one hurled darts with greater speed or struck the mark more accurately); Lolli, "Ausonius," 711–12.

62. Amm. Marc. 27.6.15 ("Consurrectum est post haec in laudes maioris principis et novelli, maximeque pueri, quem oculorum flagrantior lux commendabat, vultusque et reliqui corporis iucundissimus nitor, et egregia pectoris indoles: quae imperatorem implesset cum veterum lectissimis comparandum, si per fata proximosque licuisset, qui virtutem eius etiam tum instabilem obnubilarunt actibus pravis"). See also Rohrbacher, "Physiognomics in Imperial Biography"; Humphries, "Body Politic," 190–200.

Song of Songs: "Oh my Valentinian, you are 'my youth radiant and ruddy,' bearing a likeness of Christ in himself."[63] His head was golden, his eyes shone like those of a dove, his belly gleamed like an ivory casket, his cheeks were like vials of spice, his lips were dripping lilies, his hands were round and golden, and his conversation was fervently desired. The young emperor's striking though chaste beauty was central to this lament, with which the bishop turned him into a Christian martyr and, as Neil McLynn has so memorably observed, "discreetly concluded the earthly affairs of the house of Valentinian."[64]

Good, legitimate emperors were extraordinarily beautiful and thus desirable, and so were young boys. Consequently, an emperor, the top of everything, *apex omnium*, as a boy was the most beautiful, radiant, and desirable of all. Such an imperial boy's beauty literally conquered: "The barbarians too have fallen in love with Gratian's splendor, and willingly surrender and bow low."[65] Imperial beauty was central to military victory because erotic desire overwhelmed even the fiercest barbarians, as Themistius and Symmachus had so eloquently illustrated earlier.[66] Assuming that the young Gratian's imperial beauty forced barbarians into submission as effectively as (or even more effectively than) his sword—willingly and without bloodshed, simply out of burning desire—then the military prowess of even younger imperial boys was exercised through more than one kind of weapon.

BATTLE-READY BOYS

In 396, the poet Claudian, who will return in the chapters that follow, praised the eleven-year-old Honorius on the occasion of his third consulate. Not surprisingly, the young emperor and consul appeared in splendid beauty, conquering young men and chaste matrons alike.[67] More to the point, "through his happy influence

---

63. Ambr., *De ob. Val.* 58 ("Valentinianus meus, 'iuvenis meus candidus et rubens,' habens in se imaginem Christi"), quoting Song of Songs 5:3. According to Faller (358, n. to 60.1), Ambrose's citations of the Song of Songs derive from Origen, not the Vulgate (5:10), and are occasionally closer to the Septuagint; see also Liebeschuetz, *Ambrose of Milan*, 361–63, 390–91.

64. Ambr., *De ob. Val.* 59–63, quoting Song of Songs 5:10–16; for chastity and restraint, see, e.g., *De ob. Val.* 16–17. McLynn, *Ambrose*, 335–41, quote at 341; see also Duval, "Formes profanes," 260–74; Lunn-Rockliffe, "Ambrose's Imperial Funeral Sermons"; Croke, "Arbogast," 237–44; Salzman, "Ambrose," 196–97; Santini, "Martyr of Civil Wars."

65. Them., *Or.* 13.176b.

66. Them., *Or.* 13; Symm., *Or.* 3; see also Jussen, "Enduring the Dust," 256–66: G. Kelly, "Pliny and Symmachus," 269–71.

67. Claud., *III Cons. Hon.* 126–130:

Quanti tum iuvenes, quantae sprevere pudorem
spectandi studio matres, puerisque severi
certavere senes, cum tu genitoris amico
exceptus gremio mediam veherere per urbem
velaretque pios communis laurea currus!

See also IV Cons. Hon. 639–645.

[*fatis*]," Honorius won fierce battles.[68] Should any in the audience doubt the victorious force of Honorius's beauty, Claudian reminded them that the emperor and consul had accompanied his father Theodosius in the field since infancy, preparing him for his own campaigns. "As a little boy, you crawled over shields, and freshly seized royal plunder furnished your toys. You were the first to embrace your fierce father Theodosius after his bitter battles whenever he came home hot with northern slaughter. . . . You had no fear of his sword, and his helmet's grim brilliance did not frighten you. . . . How mad for war were you at that time, Honorius, how ardent to follow your father!"[69] As soon as "[your] legs grew strong," Claudian tells Honorius,

> and you walked straight, your father permitted neither unmanly laziness nor rest made weak by luxury nor lazy sleep. Rather, he guided your young limbs through hard labors and built up your tender strength into a tough nature. You endured savage cold, did not yield to heavy rainstorms, tolerated the summer sun, and swam across madly roaring torrents. Your climbing mastered the mountains, your running the plains, your leaping the valleys and hollows. You also passed the nights awake, lying on your shield, drinking melted snow from your helmet. Now you shot arrows from your bow, now missiles from your Balearic sling.[70]

68. Claud., *III Cons. Hon.* 87 ("Victoria velox / auspiciis effecta tuis. Pugnastis uterque: / tu fatis genitorque manu") (Under your auspices victory was speedily won. You both participated in battle: you in the form of your fate and you father with his hand)."

69. Claud., *III Cons. Hon.* 22–26, 31–32, 73–74:

Reptasti per scuta puer, regumque recentes
exuviae tibi ludus erant, primusque solebas
aspera complecti torvum post proelia patrem,
signa triumphato quotiens flexisset ab Histro
Arctoa de strage calens . . .
intrepidum ferri galeae nec triste timentem
fulgur. . . .
Quae tibi tum Martis rabies quantusque sequendi
ardor erat!

The last sentence alludes to Hector and Astyanax.

70. Claud., *III Cons. Hon.* 39–50:

Mox, ubi firmasti recto vestigia gressu,
non tibi desidias molles nec marcida luxu
otia nec somnos genitor permisit inertes,
sed nova per duros instruxit membra labores
et cruda teneras exercuit indole vires
frigora saeva pati, gravibus non cedere nimbis,
aestivum tolerare iubar, trasnare sonoras
torrentum furias, ascensu vincere montes,
planitiem cursu, valles et concava saltu,
nec non in clipeo vigiles perducere noctes,
in galea potare nives, nunc spicula cornu
tendere, nunc glandes Baleari spargere funda.

Themistius, Ausonius, Ambrose, and Claudian used highly evocative language to make vivid the splendid, glittering, overwhelming beauty and the battle-readiness of the most sacred emperors, especially the young emperors, often with erotic overtones. This splendor was reflected in the brilliance of their sumptuous gilt and jewel-encrusted vestments, their diadems, brooches, and ornamented boots, and mirrored in the glittering titles of the senators, military officers, and other elites, who also wore elaborate cloaks, brooches, and sparkling boots and trousers. However, the appropriate clothing for a Roman or Constantinopolitan senator, as the emperors reminded them, was the plain and severe toga—or failing that, a chlamys. Senators and other elite *viri* could, of course, shimmer and glitter, but they had to make sure at all times that their splendor remained visibly distinct from that of their divine sovereign, never as worth looking at as the unattainable, sublime beauty of the emperor, whom they longed for as a matter of state: the desire of Roman men for an unattainable Roman emperor was equated with Roman might, and Roman might meant proper Roman manliness.

Although the emperor's beauty was thus designed to elicit a unifying desire, reflected and magnified by the extension of his affection to everyone in the realm, these reciprocal bonds of love managed and balanced an economy of power in which difference and distinction were highlighted rather than erasing status, either that of the most sacred ruler beyond the bounds of other mortals or that of anyone else. Roman senators knew that their splendor as a *clarissimus, spectabilis*, or *illustris vir* brought them close to the ruler—and the closer they were, the greater their prestige. But no amount of metaphorical desire ought to tempt them to forget at any moment what separated them from the divine emperor, whatever his age. Likewise, "barbarians" retained their ethnic characteristics even when overwhelmed by love for the emperor. Nevertheless, this love and the emperor's reciprocal affection had the power to make anyone, regardless of distinction, into a Roman, and this centripetal force, melding all the empire's people into one Roman whole, could be even greater if the emperor was a boy, because a young boy's "natural" desirability further enhanced the beauty inherent in the *sacratissimus imperator*.

All of the authors mentioned so far, themselves members of the elite, scrupulously stressed the coalition of beauty and military prowess, much as Pacatus did for Theodosius. This pairing worked even more dramatically with young emperors, gloriously beautiful boys who were also portrayed as battle-hardened or at least battle-ready, because by definition no one could claim the imperial purple without military prestige, *virtus*.[71] These authors refracted imperial intent when they paired the young rulers with their valiant fathers (or uncles), showed them growing up amid soldiers and the clamor of camps, or emphasized their personal soldierlike exploits. This is corroborated by coins that likewise presented these

71. *Pace* McEvoy, *Child Emperor Rule*, 109–13, the military aspect never subsided; see also Icks, Jussen, and Manders, "Generaals," 543–57; Stewart, *Soldier's Life*, 61–71; Hekster, *Caesar Rules*, 109–32.

very young rulers as victorious and stressed the expectation of imminent victories, the hope of the republic, *spes rei publicae*.[72] In other words, by presenting Gratian, Valentinian II, and Honorius as beautiful yet rustic, hard, austere, and dignified young rulers, these authors acted in the interest of stability and dynastic continuity and thus amplified imperial messages promulgated on coins. They too had experienced civil war and knew what it could do to Roman *viri*, senatorial and otherwise. And they understood how fine a line separated exemplars of Roman manly excellence from the less-than-manly supporters of a losing emperor, never mind the shameful degradation of the loser, now a tyrant, monster, and ambiguously gendered (because sexually available) slave by birth and hence nature, and of his closest allies, now infamous bandits and fellow slaves. Thus they signaled the continuity of existing virtues such as military prowess and dynastic lineage but also stressed unifying strategies such as clemency, mildness, forgiveness, and reciprocal desire, love, and affection.

Not surprisingly, not all members of the highly competitive elite were persuaded.[73] The Roman senators maintained a skeptical distance—particularly with regard to child emperors, as the next chapter will illustrate—though they expressed such views officially only in regard to Theodosius's triumphal message. For example, in the public monuments, statues, and inscriptions that Roman senators had installed along Theodosius's triumphal route in 389, they acknowledged his victory over Magnus Maximus but also pointed out that liberating Rome from tyranny (when necessary) was exactly the emperor's job. Theodosius had done what was expected of him, and Rome was grateful: he had acted as divinely authorized *restitutor*, or restorer, of the Eternal City, the head of the *imperium Romanum*. In short, on monuments that Theodosius was sure to see, the Roman Senate reminded everyone that bestowing imperial legitimacy and delineating the parameters of true Roman *vir*-ness were the prerogative of the Eternal City. Its senators (and other elites) influenced the legitimacy of an emperor and what he should look like—or so they maintained. Indeed, however successfully Pacatus, Ausonius, Ambrose, and Themistius mediated among their personal interests, the elites in Milan and Rome, and the expectations of a victorious ruler, his adolescent son, his court, and military leaders, it was impossible to convince everyone—particularly those who claimed the mantle of the ancient, time-honored "Republican" arbiters of Rome's prestige, power, and hence manly excellence—that a splendidly beautiful imperial boy was the apex of Roman virtue. Critical voices greeted imperial children and accompanied their transitions into adolescence and beyond, especially if the young emperor continued to be

---

72. Icks, Jussen, and Manders, "Generaals," 551–56, point out that 50 percent of the coins minted under Honorius refer to his military role and that between 395 and 403, 40 percent bear the legend *virtus exercitus*.

73. Thus, at *Or.* 13. 170c, Themistius stated that child rulers were hated, with Gratian being the exception.

very close, even past puberty, to a strong older man who was not his father. The following chapter addresses one of these cases and presents a source that reveals some of the representational challenges confronted by child emperors and those who spoke on their behalf when addressing an elite audience: the *Life of Heliogabalus* in the *Historia Augusta*.

3

Top Boys

The Life of Heliogabalus *in the* Historia Augusta

[Alexander Severus] forbade men to call him dominus. *He ordered that he be addressed in letters as if he were a private citizen, retaining only the title* imperator. *He removed all the jewels from the shoes and garments, as Heliogabalus used to wear them. Instead, he wore, as his portraits also show, a white robe without any gold, as well as ordinary* paenula *[cloaks] and togas.*[1]

The *Historia Augusta*, which contains the *Life of Heliogabalus*, is a highly entertaining mixture of fact and fiction. It offers invaluable insights into elite concerns regarding Roman *vir*-ness at the top of the social pyramid during the early decades of the Theodosian age, with its civil war triumphs, imposition of less-than-manliness on vanquished Roman elites, and child emperors. While not responding directly to any of the authors discussed so far, the *Historia Augusta* belongs to the chorus of elite voices grappling with shifting notions of imperial virtues, including manliness, and their reverberations, and the *Life of Heliogabalus* in particular makes vivid some implications of what boys as emperors could represent, in ways rarely addressed in scholarship.

The *Historia Augusta*, or *Imperial History*, is a notoriously difficult source that has been subject to a host of interpretations. Written as if six historians were presenting the emperor Constantine with a collection of biographies of his predecessors from Hadrian to Carinus, it was established as the work of a single late fourth-century author by Hermann Dessau in a foundational article from 1889.[2] Since Dessau, scholars have vigorously debated every other aspect of

---

1. *HA, Alex. Sev.* 4.1–2 ("Dominum se appellari vetuit. Epistulas ad se quasi ad privatum scribi iussit servato tantum nomine imperatoris. Gemmas de calciamentis et vestibus tulit, quibus usus fuerat Heliogabalus. Veste, ut et pingitur, alba usus est nec aurata, paenulis togisque communibus").

2. Dessau, "Über Zeit und Persönlichkeit." For a recent survey of scholarship regarding the *HA Aug.*, see Fündling, *Kommentar zur Vita Hadriani* 1, 3–87; Haake, "'In Search,'" 271–72, esp. n19; Johne, *Kaiserbiographie und Senatsaristokratie*, 11–46. Zinsli, *Kommentar*, 5–34, offers a detailed analysis of the history of scholarship on the *Historia Augusta*.

this extraordinary collection. The consensus holds that the author was pagan—although there is disagreement on whether he was part of a pagan resistance to Rome's official Christianity, if such a resistance existed—and that he wrote from a pro-senatorial perspective with a rather jaded view of imperial governance.[3] Much research, drawing on meticulous analysis of his sources, has focused on the anonymous author's identity and on when he might have completed his collection.[4] Equally hotly contested are attempts to extract accurate data about the second- and third-century emperors memorialized, for whom the *Historia Augusta* is often our sole extant source, or one of very few.

Hand in hand with these discussions go different assessments of the collection's structure and message. Following Ronald Syme and André Chastagnol, most scholars have divided the *Lives* into primary, secondary, intermediate, and late.[5] The complementary histories of Heliogabalus and Alexander Severus are longer than any of the others and positioned as a pair at the center of the collection as we now possess it. More recently, the focus has shifted to the philological and literary aspects of the *Historia Augusta* as a unique endeavor with its own style and genre.[6] This approach is particularly relevant for what follows, because I consider the *Historia Augusta* a literary work composed in the late fourth to early fifth century, and my discussion thus examines the literary character "Heliogabalus" rather than the third-century emperor Marcus Aurelius Antoninus, known as Elagabalus.[7] In short, I read the *Historia Augusta* and especially the *Life of Heliogabalus* in light

3. See Haake, "'In Search,'" 273; Nardelli and Ratti, "*Historia Augusta Contra Christianos*," 143–44; Straub, *Heidnische Geschichtsapologetik*, 137. On the title, see Paschoud, "*Historiae Romanae Scriptores Latini Minores*." Another central question has been whether the author used forgery—or as I would prefer to call it, fiction—to hide his personal bias, or *Tendenz*, or simply to amuse himself. Paradigmatic of the first view is Seeck, "Politische Tendenzgeschichte." Syme, in contrast, thought that the rogue scholar lacked all political motive: see, e.g., *Ammianus*, 191. Now the consensus is that the author expressed political views: see Haake, "'In Search,'" 269–74; Scheithauer, *Kaiserbild*, 39–64.

4. Because Ratti (*Antiquus error*, 220–22; *Polémiques*, 111–27) argues for Nicomachus Flavianus Senior as the author, he has to posit 394 as the *terminus ad quem*. In contrast, Cameron, *Last Pagans*, 745–82, proposes a date before 375 because he considers *HA* a continuation of Marius Maximus, as does Kulikowski, "*Historia Augusta*." Savino, *Ricerche*, 44, thinks that a certain Tascius Victorianus was the author and therefore requires a time after Stilicho's death in 408 (22–24, 256–58); similarly, Neri, "L'imperatore come *miles*," and Rohrbacher, *Play of Allusion*, 158–69. Zinsli, *Kommentar*, 281–90, 656, dates the *Life of Heliogabalus* specifically between 394 and 405; I adopt a slightly broader range.

5. Syme, *Emperors and Biography*, 56; Chastagnol, *Histoire Auguste*, xxxvii–xlvi; see also Rohrbacher, *Play of Allusion*, 3–16. Primary (with numerous details verifiable through other sources): Hadrian, Antoninus Pius, Marcus Aurelius, Verus, Commodus, Pertinax, Julianus, Severus, and Caracalla; secondary (usurpers and caesars): Aelius, Avidius Cassius, Pescennius Niger, Clodius Albinus, Geta, Macrinus, and Diadumenianus; intermediary (group histories): the Maximini, the Gordians, and Maximus and Balbinus; late: the nine *Lives* after the two Valerians.

6. See Thomson, *Studies*; Burgersdijk, "Style and Structure"; Burgersdijk, "Praise through Letters"; Rohrbacher, *Play of Allusion*, 11–14; Chastagnol, *Histoire Auguste*, 17–56.

7. Following Mader, "History as Carnival," 131n2; Zinsli, *Kommentar*, 2; Rohrbacher, *Play of Allusion*, 14. See also Icks, *Crimes of Elagabalus*, 7.

of the contemporary concerns with *vir*-ness, imperial power, and child emperors detailed above.

As literary fiction, the *Historia Augusta* may certainly be considered, in the words of Alan Cameron, "as trivial a product as everyone used to think. Its author was just not interested in heresy, [the Roman emperor] Julian, Germans, or Constantinople. His political views, if they deserve to be so described, were utopian fantasies such as good emperors respecting the senate and choosing the best men to succeed them. The author of the *HA* was a frivolous, ignorant person with no agenda worthy of the name at all."[8] However, although heresy, Julian, Germans, and Constantinople might not have dominated the author's agenda, he lavished considerable attention on subjects that I would characterize as eminently political—manliness, or *vir*-ness, prominent among them. Further, even a "frivolous, ignorant person" may be exquisitely attuned to what Chastagnol has called the ambience or atmosphere of their time, to the issues that deeply preoccupied their audience.[9] Hence, I treat the *Life of Heliogabalus* as a significant source, which responded to, satirized, and illuminates the atmosphere and the *realia* of its time and place—Italy in the later fourth and early fifth centuries—as seen by a man who had a particular view of Roman imperial power and the Roman Senate and wished to look at their dark side while entertaining himself and his audience with humor.[10]

LIFE OF HELIOGABALUS

The *Lives* of Heliogabalus and Alexander Severus are matched, distinct from the others, and marked as central to the collection of imperial lives as we now possess it.[11] Pretending to write as someone named Aelius Lampridius, the author, inspired by Suetonius, used a wide array of sources, such as Dio Cassius, Herodian, a collection of biographies attributed to Marius Maximus, Aurelius Victor, Eusebius's *Life of Constantine*, and Ammianus Marcellinus's *Res gestae*, whose content he creatively altered to shape these two complementary and exemplary imperial biographies. The backbone of the *Life of Heliogabalus* is the historical narrative, but the text is fleshed out with allusions to Cicero, a collection of culinary recipes associated with Apicius, Pliny the Elder's *Natural History*, and Juvenal's *Satires*, all

8. Cameron, *Last Pagans*, 781.

9. Chastagnol, *Histoire Auguste*, cxxxiii. See also Molinier Arbo, "L'*optimus princeps*," 87; Thomson, *Studies*, 115–17.

10. Thus, while I concur with Rohrbacher, *Play of Allusion*, 21, that the collection is a highly erudite and allusive work created for the sake of "comic anarchy," I agree with Zinsli's review of Rohrbacher that the *HA*'s author's choice of what specifically to allude to was informed by contemporary concerns. See also Rohrbacher, *Play of Allusion*, 2–22, 170–75; D. Pausch, "*Libellus*"; den Hengst, "Author's Literary Culture."

11. For an overview of the structure, models, and sources of the whole collection, see Rohrbacher, *Play of Allusion*, 3–16; Burgersdijk, "Style and Structure," 28–46, 251–65.

combined to create the figure of "Heliogabalus," the last of the Antonines.[12] The author presents this *ultimus Antoninorum* as the climax of an inexorable march toward more and more excessive tyranny.[13] "Heliogabalus," the nadir of imperial aberration, is then juxtaposed to his polar opposite, "Alexander Severus," as optimal an *imperator* as the anti-imperialist author was willing to conceive.[14] As the ultimate tyrant, *princeps pessimus*, and the ideal ruler, *princeps optimus*, Heliogabalus and Alexander Severus also embody two contrasting and complementary versions of male gender performance at the outer edges of the possible.[15]

The Heliogabalus of "Lampridius" is an übertyrant, the tyrant to end all tyrants. The writer exaggerates almost every topos denigrating the tyrannical ruler (except cruelty) to create the most *prodigiosus tyrannus*, the most monstrous of them all.[16] In good invective tradition, two related themes already familiar from the previous chapters structure Heliogabalus's portrait. First, tyrants are of ambiguous manliness and hence of indeterminate or compound gender, neither male nor female or both male and female. Second, because they are not *viri*, they lack manly rigor and strength, which makes them unable to control their desires (*libidines*), so they do everything to excess: the luxuriousness of their clothing, the extravagance of their banquets, the dimensions of their greed, the scope and variety of their sexual partners and positions. Moreover, as less-than-manly men, tyrants are soft and brittle, easily manipulated by women and those other fluid and compound beings, eunuchs.[17] Heliogabalus, *ultimus Antoninorum, homo omnium impurissimus*, embodies all this to the extreme.[18] The way in which Lampridius constructed his *Life* reflects these traits: it too is characterized by excess, *amplificatio*, and seeming disorder, producing a carnivalesque, Saturnalian farce, a caricature.[19] To be sure, Heliogabalus's exaggerated features only appear to be randomly assembled. In fact, the aspects of his persona that are amplified to such biting effect were chosen carefully to reflect real anxieties and tensions, the ambience of the time.

---

12. For discussion of the sources, see Zinsli, *Kommentar*, 35–140; Fündling, *Kommentar zur Vita Hadriani*, 1, 152–53 (use of Ammianus); Alföldi-Rosenbaum, "Apicius, *De re coquinaria*," 5–10; Vössing, *Mensa regia*, 415; Barnes, "*Ultimus Antoninorum*"; Burgersdijk, "Style and Structure," 118–210.

13. *HA, Heliogab.* 1.7. See also Mader, "History as Carnival," 131.

14. Haake, "'In Search,'" 273–74, calls the author "antimonarchic," echoing the title of the volume in which his contribution is published, but what he describes is an anti-imperial stance. See also Chazan, *Rhétorique du blâme*, 1–41, 313–45, 397–405.

15. Bertrand-Dagenbach, *Alexandre Sévère*, 94–102.

16. *HA, Heliogab.* 1.2.

17. Scheithauer, *Kaiserbild*, 13–27, 54–64, 73–87, 165; Gualerzi, *Né uomo, né donna*, 26–32.

18. *HA, Macr.* 7.7–8; *HA, Heliogab.* 24.4 ("cenas vero et Vitellii et Apicii vicit"), 33.1 ("Libidinum genera quaedam invenit, ut spinthrias veterum malorum vinceret, et omnis apparatus Tiberii et Caligulae et Neronis norat"), 26.1 ("Primus Romanorum holoserica veste usus fertur"); see also Scheithauer, *Kaiserbild*, 59.

19. Turcan, *Histoire Auguste*, 62; Mader, "History as Carnival," 158–65, 167.

In keeping with the biographical genre, Lampridius opens with Heliogabalus's birth, his *origo*.[20] No one knew who his father really was, least of all his "oriental" Syrian mother, Symiamira, a woman worthy of her depraved son.[21] Perhaps it was Caracalla, since he was known to have committed *stuprum*—a form of intercourse outside acceptable norms—with Symiamira, but since she lived *meretricio more*, like a prostitute, Heliogabalus was in effect fatherless, illegitimate from birth.[22] His sordid origin foretold his end. Eventually Heliogabalus's Praetorian guards, tired of his perversities, rose up to "liberate the republic" (ad liberandam rem publicam). They executed his cronies in such a fashion "that their death matched their life" (ut mors esset vitae consentiens), for example by perforating the anus.[23] Next, they "killed the emperor in a latrine [*latrina*] to which he had fled" and dragged his corpse through the streets.[24] Then they tried to stuff the body into a muddy sewer (*cloaca*), which was, however, too narrow, so they instead weighed it down and threw it into the Tiber—the first emperor's corpse to suffer such *iniuria*. His mother was also killed and his name erased by order of the Senate ("nomen eius, id est Antonini, erasum est senatu iubente"), his memory denigrated and condemned.[25]

Heliogabalus's life conformed to its beginning and end, as the author gradually reveals. He became emperor at a young age (the actual Marcus Aurelius Antoninus Elagabalus had been fourteen), so he was utterly dependent on his mother and grandmother, without whom he could not even enter the Senate.[26] Indeed, he was the first emperor to make his mother a senator, a *clarissima* who sat in the senate as a *clarissimus vir* and participated in the drafting of decrees.[27] He then proceeded

20. *HA, Heliogab.* 1.4–2.3.

21. *HA, Heliogab.* 18.2 ("probrosissima mulier et digna filio"). For allusions to Semiramis, see Zinsli, *Kommentar*, 339–41; Vout, *Power and Eroticism*, 22.

22. *HA, Heliogab.* 2.1; Zinsli, *Kommentar*, 180. *Coll. Mos.* 5.3.1–2 also uses *stuprum* as a term for sexual acts between adult men.

23. *HA, Heliogab.* 16.5–6: "Sed milites et maxime praetorianus . . . factaque conspiratione ad liberandam rem publicam primum . . . cum alios vitalibus exemptis necarent, alios ab ima parte perfoderent, ut mors esset vitae consentiens" (The soldiers, however, and particularly the members of the Praetorian guard . . . formed a conspiracy to free the republic, . . . killing some [of Heliogabalus's followers] by tearing out their vital organs and others by piercing their anus, so that their deaths conformed to their lives). Earlier, these soldiers had demanded that he dismiss his courtiers: *HA, Heliogab.* 15.1–4; see also Chastagnol, *Histoire Auguste*, 57–67.

24. *HA, Heliogab.* 17.1 ("Post hoc in eum impetus factus est atque in latrina, ad quam confugerat, occisus").

25. *HA, Heliogab.* 17.2–4, 18.23 (his mother's death).

26. Zinsli, *Kommentar*, 237, rightly cautions that *HA, Heliogab.* 2.1 merely hints at his young age, which is otherwise not emphasized; as Hartke, *Römische Kinderkaiser*, 203, points out, the actual Elagabalus would have been under his mother's guardianship. Still, the audience of the *Historia Augusta* would have been aware of Elagabalus's youth.

27. *HA, Heliogab.* 4.1–2: "Deinde ubi primum diem senatus habuit, matrem suam in senatum rogari iussit. . . . Solusque omnium imperatorum fuit, sub quo mulier quasi clarissima loco viri senatum ingressa est" (Next, when he held his first audience with the Senate, he gave orders that his mother should be asked to come into the Senate chamber. . . . He was the only one of all the emperors under

to form a new Senate on the Quirinal Hill, consisting entirely of women, a "sena-culum, id est mulierum senatum." Under Symiamira's leadership, this new, second Senate immediately proceeded to enact "ridiculous laws" (*senatus consulta ridicula*), which sound very much like the boot and trouser laws discussed in chapter 2. In this case, they addressed matrons—elite married women—and decreed who could wear what clothes in public, who should kiss whom first, who could ride a horse versus a mule, what kind of chariot could be used, who could wear gold and who jewels on their boots ("quae aurum vel gemmas in calciamentis haberent").[28] Real senators, actual *viri clarissimi*, meanwhile, were derided as *mancipia togata*, toga-wearing slaves. It was an upside-down world, in which women were treated as senators, as *clarissimi viri*, and senators, dignified *gravissimi viri*, as if they were enslaved.[29]

THE EMPEROR AS *EXOLETUS*

When women acted as and hence "became" men and were masculinized, the classic rules of Roman gender—and power dynamics—demanded that the men associated with them act as and "become" women.[30] Lampridius's Heliogabalus went further by creatively combining his dependence on his grandmother and mother, the *clarissima vir*, with an all-encompassing gender performance to build his status as tyrant extraordinaire.[31] According to Lampridius, the young Heliogabalus exulted in intercourse as "a ruler who satisfied his lust through every cavity of his body" (principem per cuncta cava corporis libidinem recipientem).[32] Indeed, the emperor consistently presented himself as a woman, and this in ways that transcended gendered binaries, thus making him nonbinary or gender-indeterminate. That is, Lampridius's Heliogabalus embodied a form of less-than-manliness that encompassed acting as and even being a woman.[33] For example, Heliogabalus

---

whom a woman attended the Senate as if she were a *clarissima* in the place of a *vir*); see also 12.3, 15.6. The first act following the deaths of Heliogabalus and his mother was a decree outlawing women in the Senate: see *HA, Heliogab.* 18.3; E. Elm, *Damnatio memoriae*, 133–56.

28. *HA, Heliogab.* 4.2–3.

29. *HA, Heliogab.* 20.1: "Senatum nonnumquam ita contempsit, ut mancipia togata appellaret" (He often showed such contempt for the Senate that he called [senators] togaed slaves); 10.6: "gravissimis viris"; 11.2.

30. See Späth, *Männlichkeit und Weiblichkeit*, 339–46; with a different emphasis, Kuefler, *Manly Eunuch*, 19–96; Gunderson, *Staging Masculinity*, 59–86; Gardner, "Sexing a Roman," 136–52.

31. Suetonius's Nero is alluded to throughout as a forerunner: see Charles and Anagnostou-Laoutides, "Unmanning an Emperor," 203–8; for Neronian taste as an indication of illegitimate imperial behavior, Gowers, "Persius"; Dench, *Romulus' Asylum*, 279–92.

32. *HA, Heliogab.* 5.2.

33. Gleason, *Making Men*, 62–67. Gleason observes, "A man who actively penetrates and dominates others, whether male or female, is still a man. A man who aims to please—anyone, male or female—in his erotic encounters is *ipso facto* effeminate" (65); here Gleason uses "effeminate" to translate *androgynos*, or being a *cinaedus*, terms of gender indeterminacy that had become indistinguish-

chose the role of Venus in plays reenacting the story of Paris, in which the goddess delighted in letting her clothes slip down to her feet. Naked, on her knees, and with one hand on her breasts and the other on her genitals, Heliogabalus-as-Venus thrust his considerable derriere at his suitor.[34] On other occasions, s/he "became" Salambo, supposedly a Syrian goddess associated with the worship of the castrated Adonis, and dressed, bathed, and shaved as a woman with women, always eager to enhance the feminine appeal.[35] Indeed, Heliogabalus was the first emperor to wear the jeweled diadem, not because of its Persian royal association but because s/he thought it "more becoming for a woman's face."[36]

Second, with advancing age, Heliogabalus increasingly enjoyed being a *meretrix*, a prostitute who acted sexually as a woman, for example when publicly fellating his/her lover Hierocles.[37] Here he demonstrated an absolute preference for being penetrated by men with extra-large genitals.[38] "In fact, in Rome he did nothing but sent out agents to find for him men with large genitals [*bene vasatos*] and bring them to the palace so that he could enjoy their special endowments."[39] Furthermore, "he made public a bath in the palace and at the same time opened that of Plautinus to the populace, so as to recruit in this way the service of particularly well-hung men. Careful attention was given to searching the whole city [*tota penitus urbe*] in depth and among the sailors for *onobeli* [men hung like asses], which is what they called those who looked extra virile [*viriliores*]."[40] Heliogabalus used

---

able in her second-century CE context. Betancourt, in *Byzantine Intersectionality* (106–8), taking his cues from his reading of Dio Cassius as describing Elagabalus as a transgender woman in *Roman History* 80.11–17 and from Dio's later Byzantine reception, which suggests that Elagabalus sought gender-affirming surgery (by means of an incision that would create a vagina), uses *she/her* pronouns; see also his discussion of gender indeterminacy in the context of Byzantine transgender lives (89–91). In what follows I will use the pronouns that conform to Heliogabalus's comportment as Lampridius portrayed it, always in a derogatory fashion. I do not seek to reconstruct what Marcus Aurelius Antoninus (Elagabalus) might have wished to express.

34. *HA, Heliogab.* 5.4–5 ("Agebat praeterea domi fabulam Paridis ipse Veneris personam subiens, ita ut subito vestes ad pedes defluerent nudusque una manu ad mammam altera pudendis adhibita ingenicularet posterioribus eminentibus in subactorem reiectis et oppositis").

35. *HA, Heliogab.* 5.4–5, 7.3. According to later sources, these festivals included lamentations for the death of Adonis or Attis, celebrated by the Galli, the castrated priests of the Great Mother Goddess: see Turcan, *Histoire Auguste,* 174–75; Zinsli, *Kommentar,* 190, 386 (K 115 Venus), 417–18 (K 149 Salambo). See also Tougher, "Aesthetics of Castration," 51–56; Beard, "Roman and the Foreign"; Latham, "'Fabulous Clap-Trap.'"

36. *HA, Heliogab.* 23.5 ("magis ad feminarum vultum aptus").

37. See Gleason, *Making Men,* 66–67, for the astrological twinning of *meretrices* and *cinaedi.*

38. *HA, Heliogab.* 6.5, 26.3–5, 31.7.

39. *HA, Heliogab.* 5.3 ("Romae denique nihil egit aliud, nisi ut emissarios haberet qui ei bene vasatos perquirerent eosque ad aulam perducerent, ut eorum condicionibus frui posset").

40. *HA, Heliogab.* 8.6–7 ("Lavacrum publicum in aedibus aulicis fecit, simul et Plautini populo exhibuit, ut ex eo condiciones bene vasatorum hominum colligeret. Idque diligenter curatum est, ut ex tota penitus urbe atque ex nauticis onobeli quaererentur: sic eos appellabant, qui viriliores videbantur"); cf. Apul., *Met.* 3.24–25.

a man's endowment as the principal criterion for appointment to offices that carried the highest senatorial rank, *illustris vir*—"praesides, legatos, consules, duces omnesque dignitates"—which led to the formation of rival political factions based on penis size.[41] Of course, he was always accompanied by large numbers of men chosen for this very characteristic.[42]

According to Lampridius, the desire and the search for strong and extremely well-hung men were distinct, even central features of Heliogabalus's character. They found their apogee in Heliogabalus's marriage to Zoticus. Here, the *Historia Augusta*'s author took an episode reported of Marcus Aurelius Antoninus (Elagabalus) by Dio Cassius to new heights, making it a constitutive event of his rule, "imperial politics . . . [as] an extension of the tyrant's sexual preferences."[43] In Lampridius's telling, Zoticus, originally an athlete from Smyrna to whom Heliogabalus had taken a shine because of the size of his genitals, had gained such immense power that all the chief officeholders (*omnes officiorum principibus*) considered him the emperor's husband (*quasi domini maritus*).[44] Of course, Zoticus utterly abused his intimacy with the ruler (*hoc familiaritatis genere*), selling access at exorbitant prices and dictating policy. Before long, Heliogabalus proceeded to consummate a marriage with Zoticus (*nupsit et coit*), for which the emperor assumed the role of the bride accompanied by her maid (*ita ut et pronubam haberet*).[45] "After that he would ask philosophers and *gravissimi viri* whether they in their adolescence had also passively enjoyed what he was now enjoying [*et ipsi in adulescentia perpessi esset quae ipse pateretur*], and this with the greatest impudence."[46]

Wedding ceremonies between emperors and their often low-status lovers were not new, neither in actuality nor as a trope of invective.[47] Thus, Suetonius and Dio

41. *HA, Heliogab.* 9.3: "Prodebatur autem per eos maxime, qui dolebant sibi homines ad exercendas libidines bene vasatos et maioris peculii opponi" (But this report was spread most of all by those who were aggrieved that they were opposed by well-hung men equipped to gratify his lusts and with larger resources); well-hung men elevated to offices carrying the rank of *illustris* at 11.1, 12.1–2 ("Ad honores reliquos promovit commendatos sibi pudibilium inormitate membrorum").

42. *HA, Heliogab.* 31.6; Mader, "History as Carnival," 146–47; Williams, *Roman Homosexuality*, 86–91.

43. Dio Cass. 80.13.4, 80.15–16; quote in Mader, "History as Carnival," 145.

44. *HA, Heliogab.* 10.2; Dio Cass. 79.16 describes Zoticus's origins.

45. *HA, Heliogab.* 10.3; 10.5. *Nubere* designates the woman's part in a wedding. The author of the *Historia Augusta* here alludes to Juv. 2.117–38, esp. 120: "gremio iacuit nova nupta mariti."

46. *HA, Heliogab.* 10.6 ("Quaerebat deinde a philosophis et gravissimis viris, an et ipsi in adulescentia perpessi essent quae ipse pateretur, (et) quidem inpudentissime").

47. CTh 9.7.3, issued in 342 by Constantine II and Constantius, addresses such marriages: "Cum vir nubit in feminam, femina viros proiectura quid cupiat, ubi sexus perdidit locum, ubi scelus est id, quod non proficit scire, ubi Venus mutatur in alteram formam . . . iubemus insurgere leges . . . ut exquisitis poenis subdantur infames" (When a man weds as a woman, what should this "woman," who would abandon *viros*, "men" [or "being a man"], want when sex has lost its place? When there is this crime . . . when Venus is changed into another form . . .). The guilty parties were to suffer "exquisite punishments." The interpretation of this law is contested. Most likely, the voluntary abandonment of the dominant male gender rather than the act of marriage was the punishable offense; see Dalla, *Ubi Venus*, 167–70; Masterson, *Man to Man*, 23–25 and n53. *Pace* Harper, *Shame*, 152–53, there are no particularly Christian

Cassius mention Nero's wedding to the beautiful Sporus and Domitian's love for the celebrated Earinus.[48] However, Sporus and Earinus were eunuchs (and slaves), persons whom the sources describe as both female and male, neither male nor female, or on occasion a third sex (*tertium genus*). In other words, while Nero performed marriage rituals with admittedly unsuitable lovers (and while still married to his wife, of course), he married Sporus, widely praised for his exquisite beauty, in the role of the groom.[49] Nero was the husband to his eunuch bride or wife, and Domitian's role in relation to the gorgeous Earinus was also clear. In contrast, Lampridius left no doubt that Zoticus was fully male and performed sexually as a man—that in fact, from the perspective of Heliogabalus, Zoticus's most desirable feature was his majestic cock. There could be no doubt whatsoever about who penetrated whom in this union: Zoticus was the *dominus* of Heliogabalus.

Lampridius's *Life of Heliogabalus* carefully constructs the (fictional) emperor's gender performance as absolutely comprehensive: he was all things to all women and all men. However, as Heliogabalus grew older (than his fourteen years of age on assuming the imperial throne), a distinct preference for penetration by strong, well-endowed men emerged. The emperor was a (freeborn) young man who even after passing adolescence (when such behavior was acceptable, if perhaps not exactly praiseworthy for a future *gravissimus vir*) never fully and certainly not exclusively took on the sexual role of a *vir* and instead continued to assume the passive role of a woman with great enthusiasm. According to Lampridius, Heliogabalus had therefore been an *exoletus*, and surrounded himself with troops of other *exoleti*, as well as the most voluptuous little boys and youths.[50]

Exoletus or *exsoletus*, literally "outgrown (male)," like other Latin and Greek technical sexual terms, is hard to translate. As a rule, *exoleti* were late- and post-adolescent males, usually of servile status and often working as prostitutes, who assumed the passive sexual role in intercourse with adult men.[51] These were the

notions at stake. For formalized male partnerships in Byzantium, see Rapp, *Brother-Making*, 40–47; Masterson, *Between Byzantine Men*, 121–54.

48. For Nero and Sporus, see Suet., *Nero* 28, 46, 48, 49; Dio Cass. 62.18, 62.28. Earinus was praised by Martial (Mart., *Epigr.* 9.11, 12, 13, 16, 17, 36) and Statius, who portrayed him as a bride offered to Domitian (Stat., *Sil.* 3.4.50–56). See also Dio Cass. 67.2.2–3; Tougher, "Aesthetics of Castration," 56–66; Richlin, "Not Before Homosexuality," 550–54; Vout, *Power and Eroticism*, 168–202.

49. According to Suet., *Nero* 29, however, Nero married Doryphorus while imitating the moans of a virgin—that is, in the role of the bride; Tac., *Ann.* 15.37.4, reports that he did the same with a certain Pythagoras. See also Dalla, *Ubi Venus*, 63–69; Vout, *Power and Eroticism*, 136–38.

50. *HA, Heliogab.* 26.4–5 ("Exsoletos undique collectos et luxuriosissimos puerulos et iuvenes . . . exsoletos habitu puerorum, qui prostituuntur"); 31.6 ("Causa vehiculorum erat lenonum, lenarum, meretricum, exoletorum, subactorum etiam bene vasatorum multitudo"); 12.4 ("In conviviis exsoletos maxime iuxta se ponebat eorumque adtrectatione et tactu praecipue gaudebat"). According to Suet., *Tit.* 7, Titus also enjoyed *exoletorum et spadonum greges*, "troops of *exoleti* and eunuchs."

51. It is hard to pinpoint what exactly distinguished *cinaedi* and *ex(s)oleti* from each other. Magie and Turcan translate *exsoletus* as "pervert" and "catamite," the latter the Latin translation of *Ganymede*—that is, a young boy used sexually. On the richness of the essentially untranslatable vocabulary denoting Roman male sexual passivity, see Zinsli, *Kommentar*, 197–99, 500–1; Taylor, "Two

persons specifically targeted by Nicomachus Flavianus's imperial constitution of 390. However, as that same constitution makes clear, freeborn adult men likewise assumed such positions, and the opprobrium they faced was significant, especially for a *vir*. Such behavior, a *vir*'s voluntary abdication of his proper sexual role and hence his elite manliness, was already proscribed in the Republican Lex Scantinia.[52] This law—which is not extant—was in all likelihood no longer enforced toward the end of the fourth century, if indeed it ever was. But it was known and might have been retained as an ostentatious deterrent similar to the *Collatio* of 390, which likewise served as a stern reminder of where the boundaries of appropriate elite male gender performance were drawn. This forms the context in which Lampridius's Heliogabalus had become emperor as an adolescent and then failed to pass through the proper transformation from boy (*puer*) to man (*vir*). He remained enthralled to his mother and received grown men, who were not only more virile than most but grotesquely so, and who dominated his court. Most prominent among them was Zoticus, who lorded it over even the chief officeholders, regulated access to the imperial person, and enjoyed a familiarity with the ruler that resembled that of a husband with his wife, as indeed showcased by their wedding, in which the emperor was the bride.[53]

THE AMBIENCE OF THE TIME

The author of the *Historia Augusta*, as has become apparent, was a deeply allusive writer whose wordplay and intertextual references are legion. But while literary games were central to his endeavor, he also had a distinct political agenda. No friend of Roman imperial rule, the author aimed greater venom at some emperors than at others.[54] One object of his derision and a potential foil of the *Life of*

Pathic Subcultures," 358–63; Richlin, "Not Before Homosexuality," 531. See also Adams, "Use and Meanings," 144–69; Gunderson, *Staging Masculinity*, 149–86; Williams, *Roman Homosexuality*, 83–84; Williams, "Language of Gender."

52. The opprobrium was such that even slaves were not to be forced into such a position. For the Lex Scantinia, which appears to have punished nonconsensual sex with a free boy or young man, see, e.g., Juv. 2.43–45; Suet., *Dom.* 8; Tert., *De monog.* 12; Auson., *Epigr.* 92; Prud., *Perist.* 10.203–204; Dalla, *Ubi Venus*, 82–99 (for examples of legislation concerning slaves, 7–35, 41–49); Richlin, "Not Before Homosexuality," 530–541; Frakes, *Compiling the Collatio*, 265. For other aspects of a free man's sexual relationship with another one of lower status, see Juv. 9; Nappa, *Making Men Ridiculous*, 100–4, 121–26, 179–90.

53. Alexander Severus, in contrast, immediately removed all *exoleti* (and infamous women) from court (*exoletis omnibus deportatis*): HA, *Alex. Sev.* 34.4. The author of the *Historia Augusta* downplays Heliogabalus's dependence on eunuchs, another standard of anti-tyrannical invective, opining on it only through Alexander Severus's entirely different behavior: like the emperor Julian, Alexander considered eunuchs slaves for women and dismissed them from all prestigious positions at court: HA, *Alex. Sev.* 23.4–8, 34.3, 35.5–36, 45.2–5, 66.3–67.2; Bertrand-Dagenbach, *Alexandre Sévère*, 100; Guyot, *Eunuchen*, 157–63.

54. Scheithauer, *Kaiserbild*, 39–64; Chazan, *Rhétorique du blâme*, 339–43.

Heliogabalus was the emperor Constantine.[55] But the ambience of the time also allowed for other targets. Another of the author's more pronounced pet peeves was child emperors. Thus, writing as Flavius Vopiscus of Syracuse, he lavishly praised the fact that Marcus Claudius Tacitus had become augustus in 275 as a grown man, in contrast to "those monsters [*prodigia*] of times past—Nero, Heliogabalus, Commodus," whose innate flaws were amplified by their youth on their elevation to imperial rule. At the moment of Tacitus's election, Vopiscus reports, Maecius Faltonius Nicomachus, another fictional character, addressed the new augustus and the Senate as follows:

> May the gods save us, [conscripted fathers (*patres conscripti*)], from boy emperors [*principes pueros*] and prepubescent boys as fathers of the fatherland [*patres patriae dici impuberes*], whose hand a schoolmaster must guide for the signing of his name and who is induced to confer a consulship by sweets or toys. . . . What wisdom is . . . in having as emperor one who . . . fears his guardian, . . . who appoints as consuls or generals or judges men whose lives, whose merits, whose years, whose families, whose achievements he does not know at all? . . . I appeal to you, Tacitus Augustus, . . . in the name of our common fatherland and our laws, that, if Fate should overtake you too swiftly, you will not name your young sons as heirs to the Roman Empire, so that you will not bequeath to them the republic, the conscripted fathers, and the Roman people like your little villa, your *coloni*, your slaves. . . . It is the great glory to a dying emperor to love the republic more than his own sons.[56]

Child emperors, so young that they feared their guardians and could not sign anything into law unless their schoolteachers guided their hands, were one bone of contention. The *Life of Heliogabalus*, complemented by the *Life of Gordian III*, addressed another, of perhaps even more significant contention: what would happen when these schoolboy emperors grew into adolescents and young adults and *still* feared their guardians, strong men who were not their fathers, so that they failed to transition properly from *puer*—another technical term for the passive sexual role—to *vir*?

In the case of Gordian III, who was elevated to caesar and shortly thereafter to augustus in 238 at eleven or thirteen, all went more or less smoothly. The emperor married very young (*Gordianus adolescens*) and was thus in a position to demonstrate in due (and hopefully short) course his successful transition from *puer* to *vir* by becoming a father. Moreover, after his wedding he was counseled by his (fictional) father-in-law, Misitheus. Under the guidance of this *doctissimus vir* and prefect, the emperor stopped ruling in a puerile manner, tempered the influence of his mother, and removed from his court both those who were loyal to her and the eunuchs (*spadones*), who were accustomed to selling offices.[57] Indeed, an entirely

55. Zinsli, "Gute Kaiser, schlechte Kaiser"; Zinsli, *Kommentar*, 255–64; Neri, *Medius princeps*.

56. *HA, Tac.* 6.4–9; cf. 4.1–8. For a discussion of the dynastic implications, see Icks, "Inadequate Heirs."

57. *HA, Gord.* 22.2–6, 23.6–7.

fictional letter exchange between the emperor and Misitheus dramatizes how vital the removal of these eunuchs was for the realm's stability. Only then, enlightened by his father-in-law, did Gordian III realize the perils he had escaped: "Now at last I know that no Felicios should have been put in command of the Praetorian guard and that I should not have entrusted the Fourth Legion to Serapammon." In other words, no one with the name of a eunuch or an Egyptian (slave) should ever hold high office or military command.[58] Writing here as Julius Capitolinus, the author of the *Historia Augusta* forcefully reiterated that young emperors were a risky proposition. However, he conceded that things might function tolerably well as long as such a ruler married as soon as possible and was handled by a true *vir*, preferably a *doctissimus* one, who was, moreover, a relative—echoes of Honorius and Stilicho, as will become apparent below and in the next chapter.

Heliogabalus had not been counseled by a *doctissimus vir*, had been left to the influence of his mother and to his own devices, and had mightily indulged the attentions of strong men selected solely on the merits of their members. He had not transitioned properly from *puer* to *vir*; on the contrary, he had married his strong man as a woman, which made him an *exoletus*. An emperor as an *exoletus* was a *prodigium*, a monster of extraordinary proportion, because he joined together the two outer extremes of Roman manliness: the *sacratissimus, divinus imperator* and *dominus*, and the *exoletus*, the lowest of the low.[59] Such a vision, this nadir of Roman manliness and hence of Roman imperial power and might, indeed could be imagined only as satire and carnivalesque, Saturnalian farce. It had no place in any other genre, least of all history, not to mention reality.[60] Yet Lampridius's "history," his *Life of Heliogabalus*, does make visible just such a nadir—albeit in a mixture of horror and comedy. If emperors defeated in civil wars became purple-clad homegrown little slaves and if very young boys were emperors, then it did not require an enormous leap of imagination to think of such little rulers as growing into *exoleti* when they became *adolescentes* (and passed that age). And if one could think thus about less-than-manly men, then imperial representation itself came close to its limits on either end of the spectrum because such thoughts significantly expanded who could (and did) embody imperial virtue, dignified manliness: a broad range of men, beginning with small boys, progressing to adolescent youths who had barely grown beards and had not shed their soft and subtle attributes, and ending—where?[61]

---

58. *HA, Gord.* 24.1–25.2. For a succinct overview of the immense scholarship on the *Life* and especially these passages, see Paschoud, *Histoire Auguste*, 251–62.

59. *Prodigia* and monsters as mixtures of opposing elements will be discussed in greater detail in chapter 6.

60. For Roman satire more generally, see Habinek, "Satire as Aristocratic Play," 177–91; Rimmel, "Poor Man's Feast," 81–94; Nappa, *Making Men Ridiculous*, 35–72.

61. Gallienus's decision at some point between 260 and 268 to represent himself on coins as Galliena Augusta, with a beard (*RIC* V.1, nos. 74, 82, 87, 128, 359–360), further indicates a broad spectrum of imperial *vir*-ness: see MacCoull, "Gallienus the Genderbender."

Assuming that the *Life of Heliogabalus* was written in the late fourth or early fifth century, the author and his audience had witnessed instances when the experiment of young boys as emperors had gone wrong once they grew into young men, for example in the case of Valentinian II. Honorius, who at ten years old became the sole ruler of the west in 395, and his *magister militum* Stilicho, whose daughter Honorius married in 398, had to learn how to manage their relationship and its representation through trial and error. By the early fifth century, they were doing far better than Valentinian II and his court had done (at least until Stilicho's ouster in 408), but at the time that Honorius became the sole augustus, the verdict was still out. Unless the author of the *Historia Augusta* wrote as late as 424, he could not have known how long lived and successful Honorius's reign would turn out to be. At any rate, in the 390s and early 400s, Honorius and Stilicho, residing first in Milan and later in Ravenna, had a good sense of the "ambience" of the western elites and the *urbs aeterna*. Honorius had participated in Theodosius's Roman triumph of 389 and visited the city in 403–4; he may also have been there briefly in 395 and 397.[62] With the help of the poet and panegyrist Claudian, who also addressed the Roman Senate, Honorius and Stilicho tackled head on the issue of the emperor as *puer* who ruled with his military leader and guardian. As the next chapter will discuss, Claudian portrayed Honorius as a beautiful and battle-hardened youth, full of hope and the promise of a shining future, while shaping Stilicho into his father and father-in-law and the future grandfather of many more emperors—the quintessential imperial family man.[63]

However successful the works of those who wrote for imperial boys might have been, the author of the *Historia Augusta* and those whose views he expressed were having none of it. For them, a boy on the throne as the *sacratissimus imperator*, whose divine majesty emanated from his ornate vestments and who was guided and supervised by a military commander who fought the actual battles, remained anathema. That arrangement negated Roman *vir*-ness and hence imperial power. Such constellations, the *Life of Heliogabalus* declared, violated the *ordo rerum* and turned the world upside down. If emperors were no longer hardened, austere, blood-splattered men (*viri*) wearing simple cloaks (*paenulae*) but instead were silk-encased, jewel-encrusted boys (*pueri*)—perhaps even *pueri* who liked being fucked by their generals (metaphorically speaking, of course)—then what were the chances that the entire *orbis Romanorum*, the *imperium Romanum*, would suffer the same fate (metaphorically speaking, of course)?

It was a monstrous thought, worth thinking with in a manner as exaggerated as the behavior of its objects. Heliogabalus, for instance, as befit an imperial *exoletus* and most tyrannical tyrant, triumphed not on the battlefield but in the banquet

---

62. As Gillett ("Rome, Ravenna") has shown, the court did not move to Ravenna before 408. For Honorius's Rome visits, see pp. 137–38; Lejdegård, *Honorius*, 45–59.

63. Claud., *VI Cons. Hon.* 77–91, 127–330, 384–406; *Cons. Stil.* 1.71–73, 3.176–81: see Straub, "*Parens principum*"; Coombe, "Hero in Our Midst"; Coombe, *Claudian the Poet*, 123–46; Gualandri, "Un 'generalissimo' semibarbaro."

hall, outfeasting all who came before him.[64] His dinners never cost less than one hundred thousand sesterces, and included exotic fare such as flamingo brains and the heads of parrots. To make manifest his monstrosity, his combination of incompatibles into one abominable whole, these banquets too mixed incompatible ingredients: peas with golden nuggets, lentils with pieces of onyx, rice with pearls.[65] Heliogabalus demonstrated his divine imperial *virtus* by outdoing his tyrannical precursors through the all-encompassing nature of his *luxuria* (*totus, cuncti, omnis*): the entire *orbis Romanorum* furnished his pleasures.[66] His clothes likewise expressed such *amplificatio*. "He was the first of all Romans, it is said, who wore clothing wholly of silk, though garments partly of silk were in use before his time. Washed linen he would never touch, saying that it was for beggars."[67] "He would wear an entirely golden tunic. He also wore one of purple, and a Persian one studded with jewels, of which he said that it weighted him down through his pleasures. He wore jewels even on his shoes, sometimes engraved ones, which would make everyone laugh—as if one could see the engravings of famous artists on jewels attached to feet! He also wanted to wear a jeweled diadem, which he considered more beautiful and becoming for a woman's face."[68] Further, Heliogabalus delighted in wearing a Dalmatian tunic—popular toward the end of the fourth century as a distinct garment of the Christian clergy but here associated with wayward young boys in need of correction.[69] Covered thus from head to toe in silk, gold, and jewels, he sparkled, glittered, and made himself well worth looking at as a *clarissimus, illustris, spectabilis . . . exoletus.*

64. *HA, Heliogab.* 24.1, 30.4–5.

65. *HA, Heliogab.* 19.3–7, 21.1–4, 24.3, 28.6. He further violated the natural order by bringing the sea inland, erecting mountains of snow in the summer, feeding fish to peasants, and never eating fish while near the sea (23.7–8). As Zinsli, *Kommentar*, 186, points out, many of these transgressions poke fun at cherished Roman traditions; see also Mader, "History as Carnival," 160–62.

66. Mader, "History as Carnival," 166–68.

67. *HA, Heliogab.* 26.1–2. See also Neri, "Considerazioni"; for the foreign-luxury connotations of silk, L. P. Eberle, "Foreign Silk"; for legislation regulating the wearing of silk, Nardi, "La seta." For the Orientalizing aspects of such criticism see e.g. Chazan, *Rhétorique du blâme*, 203–20.

68. *HA, Heliogab.* 23.3–5 ("Usus est aurea omni tunica, usus et purpurea, usus et de gemmis Persica, cum gravari se diceret onere voluptatis. Habuit et in calciamentis gemmas, et quidem scalptas. Quod risum omnibus movit, quasi possent scalpturae nobilium artificum videri in gemmis, quae pedibus adhaerebant. Voluit uti et diademate gemmato, qui pulchrior fieret et magis ad feminarum vultum aptus"). For discussion of the diadem, see Turcan, *Histoire Auguste*, 207–8.

69. *HA, Heliogab.* 26.2: "Dalmaticatus in publico post cenam saepe uisus est, Gurgitem Fabium et Scipionem se appellans, quod cum ea veste esset, cum qua Fabius et Cornelius a parentibus ad corrigendos mores adulescentes in publicum essent producti" (He would often appear in public after dinner dressed in a Dalmatian tunic, and call himself Fabius Gurges or Scipio, because he was wearing the same kind of clothing that Fabius and Cornelius wore when they were brought out in public as adolescents by their parents in order to have their manners corrected), alluding to Juv. 6.265–267. In Gell., *NA* 6.12, Scipio accuses a certain Gallus of wearing a *dalmatica* as a sign of being a *cinaedus*; see also Val. Max. 3.5.1; Zinsli, *Kommentar*, 643–49, 681–93; Neri, "Considerazioni," 219, 230.

4

Epic Warriors and Imperial Father (Figure)s

Claudian's Panegyrics *on the Consulships of Honorius and Stilicho*

It is difficult to imagine a clearer challenge to early Theodosian imperial representation than the one so bitingly formulated by the author of the *Life of Heliogabalus*. In his view, emperors were free to elevate their young sons as fully fledged augusti, but that did not make this action anything but preposterous. Of course, imperial sons had succeeded their fathers throughout Rome's history, but usually only after undergoing a period of "probation" during which they were trained and assessed; that is why imperial princes received the title "caesar." Valentinian I's decision to elevate Gratian directly to coruler skipped that step, removing the possibility that an unfit son would not be considered worthy.[1] The author of the *Historia Augusta* responded to such blatant disregard of established mores with two (fictional) scenarios envisioning likely outcomes of this novel imperial practice: either the young ruler transitioned successfully from *puer* to *vir* and demonstrated this by, for example, getting married (and becoming a father), as in the *Life of Gordian III*, or he failed to mature and remained beholden to a strong man (other than his father), with the catastrophic result of the emperor as *exoletus*. Ammianus's criticism of Valentinian I (see chapter 2) confirms that the author of the *Historia Augusta* was not alone in his assessment. More to the point, Honorius's court at Milan too was aware of the ambience of the time, of the potential implications (as presented by the author of the *Historia Augusta*) of a one-year-old consul, eight-year-old coaugustus, and ten-year-old ruler of the western empire under the guardianship of a powerful general. The court responded by expanding his family and creating a new father for the young emperor: Stilicho.

---

1. Constantine's elimination of Crispus and Constantius's execution of the caesar Gallus demonstrate that the succession of a son or close relative was not automatic.

93

Theodosius had also used family ties to further his legitimacy and strengthen his dynastic position. For him, the expansion of the core family played a pivotal role.[2] After becoming the eastern ruler, and especially once Magnus Maximus, who claimed blood ties to the Theodosians, emerged as a serious counterweight in the west, Theodosius extended his family, and thus his dynastic power base, through adoption and marriage.[3] In the early 380s, he persuaded the African leader Gildo to marry his daughter to a relative of the augusta Aelia Flaccilla; he pressured Olympias, a young Constantinopolitan heiress and the widow of the praetorian prefect Nebridius, to marry one of his relatives; and he adopted his niece Serena as his daughter and in 384 married her to a promising young military man, Stilicho.[4] When Stilicho became Honorius's guardian in 395, he was not only the empire's highest-ranking general but also the emperor's brother-in-law. The court immediately emphasized this bond. Moreover, the next five years witnessed a startling, albeit gradual, transformation.

By 400, Stilicho had replaced Theodosius as the father of Honorius and Arcadius and as the grandfather of all future emperors of the gens Ulpia, the house of Theodosius: that house was now the house of Stilicho. Thanks to the fortuitous presence in Milan of the brilliant poet Claudian, whom Stilicho sponsored, this transformation was propagated on a sophisticated literary level with lasting impact. Guided and advised by a "father" who was alive and present, Honorius—and Arcadius, because Stilicho claimed to be his guardian too—could mature into excellent princes, devoting themselves to peacetime governance while Stilicho took care of the arts of war. According to Claudian, this division of imperial power was nothing new, since good imperial fathers had always instructed their sons in the virtues of war and the self-mastery necessary to govern in periods of concord. Moreover, a powerful father was the ultimate arbiter of a son's successful transition from child to man, *puer* to *vir*. Indeed, Theodosius himself had asked Stilicho to assume the role of father to Honorius (and Arcadius), and by transferring the role of arbiter of that crucial transition to Stilicho as "father," he had banished the specter of the emperor Honorius as *exoletus*.

Claudian, a native Greek speaker from Alexandria, had arrived in the west in 394 either directly or via Constantinople together with Theodosius, Honorius,

---

2. According to *Epit. de Caes.* 48.18, Theodosius particularly emphasized these ties, or *adfinitates*: "Patruum colere tamquam genitorem, fratris mortui sororisque liberos habere pro suis, cognatos affinesque parentis animo complecti" ([Theodosius] nurtured his paternal uncle as if he were a father, treated his deceased brother's and sister's children like his own, having embraced cognates and relations by marriage with the mind of a parent). See also Matthews, *Western Aristocracies*, 109n2.

3. See chapter 1; also Rees, *Commentary*, 353.

4. Hieron., *Ep.* 79.2; Anonym., *Olymp.* 3; Claud., *Laus Ser.* 104. As mentioned in chapter 2, n. 26, despite Cameron's doubts ("Status of Serena," 509–16), scholars accept Serena as Theodosius's adopted daughter: see, e.g., Gualandri, "Un 'generalissimo' semibarbaro," 34, 37; Brändle and Leppin, "Olympias 4"; Matthews, *Western Aristocracies*, 107–12.

Honorius's sisters Galla Placidia and Serena, and Stilicho.[5] Already by January 395, Claudian had been invited to praise the two teenage consuls of that year.[6] The following year, he composed a panegyric praising the third consulship of Honorius in Milan, a performance he repeated in 398 to honor Honorius's fourth consulship. In 399 he praised the western consul Manlius Theodorus, and in 400 the first consulship of Stilicho. Two central themes emerge throughout these panegyrics. First, Claudian presented Honorius as fully capable of exercising his duties as a battle-ready imperator, due to his upbringing by Theodosius and Stilicho. The dying Theodosius had entrusted Stilicho with guarding his two sons and therefore made him alone responsible for both halves of the empire. Theodosius had done this because of Stilicho's military valor and, more important, his family ties: they were blood relatives.[7] Second, Claudian gradually and inexorably expanded and transformed the nature of these familial bonds to change Stilicho from Theodosius's son-in-law into the emperors' father.[8]

STILICHO, THE OTHER THEODOSIUS

Praising Honorius as a consul meant, first, representing an eleven-year-old as the epitome of imperial *virtus*, including imperial *vir*-ness in all its sacred glory. As chapters 1 and 2 discussed, Roman emperors had to be victorious in battle and showcase superior martial qualities, accomplishments nearly impossible to claim for a child. At the same time, the young ruler had to be shown transitioning successfully through adolescence into adulthood—a precarious process, as the *Life of Heliogabalus* so vividly illustrates. Claudian confronted both challenges with a poetic epic in which fathers play a crucial role: he began his celebration of the eleven-year-old consul by praising Theodosius.

Young Honorius could proudly wear the trabea, the time-honored consular robe symbolizing peace after victorious battle (*succedant armis trabeae*), because his father had prepared him for war since infancy. Raised in his father's camps, Honorius had learned to crawl among bloodied weapons, and—as discussed in chapter 2—soon began to steel himself with exercise in scorching heat and freezing cold. Such a child did not hesitate to embrace his father returning blood-splattered

---

5. Guipponi-Gineste, *Claudien*, 8, cautions that we know little of Claudian's life; Cameron, *Claudian*, 1–29, thinks he arrived directly from Alexandria. See also Cameron, "Claudian Revisited"; Charlet, "La romanité de Claudien." As a member of the elite, Claudian differs from Cameron's classic model of the wandering poet: see his "Wandering Poets"; Gillett, "Epic Panegyric and Political Communication," 266–71; Gualandri, *Aspetti della tecnica compositiva*, 8–9.

6. Claud., *Prob.*; see also Charlet, *Claudien* I, 1–23.

7. Claud., *III Cons. Hon.* 142–62; Ambr., *De ob. Theod.* 5; Cameron, *Claudian*, 39; McEvoy, *Child Emperor Rule*, 141–44; Vannesse, "La militarizzazione," 89–95; Sánchez-Ostiz, "Claudian's Stilicho," 310–30.

8. As demonstrated by Gualandri, "Un 'generalissimo' semibarbaro," 39–54.

from the battlefield.[9] No learned member of the audience would fail to recognize the allusion here to young Astyanax greeting his father, the mighty Hector. Like Hector, Claudian's Theodosius hoped that his infant son would one day surpass him as a fierce warrior. But everyone also knew Astyanax's fate: he had been thrown to his death from the walls of Troy.[10]

By evoking Astyanax, Claudian acknowledged the consul and emperor's youth, and its danger. Every boy's transition into adulthood, regardless of his birth and training, was fraught. To emphasize the point further, Claudian added a second allusion, to a certain Parthenopaeus, who had perished because he was too young when exposed to the brutal realities of war. Parthenopaeus had forced his mother to let him participate in a battle against Thebes, like a lion cub eager for the hunt before it was weaned. Because his mother was unable to restrain him, he died on the battlefield.[11] Young Honorius had also been spoiling for a fight like a young lion, impatiently demanding his own weapons.[12] Unlike Parthenopaeus, though, he had a powerful father, who tempered his "rage for battle," *Martis rabies*.[13] Theodosius simply said no: "ille vetat" ("he forbade it").[14] Future epic warriors, just like young Roman emperors, had to be prepared for battle from infancy. However, such upbringing must never lead to a *puer*'s unrestrained thirst for military glory; that was ill advised, potentially fatal, and certainly not a virtue. Instead, to become truly virtuous, battle-ready imperial boys required a strict fatherly hand.

Claudian's third exemplar for Honorius to emulate was the most valiant warrior whom epic had to offer: Achilles. Achilles had survived his adolescence because he too had been firmly guided and taught patience and restraint. Significantly, though, his guide had not been his father but instead the wise centaur Chiron. First, Chiron taught Achilles the arts of governance, as well as music and healing, and only then was the latter allowed to unleash his tremendous powers.[15] Honorius, like Achilles, had been guided, restrained, and directed by his own Chiron, the warlike (*bellipotens*) Stilicho, and—unlike Achilles—by his own divine father. Thus trained, Honorius could wait for his innate divine qualities (*auspicies*) to mature while he too acquired the art of governance, making him even more

<hr>

9. Claud., *III Cons. Hon.* 5, 24, 43 ("cruda teneras exercuit indole vires"); Schindler, *Per carmina*, 76–80; Gualandri, "Un 'generalissimo' semibarbaro," 39–41.

10. Claud., *III Cons. Hon.* 22–32; Hom., *Il.* 6.394–502; Virg., *Aen.* 12.433–34; Ov., *Met.* 13.413–17. See also Schindler, *Per carmina*, 79–85; Ware, *Claudian*, 90–95; Gualandri, "Claudian," 119–22; Parkes, "Model Youths?" In contrast to Honorius, Astyanax shied away from his father in armor.

11. Claud., *III Cons. Hon.* 39, 62, 73–82; Stat., *Theb.* 9.739–43 (lion analogy).

12. Claud., *III Cons. Hon.* 22, 26–28 (weapons and booty).

13. Claud., *III Cons. Hon.* 73. *Rabies*—rage, madness, fierce eagerness—has negative connotations (*OLD*, s.v.).

14. Claud., *III Cons. Hon.* 83.

15. Allusion to Stat., *Achil.* 1.116–18, 2.154–56, 2.157–62, at Claud., *III Cons. Hon.* 22–23, 60–63. See also Parkes, "Model Youths?," 74, 76.

worthy of the sacred diadem that he already wore.[16] Theodosius and now Stilicho guaranteed Honorius a path to imperial *vir*-ness that was Achilles-like.[17]

While Claudian—and therefore Stilicho—acknowledged the imperial consul's precarious age, he stressed two interrelated points. First, Honorius was ready for battle. But second, to unleash that force too early, to expect *this imperator* to fight, would be a mistake. Battle-readiness in adolescents and very young men was a double-edged sword that could lead to disaster if unchecked, as Parthenopaeus and Achilles demonstrated. During his lifetime, Theodosius had been the perfect arbiter of his son's maturity, and now Stilicho had inherited that parental responsibility. Consequently, the transfer of power from Theodosius to Stilicho was one of the panegyric's central themes.[18] Claudian used direct speech to personify the dying Theodosius, giving him the most forceful voice. On his deathbed, the emperor exhorted Stilicho to "put on a father's mind" (*indue mente patrem*) and assume the care of his sons Honorius and Arcadius.[19] Stilicho's enduring loyalty (*fides*) and military prowess (*bellipotents, robur*) alone made him the perfect arbiter of the young emperors' transitions into adulthood, but in addition he was an imperial son-in-law, or *gener*.[20] Claudian's Theodosius vividly recalled Stilicho and Serena's wedding and expressed confidence that he would be untroubled once received among the gods (*divi*), knowing that the united brothers (*unanimi fratres*) Honorius and Arcadius were worthy peacetime rulers because of a father (figure) who shared their blood (*consanguineus*).[21]

Although Honorius was the principal addressee of Claudian's first panegyric, the focus was on the divine Theodosius and on Stilicho.[22] Because success in the vital quest for imperial *vir*-ness was difficult to achieve even for those blessed with divine parentage, fatherly guidance was crucial. Achilles had become the greatest hero only because he had been taught restraint as a youth. If such fatherly guidance was assured, an emperor's age was immaterial; indeed, extreme youth could be advantageous under the right circumstances. Therefore, in an innovative poetic move, Claudian's preface to the panegyric opens with the rearing of eagles. These birds allow to live only those of their young who pass the judgment (*iudicium*) of the sun and the sky. The eaglets must endure the sun's brilliance by staring directly at it, and the father eagle must tear the unworthy (*degener*) to shreds.[23] Theodosius,

16. Claud., *III Cons. Hon.* 60–62, 88–84 ("victoria velox / auspiciis effecta tuis. Pugnastis uterque: / tu fatis genitorque manu"), 144; see also *IV Cons. Hon.* 639–45.

17. Claud., *III Cons. Hon.* 42–44, 49–50; Ware, *Claudian*, 93–94.

18. Claud., *III Cons. Hon.* 142–62.

19. Claud., *III Cons. Hon.* 157. *Induo* as in putting on a dress (*OLD* s.v.).

20. Claud., *III Cons. Hon.* 142–62.

21. Claud., *III Cons. Hon.* 7–8, 105–10, 144, 154–58 ("Per consanguineos thalamos noctemque beatam, / per taedas quas ipsa tuo regina levavit / coniugio sociaque nurum produxit ab aula, / indue mente patrem, crescentes derige fetus / ut ducis, ut soceri"), 189–211. See also Ware, *Claudian*, 51–52, 81–88; Gualandri, "Un 'generalissimo' semibarbaro," 39–41.

22. Müller, *Lectiones*, 92.

23. Claud., *III Cons. Hon. Pref.* 1–14; see also Roche, "Staring at the Son."

of course, was that eternal, glittering sun, a divine Jupiter who ruled the world with his legionary eagles.[24] Because Honorius lived, that proved that he (and Arcadius) had shown innate strength (*vires*) and been confirmed (*fides*) as worthy, as Claudian reemphasized when describing the joint triumphant entry into Rome in 389 of Theodosius and Honorius, whom he compared to Bacchus at that moment.[25] The preface ends with the same solar metaphor. This time, however, the divine, Jupiter-like augustus is Honorius, called on to ascertain whether the fledgling poet Claudian too can stare at the brilliant imperial sun: "Now we are granted our lord's ears and the royal palace, and our lyre resonates with Augustus as its judge."[26]

Claudian's panegyric responded to the circumstances of 396. Like Pacatus before him, he spoke simultaneously for himself and for others—in this case, Honorius and Stilicho. His audience included supporters of Eugenius and Arbogast, whom Theodosius had defeated in another bloody civil war, in 394, a victory that Claudian also mentioned.[27] Theodosius had died suddenly in January 395, leaving Honorius, who had only just arrived in Milan, and the members of the eastern elites whom he had brought along, to collaborate with the western administration and an army that included soldiers conquered in civil war. Theodosius's decision to strengthen his ties with the Valentinians before moving against Maximus helped: Honorius had been accompanied by Galla Placidia, his half sister and Valentinian I's grand-daughter.[28] But such western connections could mitigate the formidable challenges only slightly. Faced with uncertainties, Claudian emphasized dynastic legitimacy: Honorius was a worthy heir and Stilicho Theodosius's "blood" relative. True, the emperor was young, but youth represented hope. Everyone in the audience, more-over, had successfully transitioned from *puer* to *vir*: they all, as elite fathers, knew how to manage that process. Plus, another civil war would bring the kind of disas-trous instability that no one could control. Therefore, everyone who wished to avoid that prospect had better support the divine augustus, who was guided by the strong father figure whom the *divus* Theodosius had chosen, and enjoy the peace inaugurated by Honorius's third consulate.

MARRIAGE TO MARIA

Two years later, in January 398, Claudian was again called upon to praise Honorius, now consul for the fourth time. Circumstances had changed. The augustus was

24. Pacatus also compared Theodosius to the sun: *Pan. lat.* 2(12).10.1.

25. Claud., *III Cons. Hon.* 8–9, 45, 130–32, 134–36.

26. Claud., *III Cons. Hon. Pref.* 17–18 ("Iam dominas aures, iam regia tecta meremur / et chelys Augusto iudice nostra sonat").

27. Claud., *III Cons. Hon.* 90–105.

28. Galla Placidia was Theodosius's daughter with Galla, his second wife, and hence Honorius's and Arcadius's half sister. Galla was the daughter of Valentinian I and his second wife, Justina, and thus Valentinian II's sister. In 396 she lived in Stilicho's household. See Consolino, "La prosopopea," 15; Icks, "Inadequate Heirs," 76; McLynn, *Ambrose*, 355–56; Matthews, *Western Aristocracies*, 258–64.

just shy of his fourteenth birthday, the official beginning of adulthood, signaled by the exchange of the bulla for the *toga virilis*.[29] More important, as Claudian joyfully announced, within a month Honorius would marry Maria, Stilicho's twelve-year-old daughter, a glorious union manifesting his transformation from *puer* into *vir*.[30] Stilicho, already Honorius's brother-in-law, would now be his father-in-law as well, and his adopted sister Serena his mother-in-law.[31] Claudian could thus celebrate the emperor as a four-time consul, (almost) married imperial *vir*, and, best of all, (almost) father who would guarantee the continuity of the glorious gens Ulpia.[32] Born to the imperial purple, Honorius was Trajan's worthy successor: "The day that gave you birth also gave you *imperium*: while still in the cradle you were raised a consul."[33] All he had to do to become an *optimus princeps* like his illustrious ancestor was produce an heir. "What joy for the world when the down begins to overspread your cheeks! . . . O that it might be granted to me to provide the wedding song for your nuptial bed, to hail you soon as 'father'!"[34]

Meanwhile, Honorius was a brilliant emperor and shining consul. His beauty (*decor*) sparkled like his father's gold-plated helmet, spear, and shield, dazzling all who beheld him, while his august cheeks blushed with majestic modesty. Soon this beauty would overwhelm Maria.[35] For now, young men carried Honorius, whom Claudian again likened to Bacchus, on his golden throne. He was a god all could see, made even more dignified, or "weightier" (*gravior*), by his spectacular trabea: "Indian jewels roughen your robe, and emeralds glow amid the fabric's precious threads. It contains amethysts and shining Spanish gold, whose hidden flames balance dark-blue jacinth [sapphires]. The appeal of the cloth's raw material would not suffice for such a garment: the needle enhances its merit, and metals bring the pictured work

29. The bulla was an amulet indicating a boy's citizen status: see Laes, *Children in the Roman Empire*, 278–80.

30. Technically, Honorius was too young to marry, but there had been other imperial exceptions, like Nero's assumption of the toga virilis at thirteen: see Tac., *Ann.* 12.41.1; McEvoy, *Child Emperor Rule*, 160; Gualandri, "Un 'generalissimo' semibarbaro," 42; Busch, *Die Frauen*, 54–56; Cameron, *Claudian*, 109.

31. Claud., *carm. min.* 10.41.

32. Claud., *IV Cons. Hon.* 18–20: "Haud indigna coli nec nuper cognita Marti / Ulpia progenies et quae diademata mundo / sparsit Hibera domus" (The Ulpian clan was not unworthy of respect, nor known just recently to Mars for warfare. This Spanish house has spread diadems throughout the world).

33. Claud., *IV Cons. Hon.* 122–27: "Hoc nobilis ortu / nasceris aequaeva cum maiestate creatus / nullaque privatae passus contagia sortis. / Omnibus acceptis, ultro te regia solum / protulit et patrio felix adolescis in ostro, / membraque vestitu numquam temerata profano / in sacros cecidere sinus" (From this origin, Honorius, you were nobly born, given life along with your majesty, and you endured none of the commoner's pollution. Your palace admitted everyone but produced you alone of its own accord, and you grew up fortunate in your father's imperial purple. Profane clothing never soiled your limbs; they rested in holy folds of fabric); 154–55: "Vitam tibi contulit idem / imperiumque dies. inter conabula consul / proveheris." Honorius first became consul in 386, at about fifteen months old.

34. Claud., *IV Cons. Hon.* 641–42, 650–51 ("quae gaudia mundo, / per tua lanugo cum serpere coeperit ora, ... o mihi si liceat thalamis intendere carmen / conubiale tuis, si te iam dicere patrem").

35. Claud., *IV Cons. Hon.* 518–26.

FIGURE 11. Roman emperor Constantius II in consular robe. From the Codex Calendar of 354. Romanus I ms., Barb. Lat. 2154 fol. 13. Inv.: 231.549. Palazzo Corsini, Rome, Italy. © Bildarchiv Foto Marburg / Art Resource, NY.

to life. Many a jasper ornaments the portrait, and Red Sea pearls breathe amid various figures. . . . The Phoenicians bestowed the coloring, the Chinese the silk threads, the Hydaspes River the weight of the jewels."[36] Honorius's consular robe emphasized his own divine majesty and that of his Spanish house, which had triumphed over peoples near and far—indeed, over the entire world—and whose eternal might, just like that of the empire, the young prince would soon guarantee with his offspring.

Nevertheless, though his marriage was imminent, the scion of the house of Trajan was still young. Despite his exalted birth and divine person, Honorius had to be further instructed in how to perfect the virtues that an emperor embodied. Claudian thus returned to Theodosius and Honorius's triumphant entry into Rome, now in the form of a divine teaching moment: Theodosius—in a long speech inspired by Pliny's panegyric for Trajan and echoing Pacatus's praise—presses home the importance of merit, of doing the labor necessary to deserve the imperial throne that has been inherited.[37] Had Honorius been born to the tiara of a Persian ruler, elevated birth would have sufficed and he could have whiled away his days in soft, fluid luxury (*luxuque fluentem*).[38] But every student of Rome's history knew that no one, regardless of exalted status, could rule true Romans unless he had hardened his mind and body through strenuous discipline from earliest youth. Honorius should listen to the Greek Muses but focus on Latin exemplars such as Camillus, Regulus, Mucius Scaevola, and Cato the Younger. Those consuls of old had worked the land as farmers (*trabeato rura colono*) and modeled patience, insight, chastity, restraint, and austerity.[39] Indeed, these virtues had made Honorius's father as great

---

36. Claud., *IV Cons. Hon.* 565–76, 584–601:

Portatur iuvenum cervicibus aurea sedes
ornatuque novo gravior deus. Asperat Indus
velamenta lapis pretiosaque fila zmaragdis
ducta virent; amethystus inest et fulgor Hiberus
temperat arcanis hyacinthi caerula flammis.
Nec rudis in tali suffecit gratia textu.
Auget acus meritum picturatumque metallis
vivit opus: multaque animantur iaspide cultus
et variis spirat Nereia baca figuris.
. . . Tribuere colorem
Phoenices, Seres subtegmina, pondus Hydaspes.

The Hydaspes, in Punjab, was the site of a battle between Alexander the Great and Porus: see Plut., *Alex.* 62. See also Guipponi-Gineste, "Pierres précieuses," 95–100; Guipponi-Gineste, *Claudien*, 381–95 (Claudian's sophisticated use of *ornatus* as a stylistic element); Dewar, "Spinning the *Trabea*." For the significance of colors to evoke the divine in mosaics and other forms of material representation, see Kiilerich, "Picturing Ideal Beauty."

37. Claud., *IV Cons. Hon.* 214–418. Claudian also alludes to Dio Chrysostom's kingship orations: see Ware, "Learning from Pliny."

38. Claud., *IV Cons. Hon.* 214–18.

39. Claud., *IV Cons. Hon.* 396–418. Livy and Virgil used the same canon of exemplars: see Eigler, *Lectiones vetustatis*, 12–18. For the significance of the Muses, see Zarini, "Culture grecque," 27–31. One of the earliest consular diptychs and the lost consular spoons from Aquileia also represented the Muses: see Cameron, "Origin," 178–79, 188–89.

an emperor as Trajan and allowed him to liberate Rome twice from tyrants, those raging beasts ("immanis . . . belua") who incited civil wars. As one of the gods who were present ("praesentes . . . deos"), Theodosius had shown the vanquished justice and clemency and thus had shared his victory with the defeated.[40]

Honorius then reminds his father that he is of the age when Achilles's son Pyrrhus was allowed to join in battle. Again, Theodosius restrains him: "Your love [of battle] is too hasty; the stronger time of your life will come: do not hurry."[41] Honorius should not fight just yet. Pyrrhus had fought too soon and could not control himself, which had led him to brutally slay Priam while the old king was kneeling at the altar. Such impious fury was abhorrent. Martial valor combined with beauty, education, clemency, and justice had brought Rome the peace that Honorius must now preserve; those virtues would make him a Roman Achilles, who knew how to restrain his rage. Meanwhile, as Theodosius observed from the heavens, Stilicho, the emperor's father- and brother-in-law, won the victories that were the gens Ulpia's due.[42]

THE EPIC WARRIOR'S SOFT YOUTH: HONORIUS AS ACHILLES

In February 398, Claudian praised Honorius and Maria's wedding in five poems.[43] This joyful occasion must have been particularly welcome, because Honorius and Stilicho had little else to celebrate. In the summer of 397, Stilicho had failed to subdue the Gothic troops under Alaric who were ravaging Greece and Illyricum. In the fall the African *comes* Gildo, whom Theodosius had appointed and whose daughter had married a relative of Aelia Flaccilla's, had rebelled and shifted his allegiance, together with his grain shipments, from the west to Constantinople: a serious threat.[44] Interpreting Stilicho's actions in Illyricum and Greece as attempts to wrest control of these provinces from the east, the court at Constantinople declared him a public enemy, *hostis publicus*, in late 397 or early 398.[45] The court in Milan reacted by intensifying the dynastic links uniting Stilicho, Theodosius, and Honorius with another marriage.

All five wedding poems highlight the tight family bonds inaugurated by the divine Theodosius but focus on Stilicho as his *gener*, or son-in law, and Honorius's

---

40. Claud., *IV Cons. Hon.* 55–64 (for Theodosius's *civilitas*), 72–73, 98–99 (*deos*), 111–21, 250 (alluding to Pliny's characterization of Domitian as *belua*). See also Bönisch-Meyer, *Dialogangebote*, 210–12, for *deus praesens*.

41. Claud., *IV Cons. Hon.* 353–69, 371–72 ("Sed festinus amor. Veniet robustior aetas; / ne propera").

42. Claud., *IV Cons. Hon.* 18–20, 430–34, 505–17.

43. Claud., *carm. min.* 9–14: preface to the epithalamium (9), epithalamium (10), *fescennines* (11–14); Gineste, "Poésie," for the evolution of the genres epithalamium (271–73) and *fescennina* (274–75). In what follows, I adapt Bernstein's translation.

44. Matthews, *Western Aristocracies*, 268–73.

45. Börm, *Westrom*, 42–48; Kulikowski, *Rome's Gothic Wars*, 164–68; Cameron, *Claudian*, 93–95.

FIGURE 12. The Monza Diptych, ca. 400 CE, ivory, probably representing Stilicho, Serena, and Eucherius. Duomo, Monza, Italy. White Images / Scala / Art Resource, NY.

socer, or father-in-law. As Honorius proclaims in one, "I did not rush to seize a bride already betrothed to someone else in marriage, but the bride long since engaged to me, and left to me by my father's orders, and who through her mother shares with me a common grandfather and a single origin."[46] Claudian dedicated the wedding poem *Fescenninum* 13 entirely to Stilicho, asking him to change his armor for a soft, subtle flower garland (*molli necte corona*) to celebrate the day

46. Claud., *carm. min.* 10.29–31:

Non rapio praeceps alienae foedera taedae,
sed quae sponsa mihi pridem patrisque relicta
mandatis uno materni sanguinis ortu
communem partitur avum.

that made him the emperor's father: "Stilicho socer est, pater est Stilicho."[47] That day, Serena also became Honorius's mother (*mater*). Honorius asks her to hasten the wedding as his cousin and sister but makes it clear that although Flaccilla had borne him, Serena was his true mother ("pietate parens . . . partuque remoto / tu potior Flaccilla mihi").[48] Slowly but surely, Stilicho and Serena replace Theodosius and Flaccilla as Honorius's (and Arcadius's) true parents.

In the poems celebrating Honorius and Maria's wedding, Claudian brings to the fore another theme already present in his two prior panegyrics: Honorius as a young Achilles ("iam spondet Achillem").[49] Alluding throughout to Statius's *Achilleid* and *Thebaid*, he models Honorius's impatience, uncertainty, and mood swings—that is, his awakening erotic desire for Maria—on Achilles's desire for Deidameia.[50] When Achilles was asked to join the Greek expedition against Troy, his mother Thetis begged him to hide on the island of Skyros instead, camouflaged as a young girl. Achilles rejected her subterfuge, but Thetis persuaded him that many gods had also worn women's clothes, including Jupiter, Bacchus, and his half brother Hercules (to whom Claudian had already compared Honorius).[51] Convinced, Achilles went to Skyros dressed as a young girl, where he met Deidameia, the king's daughter, as she was playing with her sisters. That vision awakened his erotic desires, and he pursued her, still wearing a young woman's clothing, until he finally caught and raped her during a festival in honor of Bacchus (or Dionysus), resulting in the birth of Neoptolemus. Eventually Odysseus, also wearing women's clothing, exposed Achilles, who then joined the battle.[52]

Claudian's poems follow the same narrative arc. The opening verses of the *Epithalamium*, or wedding poem, present Honorius as a young Achilles enmeshed in a dance of love and war. Like Achilles, Honorius in love forgot about horses and hunting and thought only about selecting wedding presents for Maria, including the jewels that Augustus's wife Livia had worn. Like Deidameia, Maria had put a spell on her young Achilles.[53] Venus took pity on Honorius's

47. Claud., *carm. min.* 13.12. See also Gualandri, "Un 'generalissimo' semibarbaro," 42–43.

48. Claud., *carm. min.* 10.38–42. As Cameron, *Claudian*, 58, notes, from then on Serena is mentioned only as Honorius's mother.

49. At *carm. min.* 9.19, Claudian compares Honorius and Maria to Achilles's parents, Peleus and Thetis, but melds Peleus with Achilles; see also Wasdin, "Honorius Trimphant," 59–60.

50. Statius reworked the Epic Cycle, especially the *Cypria*, but also alluded to Ov., *Ars am.* 1.695–96, and to Dido and Aeneas (Virg., *Aen.* 1.498–502): see McNelis, "Statius' *Achilleid*," 588–95; Parkes, "Model Youths?," 73–80.

51. Stat., *Achil.* 1.254–65; see also McNelis, "Bacchus"; Heslin, *Transvestite Achilles*, 240–41. In a different version, Thetis plays no role, so it is Achilles himself who decides to wear women's clothing: see Fantuzzi, "Achilles at Scyros," 295–305.

52. Stat., *Achil.* 1.593–618. As Waldner, *Geburt*, 82–101, has shown, the story goes back to the fifth century BCE.

53. Claud., *carm. min.* 10.16–19.

suffering and hastened to Milan to advance the wedding day.[54] At court, she first encountered Stilicho's splendid soldiers, ready to conquer Gildo. All dressed in triumphal white, the soldiers immediately obeyed her command to suspend the war for love. Honorius roamed the fields like a lovesick stallion while the soldiers composed wedding songs praising Stilicho as the best leader and a fortunate father about to bounce imperial grandchildren on his knees.[55] The *Fescennines* continue where the *Epithalamium* leaves off, culminating in the wedding night. In the concluding poem, Claudian praises Maria's exceptional modesty (*pudor*) by evoking Achilles's rape of Deidameia: the marriage was consummated in a battle in which Honorius celebrated a bloody triumph.[56]

The story of Achilles playing with Deidameia and her sisters enjoyed immense popularity in the later Roman Empire. A frequent decorative motif, mosaics, frescoes, vases, and silverware portrayed Achilles wearing women's clothing while wielding a sword and shield, dramatizing the moment of his exposure by Odysseus.[57] Like Claudian's description of Honorius's erotic triumph, these scenes celebrated the time-honored trope of love as war, or *militia amoris*.[58] For my purpose, the other theme of Claudian's analogy of Honorius as the young Achilles, enhanced through comparisons with Bacchus and Hercules, is more important: divinely beautiful heroes, whose embodiment of manliness includes the subtle softness of (looking like) a young woman. Claudian's praise of Honorius's beauty via the young Achilles emphasized their adolescent softness and smooth gorgeousness, which transcended gendered binaries, as befitted those who were divine. Bacchus, Hercules, and Achilles signaled their expansive, capacious fluidity with female dress, while the glitter of consular and imperial robes accentuated Honorius's youthful beauty.[59] Both young Achilles and Honorius had conquered a chaste young woman through their erotic power. Yet their immense desirability to men and desire for men was equally prominent: everyone knew of Achilles's love for Patroclus.

Like Themistius, Ausonius, and Ambrose, Claudian paired the young emperor's gorgeous beauty with martial valor. However, by comparing Honorius to Bacchus,

---

54. Claud., *carm. min.* 10.180–227. See Elsner, "Visualising Women," 22–36, for contemporary representations of Venus as an embodiment of the sexual pleasures of marriage.

55. Claud., *carm. min.* 10.289–94, 334–41.

56. Claud., *carm. min.* 14.3–6, 25–30. This particular Claudianic move has received comparatively little scholarly attention.

57. Cameron, "Young Achilles," 2–4; Guidetti, "Hero's White Hands"; Guidetti, "'First-Generation Diptychs,'" 220. This image forms the center of the famous fourth-century CE silver Achilles plate, probably an imperial donative made in Thessalonica, from Kaiseraugst (Römermuseum, Augst, inv. 1962.1): see Guggisberg, *Der spätrömische Silberschatz*, 255–56, 263 (*largitio*), 263–66 (popularity of the young Achilles motif). Achilles's exposure in Skyros is also the theme of the central medallion of a silver plate from the Sevso treasure (263).

58. Wasdin, "Honorius Triumphant," 57–60.

59. Hostile Christian responses (see Eppinger, "*Hercules Cinaedus?*," 202–11), did little to dent the popularity of Achilles or Hercules in women's clothes.

FIGURE 13. Central medallion of the Achilles platter dish, 330–340 CE, silver, diameter: 53 cm. The scene shows Achilles being discovered by Odysseus. From Kaiseraugst, inventory number: 1962.1. © Augusta Raurica. Photo: Susanne Schenker.

Hercules, and the young Achilles in love, Claudian rendered the emperor's youthful male beauty more subtle by adding the erotic power of a young woman to the transcendent whole. Such exuberantly gendered beauty went hand in hand with extraordinary martial valor, the height of imperial *vir*-ness, also signified by Achilles, Bacchus, and Hercules: all of Claudian's exemplars for Honorius amplified this point. Becoming a world-conquering hero required a softness in youth that incorporated the subtleness of a young woman. This expansiveness permitted the hero—or young emperor—to marshal an immensely capacious *vir*-ness and to explode into combat when called for.[60] As Claudian's intertexts make clear, Achilles, Bacchus, and Hercules, all of whom spent time in women's clothing, stood for Rome's world-conquering power as well, just like the young consul,

60. Williams, *Roman Homosexuality*, 125–32, surveys descriptions of softness in several first- and second-century CE Latin sources, including those that advocate a golden mean of grooming (soft the right way). He does not, however, address the positive military implications or soft power.

whose trabea also signaled triumph.[61] Indeed, the insignia and vestments of their soft, womanly side could turn instantaneously into weapons. Thus, Statius's Bacchus wears his *mitra*, a headband associated with women and "Persian" men, while using his staff to conquer India.[62] Claudian further compared Honorius to Alexander, whose military triumphs matched his beauty and same-sex desirability.[63]

Indeed, Claudian consistently paired Honorius's soft beauty, enhanced by his downy beard, with the language of conquest. The emperor celebrated his wedding in gleaming armor, triumphant soldiers sang his wedding songs, and Venus's gift was war booty.[64] The first *Fescennine* celebrates his beauty's domination of the *orbis terrarum*, the entire world: "bellumque solus conficeret decor" (your beauty alone would end a war).[65] It glittered fiercer than the stars, was hotter than fire and so amazing that Thetis (!) would have preferred him to Achilles, and made him more desirable than Bacchus and Adonis.[66] Lions welcomed the thrust of his lance, and fierce Scythians longed to be enslaved by his beauty, which persuaded wild Amazons to sue for peace.[67] Finally, even chaste Maria succumbed to the beautiful Honorius ("formosus Mariam ducit Honorius").[68] The capacious, subtle beauty of the greatest warriors whom epic and history had to offer, which included the beauty and virtues of a young woman, was universal and divine and, embodied by a young *sacratissimus imperator* such as Honorius, all but guaranteed commensurate martial valor. It was beauty as a weapon powerful enough to overwhelm lions, Scythians, Amazons, and imperial brides to preserve Rome's eternal greatness.

Scholarly analysis has rightly stressed the degree to which Stilicho dominates Claudian's two panegyrics and his wedding poems, with Honorius relegated to the margin as a perennial son, merely signaling future potential.[69] Stilicho's powerful position as a military leader and guardian was undoubtedly important. However, such readings underestimate the degree to which the language of youth, beauty, and same-sex erotic desire was also a language of power. Like Ausonius, Themistius, and Ambrose before him, Claudian combined his praise of the young augustus's beauty with tributes to a military valor that operated in the present

61. Virg., *Aen.* 6.801–5, compares Augustus's conquests to those of Bacchus and Hercules in Persia; according to Plin., *HN* 7.191, Bacchus invented the Roman triumph. After Commodus, emperors were acclaimed as *Hercules pacator orbis*, implying conquest but also negotiation or labor that benefited the world: see Bönisch-Meyer, *Dialogangebote*, 229–34.

62. Stat., *Achil.* 1.615–18; *Theb.* 7.149–50. See also McNelis, "Bacchus," 449–540; Heslin, *Transvestite Achilles*, 238–54.

63. Claud., *IV Cons. Hon.* 257–60, 374–78; see also Parkes, "Model Youths?," 71–72.

64. Claud., *carm. min.* 10.16–19, 289–94, 334–34; Gualandri, "Un 'generalissimo' semibarbaro," 45–47.

65. Claud., *carm. min.* 11.39.

66. Claud., *carm. min.* 11.6–9. In *IV Cons. Hon.*, Claudian likens Honorius to Hercules (206–11) and to the sons of Leda and Jupiter (532–36).

67. Claud., *carm. min.* 11.13–15, 25–34.

68. Claud., *carm. min.* 14.37.

69. See, e.g., Wasdin, "Honorius Triumphant," 60–61; Parkes, "Model Youths?," 78–82; Roche, "Staring at the Son," 143; Müller, *Lectiones*, 167–73; McEvoy, *Child Emperor Rule*, 160–61; Nathan, "Ideal Male in Late Antiquity," 10–17.

while also signaling future might. Honorius's beauty, like that of Gratian (or Achilles), slayed—literally. Comparing Honorius to epic warriors famous for complex gender performances allowed Claudian to emphasize the unifying force that the immense desirability of a youthful emperor exercised on everyone: old, young, male, female, Roman, non-Roman, even the animal world. Overwhelming male beauty was as powerful a weapon as the actual sword of a Stilicho or any other military leader. In 398, then, Claudian's Honorius and his Stilicho complemented each other perfectly, the sum of their powers vastly exceeding its parts.[70]

The interconnectedness of beauty, same-sex erotic desire, martial valor, and a fluid, expansive manliness—including dressing in women's attire—is a central theme of the works discussed in the previous chapters. The author of the *Life of Heliogabalus* acknowledged the full force of the emperor's erotic power by illustrating the many ways it could be abused if allowed to go unchecked. Pacatus's praise showed that a supremely beautiful legitimate ruler of mature age, by modulating his erotic attraction through physical hardness, discipline, and self-restraint, was more than capable of regulating the desire of others.[71] Indeed, as the emphasis of Ausonius and Ammianus on the chaste modesty (*pudor*) of supremely gorgeous young emperors indicates, it was necessary to harness the power of their attractiveness. The boundary between desire and fulfillment had to be firm: you could look at the divine, you should desire it, but you must never touch it. Only bad emperors like "Heliogabalus" allowed this line to be crossed. While a *sacratissimus imperator* was young and his naturally soft beauty even more sublimely dangerous for those who desired him, it was his father's duty to step in as teacher and arbiter. Just as he did when curbing excessive exuberance in warfare, a good father enforced firm boundaries of male erotic desire and preserved the young emperor's modesty. Because Honorius had been guided by the firm hand of "the law's most just arbiter, and most faithful guardian of splendid peace," Stilicho, his *pudor* had remained intact.[72] His transition from *puer* to married *vir* and *sacratissimus divinus imperator* was on the right track, channeling his erotic power into mature leadership, marriage, and fatherhood.

PROGENITOR OF EMPERORS
AND FATHER OF THE PRINCE

In 400, in Milan and then Rome, Claudian was finally able to celebrate the first consulate of his hero Stilicho.[73] His panegyric in three books concluded Stilicho's assumption of Theodosius's place as father, further expanding imperial

70. Ware, "Learning from Pliny," 329–31.

71. *Pan. lat.* (2)12.8.3–4, (2)12.9.4–7, (2)12.20.46. See chapters 1–2; also Aus., *Grat. Act.* 13.62; Amm. Marc. 27.6.15.

72. Claud., *carm. min.* 10.332–33 ("Iustissime legum / arbiter, egregiae pacis fidissime custos").

73. Schindler, *Per carmina*, 109–37; Garambois-Vasquez, "L'éloge de Stilichon"; Cameron, "Origin," 205.

fatherhood.[74] Two years after Honorius's wedding, Claudian had to moderate the hopeful exuberance of his earlier poems. Honorius and Maria had not yet produced children, and tensions with the east continued to increase. As a countermeasure, Claudian redirected his focus on dynastic lineage to Stilicho, as the model of imperial fatherhood. Stilicho's consular trabea became the canvas for a rich word picture celebrating Honorius's (but really the new consul's) court. In Claudian's depiction, Honorius's consular robe had added gravitas, literal weight, to the young emperor's youthful beauty to enhance his (as yet only potential) martial significance. This time, the trabea honored a mature *vir* and military leader who had actually fought. Here too, however, Claudian used the garment to emphasize contrasting valor: rather than a *bellipotens* warrior, he painted Stilicho as the quintessential imperial family man, the father and grandfather of many future augusti born to the house of Stilicho.[75]

Eliding Honorius and Maria's childless union, Claudian assembled Stilicho and Serena's offspring to portray an extended imperial family with numerous grandchildren (*dominis avus*) as the centerpiece of the consular trabea.[76] The goddesses Roma and Minerva had woven this trabea with purple and golden threads, and they gave it to their hero just as Venus had presented Aeneas with arms and a shield (*clipeus*).[77] Roma and Minerva's robe announced a golden age, which Jupiter had promised Aeneas and which Augustus, who later received Aeneas's golden shield, had realized.[78] Both goddesses and all the deities representing Rome's western and eastern provinces were overjoyed that Stilicho had finally set aside his modesty (*pudor*) and accepted the office that would bring back Rome's liberty.[79] Now Stilicho would inaugurate a new golden age through unsurpassed domesticity. The goddesses' trabea had three embroidered panels (*segmenta*) with vistas of the imperial palace's interior. The first showed Maria giving birth to Honorius's first son, anxiously watched by Serena and aided by the goddess of childbirth.[80] The second depicted that little Honorius happily bouncing on the knees of Stilicho,

---

74. Claud., *Cons. Stil.* 1–3 (bks. 1–2: Milan; bk. 3: Rome). See also Müller, *Lectiones*, 91–182; Coombe, *Claudian the Poet*, 124–46; Sánchez-Ostiz, "Claudian's Stilicho," 315–28. Coombe, "Hero in Our Midst," discusses the political implications of Claudian's style, focusing on *In Rufinum*.

75. Gualandri, "Un 'generalissimo' semibarbaro," 48–53; Cameron, *Claudian*, 47, 95, 98–99, 154.

76. Claud., *Cons. Stil.* 2.233–40; see also *carm. min.* 10.340–41.

77. Claud., *Cons. Stil.* 2.218–329; cf. Virg., *Aen.* 8.731. See also Consolino, "La prosopopea"; Feldherr, "Viewing Myth."

78. Claud., *Cons. Stil.* 2.278–81, 331–33, 339–41 ("Dixit gremioque rigentia profert / dona, graves auro trabeas. Insigne Minervae / spirat opus.")

79. Claud., *Cons. Stil.* 2.330–76.

80. Claud., *Cons. Stil.* 2.341–44:

Rutilis hic pingitur aula columnis
et sacri Mariae partus. Lucina dolores
solatur; residet fulgente puerpera lecto;
sollicitae iuxta pallescunt gaudia matris.

See also Schmidt, *Politik und Dichtung*, 39.

who used the playtime to instruct the future ruler in the art of war. The third panel celebrated the anticipated imperial wedding of Stilicho and Serena's son Eucherius to Honorius's half sister Galla Placidia. That union would further strengthen the links to the Valentinian dynasty, through a bride "born from emperors, sister to emperors."[81] Stilicho and Serena's daughter Thermantia completed the picture, smiling happily on her brother's wedding day.

Three weddings—that of Stilicho and Serena, that of Honorius and Maria, and the imagined one of Eucherius and Galla Placidia—were thus central to Stilicho's consulship. They morphed the united houses of Valentinian and Theodosius into that of Stilicho, whose *domus* "now claims diadems for both sexes, and gives birth to queens and husbands of queens."[82] He embodied mature, adult Theodosian Roman imperial manliness and virtue, combining ferocious military powers with *clementia* and *fides*. Chosen by Theodosius as a father for his two sons, Stilicho was now the father of the ruler, *parens principis*. As such, he could guide Honorius without threatening or displacing the actual augustus.[83] Stilicho and Honorius shared the gens Ulpia and formed one *domus*.[84] As the father of Honorius and Maria, Eucherius and Galla Placidia, Stilicho was *verior Augusti genitor*, the true procreator of the current augustus and all future ones. Moreover, he was also the father of future empresses: just like their brothers and husbands, Serena and Maria, Galla Placidia and Thermantia were indispensable guarantors of Rome's eternal future.[85] Stilicho, that phoenix risen from the ashes of civil war, advanced the Theodosian golden age as arbiter and teacher, guide and military leader, father and grandfather of augusti, promising a Theodosian *imperium sine fine*.[86]

Claudian's achievements were remarkable. In 398, the not-yet-married, thirteen-year-old Honorius became an exemplary peacetime ruler, whose sublime, expansively gendered beauty complemented the (moderate) military success of his general and "father." Just two years later, Claudian celebrated Stilicho's consulship via images of motherhood and fatherhood, with the consul as true father guaranteeing Rome's *aeternitas* through three generations. Emperor and consul formed the perfect Roman imperial gens, united by sacred family bonds. Alas, the actual bodies beneath the shimmering consular robes failed to perform as advertised. Honorius remained childless with both Maria and Thermantia, whom he wed after Maria's death in 407, and Eucherius never married Galla Placidia. However, in 398 and 400

---

81. Claud., *Cons. Stil.* 2.357 ("Progenitam Augustis Augustorumque sororem"). As mentioned in n. 28 above, Galla Placidia had grown up in Stilicho's household.

82. Claud., *Cons. Stil.* 2.360–61 ("Iam domus haec utroque petit diademata sexu / reginasque parit reginarumque maritos").

83. Claud., *Cons. Stil.* 3.113–30.

84. Claud., *Cons. Stil.* 1.30–34.

85. Claud., *Cons. Stil.* 3.122, 113–23 (for *socer*).

86. Claud., *Cons. Stil.* 2.409–23. See also Coombe, "Hero in Our Midst," 170–76; Coombe, *Claudian the Poet*, 128, 132–43; Lecocq, "Le phénix chez Claudien," 138–46.

this was the future, and the strategy worked. In 405/6, Rome's Senate dedicated an inscription to Stilicho praising his *adfinitas regiae* as Honorius's *progener* and *socer*.[87] Another inscription declares him *parens* to Honorius; the poet Prudentius called him *parens* and Symmachus *parens publicus*.[88] These were powerful honorifics, evoking Romulus as the *pater patriae*: father, liberator, and savior of the realm, a title that Augustus had first claimed, followed by all the subsequent emperors.[89] Stilicho now took on that mythical sheen, which brought him even closer to the actual emperor, his "son." The *parens principis* Stilicho could declare the same bond with Arcadius in Constantinople as the one that united him with Honorius. Indeed, that had been Stilicho's claim all along: to guide the entire *imperium* of the united divine brothers for the greater glory of Rome.

Arcadius, however, had no interest in Stilicho's demand that he be recognized as the father of both princes and as such a new Theodosius. To the eastern court he was a public enemy, his consulship meritless. Claudian's creation of Stilicho as a true progenitor of future augusti, as the father and continuator of the Theodosian dynasty, was aimed at a western audience. In Milan and Rome, tensions with the eastern court and unrest caused by Gothic federations required constant reminders that the young augustus was powerful and his rule secure. Presenting Stilicho as Honorius's father allowed the court at Milan to take full advantage of the erotic power of the youthful emperor's softness while highlighting the unique bond that tied his leading general to the house of Theodosius, which continued unabated as the house of Stilicho. The emperor and his general formed a perfect union: as father and teacher, Stilicho supervised Honorius's transition to full imperial *virness* while maintaining peace, and together they preserved Rome's eternal glory. Potential usurpers were put on notice that Stilicho was no random military leader controlling a weak emperor. Moreover, Stilicho as father countered—at least from the representational perspective—the specter of the *exoletus*. At a minimum, their relationship resembled the scenario that the author of the *Historia Augusta* had imagined for Gordian III, in which a mature father-in-law guided a married and hence tolerable young ruler. Claudian highlighted that Stilicho was already a father of three, while Honorius was capable of becoming a father at any moment.

87. *CIL* 6.1730, ll. 1, 6–14 ("[Flavio Stilichoni, inlustrissimo] [. . .] ab ineunte aetate per gradus clarissimae militiae ad columen gloriae sempiternae et regiae adfinitatis evecto, progenero divi Theodosi, comiti divi Theodosi Augusti in omnibus bellis atque victoriis, et ab eo in adfinitatem regiam cooptato, itemque socero domni nostri Honori Augusti"). See also *CIL* 6.1731; for the date, Orlandi in *EDR* 111525. These inscriptions survived the memory sanctions following Stilicho's execution in 408. See also Lizzi Testa, "I vescovi, i barbari e l'impero di Roma," 27–34.

88. *CIL* 9.4051; Prud., *Contra Symm.* 2.709 ("comes eius / atque parens, Stilicho") (402); Symm., *Ep.* 4.12.1 (400), 4.1.4.2 (401). See also Matthews, *Western Aristocracies*, 265; Gualandri, "Un 'generalissimo' semibarbaro," 37, 51–52; McEvoy, *Child Emperor Rule*, 169; Straub, "*Parens principum*," 94–111; Marcone, "Stilicone *parens publicus*."

89. Cic., *Rep.* 1.41.64; Livy 7.1.10; Consolino, "La prosopopea," 15–16; Bönisch-Meyer, *Dialogangebote*, 246–52.

This, then, was the message: the Roman emperor, the most sacred, divine apex of imperial virtues, might be a child or an adolescent, but if he was guided by a father(figure) and could become a father, he would be a proper imperial *vir*.

FOREVER YOUNG: PAIRING THE RULER

As the preceding chapters have shown, during the reign of Theodosius and the early years of Honorius's and Arcadius's rule, the meaning of being a *vir*, an elite Roman man, shifted under intense pressure. Pacatus, Themistius, Ausonius, Ambrose, the author of the *Historia Augusta*, Claudian, and others—all members of that elite and, as such, highly attuned seismographs of power—sensed these shifts and reflected them in their writing. Although each author was reacting to specific situations and had his own agenda and point of view, their individual voices combined into a choir that expressed a gradual expansion of elite manliness centered on the imperial person. Beginning with Gratian and Valentinian II, significantly adjusted and redirected by Theodosius, and further extended by his sons, a concept of divine imperial *vir*-ness emerged that progressed toward an expansive form of manliness best described as queer. The queerness at the center of power that I am trying to capture resembles what Eve Kosofsky Sedgwick has called "the open mesh of possibilities, gaps, overlaps, dissonances and resonances, lapses and excesses of meaning when the constituent elements of anyone's gender, of anyone's sexuality aren't made (or *can't be* made) to signify monolithically."[90] This capacious manliness was distinctly imperial and reflected a series of representational experiments and choices through which Theodosius and his sons gradually made the *divinus, sacratissimus imperator* into a supremely gorgeous *vir* who could be hard, robust, battle-proven, soft, subtle, smooth—as smooth as a young girl or woman—and eternally young: all this, to reiterate, as a *vir*.[91]

The choir of texts analyzed in these chapters also illuminate why first Theodosius and later his sons found this exuberant, capaciously gendered language of manly beauty useful. Most importantly, it augmented the emperor's attractiveness to and erotic desirability for everyone—and above all, other (predominantly male) members of the elite. This was a trait that could be deployed to address a series of challenges. Repeated usurpations had caused civil wars that set Romans against Romans, with each side augmenting its fighting force with Gothic, Alan, Frankish,

---

90. Sedgwick, *Tendencies*, 8 (emphasis hers). In the introduction to the revised edition of *Epistemology of the Closet*, Sedgwick says, "So what is queer about [*Epistemology of the Closet*]? Retrospectively, I would say it's exactly [the] resistance to treating homo/heterosexual categorization . . . as a done deal, a transparently empirical fact about any person" (xvi). See also Varner, "Transcending Gender," 189–93, 196–202.

91. "Gender indeterminate" and "nonbinary" (which I use sparingly) partly capture what I see here, but not all of it, because this capaciousness is an expansion of being male. This is also why I avoid the term *effeminate*, unless it is used in the sources.

or Hunnic troops. Even nonfighting members of the empire-wide elite, particularly in the west, where most of the battles were fought, were forced to choose sides as legitimate Roman emperors opposed each other. The loser and his supporters faced death and ignominy. At the moment of loss, emperors who had been the apex of Roman *vir*-ness instantly became less-than-manly tyrants and monsters, while their surviving supporters suffered a near complete forfeit of status, including their manliness or *vir*-ness: they were denigrated as soft, fluid, delicate beings devoid of hardness, vigor, restraint. The victor's imperial clemency could, however, equally instantaneously revert that loss. Clemency restored *vir*-ness; indeed, it reconstituted unity by turning defeat into victory for all.

Pacatus's praise of Theodosius's civil war victory through the contrast of two forms of imperial *vir*-ness—beautiful, clement victor versus monstrous loser—reflects this fragile or malleable manliness in two interrelated ways. First, it was now openly acknowledged that civil wars pitted Romans against Romans (rather than solely against Romans denigrated as lesser others)—in Theodosius's case an eastern Roman, Constantinopolitan ruler against a western Roman contender. Therefore victory equated "being Roman" and loss "being non-Roman," regardless of ethnic considerations. Being Roman meant being a true *vir*, and, conversely, being a true *vir* meant being Roman, so the victorious emperor became the arbiter of both Romanness and *vir*-ness, deciding who was a *vir* and Roman, and who was less-than-manly and non-Roman, at least in the immediate aftermath of a civil war.

The emperor's ability to make men instantly into elite Roman *viri* or the reverse intersected with a second phenomenon, which predated Theodosius's reign but presented a significant challenge for him and his sons: children as emperors, a practice initiated by Valentinian I's elevation of Gratian as fully fledged coruler at age eight, followed by that of Valentinian II, aged four. Valentinian I might have been influenced by military officers' custom of bringing along their sons, who were enrolled in the army's lists, whenever they moved, but his decision was unprecedented and caused friction.[92] Theodosius continued the practice and introduced it into the eastern part of the empire when he made coaugusti of Arcadius at six and Honorius at eight. Declaring a child an augustus manifested the ruling emperor's power as the arbiter of *vir*-ness, here imperial *vir*-ness. Because a legitimate Roman emperor embodied Roman virtues, he was by definition a splendid *vir*, irrespective of age. The moment the emperor decided that his son was an augustus, that son became an imperial *vir*, whether at four or forty-five years old.

Nevertheless, elevating a child to augustus was risky, as the *Historia Augusta* illustrates. Making children consuls might have been one way to test the waters. As mentioned briefly above, Gratian, Valentinian II, Valens's deceased son Valentinian Galates, and Arcadius and Honorius all became consuls while very young,

---

92. See chapter 2; McEvoy, *Child Emperor Rule*, 326, for the utter novelty of this imperial action.

at ages ranging from under two to seven years old.[93] Moreover, there were other examples of very young members of the senatorial elites in Rome, Milan, Constantinople, and elsewhere who were appointed to high-ranking offices, particularly those that provided games. As Alan Cameron has emphasized, in the late fourth century a young boy's accession to such a position (e.g., the quaestorship) afforded his father, who had paid for the privilege, a welcome occasion to show off his wealth and standing through lavish gifts distributed to friends and acquaintances. These adolescent officeholders, often represented together with their fathers—for example, on the newly fashionable presentation diptychs—enhanced the standing of their families and especially that of the father with whom they were joined.[94]

For the emperor's family, father-son pairings were advantageous because they significantly broadened the representational possibilities. Through doubling, a father's *vir*-ness expanded toward the capaciously soft and smooth, in ways that could be as experimental and gradual as the circumstances (and the experiment's reception) demanded. Symmachus, the first panegyrist to praise a nine-year-old augustus, mentioned the boy's father, Valentinian I, but rather than emphasize the father-son couple he concentrated on portraying Gratian as an ideal emperor.[95] Themistius in 376 and then Ausonius in 379 focused on the beauty, splendor, and desirability of the still young Gratian, because in 376 his father had just died and in 379 he was the senior emperor, but Valens (Gratian's uncle) was ever present.[96] Pacatus's panegyric to Theodosius mentions Arcadius and Honorius, though only in passing, first because the emphasis is on the contrast between the emperor and Maximus, and second because although Honorius was present, focusing on him would have called unwanted attention to the absent senior western augustus, young Valentinian II.[97] Nevertheless, at the moment of triumph, this Theodosius oscillates between the more traditional, mature beauty of the battle-proven emperor in the Republican register and a softer side. This is expressed both in his benevolent clemency and compassion, or *misericordia*, which enveloped all in his maternal bosom, and in the ways he loved his friends (*amicitia*)—"a humble [*humilis*] virtue, and it is doubtful whether it was judged a virtue—worthy not of palaces but of sheds"—which exceeded the more formalized companionship of the *princeps civilis*.[98]

---

93. Jovian's son Verronianus was made a consul at about age one, when his father became augustus; Gratian was seven; Valentinian II became a consul for the first time at five, when he was already augustus; Valentinian Galates was likewise five; Arcadius also became a consul as augustus, at seven; Honorius was barely two. See McEvoy, *Child Emperor Rule*, 326–27.

94. Cameron, "Origins," 179–85; see also Guidetti, "'First-Generation Diptychs,'" 212–15.

95. Symm., *Or.* 3. See also Mleczek, "Gratian," 359–69; Sogno, *Q. Aurelius Symmachus*, 15–19; McEvoy, *Child Emperor Rule*, 309.

96. See chapter 2; Jussen, "Enduring the Dust;" G. Kelly, "Political Crisis."

97. *Pan. lat.* 2(12).11.4–5; see also Rees, *Commentary*, 262–63, and 15–16.

98. *Pan. lat.* 2(12).16.1. See also chapter 1; Ch. Kelly, "Pliny and Pacatus," 233.

Pacatus could call attention to Theodosius's softer side even without emphasizing it through a pairing with Honorius because the emperor had done so himself, as the next chapter will discuss in detail. Here, I want to point to the famous Madrid *missorium*, a larger silver plate presented by Theodosius to a high-ranking official in 388 in celebration of the *decennalia*, or ten-year anniversary of his rule.[99] All three of the then-emperors (Valentinian II, Theodosius, and Arcadius) are present, with Valentinian II clearly marked as the senior augustus. Theodosius, offering the documents of appointment, or *codicilli*, to an imperial official, is central.[100] Although in his forties, the emperor appears young, with a shiny, unlined, elongated face, just as youthful as the sixteen-year-old Valentinian and the soft, round-faced Arcadius; all three have regular, harmonious features, radiating divine perfection. As Martin Kovacs and Fabio Guidetti have shown, this *missorium* is among the earliest examples of a new Theodosian visual language. Originating in Constantinople, it departs markedly from the more expressive, fleshy, stocky, age-appropriate representations of the Valentinians, in a return to and reinterpretation of a classicizing style, already noticeable on coins that predate the *missorium*.[101]

Theodosius, in other words, chose to present himself as both mature and eternally young, indistinguishable from his two young corulers except in their different dimensions. In their youthful smoothness, the *missorium*'s emperors evoke a transcendent "aura of sanctity," which the imperial official is allowed to share.[102] At the same time, as Mark Masterson has pointed out, this aura of transcendence is enhanced by the other divine figures on the plate, above and below, which are associated with desire and fertility: the reclining figure of the goddess Earth and the surrounding naked cupids. The plate thus suggests a double pairing. One connects the mature emperor with the two youthful rulers, while the other creates "representation along a circuit of erotic desire (i.e., the cupids) [and] generates a narrative of masculine grandeur . . . offer[ing] a picture of relations between men whose closeness and genuineness has the liveliness of actual sexual release. . . . Erotics . . . heighten glamorous transcendence."[103]

With Honorius, the expansion of imperial *vir*-ness through layers and parings accelerated markedly. In Claudian's hands Theodosius, the mature (though also soft) father, morphed into the predominantly Republican and Augustan Stilicho, a mighty, battle-proven imperial *vir* and father, progenitor of the gens Ulpia's future augusti and augustae—except that Stilicho was not Honorius's father, and this

---

99. Most scholars (e.g., Kiilerich, "Representing an Emperor," 273–80) favor 388, as pointed out by Guidetti, "Between Expressionism and Classicism," 156–57n22; while Kovacs, *Kaiser, Senatoren*, accepts 393 (91n1). See also Kiilerich, *Late Fourth Century Classicism*, 19–26.

100. Ch. Kelly, *Ruling*, 19–22, 193–94.

101. Kovacs, *Kaiser, Senatoren*, 66–69, 91–96; Guidetti, "Between Expressionism and Classicism," 155–64, 169–71; Guidetti, "'First-Generation Diptychs,'" 219–21.

102. Quote in Ch. Kelly, *Ruling*, 188.

103. Masterson, *Man to Man*, 87.

FIGURE 14. *Missorium* of Theodosius I the Great and his son, 387–388 CE, silver, diameter: 74 cm (29 in.), weight: 16.13 kg (35.56 lbs). Academia de la Historia, Madrid, Spain. Scala / Art Resource, NY.

family, in a queering move, had been fluidly created.[104] Theodosius's metamorphosis occurred in tandem with the expansion of Honorius as supremely gorgeous and battle-ready yet smooth, further enhanced in 398, on the cusp of his marriage, through the analogy with the cross-dressed Bacchus and young Achilles.

Other pairings of youthful and mature beauty emphasize this development. For example, after Honorius's second term as a consul—in 394, the year in which Theodosius beat Eugenius—he was succeeded in 395 by two teenage brothers from the prominent Roman aristocratic family the Anicii. This gesture of reconciliation, directed at their father Probus, also witnessed the discovery of Claudian's poetic

104. Reminding me of Sedgwick's analysis of Oscar Wilde's multiple aunts and uncles: "Tales of the Avunculate," 52–72. This also corresponds to J. Butler's description of kinship as potentially "a site of queer coinage, of a performative re-elaboration, and the recognition of binding ties made and remade" ("Kinship Beyond the Bloodline," 41).

talents in Milan: his first panegyric celebrated the emperor Theodosius in tandem with the beautiful young brother consuls, whose divinely approved selection occurred in the camp of the victorious army (about two weeks before Theodosius's death on January 17, 395)—youthful beauty meets battle-readiness.[105]

BOOTS AND TROUSERS REDUX: MANLIUS THEODORUS

Claudian's praise for the consul of 399 presented yet another pairing. The consul in question was Manlius Theodorus, who gave his name to the year that witnessed the second iteration of the boots and trousers law.[106] Tensions continued unabated with the eastern court, which still considered Stilicho a public enemy; in response the court in Milan refused to acknowledge the eastern consul of 399. Manlius Theodorus, the prefect of Italy and a well-known author of philosophical treatises with a large circle of acquaintances who included Augustine, was one of Stilicho's loyal supporters and might have stepped up to spare him the humiliation of being rejected as a consul by the east.[107]

Claudian could thus celebrate an *illustris vir* who embodied all the traditional virtues in the most traditional ways, a mature, learned "Republican" to complement the young married emperor. Theodorus was a model Stoic in the Ciceronian mold, his life of *otium cum dignitate* the perfect combination of active service and intellectual engagement. He proved that age-old Roman ideals were alive and well at Honorius's Milanese court.[108] Personifications of the central Theodosian virtues—*iustitia, clementia, pax,* and *fides*—saluted this *auctor* and *doctus vir* of thoroughly Latin erudition. Like Cicero, Manlius Theodorus possessed a Latin clarity that penetrated obscure Greek wisdom, helping reason to dominate fear, virtue to subdue vice, and restraint to temper lust.[109] In short, the consul Theodorus was an exemplary Roman senator, *fortis vir,* and father of sons who would in turn give their names to future years. He was the perfect mature representative of the youthful Honorius, a pairing that enhanced the other paired exemplar of traditional virtues, Stilicho, and signaled what was bound to happen soon: imperial children (*proles*).[110]

---

105. Claud., *Prob.* 8–75 (the young consuls' *gens* and their father as guarantor of their suitability), 67–70 (the consuls' youth), 113–73 (praise of Theodosius as victor to link the military camp with the future consuls), 175–206 (the trabea made by the boys' mother). See also Claud., *carm. min.* 40–41.

106. Claud., *M. Theod.*; see Müller, *Lectiones,* 37–60.

107. Augustine dedicated his *De beata vita* to Manlius (or Mallius). See also Matthews, *Western Aristocracies,* 74–75, 256, 262–66 (career of Manlius, who became prefect in 397); Döpp, *Zeitgeschichte,* 150–58.

108. Claud., *M. Theod.* 1–3, 10–15, 115, 159–63, 335.

109. Claud., *M. Theod.* 84–99. See Zarini, "Culture grecque," 31–43, for Theodorus's education.

110. Claud., *M. Theod.* 116–17, 135–73, 240–50, 257–60, 266–69. *Proles* is the panegyric's closing word.

In early June 399, Honorius and Arcadius reissued the law prohibiting the wearing of "oriental" boots and trousers, *tzangae* and *bracae*, in the *urbs Roma*, now with increased sanctions that included expulsion from the sacred city.[111] The law must have originated in Milan, because the only consul it recognizes is Manlius Theodorus. Why Honorius and his court reissued this ostentatious law remains subject to conjecture, but the tensions with Constantinople doubtless played a role. Quite possibly, *illustres viri* in Milan and the Eternal City were neither sufficiently outraged at the machinations of the eastern court nor sufficiently unanimous in their support of Stilicho's claim that he oversaw the entire empire.[112] The court in Milan might have wanted to let all members of the elite know that parading around in boots and trousers with eastern connotations could be taken as a lack of loyalty. The emperor might be gorgeously soft, but that should not encourage shining, splendidly illuminated Roman *viri* to be too "eastern," lest they be tempted to exploit the current tensions for their own interests. Once again, therefore, the court in Milan considered it opportune to impress upon elite *viri* in Rome, and through them all members of the elites, who it was that defined proper western Roman *vir*-ness: their emperor.

However, as much as the court in Milan might have liked to suggest otherwise, Honorius was not Rome's only emperor. Even though the focus of the preceding chapters has been the west, Arcadius, the senior emperor, ruled in Constantinople. Theodosius, moreover, had spent nearly his entire reign in Constantinople. The next chapter thus steps back to examine how Theodosius developed his imperial virtues and their representation in the Constantinopolitan context and how these developments influenced what happened in the west.

111. CTh 14.10.3; for text see chapter 2, n. 12, above.

112. Symmachus addressed several letters to Theodorus without mentioning the east: Symm., *Ep.* 5.6, 5.10–11. See also Cameron, *Claudian*, 126; Döpp, *Zeitgeschichte*, 150–52; Long, *Claudian's "In Eutropium,"* 157–59.

5

Love of Mankind

Theodosius in Constantinople

Claudian's literary brilliance, combined with the voices of Pacatus, Ammianus, Ambrose, and Ausonius, has ensured that our perspective on the early Theodosian age is predominantly that of the Latin west. These authors, together with the anonymous *Life of Heliogabalus* in the *Historia Augusta*, Nicomachus Flavianus's legal rhetoric, and the boots and trouser laws, offer a remarkably consistent message. Though writing in a distinct genre and for his own purpose, each author traced changes that both expanded Roman *virtus*, elite manliness, toward greater softness and capaciousness and dictated how Roman emperors and other members of the elite should embody and display such *vir*-ness. Except for the *Historia Augusta*, these voices mediated the interests of the ruling emperors with a keen awareness of their principal audience, the elite to which they all belonged. As such, they functioned as highly attuned seismographs of power and inner-elite competition, because rival claims of imperial legitimacy and of elite status were expressed through contested notions of *vir*-ness.

Two intertwined themes emerge from this choir. First, these authors emphasized the emperor's beauty—his *forma*, *decus*, and *pulchritudo*, physically expressed in variations of hardness increasingly combined with those of youthfulness. To be sure, emperors continued to embrace a constant kaleidoscope of many excellences that had been admired since Republican and especially Augustan times, including a commitment to renewal. The promise to restore a lost golden age was de rigueur for those claiming, like Theodosius and Stilicho, to be the heirs of Aeneas and Augustus (an inheritance claimed by reference to the golden shield of virtues, *clipeus virtutis*, that had been gifted to them both), and youthfulness was an apt expression of such renewal.[1] Success in battle remained central, but the emphasis could change. Like their precursors, the emperors Gratian and Theodosius highlighted virtues they considered key, above all clemency and benevolence, which were especially apt for celebrating peace and reconciliation in times of civil war.[2]

Gratian and Theodosius were also both characterized as immensely beautiful. Here, however—and this is the second theme—the descriptions diverge. Pacatus's Theodosius was a triumphant commander who had hardened his body in the strict discipline of military camps. Between campaigns, though, he traded his armor for the toga and became a true *civilis princeps* who excelled in the arts of peace. Theodosius's immense beauty (*forma*) combined hard military vigor with civilian *decus*—beautifully appropriate behavior, such as mingling with the inhabitants of the *urbs Roma*—and was softened by his exhibition of not only uncommonly humble love (*amicitia*) for his friends but also motherly mildness and mercy (*misericordia*) on the battlefield. Pacatus's Theodosius was thus a beautifully hard warrior with a distinctly gentler side. Ultimately, he was utterly beautiful because he was divine, a *deus praesens*, or god one can see, as his soldiers attested when swearing their loyalty oath.[3] In Gratian's case, the equation was reversed. He was the first emperor to receive praise while still a child or preteen. Even at that age, Gratian too was battle-ready, clement, benevolent, and just. Restraint was also one of his key excellences, as it would be for Theodosius. For Gratian, however, restraint and chastity assumed a different flavor, because the emperor was sublimely gorgeous as only a young man whose beard is just about to sprout can be, as Themistius made vividly clear. Such beauty rendered the emperor immensely desirable, in ways unmoderated by mature hardness. It therefore had to be fenced in through commensurate chastity—which, of course, made him infinitely more desirable, but also confirmed the lines that could never be crossed without threatening his legitimacy.

1. For a discussion of the stone copy of the shield from Arles, the *clipeus* awarded to Augustus by the Senate, see the introduction; see also Zanker, *Power of Images*, 95, fig. 79; S. J. Harrison, "Survival and Supremacy," 70–76; Welch, "Shields of Virtue(s)"; Hekster, *Emperors and Ancestors*, 5–12.

2. See Hekster, *Emperors and Ancestors*, 317, for the flexibility in imperial selection and presentation of ideas; Bönisch-Meyer, *Dialogangebote*, 227–34, shows that after Septimius Severus, emperors who had won civil wars were praised by unofficial epithets as *restitutor* (restorer) of peace or *pacator orbis*, bringer of universal peace. In the latter case, the emperors were associated with Hercules.

3. Veg., *Mil.* 2.5: "Nam imperator cum Augusti nomen accepit, tamquam praesenti et corporali Deo fidelis est praestanda deuotio, inpendendus peruigil famulatus. Deo enim uel priuatus uel militans seruit, cum fideliter cum diligit qui Deo regnat auctore" (For since the Emperor has received the name of the 'August', faithful devotion should be given, unceasing homage paid him as if to a present and corporeal deity. For it is God whom a private citizen or solider serves, when he faithfully loves him who reigns by God's authority). Vegetius's *Epitoma rei militaris* was most likely dedicated to Theodosius I: see Milner, *Vegetius*, xxxvii–xliii.

Pacatus's characterization of Theodosius, with its careful gestures toward his softer, motherly side, demonstrates that the ruler's youthful gorgeousness, as embodied by Gratian, could be useful when properly combined with hardness. The contrast with Magnus Maximus said it all: he was the exemplar of soft, fluid, delicate manliness gone wrong. After his defeat, Maximus was no longer an illuminated *vir* well worth looking at but instead a less-than-manly monster. Moreover, Pacatus's innovative juxtaposition of two opposing models of imperial *vir*-ness exemplifies the second theme: pairing, which pointed the way forward. Pacatus had paired a perfect, hard, mature, and appropriately soft emperor with his opposite, Maximus, rather than with his very young coaugustus. The panegyrist mentioned Theodosius's sons only briefly, because for political reasons he could not acknowledge the young Valentinian II. As for Gratian, as the sole ruler he could not easily be paired with a more mature figure, with the exception of his tutor: Ausonius thus cast himself as the most learned man, or *doctissimus vir*, who had successfully inculcated the young emperor's exemplary comportment. Claudian finally had all the requisite pieces in place. He combined Theodosius's mature, hard, battle-proven *vir*-ness with Honorius's youthful gorgeousness without having to fear softness gone wrong—the dangers of the *Life of Heliogabalus* were ever present—because a strong father figure held it firmly in check. In five years, Claudian first successfully transformed Stilicho into an ideal father figure in Theodosius's mold and then made him the de facto father of the ruling house, paired at each transformative step with the ever more capaciously soft, youthfully smooth, and finally married Honorius to create a vastly expanded and far more flexible ideal of imperial *vir*-ness.

Here Theodosius's rule was pivotal, because it was during his reign that child emperors became institutionalized. Theodosius was a newcomer, but once he established himself independently in Constantinople he strengthened his links with the Valentinian dynasty, including at the crucial moment when he decided to move against Magnus Maximus on behalf of Valentinian II. Already in 383, he adopted the Valentinian precedent of making his very young sons augusti—but he could have chosen a different play. This one required the incorporation of child emperors into the construction of imperial *vir*-ness, which in turn meant a conscious strengthening of the language of smooth, soft, gorgeous youthfulness as a language of supreme (military) power. So far, I have focused on the western empire, on Milan and Rome, where Theodosius's influence is less directly visible in the sources. He was, after all, the eastern emperor. Thus, to tease out his intentions and to reconstruct his representational program—which Honorius and Arcadius expanded and refined—it is crucial to turn to Constantinople. Only once the eastern, Constantinopolitan Theodosius emerges will it be possible to see what he wanted to convey and to assess its effects on Rome and Milan.

THE WEAPON OF PHILANTHROPY:
MILITARY VICTORY RECAST

Victory in battle, as has been discussed, remained essential as a Roman imperial virtue.[4] The *imperator* was a battle-hardened commander (the original meaning of the title) who crushed the empire's foes—or would crush them when necessary—and Theodosius had certainly done so. However, his record against foreign opponents was decidedly mixed, and he had won his most consequential victories in civil wars, against Roman opponents. His less than stellar external success had repercussions for the crucial imperial virtue of victory. To be sure, Theodosius's record could be considered less mixed if the inauspicious conditions he inherited were taken into account, but supreme, most sacred divine rulers should not require such all too human excuses.

Theodosius was recognized as an augustus in 379, about five months after Rome's defeat at Adrianople.[5] That loss had revealed structural inadequacies in Rome's defenses along the lower Danube, which were meant to safeguard access to Constantinople and to the important trading routes into the Black Sea region. In the 360s Valens, forced to pay for the reconstitution of the eastern army after Persia's victory over Julian in 363, suspended long-standing arrangements by which Gothic peoples across the Danube—the Greuthungi and the Tervingi in what are roughly modern Romania, Moldova, and southern Ukraine—provided auxiliary troops on demand and against payment, among other agreements.[6] Those troops would have reinforced Valens's army but instead now roamed in search of booty through Thrace and Illyricum as far as Constantinople, together with Taifals, Alans, and some Hunnic federations. Regaining control over these rogue contingents was Theodosius's first task, which is why he made his headquarters in Thessalonica, close to the endangered areas. The new emperor had to rely on a diminished and demoralized army: legislation from 379 speaks volumes about deserters, minors and peasants forcibly conscripted, and a general eagerness to avoid military service at all costs.[7] Indeed, according to Zosimus—our principal source, though hostile—Theodosius's army operated haphazardly and often crumbled under Gothic attacks.[8] Gratian's decision to halt the offensive of his commanders Bauto and Arbogast, who had pushed Gothic troops from Illyricum into Thrace—that is, from a western into an eastern province—further signaled that the east would have to fend for itself.[9]

---

4. Unofficial imperial epithets show that the emperor's subjects considered him always victorious: see Bönisch-Meyer, *Dialogangebote*, 222–27.

5. As mentioned in chapter 1, with Gratian's grudging support; see also Sivan, "Was Theodosius I a Usurper?," 198–206.

6. See Batty, *Rome and the Nomads*, 11–52, 77–150; Lenski, *Failure of Empire*, 139–417, esp. 308–19.

7. CTh 7.13.8–11, 7.22.9–19.

8. Zos., *HN* 4.25.2–4, 4.31.2–4. See also Heather, *Goths and Romans*, 150–55.

9. Kulikowski, *Rome's Gothic Wars*, 149–52; Williams and Friell, *Theodosius*, 28–35; Errington, "Theodosius and the Goths," 1–5.

Theodosius spent nearly four years attempting to control these Gothic contingents, but victory proved elusive. Destruction was widespread, even halting overland communication between east and west through the Balkans.[10] The emperor needed to shore up his army's morale, which he tried to do by celebrating each advance, however moderate, as a victory against "Goths, Alans, and Huns," especially in an *adventus* into Constantinople in late 380.[11] Only in October 382, after another two moderately successful fighting seasons, could Theodosius finally announce a peace treaty. Much analyzed in scholarship, that agreement can best be described as the result of realpolitik after four years of war. Formally, the Goths surrendered. However, they retained an unprecedented degree of autonomy within the empire, including their own land in Thrace and the incorporation into the army and as auxiliaries of unified contingents under their own commanders; these were the Goths, Alans, and Huns who later granted Theodosius victory over Magnus Maximus and Eugenius.[12]

Unsurprisingly, then, this peace agreement was deeply controversial. Contemporaries were quick to point out that the emperor had insufficiently crushed Rome's enemies and had granted far too generous terms to barbarians so recently hostile.[13] In response, Theodosius turned to Themistius, whose support during the emperor's difficult earlier years had been crucial. Themistius's orations 14, 15, and 16, delivered in praise of Theodosius between 379 and 383, offer a master class in persuasion, turning moderate success into lasting advantage: the emperor and the acclaimed orator collaborated to transform the key imperial virtue of victory in battle against a foreign enemy into a celebration of diplomacy.[14] True victory was no longer won on the battlefield but rather through the "soft" weapons of imperial clemency and "love of mankind," or philanthropy.[15]

Themistius delivered his first panegyric to Theodosius in early summer 379 in Thessalonica, where he had arrived with other Constantinopolitan senators to present the new augustus with the so-called crown gold, a "voluntary" celebratory tax.[16] Themistius's speech began entirely traditionally. He praised the new emperor as perfect in mind and body and as the restorer of Rome's golden age, who would

---

10. Them., *Or.* 16.212b.

11. *Cons. Const.*, s.a. 379. For the increased frequency of triumphal celebrations between 378 and 382, see McCormick, *Eternal Victory*, 41–46; Lenski, "*Initium mali*," 138–41.

12. See Zos., *HN* 4.24.3–6 for Theodosius's policy in 379–382, especially the treaty of October 3, 382; also Heather, *Goths and Romans*, 158–92; Heather and Moncur, *Politics*, 199–207; Lenski, "*Initium mali*," 142–45; Elton, *Roman Empire*, 130–34. See also Greatrex, "The Background," 41–44.

13. Heather, *Goths and Romans*, 165–77.

14. See esp. Them., *Or.* 14.183b, 16.207b–c, 16.208b, 16.210a–c. In what follows, I adapt the translations of Heather and Moncur. For the collaboration, see Heather and Moncur, *Politics*, 27–28, 33–34; also Brown, *Power and Persuasion*, 105–8.

15. Caner, *Rich and the Pure*, 35–43. I will discuss additional changes to imperial philanthropy in chapter 8.

16. Zos., *HN* 4.25.1, 4.28.1–4; Heather and Moncur, *Politics*, 30 (pointing out that Themistius arrived late), 218; Klauser, "*Aurum coronarium*," 292–309; Jones, *Later Roman Empire*, 1:430–31.

soon vindicate its power with a decisive victory over the "Scythians"—that is, the Goths. As a battle-hardened commander, Theodosius would transform farmers and miners into strong Roman soldiers, creating an army that had never tasted weakening luxury. Like the terror-inspiring Achilles, the emperor spread fear just by pitching his tents near the Scythians.[17]

More important than imminent victory over the Goths was Themistius's second theme: Constantinople, the New Rome and Theodosius's ideal capital. Constantinople, the other Rome, had risen to its current prominence on merit, just like the new augustus. Both shared virtues that made them Rome's equal, which meant that the eastern augustus was also at least equal to his western counterpart, even though he was technically the junior emperor. Of course, Themistius also praised Gratian, the senior emperor, because he had shown such excellent judgment in making Theodosius his father: chosen fathers could be better than biological ones. Theodosius reciprocated by gaining the goodwill of a son.[18] In sum, in 379, Themistius's priority was to clarify for the eastern but also the western audience the relationship between the two augusti. The experienced Theodosius was in fact the senior augustus, by merit rather than dynastic precedence. Valentinian II, the second senior augustus, received no mention.

Theodosius finally arrived in Constantinople in late 380, "as if celebrating a triumph for some famous victory."[19] Not long after, in January 381, Themistius delivered his second panegyric. His oration 15 reveals a noticeably different understanding of victory than that of oration 14.[20] Alluding to Homer, Themistius once more expressed all confidence that Theodosius would chase the Goths, these "hounds of hell," to the "far hereafter" as soon as the army had left its winter quarters.[21] However, still referring to Homer but now also to Hesiod's *Works and Days*, this time he focused on Theodosius as an ideal peacetime ruler.[22] Of course an emperor should conquer if the necessity arose. But his foremost duty was to govern, just as a shepherd's duty to protect his flock involved more than throwing sticks and unleashing his dogs. The divinely born Theodosius, beautiful and swift, equaled Zeus because he carried the supreme god in his soul and, like him, had been entrusted with safeguarding the entire world.[23] That was a task only a divine emperor could accomplish, while his generals could win battles.[24]

17. Them., *Or.* 14.180c–181c.

18. Them., *Or.* 14.181d–183a. See also Lenski, "Constantine and the Tyche," 337–48.

19. Quote in Zos., *HN* 4.33.1, citing Eunapius. Heather and Moncur, *Politics*, 212, 230, date *Or.* 15 to January 19, 381.

20. Heather and Moncur, *Politics*, 212–13.

21. At *Or.* 15.185a–c, Themistius indicates that the army was then in winter quarters. He returns to the Gothic campaign theme only at 15.197b–199a, with the hounds of hell and the hereafter (cf. Hom., *Il.* 8.527–29, 3.353–54).

22. Them., *Or.* 15.184d.

23. Them., *Or.* 15.186b–187d, 188b–189b.

24. Them., *Or.* 15.188b–c.

Theodosius must preserve justice, righteousness, and free speech, which required choosing the right friends as advisers—men willing to shoulder their part of governing the empire by acting as his eyes and ears (an allusion to Xenophon's *Cyropaideia*).[25] Therefore, he should immediately demonstrate clemency and rehabilitate all the good men who had suffered under Valens. Gratian, who otherwise deserved praise—both emperors were equally beautiful, even if their beauties were of different kinds—had fallen short in some of these peacetime virtues because he was too young and inexperienced.[26] In contrast, Theodosius knew how to govern with piety, mildness, and "love of mankind, the most regal of all virtues."[27] Love of mankind, or philanthropy, was an immensely powerful weapon, far more potent than jewel-encrusted swords and shields, because it was a weapon of the gods. The recent surrender of the Gothic leader Athanaric made that power manifest: philanthropy had "defeated many hands and preserved them too."[28]

The victorious power of philanthropy and mildness was Themistius's principal theme in oration 16, delivered two years later, on January 1, 383, in the Senate and with the emperor present. The occasion was the beginning of the consulship of the general, or *magister militum*, Flavius Saturninus.[29] Saturninus had been instrumental in brokering the peace agreement of 382, and the consulship was his reward; Richomeres, his collaborator, was guaranteed the same for the subsequent year.[30] Themistius began by praising Theodosius on behalf of the Senate because the emperor had foregone the recent Valentinian custom of either claiming the honor for himself or designating a "child in its swaddling to put on the toga" as consul, even though he could have honored the then five- or six-year-old Arcadius in this way.[31] Themistius was criticizing the child consuls mentioned in chapter 4, of which Gratian had been one.[32] Theodosius, however, was instead rewarding a seasoned general who had accomplished the emperor's most important command.[33]

25. Them., *Or.* 15.196c–197a. I will return to Xenophon in chapter 7.

26. Them., *Or.* 15.198b.

27. Scribes later gave *Or.* 15 the title "The Most Royal [*or* Regal] of the Virtues."

28. Them., *Or.* 15.191b–c, 196c–197b, 197b–c (quote). Theodosius had received Athanaric, old and infirm, eight days before the speech was delivered, and Themistius might have inserted the episode, which he characterized as a surrender and hence another Roman victory, at a later date. Athanaric died within days, and Theodosius gave his new subject a splendid funeral. See Heather and Moncur, *Politics*, 212, 217, 230, 234–35.

29. Heather and Moncur, *Politics*, 255.

30. Them., *Or.* 16.201b; Heather and Moncur, *Politics*, 267n200.

31. Them., *Or.* 16.202d–203b, 204b–205a.

32. Gratian had become a consul at six, Valentinian II at five, and the sons of Jovian and Valens too had been child consuls—but so had Honorius. See *PLRE* 1:946, 381, 401; Heather and Moncur, *Politics*, 256, 271n17–18.

33. Them., *Or.* 16.204d–205b.

When Rome faced hostile barbarians who attacked it on all sides, when Thrace and Illyricum were laid waste and "whole armies had vanished completely like a shadow,"

> God summons to leadership the only man capable of resisting such an inundation of misfortunes. . . . [Theodosius] was the first who dared entertain the notion that the power of the Romans did not lie in weapons nor in breastplates, spears nor unnumbered manpower, but that there was need of some other power and provision which, to those who rule in accordance with the will of God, comes silently from that source, which subdues all nations, turns all savagery to mildness and to which alone arms, bows, cavalry, the intransigence of the Scythians, the boldness of the Alans, the madness of the Massagetai yield.[34]

Theodosius "realized that forgiving those who had done wrong was better than fighting to the bitter end." Thus, he dispatched Saturninus, just as Achilles had sent his beloved Patroclus (but with a better outcome), to gain "this victory and win the day through his intelligence and goodwill." Theodosius arrayed Saturninus, as Achilles "the son of Peleus had done [with Patroclus,] . . . in his own truly heavenly armor: patience, gentle mildness [*praotes*], and love of mankind."[35]

> [Saturninus] needed no time at all to achieve this victory, but had only to reveal and proffer the goodwill of the man who sent him for the arrogance of the Scythians at once to bow before him, their boldness to be cut short, their spirit humbled, the sword to fall voluntarily from their hands and for them to follow as he led them . . . carrying only their short swords which they intended to present to the king in place of suppliant offerings. . . . Wafting the king's love of mankind before them like an olive branch, [Saturninus] led them docile and amenable, all but twisting their hands behind their backs, so that it was a matter of doubt whether he had beaten the men in war or won their friendship.[36]

Theodosius's philanthropic victory was complete because he had beaten not merely barbarians like the Armenians, who were predisposed to servitude, but "those in whom is bred from childhood an unyielding spirit, and for whom the slightest submission is worse than death." To turn such fighters into "docile and amenable" friends was nearly unimaginable and hence further testament to the

---

34. *Massagetai* is a literary term for Huns, like *Scythians* for Goths. Them., *Or.* 16.206d, 207b–c (ἐθάρρησε πρῶτος εἰς νοῦν ἐμβαλέσθαι μὴ κεῖσθαι Ῥωμαίοις τὴν δύναμιν τανῦν ἐν σιδήρῳ μηδὲ ἐν θώραξι καὶ ἀσπίσι, μηδὲ ἐν σώμασιν ἀναριθμήτοις, ἀλλὰ δεῖν γὰρ ἑτέρας δυνάμεως καὶ παρασκευῆς, ἢ τοῖς κατὰ νοῦν τοῦ θεοῦ βασιλεύουσιν ἐκεῖθεν ἀψοφητὶ παραγίνεται, καὶ πάντα μὲν ἔθνη χειροῦται, πάντα δὲ ἥμερα καθίστησιν ἐξ ἀγρίων, εἴκει δὲ αὐτῇ μόνῃ καὶ ὅπλα καὶ τόξα καὶ ἵπποι καὶ αὐθάδεια Σκθυικὴ καὶ τόλμα Ἀλανῶν καὶ ἀπόνοια Μασσαγετῶν). See also *Or.* 15.191a–c, 192d, 193b, 194a, 197a–d; Heather and Moncur, *Politics*, 261–63.

35. Them., *Or.* 16.208b–d (Καὶ πέμπει καθάπερ Ἀχιλλεὺς τὸν ἑταῖρον [Patroclus] . . . πέμπει δὲ ὥσπερ ὁ Πηλέως ἐνσκευάσας τοῖς ὅπλοις τοῖς ἑαυτοῦ τοῖς ἀτεχνῶς οὐρανίοις, ἀνεξικακίᾳ, πρᾳότητι, φιλανθρωπίᾳ).

36. Them., *Or.* 16.209a, 210a.

emperor's immense, divine powers of kindness, benevolence, peace, and "the remitting of sins," which rather than slaughtering bodies won over hearts and minds.[37]

Orations 14, 15, and 16 perform and reveal a transformation of imperial victory. As Heather and Moncur have demonstrated, Theodosius propelled that transformation through Themistius's rhetoric brilliance. Crushing foreign enemies in victorious combat remained the key virtue it had always been; indeed, in 383 Themistius made it clear that the Goths had surrendered. At the same time, however, he left no doubt that the emperor's true power resided elsewhere: others could win victories on his behalf, but he was the sole, divine ruler, and as such uniquely capable of governing in peacetime. As a perfect sovereign, Theodosius knew how to choose his friends and advisers, including his generals, to ensure the proper governance and defense of the realm. So far, the picture of the emperor that Themistius projected onto Theodosius largely conformed to prior expectations. However, beginning with oration 15, he claimed that clemency, good judgment, mildness, and, above all, love of mankind, or philanthropy, were more than peacetime virtues. They were in fact the divine emperor's most effective weapons of war, far more potent than mere force.

Oration 15 prepared what oration 16 brought to fruition. In Themistius's telling, the treaty of 382 manifested Rome's true power as diplomatic. This was peace won through the emperor's forgiveness, mildness, and love of mankind. Though these were the most powerful weapons that God had granted Rome, only the divine Theodosius had possessed the foresight and audacity to recognize their might.[38] Only Theodosius had been able to choose a general endowed with intelligence and goodwill as well as supreme courage, willing to confront the enemy without any accompanying generals or troops, clad only in the emperor's heavenly weapons of mildness and philanthropy.[39] Together they had won victory without shedding blood. Now mildness and love of mankind carried the day, changing roving barbarians into settlers who "turned the metal of their swords and breastplates into hoes and pruning hooks."[40] Victories won through intelligence and philanthropy pacified barbarians and accelerated a process that otherwise would have taken far longer. Rather than filling provinces with corpses, these weapons persuaded the newly friendly Scythians to pay the same taxes, follow the same laws, and serve in the same army as the Romans—in short, they made them almost instantly "thoroughly Roman." "For such are the triumphs of reason [*logos*] and universal love [*philanthropia*]."[41]

In addition to his benevolent, fatherly love of mankind, however, Themistius's Theodosius deployed erotic power. In 376, Themistius had praised Gratian's exceptionally gorgeous beauty as a weapon that conquered fierce, recalcitrant barbarians.

---

37. Them., *Or.* 16.210b–c; see also 16.211a–b.
38. Them., *Or.* 16.206d.
39. Them., *Or.* 16.208d.
40. Them., *Or.* 16.211b.
41. Them., *Or.* 16.211d–212a, quote at 16.211a.

Now Saturninus, acting on Theodosius's behalf, used erotic desire to intensify the persuasive force of the emperor's universal love. Saturninus was Theodosius's far more fortunate (as Themistius hastened to add) beloved Patroclus. His seductiveness vis-à-vis the Goths equaled that of Aphrodite's girdle, and his honeyed words were more soothing than the drug that Polydamna had given to Helen. He put a potent spell on the hard barbarians, which made them docile, amenable, and willing to yield and rendered these human "towers more solid than adamant [or diamonds] softer than wax."[42]

Oration 16 also praised Arcadius for the first time. As part of a series of digs against Gratian, including the criticism of Valentinian infant consuls, Themistius said that no one would have complained if Theodosius had raised Arcadius, "the beloved beacon of the world" and a new Alexander, to that office, but he preferred Saturninus.[43] Arcadius also received the panegyric's last words.[44] Once more evoking Theodosius's mildness and philanthropy, which allowed the realm's inhabitants to again draw a common breath as one unified organism after a victory won without soldiers, Themistius expressed his fervent hope that Arcadius would share his father's virtues. Theodosius's example would be the guiding light of this "beloved star of the world" if, as he anticipated, Themistius was allowed to tutor Arcadius, to fill not his stomach with sweet delicacies but his mind with his father's indelible manly deeds.[45] Eighteen days later, on January 19, 383, the fifth anniversary of his own election, Theodosius elevated the five- or six-year-old Arcadius as coaugustus. Gratian, whom Themistius had slyly attacked and studiously silenced in oration 16 (in contrast to oration 15, where he presented both emperors as equals, despite their differences), did not acknowledge Arcadius prior to being fatally defeated by Magnus Maximus in the summer of 383.[46] Meanwhile, also in early 383, Theodosius granted the title *augusta* to his wife Aelia Flaccilla.[47]

ALL PEOPLES (*CUNCTOS POPULOS*) UNITED BY LOVE OF MANKIND

Themistius's speeches demonstrate that Theodosius arrived in Constantinople in fall 380 with changed notions of imperial victory sufficiently formulated to convey them to the philosopher and rhetorician in time for oration 15, delivered early

42. Them., *Or.* 16.209b. See Hom., *Il.* 14.159–221, for the seductive potency of Aphrodite's girdle; *Od.* 4.227 describes how Helen gave the visiting Telemachus a drug she had received from Polydamna that took away painful memories.

43. Them., *Or.* 16.204c-d.

44. Them., *Or.* 16.213a-b.

45. Themistius did indeed become (or was already) Arcadius's tutor: see Heather and Moncur, *Politics*, 19, 271n217.

46. Ambr., *Ep.* 24.9; Heather and Moncur, *Politics*, 255–57. Arcadius does not appear on Gratian's coins: see *RIC* 9, xix–xxi, 72.

47. Holum, *Theodosian Empresses*, 31.

in 381. The idea that mildness and philanthropy were the most important imperial weapons was novel, and the emperor and Themistius were aware that convincing their audience of its merit would be difficult. After all, it rendered the emperor's active participation in battle—the age-old manifestation of his divine mandate—secondary to his peacetime acumen and delegated military command to generals. Indeed, emperors who insisted on bloodying their hands could be considered derelict in their duty—governing the entire world—for the sake of personal glory. What had been the foundation of imperial *vir*-ness morphed almost into self-indulgence, a youthful lack of restraint. At the same time, mildness, forbearance, and philanthropy were weapons that the emperor could wield even if he was very young, provided he was surrounded and instructed by mature friends (such as Themistius). In oration 16, the philosopher (as tutor) mentions Arcadius for the first time, together with Theodosius, while relegating Gratian to the sidelines. Thus, when Themistius presented his senatorial audience in 383 with the most elaborate version to date of Theodosius's new, softer understanding of imperial victory, he paired the emperor with the beloved, seductive general Saturninus but also with the (imminent) augustus Arcadius.[48]

One aspect of the persuasive love of mankind as a weapon that Themistius particularly highlighted was its ability to transform hostile, unyielding barbarians almost instantaneously into Romans. This suggests an altered assessment of the conquered. Certainly, Scythians were intransigent, Alans bold, and Massagetai—Huns—mad, and they had to be beaten and subdued, but they did not have to be crushed. If they were instead persuaded to repent their sin (that is, opposing Rome in the first place) and yield to the powerful love of mankind, then victories could be won without costly, bloody battles. In addition, those thus subdued could become thoroughly Roman with far greater ease and begin acting as all other Romans did far sooner. Indeed, if even exceptionally hard, adamantine barbarians could become so amenable, so civilized, then everyone—all people everywhere— had the potential to become thoroughly Roman, united in one common breath, once an emperor's divine philanthropy had conquered them.

As Pacatus illustrated six years later, in 389, Theodosius's recasting of victory as a triumph of philanthropy, mildness, and forgiveness emphasized qualities desired in the winner of a civil war. Clemency, or mildness, and forgiveness were particularly important when the losers were Romans. As chapter 1 discussed, the defeat of fellow Romans required the denigration of their commander as monstrous and less-than-manly, but the emperor's immense, clement love of mankind instantly converted the former's less-than-manly followers back into true Roman manly men. Themistius's description of Theodosius's power over barbarian opponents anticipated a similar transformation. Here too a "loving" victory accelerated the

---

48. Heather and Moncur, *Politics*, 283n263, suggest that Themistius must have known about Arcadius's forthcoming elevation.

process of becoming Roman, this time by softening too much hardness. Ethnicity became sufficiently malleable to integrate foreigners fast, to allow them to become Roman *viri* regardless of their origin, especially if they served the emperor's needs.[49]

Further, and this also applies to post-civil-war reconciliation, Theodosius's mildness extended to all Romans, especially the inhabitants of his new capital. In this context, Themistius and Theodosius downplayed the latter's dynastic relations with the Valentinians, Gratian in particular. Already in 379, in oration 14, Themistius had signaled a respectful yet reserved relationship by stressing that Theodosius was senior in every respect and intended to act accordingly, especially in the east. His capital, Constantinople, was the equal (at the very least) of Rome, and the emperor lost no time in further elevating its status. Among his first steps were the rehabilitation of those who had suffered under Valens and, relatedly, the expansion of the Constantinopolitan Senate, moves that solidified his power base.[50] These were the new senators and officials whose dress the laws of 382 regulated to align with their counterparts in Rome.[51] Further, Theodosius offered reconciliation to those who had supported his precursor.[52] In other words, the new eastern emperor truly wished (*volumus*) to integrate all peoples (*cunctos populos*) in one united realm that was unmistakably his.[53]

In February 380, before setting off from Thessalonica for another season of Gothic campaigns, Theodosius sent an edict to Constantinople in response to requests that he clarify his position regarding Christianity for the benefit of his future subjects. At that point, the emperor had never been to the east and knew as little about Constantinople as its inhabitants knew about him. The law, issued in the names, in order of seniority, of Gratian, Valentinian II, and Theodosius, has been preserved only in excerpts and without an accompanying imperial letter, so we must surmise its exact content and intent. In the version extant in the Theodosian Code, it declares that "all the peoples subject to the moderation of [his] Clemency should continue to dwell in that religion which was handed over to the Romans by the divine Apostle Peter as it has been preserved, and which is now professed by the pontifex Damasus of Rome and by Peter, bishop of Alexandria, a man of apostolic holiness; that is, that in accordance with apostolic teaching and evangelical doctrine we should believe in one godhead of Father and Son and Holy Spirit under a like majesty and a holy trinity. We command persons accepting

49. Salzmann, "Symmachus and the 'Barbarian' Generals," 352–67. Recent scholarship has emphasized that the proportion of "barbarians" in the late Roman army was not nearly as high as the literary sources suggest: see Elton, *Warfare in Roman Europe*; Emion, "Des soldats," 11–15 (bibliography), 327–56. See also Maas, *Conqueror's Gift*, 99–122.

50. CTh 9.42.8–9; Them., *Or.* 14.183b; Amm. Marc. 28.1.2–56, 29.1.6–2.27; Heather, "Liar in Winter," 191–201; Matthews, *Roman Empire*, 209–28.

51. See chapter 2; CTh 14.10.1, 14.12.1; Arce, "Dress-Control," 38–40; Kovacs, "*Praeclara in veste*," 402–18; Heather, "New Men," 11–33.

52. Croke, "Reinventing Constantinople," 243.

53. CTh 16.1.2.

this rule to embrace the name catholic [or universal] Christians," while dissenters would be considered heretics and no longer permitted to call their meeting places churches.[54]

This edict has enjoyed an illustrious history, in part because it opens emperor Justinian's Codex of 534 under its first two words, *cunctos populos*.[55] That is an unusual phrase in Roman legislation. It echoes the commandment of the resurrected Christ according to Matthew 28:19 and Luke 24:47 that his followers spread his message to *panta ta ethne*, "all peoples."[56] Theodosius's legal staff used this wording intentionally. To what end? Earlier scholarship assumed that the edict introduced Catholic Christianity to the empire by fiat, but more recent work has highlighted how meticulously Theodosius and his jurists crafted their words to signal to the addressees in Constantinople the emperor's desire for consensus and unity.[57] Theodosius made it clear that his preferred Christianity was not the Homoian, or "Arian," version, which declared God the Father and his Son alike but not the same in essence—and which Valens (and Gratian) had sponsored.[58] Instead, he would follow the version (known as Nicene and represented by the bishops of Rome and Alexandria) in which he had been raised and for which he intended to claim Constantinople's major churches.[59] However, as Neil McLynn has shown, those schooled in parsing imperial legal nuances could see that the emperor wished to initiate discussion and negotiation as to how to implement his preference and what exactly those who disagreed with it would face: the details would be determined if and when the new augustus arrived in the city.[60]

<hr>

54. CTh 16.1.2, trans. Pharr with my modifications. See Letteney, *Christianization of Knowledge*, 231–62, for a discussion of the Theodosian Code and its fourth-century antecedents, including new legal language introduced to reflect Christian concepts.

55. *CJ* 1.1. The edict has been considered among the most significant documents in European history: see (critically), e.g., McLynn, "'*Genere Hispanus*,'" 79–89; S. Elm, "Late Roman Toleration"; Humfress, "Ordering Divine Knowledge," 162–74; Williams and Friell, *Theodosius*, 52–53.

56. The Vulgate and the Vetus Latina translate this as "omnes gentes" or "omni gente"; Errington, *Roman Imperial Policy*, 217, translates it as "citizens of all cities," which accords with customary legal language but is not what this law used. See also Stubblefield, "*Africa catholica*"; Letteney, *Christianization of Knowledge*, 234–45, for other instances in the Theodosian Code of specifically Christian and not customarily legal terminology.

57. McLynn, "'*Genere Hispanus*,'" 79–88; Hunt, "Imperial Law," 57–62; S. Elm, "Late Roman Toleration." See Drake, "Constantine and Eusebius in Antioch," 106–36, and Humfress, "'Cherchez la femme!,'" 53–59, for other examples of such negotiations.

58. After Adrianople, "Nicene" Christian authors portrayed the defeat as a divine punishment for Valens's "Arianism": see Gr. Naz., *Or.* 33.2, 32.4; Ambr., *De spiritu sancto* 1 praef. 17; *De fide* 2.141–142. Before the battle, however, Valens had pardoned Nicene Christians, and during his temporary rule over the east after the battle, Gratian had granted most eastern Christians the freedom to worship in whatever fashion they chose: see Brenneke, *Studien zur Geschichte*, 181–242; Lenski, "*Initium mali*," 149–55; McLynn, *Ambrose*, 91–92, 104–10.

59. See McLynn, "'*Genere Hispanus*,'" 102–8, for Theodosius's religious formation.

60. McLynn, "'*Genere Hispanus*,'" 82–89.

In other words, this edict functioned as ostentatious legislation intended for Constantinople.[61] Even if Theodosius did not seek to echo the scriptural message, he conveyed his desire to unify, first, Christians in his new capital who had long been at odds and, second, *all the peoples* through the cohesive power of a universal majesty in which father(s) and son(s) were in essence equally divine.[62] After all, integrating everyone into the divinely sanctioned Roman Empire was central to Roman rule, as Virgil had made clear.[63] The same *virtus*, or manly courage, that granted imperial victory also guaranteed good governance. Theodosius, as a most sacred divine Roman emperor, evidently considered it his mandate to adhere to the command of the resurrected Christ to make his *religio* universal (the translation of *catholicos*). Soon after his accession, he took the appropriate steps to communicate as fast and as widely as possible his understanding of Rome's purpose: to bring just rule to all the (conquered) peoples through the unifying power of his divine love of mankind, made manifest in his imperial softness.

Within months of his arrival in Constantinople (that is, around the time of oration 15), Theodosius called all the eastern and selected western bishops to a council there, which convened in May 381, presided over by the new emperor's bishop, Gregory of Nazianzus.[64] It was tasked with reaching a consensus regarding the details of the relationship between Father, Son, and Holy Spirit as agreed upon at the council of Nicaea in 325. Deep divisions between those in the east, especially in (and between) Antioch and Alexandria, made for slow progress.[65] Gregory resigned, and Theodosius replaced him with the (unbaptized) senator Nectarius, a consummate insider and power broker supported by the bishops.[66] In 382, the council achieved a resolution that reflected the edict *Cunctos populos* as, in the words of Gregory of Nazianzus, the "written law of persuasion" which Theodosius had intended.[67] It also decreed Constantinople's bishop second only to the one in Rome and supported an adjusted Nicene definition of the Christian Trinity as three in one, each member of the same divine essence. Even so, it was flexible enough to accommodate Homoians and others who continued to hold

61. Schmidt-Hofner, "Ostentatious Legislation," 89–96.

62. Humfress, "Ordering Divine Knowledge," 116; Berzon, "Strategies of Containment," 124–49; Escribano Paño, "Social Exclusion," 39–69.

63. Virg., *Aen.* 6.851–853; cf. August., *De civ. D.* praef.: "Hoc vero, quod Dei est, superbae quoque animae spiritus inflatus adfectat amatque sibi in laudibus dici: Parcere subiectis et debellare superbos" (But the swollen fancy of the proud-spirited envies even this utterance, which belongs to God, and loves to hear the following words spoken in its own praise: 'to spare the humble and to subdue the proud').

64. McLynn, "Moments of Truth," 217–38.

65. Ayres, *Nicaea*, 253–61.

66. Errington, "Church," 57–59; Hebblewhite, *Theodosius*, 50–61.

67. Gr. Naz., *De vita sua* 1304. See also Them., *Or.* 15.190a (mildness), 16.212c (persuasion); Theod., *HE* 5.9.15; McLynn, "Moments of Truth," 238–39; Errington, "Church," 60–62, 66; van Nuffelen, "Episcopal Succession," 441–47.

the Son subordinate to the Father, who were the majority at Theodosius's court, among his eunuchs, his Gothic military, and the city's elite.[68]

THREE IN ONE: REPRESENTING THE AUGUSTI, OR AELIA FLACCILLA'S MILITARY LOOK

Theodosius's declarations of the importance of unity and the triumphant power of mildness, forbearance, and philanthropy began soon after his accession and steadily intensified until reaching their first inflection point in 383. By that time, as immortalized in Themistius's oration 16, the emperor had announced his religious preference, assembled a council that had formulated its details, added members to the Senate, and concluded a peace agreement with the Goths. He had also continuously adjusted his relations with his coemperors Gratian and Valentinian II. The year 383, however, witnessed a decisive turn. Theodosius declared that he alone deserved credit for all the recent advances, by God's will. He could thus rightly claim the imperial throne independent of the Valentinians.[69] Eighteen days later he made Arcadius an augustus, the first child emperor of the east, and soon thereafter, as mentioned above, Aelia Flaccilla an augusta.

During a nearly uninterrupted residence between 380 and 394, as the first emperor to live permanently in Constantinople, which he left only to fight Magnus Maximus and Eugenius, Theodosius defined the features of his *domus*, his dynasty, as Constantinopolitan and, following Constantine's precedent, adjusted the cityscape to his vision.[70] The transformation began with his family.[71] As soon as he arrived, Theodosius established his uncle Eucherius as a consul of 381 and another relative, Antonius, as a consul of 382 (followed by his generals Saturninus and Richomeres). Also in 382, Nebridius, the empress's brother-in-law, became the *comes rerum privatarum*, in charge of the emperor's estates.[72] Serena and her sister Thermantia were called to Constantinople from Spain. Theodosius adopted both as daughters and used them to secure ties with the military elite through marriage: Serena in 384 or 385 with Stilicho, and Thermantia with an unnamed dux.[73] After elevating Arcadius as augustus, Theodosius significantly and visibly expanded the role of the empress. Granting Aelia Flaccilla the title *augusta* signaled a rare honor. Constantine had made his mother Helena and wife

---

68. For the nuances of Gregory of Nazianus's definition of the Trinity, which became foundational for the council, see Ayres, *Nicaea*, 245–50; Falcasantos, *Constantinople*, 77–84.

69. Heather and Moncur, *Politics*, 217.

70. Croke, "Reinventing Constantinople," 242–43. I follow Croke in emphasizing the different stages of this development, whose actors are too often elided into "the Theodosians" (379–450).

71. Matthews, *Western Aristocracies*, 101–45, remains foundational.

72. Bagnall et al., *Consuls*, 296–97 (Eucherius); Antonius 5, *PLRE* 1:77; Nebridius 2, *PLRE* 1:620.

73. Thermantia 2, *PLRE* 1:909.

FIGURE 15. Solidus of Aelia Flaccilla, obverse, gold, weight: 4.46 g, Constantinople, British Museum, 1867, 0101.945. © The Trustees of the British Museum.

Fausta augustae, but since then no imperial consort had received the title.[74] Aelia Flaccilla's new rank, as Keith Holum points out, "must have impressed contemporaries as a dramatic innovation."[75] Newly minted gold, silver, and bronze coins featured an even more astonishing novelty: the augusta Aelia Flaccilla wearing the paludamentum, a military cloak like the chlamys, secured by a fibula with triple-chain pendants.[76] She also carried a scepter and wore a diadem with a large jewel at the center of her forehead. Before her, these insignia had been reserved solely for the emperor. The new augusta, in short, wore the regalia of the augustus.[77]

To represent an augusta as an emperor was unheard of. Here too, Theodosius reached back to Constantine, but he took the implications further.[78] Constantine had significantly enhanced the position of his women relatives, a deliberate move in contrast to the practices of his erstwhile tetrarchic colleagues and later opponents, whose consorts had played no public role to speak of. Representations of the augusta Fausta show her with a distinct Constantinian hairstyle, which downplayed her connection to her brother, the defeated Maxentius.[79] Constantine's

74. Augustus's wife Livia had also been an augusta, but only very few imperial women after her prior to Helena and Fausta. See Hillner, *Helena Augusta*, 111–39.

75. Holum, *Theodosian Empresses*, 31. See also McEvoy, "Orations," 119.

76. Coins include *RIC* 9:13, 17, 23, 25 (Heraclea), 48–49 (Constantinople); see also Bastien, *Le buste monétaire*, 1:235–56, 2:637–40. Ammianus Marcellinus (23.3.2, 26.6.2) considered the dying Julian's handing his personal paludamentum to Procopius a legitimate transfer of power; see also Kolb, "Römische Mäntel," 69–167; Delmaire, "Le vêtement dans les sources juridiques"; R. R. R. Smith, "Late Antique Portraits"; F. Morgan, *Dress and Personal Appearance*, 15–16; Olson, "Toga and Pallium"; MacCormack, *Art and Ceremony*, 263–64.

77. Angelova, "Ivories," 3–8.

78. Busch, *Die Frauen*, 26–27.

79. Maxentius was fatally defeated in 312, and after 318 Fausta and Helena are represented on coins with a specific braid-wreath hairdo: see Eus., *Vit. Const.* 1.43.2, 1.17.1, 2.56.1; Schade, "Die bildliche

daughter Constantina was frequently portrayed independent of her male relatives, and an inscription in a basilica she had built on her estate commemorates her with the language of imperial victory.[80] While still a caesar, the later emperor Julian characterized Eusebia, Constantius's wife, as an "image of philanthropy" and "partner in the imperial rule" (*koinonos . . . ton basileias*), who encouraged her husband's benevolent judgment. According to Ammianus Marcellinus, Eusebia participated in imperial deliberations, *consulens in commune*, and interceded with Constantius on Julian's behalf as *regina* (queen), a term he used for female rulers governing non-Romans.[81]

When Theodosius made Aelia Flaccilla an augusta and awarded her the insignia of the emperor, he significantly advanced such notions of partnership and agency. Paludamentum, diadem, and scepter symbolized the supreme imperial powers of jurisdiction and military command. Representing the augusta with these regalia implied that she participated in a joint imperial endeavor in ways that exceeded a consort's central role as a mother of future emperors.[82] In aligning Flaccilla's image with his own while also making his very young son an augustus, Theodosius expanded imperial womanness as well as imperial *vir*-ness. Together, the triad expanded gender performance or gender representation by adding manliness to the empress and softness to Theodosius, at the same time strengthening the imperial union through the enhanced partnership at its center.[83] Public statues emphasized this new ensemble. In an oration delivered in 384, which was once again dedicated to Theodosius's love of mankind, Themistius mentioned a statue (*agalma*) of Aelia Flaccilla recently erected in the Senate house, "where there is also one of the emperor, and one of the emperor's son, and thus will the majesty of [the imperial] choir be increased by this partnership [*koinonia*]."[84] As the iconography of the ruling augusti included Flaccilla, the emperor, his son, and his consort were merging into one "multigendered" or fluidly gendered imperial union. Officials, provincial authorities, and private individuals got the message

Repräsentation," 43–44 (*Zopfkranzfrisur*); Hillner, "Woman's Place," 76–78 (the many imperial consorts related to defeated "usurpers"); Holum, *Theodosian Empresses*, 29–43; Busch, *Die Frauen*, 25–34, 59–85, 189–207; Icks, "Inadequate Heirs," 81–83.

80. *ICUR* 8.20752 in S. Agnese; see also Harries, "Empress's Tale," 210–12; Hillner, "Woman's Place," 85–88.

81. Jul., *Or.* 3.106 a–b, 114b–c, 115a–c; Amm. Marc. 15.2.7–8, 15.8.1–3. See also Wieber-Scariot, "Im Zentrum der Macht," 104–14. An analysis of the terminology denoting female members of the imperial family remains a desideratum.

82. See Hillner, "Empresses, Queens," 354, for early medieval continuity.

83. Angelova, *Sacred Founders*, 186, 199, emphasizes the masculinization of the empress, while I am stressing the softening of the combined imperial characteristics. See also Croke, "Ariadne"; Schade, "Female Body," 227–30; Schade, "Women."

84. Them., *Or.* 19.228b, trans. adapted from Holum, *Theodosian Empresses*, 41. See also Zos., *HN* 5.24.6; Eus., *Vit. Const.* 3.54.2; Holum, *Theodosian Empresses*, 34–41; Vanderspoel, *Themistius and the Imperial Court*, 213–15; Angelova, *Sacred Founders*, 183–202.

of Flaccilla's enhanced role: on newly erected statutes, the augusta was praised as "mistress of the entire world."[85]

On September 9, 384, a few months after Themistius's oration 19, Flaccilla gave birth to Honorius. Only about two years later, in 386, the empress's death rocked that entire world, as Gregory of Nyssa declared in his funeral oration for her.[86] By divine design, Gregory emphasized, Aelia Flaccilla had been Theodosius's partner in life and rule (*biou kai basileias koinonias*).[87] "This ornament of empire has gone from us, this rudder of justice [*dikaiosyne*], this image of philanthropy, or, rather, its archetype."[88] Flaccilla and Theodosius were of one mind and equal in their love of mankind, piety (*eusebeia*), and justice (*dikaiosyne*), and she participated in his governance (*arche*).[89] The virtues for which Gregory praised the augusta were particularly relevant for the emperor, justice above all: traditionally, they were connoted as male. Of course, Flaccilla also excelled as a more typical empress: "This model of wifely love [*philandria*] has been taken away, this pure ornament of self-restraint [*sophrosyne*]. . . . Gone is this zeal of faith [*pistis*], this pillar of the church, and adornment of the altars."[90]

Gregory's emphasis on Flaccilla's philanthropy assumes additional significance in the context of Theodosius's recasting of imperial victory. As a rudder of justice and archetype of philanthropy, the empress shared Theodosius's peacetime qualities, but because love of mankind had by 386 become a central, powerful weapon, his military virtues were also hers—as the coins featuring her in the paludamentum made visible.[91] Flaccilla was presented as a real partner in Theodosius's *basileia* and *arche*, initiating a process that made future Theodosian empresses "into . . . victorious sovereign[s]."[92] Here it is worth noting that Gregory of Nyssa and Gregory of Nazianzus were at that time championing extraordinary Christian women—including their own relatives, especially their sisters Macrina and Gorgonia—as "men of God." They achieved this by layering manly virtues

85. E.g., *I Ephesos* 314. See also Roueché, "Image of Victory," 531; Bönisch-Meyer, *Dialogangebote*, 118–20, for earlier versions of this title.

86. Gr. Nyss., *Flac.* 478–79 = 3.1–38, 488–89 = 10.1–19, in Maraval (SC 606), 76–78, 96–98. See also Holum, *Theodosian Empresses*, 23, 27; Hillner, *Helena Augusta*, 309–46.

87. Gr. Nyss., *Flac.* 478–79 = 3.14–20.

88. Gr. Nyss., *Flac.* 480 = 4.17–20. See Holum, *Theodosian Empresses*, 23.

89. Gr. Nyss., *Flac.* 488 = 10.3–4. Holum renders *arche* as "office." According to Pl., *Rep.* 615c, *eusebeia* denotes "reverence toward gods or parents"; see also Dion. Halicar., *Ant. Rom.* 1.4.2. From Augustus onward, the Latin *pietas* as (the emperor's) reverence toward the gods became a central imperial virtue. At the same time, the emperor's subjects were expected to revere (with *pietas*) the current ruler as a god and the father of the *patria*: see Cic., *Har.* 19; Zanker, *Power of Images*, 96; Manders, *Coining Images of Power*, 178.

90. Gr. Nyss., *Flac.* 480 = 4.20–25.

91. Theodosius's expansion of philanthropy as a weapon altered its valence for the empress—that is, it now differed from Eusebia as its image: see McEvoy, "Orations," 123.

92. Angelova, *Sacred Founders*, 199 (quote), calls this an increase in masculinization.

with those associated with elite women, as in Gregory of Nyssa's characterization of the empress: these women became men while staying women.[93]

Gregory's funeral oration for Flaccilla not only confirmed the enhanced capaciousness of her imperial role but also pointed to additional possibilities for recasting imperial rule (as Christian). If the empress as an equal partner embodied expansions of and other changes to imperial virtues traditionally associated with the ruler, then the emperor could, by the same logic, likewise embrace those usually associated with his consort.[94] Self-restraint, or *sophrosyne*, was a preeminent virtue for all elite women, but, as has become apparent, it was also important for elite men, especially while they were young and particularly beautiful.[95]

In our context, Gregory's celebration of Flaccilla's humility (*tapeinophrosyne*) is even more interesting.[96] He declared it crucial without offering guidance on how to recognize it. However, Gregory did invite his audience to remember what he considered Flaccilla's miraculous *adventus* into Constantinople. As the empress, dressed in purple decorated with gold, was carried through the streets on a gilded litter while surrounded by her bodyguards, the city's dignitaries in their finery, and throngs of people, a cloud suddenly shrouded her face. When it parted, its lingering shadow dulled the brilliance of her jewels, suddenly allowing the people to see the empress's face, which was covered in raindrops as if stained by tears. This moved everyone else to tears: an empress revealed as a human being who could suffer just like all other human beings was a miraculous sight.[97]

That miracle, Gregory implied, was imperial humility, a moment of shared humanity manifested in drops of rain evoking suffering on the face of the ineffable imperial person. This humility was akin to the humble love that Pacatus praised three years later and differed from Pliny's imperial *civilitas*, which Pacatus also praised as an essential imperial virtue. Civility meant moments when the ruler set aside his divine aloofness out of affectionate love for his elite subjects.[98] Calling a member of the imperial family humble, *tapeinon* or *humilis*, was different—and

93. Stefaniw, "Becoming Men," 341–55; Frank, "Macrina's Scar"; S. Elm, "Family Men"; Burrus, *Sex Lives of Saints*, 154–59. The bibliography on the topic of manly Christian women is vast and includes discussions of transgender saints who mark becoming men through dress, which is not the case for Macrina and Gorgonia, as Stefaniw's wonderful title makes clear; although Christian manly women are attested in the early third century (Perpetua is the best known), they take off in the fourth. Transgender saints are the next step in the evolution and mostly date from the early fifth century onward. See S. Elm, "Marking the Self"; Gold, "Transgender Saints," 562–71; Franco, "Byzantine Lives"; Cobb, *Dying to Be Men*, 92–123.

94. Noreña, "Hadrian's Chastity," has shown that previous emperors also assumed virtues associated with women, often to signal shifts in their self-understanding and representation.

95. McDonnell, "Roman Men and Greek Virtue."

96. McEvoy, "Oration," 123–26.

97. Gr. Nyss., *Flac.* 481–83 = 5.1–6.5, 486–87 = 8.

98. Gr. Nyss., *Flac.* 480 = 4.27; *Pan. lat.* 2(12).16.1, 2(12).9.47, 2(12).21.2–22.1; *HA, Pert.* 9.9; *HA, Alex. Sev.* 20.1, 60.3; Wallace-Hadrill, "*Civilis Princeps*"; Noreña, *Imperial Ideals*, 36–38; Schmidt-Hofner, "Trajan und die symbolische Kommunikation," 43–50.

riskier. *Humility* denoted low social status, with all the legal opprobrium associated with those who were less-than-elite, compromised bodily autonomy included.[99] However, it is easy to see why a Christian author like Gregory might want to make lowness or humility an imperial virtue. In his view, "the [imperial] purple down here derives its color from the blood of a sea snail, but the purple in the heavenly realm," where the empress now resided, "is made splendid through the blood of Christ," who was humility incarnate.[100] In this instance, Gregory praised Flaccilla as humble, but since the emperor shared her mind, he too could (indirectly) claim such divine humility made splendid through the blood of Christ.[101]

The close pairing of Theodosius and Flaccilla, in short, allowed Gregory to expand an array of imperial virtues with gendered connotations such that both partners embodied them. At the same time, he resorted to time-honored rhetorical devices like praising or criticizing the consort to target the emperor, for example when he used the empress's faith (*pistis*) and imperial liberality as a "pillar of the church, [an] adornment of the altars, the wealth of the poor, the generosity of the law, and a heaven for the afflicted" to chastise Theodosius for lack of efficiency in tempering various "Arian" heresies that continued to flourish in Constantinople. Flaccilla had expressed "disgust" at the sight of such impiety, or *asebeia*, widespread despite several synods and various pieces of legislation.[102] Further, at its core, Flaccilla's role in the imperial partnership remained that of a mother, the most splendid manifestation of her exceptional love for her husband, or *philandria* (Gregory did not mention the erotic attraction that Julian had praised in Eusebia's *philandria*).[103] She loved her husband so much that she chose to take their daughter, Pulcheria, with her to the heavenly realm and left Theodosius with her most important possessions, their two sons, "to serve as bulwarks of the *basileia*."[104]

THEODOSIUS'S CONSTANTINOPLE: THE EMPEROR IN HIS CITY

In the 380s, Constantinople witnessed the emergence of a new, Theodosian imperial image.[105] The emperor asserted himself as Constantinopolitan and Christian through an expanded vision of imperial virtues, embodied in a more capacious

---

99. I will return to this topic in chapter 8. See also Diefenbach, "Zwischen Liturgie," 31–39; Diefenbach, "Frömmigkeit," 51–52; McLynn, *Ambrose*, 323–30; Ch. Kelly, "Stooping"; Pfeilschifter, *Kaiser und Konstantinopel*, 95–104.

100. Gr. Nyss., *Flac.* 487 = 8.

101. Gr. Nyss., *Flac.* 488 = 10.

102. Gr. Nyss., *Flac.* 481 = 4.30–35, 487 = 9; Maraval (SC 606) 82n1.

103. Jul., *Or.* 3.106a, 113c–114a, 127c; Schade, "Female Body," 227–30.

104. Gr. Nyss., *Flac.* 488 = 10.10–15. See also Holum, *Theodosian Empresses*, 27–28.

105. Diefenbach, "Zwischen Liturgie," 21–27; Diefenbach, "Frömmigkeit," 42–45.

imperial *vir*-ness: the layering of several traits added softness to this *vir*-ness and made it more inclusively gendered. First, with Themistius's help, Theodosius recast philanthropy, mildness, and forgiveness as the most powerful imperial weapons. Enemies whom they subdued became thoroughly Roman in a short time, because these arms civilized intransigent hardness into amenable softness. Second, the moment that he won such a philanthropic victory over the Goths, Theodosius elevated young Arcadius and Aelia Flaccilla as augusti and partners of his rule—both of them further softening the new imperial triad, one because of his youth, the other because of her gender. This novel expansion of the empress's role set the stage for an intensified partnership, which differed rather markedly from Claudian's later characterization of Serena as (Honorius's) mother (the sole task he also expected of Maria, the emperor's very young bride).[106] Third, the strong union at the imperial center was expressed in the terminology of love, which was extended to all peoples, such as those recently subdued and those affected by the repercussions of a changed dynasty, which privileged a different interpretation of Christianity. (Theodosius expressed his desire to unite all peoples in his preferred version of one universal religion but left room to negotiate a consensus.) Fourth, statues and other forms of visual display emphasized a soft, sublime youthfulness that was shared by each member of the augustan trinity: Theodosius, Arcadius, and Aelia Flaccilla (later joined by Honorius and Galla).[107] This new Theodosian imperial language, further consolidated by Arcadius and Theodosius II, gradually transformed the Constantinian legacy it consciously evoked to create a Constantinople that not merely equaled Rome but surpassed it as the Christian capital, a development that dawned only gradually on the Latin west.[108]

When Theodosius and his court arrived in Constantinople, they moved into a crowded space. The imperial palace was already home to the widows and children of Jovian, Procopius, and Valens, as well as to palace eunuchs and other staff.[109] Many of them, together with sections of the army, most of the clergy, and a significant portion of the city's elite, as mentioned above, adhered to the non-Nicene forms of Christianity that so irked Gregory of Nyssa. They were thus among those to whom Theodosius offered his imperial mildness, because they could not simply be purged but had to be persuaded and instructed, and doing so in person was powerful.

As Neil McLynn has highlighted, Theodosius continued the Valentinian practice of regularly attending church and introduced such imperial presence to his

---

106. See chapter 4. See also McEvoy, "Orations," 127–34.

107. Kovacs, *Kaiser, Senatoren,* 91–96; Guidetti, "Between Expressionism and Classicism," 155–64.

108. Bauer, *Stadt,* 28–32, 262–67; Bassett, *Urban Image,* 21–38; Falcasantos, *Constantinople,* 46–62, 72–73; Guidetti, "Between Expressionism and Classicism," 169–71; Machado, "Aristocratic Houses," 137–58. See also Ando, "Palladium," 375–86.

109. Croke, "Reinventing Constantinople," 244–45; Matthews, *Western Aristocracies,* 111.

new capital.[110] Unlike his mobile precursor, who spent more time in Antioch than in Constantinople, Theodosius had an uninterrupted initial seven-year span there, during which he privileged the Church of Holy Wisdom, even on ordinary Sundays. His presence further enhanced the merging of Christian, imperial, and civic (begun by Constantine, who had integrated the city's important churches into civic monumental ensembles) and gave his new imperial language weight.[111] Each church visit was a carefully scripted ceremony that offered the emperor and his court a routine means of interacting with the Constantinopolitan people outside the palace and performing "a partnership between church and state" that displayed Theodosius's preferences.[112] Thus, together with Bishop Nectarius, his chosen successor to Gregory of Nazianzus, who claimed to have resisted imperial interference, Theodosius began to tailor the liturgy to his needs.[113] For example, every time he and his court attended services at the Great Church, the emperor stood next to the bishop and priests at the altar during the Eucharistic rites.[114]

This merging of imperial and church ceremonial extended to high-profile occasions such as baptisms, marriages, and funerals. Theodosius had two children in Constantinople with Aelia Flaccilla (Pulcheria and Honorius) and three with Galla. Among the marriages were that of the emperor to Galla and those of Serena and Thermantia, while the funerals included those of Pulcheria, Flaccilla, Athanaric, the bishop Meletius, and Galla, who died in childbirth in 394.[115] In addition, as early as 382 the emperor began to convert Constantine's mausoleum, adjacent to the Church of the Holy Apostles, into a resting place for the Constantinian and Valentinian dynasty, transferring the remains of Valentinian I, Constantia (Gratian's first wife), Julian, his wife Helena, and Jovian there.[116] All of these occasions included processions.[117] Each time, "the marketplaces were full, the colonnades, streets, every place, two- and three-story houses were full of people leaning out, men, women, children, the very aged," and "people in their myriads, so densely crowded together as to look like a sea of heads, became all one continuous body."[118]

110. McLynn, "Transformation," 250–55, 258–62.

111. Bassett, *Urban Image*, 33–35.

112. McLynn, "Transformation," 255.

113. Gr. Naz., *Or.* 37.22–23; McLynn, "Transformation," 261–62.

114. Soz., *HE* 7.25.9; Theod., *HE* 5.18.20–24.

115. *Cons. Const.* 387.1. Theodosius's two sons with Galla died young, Gratian in 388 and John in 394, but Galla Placidia survived: see Busch, *Die Frauen*, 37–38.

116. Valentinian I's remains were transferred from a different resting place in Constantinople, Constantia's perhaps from Milan, Julian's from Tarsus, Helena's from Rome, and Jovian's from Asia Minor: see Croke, "Reinventing Constantinople," 253.

117. Holum and Vikan, "Trier Ivory," 113–33; Andrade, "Processions," 161–89.

118. Gr. Naz., *Poem.* 2.1.1331–1335:

Πλήρεις ἀγοραί, δρόμοι, πλατεῖαι, πᾶς τόπος,
διώφορα, τριώφορα νευόντων κάτω

Theodosius also introduced a novel form of procession that emulated the imperial *adventus* and offered excellent opportunities to showcase his faith: the transfer of the remains of exceptional Christians. When those of Bishop Meletius were returned to Antioch in 381, the emperor declared that each city along the route should receive the casket as if the deceased were an emperor or governor.[119] For his city, Theodosius acquired the relics of martyrs and other holy persons, which were introduced to Constantinople in an *adventus* in which he participated, and laid to rest in newly erected sanctuaries, changing the cityscape and adding festival days to the liturgical calendar.[120] The most important translation was that of John the Baptist's head, brought to a church built in 392 in the Hebdomon, where the emperor had already founded one dedicated to John the Evangelist.[121]

With Theodosius, the Hebdomon—the military training ground, or *campus*, about four kilometers (two and a half miles) outside the city—assumed a central place in the imperial ceremonial. It was there that the troops proclaimed Arcadius emperor in 383, followed by Honorius in 393 and probably all subsequent emperors.[122] From there, the new augustus advanced in an *adventus* into Constantinople, after the late 380s or early 390s through a freestanding triumphal arch erected by Theodosius, the Golden Gate.[123] In the city, the route continued along the principal east-west axis, the Mese, passing through the Forum of Constantine and the Forum of Theodosius before reaching the capitol.[124] In 393 Theodosius inaugurated his new forum, also known as Forum Tauri, whose construction must have begun around the mid-380s, including a basilica erected alongside it. At the forum's center stood a carved spiral column flanked by two equestrian statues, of Theodosius and Arcadius.[125] The forum and the column evoked those of Trajan in Rome, accentuated by decorative elements with motifs of Hercules, one of Trajan's patron gods. On the pedestal of Theodosius's statue, an inscription declared him

ἀνδρῶν, γυναικῶν, νηπίων, παλαιτάτων·

πόνος, στεναγμός, δάκρυα, βρυχήματα,

εἰκὼν ἁλόντος ἄστεος κατὰ κράτος·

Also Gr. Nyss., *In Meletium* (Εἰς θαλάσσης ὄψιν καταπυκνωθέντες ὁ μυριάνθρωπος δῆμος ἐν ἦν κατὰ τὸ συνεχὲς σῶμα οἱ πάντες οἷόν τι ὕδωρ περὶ τὴν τοῦ σκηνώματος πομπὴν πελαγίζοντες) (trans. Croke, "Reinventing Constantinople," 246).

119. Soz., *HE* 7.10.5; Croke, "Reinventing Constantinople," 247.

120. Beginning with Bishop Paul in 381, and the African martyrs Terentius and Africanus; Paul was incorporated into the liturgical calendar. See CTh 2.8.19, 2.8.20, 8.1.11.4; Croke, "Reinventing Constantinople," 248–49; Errington, "Themistius and His Emperors"; Angelova, *Sacred Founders*, 185–94; Angelova, "Relics"; Diefenbach, "Zwischen Liturgie," 21–45; Holum, *Theodosian Empresses*, 6–78, 29–44.

121. Soz., *HE* 7.21.

122. Amm. Marc. 26.4.3 attests that Valens was the first to be proclaimed emperor at the Hebdomon in 364; see also McCormick, *Eternal Victory*, 67–68, and 155–57, 212–16.

123. This gate was later incorporated into the western city walls: see Bardill, "Golden Gate," 673–95.

124. Bassett, *Urban Image*, 82–83.

125. *Chron. Pasch.* 393 (565.6–7); Bauer, *Stadt*, 187–203, and figs. 63, 65; Croke, "Reinventing Constantinople," 258–59; Bardill, "Golden Gate," 696.

"shining on all sides" as a "second light-bringing Helios" rising in the east. The wording echoes the praise of Constantine on his porphyry column in his forum and thus heralds Theodosius as the city's second founder.[126]

The Golden Gate and the Forum of Theodosius formed, in Sarah Bassett's words, "a thematically coherent" vision, whose expression included strategically placed triumphal monuments commemorating victory over the Goths in 386 and Magnus Maximus in 391.[127] Equally important was the gradual crescendo of dynastic imagery: the arch memorializes Theodosius alone *post fata tyranni*, "after the death of the tyrant," and in the forum he is joined by Arcadius.[128] The finale was the hippodrome, adjacent to the imperial palace. Imperial birthdays, anniversaries of imperial elevations, or *dies imperii*, and imperial consulships were celebrated there, as well as at least three victories, in 380, 386, and 391.[129]

Between 390 and 392, Theodosius erected his best-known monument in the hippodrome, deploying the complete tableau of the emperors to proclaim the extinction of tyrants and affirm that "everything cedes to Theodosius and his eternal offspring."[130] The monument is an Egyptian obelisk, with four imperial persons pictured at its base. It has received intense scholarly attention, not least because identifying these figures is not easy. As in the contemporary Madrid *missorium* (see chapter 4), all of the portrayed persons are clothed in elaborate vestments and have polished, unlined, and uniformly youthful faces. Their sole distinction is size. In all probability, the largest emperor is Theodosius, flanked by Valentinian II, Arcadius, and Honorius, but other Theodosian arrangements are possible.[131] Representations of recognizably old high-ranking officials further emphasize the emperors' eternal youth.[132] The richly decorated base also depicts the erection of the obelisk itself, chariot races, and, on two sides, supplicating barbarians, recognizable as such because they wear pelts and "Persian" outfits.[133] The monument's triumphal aspects are evident, but scholars have noted the absence of fighting scenes and emblems of victory such as captured cities and other

126. *Anth. Pal.* 16.65; Bauer, *Stadt*, 172–77, 200–201; Croke, "Reinventing Constantinople," 259; Maier, *Palastrevolution*, 401–2.

127. Bassett, "Topography," quote at 529, see also 533–34; Bassett, *Urban Image*, 80–82.

128. For the inscription, see Bardill, "Golden Gate," 683.

129. Diefenbach, "Frömmigkeit," 64–66; Bauer, *Stadt*, 247–54; McCormick, *Eternal Victory*, 42–64.

130. *CIL* 3.737: "Iussus et extinctis palmam portare tyrannis. / Omnia Theodosio cedunt subolique perenni" (I have been ordered to carry the palm [of victory] over extinct tyrants. Everything cedes to Theodosius and his eternal offspring). See Kiilerich, *Obelisk Base*, 19–66, inscription at 26; Bassett, "Topography," 530; L'Orange, *Roman Empire*, 180 and plate 98.

131. Arcadius has also been suggested as the largest figure, and one of the others might have been Galla: see Kovacs, *Kaiser, Senatoren*, 91–2; Guidetti, "Between Expressionism and Classicism," 157; Maier, *Palastrevolution*, 401–12; Croke, "Reinventing Constantinople," 262; Kiilerich, *Obelisk Base*, 137–38; Kiilerich, *Late Fourth Century Classicism*, 12–18, 31–43.

132. Kovacs, *Kaiser, Senatoren*, 107–9.

133. Von Rummel, *Habitus barbarus*, 199–200; Bassett, "Topography," 530–34.

FIGURE 16. Obelisk of Theodosius, Istanbul, detail of imperial family. Photo: Lily Callender.

symbols indicating conquests.[134] Instead, the enemies are shown as already subdued, and their images form part of a cycle dedicated to the emperors' interactions with all their people, on whom they bestow their liberality, generosity, and love of mankind. Vanquishing foreign enemies remained a central duty of imperial rule, but it was only one in the array that God had entrusted to the divine, eternal, and eternally young emperor Theodosius and his equally divine, soft, and smooth sons, Arcadius and Honorius.

BACK TO THE WEST

When Pacatus celebrated Theodosius's victory over Magnus Maximus in Rome in 389, the emperor had spent a decade creating a cohesive vision of himself, his dynasty, and his imperial capital. He made this vision legible through Themistius's orations, his own ostentatious legislation and interaction with his bishops, a host of statues and strategically placed building projects, and his sheer presence among and frequent encounters with Constantinople's inhabitants. The

134. Maier, *Palastrevolution*, 407–11, 417–18, with literature.

Constantinopolitan Theodosius emphasized governance as the quintessential imperial virtue, while victory in battle, though central, could—and should—be delegated to generals. In any case, bloodless victories were preferable and possible only through the emperor's divine love of mankind. Representations of Theodosius conveyed this type of soft power through pairing with his very young sons, "classicizing" portraits that highlighted his smooth agelessness, and a close alignment between himself and the augusta in imperial military regalia.

The western elites in Milan and Rome were aware of Theodosius's general tenets. After the peace of 382, the flow of information between the empire's two halves resumed, and from 384 to 391 Theodosius spent time in northern Italy, Milan, and Rome.[135] Still, Pacatus's panegyric offered an opportunity to relate the emperor's virtues to audiences for whom some Constantinopolitan innovations might have come as a surprise. Thus, the orator highlighted Theodosius's presence as novel: in Rome as in his own capital, the emperor "frequently allow[s] [himself] to appear before the people as they wait for [him] to emerge, and granting not only that [he] be seen but easily approached. . . . Whoever he is who consults you [Theodosius] . . . takes away the awareness of having seen a divine spirit."[136] Further, Pacatus focused on the emperor's extraordinary clemency and compassion, which together with his humble love for his friends constituted the civil war victor's softer side.[137]

Theodosius's victory over Eugenius in 394 provided the next major opportunity to present his Roman (and Constantinopolitan) imperial virtues to western elites. This time, however, the occasion was somber. Rather than return to Rome in another triumphal *adventus*, Theodosius died in Milan of complications from edema on January 17, 395.[138] On February 25, Ambrose, the bishop of Milan, praised the deceased, whose casket was displayed in the city's cathedral, in the presence of the ten-year-old Honorius, Stilicho, and military and civilian elites, including those just defeated. Ambrose's oration—a lament, consolation, and funeral mass—sought to consolidate Theodosius's legacy and facilitate a smooth transition to Honorius by announcing, for the first time, Stilicho's claim to be the guardian of both Honorius and Arcadius, who were now "under the protection of a close relative who [is] present."[139]

To this end, Ambrose, like Pacatus, emphasized Theodosius's Constantinopolitan themes, in particular his extraordinary clemency and love of mankind. This was all the more trenchant because many in the audience had witnessed tensions

135. Lenski, "*Initium mali*," 136–41; McLynn, *Ambrose*, 342–53.

136. *Pan. lat.* (2)12.21.2–3; see also Ruf., *HE* 2.19. Rees, *Commentary*, 300, points out that the notion of "easy approach" ("patiens sed facilis adiri") had erotic overtones.

137. See chapter 1.

138. For Theodosius's preparations for another Roman triumphal entry, see Ambr., *Ep.* 74(40).1; Williams and Friell, *Theodosius*, 139.

139. Ambr., *De ob. Theod.* 5 ("Nisi ut eos praesenti commendaret parenti"). For the interweaving of literary genres, see Lizzi Testa, "Memorie."

caused by the emperor's Constantinopolitan habits that the Milanese bishop had not appreciated during Theodosius's stay between 388 and 391. For example, when Theodosius attended a service in Milan's cathedral for the first time, he advanced to participate in the Eucharist among the priests at the altar, as was his custom, but was sent back by Ambrose.[140] Other drama-filled moments followed, most famously after a massacre by imperial troops in a mismanaged response to a riot in Thessalonica in 390, which ended with the emperor performing a public act of penitence in Ambrose's church.[141] This event is probably the most analyzed of Theodosius's entire reign, in part because our knowledge of it depends heavily on later sources intent on praising the bishop.[142] It seems clear that the retaliatory killings, which caused an outcry because innocents also suffered, exceeded the emperor's intended punishment for the disturbance of public order and went against his frequently proclaimed policy of clemency and philanthropy. As Neil McLynn has shown, Ambrose offered a way out of this public relations debacle by exhorting Theodosius to restore his reputation by performing a public act of penitent humility that emphasized his humanity as well as his imperial mercy.[143] Elements of this staging of imperial humility are familiar: they echo Gregory's description of Flaccilla and Pacatus's celebration of Theodosius's humble love and mercy, or *misericordia*.

I mention this episode here because Ambrose explicitly referred to it in his funeral oration. Theodosius had done in public what most were ashamed to do in private: he had humbled himself by throwing his imperial regalia (*insigne regium*) to the ground, weeping in the church, and praying with groans for forgiveness, and in so doing had "placed his kingdom under God."[144] Ambrose included *De obitu Theodosii* in book 10 of his letter collection, which he published after the emperor's death. Echoing Pliny's collected letters, whose tenth book focuses on the latter's interactions with Trajan, book 10 of Ambrose's collection is arranged to showcase his relationship with Theodosius, demonstrating how he, the bishop, had succeeded in uniting the Roman Empire under the Nicene God.[145] To be sure, Ambrose's funeral oration translated Theodosius's Constantinopolitan virtues for a broad western audience. However, just like Pacatus, the bishop and senator, or *vir clarissimus*, also spoke for himself—and he could do so with great assuredness

---

140. At least in Sozomen's characterization in *HE* 7.25.9; see also McLynn, *Ambrose*, 298.

141. Liebeschuetz, *Ambrose of Milan*, 18–19; McLynn, *Ambrose*, 315–30; Hebblewhite, *Theodosius*, 102–11.

142. I.e., Ruf., *HE* 11.18; Paulin., *V. Amb.* 24; August., *De civ. D.* 5.26; Soz., *HE* 7.25; Theod., *HE* 5.17–18.

143. McLynn, *Ambrose*, 323–28.

144. Ambr., *De ob. Theod.* 27–28 ("regnum suum Deo subiecit"), 34. I use Liebeschuetz's translation, with modifications.

145. Nauroy, "Letter Collection," 154–55; Liebeschuetz, *Ambrose of Milan*, 27–28, 31–32, 35–38 (Pliny's model), 176 (publication as part of Ambrose's letter collection).

because he praised a ruler who was deceased.[146] In the process, Ambrose amplified and shaped virtues that the emperor had already embraced to paint the ideal Christian emperor as one who had firmly placed himself under God and his bishop.[147] Ambrose did this by assuming the role that I have claimed the emperor took for himself: arbiter of Christian imperial *virtus*, and thus of Christian imperial manliness.

Most scholars regard the bishop's portrayal of Theodosius as quintessential Christian emperor not only as exemplary but normative; that is, they interpret it as a direct and consistent reflection of the emperor's intent.[148] However, assuming that Ambrose provided in effect the only relevant characterization of Theodosius as a Christian ruler does a real disservice to both emperor and bishop. Each had distinct ideas of what being a Christian sovereign entailed, although it is harder to specify what they were for Theodosius: he merely ruled, while Ambrose wrote, and the bishop was eminently capable of shaping an imperial portrait that served his own interests just as much as (if not more than) those of the imperial house.

AMBROSE'S THEODOSIUS FOR THE BENEFIT OF HONORIUS

"This is what severe earthquakes and incessant rain were threatening, and a darkness gloomy beyond experience was foretelling, that our most merciful [*clementissimus*] emperor Theodosius was about to withdraw from this earth. Thus the very elements were mourning his passing."[149] *Clementissimus imperator*—that was Theodosius's central legacy.[150] He had been extraordinarily clement, mild, benevolent, and indulgent. In Ambrose's interpretation, the emperor was *clementissimus* because he excelled in two other imperial virtues, piety (*pietas*) and faith (*fides*). *Pietas*, loyalty to God and to one's family or dynasty, and *fides*, trust, the military oath of loyalty, (good) faith (*bona fides*) guaranteed by imperial authority, and

---

146. McLynn, *Ambrose*, 291–92, 330–31, 341–57.

147. Imperial virtues (especially *fides*) were one of Ambrose's themes since writing *On Faith* at Gratian's request in 378: see Ambr., *De fide* 1.3, 2.136; *Ep.* 33.1–2; *Off.* 3.2. See also Lizzi Testa, *Vescovi e strutture ecclesiastiche*, 20–22; Consolino, "L'optimus princeps," 1031–32; Stewart, *Soldier's Life*, 150–60.

148. For the literature, including voices critical of Ambrose's influence, see Moreau, "Le *De obitu Theodosii*"; Maier, *Palastrevolution*, 386; Biermann, *Die Leichenreden*, 13; Groß-Albenhausen, *Imperator christianissimus*, 125–33; Lunn-Rockliffe, "Ambrose's Imperial Funeral Sermons," 192–205; McLynn, *Ambrose*, 292–360; Consolino, "Teodosio."

149. Ambr., *De ob. Theod.* 1.

150. Bönisch-Meyer, *Dialogangebote*, 253, 255, 271–74, points out that *clementissimus* was a rare descriptor, but she ends her analysis in the third century; at 15–16, 135–41, she shows that Trajan was a trendsetter with *liberalissimus*, *fortissimus*, and the frequency of *sanctissimus* and *sacratissimus*; see 74–83 for the complex relationship between Greek and Latin epithets, which were culturally specific translations and adaptations. This is especially relevant for the increase in peacetime or civilian virtues from the second century onward. For instance, there is no Greek equivalent for *clementissimus* (81)— *euergetes*, "most benevolent or indulgent," and *philanthropos*, "philanthropic," come closest.

faith in God, were imperial virtues now being Christianized.[151] Theodosius's *pietas* and *fides* guaranteed the continued security of the empire, because

> he has left behind . . . his sons . . . as heirs of his piety [*pietas*]; they are not cut off [from their father and his support], for he has won them the favor [*gratia*] of Christ and the loyalty [*fides*] of the soldiers to whom he was proof that God upholds piety and avenges treachery. . . . An emperor of such greatness, then, has withdrawn from us. But he has not wholly withdrawn; for he has left us his children, in whom we can both see and embrace him. Their age should not trouble us! The loyalty of his soldiers [*fides militum*] makes the emperor's age fully grown [*perfecta*]. For age is fully grown when strength [*virtus*] is. This is reciprocal. For the faith [*fides*] of the emperor produces strength [*virtus*] in his soldiers. You are calling to mind, no doubt, what triumphs Theodosius's faith gained for you [*vobis Theodosii fides triumphos adquisiverit*]. . . . Theodosius's faith [*fides*] thus was your victory; let your faith be the courage [*fortitudo*] of his sons. Thus does faith [*fides*] augment age.[152]

Theodosius's *fides* had made him victorious. It had subdued Eugenius and guaranteed Honorius's position as an augustus because the emperor's faith had given his sons as much strength and courage, *virtus* and *fortitudo*, as he himself had enjoyed. Their combined manly strength and courage was fortified by their soldiers' faith, the *fides militum*, which in turn drew its power from the emperors. Thus, the emperor's piety and faith, both of which Honorius had inherited, guaranteed victory and, moreover, rendered the new emperor's age immaterial: the augustus perpetuated the peacetime virtues of the departed Theodosius, which were, in fact, also the emperor's most powerful weapons in war. Thus—such, presumably, was Ambrose's rationale—it had been entirely appropriate for the bishop to put the letter informing him of the emperor's victory in another bloody civil war on his church's altar: an unprecedented move, but conforming with the idea that Theodosius had placed his kingdom under God—very much on his own imperial terms, however.[153]

Now, after Theodosius's death, Ambrose made the durability of an emperor's faith, his *fixa fides*, into a barometer of imperial manliness, including courage in battle.[154] As Themistius had also stressed, victory as proof of divine favor no longer required that the emperor participate in combat: he could be victorious without shedding blood. Indeed, bloodless victory (*victoria incruenta*) through piety and faith became an important sign of Christian imperial rule, as Sulpicius Severus's

---

151. See Moreau, "Le *De obitu Theodosii*," 36–40; Raspanti, "*Clementissimus Imperator*," 48–54; Consolino, "Teodosio," 257–77; Maier, *Palastrevolution*, 388; McEvoy, *Child Emperor Rule*, 145–46; Meyer, *Legitimacy and Law*, 5, 250–93, and passim for *fides* as good faith in the legal-financial-contractual sense and its transformations in late antiquity as an aspect of imperial authority; T. Morgan, *Roman Faith*, 129–37, on the *Fides Augusta* and other instances of *fides* as a divine and human attribute.

152. Ambr., *De ob. Theod.* 2, 6, 7, 8.1 ("Theodosii ergo fides fuit vestra victoria: vestra fides filiorum eius fortitudo sit").

153. Ambr., *Ep. extra coll.* 2(61).2; McLynn, *Ambrose*, 353–354; Lizzi Testa, "Memorie," 4–5.

154. Ambr., *Ep.* 51(15).5–7.

Life of Saint Martin of Tours attests.[155] However, in Ambrose's hands, the emperor's peacetime weapons underwent a significant change. Unlike imperial philanthropy and extraordinary clemency, both of which were the emperor's to give or withhold, piety and durability of faith, as Ambrose saw it, were judged by the bishop as God's representative, not by the emperor. In short, bishops as arbiters of faith and piety decided whether the *fides* of an emperor merited victory and thus whether he possessed manliness. By the same logic, those who opposed a sufficiently faithful, pious, and therefore manly emperor were by definition unfaithful (*infidelis*), whatever their religious affiliation, and less-than-manly, "rush[ing] headlong into vice, and defil[ing] themselves with rampant lust like cattle [*vaga sese libidine polluebant*] . . . in their fall into wickedness [*perfidia*]."[156]

Such forms of episcopally sanctioned imperial manliness had to overcome the hesitations of the more tradition-bound, and the senator Ambrose knew this quite well: active participation in battle was still a significant proof of imperial manliness, as his frequent references to Theodosius's triumphs show.[157] Like Claudian a few years later, Ambrose also responded by making his Theodosius the model for Honorius, thereby imbuing the ten-year-old, who now stood next to him at the altar (*adsistente sacris altaribus Honorio principe*), this time obviously with the bishop's permission, with all the virtues his father had embodied.[158]

Having emphasized the bond between Theodosius's army (including the defeated who had then joined it) and Honorius, Ambrose turned to reconciliation and imperial benevolence. As Theodosius had done, Honorius (and Arcadius) should grant *indulgentia* to Eugenius's supporters and pardon those who had sought asylum in the churches.[159] Here again, Ambrose gave a Theodosian virtue his own twist, because emperors considered the granting of asylum their prerogative and did not look benevolently on bishops lobbying for it, even for others, a topic to which I will return in chapter 8. In this case, however, Ambrose succeeded, as two laws issued in 395 confirm.[160]

---

155. See Zecchini, "S. Ambrogio," 110–13; Sághy, "*Veste Regia Indutus*," 47–56; Lizzi Testa, "Martino vescovo santo"; Maier, *Palastrevolution*, 383–98.

156. Ambr., *De ob. Theod.* 39, 51, see also 4: "Subplantavit perfidiam tyrannorum" ([Theodosius] supplanted the faithlessness/wickedness/perfidy of the tyrants).

157. Ambr., *De ob. Theod.* 56.1–2: "Italia, quae claros spectavit triumphos, quae a tyrannis iterum liberata concelebrat suae libertatis auctorem" (Italy, which witnessed his spectacular triumphs, and which, set free from tyrants once more, acclaims the author of her freedom).

158. Ambr., *De ob. Theod.* 3. For detailed analysis, see McLynn, "Transformation," 261–65.

159. Ambr., *De ob. Theod.* 4–5; *Ep. extra coll.* 3(62).3: "Qui ad matrem pietatis tuae ecclesiam petentes misericordiam confugerunt" (Those who fled to the church, mother of your piety, begging for mercy).

160. CTh 15.14.11–12; Lizzi Testa, "Memorie," 8–11; McLynn, *Ambrose*, 354; Ducloux, *Ad ecclesiam confugere*, 64–80, 267–68.

Ambrose further adjusted Theodosian representation by integrating deceased members of the imperial household, including the emperor Gratian, into the funeral liturgy. Gratian, Theodosius the Elder, Pulcheria and the infant Gratian, Aelia Flaccilla, and Constantine and Helena formed a sacred assembly (*sanctorum consortia*) to receive Theodosius of *augusta memoria* in the kingdom of heaven.[161] These heavenly presences served to strengthen and deepen the dynasty, tying Honorius (and Arcadius) all the way back to Constantine, and offered Ambrose the occasion to discuss Helena's discovery of the true cross, the earliest version of the story.[162] He might have inserted this lengthy episode after delivering the funeral oration, but it connects to the dynastic theme—Helena prefigured Flaccilla, therefore Constantine prefigured Theodosius—with an emphasis in the bishop's favor: demonstrating the inevitable success of the Nicene faith.[163]

Echoing Gregory of Nyssa's lament for Flaccilla, Ambrose praised Helena Augusta as the mother of future augusti and as a partner in Constantine's rule.[164] She, rather than her son, had been chosen to direct imperial liberality to the poor and the churches, to safeguard piety, and to establish the right faith.[165] The divine sanction of Helena's central role was manifested in her discovery of the cross and its nails. She shaped the latter into a bridle for the emperor's horse and, "brilliant with jewels," the diadem that Constantine introduced as an imperial headdress.[166] Helena's extraordinary piety made her the guarantor of the emperor's faith. As his *conregnans*, to use Paulinus of Nola's term, she embodied justice and self-control (*temperantia*) while guaranteeing, as his mother, the continuity of the imperial house.[167] Ambrose, similar to Gregory, made Helena—and by analogy Aelia Flaccilla—the principal imperial carrier of the virtues of faith and piety, here understood as the correct interpretation of Christianity. At the same time, he emphatically established humility, through Theodosius's fulsome display —*humilem se praebuit Theodosius imperator*—as a male imperial virtue, while Gregory had more tentatively assigned it to Flaccilla and allowed the emperor to

161. Ambr., *De ob. Theod.* 39–40. Ambrose did not mention Valentinian II or the recently deceased Galla, the latter's sister and Theodosius's wife: see Zos., *HN* 4.57.3. For Gratian's rehabilitation, see Cameron, *Last Pagans*, 96–97; Lizzi Testa, "Memorie," 2–4; McLynn, *Ambrose*, 155. For Galla, see Hillner, "Woman's Place," 77–78, 83–89; Busch, *Die Frauen*, 38.

162. Ambr., *De ob. Theod.* 41–51; Hillner, *Helena Augusta*, 309–316; Drijvers, "Helena Augusta"; Bojcov, "Der heilige Kranz."

163. Liebeschuetz, *Ambrose of Milan*, 175–76.

164. Helena was, of course, Constantine's mother, but her representation appears to have suggested otherwise: *CIL* 1.517 and 10.1438 address her as his wife. His actual wife Fausta was killed in 326 together with his eldest son, Crispus: see Drijvers, "Helena Augusta," 137.

165. Ambr., *De ob. Theod.* 42.

166. Ambr., *De ob. Theod.* 47.

167. Paulinus of Nola, *Ep.* 31 (405); Ambr., *De ob. Theod.* 26; Angelova, *Sacred Founders*, 184.

claim it in a far more indirect way.[168] This was a bold and lasting move: Ambrose's funeral oration may well have been the watershed moment that set humility on the path to becoming a central—male—Christian imperial virtue.

DILEXI: I LOVED THE MAN AND HE LOVED ME BACK

However dramatic his appraisal and transformation of humility, Ambrose most strikingly imbued traditional imperial virtues with Christian meaning through the explication of Psalm 116 (114 in the Vulgate) at the core of his funeral lament.[169] This psalm celebrates a just and merciful God as the "lord of virtues" (*dominus virtutum*). It opens with the word *dilexi*, "I have loved": "I have loved, seeing that the Lord will hear the voice of my prayer." In his exegesis of the opening word, Ambrose transformed the emperor, ascending to heaven, into the psalmist while intimating the closeness of his own relationship to the departed. Through Ambrose's voice, Theodosius addressed God directly: "In this psalm . . . we seemed to hear Theodosius himself speaking. 'I have loved,' he says; I [Ambrose] recognize that pious voice. . . . He [Theodosius] did truly love, he who fulfilled the duties of one who loves." "You know, Lord, that I love you. . . . I have loved."[170] Ambrose reiterated "I have loved" twenty-two times in six short paragraphs.[171] Speaking through the bishop, Theodosius declared love the guiding principle of his rule, his most enduring imperial virtue: love for God and love for all the people, love of (hu)mankind. "Because Theodosius of revered memory loved the Lord his God he has earned the fellowship of the saints."[172]

And just as God's love is reciprocal and reciprocated by all good men, so was Theodosius's love answered in kind. All who were embraced by Theodosius's love loved him in return. Ambrose was the first to confess his love for the departed. Seven times in three paragraphs, the bishop declared that he too had loved. "I have loved [*dilexi*] a man who valued a critic more than a flatterer." "I have loved [*dilexi*] a man who in his last moments and with his last breath kept asking for me." "I have loved [*dilexi*] a merciful man, humble in power, endowed with a pure heart and a gentle disposition. . . . I have loved [*dilexi*]. . . . Yes, I have loved [*dilexi*], I admit it, and for that reason my grief has pained me to the core of my being."[173]

"I have loved" was proclaimed nearly thirty times by the bishop mourning the emperor in the great church in Milan, standing next to the young son and heir. Of

168. Ambr., *De ob. Theod.* 26–28; *Ep. extra coll.* 11 (51).

169. It is possible that Ambrose's church already used a lectionary with established readings, but he more probably selected this psalm for the occasion: see Lunn-Rockliffe, "Ambrose's Imperial Funeral Sermons," 195–97.

170. Ambr., *De ob. Theod.* 17–23.

171. McLynn, *Ambrose*, 358.

172. Ambr., *De ob. Theod.* 32.

173. Ambr., *De ob. Theod.* 33–35, 37.

course, Ambrose spoke of Theodosius's all-embracing, merciful, and forgiving love in the voice of the psalmist. But it was also Ambrose the senator and *clarissimus vir* who spoke that day of love of men, from man to man, with all the force of desire for the emperor whom he had loved and who had loved him: *dilexi*.[174]

Ambrose concluded his lament and memorial sermon for the deceased emperor by turning directly to the weeping Honorius. They were bidding farewell to the casket that would convey the imperial body to "the tomb of his fathers," Constantine's mausoleum that Theodosius had transformed in Constantinople. Honorius, weeping, had to stay behind. "The good of the republic . . . hold[s] you back. . . . Your father made you emperor; the Lord confirmed you." The young ruler could rest assured that his father's "triumphal relics will be received with . . . conspicuous honor. . . . Theodosius is returning there more powerful, more glorious. . . . Constantinople, you are surely blessed, you who are receiving a citizen of paradise, and will possess in the august lodging of his buried body an inhabitant of the kingdom of heaven."[175]

174. For Ambrose's erotic language in Valentinian II's funeral oration, see Santini, "Martyr of Civil Wars."

175. Ambr., *De ob. Theod.* 54–55.

PART II

Soft Power

Arcadius and Eutropius in Constantinople, 399

6

———

Eutropius the Consul,
Eutropius the Eunuch

Claudian's Palimpsest Against Eutropius

It would have been less shameful if a woman illegally took up the fasces. That sex rules the Medes and the lightweight Sabaeans, and a great part of the barbarian world lies under the arms of queens. But there is no evidence of a people who endure the scepter of a eunuch.[1]

The year was 399 CE, the venue Constantinople. Imagine the newly anointed consul of the eastern empire clad in the consular trabea—heavily embroidered with gold, glittering with multicolored jewels, and draped with artful bands (*claves*)—holding the scepter (*scipio*) of office, and riding in a special carriage.[2] He and his colleague in the west, Manlius Theodorus, will be inscribed in "the *fasti* of the entire world," surpassed in honor and importance only by the sacred Christian emperors in Milan and Constantinople—Honorius, age fourteen, and Arcadius, twenty-two.[3] As befit his exalted position, the eastern consul had already received

---

1. Claud., *Eutr.* 1.320–24:

Sumeret inlicitos etenim si femina fasces,
esset turpe minus! Medis levibusque Sabaeis
imperat hic sexus reginarumque sub armis
babariae pars magna iacet: gens nulla probatur,
eunuchi quae sceptra ferat.

In what follows I use the text of Charlet and I modify the translation of Bernstein, who claims that the poem is unfinished (248).

2. Claud., *IV Cons. Hon.* 565–67, 564–601; Claud., *Cons. Stil.* 2.339; CTh 14.12.1; Dewar, "Spinning the *Trabea*," 217–37. For representations of the consular insignia, see fig. 11; chapters 2 and 4; Olovsdotter, *Consular Image*, 61–90; Roberts, *Jeweled Style*, 111–15, with fig. 23; for the relation between the *tunica palmata* and the trabea, M. Pausch, *Die römische Tunika*, 163–68.

3. Amm. Marc. 29.2.15 ("Consulares, post scipiones et trabeas et fastorum monumenta mundana"). For honors, see Schlinkert, *Ordo senatorius*, 162–77. For Manlius Theodorus, see chapter 4; Müller, *Lectiones*, 37–60; Matthews, *Western Aristocracies*, 215–20, 258–61.

155

an extraordinary honor in the preceding year, when the emperor had made him a *patricius*, a title expressing the highest esteem.[4] In this case, the esteem was well merited. The new consul had long served the imperial court, in just the previous two years repelling Gothic and Hunnic incursions into Asia Minor and Armenia. He had carried out diplomatic missions for Theodosius, supported Constantinople's recently ordained bishop, and was a confidant of the empress.[5] This is the man we should visualize: a *patricius* and Roman senator, or *illustris vir*, a victorious military commander, a member of the sacred council (*sacer comitatus*), a consummate palace insider and trusted adviser of the imperial couple, considered the "father of the emperor," *pater principis*, by contemporaries, and a vital supporter of John Chrysostom—in sum, an exemplary representative of the highest elites.[6] How do we picture such a man? What would he wear when not clad in the consul's jewel-encrusted trabea? What might he have looked like?

Here is one description:

> Now old age had loosened his skin. His face, more wrinkled than a raisin, had collapsed into deep furrows in his cheeks. The plough cuts fallow fields less deeply, and the folds of sails tremble less in the wind. Disgusting moth larvae had eaten away at his head, and bare patches appeared in his hair, as on parched fields a barren crop shows tiny stalks here and there, or as a swallow sitting on a tree trunk dies in winter, its feathers falling in the frost. Just to increase future damage to the trabea, Fortune added to her excess this brand [*nota*] on his forehead, this disgrace to his face. When his pallor and nearly bare bones horrified his master and his pale complexion and emaciated body offended all, filled children with fear, disgusted those who sat at table [with him], shamed the slaves, and terrified passersby like a bad omen, and no one could profit from his exhausted trunk . . . they all chased him from their home like a premature corpse or a sinister shadow.[7]

---

4. *Patricius* did not correspond to a specific office: see Jones, *Later Roman Empire* 1:176; Dillon, "Inflation of Rank," 60–62; Guyot, *Eunuchen*, 136–37; Schlinkert, *Ordo senatorius*, 248–50; Scholten, *Der Eunuch in Kaisernähe*, 46–50.

5. Soz., *HE* 7.22.7–8, 8.2; Soc., *HE* 6.2; Theod., *HE* 5.27; Pall., *Hist. Laus.* 35; Pall., *Dial.* 5.55–57; Pall., *Hist. mon.* 1.64; Claud., *Eutr.* 1.311–316; Cameron, *Claudian*, 124–29, 132; Tiersch, *Johannes Chrysostomus*, 31–41; Malingrey, *Dialogue* 1:112–14.

6. Claud., *Eutr.* 2 praef. 2.50 ("principis esse pater"); Philost., *HE* 11.4.

7. Claud., *Eutr.* 1.110–131:

> Iamque aevo laxata cutis sulcisque genarum
> corruerat passa facies rugosior uva:
> flava minus presso finduntur vomere rura,
> nec vento sic vela tremunt. Miserabile turpes
> exedere caput tineae. Deserta patebant
> intervalla comae, qualis sitientibus arvis
> arida ieiunae seges interlucet aristae
> vel qualis gelidis pluma labente pruinis
> arboris inmoritur trunco brumalis hirundo.
> Scilicet ut trabeis iniuria cresceret olim,

And here is the characterization of the ruling consuls of 399 in the succinct words of the sixth-century *Chronicle of Marcellinus*: "12th indiction, the consulship of Theodorus and Eutropius the Eunuch. This Eutropius was the first and the last eunuch to be consul. The poet Claudian says of him: 'all portents pale before our eunuch consul, *omnia cesserunt eunucho consule monstra*,'" quoting the poem I just cited.[8]

Claudian wrote his two invectives, "the cruelest . . . in all ancient literature," against the consul of 399 in that very year.[9] With them, he created the iconic picture of the powerful court eunuch, one of antiquity's most enduring literary portraits of ugliness; indeed, here he made ugliness iconic.[10] Weaving together all the well-known tropes to denigrate eunuchs, Claudian created a dense palimpsest.[11] He ripped apart the beauty of the trabea to reveal a monster. The impact was lasting.[12] Claudian's Eutropius became the epitome of the pernicious court eunuch dominating a passive emperor, making both paradigmatic of an empire in decline.[13] But this "Eutropius" was a western construct. Claudian paired him with the model republican consul Manlius Theodorus to emphasize the starkness of the contrast between the Roman Empire's two halves: to make Stilicho into the father of Honorius was one thing, but to make a eunuch the father of Arcadius was something else entirely. Hammering that difference home was one of Claudian's tasks,

> has in fronte notas, hoc dedecus addidit oris
> luxuriate Fortuna suae: cum pallida nudis
> ossibus horrorem dominis praeberet imago
> decolor et macies occursu laederet omnes,
> aut pueris latura metus aut taedia mensis
> aut crimen famulis aut procedentibus omen,
> et nihil exhausto caperent in stipite lucri
> . . . tandem ceu funus acerbum
> infaustamque suis trusere Penatibus umbram.

Tinea is a worm that eats away at things such as books or cloth, hence a moth; in modern medical terms, however, it denotes ringworm: see Schweckendiek, *Claudians Invektive gegen Eutrop*, 74; Long, *Claudian's "In Eutropium,"* 1; Ware, *Claudian*, 3–6.

8. Marc., *Chron.* 2.66, quoting Claud., *Eutr.* 1.8.

9. Cameron, *Claudian*, 126 (quote), 140–42 (date); Long, *Claudian's "In Eutropium,"* 13–14, 35–50; Schweckendiek, *Claudians Invektive gegen Eutrop*, 18–28; Garambois-Vasquez, *Les invectives*, 18–20 (highlights Claudian's creation of a poetics of violence).

10. S. Elm, "Icon of Ugliness."

11. Claudian's highly allusive and innovative genre could have been a model for Genette, *Palimpsests*, and I have structured this chapter like a palimpsest as well. For Claudian's intertexts, see Roche, "Lucan"; Ware, "Eutropius, Lucan,"; Colton, "Echoes of Juvenal."

12. For example, when describing a parasitic courtier of Theoderic II, Sidonius Apollinaris (*Ep.* 3.13.5–9), evoked Claudian's Eutropius. Scholarship on that influence is scarce. Colton, *Some Literary Influences*, has no mention, but see Neri, *La bellezza*, 212–13; G. Kelly, "Sidonius and Claudian"; Schindler, *Per carmina*, 59–172.

13. Schlinkert, *Ordo senatorius*, 266; Kuefler, *Manly Eunuch*, 65–69; Cameron, *Claudian*, 126–29; Scholten, "Der oberste Hofeunuch," 51.

and he successfully created what Stilicho and the court in Milan wanted the western elites to see. His invectives against Eutropius are two of our most important contemporary sources for the history of Arcadius and his court in Constantinople in the late 390s. Thanks to Claudian's rhetorical brilliance, his "western" Eutropius has dominated how scholars interpret the eastern emperor's rule. And the most important aspect of Claudian's Eutropius was his physical condition as a eunuch, which fundamentally differentiated him from all other less-than-manly monsters, such as public enemies and civil war opponents.

However, eunuchs were part of every late Roman court. What made Eutropius extraordinary was his office. What requires explanation is the emperor Arcadius's choice to make a eunuch *consul*—unless one is content with the standard scholarly view, helpfully suggested by Claudian and later historians beginning with Eunapius, that Arcadius was simply weak "like a fatted animal," if not downright stupid.[14] I think the opposite was the case.[15] Arcadius was entirely aware of the imperial *vir*-ness that his dynasty—in which I include Gratian—had gradually assembled and propagated in the preceding decades. He understood the implications of capacious, expansively fluid, soft, and flexible manliness as a power language.[16] Had he been in Milan when Ambrose immortalized his father, he would, I think, have appreciated the multivalent power of an elite *vir*'s declaration of reciprocated love for his emperor (see chapter 5). Further, unlike Honorius, whom Claudian paired with Theodosius and Stilicho, carefully layering maturity and softness because the emperor was still very young, Arcadius was an experienced ruler when he chose Eutropius as a consul. At twenty-two, he was the father of Flaccilla, with Pulcheria on the way.[17] During Theodosius's stays in the west, Arcadius had been in charge of the east, governing with the support of a stable administration.[18]

For Arcadius in Constantinople, evidently, the youthful, soft, capacious Theodosian imperial *vir*-ness, which included the empress, was sufficiently established, sufficiently self-evident to encompass a eunuch as consul. This was a move both queering (Eutropius as consul manifested the queer aspects of imperial *vir*-ness that I have described in the previous chapters and further expanded the forms of soft manliness associated with the emperor) and unqueering (by placing the marginal at the center of power). As such, Arcadius's choice was risky. It made visible to all the gradual evolution and achievement of smooth manliness as a language of imperial sovereignty. Eutropius as consul was proof of this transformation and

14. Eunap., *Hist.* 64–66; Zos., *HN* 5.1–19.5; Philost., *HE* 11.3. For recent negative assessments of Arcadius, see Icks, "Keeping up Appearances," 165–66; Pfeilschifter, *Kaiser und Konstantinopel*, 477 n56, 487–90, with literature; see also chapters 7 and 8.

15. McEvoy, "Imperial Jellyfish," 188–90, is also a reassessment of Arcadius; and see Stewart, *Soldier's Life*, 8–6, 130–37.

16. Masterson, *Man to Man*, 35.

17. *Chron. Pasch.*, a. 395; Soc., *HE* 6.1.4.

18. Liebeschuetz, *Barbarians and Bishops*, 132–45; Hagl, *Arcadius*, 45–46.

FIGURE 17. Solidus of Arcadius, obverse, 393–395, gold, Constantinople, minted in Sirmium or Constantinople, British Museum, 1843, 0116.23. © The Trustees of the British Museum.

further cemented the emperor's position as arbiter of who possessed *vir*-ness, which included infants, father (figure)s, and now also eunuchs. Claudian's invectives demonstrate one reaction, that of Milan and the west, while the chapters that follow will investigate others, by analyzing two contemporary voices from Constantinople that illuminate Eutropius in the east.

CLAUDIAN'S PALIMPSEST: BEAUTY AND THE CONSUL

Because of its relation to the sacred in the ancient world, beauty functioned as a public barometer of moral fitness and hence the ability to govern, so shifting ideas of what was ugly or beautiful reflect new ways of thinking about governance and what being sacred, holy, or divine should look like. In turning Eutropius into an icon of ugliness, Claudian targeted the eastern consul, but he never lost sight of the fact that this inevitably reflected on Arcadius, the emperor who had elevated the eunuch.[19] Emperors frequently made themselves consuls, and these roles were deeply intertwined, a nexus that may have made children as consuls a gateway to child emperors. Each January, the new consuls gave their name to the year and celebrated their accession with great pomp, which by the late fourth century included distributing costly ivory diptychs to their peers.[20] Indeed, the office was expensive, requiring the financing of public entertainments such as chariot races, games, and theater productions, which explains why emperors chose to hold it: it

---

19. G. Kelly, "Claudian and Constantinople," 250–61.

20. For consular diptychs—e.g., from Halberstadt—see Delbrück, *Die Consulardyptichen*, 87–93, nr. 2*; Volbach, *Elfenbeinarbeiten der Spätantike*, 42 nr. 35, with plate 19; Guidetti, "'First-Generation Diyptychs'"; Cameron, "Origin," 178; Shelton, "Diptych"; Matthews, "Roman Empire and the Proliferation of Elites" (diptych of Athanasius from 517, Bibliothèque national, Cabinet des Médailles, inv. 55, no 296 bis).

offered opportunities to show their largesse and commemorate important events.[21] Further, with the year carrying his name, the consul formed part of the sacred chain connecting the present to Rome's past and ensuring its future, portending peace and prosperity.[22] Thus, "the greatest of all human honors is the consulship, by which time itself is measured."[23] This highly sought-after office assumes its full weight in our context, because in addition to giving his name to the emperor's rule, the consul took the sovereign's place whenever the latter was absent: the consul *became* the emperor—and in 399 that consul was a eunuch.

The trabea manifested the merging of the *sacratissimus imperator* and his consul. When Ausonius thanked Gratian for granting him the consulship in 379, he described his consular vestment as follows:

> In the letter you sent me you . . . condescended so far as to ask me what kind of consular robe should be sent to me. With this concern for me you have exhausted the entire staff of your officials in charge of largesse. Over and above the consulship, then, have I not been shown a thoughtfulness that cost you much labor and that brought me much happiness? Arms are being brandished in Illyricum, but for my sake . . . you handle the matter of my toga; . . . at the very moment when you are about to engage in battle, you see to the arrangements for the decoration of my palm-embroidered robe. And with happy and auspicious omen do you do it. For just as that vestment belongs to the consul in peacetime, just so in victory it belongs to the triumphant. You think it too small a gift if you were to ask me what kind of robe should be sent to me: you bid that it be brought before your very eyes. . . . You yourself select one from many, and, when you have made your selection, you provide your gift with the honor of an escort of words. "I have sent you a palm-embroidered robe," you say, "worked with an image of my father, the divine Constantius." What happiness is mine, that such care is given to my honors! This is certainly a "broidered" robe, as the phrase has it: this is a robe broidered no less with your words than with gold. But there is much more to its decoration, which, instructed by you, I can understand. For in this single garment there shines forth the radiance of not one emperor but two. Constantius is woven into the decoration of the robe, and Gratian's presence can be felt in the honor that the gift bestows.[24]

---

21. As Symmachus confirms: *Ep.* 2.62, 7.4 (consular games). See also Salway, "Roman Consuls"; Mitchell, "Eastern and Western Consulship"; Cameron and Schauer, "Last Consul," 138–42 (continuation of the office into the sixth century).

22. Prud., *Contra Symm.* 1.59–62; Claud., *Eutr.* 1 praef. 1.1–23; Bowes, "Ivory Lists," 338–47; Eastmond, "Consular Diptychs"; Sguaitamatti, *Der spätantike Konsulat,* 7–26.

23. Them., *Or.* 16.203c.

24. Aus., *Grat. Act.* 11.51–54:

> Ab hac enim litterarum ad me datarum parte digressus eo quoque descendisti, ut quaereres qualis ad me trabea mitteretur. omne largitionum tuarum ministerium sollicitudine fatigasti. non ergo supra consulatum mihi est adhibita per te cura tam diligens, pro me cura tam felix? in Illyrico arma quatiuntur: tu mea causa per Gallias civilium decorum indumenta dispensas, loricatus de toga mea tractas, . . . cum maxime dimicaturus palmatae vestis meae ornamenta disponis, feliciter et bono omine: namque iste habitus, ut in pace consulis est, sic in victoria triumphantis. parum est si qualis ad me trabea mittatur interroges; te coram promi iubes. . . . Eligis ipse de multis et cum elegeris munera tua verborum honore prosequeris. "palmatam,"

Ausonius's trabea, the short, colorful, richly decorated coat retaining echoes of the original triumphal vestments, the *tunica palmata* and the *toga picta*, featured embroidered embellishments, or *segmenta*, like those on the one presented to Stilicho. In his word picture of the scene, Ausonius focused on what was most relevant to himself: Gratian's personal care had ascertained that whenever the consul appeared in public wearing the trabea, the divine augustus and his equally divine ancestors would be present, woven into the robe ("in qua divus Constantius parens noster intextus est").[25]

The consul, heavy with gold (*graves auro*), participated in the staging of the emperor as sacred.[26] The trabea carried greater significance than the body of the wearer—which was increasingly that of a very young child—and the same was true for the garb of the imperial person. As Ausonius and Claudian make clear, the trabea embodied the office of the consul just as the imperial vestments stood for the ruler. John Chrysostom formulated it most succinctly: "The imperial mantle (*himation basilikon*) is the ruler's body (*soma despotikon*)."[27] The emperor in his glittering regalia, with his high-ranking courtiers, gleaming bodyguards, and beautiful eunuchs arrayed around him, composed a living picture that made divine beauty manifest every time he "appear[ed] in the midst of his followers like an angel of God descended from heaven."[28] Together, they made the divine present and brought it to life: a god one can see.[29]

---

inquis, "tibi misi, in qua divus Constantius parens noster intextus est." me beatum, cuius insignibus talis cura praestatur! haec plane, haec est picta, ut dicitur, vestis non magis auro suo quam tuis verbis. sed multo plura sunt in eius ornatu, quae per te instructus intellego. geminum quippe in uno habitu radiat nomen Augusti: Constantius in argumento vestis intexitur, Gratianus in muneris honore sentitur.

Gratian's father was Valentinian I, but Constantius was his father-in-law. Green, *Ausonius*, 51, suggests that this consular robe might have been one that was stored in Sirmium and belonged to Constantius, who had been consul ten times.

25. See chapter 4; Hildebrandt, "Das Gewand des Honorius," 68–70; Rollason, *Gifts of Clothing*, 89–128; Dewar, "Spinning the *Trabea*," 219–20; F. Morgan, *Dress and Personal Appearance*, 15–17.

26. Claud., *Cons. Stil.* 2.339; Claud., *Eutr.* 1.301; Aus., *Grat. Act.* 1, 11; Rees, *Layers of Loyalty*, 12–17; Ivanovici, "Iconic Presences," 130; Rollinger, "Importance."

27. J. Chrys., *De sanct. Mart.* 3 (*PG* 50.650): ἱμάτιόν ἐστι βασιλικὸν τὸ σῶμα τὸ δεσποτικόν· τὴν δὲ ἁλουργίδα τὴν βασιλικὴν καὶ ὁ διαρρήξας καὶ ὁ χερσὶν ἀκαθάρτοις μολύνας ὁμοίως ὕβρισαν· διὸ καὶ ὁμοίως κολάζονται· οὕτω καὶ ἐπὶ τοῦ σώματος τοῦ Χριστοῦ γίνεται (The ruler's body is an imperial mantle. The one who tore the imperial purple robe and the one who defiled it with unclean hands both have insulted it equally; therefore, they are punished equally. The same applies to the body of Christ). See also Delmaire, "Le vêtement, symbole de richesse," 85–98.

28. J. Chrys., *De Macc.* 1.1. See also Eus., *Vit. Const.* 3.10.3; Ambr., *Exp. ps.* 118.8.19 ("Procedit imperator . . . concurrunt omnes et in tanta multitudine illum solum aspicere gestiunt et de fulgore purpurae plus quiddam esse in vultu imperatoris existimant"); Zos., *HN* 4.28.2 (praise for the beauty of Theodosius's eunuchs); Ch. Kelly, "Emperors as Gods"; R. R. R. Smith, "Public Image of Licinius."

29. The analogy between the ruler, his vestments, and his divine mandate remained in place, *mutatis mutandis*, until the French Revolution: see Weber, *Queen of Fashion*, 3–9, 13–74, 85–87, 151–63; S. Elm, "Emperor Julian on Statues," 131–35.

Conversely, if one wanted to portray the nature and presence of god, the emperor's beauty was an apt analogy to illustrate the divine and make the transcendent material.[30] Thus, the Neoplatonic philosopher Plotinus compared the advent of the divine Mind to that of an emperor:

> And the god is nature itself, a god manifesting himself before we can see him. And he watches from above and sits, transcendent, upon a fair pediment. . . . There is an irresistible beauty going out before him. As before a great emperor there go first, in those preceding him, the lesser ranks, and the always more important ones and more lofty ones come after these. The ones near to the emperor are all the more imperial, and next come the honoured ones with him, and suddenly the great emperor himself appears amid all these others. All utter prayers and bow down.[31]

The emperor was sacred, his purple adored (*adoratio purpurae*), his majesty revered, his law-giving hand divine, his countenance heavenly, his beauty (*forma, decus*) irresistibly sublime—and his court further enhanced the sacred beauty of the most beautiful ruler, *pulcherrimus imperator*.[32] The multifaceted luminosity of the ensemble revealed the *animus divinus* of the emperor as *deus* and *deus consors*, companion of god.[33]

This was also the case every time Eutropius appeared in public and at court. As Claudian's brilliant palimpsest illustrates, the resplendent consul and the abominable monster were one and the same. The nexus between beauty, the divine, and the imperial underscores the poet's immense challenge: making Eutropius ugly risked tarnishing the divine spirit (*numen*) whom the consul embodied, the emperor himself. Granted, that emperor was Arcadius. However, irrespective of the rivalry between east and west, Arcadius and Honorius were united brothers. Each emperor's choice of consul ought to have been inviolable. Declaring a *patricius, illustris*

---

30. For the interplay between body, vestments, representation, relics, and divine materiality between the fourth and sixth centuries, see Krueger, "Liturgical Time"; Cox Miller, "Figuring Relics"; Fricke, "Tales from Stone"; Röckelein, "Die 'Hüllen der Heiligen.'"

31. Plotinus, *Enn.* 5.5.3 (ἀλλ᾽ εἶναι αὐτῷ κάλλος ἀμήχανον πρὸ αὐτοῦ προϊόν, οἷον πρὸ μεγάλου βασιλέως πρόεισι μὲν πρῶτα ἐν ταῖς προόδοις τὰ ἐλάττω, ἀεὶ δὲ τὰ μείζω καὶ τὰ σεμνότερα ἐπ᾽ αὐτοῖς, καὶ τὰ περὶ βασιλέα ἤδη μᾶλλον βασιλικώτερα, εἶτα τὰ μετ᾽ αὐτὸν τίμια· ἐφ᾽ ἅπασι δὲ τούτοις βασιλεὺς προφαίνεται ἐξαίφνης αὐτὸς ὁ μέγας, οἱ δ᾽ εὔχονται καὶ προσκυνοῦσιν). Trans. Masterson, *Man to Man*, 85–86, with further discussion.

32. *Pan. lat.* 12(9).7.5, 12(9).19.6 ("vulgor occulorum"), 12(9).19.5 ("oculis ferre gestivit"); CTh 6.24.4, March 6, 387 (*osculatio*); *Notitia Dignitatum* 39.37 (*adoratio*); R. Smith, "Measures of Difference"; Noethlichs, "Hofbeamter"; Noethlichs, "Strukturen und Funktionen," 16–35; Avery, "*Adoratio*"; Masterson, *Man to Man*, 138–40; Näf, *Senatorisches Standesbewusstsein*, 28–48; Löhken, *Ordines dignitatum*, 48–68; Matthews, *Roman Empire*, 244–47.

33. J. Chrys., *De perf. car.* 6; J. Chrys., *In Rom.* 14.10; J. Chrys., *Ad vid. iun.* 4; Ambr., *De Noe* 7.17; Amm. Marc. 16.10.7–10; Pacatus, *Pan. lat.* 2(12).6.2–4, 6(7).17.3–4; Neri, *La bellezza*, 133–43, 161–65; Scheithauer, *Kaiserbild*, 36–39; Mause, *Die Darstellung des Kaisers*, 151–62.

vir, and consul a worse monster than a civil war tyrant or usurper was very difficult without also attacking the ruler he represented.[34] Claudian maintained that precarious balance by creating a monster that transgressed all limits of power and its representation. He could do so because Eutropius lacked what the purple-clad little homegrown slaves and august *exoleti*, those other emblems of illegitimately soft and fluid manliness, unquestionably possessed: balls. To illustrate that vital absence, Claudian ripped apart the seams of the trabea to reveal vileness underneath. It was a bold move, returning to center stage the physical body of the one wearing the regalia of office, consular and by analogy imperial. Of course, Claudian did this to emphasize over and over that Eutropius was an exception, but to what rules?

EUTROPIUS THE *ILLUSTRIS VIR*

Before addressing how Claudian made Eutropius ugly, it is important to briefly review the consul's career path as a late Roman *illustris vir* who made his fortune through merit and imperial favor, facts that not even the cruelest invective could hide. According to Claudian, Eutropius was born in Assyria, a region far from the ones customarily inhabited by "true" Romans. Claiming distant eastern lands as birthplaces for eunuchs was an invective trope that reflected reality, because that is where most of them came from; castrating Roman citizens was outlawed.[35] Mutilated as an infant, Eutropius was sold to several Roman owners before the general Flavius Abundantius, consul of 393, sponsored his entrance into Theodosius's *sacrum cubiculum*, the department in charge of the civil administration.[36] When Theodosius moved west in 394 to confront Eugenius, Eutropius remained in Constantinople with Arcadius and advanced to *praepositus sacri cubiculi*.[37] This office first appeared under Constantine.[38] At the helm of a sizable apparatus of slaves and other eunuchs, the grand chamberlain was responsible for the personal affairs of the emperor, endowed with highest honors, *primae dignitates*, and exempt from all

34. See chapter 1; Szidat, *Usurpator*, 25–42; Wienand, *Der Kaiser als Sieger*, 246–80, 421–82; Sguaitamatti, *Der spätantike Konsulat*, 125–36.

35. Constantine reissued earlier laws against the castration of Roman citizens, though they were not strictly enforced: see CJ 4.42.1; August., *Quaest. vet. et novi test.* 115.17. Slave merchants had to declare where their wares came from, because the region of origin was associated with specific characteristics that determined their value: see *Dig.* 21.1.31.21 (Ulpian); Guyot, *Eunuchen*, 28–36, 45–51; Tougher, "In or Out?," 144; Sidéris, "Rise and Fall," 69–74.

36. For Abundantius, see *PLRE* 1, s.v. 4–5; Jones, *Later Roman Empire*, 2:425–26, 566–71, for the *sacrum cubiculum*.

37. McEvoy, *Child Emperor Rule*, 135–71.

38. Zos., *HN* 5.12.1, 5.9.2; Philost., *HE* 11.4; Eunap., *Hist.* 65.8, 66; Matthews, *Western Aristocracies*, 249–50; Guyot, *Eunuchen*, 130–32, 136–57; Noethlichs, "Hofbeamter," 1127.

unbecoming burdens, *sordida munera*.[39] Theodosius granted the *praepositus sacri cubiculi* senatorial rank as a *clarissimus et illustris vir*, equal to the highest-placed palace officials, the *comites consistoriani*. He also made the chamberlain a member of the *sacer comitatus*, his advisory council, "because of the great and assiduous service to our divine person."[40]

Eutropius merited that praise. After Theodosius's death, Arcadius's praetorian prefect, Rufinus, had made the same claim as Stilicho: Theodosius had made *him* the emperor's caretaker (*epitropos*) before moving against Eugenius. Of course, this caused immediate tensions with the west.[41] Within months, however, Rufinus, now without Theodosius's support, began to lose power in Constantinople. Gothic troops under the leadership of Alaric, who had participated in the emperor's victory over Eugenius, rebelled in Greece and the Balkans and besieged Constantinople. The bulk of the eastern army was still in Italy and thus under Stilicho's control, which left Arcadius and Rufinus exposed to Alaric. Rufinus rejected an offer of help from Stilicho, who nevertheless began to move east with both the eastern and the western armies.[42] Initially, Rufinus was able to diffuse Alaric's threat, probably by paying him large sums of money, but only with regard to Constantinople: the Goths continued to devastate Illyricum, which further weakened Rufinus's influence.[43] He sought to remedy this by joining the imperial family through marriage, but where Stilicho had so splendidly succeeded, he failed: Eutropius intervened, and instead of Rufinus's daughter, in 395 Arcadius married Eudoxia, the daughter of Gratian and Valentinian II's general Bauto, whom Theodosius had made the western consul in 385.[44] After her father's death later that year, Eudoxia had moved to Constantinople, into the household of Promotus, another Theodosian general and one of Rufinus's rivals.[45]

Thus, immediately after Theodosius's demise, Eutropius helped Arcadius ensure the support of Theodosian generals as a counterweight to the compromised prefect. This was a prescient move. In September 395, Stilicho encountered Alaric

39. CTh 11.16.15 (382); Guyot, *Eunuchen*, 136.

40. CTh 7.8.3 (384) ("Ex praepositis quoque sacri cubiculi, quos tanta et tam adsidua nostri numinis cura inter primas posuit dignitates"). See also Schlinkert, *Ordo senatorius*, 243–51; Jones, *Later Roman Empire*, 2:557–58; Scholten, "Oberste Hofeunuch," 64–65; Bileta, "*Venatio*."

41. Claud., *Ruf.* 1–2; Müller, *Lectiones*, 119–62; Coombe, *Claudian the Poet*, 33–35; Ware, *Claudian*, 69–72, 124–28.

42. Zos., *HN* 5.5.1; Claud., *Ruf.* 2.130; Claud., *Eutr.* 2.539, 2.550; Cameron, *Claudian*, 63–87, 156–68; Heather, *Goths and Romans*, 193–202.

43. Zos., *HN* 5.1–3; Cameron and Long, *Barbarians*, 112.

44. According to Claud., *Carm. min.* 10.23, Arcadius had been too moved by Eudoxia's beauty; see also Zos., *HN* 5.3.2; Ambr., *Ep.* 30; Symm., *Rel.* 47.2; Neri, *La bellezza*, 158–59; Long, *Claudian's "In Eutropium,"* 10. Augustine delivered the panegyric celebrating Bauto's consulship: see August., *C. litt. Petil.* 3.25.30; cf. August., *Conf.* 6.6.9.

45. Promotus, *PLRE* 1:750–51; Matthews, *Western Aristocracies*, 177, 214; Rebenich, "Beobachtungen"; Vannesse, "La militarizzazione," 87–89; Lizzi Testa, "I vescovi, i barbari e l'impero di Roma," 31.

in Thessaly, but dissension in the ranks prevented victory and prompted him to release the eastern army.[46] When that force, now under the command of a certain Gainas, returned to Constantinople in November 395, some of its soldiers killed Rufinus in the presence of Arcadius, who had ridden out to the Hebdomon to salute the troops.[47] Who instigated the brazen attack remains difficult to disentangle, but the emperor used it to purge three high-ranking commanders with long and illustrious careers under Theodosius, including Abundantius.[48]

In short, 395 was a dramatic year for Arcadius, and Eutropius helped him through it. Together they restructured the western and eastern armies and reshuffled leading members of the military and the court, removing those who might pose threats and advancing supporters. Though most scholars attribute these actions to Eutropius's inordinate influence and Arcadius's corresponding weakness, they were standard for the transition to a new emperor and inconceivable without his consent.[49] Purges of leading personnel are attested after the accessions of Constantius, Julian, and Valens, and Honorius's court similarly realigned civilian and military leadership.[50]

Stabilizing Arcadius's regime came at the expense of escalating tensions with the western court. In 397, Eutropius halted the Gothic incursions into Illyricum with the help of Alaric, whom he had promoted to *magister militum per Illyricum* with the rank of *illustris* and a corresponding income, a move that irked the less successful Stilicho.[51] In the fall of that year, Gildo, as mentioned in chapter 4, rebelled against the western empire and diverted its grain supply to Constantinople.[52] Honorius declared him a public enemy, *hostis publicus*, to which the east responded in kind by declaring Stilicho a public enemy also. In early 398, Gildo was defeated.[53] When Hunnic federations invaded Armenia that summer, Eutropius

46. Eunap., *Hist.* 62–63; J. Antioch, frags. 188, 190.

47. Claud., *Ruf.* 2.343–349, 2.380–420; Heather, *Goths and Romans*, 138–46; Bileta, "*Venatio*," 90; Garambois-Vasquez, *Les invectives*, 138–49 (shows that Claudian described the killing as a tyrannicide).

48. Eunap., *Hist.* 65; Zos., *HN* 5.8.3–9, 5.10.4–5; Claud., *Eutr.* 1.154; Soc., *HE* 8.7.2; Cameron, *Claudian*, 63–67; Liebeschuetz, *Barbarians and Bishops*, 48–85, 96; Janssen, *Stilicho*, 22–69; Hagl, *Arcadius*, 34–46; Albert, *Goten*, 108; Lee, "Emperors and Generals," 100–18.

49. Zos., *HN* 5.3.1–6, 8.1–10.5; Eunap., *Hist.* 65. Recently, scholars have offered a more nuanced assessment of the interaction between Eutropius and Arcadius: see Sidéris, "Rise and Fall," 72–73; Charles and Anagnostou-Laoutides, "Polemical Poetry."

50. According to Amm. Marc. 29.2.6, the *praepositus sacri cubiculi* Heliodorus, like Eutropius, proceeded against persons accused of high treason; see Guyot, *Eunuchen*, 144–45. See also McEvoy, *Child Emperor Rule*, 144–52; Lizzi Testa, "I vescovi, i barbari, e l'impero di Roma," 28–30; Salzman, "Symmachus and the 'Barbarian' Generals," 356–60; Schlinkert, *Ordo senatorius*, 168–69 (Heliodorus), 267–70.

51. Them., *Or.* 15–16; Heather, *Goths and Romans*, 158, 171–72; Greatrex and Greatrex, "Hunnic Invasion," 65–75.

52. Zos., *HN* 5.11.2; Oros. 7.36.2; Claud., *Bell. Gild.* 66–75; Claud., *Eutr.* 1.399–404.

53. In fact, Gildo's brother bested him on Stilicho's behalf in the battle of Theveste in March or April: see Claud., *Eutr.* 1.242–251, 2.194–218; Claud., *Bell. Gild.* 379–414; Zos., *HN* 5.11.1. It is not clear when

assumed military command and repelled them.[54] He was granted a triumph in Constantinople, the first such celebration for someone who was not an emperor since Augustus, although in Constantinople and not in Rome; was given the title *patricius*; and became the consul designate.[55]

Honorius and his court did not acknowledge Eutropius as a consul and chose the eminently traditional Manlius Theodorus, the father of several sons, as the western consul.[56] In spring and summer 399, Gothic auxiliaries in Phrygia threatened Constantinople. This time, Eutropius was less successful as a commander. Tensions with Gainas and, allegedly, Eudoxia, who had by then assumed the Theodosian name Aelia, led to his fall in the summer.[57] A law dated August 17, 399, exiled Eutropius to Cyprus, declared his legislative acts void, confiscated his possessions, removed his titles, and ordered his name excised from all statues and inscriptions.[58] A few months later, he was recalled to Constantinople and executed.[59] Thus ended the consul's career, which was at its zenith when Claudian immortalized him as the epitome of ugliness.

EUTROPIUS THE MONSTER

What is ugly? The earliest aesthetic theories argue that ugliness is more than the opposite or absence of beauty.[60] Rather, beginning with the Greek term *aischros*, usually translated as "shameful," ugliness connotes formlessness as an absence of moral value, in Latin expressed as *deformitas* and *turpitudo*. Because beauty, or harmony of form, was intrinsic to the good, the sublime, and the sacred, ugliness

---

Stilicho was declared a *hostis publicus*: see McEvoy, *Child Emperor Rule*, 156–59; Cameron, *Claudian*, 168–85; Long, *Claudian's "In Eutropium,"* 9–13; Cameron and Long, *Barbarians*, 109–26; Heather, "Anti-Scythian Tirade," 167–68.

54. Heather, *Goths and Romans*, 202.

55. Claud., *Eutr.* 1.252–286. L. Cornelius Balbus's triumph 19 BCE had been the last before Augustus monopolized the ceremonial for the princeps: see Rüpke, *Domi militiae*, 233–34; McCormick, *Eternal Victory*, 48–50.

56. Cameron, *Claudian*, 128–35, 176–80; Janssen, *Stilicho*, 70–103.

57. Zos., *HN* 5.14.5–7; Liebeschuetz, *Barbarians and Bishops*, 103–4 (cautions against overestimating Eudoxia's influence); Lizzi Testa, "Significato filosofico," 49–62.

58. CTh 9.40.17; Zos., *HN* 5.17.2–5; Philost., *HE* 11.6; Soz., *HE* 8.7.3; Seeck, "Arkadius," *RE* 2.1, 1146, 1895; Hillner, "Confined Exiles," 393–99, 409–10; Hillner, *Prison*, 195–99; E. Elm, *Damnatio memoriae*, 154–63.

59. Döpp, *Zeitgeschichte*, 159–74; Schweckendiek, *Claudians Invektive gegen Eutrop*, 16–18; Scholten, *Der Eunuch*, 223–27; Garambois-Vasquez, *Les invectives*, 18–20.

60. Rosenkranz, *Ästhetik des Häßlichen*, is seminal; he declared ugliness a central category of aesthetics (p. 5), expanding Lessing's assertion (in his *Laokoon*) that the beautiful is not per se the equivalent of the good and the true, but rather an expression of taste. Nevertheless, Rosenkranz retained "classic" notions according to which ugliness reveals moral failures; see also Kliche, "Häßlich," 26–33; Bancaud, "L'esthétique du laid," 900–4, 908–17.

stood for the absence of all three.[61] Latin provides a rich arsenal to describe this condition and the emotions it evoked—horrendous, obscene, monstrous, grotesque, terrible, savage, cruel, wild, unlovely, repellent, disgusting, despicable, loathsome, filthy, polluted and polluting, barbarous, beastly, curious, and so forth—even if, as was freely acknowledged, the sculptor, painter, or poet could make the ugly beautiful through the mastery of their representation. In sum, ugliness, perhaps more than beauty, is culturally determined: it lies in the eye of the beholder.[62] Xenophon of Colophon had quipped that if oxen and lions had hands like humans and could sculpt, they would represent their gods as oxen and lions: one person's god is another person's ox.[63]

To make Eutropius ugly, Claudian layered and intertwined three social categories that best expressed for his audience deformity and hence turpitude: *semivir*, neither male nor female or both male and female; "slave"; and "old," especially "old woman."[64] In nearly every line of his invective, he combined these categories with illness- or nature-derived metaphors implying aridity and infertility to paint the picture of a deformed and thus depraved hybrid. His Eutropius was *nec utrum*, neither one nor the other. During his life, he had moved down the sliding scale of honor and virtue to become animal-like. In short, Claudian created a *monstrum*.[65] *Monstra* came in many forms. One of their principal characteristics was hybridity, a physical melding into something novel of things not meant to be conjoined

61. Pl., *Hp. mai.* 1.286c–289b; Pl., *Rep.* 3.401b–c; Arist., *Poet.* 1448b; Kaster, *Emotion*, 158–204 (on disgust, or *fastidium*); Porter, *Sublime*, 5–25, 33–34, 51–53, 402–4 (on "majestic grandeur of any kind"; quote at 11).

62. Theorists also discuss the Renaissance as a period when ugliness began to be perceived as its own form rather than primarily a negation or absence of beauty. I think that the sheer intensity of Claudian's Eutropius reflects earlier considerations of the ugly as something sui generis, because, first, he had to mediate the tension between the beauty of a consul (representing the emperor) and the eunuch's amoral ugliness at a moment when, second, Christian humility must also find expression (as I indicate in chapter 8 and in the conclusion). See also Santorius, *Zerrbilder des Göttlichen*, 9–45; Henderson, *Ugliness*, 25–107; Gronow, *Sociology of Taste*, 1–46 (on "group taste").

63. Quote in Clem. Alex., *Strom.* 5.109–110; see also Corbeill, *Sexing the World*, 5–11, 123.

64. Claud., *Eutr.* 1.170, calls Eutropius a *semivir*. Scholars debate whether this indicates a separate gender, or *tertium genus*, and whether eunuchs should be considered a third sex, a category used in the ancient world mostly in medical literature. Sidéris ("Rise and Fall," 64–69) favors eunuchs as a third sex or gender; Tougher ("Aesthetics of Castration," 54–55), Kuefler (*Manly Eunuch*, 249–50), and Messis (*Les eunuques*, 23–24, 53–59, 95–96) are undecided; Carlà-Uhink ("'Between the Human,'" 14–17) resists the notion of eunuchs as a separate gender and finds no evidence for anything comparable to gender-reassignment surgery. In my view, Claudian's description of Eutropius is concerned with making him not a third sex but rather an utterly degraded being. Laqueur, *Making Sex*, and King, *The One-Sex Body on Trial*, remain foundational for ancient constructions of gender.

65. Claud., *Eutr.* 1 praef. 1.8 ("Omnia cesserunt eunucho consule monstra"). See Coombe, *Claudian the Poet*, 93–122, for other instances in which Claudian creates the monstrous, including with regard to some barbarians; see also Guipponi-Gineste, *Claudien*, 191–96.

and thus both exciting and terrifying.[66] Hybridity, or more precisely *strangeness*—literally *aligenia*, as the fruit of a marriage with another gens—could simply mean the crossbreeding of a horse with an ass.[67] A monster required a more drastic conjoining of truly disparate species or categories, such as male and female, or human and animal, as exemplified by the Hydra or the centaur Chiron.[68] Such merging could be positive—as with Chiron, or when an enslaved person was revealed as nobly born, when the divine mixed with the human, or even when male and female were intermingled. Whether these forms were considered positive or negative, moreover, was not stable and could change over time. Thus, as Pliny the Elder observed, in his day persons called hermaphrodites had become curiosities and playthings for the wealthy and were no longer considered monstrosities.[69]

As a rule, however, the monstrous was considered terrifying and scandalous because it overturned the divinely created laws of nature.[70] Monsters were closely aligned, even synonymous, with portents, *prodigia*, which might announce good fortune but usually indicated that all was not well with the world.[71] Because a *prodigium* was a warning, it allowed disasters to be averted through prompt action. The opening lines of Claudian's first invective urged such action. Talking cattle, wolves in cities, rains of stones, and clouds of blood predicted utter disaster unless Eutropius was removed as consul: he was a *prodigium*, a monster.

> The world shouldn't wonder any longer at half-animal children that terrify their mothers, wolves howling at night in the middle of the city, or cattle speaking to their astonished herdsman. Dire showers of stones, bloody clouds reddening a menacing sky, gore polluting wells, moons colliding in the sky, or double suns—all these monstrous portents yield their place to a eunuch consul! Alas! Earth and heaven's shame! An old woman in the trabea parades through the cities, whose name makes

66. Li Causi, "Mostri propriamente detti"; Maiuri, "Il lessico latino del mostruoso"; Segarra Crespo, "L'androgino biforme"; Lowe, *Monsters and Monstrosity*, 6–34; Emmrich, *Ästhetische Monster-politiken*, 36–69, 58–59, 87 (discusses Foucault's *Les anormaux*); Murgatroyd, *Mythical Monsters*, 1–15.

67. Lhuillier-Martinetti, *L'individu dans la famille*, 105–17, 136–45, relates that Ambrose chastised a Roman woman's marriage to a barbarian as *turpitudo*, since their children would be *aligenus*.

68. Claud., *Eutr.* 1.1, opens the invective with *semiferos partus*, half human, half animal, the description he used for Chiron in *carm. min.* 10. 145. See also Li Causi, *Generare*, 93–183, 185–88.

69. Plin., *HN* 7.34 ("Gignuntur et utriusque sexus quos Hermaphroditos vocamus, olim androgynos vocatos et in prodigiis habitos, nunc vero in deliciis"). See also Corbeill, *Sexing the World*, 150–68; Hagner, "Monstrositäten haben eine Geschichte" (focuses on the eighteenth and nineteenth centuries to show that each epoch adapts the monstrous to its own requirements); Brisson, *Sexual Ambivalence*, 7–40; Marchal, *Appalling Bodies*, 37–45 (a more recent discussion of *androgynos*).

70. As Li Causi, *Generare*, 154, points out, "L'ibrido di uomo e animale non è, nel mondo antico, uno scandalo biologico, quanto piuttosto uno scandalo etico e antropologico (o, anche, un segnale degli dei)." See Barton, *Sorrows*, 85–175, for emotional reactions to the monstrous.

71. Etymologically, the terms are related: *monstrum*, from *monstrare* and *monere*, is a warning sign from the gods, often in the form of an event that violates the laws of nature, while a *progidium* is an unnatural event that functions as a warning (*OLD*, s.vv.).

the year effeminate. . . . What sacrifice will placate the gods' vast anger? Whose neck should we cut to appease them at the dire altars? Sprinkle the consul's blood on the fasces, let the prodigy himself make atonement. Make Eutropius's neck expiate whatever this omen says Fate's preparing.[72]

ORIGIN AND RISE

Abject powerlessness was the key characteristic uniting the three social categories that Claudian employed to make Eutropius into a monster.[73] He embodied the greatest deformity and hence turpitude, the height of ugliness, because he was abjection personified, yet he had risen to supreme power: a hybrid and a paradox. A foreign-born, frequently sold slave of indeterminate gender, he had progressed from half man to decrepit old woman and resembled an ape when he assumed a position that belonged by right to the beautiful and the good. As a consul, Eutropius made the office itself into a hybrid monstrosity, because nothing could be more deformed than abject powerlessness ruling supreme.

Following the rules of the invective genre, or *psogos*, Claudian described Eutropius's origin, deeds or misdeeds, and honors or their opposite in comparison with appropriate exemplars. At the same time (and like the author of the *Life of Heliogabalus*), he amplified his allusions and mixed high and low styles with abandon to create a satire or grotesque that reflected Eutropius's monstrosity.[74] Evoking

---

72. Claud., *Eutr.* 1.1–10, 1.19–22:

Semiferos partus metuendaque pignora matri,
moenibus et mediis auditum nocte luporum
murmur et adtonito pecudes pastore locutas
et lapidum duras hiemes nimboque minacem
sanguineo rubuisse Iovem puteosque cruore
mutatos visasque polo concurrere lunas
et geminos soles mirari desinat orbis!
Omnia cesserunt eunucho consule monstra.
Heu terrae caelique pudor! Trabeata per urbes
ostentatur anus titulumque effeminat anni. . . .
An morbi ventura lues? An nulla colono
responsura seges? Quae tantas expiet iras
victima? Quo diras iugulo placabimus aras?
Consule lustrandi fasces ipsoque litandum
prodigio. Quodcunque parant hoc omine fata,
Eutropius cervice luat.

See also Claud., *Eutr.* 2.1–58; Dorfbauer, "Die *praefationes*," 204–9.

73. C. Edwards, *Politics of Immorality*, 137–72.

74. Ware, "Eutropius, Lucan," 268–69; Long, *Claudian's "In Eutropium*," 17–50; Garambois-Vasquez, *Les invectives*, 124–90; Roche, "Lucan"; Charlet, "Lucain et Claudien"; Flower, *Emperors and Bishops*, 33–77; Koster, *Die Invektive*, 314–51.

most frequently Horace, Juvenal, and Lucan, Claudian juxtaposed every mention of Eutropius's honors and achievements to revelations of his hideous, despicable body in a scathing indictment of those who had allowed him to rise at the court of the most sacred emperor.[75] Torn apart, Eutropius's magnificent robes revealed an affront to nature, an illness that Claudian the physician diagnosed in the hope of excising it from the body politic which it now polluted. Eventually, this contamination might even reach the sacred, sublime Arcadius. Although the emperor had so far been spared, the risk of infection increased the longer this monstrosity was allowed to exist.[76]

> Is this how you govern, Fortune? What vicious joke is this? . . . If it was your pleasure to disgrace the consul's curule chair with the crime of slavery, then let someone come forward as consul who has just broken his foot chains. Open the slave workhouses and dress them in the consular robes of Quirinus. Give us anyone—but give us a man! Even slaves have their own grades of dignity and splendor. He who lived with only one master bears a lesser mark of his condition. But if you can count the waves of the seas and the sands of Libya, then you know how many masters Eutropius had. How often has he changed his status, in how many sales registers has he appeared, how many times changed his name! How often has he stood naked while the buyer consulted the doctor to make sure that no concealed defect would bring hidden loss! . . . After he was nothing more than a deformed cadaver, and an old woman's wrinkles covered him . . . [his masters] foisted him as a disgusting present on the unsuspecting. So often transferred, he bent his neck again and again to the yoke; his enslavement was old but constantly renewed, and it never stopped, though it often began anew.[77]

75. Colton, "Echoes of Juvenal"; Guipponi-Gineste, *Claudien*, 400–2.

76. Scholars disagree on whether Claudian implicated Arcadius: see Long, *Claudian's "In Eutropium*," 221–22, 235–60; Schweckendiek, *Claudians Invektive gegen Eutrop*, 18–23; Cameron, *Claudian*, 128; G. Kelly, "Claudian and Constantinople," 250–61.

77. Claud., *Eutr.* 1.24–43:

Hoc regni, Fortuna, tenes? Quaenam ista iocandi
saevitia? . . .
Si tibi servili placuit foedare curules
crimine, procedat laxata compede consul,
rupta Quirinales sumant ergastula cincti!
Da saltem quemcumque virum. Discrimina quaedam
sunt famulis splendorque suus, maculamque minorem
condicionis habet, domino qui vixerit uno.
Si pelagi fluctus, Libyae si discis harenas,
Eutropii numerabis [a)]eros. Quot iura, quot ille
mutavit tabulas vel quanta vocabula vertit!
Nudatus quotiens, medicum dum consulit emptor,
ne qua per occultum lateat iactura dolorem!
. . . Postquam deforme cadaver
mansit et in rugas totus defluxit aniles,
iam specie doni certatim limine pellunt

Eutropius was destined from birth to suffer torture. Ripped from his mother's uterus, he was cruelly castrated ("cunabula prima cruentis debita suppliciis: rapitur castrandus ab ipso ubere").[78] His vital force was thus excised before it could warm him, and he became cold to the core (*frigidus*). Forever robbed of his generative fires, he could never become a husband or father.[79] Rendered soft (*mollis*) by the knife, Eutropius was condemned to be neither male nor female or both male and female, a *semivir* or half-man, who became all things to all men and women.[80] As he was dragged through the markets of Assyria and Galatia, the young Eutropius's rosy cheeks and soft, youthful beauty (*forma*) garnered him many buyers looking for a *delicatus* (or *deliciae*), a sweet plaything or catamite.[81] He became the concubine (*paelex*) of a certain Ptolemy. They shared the marriage bed until Ptolemy tired of Eutropius and gave him as a present to (the former consul) Arinthaeus, since the slave was now too old to fetch top prices.[82] The abandoned Eutropius bemoaned his harsh fate: he had become a widow (*viduus*), but without being granted the dignity (*decus*) due to old women who have borne children.[83] Because

------

et foedum ignaris properant obtrudere munus.
Tot translata iugis summisit colla vetustum
servitium semperque novum! Nec destitit umquam,
saepe tamen coepit.

78. Claud., *Eutr.* 1.44–45. The removal of the genitals or the crushing of the testicles at birth was the most radical kind of castration, creating a man of distinct physical features; other methods, done later in life, had less dramatic consequences for maturation. Some authors use *eunuch* for persons castrated as infants and *spado* for those cut around puberty or later. Men made impotent by an accident or for medical reasons were called "eunuchs by nature." See Messis, *Les eunuques*, 31–45; Kuefler, *Manly Eunuch*, 32–36.

79. Claud., *Eutr.* 1.47–53: "Advolat Armenius certo mucrone recisos / edoctus mollire mares damnoque nefandum / aucturus pretium; fecundum corporis ignem / sedibus exhaurit geminis unoque sub ictu / eripit officiumque patris nomenque mariti . . . in cerebrum secti traxerunt frigora nervi" (An Armenian came running, his precise blade skilled at making men soft to increase his cursed earnings through their loss. He drained the body's generative heat from its twin seats, and in one blow he took away a father's capacity and a husband's title, . . . his severed nerves leading the cold deep into [Eutropius's] brain).

80. Claud., *Eutr.* 1.171 ("semivir"), 1.461–62 ("ambigui . . . mares"), 1.223: "nubas ducasve licebit" (a wife as well as a husband).

81. Claud., *Eutr.* 1.58–62, 1.75–76 ("Cum forma dilapsus amor. Defloruit oris / gratia"), cf. 1.342–345. See also Amm. Marc. 29.1.8; J. Chrys., *Ad vid. iun.* 4; Theod., *HR* 3.2. Zos., *HN* 4.28.2; *Anth. Graec.* 16.33; and Coripp., *In laud. Iust.* 1.86–88, 3.224–230, praise the beauty of eunuchs such as Justinian's *praepositus sacri cubiculi* Callinicus; later, they were compared to angels. See Ringrose, "Eunuchs as Cultural Mediators," 86–89; Tougher, "Aesthetics of Castration," 50–51; Neri, *La bellezza*, 164–65.

82. Claud., *Eutr.* 1.66–77. Ptolemy was probably the *tribunus stabuli*, in charge of the imperial stables, under the *magister peditum* Flavius Arinthaeus, consul in 372: see Charlet, *Claudien, Œuvres 3*, 275n14.

83. Claud., *Eutr.* 1.72–74, 1.69. *Viduus, -a, -um*, more often seen as a feminine noun, *vidua, -ae*, is here adjusted for Eutropius as male. See also Corbeill, *Sexing the World*, 143–69; Ware, "Eutropius,

he could no longer please sexually, Eutropius moved on to become a pimp (*lenonis opus*)—a perfect profession for him, since he knew all the tricks of the trade. He soon became a virtuoso, corrupting even the most chaste matrons, though eunuchs normally considered the protection of their mistresses' chastity their highest duty and sole *virtus*.[84] Eutropius's efforts earned him numerous lashings until he was handed over to yet another master, to serve as his daughter's attendant, or *nutritor*: "The future consul, ruler of the east, combed his mistress's hair and was often naked before her while bringing her water in a silver jug to wash with. When she threw herself down exhausted from the consuming heat, he cooled her with a rose-colored peacock-feather fan, this future *patricius*!"[85]

Each step brought Eutropius closer to the inner circles of power, but each new master also made him less beautiful and desirable, turned him further into an old woman condemned by the mirror (*speculo damnante*), until he became animalesque.[86] Chased away like a half-frozen swallow, a mangy (*scabie*) dog, or an old fox, this venal cadaver—no longer tolerated as a household slave—was placed in charge of the imperial court.[87] When Eutropius finally assumed the consular robe, in a caricature of the *processus consularis*, he had become an ape:[88] "How beautiful was the sight when he stretched his bloodless limbs to load them with the toga, weighed down by the belt heavy with gold, made more obscene by his old age! Like an ape imitating a human, whom a laughing slave boy has dressed in precious silks, leaving the back and buttocks bare to amuse the guests at the banquet table, he struts his stuff richly dressed, chest held high, even more deformed by his

---

Lucan," 260–63 (shows how Claudian satirized Eutropius by alluding to elegiac heroines lamenting their fate, just as Pacatus had done with Magnus Maximus: see chapter 1).

84. Claud., *Eutr.* 1.78–98, 1.98–101:

Hinc honor Eutropio cumque omnibus unica virtus
esset in eunuchis thalamos servare pudicos,
solus adulteriis crevit. Nec verbera tergo
cessavere tamen.

85. Claud., *Eutr.* 1.104–9:

. . . nutritoremque puellae
tradidit. Eous rector consulque futurus
pectebat dominae crines et saepe lavanti
nudus in argento lympham gestabat alumnae.
Et cum se rapido fessam proiecerat aestu,
patricius roseis pavonum ventilat alis.

86. Claud., *Eutr.* 1.94.
87. Claud., *Eutr.* 1.117–18, 1.130–37, 1.142–47.
88. See Charlet, *Claudien III*, 280–81n63, for the caricature of the *processus consularis*; Schweckendiek, *Claudians Invektive gegen Eutrop*, 88–89.

brilliant vestments. The shining court accompanied the polluted fasces—perhaps even the emperor."[89]

RULE

In the moral economy of the later Roman Empire, abject powerlessness implied, as we have seen, complete absence of virtue. Without virtue, one could not comport oneself as a *vir*, and hence lacked manliness and self-control, allowing one's basest desires to flourish without restraint and leading everything to be done to excess: excessive greed, excessive cruelty, and excessive sexual activity.[90] As soon as he became powerful, Claudian's Eutropius turned rapacious to the utmost. Just as he had been sold to countless masters, he now sold everything, including entire provinces.[91] Cut at birth, he ruled with bloodthirsty cruelty, directing his most vengeful ire against his former masters—that is, the Constantinopolitan elites.[92] Once used as a sexual plaything, Eutropius was driven in his every move by his

89. Claud., *Eutr.* 1.300–9:

Quam pulchre conspectus erat cum tenderet artus
exangues onerare toga cinctuque gravatus
indutoque senex obscaenior iret in auro!
Humani qualis simulator simius oris
quem puer adridens pretioso stamine Serum
velavit nudasque nates ac terga reliquit.
Ludibrium mensis, erecto pectore dives
ambulat et claro sese deformat amictu.
Candida pollutos comitatur curia fasces,
forsitan et dominus.

Weiß and Wiener, *Claudianus*, have the plural *domini*, translated as "his former masters," that is, relating it to members of the curia rather than implying the presence of the emperor.

90. Prud., *Ham.* 279–99; Kuefler, *Manly Eunuch*, 55–69, 96–102; Müller, *Lectiones*, 227–31.

91. Claud., *Eutr.* 1.190–93: "Sed peius in aurum / aestuat: hoc uno fruitur succisa libido. / Quid nervos secuisse iuvat? Vis nulla cruentam / castrat avaritiam" (Yet he burned even worse for gold: the sole desire his mutilated body can enjoy. What good did it do to cut his nerves? No violence could castrate his cruel avarice). This was a common accusation against eunuchs: see also Claud., *Eutr.* 1.193–98, 1.207, 1.221–29, 2.87, 2.585–88; Guyot, *Eunuchen*, 164–76; Ch. Kelly, *Ruling*, 166–68.

92. Claud., *Eutr.* 1.177–85: "Procerum squalore repletus / carcer et exulibus Meroë campique gemiscunt / Aethiopum. Poenis hominum plaga personat ardens; . . . Asperius nihil est humili cum surgit in altum. / Cuncta ferit dum cuncta timet, desaevit in omnes / ut se posse putent, nec belua taetrior ulla / quam servi rabies in libera terga furentis; / agnoscit gemitus et poenae parcere nescit / quam subiit, dominique memor quem verberat odit" (Filth-covered nobles filled up the prisons, exiles groaned in Meroë and Ethiopia's fields. Men's punishments resounded through the burning desert. . . . No one is more bitter than a lowly man rising high. He is afraid of everything, so he strikes out at everything. He savages everyone, just so they know he can. There is no beast more vicious than a maddened slave raging on free men's backs. He recognizes their groans, but he cannot imagine sparing them the punishment he once endured. He remembers his own master and hates the men he beats). See also 1.167–69.

boundless sexual desires, as Claudian showed with constant double entendres. Eutropius had been the slave of many masters, *eros*, and thus of Eros.[93] When he became consul, he was a "a mass of senile, pendulous flesh [*defluxit aniles*]" who forced "our cities" to watch an old woman (*anus*) in the trabea make "the year [*annus*] effeminate"—an untranslatable chain of wordplay that leaves nothing to the imagination.[94] Eutropius accepted the trabea as compensation for his wily right hand, which he frequently offered to grant everything someone might "love"; he feared nothing behind his back and, ever vigilant, lay night and day with his legs spread open, the literal meaning of *pateo* ("I endure").[95]

Claudian's sexualized double entendres include tropes of old age, especially those associated with women.[96] Both *senex*, "old," and *anus*, "old woman," are grammatically ambiguous and were staples of satire, in which old women epitomized the repulsive.[97] Martial, Horace, and Juvenal selected distinct parts of an old woman's body, especially her genitalia, and compared them to animals or excrement, portraying old women as completely severed from their former generative roles in the family, neither wives nor mothers and thus free to search incessantly for intercourse in all its variations. Thus, Martial chastised an old woman's temerity in expecting to be fucked gratis even though she was ugly and old (*anus*), while Horace informed another that her anus was like that of an old cow with diarrhea— tropes and allusions that Claudian used to excellent effect in satirizing Eutropius as a repulsive old woman.[98]

Resorting to the *amplificatio* of satire in addition to other literary techniques, Claudian portrayed Eutropius as the lowest slave, who was despised even by his fellow slaves and whose disappointed masters had sold him time and again. That slave had become the *patricius* of the east. Had Eutropius been merely an enslaved

93. Claud., *Eutr.* 1.33, alluding to Juv. 8.65–66, which plays with horses no longer fit for racing, and to the Greek god of desire, Eros. For Claudian's use of Greek, see G. Kelly, "Claudian and Constantinople," 249; Gualandri, "Claudian," 116–24.

94. Claud., *Eutr.* 1 praef. 1.9–10 ("Trabeata per urbes/ ostentatur anus titulumque effeminat / anni"), 1.38–39 ("deforme cadaver / mansit et in rugas totus defluxit aniles").

95. Claud., *Eutr.* 1.370 ("Accipit et trabeas argutae praemia dextrae"), 1.367 ("Quidquid amas, dabit illa manus"), 1.362 ("Nil timet a tergo"), 1.363–364 ("Lenis facilisque moveri / supplicibus" [He was mild toward those who supplicated/bowed down/wiggled their behinds before him]). See Masterson, *Man to Man*, 159–61, for an excellent discussion of the passage; see also Long, *Claudian's "In Eutropium,"* 143; and Kamen and Levin-Richardson, "Revisiting Roman Sexuality."

96. See Claud., *Eutr.* 1.10, 1.240, 2.398, for further use of *anus, -a*. He also feminized Eutropius by comparing him to an alcoholic mother-in-law, *socrus* (1.269), mocking him for trading a eunuch's fan (*flabella*) for the consul's cloak, and a girl's sunshade (*umbracula . . . virginibus*) for the fasces (1.463– 465), and declaring that eunuchs now followed the chairs of senators rather than the litters of matrons ("Verso iam discite more curules, / non matrum pilenta sequi") (1.472–74).

97. See, e.g., Claud., *Eutr.* 1.77, for *senex, -is*, a generic masculine also used for women (*OLD*, s.v. "senex", 1734) in the same way that *verna* is used for male persons.

98. Mart., *Epigr.* 7.75.1 ("Vis futui gratis, cum sis deformis anusque"); Hor., *Epod.* 8 and 12; Catul. 97.7–8; Fuhrer, "Alter und Sexualität," 50–55; Richlin, "Invective against Women," 71–78.

person, however, he never would have risen to such power. Only his condition as a eunuch made his spectacular career possible—and thus exposed the monstrosity of his consulship. Because he had been a beautiful young eunuch, Eutropius became the lover of powerful men, who propelled him higher and higher as their widow, pimp, maid, and old woman. "It would have been so much better had he remained a man! He would be happier in his disgrace. Had he been stronger, he would still be a slave!"[99] Each step up the career ladder made him more powerful and more repulsive, more desiccated, deformed, diseased, and hideous, as the bodies of old women are wont to be, and more animal-like: ugliness revealed through tears in the shining consular robe.

THE TRABEA AS PALIMPSEST: BEAUTY AND FATHERHOOD

Claudian made Eutropius's ugliness iconic by layering notions of deformity into a palimpsest that focused relentlessly on the ambiguous body exposed by the consul's regalia. His focus on Eutropius's physical traits as a desiccated old woman–eunuch–slave was deliberate and more consequential than the exuberant amassing of satirical allusions and tropes.[100] Three considerations lead me to this conclusion. First, Claudian's focus on the ugliness of Eutropius's body in contrast to the beauty of his trabea exposed a tension implicit in the tendency in literary and material representations to foreground the emperor's vestment rather than his body as a symbol of imperial legitimacy.[101] If, as John Chrysostom pithily observed, his clothes made the emperor, and if, as Eusebius of Caesarea implied, the splendid robes rather than the physical person channeled the divine—"at last [Constantine] himself proceeded through the midst of the assembly, like some heavenly messenger of God, clothed in raiment which glittered as it were with rays of light, reflecting the glowing radiance of a purple robe, and adorned with the brilliant splendor

99. Claud., *Eutr.* 1.56–57 ("Profuerat mansisse virum; felicior extat / opprobrio; serviret adhuc, si fortior esset!") See also Garambois-Vaquez, *Les invectives*, 91–92.

100. When Sidonius Apollinaris denigrated Theoderic II's parasite (*Ep.* 3.13.5–9), he too focused on the body to make him repellent: more deformed than a cadaver, with a head disfigured by bald patches and exceedingly deep lines in his face, an old, impotent man resembling an old woman with the pendulous breasts of a nursing mother. See Gualandri, "Sidonius' Intertextuality," 279–316; van Waarden, "Sidonius"; Harries, *Sidonius Apollinaris*, 396–401; Gillett, *Envoys*, 92; Neri, *La bellezza*, 211–13; Damon, *Mask of the Parasite*, 172–91.

101. Flower, "*Tamquam figmentum hominis*," 822–35; Francis, "Verbal and Visual Representation"; Guipponi-Gineste, "Pierres précieuses," 86–100; Neri, *La bellezza*, 133–51; Neri, "Dialettica politica"; R. R. R. Smith, "Public Image of Licinius"; Kristensen, "Embodied Images"; Cox Miller, *Corporeal Imagination*, 9–11, 79; S. Elm, "What the Bishop Wore," 156–69; Meister, *Körper*, 109–270 (early empire).

of gold and precious stones"[102]—did the actual body of the ruler matter?[103] Every time Claudian allowed Eutropius's repulsive body to break through the gold-encrusted trabea, he emphasized the gulf separating body and vestment. But if jeweled clothes represented sacred imperial majesty, then it was less crucial who wore them. It could be a child, a woman—or a eunuch.

Second, the same move that revealed this tension also allowed Claudian to counter it. By emphasizing the ugliness of Eutropius's hybrid and hence monstrous body in stark contrast to his gorgeous robes, Claudian strengthened the analogies among shiny clothes, radiant beauty, virtue, *vir*-ness, and fitness to govern—that is, imperial legitimacy.[104] The bodies of those who ruled could and even should be, as Claudian had already made clear, capaciously ambiguous in their gender expression. Only one year earlier, in 398, he had used wedding poems to praise Honorius as extraordinarily, powerfully beautiful and universally desired through comparison with the young Achilles in love and wearing women's clothing (see chapter 4). However, Claudian—which means Stilicho and the western court—also insisted with great firmness on one capacity that was essential for the body of the ruler: the divine emperor—however his gorgeous beauty was expressed—*and* the consul representing him had to be or have the potential to become fathers. Because Honorius was still not a father in 399, Arcadius's decision to make a eunuch into a consul gave Claudian—and thereby the western court—the perfect opportunity to delineate with absolute clarity their understanding of where the outer edge of the capaciously expanding imperial *vir*-ness had to be located: the emperor and his consular embodiment could be children and even, under exceptional circumstances, as the epitaph to this chapter shows, women—but not eunuchs.[105]

Third, that outer edge—no eunuchs—allowed Claudian to draw clear distinctions between Eutropius the consul and Eutropius the possible instigator of a civil

102. Eus., *Vit. Const.* 3.10.3 (αὐτὸς δὴ λοιπὸν διέβαινε μέσος οἷα θεοῦ τις οὐράνιος ἄγγελος, λαμπρὰν μὲν ὥσπερ φωτὸς μαρμαρυγαῖς ἐξαστράπτων περιβολήν, ἀλουργίδος δὲ πυρωποῖς καταλαμπόμενος ἀκτῖσι, χρυσοῦ τε καὶ λίθων πολυτελῶν διαυγέσι φέγγεσι κοσμούμενος). See also Masterson, *Man to Man*, 138–54, 164–69, for the centrality of imperial grandeur displayed, *inter alia*, through vestments; Roberts, "Light, Color, and Visual Illusion," discusses Mary in all her jeweled finery designed "to communicate the glory of Christ's court and all its occupants" (120).

103. For the complex relationship between masculinity and sanctity in the later Roman Empire, see Gleason, *Making Men*, 166; Kuefler, *Manly Eunuch*, 70–76, 209, 282; Burrus, *Begotten, Not Made*, 138–40; S. Elm, "Emperor Julian on Statues."

104. See Masterson, *Man to Man*, 166, for shine; Bildhauer, *Medieval Things*, 19–58, for the intense interaction between bodies and things produced by a visually powerful shine; Weber, *Queen of Fashion*, 3–9, 13–74, 85–87, 151–63.

105. Claud., *Eutr.* 1.320–24; see also 1.427–29: the east enjoys soft rule, and some cities there are used to women holding the scepter ("sceptris muliebribus"). McCall, *Brilliant Bodies*, 8–10, mentions *aristophilia* as a major reason why elite women could be part of homosocial groups in certain situations (here, Renaissance courts). Representations of imperial women always oscillated between praising them as perfectly restrained and criticizing them as too outspoken and hence manly: see Boatwright, *Imperial Women of Rome*, 281–88; Hillner, "Empresses, Queens."

war and as such a public enemy. This was important because in 398 Arcadius had declared Stilicho a *hostis publicus* in retaliation for Honorius's doing the same to Gildo. Public enemies were characterized in the language of defeated civil war opponents, which meant, as discussed in chapter 1, that they became less-than-manly monsters, furious beasts, and raging pestilences. From this perspective, the difference between Stilicho and Eutropius was not that great: many tropes that denigrated eunuchs were also used to malign civil war opponents, especially once they were defeated.[106] However, Magnus Maximus and the fictional Heliogabalus were certainly in possession of their testicles, as was Stilicho: they were all fathers or had the potential to become such. Thus, in a situation of crisis and mutual recrimination between the courts of Honorius and Arcadius, Claudian's emphasis on Eutropius's body, on his physical condition as a eunuch, was an excellent way to clarify who was a monster and who was most emphatically a Roman *vir*.

Claudian's Eutropius, his literary creation of ugliness personified, was designed to address problems and tensions in Honorius's court. For Arcadius, the situation was markedly different. As mentioned above, he was already a father and seasoned ruler who had governed the east alone during Theodosius's absences and consolidated his policies, rather than the infantilized minor that scholars still portray.[107] He did not have to fear the *exoletus* issue when making Eutropius his general—and even if it had reared its head, Eutropius the eunuch would have been an excellent solution. Further, Arcadius's consort Eudoxia embraced Aelia Flaccilla's precedent and dressed in the emperor's regalia, as made manifest in her adoption of the name Aelia and the images on her coins, while eastern authorities such as Gregory of Nazianzus and Gregory of Nyssa characterized their sisters and other exceptional women as exemplars of Christian manliness.[108] For Arcadius, evidently, choosing a eunuch as a consul did not compromise soft, capacious imperial *vir*-ness, because, as I will discuss in the chapters that follow, the office surpassed his physical condition. Moreover, even though a consul embodied and represented the emperor, he did remain a consul: Arcadius could make Eutropius "father of the ruler" because there was no doubt who was, as an actual father, the *pater patriae*.

ALTER SEXUS, ALTERA ROMA:
THE EUNUCH VANISHES

Claudian's ferocious focus on Eutropius as a eunuch insisted that, from the western perspective, his appointment as a consul had crossed, to use Peter Brown's words, the invisible frontier of physical integrity.[109] Demanding the immediate removal

106. Thome, "Crime and Punishment"; Jal, "*Hostis (publicus)*"; Masterson, *Man to Man*, 138–39, 156–64.

107. Icks, "Keeping up Appearances," 165; McEvoy, "Imperial Jellyfish," 182–84.

108. S. Elm, "Family Men"; Neville, *Byzantine Gender*, 33–58.

109. Brown, *Body and Society*, 362.

of that abomination was done to safeguard the entire Roman Empire. Addressing Stilicho and hence the audience with the words of Aurora, the personification of eastern Rome, Claudian declared that "the world had begun to unite under the brothers' rule. . . . Then suddenly, Rufinus's castrated successor leaped forth—a monstrous story I'm ashamed to tell. Fortune brought similar grief upon us once more: it seemed our new master had only changed his sex."[110] This *castratus* differed from all others who had imperiled Rome's unity, because as consul he suddenly posed an alarming, unheard-of question, threatening everything that had been self-understood—namely, that elite *vir*-ness required the capacity to generate offspring, the ability to become a father.[111] An arid, frigid, infertile monster had been admitted to the ranks of Rome's most venerated fathers, the *patres conscripti* of the Senate. There he now sat, a false father called "the emperor's father," a sterile senator, forever unable to be a "generator" of princes (*genitor principis*).[112] The east might have made Eutropius a consul, *patricius*, and *illustris vir*, but for the west that Eutropius did not exist. It knew only Eutropius the monster and icon of ugliness that Claudian had created.

Claudian's focus on Eutropius as a eunuch lessened quite dramatically as soon as Eutropius the consul ceased to exist. Scholars debate whether he wrote the bulk of his second attack after news of Gothic troubles had reached Milan and added the prefaces only after the consul's fall, or whether he wrote his entire second invective once Eutropius had been exiled but before his execution.[113] In either case, in his second invective Claudian turned the focus away from Eutropius the individual to condemn the eastern elites who had abetted the eunuch's rise; he also shifted the

---

110. Claud., *Eutr.* 2.546, 2.549–52:

. . . Fraterno coniugi coeperat orbis
imperio . . .
cum subito (monstrosa mihi turpisque relatu
fabula!) Rufini castratus prosilit heres,
et similes iterum luctus Fortuna reduxit,
ut solum domini sexum mutasse viderer.

See also Roberts, "Rome Personified," 535–37; Lenski, "Constantine and the Tyche," 334–39.

111. Daube, "Self-Understood," 126–34.

112. Claud., *Eutr.* 2.68–69: "Praesidium legum genitorque vocatur / principis et famulum dignatur regia patrem" (They call Eutropius the law's guardian, the emperor's father, and the court thinks a slave fit to be a senator [or father, *pater*]); see also *Eutr.* 1.109; 1.469–472: "Mixta duplex aetas inter puerumque senemque / nil medium: falsi conplete sedilia patres, / ite, novi proceres, infecunduoque senatu Eutropium stipate ducem" (You mix two stages of life, boy and old man, with nothing in between. Fill the benches, false "father" senators, go forth, new leaders, and crowd around your master Eutropius, in an infertile Senate); 1.495–496 ("sterili . . . consule").

113. Most scholars argue for a unified composition after Eutropius's fall. See Weiß and Wiener, *Claudianus*, 410–61; Charlet, *Claudien III*, xvii–xix; Long, *Claudian's "In Eutropium,"* 149–77; Felgentreu, *Claudians praefationes*, 102–8; Garambois-Vasquez, *Les invectives*, 18–20; Müller, *Lectiones*, 267–68; Dorfbauer, "Die *praefationes*," 204–9; Burrell, "Claudian's *In Eutropium liber alter*," 112–14.

genre from invective toward parody.[114] This heralded a further theme: Claudian's *Eutropius* became a means to reject all claims that Constantinople could equal or even surpass Rome.[115] To use him this way and in a tacit acknowledgment of the consul's former power, Claudian made Eutropius into a usurper as tyrant. That tyrant vanished from the second part of the invective, yielding center stage to Stilicho, whom Aurora implored to liberate her and grant her merciful protection as the victor of what was in truth a parody of civil war. Stilicho alone could unite and safeguard the empire under the protective (Augustan) shield of the *aeterna urbs*: the last word of *Against Eutropius* is *virtus*.[116]

To be sure, Claudian's second invective still denigrated Eutropius as a eunuch. However, treating him as a usurper, a *mollis tyrannus* who had effectively displaced Arcadius and ruled the empire as if it were his bedchamber, allowed Claudian to focus more on the tyrant's coterie—that is, the Constantinopolitan Senate and other elites—than on the emperor himself.[117] Arcadius could be salvaged because he had been badly advised, but the most important point was that Stilicho had to be the guardian of the entire empire, since the east was unable to rule itself in the proper Roman manner. Making Eutropius a consul confirmed that Constantinople was at best a "second Rome" (*altera Roma*).[118] And only such a second-rate capital could permit a war council (*consilium belli*) of less-than-manly (*minimeque viriles*) young and lascivious old men marked by the "battle scars" of enslavement—a parody of the Senate reminiscent of that in the *Historia Augusta's Life of Heliogabalus*—to move against the Goths without Stilicho's support.[119] Granted, those Goths, whom Claudian called Scythians, were themselves rather eunuchlike, so even a soft tyrant should have been able to subdue such malleable opponents:

114. Ware, "Claudian," 181–201; G. Kelly, "Claudian and Constantinople," 251–53; Long, *Claudian's "In Eutropium,"* 17–50, 197–200 (Claudian's eastern audience); Gnilka, "Review of Cameron, *Claudian*"; Cameron, "Claudian Revisited," 136–37; Christiansen, "Claudian and the East."

115. G. Kelly, "Claudian and Constantinople," 256; C. Edwards, "Imaginaires de l'image de Rome?," 241; Ware, *Claudian*, 121–23.

116. Favro, "IconiCITY," 30–38; Grig, "Competing Capitals," 37–38; Long, *Claudian's "In Eutropium,"* 245–60. Schweckendiek, *Claudians Invektive gegen Eutrop*, 112, considers this a so-called golden line, but see K. Mayer, "Schoolboys' Revenge," 262–69.

117. Claud., *Eutr.* 2 praef. 2. 21, 2.133: "Quam similes haec aula viros!" (How much the eastern courtiers resemble Eutropius!).

118. Claud., *Eutr.* 2.126–28. See also Optatianus Porphyrius, *Carm.* 4.5–6 (first use of *altera Roma*, under Constantine); CTh 13.5.1; Themistius, who calls Constantinople "New Rome" in Them., *Or.* 3.42a (357) and *deutera Rome*, "second Rome," in Them., *Or.* 14.184a; Bassett, *Urban Image*, 159; Elia, "Sui 'privilegia urbis Constantinopolitaneae,'" 79–98; Grig and Kelly, "Introduction."

119. Claud., *Eutr.* 2 praef. 21–22, 2.324–45; *HA, Heliogab.* 20.6, inspired by Juv. 4.72, a caricature of Domitian's Senate. See also Charlet, *Claudien III*, 295–96; Schweckendiek, *Claudians Invektive gegen Eutrop*, 142. For the long tradition of viewing cosmopolitanism, as here in Constantinople, with skepticism while also claiming world-spanning rule see C. Edwards and Woolf, "Rome as World City;" Minets, *Slow Fall of Babel*, 220–35.

"Now another sex [*alter sexus*] is up in arms, and the world has entrusted itself to eunuchs as defenders."[120]

Of course, the eastern army had the traits of its leaders—according to the playbook that Pacatus had also used—and therefore could not manage to defeat even such Scythians.[121] No wonder that the gods of Roman warfare lost patience, with Mars asking Bellona, "My sister, can't we yet cure softness in the east? Not yet? Won't the corrupt ages ever stiffen up? . . . Do you see this obscene crime? . . . Look what kind of deeds result from a little quiet, how much damage rest from warfare does. The year handed over to a eunuch was without a war."[122] *Altera Roma*, left to its own devices, had brought about the rule of an *alter sexus*. Eutropius as consul confirmed all the west's worst suspicions of the east—and allowed Claudian to make that abundantly clear. Obviously, only Stilicho could save the east, free the consulship from the marks of enslavement (*maculis servilibus*), and restore Rome's manly (Achillean) anger (*virilis ira*), which would put the barbarians back in their place.[123]

Arcadius's choice to make the eunuch Eutropius a consul reverberated in Milan because it made visible how much softness imperial manliness had acquired. Gratian's and then Theodosius's expansion of youthfully smooth imperial gorgeousness was gradual and experimental. It was also more capaciously present in Constantinople, where Theodosius had resided and governed with Arcadius, Aelia Flaccilla, and Honorius, than in the west, where Gratian's demise and Valentinian II's fate had led to the rule of the more traditionally manly Magnus Maximus. Honorius's early accession as the sole ruler of the west accelerated the expansion of gorgeous softness, which was always moderated and harnessed by constant pairing with the "hard" manliness of Stilicho. Then, rather suddenly and probably unexpectedly, a eunuch consul revealed the potential scope of such capaciously gendered imperial *vir*-ness and questioned a fundamental assumption: was the ability to become a father an essential requirement for all elite *viri* or only for the ruling emperor? The answer offered by the court in Milan—aware

120. Claud., *Eutr.* 2.223–25 ("Nunc alter in armis / sexus et eunuchis se defensoribus orbis / credidit"). See Schweckendiek, *Claudians Invektive gegen Eutrop*, 202–5, for the Virgilian allusions.

121. *Pan. lat.* (2).12.33.2–5.

122. Claud., *Eutr.* 2.112–22:

Necdum mollitiae, necdum, germana, mederi
possumus Eoae? Numquam corrupta rigescent
saecula? . . .
Aspicis obscenum facinus? . . .
. . . En quales sese diffundit in actus
parva quies! Quantum nocuerunt otia ferri!
Qui caruit belis, eunucho traditor annus.

123. Claud., *Eutr.* 2.133, 2.138–39: "Quid quod et armati cessant et nulla virilis / inter tot gladios sexum reminiscitur ira?" (What if these armed soldiers yield and no one remembers manly anger among so many swords?). See also Garambois-Vasquez, *Les invectives*, 223–28.

of Constantinople's rising power but confident in Rome's lasting uniqueness—was unequivocal.[124] Manlius Theodorus as counterconsul, the reissuing of the boots and trousers law, and Claudian's celebration of Stilicho as a consul and family man in 400 said it all: to be able in the end to become a father was the *conditio sine qua non* not only for the emperor but for elite *vir*-ness as a whole, however soft it might otherwise be.

The eastern position was in all likelihood the same with regard to the emperor, but the question was not answered with the same clarity there, because it was not posed with the same starkness. Unlike the so far childless Honorius, Arcadius was already a father twice over, so the tension for elite (rather than imperial) *vir*-ness was less evident. Indeed, as a father, the emperor could afford to appoint Eutropius as a consul because of the latter's merit. The consulship honored the exceptional achievements of an *illustris vir* and *patricius*; what mattered most was the office and not its holder's physical condition. Softness, in short, did not contradict power. Consequently, being an elite (as opposed to an imperial) *vir* no longer required actual fatherhood: one could be a powerful *vir* without being (able to become) a father. The reactions of two members of the elites in the east, Synesius and John Chrysostom, reveal that this message was understood there, even if Eutropius's condition as a eunuch was never far from the surface and demanded attention, engagement, and explanation.

---

124. Skinner, "Early Development of the Senate"; Skinner, "'Byzantine' Senatorial Perspective"; G. Kelly, "New Rome"; Ward-Perkins, "Old and New Rome Compared"; Machado, *Urban Space*, 58–83, 204–30; Brown, *Through the Eye of a Needle*, 241–58.

7

Eutropius the Scythian, Arcadius the Jellyfish

Synesius's On Kingship

Synesius of Cyrene's mirror of princes, or *basilikos logos*, known as *On Kingship*, or *De regno*, is our earliest detailed eastern assessment of Eutropius as a powerful *illustris vir* and then consul.[1] Composed between mid-398 and early 399, *On Kingship* responded to Arcadius's Constantinople "very early in the stages of a major transition in the nature of imperial rule." By then, Theodosius's building projects, especially his forum and the Golden Gate, had been completed, and his son and longtime coruler, who had grown up in the city, emerged as "an important conduit of continuity."[2] Arcadius had assembled his leading personnel and chosen John Chrysostom as the bishop of the capital's Nicene congregation, which included members of the court, the military's higher ranks, and the Senate, although many court eunuchs and parts of the populace retained older, more established forms of Christianity, as well as different Nicene versions.[3] The city had sizable Jewish and pagan communities, and its multiethnic and multilingual inhabitants—Goths, Franks, and Vandals prominent among them—enhanced its cosmopolitan character.[4]

Continuing Theodosius's practice, Arcadius often interacted with Constantinopolitans, albeit in his own way and with his own ceremonial language. Rather

---

1. For the *De regno* I use the text in Lacombrade but have also consulted Lamoureux and Aujoulat and Garzya. Note that Fitzgerald offers a useful translation, though based on an outdated text.

2. Quotes in McEvoy, "Imperial Jellyfish," 183. For Theodosius's changes in the cityscape, see chapter 5; Machado, "Aristocratic Houses," 137–58.

3. Andrade, "Processions"; McLynn, "Moments of Truth"; S. Elm, "What the Bishop Wore"; Croke, "Dynasty and Aristocracy"; Pigott, "Capital Crimes."

4. Falcasantos, *Constantinople*, 76–86; Berzon, *Classifying Christians*, 9–11; Berger, *Konstantinopel*, 49–53; Dagron, *Naissance*, 367–88.

than every week, he attended the city's main church only on major feast days such as Christmas and Easter, and he was present at shrines on highly visible occasions, such as when they received new relics. Arcadius's marriage and the birth of his first daughter (soon to be followed by a second) may have involved ceremonies in the church.[5] It is known that these events saw people dancing in the streets, and that they were accompanied by races in the hippodrome. Constantinople's inhabitants had certainly been present at Arcadius's accession as augustus in the Hebdomon in 383 (and that of his brother Honorius in 393), which also featured splendid parades along the Mese, and at its commemoration every fifth year, in 388, 393, and 398, all marked with exhibitions and games in the hippodrome. The celebrations were particularly lavish when the emperor was the consul, as Arcadius had been four times by 398/399.[6] The anniversary of Constantinople's foundation was yet another moment when Arcadius interacted with the populace, a good number of whom had seen him in a triumphal *adventus* at the side of his father in 386.

Unlike his father, however, Arcadius had never participated in a military campaign. It is important to remember that he always had the option of doing so, but Theodosius's recasting of imperial victory as philanthropy had begun to take effect.[7] By 398/399, Arcadius had left the city only for summer visits to Cappadocia. The emperor's observers noticed and reacted mostly with opprobrium, because campaigning continued to be an important aspect of imperial legitimacy—philanthropy as the most important imperial weapon was by no means universally accepted, as will become apparent in what follows. Moreover, an emperor's uninterrupted presence in Constantinople was a real novelty—and as such inherently suspect in a society that venerated tradition. Given that the emperor's lack of movement outside the capital coincided with Eutropius's rise, it is not surprising that contemporary eastern historians used the consul to hold the emperor in scorn. Eunapius described Arcadius as dominated by his wife and eunuch.[8] According to

5. J. Chrys., *De Hiero. Phoca* (PG 50. 699–706); Soc., *HE* 6.18 (Easter, Christmas), 6.23.2–6 (visit to a shrine); Soz., *HE* 8.16.1; *Chron. Pasch.*, a. 395, 565–66; McLynn, "Imperial Piety," 323–39; McLynn, "Transformation," 265–67 (church attendance only on special occasions); van Nuffelen, "Playing the Ritual Game," 193 (major feast days still offered many occasions for interaction); McEvoy, "Imperial Jellyfish," 189–91. The baptism of Theodosius II in 402 was the first of an imperial child: see Marc. Diac. 46–49; Holum, *Theodosian Empresses*, 55n31 (date).

6. Croke, "Reinventing Constantinople," 249–50, 264, points out that according to the later *Book of Ceremonies*, imperial births, marriages, and anniversaries were always accompanied by entertainments in the hippodrome and assumes (at 250) a late fourth-century precedent. See also McEvoy, "Imperial Jellyfish," 184–87.

7. J. Lydus, *De mag.* 2.11, writing in the early sixth century, mentioned a law that Theodosius had purportedly issued forbidding his sons to fight. See also Pfeilschifter, *Kaiser und Konstantinopel*, 92–98, 485–97; Holum, *Theodosian Empresses*, 79.

8. Eunap., *Hist.* 64–66, and esp. 62.3 The fragments relating to Eutropius belong to the later version, begun around 399 and published in 404. See also Blockley, *Fragmentary Classicising Historians* 1:105–6, 2:93–103; Breebaart, "Eunapius of Sardes"; Buck, "Eunapius, Eutropius"; Rohrbacher, *Historians of Late Antiquity*, 62–72; Becker, *Eunapios*, 25–35.

Philostorgius, he was "short, slight of build, weakly, and dark in complexion," while "his dullness of mind was evident in his speech and the way his eyes looked as they drooped sleepily downward beneath their drowsy lids."[9] Zosimus, who continued Eunapius's history, characterized the emperor as stupid, lethargic, and cajoled by his advisers "like a fatted animal."[10] Modern scholars followed suit and have only recently begun to question the assessment of their ancient precursors.[11]

In this context, Synesius's *On Kingship* and Claudian's *Against Eutropius* are often considered the most damning verdicts of Arcadius's reign. Both sources have been instrumental in placing the emperor deep into the shadows cast by his famous father, Theodosius I, and his son, Theodosius II, who became coaugustus at the ripe old age of eight months. However, in contrast to the ancient historians, all of whom wrote after the consul's fall and subsequent death, Synesius and Claudian wrote while Eutropius was still active. Therefore, their assessments are from a different perspective. With regard to Eutropius in particular, Claudian's characterization has prevailed over Synesius's. This is significant because Synesius presents a contemporary view, without hindsight, from the east, from Constantinople, with relatively little (if any) regard for the interests of the court in Milan. A careful analysis of his commentary on the powers that be at Arcadius's court between 398 and early 399 is even more important, because Synesius is among the few sources for the emperor's early rule. That rule, it must be remembered, was stable enough to allow for an eight-month-old coaugustus and for the six-year-old Theodosius II to succeed without a causing a ripple when Arcadius died in 408. Theodosius II ruled until his death after a riding accident in 450.[12] Arcadius therefore mastered the transition from his father's rule to his own and paved the way for the longevity of that of his son. At the very least, he should be given credit for that stability. Indeed, I hope that my reading of the emperor's dull lethargy as a later hostile characterization of the flexible and hence durable soft and capacious imperial *vir*-ness of the early Theodosians will further contribute to the reevaluation of Arcadius and his rule.

Synesius's *De regno* has received much scholarly attention, most of it related to the date of composition, which affects the interpretation of the circumstances to which it alludes.[13] Born into a wealthy landed family in Cyrene around 370 CE,

9. Philost., *HE* 11.3 (ὁ δὲ Ἀρκάδιος βραχὺς τῷ μεγέθει, καὶ λεπτὸς τὴν ἕξιν, καὶ ἀδρανὴς τὴν ἰσχύν, καὶ τὸ χρῶμα μέλας· καὶ τὴν τῆς ψυχῆς νωθείαν οἵ τε λόγοι διήγγελλον, καὶ τῶν ὀφθαλμῶν ἡ φύσις, ὑμνηλῶς τε καὶ δυσαναφόρως αὐτοὺς διικνύουσα καθελκομένους). Trans. Amidon, 146, with modifications.

10. Zos., *HN* 5.24.1–2, 5.12.1–2 (καθάπερ βοσκήματος), 5.14.1; see 5.1–19.5 for Eutropius.

11. See, e.g., Jones, *Later Roman Empire*, 1:173, and Icks, "Inadequate Heirs," 70, for negative views; McEvoy, "Imperial Jellyfish," 181, represents reassessment.

12. *Cons. Const.*, a. 402.

13. See, e.g., Schmitt, *Die Bekehrung*, 242–50, 282–88; Hoffmann, "Die Lebenswelt," date at 46; Lizzi Testa, "Significato filosofico," 49–62; Brandt, "Die Rede περὶ βασιλείας," 57–70; Tanaseanu-Döbler, *Konversion*, 155–286; Swain, *Themistius*, 100–7; Flower, *Emperors and Bishops*, 59–61.

Synesius came to Constantinople as an ambassador of Libya Superior to effect tax relief and to present the *aurum coronarium*, or crown gold, to Arcadius on his province's behalf. He remained in the city for three years.[14] Earlier scholars dated this stay to 399–402. In that case, Synesius would have composed *De regno* in late 399 or early 400, after the revolt of Tribigild and his Gothic federation, to which Claudian's second invective against Eutropius also refers.[15] Cameron and Long, together with Barnes and Heather, however, revised the dates of Synesius's embassy and subsequent stay to 397–400, largely because the crown gold was presented to emperors on their elevation and on every fifth anniversary thereafter. Arcadius became an augustus on January 19, 383, so Synesius must have arrived in Constantinople in 397, in time for the emperor's fifteen-year anniversary on January 19, 398.[16] Cameron and Long moreover concluded that Synesius composed *De regno* in the first part of 398. However, their argument also supports a date later in 398 or in early 399, before Tribigild began causing trouble. As a consequence, the Gothic leader whom *De regno* attacks was not Tribigild but Alaric, and it was written when Eutropius was the consul designate or consul.[17]

De regno has been read as evidence for the frustration that provincial elites experienced in the capital but also as a declaration of Panhellenic sentiment—indeed, as *the* manifesto of an anti-Germanic party resisting Goths who held high military and imperial positions.[18] While the idea of an anti-Germanic Panhellenic party has lost its adherents, Synesius's so-called anti-Scythian tirade in *De regno* remains one of the most widely cited passages in nearly all scholarly works on the period. "Scythians"—that is, Goths—are a central concern of the work but not its only one.

This interesting and complex example of the genre of *basilikos logos* (or *Fürstenspiegel*) presents a version of an ideal ruler and details the myriad ways that Arcadius fell short of it.[19] In a highly entertaining manner, Synesius offered a playful yet biting critique of the emperor, whom he depicted as a cartoonishly inept jellyfish.[20] Writing—and performing—the work for a circle of like-minded, highly educated

14. Klauser, "*Aurum coronarium*"; Kreikenbom, "Kyrene und die Ptolemaïs."

15. This dating has recently been maintained by Lamoureux and Aujoulat, *Opuscules II*, 11–26; Hagl, *Arcadius*, 64–65; Roques, "Synésios à Constantinople"; Roques, *Synésios de Cyrène*, 160–68.

16. Cameron and Long, *Barbarians*, 91–102, 128–30; Barnes, "Synesius in Constantinople"; Heather, "Anti-Scythian Tirade," 153–55. See also Liebeschuetz, *Barbarians and Bishops*, 106–7, and n. 20.

17. Petkas, "King in Words," 127.

18. The later dating was originally proposed by Seeck, "Studien zu Synesius," to support his view of *De regno* as the manifesto of an anti-barbarian party; Albert, *Goten*, 80, and Cameron and Long, *Barbarians*, 9–10, 91–102, successfully dismantled the existence of such a party in arguing for the earlier dates. Hagl, *Arcadius*, 27–30, accepts the dismantling but argues (63) for the later date of Synesius's stay and the composition of *De regno* in 399.

19. For the genre *basilikos logos*, see Swain, *Themistius*, 102–7; Alvino, "Osservazioni," 178–79; Schmitt, *Die Bekehrung*, 282–98; Hagl, *Arcadius*, 71–95; Gangloff, *Pouvoir imperial*, 397–456.

20. Syn., *De reg.* 14.3, refers to a jellyfish of the type known as a sea lung.

members of the elite as if the emperor were present, Synesius created a fictional "Arcadius."[21] This imagined future Arcadius would restore the empire to its former glory as soon as he had rid himself of his current advisers and replaced them with Synesius's friends and sponsors. The most prominent of the latter was a certain Aurelian, Synesius's principal addressee. Aurelian, a senator from an important Constantinopolitan family, became the praetorian prefect and consul designate for 400 in August 399, immediately after Eutropius's fall. Synesius had made the right connections.[22]

Because Synesius's main concern was his immediate audience, his friends who should replace Arcadius's current advisers as fast as possible, his attacks focused on those advisers rather than on the emperor. The most important adviser at that moment was Eutropius, who, inter alia, had been instrumental in promoting the "Scythian" Alaric (see chapter 6). Scholars have noted that Synesius was aware of Eutropius's role in Arcadius's court.[23] What continues to be underexamined, however, are the consequences of the eunuch's "presence" in Synesius's amusing yet serious creation of the ideal Arcadius.[24] Eutropius, to be sure, is veiled in eloquent silence and appears only indirectly in *De regno*. If he is taken as a principal target, however, the work's argumentative strategy reverses: rather than using the eunuch to criticize the emperor, Synesius used his fictional Arcadius to chastise the powerful eunuch, the *patricius, illustris vir*, "father of the prince," and, finally, consul. Certainly, to reiterate, any criticism of an emperor's most influential adviser indicts the sovereign for the bad choices he has made. But my shift in focus significantly alters the interpretation of *De regno*. If Eutropius played a central role, Theodosian imperial *vir*-ness was far more directly at stake. Synesius did not compare Arcadius to a soft, moist, delicate jellyfish by accident.

THE IDEAL ARCADIUS AS A STATUE
BUILT WITH WORDS

Synesius opened his performance with a subtle yet bold declaration: though only just arrived in the city, he was in fact Constantinople's new Themistius, a rustic philosopher who would speak truth to power. That was exactly the kind of

21. Some scholars (e.g., Lacombrade, *Synésios*, 87; Swain, *Themistius*, 107) continue to be attracted by the idea that Arcadius was present and Synesius performed an impressive feat of *parrhesia*, free and frank speech. Most, however, doubt that the emperor even took note of the work, although it was probably performed as well as written down: see Petkas, "King in Words," 128–32, 134–38, 146–48; Alvino, "Osservazioni"; W. Johnson, *Readers*, 61 (observes that such recitations were standard entertainment).

22. CTh 2.8.23; Syn., *Ep.* 61; Cameron and Long, *Barbarians*, 121–26, 149–67; Schmitt, *Die Bekehrung*, 255–61; Liebeschuetz, *Barbarians and Bishops*, 108–9; Lamoureux and Aujoulat, *Opuscule II*, 16–19.

23. Barnes, "Synesius in Constantinople," 108; Cameron and Long, *Barbarians*, 84–91, 107–9.

24. Cameron and Long, *Barbarians*, 103–42; Schmitt, *Die Bekehrung*, 287–88; and Heather, "Anti-Scythian Tirade," refer to Eutropius's position without exploring the implications.

person missing from Arcadius's court after Themistius died. Thankfully, Synesius was well equipped to take up his mantle, even though he had not been the young emperor's tutor. Nonetheless, as a father figure and teacher, he would now remind Arcadius of the norms (*gnomoi*) and touchstones (*basanisterioi*) foundational for good rule.[25] Sadly, while Arcadius had been without frank philosophical advice, a coterie of imbeciles, flatterers, and entertainers had filled the void, with abysmal results for the realm.[26] To reverse the damage, Synesius erected a "most beautiful statue of words" and "fashion[ed] [*plattein*] a king in speech" to model correct imperial conduct: how to be philosophically minded, active, and courageous—that is, how to be manly, or *andreios*, the Greek equivalent of being a *vir*, which encompasses a similar range of meanings associated with virtue, or *arete*, so that he would radiate divine beauty appropriately.[27] In fact, remedies were at hand. All Arcadius had to do was remove his current advisers, replace them with Synesius's friends, and emulate the statue in words that Synesius had created for him, and all would be well again.

Synesius's eagerly anticipated but presently nonexistent ideal Arcadius was a ruler who embodied divinely inspired love of mankind, *philanthropia*. In imitation (*mimesis*) of God's solicitude (*kedemonia*) for the universe, that emperor (*autokrator*) was a philosopher who combined Roman imperial might with Greek paideia to guide and safeguard all the peoples in his care.[28] The ideal Arcadius radiated sublime calm (*galene*), foresight, and self-restraint.[29] He was like a new Odysseus who knew how to control his guard dogs so that he could rid his house of noxious suitors at the right time. He was a new Achilles, a man who inspired terror (*deinos aner*) when unleashing his rage.[30] Like Cyrus, who had founded the Persian empire, he knew how to use eunuchs and to choose the right friends as advisers.[31] However, unless the real Arcadius followed Synesius's admonitions, the statue of the ideal ruler created by words would remain fictional. Instead of becoming reality once again, the "good old days" would be lost: the emperor would no longer be

25. Syn., *De reg.* 6.3 (εἷς οὗτος βασιλείας σοι γνώμων. σὺ δὲ ἤδη σαυτὸν πρόσαγε τῷ βασανιστηρίῳ). Such touchstones (*basanistes*) also form part of Cynic diatribes and are alluded to by a reference to falsified coins in Syn., *De reg.* 14.4: see S. Elm, *Sons of Hellenism*, 108–11; Muehlberger, "Wartime Effects."

26. Syn., *De reg.* 29. See also Syn., *De prov.* 1.18; Alvino, "Osservazioni," 180–81.

27. Syn., *De reg.* 1.1–2, 26.1 (Πρὶν ἐπαγγείλασθαι πλάττειν τὸν ἐν τῷ λόγῳ βασιλέα), 9.5 (φέρε δή σοι γράψω λόγῳ τὸν βασιλέα, ὥσπερ ἄγαλμα στήσας), 18.3 (πάγκαλος). The term *plattein* indicates fiction. For *andreia*, see Quiroga Puertas, "Deconstructing Praise," 454–60.

28. Syn., *De reg.* 8.4, and see 24–25, 29; Alvino, "Osservazioni," 178, 188; Petkas, "King in Words," 134–41. For parallels with Themistius, see S. Elm, *Sons of Hellenism*, 60–87; Niccolai, *Christianity*, 253–60.

29. The imperial virtues of *eusebeia* (piety), *pronoia* (foresight), *sophrosyne* (restraint), *phronesis* (prudence), *dikaiosyne* (justice), and *metriotes* (just measure) recur throughout: see, e.g., Syn., *De reg.* 7.1, 7.5, 8.4, 10.1, 10.21, 17.9, 18.1, 22.2, 25.5–26.1, 28.1.

30. Syn., *De reg.* 5.5, 13.4, 21.5: see Pl., *Rep.* 343b, 345c, 375a; Hom., *Il.* 8.527, 2.196, 11.654 (in order of occurrence); Hom., *Od.* 11.24–26, 11.31–36.

31. Syn., *De reg.* 11–12.

FIGURE 18. Statue of an early Theodosian emperor (Arcadius or Valentinian II), marble, ca. 390 CE, Aphrodisian workshop. From the so-called Place of Palms in Aphrodisias. Archaeological Museum, Istanbul, Turkey, inv.no. 2264. © Vanni Archive / Art Resource, NY Art Resources.

the "public servant of the commonwealth," nor would "God and king take charge of affairs [to] preemptively strike the killing blow against the doom which has long been in labor pangs to destroy Roman supremacy."[32] It was thus Synesius's fervent hope that the real Arcadius would step up, replace those currently in power around him, and embrace true Roman imperial virtue, *andreia*, for everyone's sake.[33]

32. Syn., *De reg.* 18.1–2 (Καὶ σύ, βασιλεῦ, τῆς ἐπαναγωγῆς τῶν ἀγαθῶν ἄρξαιο, καὶ ἀποδοίης ἡμῖν λειτουργὸν τῆς πολιτείας τὸν βασιλέα . . . καὶ δεῖ θεοῦ καὶ βασιλέως ἐπὶ τὰ πράγματα, τὴν ὠδινομένην χρόνον ἤδη συχνὸν τῆς Ῥωμαίων ἀρχῆς τὴν εἱμαρμένην προαναιρήσοντος).

33. Syn., *De reg.* 29.3–4 (Κἂν γένηται τοῦτο, δέδωκά σοι ὅπερ ἀρχόμενος ᾔτησα, λόγῳ μὲν αὐτὸς ὑποσχόμενος ἀνδριάντα βασιλέως σοι δεῖξαι - καὶ γάρ ἐστι λόγος ὄντως ἔργου σκιή -, παρὰ σοῦ δὲ αὐτὸν ἀντῄτουν ἔμβιον ἀπολαβεῖν καὶ κινούμενον).

Molded by the ragtag assembly surrounding him, Arcadius had become accustomed to "the truncated [*koloba*] thoughts and words of these people, [which] suit [his] ears more than an intellect cultivated by philosophy and expressed in lucid and terse language. This is the profit [he has] gained from [his] astonishing seclusion, suspicious of and behaving arrogantly toward the wise element of the citizenry while inviting in the mindless, and stripping down before them [*pros ekeinous apogymnoumenoi*]."[34]

Emphasizing the trope of the sealed-in ruler, *princeps clausus*, which has dominated Arcadius's scholarly assessment ever since, Synesius attacked Eutropius without mentioning his name.[35] Only the *praepositus sacri cubiculi*, or grand chamberlain, would ever see the emperor stripped naked. Such persons were normally eunuchs, whose thoughts were as truncated (*koloba*) as the parts that would have made them truly male. Here that eunuch was Eutropius, who inflicted immeasurable harm by "truncating" the emperor's reach. He concealed the imperial body (*basilikon soma*) as if it were sacred and displayed the emperor, whenever he emerged, in theatrical scenes redolent of foreign, "barbarian" pomp and glitter.[36] Secluded in the imperial bedchamber (*thalamos*), Arcadius had no opportunity to see what was going on in the empire.[37] Like a jellyfish in the sea, he was consumed by his lowest passions, surrounded by "small-headed" (*mikrokephalos*) and "pea-brained" (*oligognomos*) persons, who were the result of "nature falsified."[38] The emperor had received some of them as gifts to delight him with their disfigurement or their extraordinary beauty. These advisers were themselves enslaved, without restraint or self-control—without *andreia*—and thus dominated by their worst passions, constantly erupting in inappropriate laughter or weeping, gesticulating widely to amuse their ruler.[39]

34. Syn., *De reg.* 14.4 (Τούτων τὰ κολοβὰ διανοήματα καὶ ῥήματα ταῖς ἀκοαῖς ὑμῶν ἐναρμόζεται μᾶλλον ἢ νοῦς ἐκ φιλοσοφίας ἐν γλώττῃ περιτράνῳ τε καὶ στρογγύλῃ. ὃ δὲ τῆς θαυμαστῆς οἰκουρίας ἀπολελαύκατε, τοῦ δήμου τὸ μὲν φρόνιμον ὑποπτεύοντες καὶ πρὸς ἐκείνους ἀποσεμνύνομενοι, τὸ δὲ ἀνόητον εἰσαγόμενοι καὶ πρὸς ἐκείνους ἀπογυμνούμενοι). Trans. Petkas, "King in Words," 126.

35. Stroheker, "*Princeps clausus*," 271–83; Icks, "Keeping up Appearances," 173–77.

36. Syn., *De reg.* 14.2–3.

37. Syn., *De reg.* 14.3, 15.7. *HA, Alex. Sev.* 66.3 explicitly holds eunuchs responsible for cloistering emperors: see Zinsli, *Kommentar*, 471.

38. Syn., *De reg.* 14.3, 14. 4. At 14.3 he mentions the jellyfish, or mollusk of the sea, *thalatiou pneumonos*, alluding to Pl., *Phileb.* 21c.

39. Syn., *De reg.* 14.4 (Τοιγαροῦν ἡ σεμνότης αὕτη καὶ τὸ δεδιέναι μὴ ἐξανθρωπισθείητε σύνηθες γενόμενοι θέαμα κατακλείστους ποιεῖ πολιορκουμένους ὑφ' ἑαυτῶν, ἐλάχιστα μὲν ὁρῶντας, ἐλάχιστα δὲ ἀκούοντας, ἀφ' ὧν πρακτικὴ φρόνησις συναθροίζεται, μόνας ἡδομένους τὰς τοῦ σώματος ἡδονάς, καὶ τούτων γε τὰς ὑλικωτάτας, ὅσας ἀφή τε καὶ γεῦσις πορίζουσι, βίον ζῶντας θαλαττίου πνεύμονος … καὶ γὰρ οἷς σύνεστε παρὰ δίαιτάν τε καὶ ἄλλως, καὶ οἷς ἐστιν εἰς τὰ βασίλεια πάροδος ἀδεέστερον ἢ στρατηγοῖς τε καὶ λοχαγοῖς, τούτους οὓς χαρίεντας ἄρα παρασκευάζεσθε, τοὺς μικροκεφάλους τε καὶ ὀλιγογνώμονας, οὓς ἡ φύσις ἁμαρτάνουσα παραχαράττει, καθάπερ ἀδικοῦντες οἱ τραπεζῖται τὸ νόμισμα).

Consequently, Arcadius had forgotten "that one can advance only according to the principles that have lifted one up in the first place."[40] He should have recalled that the *mores maiorum* of Republican times had made Rome great, not robes heavier than weapons.[41] Rome's first kings had not been encased in gold and purple, nor had their heads and feet been encrusted with jewels and pearls, nor their throne adorned with gemstones assembled from the far corners of the empire. The current emperor, in contrast, would prance around like a peacock were he not so loaded down by his ornate clothes that he could barely move, unable to enter the Senate unless his path had been sprinkled with gold dust and he had donned yet another ceremonial costume. Alas, the Roman kings of old—frugal, sunburned, self-contained martial rulers who wore clothes as simple as those of the soldiers with whom they fought—were gone. One could still admire their statues in Constantinople, but with their Spartan caps they were now ridiculed as curiosities. Yet those Roman rulers did not hide inside their palaces. Instead, they had crushed barbarians from Asia and Europe before the latter could enter the empire.[42]

To create the ideal Arcadius, with an eye toward achieving a better future, Synesius contrasted forms of imperial *vir*-ness from Rome's glorious past with their less-than-manly present iteration. His exemplary Roman rulers belonged to former generations who had achieved world dominion like simple Spartan soldiers, with their *andreia*, or manly courage, on full display whenever they rode out to meet their enemies. Indeed, this glorious past, when Rome's emperors distinguished themselves through their character (*psyche*) rather than their fashion (*skeue*), was as recent as Carinus, who had ruled between 283 and 285 and so impressed his Persian opponent, resplendent in tiara and ceremonial robes, with his frugal meals and plain chiton that the latter submitted without battle.[43] Conversely, Arcadius had succumbed to fluid lassitude, *hedone*, and become a less-than-manly, spineless mollusk. No wonder that Scythians as well as Getae and Massagetai, Hunnic peoples who "falsified their appearance through artful means as if to show that a new and unusual race [*genos*] has sprung up from the earth, demanding money in exchange for peace," now terrorized Rome.[44]

40. Syn., *De reg.* 14.5 (ἔδει μὲν εἰδέναι καλῶς ὅτι ταῖς αὐταῖς παρασκευαῖς ἕκαστον αὔξεται καὶ συγκροτεῖται).

41. Syn., *De reg.* 14.5, 15.4.

42. Syn., *De reg.* 13–16. See Bassett, *Urban Image*, 50–97, for the statues in Constantinople. See also Icks, "Keeping up Appearances," 170–71.

43. Syn., *De reg.* 16.7 (Οἱ δὲ ἁπλῶς ἑαυτῶν εἶχον, οὐκ ἀπὸ τῆς σκευῆς, ἀλλ' ἀπὸ τῆς ψυχῆς βασιλεῖς ὄντες). Synesius here mistook Marcus Aurelius Carinus for his father, Marcus Aurelius Carus, who was emperor from 282 to 283 and successfully fought the Sassanian Persians. See Lacombrade, *Synésios*, 116n98.

44. Syn., *De reg.* 15.8 (Οἱ δ' οὖν ἕτερα ἀντὶ τούτων ὀνόματα θέμενοι, ἕτεροι δὲ αὐτῶν καὶ τὰ πρόσωπα τέχνῃ παραποιήσαντες, ἵνα δὴ δοκοίη γένος ἄλλο νέον τε καὶ ἀλλόκοτον ἐκφῦναι τῆς γῆς, δεδίττονται ὑμᾶς ἀντιδιαβαίνοντες, καὶ μισθὸν εἰρήνης ἀξιοῦσι πράττεσθαι). "Getae" and "Massagetai," analogous to "Scythians," were names for Goths taken from Herodotus (1.216.13), here used for Dacian and Hunnic peoples: see Lacombrade, *Synésios*, 147n90.

Synesius deployed many of the traditional tropes already familiar from the preceding chapters to form his contrasting images of imperial manliness. Arcadius in his present shape, molded by much-less-than-manly advisers, was almost as bad as a tyrant, caught up in *hedone*. Only new, better advisers, including the rustic philosopher of terse words, might instill in him a taste for the manly courage (*andreia*), forethought (*phronesis*), self-restraint (*sophrosyne*), and active participation in battle modeled by the emperors who had made Rome great.[45] But this was as yet just a hope, so Synesius arranged and combined allusions to his literary models in original ways to address the "actual condition [of Arcadius] . . . enclosed in [his] bedchamber like a lizard."[46] His most important intertexts include Dio Chrysostom's *Kingship Orations*, Xenophon's *Cyropaideia*, and works by Herodotus, Aristotle, and Plato.[47] As intertexts, they have received relatively little scholarly attention in their own right, and they assume additional relevance when read through the lens of Synesius's use of Eutropius to highlight the negative potential of imperial softness (as much as possible given the circumstances in Constantinople—that is, the power that Eutropius held, sanctioned and bestowed by the emperor). Examined more closely, these intertexts strengthen Synesius's anticipated ruler: reformed and hence able to reform—once paired with new advisers and thus shored up by their appropriately firm manliness—Arcadius would know how to use imperial softness, and his eunuchs, properly. Of course, Synesius's references and allusions to the second-most-powerful person in the east were indirect. However, given his audience's literary sophistication, the direction of his attacks, sufficiently veiled to target more than one powerful person, was evident to everyone, as the intertextual analysis of the so-called anti-Scythian tirade illustrates.

THE MOST EUNUCHLIKE PEOPLE

"The most strikingly concrete part of the *De regno*, and the most important to the historian, is the long section . . . criticizing the dependence of the Roman state on 'Scythians,' by which are meant Goths."[48] Not much needs to be added to Cameron and Long's succinct characterization. This anti-Scythian tirade has attracted a great deal of scholarship because it is one of the few contemporary passages assessing Goths and their military leaders in the eastern part of the later Roman

---

45. Schramm, "Neuplatonische Politische Philosophie"; McDonnell, "Roman Men and Greek Virtue."

46. Syn., *De reg.* 15.7 (Νῦν οὖν ἀρ' ἄμεινον πράττετε, ἀφ' οὗ περὶ τοὺς βασιλέας ἡ τελετὴ συνέστη, καὶ θαλαμεύεσθε καθάπερ αἱ σαῦραι μόλις). Synesius followed Themistius's example when addressing current political circumstances. Eunomius and his followers, on whom there is more in chapter 8, were also denounced as lizards: see Vaggione, "Of Monks and Lounge Lizards."

47. Specifically, Dio Chrys., *Or.* 1–4, plus the *Euboean Oration* (*Or.* 7); Xen., *Cyr.*, plus *Ages.*; Arist., *Pol.* and *Eth. Nic.*; Hdt. 1 and 4; Pl., *Rep.* and *Leg.* See also Lamoureux and Aujoulat, *Opuscule II*, 56–82; Schmitt, *Die Bekehrung*, 294–99; Alvino, "Osservazioni," 179–81; Petkas, "King in Words," 133–46; Amande, "Il lexikon di Sinesio."

48. Syn., *De reg.* 19–20 (Lacombrade); quote in Cameron and Long, *Barbarians*, 109.

Empire.[49] Following Peter Heather's analysis, these "Scythians" are now generally identified as a combined force of Greuthungi and Tervingi under Alaric.[50] In 397, as mentioned in chapter 6, Eutropius negotiated a settlement with Alaric, offering him the title and income of a *magister militum*. That appointment made Alaric a military leader of the first rank, able to command imperial troops, and an *illustris vir*, permitted to appear at ceremonial occasions alongside the consuls. This was an unprecedented advancement, even less favorably received than Theodosius's peace agreement of 382 (see chapter 4).[51] On first reading, Synesius's anti-Scythian tirade demands that Alaric and his Goths, whom he considered a new "race" (*genos*), be removed from the empire.[52] However, the picture assumes additional nuances once placed in the broader context of his intertexts and with a view toward his use of Eutropius. What if Synesius's anti-Scythian tirade attacked Alaric and Eutropius as sharing a certain Scythianness because they were both eunuchlike?

As every reader of Herodotus knew, the Scythians were a people (*ethnos*) or race (*genos*) from a vast area near the Borysthenes River—that is, from an outer edge of the civilized world.[53] They were nomads, superbly skilled hunters, and ferocious warriors notorious for drinking their victims' blood.[54] Some were the descendants of enslaved persons; at some point a Scythian war party, returning home after twenty-eight years, discovered that their wives had conceived with slaves in their absence, and those children were now in power. The old fighters swiftly trounced the new leaders by attacking them with whips, to which the offspring of the enslaved reacted as slaves would: they turned their backs and ran.[55] Pacatus evoked the same passage to denigrate Magnus Maximus's less-than-manly army (see chapter 1).

Further, according to Herodotus, some Scythians had pillaged a temple of Aphrodite in Syria, for which the enraged goddess had punished them and their descendants with the "female disease." Ever since, their priests and diviners had dressed and acted like women and were known as "the Enarees, the

---

49. See Hagl, *Arcadius*, 23–36, for an overview.

50. Heather, "Anti-Scythian Tirade," 159–72. Tribigild had been suggested earlier: see Albert, *Goten*, 54–55; Lizzi Testa, "Significato filosofico."

51. Rummel, *Habitus barbarus*, 148–55; Schmitt, *Die Bekehrung*, 282–99, 304–58; S. Elm, "Isis' Loss"; Kulikowski, "Nation versus Army," 75–81.

52. Syn., *De reg.* 19.6 (*homogenes*), 20.2 (*genos*). The term *genos* oscillates in meaning among "race," "people," and "ethnic group": see Dench, *Romulus' Asylum*, 257–64. See also Mac Sweeney, "Race and Ethnicity."

53. Hdt. 4.67.1–144, 1.105.131–40. See also Ps.-Hipp. 17–22. The sixth-century BCE geographer Hecataeus first described the region near today's Dnieper in Ukraine as Scythia: see West, "Herodotus and Scythia"; West, "Scythians"; Romm, *Edges of the Earth*, 67, 75n72; Hartog, *Mirror of Herodotus*, 191. See also Ziche, "Barbarian Raiders."

54. Hdt. 4.59–66; Shaw, "'Eaters of Flesh'"; Harrell, "Marvelous *Andreia*."

55. Hdt. 4.1–3.

androgynes."[56] The author of the treatise *Airs, Waters, Places* was even more explicit in describing the ambiguous manliness of the Scythians. In his view, the cold, wet climate of their inhospitable region made Scythian men likewise moist, cold, and soft, while their women became moist and fat, conditions most inauspicious for procreation.[57] Moreover, Scythian leaders were constantly jostled around on horseback, which sapped their strength so that very little was left for intercourse; only cauterization (of their joints) offered sufficient heat to bring forth occasional results.[58] In sum, "very many" Scythian men "become eunuchlike and work and converse just as women do; such men are called 'Anarieis.' Now the [Scythians] attribute the blame for this to a god [of Syrian origin] and revere and do obeisance to these men."[59] Consequently, their leaders were "among the most eunuchlike peoples on earth."[60]

These are the associations that Synesius—and his audience—had in mind when he declared that "these Scythians—as Herodotus says and we can easily see now— are all affected by the disease of effeminate weakness."[61] That disease, to reiterate, made Scythians, and particularly their leaders, eunuchlike. As such, they distinctly resembled Arcadius's most powerful adviser, who was likewise rather truncated. Whenever Synesius attacked Alaric as a Scythian, therefore, this eunuchlikeness resonated and pointed to Eutropius: both were "affected by the disease of effemi- nate weakness." Phrased differently, the "Scythian" Alaric became eunuchlike and the eunuch Eutropius was Scythianized—and their essential likeness explained the extraordinarily favorable conditions that the powerful chamberlain

56. Hdt. 1.105, 1.131–140, 4.67; Pl., *Symp.* 189e; and Plut., *Mor.* 219e, use *androgynos* as a synonym for "effeminate," whereas Origen, *c. Cels.* 3.36, uses "female illness" instead. See also Chiasson, "Scythian Androgyny"; Ballabriga, "Les eunuques Scythes."

57. Ps.-Hipp. 22.13. Women were generally considered to be wetter than men and had to dis- charge excess moisture through menstruation. To be moist was thus constitutive of women. See King, *Hippocrates' Woman*, 75–98.

58. Ps.-Hipp. 21.1 (Οὔτε γὰρ τῷ ἀνδρὶ ἡ ἐπιθυμίη τῆς μίξιος γίνεται πολλὴ διὰ τὴν ὑγρότητα τῆς φύσιος καὶ τῆς κοιλίης τὴν μαλακότητά τε καὶ τὴν ψυχρότητα, ἀπ' ὅτων ἥκιστα εἰκὸς [εἶναι] ἄνδρα οἷόν τε λαγνεύειν, καὶ ἔτι ὑπὸ τῶν ἵππων ἀεὶ κοπτόμενοι ἀσθενεῖς γίνονται ἐς τὴν μῖξιν). See also Ps.- Hipp. 20.1; Messis, *Les eunuques*, 53–61, for the medical context.

59. Ps.-Hipp. 22.1–2 (ἔτι τε πρὸς τούτοισιν εὐνουχίαι γίνονται [οἱ] πλεῖστοι ἐν Σκύθῃσι καὶ γυναικεῖα ἐργάζονται διαλέγονταί τε ὁμοίως καὶ αἱ γυναῖκες· καλεῦνταί τε οἱ τοιοῦτοι Ἀναριεῖς. οἱ μὲν οὖν ἐπιχώριοι τὴν αἰτίην προστιθέασι θεῷ καὶ σέβονταί τε τούτους τοὺς ἀνθρώπους καὶ προσκυνέουσι δεδοικότες περὶ γ' ἑωυτῶν ἕκαστοι). See also 22.8. A Syrian god (or goddess) as a cause of androgyny also informed Claudian's references (e.g., *Eutr.* 1.133–42) to Syria and Assyria, as well as the tradition that the Assyrian queen Semiramis invented eunuchs. See also Lucian, *Syr. D.* 51; Amm. Marc. 14.6.17; *HA, Heliogab.* 7.3; Guyot, *Eunuchen*, 40n.15, 77–91.

60. Ps.-Hipp. 22.13 (Ταῦτα δὲ τοῖσι Σκύθῃσι πρόσεστι καὶ εὐνουχοειδέστατοί εἰσιν ἀνθρώπων διὰ τὰς <προειρημένας> προφάσιας). See also Chiasson, "Scythian Androgyny," 41–53, for a nuanced discussion.

61. Syn., *De reg.* 21.1 (Σκύθας δὲ τούτους Ἡρόδοτός τέ φησι καὶ ἡμεῖς ὁρῶμεν κατεχομένους ἅπαντας ὑπὸ νόσου θηλείας).

and future consul had granted Alaric. Such less-than-manly men now controlled the (eunuchlike) jellyfishy emperor and the empire of the Romans.

To be sure, this was a scathing indictment of soft, youthful, capacious imperial *vir*-ness, albeit wrongly paired and hence without good advice. It had come to this because Arcadius, hiding like a lizard or spineless mollusk, had neglected the quintessential duty of a Roman emperor: military command. Rather than take part in his soldiers' exercises, steel himself in their camps, and entrust the defense of the realm to its native population, whom he ought to draft by force, he had ceded Rome's weapons to Scythians. That—and now we are in mid-anti-Scythian tirade—was an outrage. "How can we tolerate that the foreigners [*allotrioi*] are now the men among us? Is it not exceedingly shameful that in the empire that is the richest in good men [*euandrotatos*] the love of [military] glory [*philotimia*] has been handed over to others [*heteroi*]?"[62] The situation was utterly disgraceful. Rome's men were becoming progressively less manly. Even if these foreigners won victory after victory, that would be a cause for shame, because nothing, neither fraternal bonds nor a common *genos*, would prevent them from overpowering unarmed Roman civilians. These persons, so profoundly other, were now the ones who carried the weapons.[63]

Beginning with Arcadius, Rome had to reacquaint itself with the art of war. The emperor must leave the bedchamber and acquire the old Roman imperial virtues, the hard beauty of the Spartan soldier in all its simplicity, because "everything is on a razor's edge."[64] Scythians must be removed—most urgently not, as one might expect, from the army, but from high imperial office and the Senate. "I believe that today Themis, the goddess of the Senate, and the god of battle cover their heads in shame when the man in fur pelts commands those in the chlamys. And then he changes the fur for the toga and deliberates with Roman senators about politics, sitting in the place of honor next to the consuls and in front of the legitimate dignitaries. But as soon as they step outside the Senate's doors, they dress again in their furs and laugh with their companions about the toga, in which, they say, one cannot swiftly draw one's sword."[65] Such scenes caused Synesius to wonder what in the

62. Syn., *De reg.* 19.6 (Πῶς οὖν ἀνεκτὸν παρ' ἡμῖν ἀλλότριον εἶναι τὸ ἄρρεν; πῶς δὲ οὐκ αἴσχιον παραχωρῆσαι τὴν εὐανδροτάτην ἀρχὴν ἑτέροις τῆς ἐν πολέμῳ φιλοτιμίας).

63. Syn., *De reg.* 19.6 (ὅταν τὰ λεγόμενα ταῦτα, τὸ ἄρρεν τε καὶ τὸ θῆλυ, μήτε ἀδελφὰ τυγχάνῃ μήτε ἄλλως ὁμογενῆ, μικρὰ πρόφασις ἀρκέσει τοὺς ὡπλισμένους τῶν ἀστυπολούντων δεσπότας ἀξιοῦν εἶναι). Rather than an accurate description of the Goths, what mattered was their "otherness": see Gruen, *Rethinking the Other*, 1–5; Emmrich, *Ästhetische Monsterpolitiken*, 14–16, 187–98.

64. Syn., *De reg.* 16.1 (ἀληθινοῦ βασιλέως κάλλους), 18.2 (νῦν γὰρ πάντες ἐπὶ ξυροῦ ἵστανται ἀκμῆς).

65. Syn., *De reg.* 20.1 (ἐπεὶ νῦν γε καὶ τὴν βουλαίαν Θέμιν αὐτὴν καὶ θεὸν οἶμαι τὸν στράτιον ἐγκαλύπτεσθαι, ὅταν ὁ σισυροφόρος ἄνθρωπος ἐξηγῆται χλαμύδας ἐχόντων, καί, ὅταν ἀποδύς τις ὅπερ ἐνῆπτο κώδιον, περιβάληται τήβεννον καὶ τοῖς Ῥωμαίων τέλεσι συμφροντίζῃ περὶ τῶν καθεστώτων, προεδρίαν ἔχων παρ' αὐτόν που τὸν ὕπατον, νομίζων ἀνδρῶν ὀπίσω θακούντων. ἀλλ' οὗτοί γε μικρὸν τοῦ βουλευτερίου προκύψαντες, αὖθις ἐν τοῖς κωδίοις εἰσί, καί, ὅταν τοῖς ὀπαδοῖς συγέννωνται,

world Rome had come to. The overt target was Alaric, but he sat, above legitimate dignitaries, next to the consul Eutropius: two "Scythians" who should be removed from such high positions.

Synesius bristled at least as much at the following absurdity (*atopia*): Every Roman family, including his own, and even those of modest means, owned at least one Scythian slave.[66] Scythians served at table, cooked, and carried water and the litters on which Romans reclined.[67] This led to the ludicrous situation in which the same people who were slaves at home were masters in public. It also reversed the laws and norms that regulated Roman family and society, according to which men were in charge of external affairs, while women and eunuchs looked after the home. Instead, now young (eunuchlike) Scythian men with long blond hair worn "in the Euboean style" controlled Rome's security. These un-Roman men, whose Scythian nature made them inherently untrustworthy, since they were inclined toward enslavement, lacked manly restraint and were likely to erupt in revolt at the slightest provocation.[68]

EUTROPIUS THE SCYTHIAN AND ARCADIUS
THE NEW ACHILLES

Read together with the descriptions of Scythians offered by Herodotus and by *Airs, Waters, Places*, Synesius's anti-Scythian tirade reveals a constant interplay between warfare and eunuchlike behavior. Scythians were prone to enslavement because they descended from slaves, and they were eunuchlike by "nature" because the moist, cold conditions of their native region combined with horse riding and divine wrath to saddle them with the "female disease": their leaders dressed and acted as women. However, this "female disease" went hand in hand with ferocious bloodthirst in battle. Alaric, dressed in fur pelts and ridiculing his fellow senators, fit the bill. Indeed, as we saw in chapter 4, being a fearsome warrior and wearing women's clothes was no contradiction and, moreover, not necessarily a negative combination: its valence depended very much on who wore these clothes.

Just as Claudian evoked Eutropius as a monstrous portent, Synesius stressed Arcadius's refusal to act as a Roman emperor as a dire warning to him to change his advisers, behave as he should, and alter the status quo for the better. Unlike

---

τῆς τηβέννου καταγελῶσι, μεθ' ἧς οὐκ εἶναί φασι ξιφουλκίας εὐμοιρίαν). See also Rummel, *Habitus barbarus*, 148–55.

66. Syn., *Enc. Cal.* 13.

67. Syn., *De reg.* 20.2 (ἅπας γὰρ οἶκος ὁ καὶ κατὰ μικρὸν εὖ πράττων Σκυθικὸν ἔχει τὸν δοῦλον, καὶ ὁ τραπεζοποιός καὶ ὁ περὶ τὸν ἰπνόν, καὶ ὁ ἀμφορεαφόρος Σκύθης ἐστὶν ἑκάστῳ, τῶν τε ἀκολούθων οἱ τοὺς ὀκλαδίας ἐπὶ τῶν ὤμων ἀνατιθέμενοι, ἐφ' ᾧ τοῖς ἐωνημένοις ἐν ταῖς ἀγυιαῖς εἶναι καθίζεσθαι, Σκῦθαι πάντες εἰσίν; ἄνωθεν ἀποδεδειγμένου τοῦ γένους ἐπιτηδείου τε καὶ ἀξιωτάτου δουλεύειν Ῥωμαίοις).

68. Syn., *De reg.* 20.3 (Τὸ δὲ τοὺς ξανθοὺς τούτους καὶ κομῶντας Εὐβοϊκῶς).

Claudian's ferocious attacks on Eutropius, however, Synesius's were veiled and meant to entertain rather than destroy. By aligning Alaric, subtly but clearly, with Eutropius, and both with "Scythians," Synesius criticized the extent (rather than the kind) of Arcadius's softness: thanks to his current, eunuchlike advisers, it was decidedly too jellyfishy. Nonetheless, Synesius did use harshness to try to shock the ruler into action so that his fictional statue of words might become animated and real. The actual Arcadius was (like Honorius) a new Achilles. But he was hesitating too long before rejoining the battle. In principle, there was nothing wrong with his being soft and capaciously manly like the young Achilles had been, in ways that incorporated the fluidity of women. But now it was high time that he erupt as a fierce epic warrior to show the world how "great is the rage [*thymos*] of the rulers [*basileis*], the sons of Zeus!"[69] Arcadius, a new Achilles and new Odysseus, must "drive away these ill-omened dogs."[70]

As the evocation of Achilles demonstrates, imperial softness was not negative per se if it was appropriately paired with hard, warriorlike firmness, as we also saw in the previous chapters. Honorius and Stilicho exemplified one such layering of soft and hard, and Synesius here proposes another one, this time through a complete change of advisers. As a father and experienced ruler, Arcadius did not need a Stilicho. On the contrary, Alaric was already too much like that deceiving, less-than-manly, "Scythian" "public enemy." Eutropius did not fit the bill as an ideal adviser either, to put it mildly. Instead, rather than rely on one or even two less-than-manly *illustres viri*, Arcadius should emulate the rulers of old and broaden the circle of his advisers, this time including only "Roman senators" and "legitimate dignitaries."[71] Indeed, a deeper dive into his intertexts suggests that Synesius did not advocate getting rid of Alaric, Goths, or Eutropius altogether. Rather, once the emperor selected the right friends, their hardness would rip him out of the lassitude of softness wrongly understood, help him adopt the ideal image that Synesius now created, and allow him to treat those two eunuchlike Scythians as what they truly were: immensely useful guard dogs.

Synesius and his audience knew perfectly well that the "Scythians" at issue were Tervingi and Greuthungi from the region north and east of the lower Danube.[72] Calling them Scythians showed literary sophistication and inserted them into the well-known ethnographic templates I have just discussed. But Synesius also made clear that these templates could be insufficient: those who now aligned to threaten the realm as Scythians, Massagetai, or Getae were even worse than those who had originally carried these names. Though some of their features were recognizable, the Massagetai in particular were unlike any foe Romans had encountered

69. Hom., *Il.* 2.196.
70. Syn., *De reg.* 21.5, quoting Hom., *Il.* 8.527.
71. Syn., *De reg.* 20.1.
72. Batty, *Rome and the Nomads*, 192–214, 387–99.

before.[73] Synesius's depiction of the Massagetai evokes Ammianus Marcellinus, who first described the new Hunnic forces that had defeated Valens at Adrianople.[74] Like Herodotus's classic Scythians, they were savage warriors, nomadic meat eaters lusting after gold and booty, unrestrained by social order, "two-legged beasts" barely able to walk because they spent their lives riding, and dressed in ragged cloaks made of mice pelts.[75] But their faces showed their difference and repelled Ammianus most: they were all as ugly as eunuchs (*spadones*) because they slashed the cheeks of their young boys with knives to prevent the sprouting of beards.[76] Whether Ammianus's work is an intertext of *De regno* is difficult to ascertain, but Synesius's description of the Massagetai as peoples who "falsified their appearance through artful means as if to show that a new and unusual race [*genos neon*] has sprung up from the earth, demanding money in exchange for peace," echoes both Ammianus and the falsified nature of Arcadius's current, truncated advisers.[77] Eunuch references abound.

At the same time, like Ammianus, Synesius left no doubt that these barbarians were fierce warriors. Indeed, their very eunuchlikeness made them more bloodthirsty, because their lack of manliness resulted in lack of restraint, even in warfare.[78] What rendered Scythians so untrustworthy—their otherness, particularly their androgynous malleability, embodied by the man in pelts who could assume and shed the toga and hence his "Romanness" at will—also made them dangerous when carrying weapons.[79] But the reverse was also true: if ferocious Scythians could be androgynous, or eunuchlike (*androgyne* was in fact a synonym for "eunuch"), then eunuchs could be ferocious warriors.[80] Eutropius, after all, had

73. Syn., *De reg.* 15.8.

74. Amm. Marc. 31.2.1–12. See also Eunap., *Hist.* 42; Burgersdijk, "Creating the Enemy"; G. Kelly, *Ammianus Marcellinus*, 13–30; Kulikowski, "Coded Polemic" (argues that Ammianus originally published his ethnographic digression on the Huns separately in Greek); Heather, "Huns and Barbarian Europe"; Lenski, *Failure of Empire*, 354–55; Matthews, *Roman Empire*, 304–82.

75. Amm. Marc. 31.2.11 ("cupidine immense flagrantes"), 31.2.12 ("aviditate flagrans immani"), 31.2.2 ("bipedes existimes bestias").

76. Amm. Marc. 31.2.2 ("Ubi quoniam ab ipsis nascendi primitiis infantum ferro sulcantur altius genae, ut pilorum vigor tempestivus emergens, corrugatis cicatricibus hebetetur, senescunt imberbes absque ulla venustate, spadonibus similes, compactis omnis firmisque membris et opimis cervicibus, prodigiose deformes et pandi, ut bipedes existimes bestias, vel quales in commarginandis pontibus effigiati stipites dolantur incompte").

77. Syn., *De reg.* 15.8.

78. Syn., *De reg.* 21.1, 21.4–5. See also Maas, "Barbarians," for the relationship between being a barbarian and being manly; Maas, "Strabo and Procopius," 77–80.

79. See McInerney, "Plutarch's Manly Women"; for the longevity of these tropes, Betancourt, *Byzantine Intersectionality*, 191–98.

80. Eunuchs often accompanied emperors into battle. Valentinian's chief eunuch, who carried the emperor's helmet, perished in a campaign against Alemanni, and Valens's eunuchs died with him at Adrianople, as did Julian's near Ctesiphon. See Messis, *Les eunuques*, 45–52; Tougher, "Eunuchs in the East," 151–55.

successfully repelled Hunnic incursions in 397 (just as Synesius arrived in Constantinople) and 398—with the help of Alaric's Goths.[81] No wonder Eutropius had treated Alaric so favorably: they had sought each other out because they were alike. But how could Synesius's Arcadius best use the "Scythian" Eutropius and the "eunuchlike" Alaric to further his ends?

CYRUS'S BEST MEN

The Persian Cyrus the Great offered the solution: Synesius's ideal Arcadius need not remove his eunuchlike Scythians, even once he finally emulated old-time "Spartan" Roman emperors and Achilles and Odysseus, as amply demonstrated by Cyrus, another time-honored model of excellent kingship. Cyrus and the Spartan king Agesilaus II had become "most famous among the barbarians and Greeks," as Synesius emphasized, because they had chosen the right friends and avoided flattering sycophants.[82] Those friends helped both rulers to become active philosopher-kings, demonstrating the virtues of piety (*eusebeia*), foresight (*phronesis*), and self-control (*sophrosyne*).[83] Xenophon had written famous guides to good kingship about these two: *Agesilaus* and (even more relevantly) the *Cyropaideia*, which Synesius mentioned directly.[84] Themistius too had evoked the *Cyropaideia* to praise Gratian, because Cyrus was a particularly apt model for young Roman emperors.[85] The Persian knew that it was impossible to rule the greatest (multiethnic) empire the world had ever seen without his friends as eyes and ears.[86] Therefore, as Synesius stressed, it had been his maxim to "decide what to do and confirm his decision with his friends, [remembering that] to act effectively he will need many hands."[87]

Digging once again into Synesius's intertexts reveals his audience's associations when he evoked Cyrus as one of (the ideal) Arcadius's most important models. Xenophon's *Cyropaideia* illustrates the Persian king's immense success in, first, creating an enormous empire and, second, preserving its stability. The latter was the truly remarkable achievement. Cyrus managed it thanks to

---

81. Sidéris, "Rise and Fall," 72–73.

82. Syn., *De reg.* 12.1–2.

83. Syn., *De reg.* 4.1–5.3, 8.1–10.6, 11.1–12.1, 13.1. For these virtues, see also Themistius (e.g., *Or.* 22, 23, 26); Gregory of Nazianzus (e.g., *Or.* 2.11–14); S. Elm, *Sons of Hellenism*, 98–106, 166–72, 206–12.

84. Synesius referred to the *Agesilaus*, which negotiates issues of Greekness, but privileged the *Cyropaideia*: see Harman, "Spectacle of Greekness"; Gray, *Xenophon's Mirror of Princes*, 278–79; Gera, *Xenophon's "Cyropaideia,"* 288; Carlier, "L'idée de monarchie."

85. Them., *Or.* 13.169c–171c. See also Dio Chrys., *Or.* 3.104–107.

86. Xen., *Cyr.* 7.5.61–65, 8.2.10–12; Gray, *Xenophon's Mirror of Princes*, 246–90.

87. Syn., *De reg.* 12.2 (Τοῦτό γέ τοι καὶ Κῦρον τὸν πάνυ καὶ Ἀγησίλαον ὀνομαστοτάτους βασιλέων ἐν Ἕλλησι καὶ βαρβάροις ἐποίησε. γνώσεται μὲν δὴ τὰ ποιητέα καὶ γνώμην ἐν τοῖς φίλοις κυρώσει· ἵνα δὲ ἔργα γένηται, χειρῶν αὐτῷ δεῖ πολλῶν). See also Xen., *Cyr.* 8.1.45–48, 8.2.10–12.

the rules he established at his court.[88] All members of the Persian elite had to maintain the virtuous habits they had acquired during the empire's expansion, including to serve and honor each other.[89] Those closest to the king had to be particularly scrupulous, because they set the example for everyone else.[90] Display was an essential tool to make these virtues visible, and Cyrus selected sumptuous, jewel-encrusted robes that made him and his courtiers look "most tall and beautiful"; only when his descendants abandoned the hard habits of old did those robes start to signal less-than-manly luxury.[91] Occasionally, Cyrus retreated inside the palace to enhance the dignity of the ruler through absence.[92] At all times, however, he overwhelmed his friends with gifts, honors, and loving affection. In response, all followed his commands willingly and acted as his eyes and ears out of devotion.[93]

Cyrus was, further, famous for the way he treated his eunuchs.[94] He considered them perfect friends and most loyal followers of exemplary faith (*pistis, fides*). "Given that eunuchs are objects of contempt to the rest of mankind, for this reason, if for no other, they need a master who will protect them, because there is no man who would not consider it good to prove his complete superiority to a eunuch if there were no superior force to oppose him. But if subjected to the [right] master, nothing prevents him, eunuch that he is, from occupying the first place [as leader] [*proteuein*]."[95]

Because Cyrus was the right master, he trusted his eunuchs with his scepter, made them his bodyguards, and charged them with administering the palace, a task to which their softness predisposed them.[96] Most important, he knew that this softness did not diminish his eunuchs' *andreia*, or manly courage. "What one might most normally think, that eunuchs are cowardly, is not how it appeared to Cyrus. . . . He observed . . . that aggressive horses if cut [castrated] no longer bite and kick, but they are nonetheless warlike, and bulls when cut no longer bully and disobey, but they still have their force and their ability to work, and

---

88. Xen., *Cyr.* 4.3.3–22, 7.5.72–86 (Persia declined under his successors because they ignored these rules and customs).

89. Xen., *Cyr.* 7.5.83, 8.7.13–16; Gray, *Xenophon's Mirror of Princes*, 243–44, 260.

90. Xen., *Cyr.* 8.1.6–8, 8.1.14, 8.1.21, 8.5.5.

91. Xen., *Cyr.* 8.1.40 (quote), 8.1.40–42, 8.8.16–19; Danzig, "Best of the Achaemenids."

92. Xen., *Cyr.* 7.37–56, 8.1.6, 8.1.16–20; Gray, *Xenophon's Mirror of Princes*, 277–82.

93. Xen., *Cyr.* 8.2.10–12, 8.1.45–48. See also Syn., *De reg.* 11.4.

94. Azoulay, "Xénophon"; Guyot, *Eunuchen*, 80–91; Messis, *Les eunuques*, 13–16; Tougher, *Eunuch*, 7–10, 43–44; Ringrose, *Perfect Servant*, 130–41 (*Cyropaideia*'s relevance for Byzantine attitudes toward eunuchs).

95. Xen., *Cyr.* 7.5.61 (Πρὸς δὲ τούτοις ἄδοξοι ὄντες οἱ εὐνοῦχοι παρὰ τοῖς ἄλλοις ἀνθρώποις καὶ διὰ τοῦτο δεσπότου ἐπικούρου προσδέονται· οὐδεὶς γὰρ ἀνὴρ ὅστις οὐκ ἂν ἀξιώσειεν εὐνούχου πλέον ἔχειν ἐν παντί, εἰ μή τι ἄλλο κρεῖττον ἀπείργοι· δεσπότῃ δὲ πιστὸν ὄντα οὐδὲν κωλύει πρωτεύειν καὶ τὸν εὐνοῦχον). See also Azoulay, "Xénophon," 19–20.

96. Xen., *Cyr.* 8.4.2–7, 7.5.6, 7.5.65, 5.5.28–29.

dogs likewise."[97] Indeed, eunuchs still excelled in "horsemanship, . . . aim, [and] love of [military] glory [*philotimia*]."[98] They were extremely effective military commanders because the cruelty they had experienced made them fight even more ferociously. Moreover, as a successful general, a eunuch demonstrated particularly clearly how well he was controlled by his king—that the latter was, in short, a very good master.[99] According to Xenophon, Cyrus even preferred eunuchs to his own sons, because their effectiveness and unconditional loyalty made them perfect servants.[100]

IMPERIAL SOFTNESS AND PERFECT SERVANTS

Herodotus's Scythians and those of *Airs, Waters, Places* were highly effective warriors with eunuchlike physical features and the disposition of the enslaved, while Xenophon's Cyrus praised eunuchs as excellent military leaders and perfect servants—provided they were controlled by the right master. Synesius's present-day Arcadius was a soft, mollusk-like ruler, truncated by his adviser, a eunuch who had shown military acumen but damaged the emperor by colluding with a Scythian military leader. This was untenable, but on closer examination, Synesius's well-known intertexts imply that in his opinion, Scythians need not be removed *tout court* from the empire's administration and military. Much like Alaric and Eutropius, they caused harm only if left unchecked and allowed to rise too high. If their powers were properly managed, however, they could be enormously useful. As soon as Arcadius remembered that he ought to be like Achilles, "youthful and valiant, a man who inspires terror [*deinos aner*]," and acted as a Roman imperial master should, he would be able to harness these powers for Rome's good.[101] For this to happen, he must pair his imperial softness—not negative per se—with new advisers who were appropriate manly, in full possession of *andreia*: men like Aurelian. Then and only then might all turn out well. Placed in the broader frame of his intertexts, Synesius's analysis reveals a larger measure of realpolitik than a first reading might suggest. Indeed, this appraisal of Rome's dependence on Goths befits a member of the eastern elite who was as astute a seismograph of power as the author of *De regno*.

97. Xen., *Cyr.* 7.5.62.

98. Xen., *Cyr.* 7.5.63 (Καὶ οἵ γε ἄνθρωποι ὡσαύτως ἠρεμέστεροι γίγνονται στερισκόμενοι ταύτης τῆς ἐπιθυμίας, οὐ μέντοι ἀμελέστεροί γε τῶν προσταττομένων, οὐδ' ἧττόν τι ἱππικοί, οὐδὲ ἧττόν τι ἀκοντιστικοί, οὐδὲ ἧττον φιλότιμοι).

99. Xen., *Cyr.* 7.5.58–60.

100. Xen., *Cyr.* 7.5.60, 8.2.9–14. See also Xen., *Anab.* 1.8.28–29; Azoulay, "Xénophon," 21–22; Börm, "Barbaren als Tyrannen."

101. Syn., *De reg.* 21.5: ἀλλ' ἐξηγεῖταί τις αὐτῶν νέος τε καὶ γενναῖος, 'δεινὸς ἀνήρ, τάχα κεν καὶ ἀναίτιον αἰτιόῳτο' (that among [the Romans] governs someone youthful and valiant, "a man who inspires terror, and can even accuse an innocent friend"). *Deinos aner* is Achilles's quintessential epithet, used by Patroclus: see Hom., *Il.* 11.654.

In such a real-political view, it was appropriate that the emperor as arbiter of *vir*-ness had made Eutropius an *illustris vir, patricius,* and even consul, because Eutropius was a successful military leader who acted with *andreia* and *philotimia.* Thus, he deserved to be honored, even with a triumphal *adventus* into Constantinople.[102] Eutropius was powerful because useful. He also made manifest the new imperial language of soft power. But even that was not negative, unless it went too far. Unfortunately, Eutropius's position *did* go too far and was a step too high, because it was uncontested—that is, not framed and controlled by other, manly advisers (who would act as his masters). Likewise, as we have seen, it was not essential that emperors fight battles to be considered victorious: that is what their military leaders were there to do. When Synesius was writing, many of those leaders were Goths, Alans, or Franks; that was by then a given. As the long list of consuls with Gothic, Frankish, or Alan names confirms, those commanders who did what the emperor asked, preferably by winning battles, became Roman, and the more successful they were the faster this happened. Their Romanness was conferred upon them by the emperor, who honored them as consuls or in similar ways—analogous to how *vir*-ness was bestowed.

But here too Arcadius had gone too far. Because he had given too much power to Eutropius, the latter had given too much power too soon to his kindred—the Scythian Alaric. As a result, persons who only pretended to be Roman men now sat next to each other in the highest positions in the Senate, above true Romans, and thus reversed the "natural" hierarchical order, according to which Roman men commanded all others. Gothic commanders could wear the toga, become Roman, as long as it was clear that they served at the pleasure of their master, the Roman emperor, and not the other way round, throwing on their Gothic pelts as they saw fit. This was not how perfect servants acted. In Synesius's view, Alaric's capacity to change from toga to pelt at his whim revealed that Arcadius in his present state had a major representation problem.

That was the great stumbling block preventing the ideal Arcadius from emerging: he did not act or look sufficiently Roman. But what would make imperial *vir*-ness look unmistakably Roman when the language of power included softness? For Synesius, imperial *andreia,* or Romanness, meant action that demonstrated domination. His ideal Arcadius signaled such active domination in ways that made him legible as a distinctly Roman Achilles and Cyrus, for example by going out and campaigning with his armies (without necessarily fighting). He would offer peace treaties only after he had crushed the enemy sufficiently to show Rome's superiority. Then he could demonstrate as much love of mankind as he chose. But even when embracing the defeated with divine philanthropy, he would be sure to settle them in an appropriate manner and keep them sufficiently distant from his person

---

102. Claud., *Eutr.* 1.252–286.

(and his residence) to avoid giving the impression of too much imperial softness. Eutropius and Alaric were simply too close for comfort.

Arcadius's insufficient demonstration of manly imperial dominance was, however, something he had inherited from Theodosius. When, as Synesius's audience recalled, certain Scythians who had been chased from their homeland arrived at Theodosius's court as supplicants, he had shown them his divine love of mankind (*philanthropia*).[103] As soon as these ignorant Scythians had discovered, to their surprise, that the feared Romans were softer, or more sexually passive (*malakoteros*), than they had anticipated, they repaid the gift (*euergesia*) of imperial philanthropy with insolence.[104] Theodosius immediately and properly crushed them. When he noticed, however, that the defeated were accompanied by their wives and children, he was moved to show them mercy (*eleos*) and in his imperial magnanimity (*megalophones*) granted them honors, citizenship, and land to settle. Alas, these uneducated barbarians failed to grasp the meaning of the manly virtue (*arete*) that Theodosius thus demonstrated. They ridiculed the emperor's kindness (*philophrosyne*) as a sign of appeasement and encouraged other Scythians to flock to Rome to abuse his charity.

This was the flip side of Theodosius's reconceptualization of imperial philanthropy as victorious weapon. In the same way that softness as a language of imperial power, or *vir*-ness, could be construed as jellyfishiness, love of mankind, when combined with too much mercy and charity, could be mistaken for weakness. First Theodosius had used imperial philanthropy correctly: he had granted it after demonstrating proper Roman harshness. But then he had allowed too much mercy, a virtue with female connotations, to enter the equation and had promptly been perceived as too soft by the uneducated, who could not parse that form of virtue, or *arete*.[105] Arcadius had augmented that softness even further. Now, to restore Romanness to philanthropy, he had to give it spine through well-placed rage. Like Achilles, he must occasionally erupt and make these Scythians "till the fields, by order, as once upon a time the Messenians served the Spartans as helots after having abandoned their arms, or else chase them away to where they came

103. Syn., *De reg.* 21.2–6.

104. Syn., *De reg.* 21.2–3 (Μαλακωτέροις δὲ ἐντυχόντες, οὐ τοῖς ὅπλοις Ῥωμαίων, ἀλλὰ τοῖς ἤθεσιν, ὥσπερ ἴσως ἔδει πρὸς ἱκέτας, γένος ἀμαθὲς τὸ εἰκὸς ἀπεδίδου καὶ ἐθρασύνετο καὶ ἠγνωμόνει τὴν εὐεργεσίαν, ὑπερ οὗ πατρὶ τῷ σῷ δίκας ἐπ' αὐτοὺς ὡπλισμένῳ διδόντες αὖθις ἦσαν οἰκτροὶ καὶ ἱκέται σὺν γυναιξὶν ἐκαθίζον· ὁ δὲ τῷ πολέμῳ νικῶν ἐλέῳ παρὰ πλεῖστον ἡττᾶτο, καὶ ἀνίστη τῆς ἱκετείας, καὶ συμμάχους ἐποίει, καὶ πολιτείας ἠξίου, καὶ μετεδίδου γερῶν καὶ γῆς τι ἐδάσατο τοῖς παλαμναίοις Ῥωμαϊκῆς, ἀνὴρ τῷ μεγαλόφρονι καὶ γενναίῳ τῆς φύσεως ἐπὶ τὸ πρᾶον χρησάμενος). For *malakos*, see Messis, *Les eunuques*, 20–22, 93–96; Martin, "*Arsenokoites* and *Malakos*;" Sapsford, *Performing the Kinaidos*, 100–1.

105. For contemporary assessments of the gendered connotations of philanthropy, see the fourth-century Ps.-Clem., *Hom.* 12.26.6–8: "Listen how this is so: *philanthropia* is androgynous, part male and part female. Its female side is called *elemonsyne* [almsgiving] and its masculine side *agape* [charity] toward our neighbor. . . . But its feminine aspect is to show mercy [*to eleein*]. This is done by feeding the hungry, visiting the sick, receiving strangers." See also Caner, *Rich and the Pure*, 45–46.

from, so that they can spread the news to those on the other side of the river that the famous beguiling sweetness [*meilichia*] no longer holds sway in Rome," which is now instead ruled by a man who inspires terror and commands true Roman men.[106]

Not surprisingly, Synesius was short on details about how Arcadius should win crushing victories in practice, but he did reiterate that using Scythians to beat Scythians was fine as long as Romanness—capaciously defined—remained indisputably visible. Achieving that visibility would require the imperial actions already mentioned—choosing the right friends, campaigning, crushing enemies sufficiently, and settling Scythians correctly, ideally in the countryside—as the quote in the previous paragraph and one further look at Synesius's intertexts indicate. Recall that he bemoaned the overinvolvement in Rome's defense of young, blond Scythians who wore their hair "in the Euboean style."[107] Everyone knew that Homer had mentioned the Euboeans' long, backward-flowing hairstyle in the *Iliad*, and Synesius's most important literary model, Dio Chrysostom, had devoted an entire oration to a "man from Euboea."[108] For Synesius, that oration was "an outline of the happy life and one most worthy of perusal for rich and poor alike."[109] Dio's *Euboean Oration* compared and contrasted (once more) two ways of being a man. Two simple, self-sufficient men "with full beards and long hair, but not in the ugly fashion of the long hair at the back as Homer presents the Euboeans who came to Ilion" (which characterized them as not Greek), embodied good manliness.[110] They lived freely on land their fathers had acquired from a bad absentee landowner, executed by a good emperor, and spent their time hunting; even their dogs

106. Syn., *De reg.* 21.5 (quoting Hom., *Il.* 2.196) (θυμοῦ οὖν ἐπὶ τοὺς ἄνδρας, καὶ ἡ γεωργήσουσιν ἐξ ἐπιτάγματος, ὥσπερ πάλαι Λακεδαιμονίοις Μεσσήνιοι τὰ ὅπλα καταβαλόντες εἱλώτευον, ἢ φεύξονται τὴν αὐτὴν ὁδὸν αὖθις, τοῖς πέραν τοῦ ποταμοῦ διαγγέλλοντες, ὡς οὐκ ἐκεῖνα ἔτι παρὰ Ῥωμαίοις τὰ μείλιχα· ἀλλ' ἐξηγεῖταί τις αὐτῶν νέος τε καὶ γενναῖος, 'δεινὸς ἀνήρ, τάχα κεν καὶ ἀναίτιον αἰτιόῳτο'). *Meilichia*, as used, e.g., by Pind., *Ol.* 1.28–32, evokes the sweetness of a myth well told or an ivory statue well executed, but also erotic delight: see Steiner, *Images in Mind*, 282–86.

107. Syn., *De reg.* 20.3. Syn., *Enc. Cal.* 13 mentions the Euboean hairstyle of his Gothic slaves. These two passages have been interpreted as proof of distinct markers signaling Gothic identity: see Seng, "An den Haaren herbeigezogen;" Şare Ağtürk, *Painted Tetrarchic Reliefs*, 65–69, with illustrations. At Syn., *Enc. Cal.* 1, Terzaghi (190) declares that *In Praise of Baldness* responds jokingly to Dio Chrys., *In Praise of Hair*.

108. Hom., *Il.* 2.540–542. In 403 or 404, Synesius devoted an entire treaty to Dio: see Schmitt, *Die Bekehrung*, 67–121; Tanaseanu-Döbler, *Konversion*, 220–25; Rummel, *Habitus barbarus*, 161–63, 219–20. For the relevance of the *Euboikos logos* for Synesius, see Seng, "Die Kontroverse," 106–9; Op de Coul, "Aspects of *Paideia*."

109. Syn., *Dion* 2 (ὡς οὗτός γε ὁ λόγος ὑποτύπωσίς ἐστιν εὐδαίμονος βίου, πένητι καὶ πλουσίῳ τοῦ παντὸς ἀνάγνωμα ἀξιώτατον).

110. Dio. Chrys., *Or.* 7.4 (ὁρῶ . . . μετ' ὀλίγον ἄνδρα, κυνηγέτην ἀπὸ τῆς ὄψεως καὶ τῆς στολῆς, τὰ γένεια ὑγιῆ κομῶντα οὐ φαύλως οὐδὲ ἀγεννῶς ἐξόπισθεν, οἵους ἐπὶ Ἴλιον Ὅμηρός φησιν ἐλθεῖν Εὐβοέας).

had evolved from herding sheep to hunting.[111] Their opponents were debauched city dwellers who had hauled one of the huntsmen before a court of law, alleging that he was squatting on land he did not own.[112] His trial allowed Dio to indict the treatment of the urban poor.[113] Ideally, poor persons should live not in a city but on land given to them by a benevolent ruler.[114] If they had to live in cities, they should not be forced to participate in the tainted ways of the rich by decorating houses with multihued colors, gold, and ivory or working as dressmakers, makeup artists, and hairstylists who fashioned elaborate coiffures using the long hair of other men and women.[115] Such luxury destroyed Greek virtue (*arete*) and manliness and corrupted everyone, although the rich more than the poor.[116] It led rich men to lose all manly self-control, so they were unable to govern their wives and daughters. That made women of all ages and social classes sexually available, an overabundance to which young men, including future magistrates, judges, and generals, responded by turning toward each other instead.[117]

This context suggests that for Synesius, too many young, blond men with Euboean-style hair lived in Constantinople—specifically, they were too enmeshed with the very rich. The emperor in particular was surrounded, night and day, by his bodyguard of "slender young men with blond, flowing hair, 'their heads perfumed with salves and with a beautiful figure,' equipped with golden shields and golden spears."[118] That proximity prevented these young men from becoming properly Greek—that is, Roman—and living the simple life on land given to them by a good ruler. Dwelling instead in the city, they were easy prey for the luxurious corruption that had already lured future high-ranking magistrates into unbecoming same-sex encounters: if real men like them couldn't resist, how much could such Scythians? Too many young men who were too blond, too rosy-cheeked, and too Scythian, with flowing hair and golden spears, were too close to the emperor Arcadius, forging images and suggestions that were too unmanly, too un-Greek, and not imperially Roman.

Synesius's *On Kingship* was meant to amuse his audience and introduce himself as a new Themistius. Thus, he used an array of literary models and allusions to compose something worth noting: an ideal Arcadius, a statue of words that the

111. Dio. Chrys., *Or.* 7.11–12, 7.17.

112. Dio. Chrys., *Or.* 7.46–67.

113. Dio. Chrys., *Or.* 7.67–80; Hutton, "Importance of Dio's Travels," 1–18; Ma, "Public Speech," 108–24.

114. Dio. Chrys., *Or.* 7.105–7.

115. Dio. Chrys., *Or.* 7.117–18.

116. Dio. Chrys., *Or.* 7.119–22.

117. Dio. Chrys., *Or.* 7.151–52. See also Plin., *Ep.* 3.4.3–6; Juv. 2.44, 9.27–54; Mart., *Epigr.* 9.47 9.57, 12.42; Lehmann, *Armut*, 119–20n180. Dio here alludes to a contemporary scandal under Domitian involving same-sex attraction among young Roman aristocrats, which led to the reissuing of the Lex Scantinia that hovered in the background of Nicomachus Flavianus's law discussed in chapter 1.

118. Syn., *De reg.* 16.6, quoting Hom., *Od.* 15.332. See also Emion, "L'empereur chrétien"; Rummel, *Habitus barbarus*, 217–25.

FIGURE 19. Priscus (with Gothic hairstyle), 4/5th CE, mosaic, panel 6 (N), Rotunda, Thessalonica. Photo: Bente Knold Kiilerich, 2009.

emperor could bring to life at any moment, should he wish. This ideal Arcadius was a manly Platonic philosopher-king, a model of courage, foresight, and virtue, exuding divine philanthropy, an Achilles ready to demonstrate Rome's superior fighting spirit. This Arcadius was as aspirational as "Arcadius the jellyfish" was a caricature: a less-than-manly lizard sequestered in his bedchamber, bejeweled like a peacock, surrounded by his gorgeous bodyguards, and ruled by advisers who constantly truncated the emperor's Roman *vir*-ness to remake him in their own (eunuch)likeness.

It is easy to read this entertaining and biting mirror of princes principally as an indictment of Arcadius as passive, boorish, and unworthy of Theodosius. It can certainly be read as satirical or ironic.[119] None of this, however, precludes seeing *De regno* as our earliest sustained assessment of Eutropius's powerful position, including his consulship, from an eastern, Constantinopolitan elite perspective. Inserted into the context of capacious Theodosian imperial *vir*-ness, Synesius's attacks on the emperor become far less devastating, because his main targets were

119. Analogous to how scholars have suggested one should read Xenophon's praise of Cyrus's treatment of eunuchs: see, e.g., Carlier, "L'idée de monarchie," 161–63; but cf. Gray, *Xenophon's Mirror of Princes*, 289 ("the belief that Xenophon is not really praising Cyrus . . . has very few legs"); Danzig, "Best of the Achaemenids."

the advisers who had become too powerful (and were the wrong ones because they were not Synesius's friends): Eutropius the eunuch and (future) consul and his ally Alaric the *magister militum*, linked by their shared Scythianness and eunuchlikeness. Synesius's "Arcadius" was no model ruler, but the actual emperor, though advised by these two, was also not identical to his caricature.

Arcadius the Jellyfish and Eutropius the Scythian reveal that Synesius and his elite audience had noted the shifts in imperial expressions of *vir*-ness, which Eutropius's rise to power had made manifest and which Synesius's language reflects. Imperial softness as a power language had taken shape and become sufficiently established: Synesius's caricature of the emperor abounds in the smooth, moist, malleable, and fluid, associated with the less-than-manly. Elite reaction, in short, was not entirely positive, because the changes diverged quite dramatically from the *mos maiorum*, the habits of old that had made Rome great and defined its *vir*-ness, or *andreia*. These changes included the gradual transformation of philanthropy into a powerful weapon, increasing reliance on diplomacy, new settlement policies, and the emperor's unprecedented uninterrupted presence in the city. Yet these developments did not herald Rome's imminent demise.

Neither did Eutropius the *patricius* nor Alaric the *magister militum*. True, for Synesius their rise had been too fast and was too risky—and as we have seen, at first glance, *De regno* advocates removing both entirely (and all Goths from the administration and the army). However, closer examination of Synesius's intertexts shows that his aversion to these two was fueled by the fact that their proximity to the emperor (and each other) was too close and excluded members of the "true" elite, like Aurelian, whose *vir*-ness (or *andreia*) was unassailable. Likewise, Arcadius's main fault was not his imperial softness but his reliance on too few advisers, and the wrong ones. Synesius's evocation of the *Cyropaideia* suggests that he was not criticizing the fundaments of Arcadius's rule. For the writer too, bejeweled imperial vestments were what emperors wore to make themselves beautiful and dignified; they simply should not be excessive. Similarly, all emperors relied on eunuchs, who enhanced the ruler's splendor with their beauty, and the best among them held very high positions.[120] That was not the issue—indeed, Synesius tacitly appreciated Eutropius's accomplishments.[121] But Arcadius had concentrated too much power in one man. Cyrus, by contrast, had succeeded in ruling a vast empire because he had many friends acting as his ears and eyes, and he showered

---

120. Zos., *HN* 4.28.2 relates Eunapius's report that Theodosius was particularly careful in selecting beautiful eunuchs. Claudian also mentioned Eutropius's youthful beauty: see Amm. Marc. 29.1.8; J. Chrys., *Ad vid. iun.* 4; Theod., *HR* 3.2; *Anth. Graec.* 16.33; Coripp., *In laud. Iust.* 1.86–88, 3.224–30. Later, angels (and their representation) were often indistinguishable from beautiful palace eunuchs: see Tougher, "In or Out?"; Hatzaki, *Beauty*, 93–106 (focusing on the eleventh to fourteenth centuries).

121. Such sentiments were not unheard of. Amm. Marc. 16.7.7, 14.6.12, praised Julian's Eutherius, and for the author of the *Mir. Th.*, Eutropius was "a good servant of his emperor" (9.19–21); Tougher, *Eunuch*, 102, 109.

them all with love and devotion: to be a conqueror was to be a seducer.[122] Arcadius had truncated his affection for others, given too much to too few. Thus, he could no longer prove that he ruled the eunuch rather than the other way round. Therefore, expanding the circle of those who received his favor, choosing those who were more worthy of the highest offices, would solve the problem: it would reveal Eutropius as a perfect servant because he was controlled by a true master advised by the right men. Those elites would also know how to reciprocate the emperor's love, taking "care that the one man, the king, is the best [*aristos*], [which] means choosing the shortest path to help restore all families and cities, all peoples, small and large, closer and farther afield, all who are by necessity under the effects of the king's soul, whatever that [soul] might be made of."[123]

Such a king—Arcadius surrounded by true Roman friends of proven *andreia*—would keep Eutropius and Alaric and his Goths as perfect servants and guard dogs.[124] And if these perfect servants and guard dogs could not demonstrate manliness by "beget[ting] even an ordinary son," that did not matter all that much.[125] In contrast to Claudian's construction of the westerner Eutropius, the eastern version did not threaten Arcadius in any fundamental way. Arcadius was already a father (even though not yet of a son), and all he needed to do to turn his perceived jellyfishiness into gorgeously soft imperial *vir*-ness was expand his circle of friends, grant them the highest honors, and thus make Synesius's statue in words come alive and move.

122. Xen., *Cyr.* 5.28–36; Carlier, "L'idée de monarchie," 147, 153–56.
123. Syn., *De regn.* 3.3 (ὁ γὰρ ἑνὸς ἀνδρός, τοῦ βασιλέως, ἐπιμεληθείς ὅπως ἂν ἄριστος εἴη, τὴν συντομωτάτην ἐβάδισεν ἐπὶ τὸ πάντας μὲν οἴκους ἐπανορθοῦν, πολεῖς τε πάσας, ἔθνη τε πάντα, καὶ μικρὰ καὶ μείζω, καὶ τὰ γείτονα καὶ τὰ πόρρω, ἃ πάντα ἀπολαύειν ἀνάγκη τῆς ὅπως ποτὲ ἐχούσης τοῦ βασιλέως ψυχῆς). See also Pl., *Apol.* 29e2–3, evoking Neoplatonic ideals of kingship.
124. See Schmitt, *Die Bekehrung*, 576–83, for Synesius's utilitarian assessment of barbarians.
125. Philost., *HE* 11.4.

8

The Adornment of the Altar

John Chrysostom on the Fallen Eutropius

Synesius and his audience represent one segment of the Constantinopolitan elites and their grappling with the mounting evidence of Theodosius's and Arcadius's shifts in the conception and representation of imperial power and hence manliness, made manifest in Eutropius the consul. Another elite perspective was given voice on a Saturday or Sunday in late July or early August 399. The voice was that of Constantinople's bishop, John Chrysostom, who faced an exceptionally large audience in the Great Church, Hagia Sophia. Despite the summer heat, John observed, "our theater is magnificent and the assembly radiant," "as great a crowd gathered here now as I saw at holy Easter."[1] Virgins had left their chambers, women their quarters, men the marketplace. All had raced to the church to witness an extraordinary spectacle: Eutropius the consul was clutching the altar, begging for refuge.[2]

John Chrysostom's sermon, known by its Latin title *In Eutropium eunuchum patricium ac consulem*, is a rhetorical tour de force.[3] Though the text as we now have it may contain later revisions, it vividly illustrates the considerable challenges confronting the bishop on that day.[4] John's audience included the consul, of course,

1. J. Chrys., *In Eutr.* 394.40 (*PG* 52.391–396). See also J. Chrys., *In Col.* 7.3, 10.4 (*PG* 62.346–347, 62.371).

2. The Great Church's exterior is estimated to have measured 66 by 120 meters, which would allow for an audience of about five thousand: see Krautheimer, *Three Christian Capitals*, 50–51.

3. The manuscript collections preserve two homilies addressed to the fallen Eutropius. Only the first, discussed in what follows, has been accepted as genuine. John did compose the first two paragraphs of the second one, titled *De capto Eutropio* (*PG* 52.395–404). However, they deal with the capture of the *comes* (or "count") John in 400. See Cameron, "Misidentified Homily"; Voicu, "La volontá," 106, 111–12; W. Mayer, "John Chrysostom as Crisis-Manager," 134–39.

4. Soc., *HE* 6.4.9, differentiates between sermons or homilies that Chrysostom published himself and those written down by stenographers as he delivered them; for a discussion of the revisions, emendations, and preservation of these manuscripts, see Crook, *Preaching*, 23–48, 201–10.

and a larger than usual share of Constantinople's ruling elites. Among those virgins, women, and men were some of the eastern empire's most influential military leaders, members of the court, wealthy sponsors of monasteries, patrons of the bishop, adherents of forms of Christianity other than John's Nicene version, and persons who were not Christian.[5] In sum, the crème de la crème of the imperial capital, including Synesius's audience and probably Synesius himself, crowded the Great Church to watch how the bishop would deal with the fallen consul. This consul had wielded tremendous power and influence, and his fall from imperial grace was barely a day old. Moreover, everyone knew that this consul was a eunuch. So what would John Chrysostom make of the person clutching the altar in this magnificent theater with the radiant assembly watching and listening to every word?

John Chrysostom made Eutropius the consul into a visible symbol, or *eikon*, of the mighty who have fallen. He used his rhetorical brilliance to create a world in words where Eutropius symbolized the fragility of power, wealth, and status, and became a warning to everyone in the audience who considered himself or herself untouchable because of their power, wealth, and status.[6] At the same time, he used the Eutropius he evoked to console those who were or felt themselves to be inferior by highlighting the dizzying heights from which they, lower down as they were, could never fall. As an icon of the transitory nature of wealth and power, Eutropius became in John's hands an adornment of the altar and a tangible trophy of the victorious powers of philanthropy, compassion, affectionate love, and mercy.

Since every powerful person in the audience, in particular every male person, knew that they too could fall at any moment, Eutropius was a formidable reminder that the mercy granted him that day might someday (soon) be extended to another one of those present. However, John Chrysostom did more. He used his brilliant rhetorical skills, honed at Antioch, to make Eutropius, the *vir illustris*, into an exemplar for all the other *viri clarissimi, spectabiles*, and *illustres* in the audience—and then he made *them* into Eutropius. John forced his audience to feel with the person at the altar, begging the emperor, God, and John Chrysostom for mercy, such that they *became* him, viscerally and emotionally. His audience, watching Eutropius tremble, cried tears of compassion because they trembled in fear for themselves, knowing that they had to entrust their fate to the trinity of bishop, emperor, and God. But thanks to John's evocative preaching, on that day they were also transformed into the merciful church, which protected and

5. For the composition of the audience in Constantinople, see McLynn, "Imperial Piety," 318–20; W. Mayer, "At Constantinople"; Falcasantos, *Constantinople*, 80–86. For a summary of recent scholarship on Chrysostom's relation to his audience, see Roskam, "Emancipatory Preaching," 176–79.

6. I find Jan Stenger's use of cognitive poetics and text world theory particularly useful: see "Text Worlds" and *Johannes Chrysostomus*, 10–14, 21–34. Equally formative for what follows are Papadogiannakis, "Prescribing Emotions," 347–60; Leyerle, *Narrative Shape*, 2–20. See also Laird, *Mindset*, 50–164; Fauconnier, *Mental Spaces*, 10–34; Gavins, *Text World Theory*, 126–64.

shielded Eutropius the fallen as if enveloped in a mother's, bishop's, and emperor's veils of compassionate love.

Nowhere in this homily does John Chrysostom characterize Eutropius as a eunuch. Scholarly consensus, reflecting the Latin title, assumes that the entire homily slanders Eutropius qua eunuch, but nothing in the text itself suggests this directly. Of course, the audience (just like us as scholars and the author of the title) knew that Eutropius was a eunuch.[7] That John failed to mention Eutropius's physical condition in any explicit form indicates that his silence was deliberate, because we know from other homilies that he was absolutely able to express his opinion regarding eunuchs and those who acted like them in no uncertain terms.[8] John wanted Eutropius's condition to be intrinsic yet subordinate to his position as a consul and powerful man, if only because while there were many powerful men in the audience, he alone was a recently all-powerful eunuch, and the moral of this particular homily applied to all powerful men, the emperor included.

John's silence, therefore, spoke as loudly as the consul and *patricius* had spoken while in office, and as Eutropius's silence at the altar spoke now: "louder than a trumpet."[9] Because everyone who had raced to that assembly, or *synaxis*, knew the consul, Chrysostom crafted Eutropius the eunuch as the ever-present subtext. By inviting all to imagine themselves in Eutropius's place, John forced everyone in the audience to transform themselves, emotionally, at the very least into a fallen rich man but ideally into this eunuch. What does Eutropius, the icon of fortune reversed and the adornment of the altar, tell us about power and manliness at the court of Arcadius according to the bishop of Constantinople?

EUTROPIUS AND JOHN CHRYSOSTOM: 397–399

John Chrysostom managed Eutropius's fall and its repercussions flawlessly. Until 401, when tensions with the court began, John enjoyed the full support of the emperor and his wife Eudoxia, whose second and third daughters he baptized in 399 and early 400.[10] John had been elected as bishop in December 397 and consecrated on February 26, 398, with the backing of Arcadius and his court. The reasons why John was chosen are difficult to parse, because the fractious end of his tenure some six years later, when the "Synod of the Oak" condemned him

7. Roskam, "Emancipatory Preaching," 188–89, states that Eutropius was "publicly humiliated before all present in the church," adding that "we may presume that many of those present at least partially knew the man and his previous career"; for cautions about assumptions as to what the audience heard, see Sandwell, "Preaching."

8. See J. Chrys., *Virg.* 8.4–5; J. Chrys., *Subintr.* 10 (uses eunuchs as a foil for men considered less than manly); Leyerle, *Theatrical Shows*, 75–99, 129–30; Dunning, "John Chryostom and Same-Sex Eros"; De Wet, "John Chrysostom on Homoeroticism," 204–5.

9. J. Chrys., *In Eutr.* 394.40 (σάλπιγγος λαμπροτέραν φωνήν).

10. He might also have baptized their eldest daughter in 397: see Barnes and Bevan, *Funerary Speech*, 25–26; Hartney, *John Chrysostom*, 79. For imperial support, see Tiersch, *Johannes Chrysostomus*, 309–26.

to permanent exile, dominates our sources, which either passionately defend or attack the Antiochene in the capital.[11] All agree that John's election had been contentious from the start, so that the voices of Arcadius and his representatives were decisive. Our most detailed source in John's defense, written after his death in 408—Palladius's *Historical Dialogue on the Life and Conduct of the Blessed John*— declares Eutropius the driving force behind his election.[12] According to Palladius, Eutropius met John while passing through Antioch on his way east, perhaps as he was preparing his Hunnic campaign.[13] Eutropius outmaneuvered the competition, in particular the contender advanced by the powerful bishop of Alexandria, Theophilus, by conveying John to Constantinople in secret, accompanied only by a eunuch and a *magister officiorum*, and presenting his election as a fait accompli. Notwithstanding, Palladius and another pro-John source from 407 or 408, Ps.-Martyrius's *Funerary Speech for John Chrysostom*, portray John as the clear consensus candidate.[14]

In other words, John was a court bishop, chosen with the expectation that he would implement Arcadius's wishes just as his precursor Nectarius had implemented those of Theodosius. Nectarius, ordained as an unbaptized senator in 381, had succeeded in managing the complex power plays of the capital while integrating the emperor into the ceremonials of church and city to reflect their shared religious preferences, as his long tenure attests.[15] Whether Arcadius and his court expected John to consolidate what Theodosius and Nectarius had established or wanted him to introduce different practices is difficult to ascertain. Arcadius's markedly less regular church attendance argues for change, but it is worth remembering that in the Constantinople of the 390s, episcopal leadership was

11. For scholarly attempts to break the pro-John lock on the narrative, see S. Elm, "Dog That Did Not Bark," 71–76; W. Mayer, "Doing Violence," 205–13; van Nuffelen, "Palladius and the Johannite Schism"; Pigott, "Capital Crimes," 737–43; Katos, *Palladius of Helenopolis*, 9–97; Barry, *Bishops in Flight*, 20–29, 76–131.

12. Pall., *Dial.* 5.55–57, in Malingrey, *Dialogue*, 1:112–14; see also Soc., *HE* 6.2; Soz., *HE* 8.2; Theod., *HE* 5.27. For the date, see Malingrey, *Dialogue*, 1:19–21. See also W. Mayer, "John Chrysostom as Bishop," 456, which advises caution when using Palladius; W. Mayer, "John Chrysostom as Crisis-Manager," which considers Eutropius pagan (at 137), perhaps because Soz., *HE* 8.7.3, declared him impious; W. Mayer, "Audience(s) for Patristic Social Teaching," 92–94.

13. Soz., *HE* 7.22.7, says that Eutropius met John while in Egypt to consult John of Lycopolis on whether Theodosius should move against Eugenius. The fullest discussion of the election is Tiersch, *Johannes Chrysostomus*, 31–41, who follows Baur, *Der heilige Johannes Chrysostomus*, 2:7, in suggesting (at 108) that Aurelian's brother Caesarius, the *praefectus praetorio Orientis* in 397, introduced John to Eutropius. For an in-depth discussion of the *Dialogue* in connection with Palladius's *Historia Lausiaca*, see Katos, *Palladius of Helenopolis*, 9–97.

14. Ps.-Martyrius 13–17. See also Pigott, "Capital Crimes," 757–58; for a comparison of Palladius and Ps.-Martyrius, Tiersch, "Wie christlich darf ein Bischof sein?"; for imperial intervention in episcopal elections, Norton, *Episcopal Elections*, 84–91.

15. Escribano Paño, "Heretical Texts," 116–17; Pigott, "Capital Crimes," 756–60; McLynn, "Voice of Conscience," 299–308.

as much a work in progress as were imperial representation and the cityscape.[16] Whatever the respective expectations, Eutropius as a powerful adviser to the emperor had played an important role in John's appointment, and the latter's public reaction to the former's fall a year and a half into his tenure as bishop was bound to set a tone.

Already prior to John's arrival, Eutropius had passed a series of laws concerning asylum in churches that continued Theodosius's and Arcadius's policies but went against the interests of the bishop in whose church he now found himself. The first, issued in 397, prevented indebted Jews from seeking asylum. In 398, a law censured clergy, monks, and cenobites who had resorted to violence to prevent the punishment of condemned criminals and then sheltered them. It also confirmed that fugitive slaves, private debtors, and decurions who had shirked their fiscal responsibilities were prohibited from seeking asylum in churches. Churches found in violation had to assume the debts.[17] These measures did not deny clergy the possibility of offering asylum but continued the imperial practice of regulating who would be entitled to it. Thus, they formed part of the imperial efforts to delineate the spheres in which bishops and other clergy could operate in a legal capacity: bishops sought to expand that sphere, while emperors wished to contain it.[18]

In a similar vein, Eutropius intensified measures targeting Eunomius and his followers. As mentioned in chapter 5, Eunomians had been subject to imperial legislation since Theodosius's arrival in the city. Indeed, for decades they had been provoking leading church figures, who lobbied the emperors in turn, and John Chrysostom was no exception.[19] On March 4, 398, Arcadius, supported by Eutropius, addressed an edict to the *prefectus praetorii* Euthychianus banning Eunomius's supporters from all cities and communities in the countryside. He also declared Eunomius's writings instruments of sorcery (*maleficia*), making their possession a *crimen maiestatis*, punishable by death.[20] It was a harsh edict, but

16. van Nuffelen, "Playing the Ritual Game"; Diefenbach, "Zwischen Liturgie"; McLynn, "Moments of Truth," 215–39; McLynn, "Imperial Piety," 323–27; McLynn, "Transformation," 258–70; Croke, "Reinventing Constantinople," 241–64.

17. CTh 9.40.16 (398) addresses condemned criminals ("Addictos supplicio et pro criminum immanitate damnatos nulli clericorum vel monacorum, eorum etiam, quos synoditas vocant, per vim adque usurpatio vindicare liceat ac tenere"); 9.45.1–3 (397–398) address asylum; 9.45.2 addresses Jews who want to convert to avoid criminal charges or debt. See 9.45.3 ("Si quis in posterum servus, ancilla, curialis, debitor publicus, procurator, murilegulus, . . . ad ecclasiam confugiens vel clericus ordinatus . . . nec statim conventione praemissa pristinae condicioni reddatur . . . manu mox iniecta revocentur . . . non patimur. . . .")

18. See also CTh 9.40.15 (392), 9.45.1 (392); Ducloux, *Ad ecclesiam confugere*, 53–67, 70–80, 266–67.

19. Vaggione, *Eunomius of Cyzicus*, 321–54; S. Elm, *Sons of Hellenism*, 396–401; Rylaarsdam, *John Chrysostom*, 14–18.

20. CTh 16.5.34; Philost., *HE* 11.5, for Eutropius's impact; Escribano Paño, "Heretical Texts," 107–18, 120–34; see also Escribano Paño, "Social Exclusion."

only one in a long series of laws that threatened Eunomius and his followers with significant punishments and removal from public spaces. Sozomen later suggested that these laws were, to use Schmidt-Hofner's term, "ostentatious legislation," intended to frighten Eunomians into adopting Nicene Christianity rather than to punish them in fact.[21]

Indeed, it would have been impossible to remove all Eunomians and others who considered Father and Son unlike in essence from Constantinople and other cities. At the very least, this would have required a great deal of diplomatic acumen, because Eunomius was popular among the elites and at court, where he had a large following in the palace administration, especially among the eunuchs.[22] Only ten years prior, while Theodosius was in Italy to confront Magnus Maximus, Eunomian court eunuchs and other Homoians had launched an uprising and burned down Nectarius's house.[23] Theodosius responded by preventing court eunuchs from making wills, rendering them intestate so that their sizable estates would revert to the emperor on their deaths; nevertheless, Eunomius remained influential.[24] Eutropius's law of 398 accusing Eunomius of magic and sorcery was the most severe, because a *crimen maiestatis* had real consequences. Coming directly after Eunomius's death, the law might signal concerns that devotion to the deceased would become even more intense. At any rate, the new measure cannot have been popular among those most affected.[25]

Though John could have had little influence on the drafting of a law issued a week after his consecration, he would have been in favor of this one. He was no friend of magic. At Antioch, he had forcefully defended the unknowability of God against Eunomius's (alleged) claim to "know" with precision that Father and Son were unlike in essence. Indeed, one of the first homilies that John preached in Constantinople attacked Eunomians.[26] Perhaps more effective were the "Nicene" nighttime processions that John introduced, and for which Eudoxia and Eutropius provided silver candelabra and other accoutrements, to counter the

21. Soz., *HE* 7.12; Schmidt-Hofner, "Ostentatious Legislation," 93; see also Escribano Paño, "Heretical Texts," 108–12; McLynn, "'*Genere Hispanus*,'" 79–88, 95–100; Hillner, *Prison*, 91–93.

22. Soc., *HE* 5.20; Soz., *HE* 7.17; Philost., *HE* 10.6. See also Syn., *Ep.* 4, for Eunomians among the elites; CTh 16.5.29, for actions taken against Eunomians under Eutropius's precursor Rufinus; Fitschen, "Der *Praefectus Praetorio* Flavius Rufinus."

23. This was the only disturbance during Nectarius's tenure. See Soc., *HE* 5.13; Soz., *HE* 7.14; Vaggione, *Eunomius of Cyzicus*, 353n245; Vera, "I rapporti"; Baldus, "Theodosius der Große."

24. CTh 16.5.17 (389). Two laws against Eunomius and his followers were addressed to Caesarius in Antioch in 387: CTh 16.5.31–32.

25. For the death of Eunomius, see Philost., *HE* 11.5; Vaggione, *Extant Works*, 359–63; Falcasantos, *Constantinople*, 122–24.

26. J. Chrys., *Hom. c. Anomaeos* 11; see also Rylaarsdam, *John Chrysostom*, 281–82; Marasco, "I vescovi," 228–33. Vaggione, *Extant Works*, 361n294, is skeptical regarding John's influence. For John's anti-Eunomian preaching in Antioch, see Shepardson, *Controlling*, 98–128.

popular "Homoian" ones.[27] Thus, by 399 John had publicly aligned himself with the emperor, his wife, and his eunuch consul. He risked the disapproval of a significant number of high-ranking persons, court eunuchs included, whose hostility had consequences once Eutropius's position began to waver, as John discovered after 401, when his position too became less stable.[28]

Eutropius fell from imperial favor in the summer of 399, but much like those for John's election, the reasons are hard to pinpoint. Christian sources in favor of John Chrysostom blame Eudoxia. Because they hold her responsible for John's eventual demise, these authors portray the empress as a domineering and nefarious meddler in her hapless husband's affairs, who for good measure also engineered Eutropius's demise.[29] Philostorgius's Homoian *History* was a defense of Eunomius (and opposed to John), which made the historian no friend of the consul or the imperial couple. According to him, Eudoxia plotted against Eutropius. In front of the emperor, clutching her crying children, she accused Eutropius of planning to chase her from the palace. Enraged, the emperor ordered the eunuch removed instead.[30] A power struggle between the military commander Gainas and Eutropius offers a more plausible interpretation. Envious of Eutropius's prior military successes against the Huns, Gainas refused to engage a Gothic uprising in Phrygia and Lydia unless the emperor removed the consul.[31] However the fall came about, in August 399 Eutropius faced exile or execution. He fled the palace and sought asylum in the Great Church.[32]

VANITAS VANITATUM: JOHN CHRYSOSTOM'S DIDACTIC THEATER

It is always opportune—but particularly at this moment—to say: "Vanity of vanities, and all is vanity" [Eccl 1:2]. Where now are the splendid trappings of the consulship?

27. Soc., *HE* 6.8.1–9; Soz., *HE* 8.8; Andrade, "Processions"; Stanfill, "Body of Christ's Barbarian Limb," 676–78; van Nuffelen, "Playing the Ritual Game."

28. Escribano Paño, "Heretical Texts," 112–20; Pigott, "Capital Crimes," 750–56; S. Elm, "What the Bishop Wore"; Liebeschuetz, *Barbarians and Bishops*, 219; Liebeschuetz, "Friends and Enemies," 96–104, esp. 96.

29. See Barry, *Bishops in Flight*, 108–17, for a detailed analysis of how Eudoxia was made monstrous; Tiersch, *Johannes Chrysostomus*, 265–81 (discussion of the homily against Eutropius at 269–79); Dewar, "Fall of Eutropius"; Ducloux, *Ad ecclesiam confugere*, 92–103.

30. Philost., *HE* 11.6; see also Zos., *HN* 5.18.1; W. Mayer, "Doing Violence."

31. See chapter 6; Claud., *Eutr.* 2.159, 2.174–237, 2.304–461; Eunap., *Hist.* 67–69; Soc., *HE* 6.6; Soz., *HE* 8.4; Zos., *HN* 5.11–22; J. Chrys., *In Eutr.* 4; Liebeschuetz, *Barbarians and Bishops*, 97–105; Kulikowski, *Rome's Gothic Wars*, 168–70; Long, *Claudian's "In Eutropium,"* 11–12; Cameron and Long, *Barbarians*, 112–16, 324–25; Halsall, *Barbarian Migrations*, 200–1; Heather, *Goths and Romans*, 74, 207; McCormick, *Eternal Victory*, 48.

32. CTh 9.40.17. The edict is probably Claudian's *exigua charta* in *Eutr.* 2 praef. 19; he may allude to Eutropius's asylum at *Eutr.* 2 praef. 27. See also Dewar, "Fall of Eutropius," 582–83; Schlinkert, *Ordo senatorius*, 268–69.

Where are the gleaming torches? Where are the outbursts of applause and the choruses and the festivities and the public holidays? Where are the crowns and the banners? Where are the uproar of the city and the acclamations during the chariot races and the flattering comments of the spectators? They've all gone. A blast of wind has blown away the leaves and revealed the tree to us—naked and shaken to its very root at this moment. For such has been the impact of the wind that it's even threatening to pull the tree up by the roots and to shake its fibers violently. Where now are those who posed as friends? Where are the drinking parties and the dinners? Where is the swarm of hangers-on . . . and the cultivators of power who would do and say anything to please him? . . . They were a shadow and melted away. They were smoke and dispersed. . . . They were a spider's web and have been torn to shreds. That's why we're chanting this spiritual maxim, saying over and over: "Vanity of vanities, and all is vanity."[33]

With these opening lines John announced his principal theme with the rhetorical brilliance (*lampros*) and attractiveness (*to epagogon*) that made him the celebrated virtuoso *Chrysostom*, Golden Mouth.[34] Deeply schooled in the rules and practices of classical rhetoric, John had developed new means of persuasion during his decades at Antioch, which he deployed to excellent effect in the sermon delivered in the presence of Eutropius.[35] Two features of his persuasive method are particularly relevant. First, as recent research on the literary dimensions of his sermons and homilies shows, John created text worlds, or didactic theaters, that drew his listeners into the narrative flow and elicited emotions different from those they would normally feel. Second, the effect, especially over time, was cognitive reordering.[36]

---

33. J. Chrys., *In Eutr.* 391.1–25:

Ἀεὶ μὲν, μάλιστα δὲ νῦν εὔκαιρον εἰπεῖν· *Ματαιότης ματαιοτήτων, καὶ πάντα ματαιότης*. Ποῦ νῦν ἡ λαμπρὰ τῆς ὑπατείας περιβολή; ποῦ δὲ αἱ φαιδραὶ λαμπάδες; ποῦ δὲ οἱ κρότοι, καὶ οἱ χοροὶ, καὶ αἱ θαλίαι, καὶ αἱ πανηγύρεις; ποῦ οἱ στέφανοι καὶ τὰ παραπετάσματα; ποῦ ὁ τῆς πόλεως θόρυβος, καὶ αἱ ἐν ἱπποδρομίαις εὐφημίαι, καὶ τῶν θεατῶν αἱ κολακεῖαι; Πάντα ἐκεῖνα οἴχεται· καὶ ἄνεμος πνεύσας ἀθρόον τὰ μὲν φύλλα κατέβαλε, γυμνὸν δὲ ἡμῖν τὸ δένδρον ἔδειξε, καὶ ἀπὸ τῆς ῥίζης αὐτῆς σαλευόμενον λοιπόν· τοιαύτη γὰρ ἡ τοῦ πνεύματος γέγονε προσβολὴ, ὡς καὶ πρόρριζον ἀπειλεῖν ἀνασπᾶν, καὶ ταῦτα διασαλεῦσαι τοῦ δένδρου τὰ νεῦρα. Ποῦ νῦν οἱ πεπλασμένοι φίλοι; ποῦ τὰ συμπόσια καὶ τὰ δεῖπνα; ποῦ ὁ τῶν παρασίτων ἑσμὸς . . . , καὶ οἱ τῆς δυναστείας θεραπευταὶ, οἱ πάντα πρὸς χάριν ποιοῦντες καὶ λέγοντες; . . . σκιὰ ἦν, καὶ παρέδραμε· καρπὸς ἦν, καὶ διελύθη· πομφόλυγες ἦσαν, καὶ διερράγησαν· ἀράχνη ἦν, καὶ διεσπάσθη. Διὸ ταύτην τὴν πνευματικὴν ῥῆσιν ἐπᾴδομεν συνεχῶς ἐπιλέγοντες· *Ματαιότης ματαιοτήτων, καὶ πάντα ματαιότης*.

34. Soc., *HE* 6.4.9 (λαμπροὶ καὶ τὸ ἐπαγωγόν).

35. For John's rhetorical mastery, see Rylaarsdam, *John Chrysostom*, 18–22; Cook, *Preaching*, 51–83; W. Mayer, "Son of Hellenism."

36. Leyerle, *Narrative Shape*, 1–20; Stenger, *Johannes Chrysostomos*, 2–17, 32–34, 62–72, 126–36; for John's use of the theater, see Bergjan, "'Das hier ist kein Theater'"; Leyerle, *Theatrical Shows*, 42–74; Jacob, *Das geistige Theater*, 94–141, 154–70.

John fashioned these participatory narratives primarily through the rhetorical technique of *synkatabasis*, or adapting his speech to the demands of each audience member. This could be achieved by using particularly apt embellishments, or literary ornaments (*ornatus, epagogon*), to persuade and convince.[37] John then recalibrated these embellishments in unexpected ways to modulate what his listeners should feel. One powerful means to redirect emotional responses was fear (*phrike*), causing trembling and awe, designed "to imbue [John's] community's socially shared beliefs and values with affective meanings, seeking to make these values salient in everyday, mundane interaction. . . . In doing so, he seeks to promote solidarity and cohesion, as well as demarcation and exclusion, and to affect what people believe, desire, and value."[38] Constantly reenacted, John's didactic theaters persuaded his listeners to imagine their city not as it was but as it should be: a heavenly metropolis on earth.[39]

Central to John's method was the use of metaphors that linked the less familiar, such as biblical passages, to the familiar, for example an imperial *adventus*. These juxtapositions prompted his audience to reevaluate their emotional responses and consequently their behavior.[40] In his last decade at Antioch, after the so-called Riot of the Statues, to which I will return, most of these metaphors derived from the public spaces of the city and those who dominated them—the rich and the powerful. John used jarring contrasts and new angles to refashion this public domain as Christian, for example by likening "rich women who claim that they 'cannot' go around the marketplace unless they are carried on mules to 'beggars who have had their feet cut off.'"[41] In sum, by forcing his audience to imagine his world pictures, John elicited emotional responses and behaviors that might over time transform the city and its inhabitants into Christians.

What do these insights into Chrysostom's rhetorical and didactic methods reveal about *In Eutropium*? Nearly all of the research on John's preaching focuses on Antioch, where he composed most of his homilies and most consistently interacted with his audience.[42] In Constantinople, his situation was different in almost

37. Roskam, "Emancipatory Preaching," 176; Rylaarsdam, *John Chrysostom*, 7–8, 17–30, 45–99, shows how John transformed the rhetorical function of *synkatabasis* into a theological concept; Brown, *Power and Persuasion*, 70–78.

38. Papadogiannakis, "Prescribing Emotions," 347 (quote), 343, inc. n. 24; see also Rylaarsdam, *John Chrysostom*, 228–82, 286, though John was harsher than Rylaarsdam suggests, 77–80; Cook, *Preaching*, 67–74, which discusses traditional uses of fear; Leyerle, *Narrative Shape*, 112–49; Mellas, "Tears of Compunction," focuses on John's liturgical dramatization to create an affective community; C. Harrison, *Art of Listening*, 150.

39. J. Chrys., *Theod.* 1.

40. Lakoff and Johnson, *Metaphors We Live By*, remains foundational.

41. J. Chrys., *Laz. et div.* 6.3; Leyerle, "Imagining Antioch," 271, quoting J. Chrys., *Virg.* 66.10–12. See also Stenger, *Johannes Chrysostomos*, 126–237; Shepardson, *Controlling*, 50–57, 160–62.

42. The same is true for studies of his audience: see W. Mayer, "John Chrysostom and Women Revisited," 221–25; W. Mayer, "Who Came"; W. Mayer, "John Chrysostom"; Maxwell, *Christianization*, 65–87; Hartney, *John Chrysostom*, 33–52; Papadogiannakis, "Homiletics."

every respect. John had arrived only a little over a year prior, too soon to establish a rapport with that audience, which was, moreover, far wealthier and included high-ranking courtiers and, for festivals and other special occasions, the emperor and his wife.[43] On the day of Eutropius's fall, that composition was even more diverse, with powerful non-Nicene elites and others who would normally never enter this church.

That Sunday, then, John had (or had the opportunity) to operate on even more levels than he normally would. In response, he composed his homily in quadruplicate. First, he reiterated and intensified themes he had honed in Antioch and expounded in Constantinople already a few Sundays prior—such as the deplorable extravagance of chariot races, for which Eutropius was responsible as a rich man and a consul, because his office financed public entertainments like races, games, and theatrical productions.[44] Second, he addressed the person at the altar as an individual, who also happened to be a consul and *patricius*. Third, he used the recently fallen to explicate scriptural passages as part of a didactic theater in which the luxuries of the rich were recast in provocative ways to elicit new emotions, while, finally, allowing Eutropius's condition as a eunuch to hover in the background.

EUTROPIUS THE RICH MAN

John's audience, at first glance, required little help to get the picture. They could see Eutropius at the altar with their own eyes.

> Yet, see! He has become more wretched even than prisoners, more miserable even than homegrown slaves, more needy even than beggars who are wasting away with hunger. Each day he's gazing at sharpened swords and the pit and executioners and being led away to his death. . . . However hard we try, we couldn't present in words the suffering which he is likely to be enduring as he expects with each hour that passes to be executed. But then, what need is there for words from us when his own affairs are clearly sketched out for us as on an icon? . . . His countenance—as even now—was for once no better than that of a corpse. His teeth were chattering, and his whole body was rattling and trembling, and his voice kept faltering, and his tongue was slack, and his appearance suggested that his heart had turned to stone. . . . Look, . . . he has become a spectacle for the world.[45]

43. Leyerle, *Narrative Shape*, 69, argues that most of the Antiochene audience was of middling means, in contrast to that at Constantinople.

44. J. Chrys., *In Eutr.* 393.29–30; J. Chrys., *C. lud. et theat.* 7 (*PG* 56.263–270), delivered in early July 399. For the immense entertainment expenses incurred by consuls, see Olympiodorus, frag. 41; Symm., *Epp.* 2.81, 6.43, 9.141; Brown, *Through the Eye of a Needle*, 3, 65–69, 85, 116–19; Cameron and Schauer, "Last Consul," 138–42 (continuation into the sixth century).

45. J. Chrys., *In Eutr.* 393.24–44, 394.30–31:

Ἀλλ᾽ ἰδοῦ γέγονε καὶ δεσμωτῶν ἀθλιώτερος, καὶ οἰκετῶν ἐλεεινότερος, καὶ τῶν λιμῷ τηκομένων πτωχῶν ἐνδεέστερος, καθ᾽ ἑκάστην ἡμέραν ξίφη βλέπων ἠκονημένα, καὶ βάραθρον, καὶ δημίους, καὶ τὴν ἐπὶ θάνατον ἀπαγωγήν. . . . Μᾶλλον δὲ ὅσα ἂν φιλονεικήσωμεν, οὐ δυνησόμεθα τῷ

The image was jarring. "After all, who was loftier than this man? Didn't he surpass all the world in wealth? Didn't he ascend to the pinnacle of the honors? Didn't everyone tremble before him and fear him?"[46] Yet although "bright and illustrious above all, [Eutropius] appear[s] rather paltry now."[47] "The man who used to shake the entire world . . . [has] become more timid than a hare or a frog, and nailed to this column without bonds, and squeezed tight by fear instead of a chain, and filled with fear and trembling."[48]

Eutropius's fall affected a unique individual in particular ways. Because he was the all-powerful consul, many people had "posed as friends" and flocked to his "drinking parties and . . . dinners," "swarm[s] of hangers-on [who enjoyed] the undiluted wine that filled glasses all day long and the varied arts of the chefs, and the cultivators of power who would do and say anything to please him."[49] Now his exalted position had turned into the source of Eutropius's terror.[50] Somehow—and John offers no details—he had insulted the emperor. This had "inflamed" the soldiers such that they were "demanding him for slaughter . . . shouting, jumping, baying for death, and shaking their spears."[51] It was the consul's very closeness to the emperor that had caused his precipitous fall.

However, Eutropius had been powerful and enormously wealthy long before he assumed "the splendid trappings of the consulship" that now set him apart from equally wealthy persons. Wine pourers, slaves clearing paths in the marketplace, chefs, banquets, hangers-on (*parasites*), flatterers were not the consul's alone; they were par for the course for everyone in the audience who was rich.[52] "That's why

λόγῳ παραστῆσαι τὸ πάθος, ὅπερ ὑπομένειν αὐτὸν εἰκὸς, καθ' ἑκάστην ὥραν ἀποκτείνεσθαι προσδοκῶντα. Ἀλλὰ γὰρ τί δεῖ τῶν λόγων τῶν παρ' ἡμῶν, αὐτοῦ ταῦτα καθάπερ ἐν εἰκόνι σαφῶς ὑπογράψαντος ἡμῖν; . . . ἦν αὐτοῦ τὸ πρόσωπον, καὶ τανῦν, νεκρωθέντος ἅπαξ οὐδὲν ἄμεινον διακείμενον· κτύπος δὲ τῶν ὀδόντων, καὶ πάταγος καὶ τρόμος παντὸς τοῦ σώματος, καὶ φωνὴ διακοπτομένη, καὶ γλῶττα διαλυομένη, καὶ σχῆμα τοιοῦτον, οἷον εἰκὸς τὴν λιθίνην ἔχειν ψυχήν . . . καὶ γέγονε τῆς οἰκουμένης θέατρον.

46. J. Chrys., *In Eutr.* 393.20–23 (Τίς γὰρ τούτου γέγονεν ὑψηλότερος; οὐ πᾶσαν τὴν οἰκουμένην παρῆλθε τῷ πλούτῳ; οὐ πρὸς αὐτὰς τῶν ἀξιωμάτων ἀνέβη τὰς κορυφάς; οὐχὶ πάντες αὐτὸν ἔτρεμον, καὶ ἐδεδοίκεισαν).

47. J. Chrys., *In Eutr.* 394.59–60 (τὸν φαιδρὸν καὶ περιφανῆ πάντων ἐποίησεν εὐτελέστερον φαίνεσθαι νῦν).

48. J. Chrys., *In Eutr.* 394.61–395.4 (ὁρῶν γὰρ ἐκ τοσαύτης κορυφῆς κατενεχθέντα τόν σείοντα τὴν οἰκουμένην ἅπασαν, καὶ συνεσταλμένον, καὶ λαγωοῦ καὶ βατράχου δειλότερον γεγενημένον, καὶ χωρὶς δεσμῶν τῷ κίονι τούτῳ προσηλωμένον, καὶ ἀντὶ ἀλύσεως τῷ φόβῳ περισφιγγόμενον, καὶ δεδοικότα, καὶ τρέμοντα). For John's use of animals to describe human nature, see Leyerle, "Locating Animals," 281–84.

49. J. Chrys., *In Eutr.* 391.11–18.

50. For terror as contagious, see Leyerle, *Narrative Shape*, 121–27, 136–37.

51. J. Chrys., *In Eutr.* 395.40–41, 395.48–49 (βοῶντες, πηδῶντες, θανάτου μεμνημένοι, καὶ τὰ δόρατα σείοντες).

52. J. Chrys., *In Eutr.* 391.2–3; see also, e.g., *In Rom.* 17 (PG 60.568); *In 2 Cor.* 6 (PG 61.440); *In Tit.* 5 (PG 62.694).

we're chanting this spiritual maxim, saying over and over: 'Vanity of vanities, and all is vanity.' For this maxim should be inscribed permanently on walls and on clothing [*himation*] and in the marketplace and in the home and in streets and on doors and in foyers and, above all, in each person's conscience; and it should be studied constantly. Since fraudulent matters and masks and acting are thought to be true by the majority, each of you should address this to your neighbor and in turn hear it from your neighbor at dinner, at lunch, and in assemblies every day: 'Vanity of vanities, all is vanity.'"[53]

Wealth and power were bubbles that could burst for every rich person. No one could hide behind Eutropius's current position. "Haven't I said to you constantly that wealth is a runaway slave? But you wouldn't put up with us. Didn't I say that it is an ungrateful homegrown slave [*oiketos*]? But you didn't want to be convinced. Look! Concrete experience has shown that wealth isn't just a runaway slave or an ingrate, but even a murderer—it is responsible for your current trembling and terror."[54] More to the point, the lessons from Eutropius's predicament were universal. Every human being was affected.

> Were a rich person to enter [the church now], they would derive considerable benefit. . . . They would check their excessive passion, deflate their haughtiness,[55] and depart, after reflecting on human affairs in the philosophical way that they should. . . . Were a poor person to enter and look at this vision, they wouldn't utterly despise themselves nor feel distress at their beggarly state. Instead they would feel grateful that their poverty offers them a protected place, a wave-free harbor, a secure wall; and, on viewing these things, would choose over and over to remain where they are. . . . Do you see how this man's flight here affords no small benefit for both rich and poor, both lowly and lofty, both slaves and free?[56]

53. J. Chrys., *In Eutr.* 391.23–34 (Διὸ ταύτην τὴν πνευματικὴν ῥῆσιν ἐπάδομεν συνεχῶς ἐπιλέγοντες· *Ματαιότης ματαιοτήτων, καὶ πάντα ματαιότης*. Ταύτην γὰρ τὴν ῥῆσιν καὶ ἐν τοίχοις, καὶ ἐν ἱματίοις, καὶ ἐν ἀγορᾷ, καὶ ἐν οἰκίᾳ, καὶ ἐν ὁδοῖς, καὶ ἐν θύραις, καὶ ἐν εἰσόδοις, καὶ πρὸ πάντων ἐν τῷ ἑκάστου συνειδότι συνεχῶς ἐγγεγράφθαι δεῖ, καὶ διαπαντὸς αὐτὴν μελετᾶν. Ἐπειδὴ ἡ τῶν πραγμάτων ἀπάτη, καὶ τὰ προσωπεῖα, καὶ ἡ ὑπόκρισις, ἀλήθεια παρὰ τοῖς πολλοῖς εἶναι δοκεῖ· ταύτην καθ' ἑκάστην ἡμέραν, καὶ ἐν δείπνῳ, καὶ ἐν ἀρίστῳ, καὶ ἐν συλλόγοις ἐπιλέγειν ἕκαστον τῷ πλησίον ἐχρῆω, καὶ παρὰ τοῦ πλησίον ἀκούειν, ὅτι *Ματαιότης ματαιοτήτων, καὶ πάντα ματαιότης*). For John's attitude toward the rich, see also Falcasantos, *Constantinople*, 115–18.

54. J. Chrys., *In Eutr.* 392.1–5 (Οὐκ ἔλεγόν σοι συνεχῶς, ὅτι δραπέτης ὁ πλοῦτός ἐστι; Σὺ δὲ ἡμῶν οὐκ ἠνείχου. Οὐκ ἔλεγον ὅτι ἀγνώμων ἐστὶν οἰκέτης; Σὺ δὲ οὐκ ἐβούλου πείθεσθαι. Ἰδοὺ ἐκ τῶν πραγμάτων ἔδειξεν ἡ πεῖρα, ὅτι οὐ δραπέτης μόνον, οὐδὲ ἀγνώμων, ἀλλὰ καὶ ἀνδροφόνος· οὗτος γάρ σε τρέμειν νῦν καὶ δεδοικέναι παρεσκεύασεν).

55. The terms that Mayer and Allen translate as "excessive passion," "haughtiness," "arrogance," and "conceit" are *phlegmone* and *physaema*, which have strong medical connotations: *phlegmone* is an inflammation or boil and hence something excessive (such as passion), and *physema* is something blown up or puffed up, hence conceit (*TLG* s.vv.); both terms imply nasty physical conditions.

56. J. Chrys., *In Eutr.* 394.60, 395.4–6, 395.13–18, 395.20–22 (Κἂν πλούσιος εἰσέλθῃ, μεγάλα κερδαίνει. . . . καταστέλλει τὴν φλεγμονήν, καθαιρεῖ τὸ φύσημα, καὶ φιλοσοφήσας ἃ χρὴ περὶ τῶν ἀνθρωπίνων φιλοσοφεῖν, οὕτως ἄπεισιν. . . . Πάλιν ὁ πένης εἰσελθὼν, καὶ πρὸς τὴν ὄψιν ταύτην ἰδών, οὐκ ἐξευτελίζει ἑαυτὸν, οὐδὲ ὀδυνᾶται διὰ τὴν πτωχείαν· ἀλλὰ καὶ χάριν οἶδε τῇ πενίᾳ, ὅτι χωρίον αὐτῷ

Here we observe John Chrysostom in action. Through his precipitous fall, Eutropius as a consul and human being has become a teaching tool to demonstrate to every rich person that their wealth is as fragile as his. Every wealthy person is Eutropius. However, John did not stop there. Those whom Chrysostom calls poor must also look and learn.[57] "He has become a spectacle for the world, and, though silent, through this experience utters words of advice to all: 'Don't do this kind of thing, in case you experience the same fate.' Through the disaster, he's shown himself to be a teacher, and the altar emits a great radiance—particularly fearsome at this moment—and shows by this that it holds the lion tied up." Eutropius, the tamed lion, has become an exemplary warning for everyone, rich and poor alike; his suffering has been universalized.[58]

To illustrate why the lessons of Eutropius's fall concerned everyone, John next traced its causes. Insulting the emperor—which John mentioned twice without giving specifics, allowing him to offer his view—had been the trigger, but the root of the problem lay deeper. In John's eyes, Eutropius had used his enormous wealth the wrong way. He had been greedy, arrogant, full of conceit, and had wasted his resources on extravagances and nefarious pleasures such as chariot races. Here John deployed the familiar traditional tropes of the luxury critique. However, in line with contemporary Christian teaching, the bishop criticized not wealth per se but rather its mistaken use.[59] Moreover, Eutropius had refused to heed John's frank advice. In other words, he had failed to surround himself with true friends. "Didn't I say to you, 'I love you more than those who flatter you. When I criticize I care more for you than those who aim to please'?"[60] It is important to remember that John and his audience were as familiar as Synesius and his circle with the classic notions of virtuous friendship (à la Xenophon's *Cyropaideia*). Indeed, as mentioned above, it is very likely that members of that circle were among those whom John addressed that day. He could assume that most were familiar with the consequences of wrong "friends."

Eutropius—similar to Synesius's Arcadius—had ignored the loving correction of a true friend and had to learn his lesson the hard way. "For when on the

γέγονεν ἄσυλον καὶ λιμὴν ἀκύμαντος; καὶ τεῖχος ἀσφαλές. . . . Ὁρᾷς ὡς οὐ μικρὸν κέρδος γέγονε καὶ πλουσίοις, καὶ πένησι, καὶ ταπεινοῖς, καὶ ὑψηλοῖς, καὶ δούλοις, καὶ ἐλευθέροις ἀπὸ τῆς ἐνταῦθα τούτου καταφυγῆς).

57. Those whom Chrysostom calls poor are not necessarily destitute—it is notoriously difficult to get a sense of what poverty implies for our mostly elite authors: see Caner, *Rich and the Pure*, 2–10.

58. J. Chrys., *In Eutr.* 394.30–36 (καὶ γέγονε τῆς οἰκουμένης θέατρον, καὶ σιγῶν ἐντεῦθεν ἀφίησι φωνὴν ἅπασι παραινῶν, Μὴ ποιεῖτε τοιαῦτα, ἵνα μὴ πάθητε τοιαῦτα. Διδάσκαλος ἀνεφάνη διὰ τῆς συμφορᾶς, καὶ λαμπηδόνα μεγάλην ἀφίησι τὸ θυσιαστήριον, νῦν φοβερὸν μάλιστα καὶ ἐκ τούτου φαινόμενον, ὅτι τὸν λέοντα δεδεμένον ἔχει). Tamed lions as emblems of the transformative power of the will to tame ferocious passions are among John's favorite metaphors: see, e.g., J. Chrys., *In Gen. hom.* 9.3; *In Matt.* 4.9; *Ne tim.* 1.1; also Leyerle, "Locating Animals," 282; Leyerle, *Narrative Shape*, 33–34.

59. W. Mayer, "Audience(s) for Patristic Social Teaching," 85–96; Brown, *Through the Eye of a Needle*, 110–47, 224–40; Caner, *Rich and the Pure*, 51–70; Bozinis, "Natural Law," 512–20.

60. J. Chrys., *In Eutr.* 392.9–13 (οὐκ ἔλεγόν σοι . . . ὅτι Ἐγώ σε φιλῶ μᾶλλον τῶν κολακευόντων).

previous day they came after him from the emperor's palace with the intention of dragging him away by force and he fled toward the sacred vessels, his countenance—as even now—was for once no better than that of a corpse."[61] After he was deserted by his false friends, only "the church you made war against has opened its arms and taken you in, while the theaters on which you lavished care…have betrayed and destroyed you . . . [and] sharpened their sword; while the church, despite enjoying your untimely rage, runs around in every direction in a desire to snatch you out of their nets."[62]

Unappreciative of John's corrections, Eutropius had waged war against the church in a hostile act that John dramatized through imagined direct speech: "'But,' someone says, 'he blocked flight here through documents and various laws!'"[63] Rather than dwell on how Eutropius might have offended the emperor, John used the moment to lobby for a bishop's right to grant asylum in churches. In this imagined dialogue, Chrysostom insinuated that Eutropius had been the first to violate his own laws (issued by Arcadius) that "blocked flight here"—that is, curtailed who could seek asylum in churches. Of course, none of these laws, discussed above, prevented people who were not in debt from seeking asylum, but John was not interested in the details of the actual legislation. Instead, he used the consul to criticize imperial measures that circumscribed his authority without mentioning the emperor himself. Eutropius's misfortune offered an irresistible opportunity to showcase the power of the church, which the emperor's legislation had attempted to diminish. Now the bishop staged the fallen consul, prostrate at the altar like a vanquished captive, as a trophy of his victory. This triumph over the rich man and consul had been achieved, of course, through the weapons of philanthropy, tender affection or affectionate love (*philostorgia*), pity/mercy (*eleos*), sympathy (*sympatheia*), and floods of tears. The altar, not imperial monuments, as the place for trophies won by the church, not the emperor, through the weapons of philanthropy, tender affection, and mercy—these were juxtapositions designed to elicit novel emotional responses.

THE ADORNMENT OF THE ALTAR

As John Chrysostom twice assured his audience, he exposed Eutropius's failures not "to trample upon someone who's lying down" nor

61. J. Chrys., *In Eutr.* 393.36–40 (Τῇ γὰρ προτεραίᾳ, ὅτε ἐπ’ αὐτὸν ἦλθον ἐκ τῶν βασιλικῶν αὐλῶν πρὸς βίαν ἀφελκύσαι βουλόμενοι, καὶ τοῖς σκεύεσι προσέδραμε τοῖς ἱεροῖς, ἦν αὐτοῦ τὸ πρόσωπον, καὶ τανῦν, νεκρωθέντος ἅπαξ οὐδὲν ἄμεινον διακείμενον).

62. J. Chrys., *In Eutr.* 392.23–32 (Καὶ ἡ μὲν πολεμηθεῖσα Ἐκκλησια παρὰ σοῦ τοὺς κόλπους ἥπλωσε καὶ ἐπεδέξατο· τὰ δὲ θεραπευθέντα θέατρα, ὑπὲρ ὧν πολλάκις πρὸς ἡμᾶς ἠγανάκτεις, προὔδωκε καὶ ἀπώλεσεν. . . . τὸ ξίφος ἠκόνησαν· ἡ δὲ Ἐκκλησία ἡ τῆς ὀργῆς τῆς σῆς ἀπολαύσασα τῆς ἀκαίρου, πανταχοῦ παρατρέχει, τῶν δικτύων σε ἐξαρπάσαι βουλομένη).

63. J. Chrys., *In Eutr.* 394.27–28 (Ἀλλ’ ἀπετείχισε, φησὶ, τὴν ἐνταῦθα καταφυγὴν γράμμασι καὶ νόμοις διαφόροις).

to reproach him nor trample upon his disaster, but out of a desire to soften your minds and to induce them to pity/mercy [*eleos*] and to persuade them that what has happened is sufficient punishment. For there are many among us who are so inhuman that they nevertheless criticized us too because we received him in the sanctuary. I parade forth this man's suffering from a desire to soften their lack of [com]passion [*pathos*] with my comments. Tell me, beloved! Why are you annoyed? "Because," you say, "the man who fled to the church is a person who constantly warred against it." So, then, we should glorify God on that account most of all—that God let him fall into such depths of necessity that he's come to know both the power [*dynamis*] and the love of mankind [*philanthropia*] of the church.[64]

Everyone, not merely Eutropius, ought to have realized, nearly two decades after Themistius's recasting of imperial victory in the context of Theodosius's Gothic peace, that philanthropy won the most triumphs. Now John Chrysostom extended the Theodosian reconceptualization of imperial victory further to demonstrate to his audience how the bishop wielded the weapon of philanthropy. John's shift of the meaning of love of mankind was subtle yet significant. As he saw it, philanthropy elicits affectionate love (*philostorgia*) in the receiver *and* the giver, which for the latter "is more illustrious than any trophy; this is a manifest victory; this undermines pagans, this shames Jews too; this shows the church with a radiant face. . . . [Eutropius has learned the church's] power from the enormous change in his circumstances. . . . [He's come to know] its philanthropy from the fact that the church he warred against is now putting forth its shield, and has taken him under its wings . . . with much affectionate love."[65] Philanthropy together with affectionate love tamed the lion. This was John's weapon, the "radiant face . . . that . . . spared its enemy when it took him captive and that, when everyone else overlooked him in his isolation . . . alone hid him beneath its veils like an affectionate

64. J. Chrys., *In Eutr.* 393.1–2, 393.45–394.1:

Καὶ ταῦτα λέγω νῦν, οὐκ ἐπεμβαίνων τῷ κειμένῳ. . . . Καὶ ταῦτα λέγω, οὐκ ὀνειδίζων, οὐδὲ ἐπεμβαίνων αὐτοῦ τῇ συμφορᾷ, ἀλλὰ τὴν ὑμετέραν διάνοιαν μαλάξαι βουλόμενος, καὶ εἰς ἔλεον ἐπισπάσασθαι, καὶ πεῖσαι ἀρκεσθῆναι τῇ τιμωρίᾳ τῇ γεγενημένῃ. Ἐπειδὴ γάρ εἰσι πολλοὶ παρ' ἡμῖν ἀπάνθρωποι, ὥστε ὁμοίως καὶ ἡμῖν ἐγκαλεῖν, ὅτι αὐτὸν ἐδεξάμεθα τῷ βήματι· τὸ ἄστοργον αὐτῶν τοῖς διηγήμασι μαλάξαι βουλόμενος, ἐκπομπεύω τὰ τούτου πάθη. Τίνος γὰρ ἕνεκεν ἀγανακτεῖς, εἰπέ μοι, ἀγαπητέ; Ὅτι, φησὶν, εἰς ἐκκλησίαν κατέφυγεν ὁ πολεμήσας αὐτὴν διηνεκῶς. Διὰ τοῦτο μὲν οὖν μάλιστα δοξάζειν ἐχρῆν τὸν Θεόν, ὅτι ἀφῆκεν αὐτὸν ἐν τοσαύτῃ καταστῆναι ἀνάγκῃ, ὥστε καὶ τὴν δύναμιν τῆς Ἐκκλησίας καὶ τὴν φιλανθρωπίαν μαθεῖν.

Roskam, "Emancipatory Preaching," 188–89, suggests that John's public humiliation of Eutropius went against his preference for private correction.

65. J. Chrys., *In Eutr.* 394.11–16 (τοῦτο φαιδρὸν αὐτῆς τὸ πρόσωπον δείκνυσιν· ὅτι τὸν πολέμιον αἰχμάλωτον λαβοῦσα, φείδεται, καὶ πάντων αὐτὸν ἐν ἐρημίᾳ παριδόντων, μόνη καθάπερ μήτηρ φιλόστοργος, ὑπὸ τὰ παραπετάσματα αὐτῆς ἔκρυψε, καὶ πρὸς βασιλικὴν ὀργὴν ἔστη, πρὸς δήμου θυμὸν, καὶ πρὸς μῖσος ἀφόρητον). Mayer and Allen translate *philostorgos* as "compassionate," but I prefer "affectionate" and "tender love," the first meanings that Lampe, *PGL*, offers s.v. I have also changed "generosity" back to "philanthropy."

mother [*meter philostorgos*], and stood up to the emperor's anger and popular rage and unbearable hatred."[66] The church, the affectionate, compassionate mother with her veil as protective shield, had won a triumphant victory through the weapons of love of mankind and tender affection. The fallen consul clutching the altar was the trophy of that triumph—a remarkable interweaving of the victorious, the military, the manly, and the motherly, all flowing together in the church and its bishop.

The motherly, compassionate church striking her weapons of philanthropy for glorious victory—that was what the icon "Eutropius prostate at the altar" illustrated and embodied. This was the didactic theater in which every member of the audience participated in their own way because each one could, at any moment, lie prostrate where Eutropius now lay. Moreover, though John was its most dramatic embodiment, every audience member was also "the church." They too participated in its victory the moment they felt affectionate love and philanthropy toward the fallen. Eutropius, for his part, became an adornment for the altar because he made that affectionate victory manifest. "'What kind of an adornment [*kosmos*] is it,' someone says, 'to have that accursed, greedy robber clinging to the altar?' Don't say that, since even the prostitute, who was exceedingly abominable and impure, touched the feet of Christ [John 12:3]; and what happened wasn't accounted to Jesus as a fault, but as a miracle and great hymn of praise. The point is that she who was unclean didn't harm him who is pure. Instead he who is pure and faultless rendered the accursed prostitute pure through the contact."[67]

One result of the church's victory through generous compassion was the purification of the fallen. The more abject the redeemed, the greater the transformative power of the redeemer. To illustrate this, John reframed the New Testament narrative of Mary Magdalene touching the savior's feet (John 12:3) by juxtaposing it to a familiar scene that continued the theme of imperial triumph. "After all, in the case of an imperial icon too, considerable adornment [*kosmos*] occurs not just when the emperor is seated on the throne dressed in purple and wearing a diadem, but also when barbarians with their hands bound behind their backs are lying beneath the emperor's foot with their heads bowed."[68] John here referred to

66. J. Chrys., *In Eutr.* 394.1–11 (τὴν δύναμιν μὲν, ἀφ' ὧν τοσαύτην ὑπέμεινε μεταβολήν . . . τὴν φιλανθρωπίαν δὲ, ἐξ ὧν πολεμηθεῖσα νῦν τὴν ἀσπίδα προβάλλεται, καὶ ὑπὸ τὰς πτέρυγας ἐδέξατο τὰς αὐτῆς . . . μετὰ πολλῆς ἁπλώσασα τῆς φιλοστοργίας. Τοῦτο γὰρ τροπαίου παντὸς λαμπρότερον, τοῦτο νίκη περιφανής, τοῦτο Ἕλληνας ἐντρέπει, τοῦτο καὶ Ἰουδαίους καταισχύνει, τοῦτο φαιδρὸν αὐτῆς τὸ πρόσωπον δείκνυσιν).

67. J. Chrys., *In Eutr.* 394.16–25 (Ποῖος κόσμος, φησὶ, τὸ τὸν ἐναγῆ καὶ πλεονέκτην καὶ ἅρπαγα ἅπτεσθαι τοῦ θυσιαστηρίου; Μὴ λέγε ταῦτα· ἐπειδὴ καὶ ἡ πόρνη ἥψατο τῶν ποδῶν τοῦ Χριστοῦ, ἡ σφόδρα ἐναγὴς καὶ ἀκάθαρτος . . . οὐ γὰρ τὸν καθαρὸν ἔβλαπτεν ἡ ἀκάθαρτος, ἀλλὰ τὴν ἐναγῆ πόρνην ὁ καθαρὸς καὶ ἄμωμος διὰ τῆς ἁφῆς καθαρὰν εἰργάσατο).

68. J. Chrys., *In Eutr.* 394.35–39 (ἐπεὶ καὶ βασιλικῇ εἰκόνι μέγας γένοιτο κόσμος, οὐχ ὅταν ἐπὶ τοῦ θρόνου κάθηται πορφυρίδα περιβεβλημένος, καὶ διάδημα περικείμενος ὁ βασιλεὺς μόνον, ἀλλὰ καὶ ὅταν ὑπὸ τῷ ποδὶ τῷ βασιλικῷ βάρβαροι τῶν χειρῶν ὀπίσω δεδεμένοι, κάτω τὰς κεφαλὰς νεύωσι κείμενοι).

the *calcatio colli*, the ritual mentioned in chapter 2, in which the emperor placed his boot on the neck of a defeated "barbarian" (or usurper) in an unmistakable act of dominance and humiliation.[69] Such complete abasement of the defeated glorified the victor and increased the immensity of the clemency he extended to bridge the gulf between them, (nearly) as wide as that separating Mary the prostitute from Christ.

Once more, however, Chrysostom pressed further and made the specific universal. At issue here were neither captive barbarians nor Mary Magdalene the prostitute nor the prostrate consul trembling in fear. Rather, they were all icons, paradigmatic of "human nature put on trial and the feebleness of worldly affairs exposed and that whorish face (the state of well-being that derives from acts of greed is such that it comes across as more deformed [*aischrotera*] than any old crone with wrinkles) as if by a sponge wiped clean of its rouge and makeup by a change of circumstance."[70] Human nature lay humiliated at the altar under the boot of the victor, slain by the detrimental passions of worldly affairs and by divine love. Humanity was the captive that the powerful weapons of motherly affection and philanthropy—truly love of humankind—vanquished and at the same time redeemed.

Those who lay prostrate at the altar, then, like abject barbarians, prostitutes, and "Eutropius," were all the members of John's audience, including the powerful and wealthy. To embrace Eutropius with affectionate love was in effect to love oneself. Everyone who had felt the desires that power and riches elicit was lying prostrate before the master. At the same time, however, all in the audience were also victorious as soon as they felt philanthropy and affectionate love toward the fallen consul. Philanthropy, according to John, was thus as much an emotion as an act, and everyone who felt the emotion associated with philanthropy—namely, love—became vanquished and victor. The audience got the message. "Have I softened your passion [*pathos*] and cast out your anger? Have I quenched your inhumanity? Have I drawn you into sympathy [*sympatheia*]? I very much think so—the faces indicate it, and the fountains of tears. Come, then, let's now prostate ourselves before the emperor. . . . Let's ask the (hu)mankind-loving [*philanthropos*] God to soften the rage of the emperor and make his heart gentle so that he'll grant our favor in its entirety."[71]

69. Malone, "Violence on Roman Imperial Coinage," 59–69.

70. J. Chrys., *In Eutr.* 394.50–55 (ἵνα τὴν ἀνθρωπίνην φύσιν ἴδητε ἐλεγχομένην, καὶ τῶν βιωτικῶν πραγμάτων τὸ ἐπίκηρον ἀπογυμνούμενον, καὶ τὴν πορνικὴν ὄψιν τὴν χθὲς καὶ πρώην φαιδρὸν ἀπολάμπουσαν (καὶ γὰρ τοιοῦτον ἡ εὐπραγία ἡ ἀπὸ τῶν πλεονεξιῶν, παντὸς γραϊδίου ῥυτίδας ἔχοντος αἰσχροτέρα φαινομένη), καθάπερ σπογγιᾷ τινι τῇ μεταβολῇ . . . ἐκμάξασαν). John often likens the repulsiveness of greed to dogs or camels: see J. Chrys., *In 1 Cor.* 9 (*PG* 61.80); *In Col.* 7 (*PG* 62–349); *In 2 Thess.* 3 (*PG* 62.483); *In Phil.* 2, 12 (*PG* 62.197, 62.274); also Leyerle, "Locating Animals," 283, 290–95.

71. J. Chrys., *In Eutr.* 395.23–34 (Ἆρα ἐμάλαξα ὑμῶν τὸ πάθος; . . . ἆρα ἔσβεσα τὴν ἀπανθρωπίαν; ἆρα εἰς συμπάθειαν ἤγαγον; Σφόδρα ἔγωγε οἶμαι, καὶ δηλοῖ τὰ πρόσωπα, καὶ αἱ τῶν δακρύων πηγαί . . .

The transformations are remarkable. His fall made Eutropius a potent symbol both of the fragility of power, status, and wealth and of the power of the weapon of philanthropy, now conceived as compassionate love and affection. As such, Eutropius had become a trophy of the church's triumph and an adornment of her altar. Shielded by her tender motherly affection, he was embraced by all who shared her generosity and extended their love to the consul, in whom they recognized our shared humanity in all its transience. Now the entire assembly, united by affectionate love and philanthropy, joined Eutropius in prostrating itself before the philanthropic God and his philanthropic emperor, shedding copious tears of compassion so that the fruit of mercy (*karpon eleemosynen*) might be granted to all.

In a subtle buildup, John progressively intertwined the language of imperial triumph and military victory, so central to Latin and Greek Roman manliness, with that of affection and love, especially motherly love. In the process, he claimed the manly imperial victory language with increasing intensity for the church as mother. Both the emperor, the apex of *vir*-ness and father of the fatherland, and the church, or *ekklesia*, as mother made use of divine philanthropy as a weapon to achieve victory though forgiveness, mercy or clemency, and affectionate love. Victory language is inevitably joined with that of defeat and humiliation, including in a civil war, and Chrysostom used it all to emphasize the power of imperial and divine clemency, now broadened into affectionate love, gentleness, and forgiveness—the last term one that Themistius had also used when recasting Theodosius's victories.[72]

In this context of military victory and the quelling of rage through forgiveness and mercy, John evoked the absent emperor for the first time. Like Ambrose, whose funeral oration for Theodosius brought the emperor back to life by speaking as him, John conveyed Arcadius's actions, thoughts, and words as if he represented the emperor and thus made the absent present. The emperor became part of that same audience and theoretically also lay prostrate at the altar—or would have, had he not anticipated everything John now prescribed for the assembly. Arcadius had already "let fountains of tears fall from his most gentle eyes" for Eutropius.[73] He had already undergone the emotional transformation enacted by John and demonstrated the capacious power of affectionate love, triumphant through divine philanthropy. Realizing that the consul had fled to "this inviolate place, in

φέρε δὲ . . . προσπέσωμεν τῷ βασιλεῖ, μᾶλλον δὲ παρακαλέσωμεν τὸν φιλάνθρωπον Θεὸν, μαλάξαι τὸν θυμὸν τοῦ βασιλέως, καὶ ἁπαλὴν αὐτοῦ ποιῆσαι τὴν καρδίαν, ὥστε ὁλόκληρον ἡμῖν δοῦναι τὴν χάριν). Mellas, "Tears of Compunction," 159–60, calls what John seeks to achieve "sacramental mimesis."

72. See chapter 5. For the church as the common mother of us all, see, e.g., J. Chrys., *De stat.* 6 (*PG* 49.81.42–43); and as mother of love (*agape*), e.g., J. Chrys., *In Tit.* 6.768a (*PG* 62.698); on fusions of father and mother language as rhetoric of leadership see S. Elm, "Family Men," and Burrus, "Reading the Bride of Christ," with further bibliography.

73. J. Chrys., *In Eutr.* 395.49–50 (πηγὰς λοιπὸν ἀφεὶς δακρύων ἀπὸ τῶν ἡμερωτάτων ὀφθαλμῶν). On tears wept on behalf of others, see Leyerle, *Narrative Shape*, 96–97; Mellas, "Tears of Compunction," 169–72; C. Harrison, *Art of Listening*, 150; McLynn, "Imperial Piety," 324.

the army's presence, while it was . . . demanding him for slaughter, the emperor made a long speech and quashed the soldiers' rage. He invited them to consider not just this person's failing [*hamartemata*] but, if he had performed any virtuous action [*katorthoma*], to take this into consideration too; and he professed himself grateful for the latter [*charis homologon*], while he pardoned the characteristics that were of contrary character as failings that were human."[74]

Because Arcadius had anticipated the change (*metabole*) that everyone else in the audience was experiencing only now, all that was required of the assembled was to emulate the emperor. In other words, their entreaties—including those of Eutropius trembling at the altar—were guaranteed to find favor. The emperor, though insulted, "bore no grudge." Therefore, the members of the audience had better restrain their anger: they had not even been insulted. "No, at the moment it isn't the time for a lawcourt but for mercy [*eleos*], [not] for accounting but for love of mankind [*philanthropia*], not for interrogation but for concession [*synchoraeseos*], not for a ballot and penalty but for pity [*oiktros*] and grace [*charitos*]."[75] Arcadius, moreover, had extended his divine philanthropy to the fallen Eutropius knowing that the *philanthropos* God had granted mercy "before the emperor even."[76]

Indeed, God in his love of humankind

> will applaud and give us in return a considerable reward for our philanthropy. I mean that in the same way as God hates and turns away a person who is cruel and inhumane, he admits and loves a person who is merciful and generous [*philanthropos*]. When a person is just, he weaves them [victory] crowns that are more radiant [*lamproteros*]; if he is a sinner, he bypasses their sins and gives them this reward in return for their sympathy toward their fellow slave. . . . By this means, then, shall we too render him merciful, in this way shall we discharge our misdeeds, in this way shall we adorn the church [*kosmesomen*]. In this way too the generous emperor will approve, as I said a moment ago, and the entire populace will applaud, and the end of the earth will marvel at the love of humankind [*philanthropia*] and the gentleness [*hemeron*] of the city, and . . . people all over the world will cry out our name. . . . Let's prostrate ourselves, let's plead, let's request, let's snatch from danger the captive, the fugitive, the suppliant, so that we too may attain the blessings that are to come, through the grace [*charis*] and love of humankind [*philanthropia*] of our lord Jesus Christ.[77]

74. J. Chrys., *In Eutr.* 395.42–46 (μακρὸν ἀπέτεινε λόγον, τὸν στρατιωτικὸν καταστέλλων θυμὸν, ἀξιῶν μὴ τὰ ἁμαρτήματα μόνον, ἀλλὰ καὶ εἴ τι αὐτῷ γέγονε κατόρθωμα, καὶ τοῦτο λογίζεσθαι, καὶ τοῖς μὲν εἰδέναι χάριν ὁμολογῶν, ὑπὲρ δὲ τῶν ἑτέρως ἐχόντων ὡς ἀνθρώπῳ συγγινώσκων). For the connection between failing, *hamartemata*, and virtuous action, *katorthoma*, in Stoic thought, see, e.g., Chrysipp., *Stoic.* 3.295; *IG* 5.2.268, l.15 (Mantinea, 1 BCE).

75. J. Chrys., *In Eutr.* 396.11–14 (Ἀλλ' οὐ δικαστηρίου καιρὸς νῦν, ἀλλ' ἐλέους· οὐκ εὐθύνης, ἀλλὰ φιλανθρωπίας· οὐκ ἐξετάσεως, ἀλλὰ συγχωρήσεως· οὐ ψήφου καὶ δίκης, ἀλλὰ οἴκτρου καὶ χάριτος). See also J. Chrys., *In Heb.* 11.10; *Compunct. Dem.* 1.4; *In Matt.* 35.4; *In Phil.* 1.5.

76. J. Chrys., *In Eutr.* 396.21–22.

77. J. Chrys., *In Eutr.* 396.22–30, 396.34–44:

John's vocabulary and the composition of the homily instantiated the trans-formations he wished his audience to undergo.[78] Chrysostom opened his sermon with the technical vocabulary of Eutropius's senatorial rank as *illustris (lampros) vir* and consul, glittering with the brilliant vestments of power and surrounded by the trappings of his office: bodyguards, torches, applauding masses in the theater and hippodrome. He concluded the sermon with the same vocabulary, *lampros* or *illustris*, now evoked to praise what is truly radiant and splendid. The gleam-ing weapons of philanthropy, affectionate love (*philostorgia*), and pity/mercy (*eleos*), plus what they brought about, charity (*charis*), adorned the altar and made everyone who embraced them radiant. All in the assembly could thus transform themselves into *illustres viri*, acclaimed and applauded in the city and in the entire world (*oikoumene*), honored not as the emperor's consul but as those redeemed by the philanthropic God.

The prerequisite for that transformation was John's adaptation, in this homily, of the Theodosian conception of imperial victory through philanthropy, which he now merged with the language of motherly love and affection, *philostorgia*, to expand it into love of humankind. The prostrate consul was paradigmatic for this transformation. In John's hands, he became an icon (*eikon*) of Theodosian victo-rious imperial manliness as the bishop saw it: meshed with the motherly affec-tion of the church. The emperor as father wielded the weapon of philanthropy while the church as mother used the veil of her love as a shield to vanquish and redeem fallen humankind. As a human being and part of John's assembly—albeit as an absent presence—the emperor participated in that fall: he too lay prostrate at the altar. As the divine emperor, however, he had anticipated the triumph of loving affection. He was nearer than the rest of the assembly to the philanthropic God—except for the bishop, who carefully concealed that he was the mastermind by speaking on behalf of the church. Eutropius as the icon of defeat as well as vic-tory also became, for those who listened carefully, an icon of a particular kind of "civil war." This was a civil war that every human being must fight against them-selves, as both winner and loser, triumphant and humiliated, as long as humans are tempted by the worldly desire for power and wealth, the soft and the luxurious, which causes them to fall like Eutropius, only to triumph against themselves with the help of divine, affectionate love. The weapons of divine love and forgiveness

καὶ μεγάλην ἡμῖν τῆς φιλανθρωπίας ἀποδώσει τὴν ἀμοιβήν. . . . οὕτω τὰ ἡμετέρα διαλύσομεν πλημμελήματα, οὕτω τὴν Ἐκκλησίαν κοσμήσομεν, οὕτω καὶ βασιλεὺς ἡμᾶς ὁ φιλάνθρωπος ἐπαινέσεται, καθάπερ ἔφθην εἰπὼν, καὶ ἅπας ὁ δῆμος κροτήσει, καὶ τὰ πέρατα τῆς οἰκουμένης τὸ φιλάνθρωπον καὶ ἥμερον τῆς πόλεως θαυμάσεται, καὶ μαθόντες οἱ πανταχοῦ τῆς γῆς τὰ γενόμενα κηρύξουσιν ἡμᾶς . . . προσπέσωμεν, παρακαλέσωμεν, δεηθῶμεν, ἐξαρπάσωμεν τοῦ κινδύνου τὸν αἰχμάλωτον, τὸν φυγάδα, τὸν ἱκέτην, ἵνα καὶ αὐτοὶ τῶν μελλόντων ἀγαθῶν ἐπιτύχωμεν, χάριτι καὶ φιλανθρωπίᾳ τοῦ Κυρίου ἡμῶν Ἰησοῦ Χριστοῦ, ᾧ ἡ δόξα καὶ τὸ κράτος, νῦν καὶ ἀεί, καὶ εἰς τοὺς αἰῶνας τῶν αἰώνων. Ἀμήν.

78. See also Leyerle, *Narrative Shape*, 7–19.

thus transformed everyone in the audience into a *vir*—that is, a virtuous person, manly and illuminated—whether male or female, rich or poor, slave or free; in other words, these weapons made the empire queer.

THE EUNUCH WITHIN: JOHN CHRYSOSTOM'S CONCEPT OF CHRISTIAN IMPERIAL PHILANTHROPY

Not once, to reiterate, did John explicitly refer to Eutropius as a eunuch. In line with the rhetorical precepts of *synkatabasis*, or the adaptation of style to each member of the audience, his silence offered choices. For those who wished to see Eutropius "merely" as a fallen *illustris vir* and consul, the spectacle of a former peer trembling at the altar was sufficiently shocking. John's rhetoric gave permission to the powerful to show compassion to such a fallen *illustris vir* and *patricius* and ignore that Eutropius was also a eunuch. However, for those with the capacity to face that fact, John made it clear that he wanted everyone, including the absent emperor, to become Eutropius as consul *and* eunuch, even if he never made the latter point explicit.

One of the principal goals of John's rhetoric was his audience's reevaluation of their own emotions, which he achieved by placing the familiar into a new, potentially jarring context to elicit cognitive shifts. Forcing each member to imagine being a fallen eunuch perfectly aligns with this method. As a fallen eunuch rather than "merely" a fallen consul, John's "Eutropius" expanded Arcadius's imperial philanthropy by adding the demand for motherly affectionate love for an abject human being. This conception of imperial philanthropy went significantly further than that elaborated by Themistius on behalf of Theodosius and reflected concepts that John had already developed in Antioch. His preaching during and after the so-called Riot of the Statues in 387 reveals important stages of that development.[79] Theodosius and Arcadius's levy of an extraordinary tax, largely to finance the eastern army, had met with resistance among the Antiochene elites. During escalating riots, statues of the imperial family were desecrated. An emperor's statue was considered the embodiment of the ruler, so their destruction was an act of treason. Everyone in the city knew that Theodosius would react with severe punishment— the question was how severe. Antioch lost its metropolitan status; rioters were prosecuted and executed; baths, theaters, and the hippodrome were closed; and many citizens fled to the countryside.

Among those who pleaded for the emperor's mercy was John Chrysostom, who preached twenty-four sermons during and after the events.[80] His portrayal

---

79. Shepardson, *Controlling*, 147–62; Stenger, *Johannes Chrysostomos*, 174–237; Quiroga Puertas, "Toying with Theodosius"; Liebeschuetz, *Ambrose and John Chrysostom*, 209–15; Groß-Albenhausen, *Imperator christianissimus*, 170–83.

80. On these homilies, see van de Paverd, *St. John Chrysostom*, xxi–xxx, 3–13, 205–364; Quiroga Puertas, "Toying with Theodosius," 199–201.

of the fall of mighty Antioch, the shining star of the east reduced to begging for mercy, anticipated that of the fallen consul twelve years later. With these sermons, John addressed a rapt audience crammed into his church, where some of the city's notables had sought asylum while Antioch feared for its very existence. However, Antioch's precipitous fall also revealed the power of a new and unexpected weapon, ready to defend the prostrate city. While fleeing to the countryside, some rich and powerful members of the city's council (*boule*) encountered an army of monks and ascetics who were racing to Antioch to do battle for the emperor's philanthropic mercy.[81] Together with Antioch's bishop Flavian and armed with copious tears, dignity, and manly *arete*, or courageous virtue, they reminded Theodosius that his most cherished imperial virtues were philanthropy and mercy/pity. Thus admonished, Theodosius curbed his anger and spared the city.[82] Indeed, so immense was his merciful forgiveness "that the city in future shall carry the name of your *Philanthropia*," John assured him.[83] Antioch, deserted by its luxury-loving elites, who had either left or sought asylum in the churches, was saved by austere Christian ascetics, who pressed the emperor to use the power of his philanthropy. In the intervening decade at Antioch, as Daniel Caner has shown, John progressively expanded this fairly traditional understanding of imperial *philanthropia* with far-reaching consequences for the appropriate use of wealth and how it should be redistributed. These developments profoundly influenced the evolution of social structures in Byzantium.[84]

John's homily for Eutropius in 399 offered the recently elected bishop of Constantinople the first occasion to present his new understanding of philanthropy as Christian imperial virtue to an elite audience in the capital. In its traditional or classic understanding, philanthropy contained a distinct concessive dimension. As Themistius's characterization of Theodosius's philanthropy toward the Goths makes apparent, this concessive aspect remained in force well into late antiquity, including in Christian contexts.[85] Philanthropy, in essence, was intended for persons who did not belong to one's family, who were not kin, and who had experienced a (dramatic) reversal of fortune. As such, it always encompassed clemency and pity in the sense of "'being benevolent to others, even if doing so goes against

81. See, e.g., J. Chrys., *De stat.* 2.1, 5.5–6, 17.2, 18.4 (*PG* 49.34–35, 49.76–77, 49.174, 49.186).

82. J. Chrys., *De stat.* 21.3 (*PG* 49.217.16) (Νῦν δὸς αὐτὴν καλεῖσθαι λοιπὸν ἀπὸ τῆς σῆς φιλανθρωπίας). See also Lib., *Or.* 20.46; Stenger, *Johannes Chrysostomos*, 223–37; Shepardson, *Controlling*, 154–60, highlights John's emphasis on reversed gender roles during the crisis, when men deserted the agora to hide in mountain caves while women were forced out of their houses.

83. That Antioch's bishop, supported by monks, succeeded in placating Theodosius is John's version of the event. According to Libanius, Antioch was instead exonerated by the report of Theodosius's *magister officiorum* Caesarius (the brother of Aurelian), who had been sent from Constantinople to investigate. See van de Paverd, *St. John Chrysostom*, 57–63, 131–49; Quiroga Puertas, "Toying with Theodosius," 205–9. See also Quiroga Puertas, *La rétorica de Libanio*.

84. Caner, *Rich and the Pure*, 64–65, 71–83, 114–22.

85. Them., *Or.* 16.207bc; Heather and Moncur, *Politics*, 208–18, 230–35, 255–64.

one's natural inclination,' or 'showing kindness to fellow humans, despite full knowledge that they do not deserve it.' This dimension gave ancient philanthropy its hard, distinctive edge, turning a lofty ideal into a provocative (and potentially burdensome) challenge."[86] Significantly, irrespective of their religious affiliation, late antique authors also stressed that philanthropy was particularly true when extended to those who did not deserve it, because it responded to the recipients as human beings rather than to their character or actions.[87]

In making the case for Eutropius, John stressed this concessive element as well. The emperor, the church, and those present in the assembly that day extended their philanthropy to someone not their kin who had experienced a dramatic fall and who, as an unscrupulous rich man, was as "deserving" as a captive barbarian or a prostitute. If one added that Eutropius was a eunuch, he made everyone's philanthropy exceedingly "true."[88] In the second part of his homily, John linked that philanthropy with pity/mercy (*eleos*) and affectionate love (*philostorgia*). Though the distinctions were fluid, *eleos*—now increasingly meaning mercy[89]—and *philostorgia* were traditionally reserved for one's family or kin. These emotions and the resulting actions were not intended for outsiders. In the sermons he preached in Antioch, especially after 387, however, John began to argue that mercy was true and Christian only if extended beyond one's family. Almsgiving, or *eleemosyne*, the practical aspect of mercy, should include everyone. Specifically, like philanthropy, mercy should be directed most to those who deserved it least: persons who were very much the other, such as prostitutes, beggars, or lepers.[90] Moreover, John insisted that Christian philanthropy, combined with mercy and almsgiving, had to have the personal dimension of affectionate love. Sending one's slaves to distribute handouts was not sufficient.

True Christian philanthropy as mercy and love thus required that the benefactor personally and physically interact with the receiver, and the more abject the latter, the better.[91] Only the voluntary abasement of the giver toward the humble, the lowly, in repeated physical acts of affectionate love (*philostorgia*) could bring

86. Caner, *Rich and the Pure*, 36 (quotation marks indicate Caner's definition of the term); see also 1–34.

87. Caner, *Rich and the Pure*, 36–43.

88. J. Chrys., *In Eutr.* 394.35–40; see also J. Chrys., *Laz. et div.* 1.6, 2.4, 6.5.

89. Building upon shifts already under way: see Konstan, *Pity Transformed*, 59; Blowers, "Pity, Empathy," 10–26.

90. John here expands Gregory of Nazianzus's theories: see Gr. Naz., *Or.* 14; J. Chrys., *In Matt.* 66.3; J. Chrys., *In 1 Cor.* 21.6; J. Chrys., *Laz. et div.* 2.4; Caner, *Rich and the Pure*, 48–59, 76–82; Wessel, *Passion*, 38–48; Holman, *Hungry Are Dying*, 143–53.

91. See, e.g., J. Chrys., *In Act.* 14.2; *In Heb.* 32.3; *In 1 Cor.* 27.1, 30.5; *De eleem.* 1, 6; *In Matt.* 88.3; *In 1 Tim.* 14.3; *In Rom.* 21.3; see also Sandwell, *Religious Identity*, 190–98; Caner, *Rich and the Pure*, 77–81; Brown, *Power and Persuasion*, 152–58; Brändle, "Sweetest Passage"; Hartney, *John Chrysostom*, 157; Tonias, "Iconic Abraham," 566–81; for the contrast to Gregory, N. V. Harrison, "Greek Patristic Perspective," 91–93.

about the cognitive reordering of the wealthy and powerful that might, over time, break their arrogance and conceit and help them to approximate the condescension, or *synkatabasis*, of Jesus Christ. That was what being Christian (and wealthy) required, in imitation of the Lord's voluntary abasement to the most abject form of humanity.[92]

In this context, John Chrysostom's conspicuous silence regarding Eutropius's well-known condition as a eunuch requires another look. In the opinion of most scholars, John chastised Eutropius but nevertheless offered a spirited defense in defiance of Arcadius.[93] In my reading, the bishop instead amplified the emperor's wishes. However, he did so very much in his own way, carefully creating spaces for Arcadius—and for himself—to maneuver; it was still early days in their relationship. Thus, John begun by stressing the military valor, the manliness, of Theodosius and Arcadius's version of victory won through the weapons of philanthropy, which allowed him—according to the logic of defeat, especially in a civil war—to highlight the magnificence of the benevolent generosity that the *clementissimus* emperor (if he so desired) would surely extend to the consul. After all, Eutropius's fortunes had reversed only on the previous day and his fate was as yet entirely undetermined: he might be pardoned, exiled, or executed.[94] Arcadius was deeply attached to Eutropius, as John emphasized, which further increased the potential reach of imperial mercy. Indeed, John's powerful portrayal of the mighty consul as a trembling frog, prostrate at the altar like a barbarian captive under the emperor's boot, dramatized the extent to which Arcadius had already shown him mercy and love. On the previous day, the tear-stained emperor had condescended in magnificent ways by extending his philanthropic, affectionate love to the fallen (who was not his kin, even though the consul was a father figure to him): Arcadius, the emperor, had performed an act of *synkatabasis* that mirrored the one Christ had shown to the prostitute and, more important, to all of humankind, simply because of his divine, benevolent love.

In classic rhetoric, as mentioned above, *synkatabasis* denoted the ability to adapt one's speech such that everyone in the audience would be persuaded according to their preferences and abilities.[95] John Chrysostom, as David Rylaarsdam has pointed out, transformed the technical meaning into a fundamental theological concept, according to which divine philanthropy expresses itself in God's

---

92. See, e.g., J. Chrys., *In 1 Tim.* 14.3; *In Jn.* 81.3; *In Eph.* 18.4.

93. This interpretation follows the tendency of the pro-John sources, which portray the bishop as an excessively frank critic of the passive emperor: see Pfeilschifter, *Kaiser und Konstantinopel*, 488–90, n. 89, 502–3; Tiersch, *Johannes Chrysostomus*, 284. McLynn, "Imperial Piety," 324–27, instead emphasizes their gradual estrangement.

94. As Hillner, "Confined Exiles," 393–415, points out, exile was a common punishment for the elite; shortly afterward, Eutropius was indeed exiled to Cyprus before being recalled and executed (409).

95. Rylaarsdam, *John Chrysostom*, 7–9, 29–30 (difficulties of translating the term), 37–48.

synkatabasis, his condescension or appropriate adaptation to the givens of each human being. Christ made this condescension manifest with his voluntary decision to become incarnate and in so doing descend to the lowest form of humanity, the enslaved persons suffering death by crucifixion.[96] Divine philanthropy as affectionate love, *synkatabasis* or condescension, and humility were thus intrinsically intertwined. "See God's appropriate adaptation [*synkatabasis*]. . . . His words are uttered not with a view to his own dignity but out of adaptation to our limitations."[97] "We can learn Christ's care for his disciples and both the humility [*tapeinon*] and the adaptation of his manner [*synkatabasis*] toward them."[98] Indeed, Christ's humility "is below his dignity . . . but is worthy of his majesty if one considers the ineffable richness of his philanthropy."[99]

IMPERIAL CIVILITY AND HUMILITY

John's development of the theological concept of philanthropy as appropriate adaptation or condescension all the way down to the humble coincided with the gradual inclusion of humility, or *tapeinophrosyne*, in the kaleidoscope of imperial virtues, at least as expressed by authors who were Christian bishops. Gregory of Nyssa's funeral oration for the empress Flaccilla and Ambrose's for Theodosius demonstrate this slow and carefully calibrated process, which required the expansion of imperial civility (*civilitas*). The inclusion of imperial "humility" began with Theodosius, but as Steffen Diefenbach and Christopher Kelly have shown, it was given full ceremonial expression only in 447, late in Theodosius II's reign, when the emperor set aside his regalia and walked barefoot in a seven-mile procession from the Great Palace to the Hebdomon, a first in Roman history.[100] To recall, imperial *civilitas* was expressed through ceremonial gestures signaling the emperor's stooping down ("Herabneigen"), such as walking about in public without imperial vestments or bodyguards, visiting sick senators, and similar acts of cordiality that ultimately reified the social distinctions they ostensibly overcame, because they were temporary.[101] In Pliny's opinion—and he was the model whom Pacatus

96. Rylaarsdam, *John Chrysostom*, 132–51.

97. J. Chrys., *In Gen. hom.* 51.8 (*PG* 54.453) (Ὅρα συγκατάβασιν Θεοῦ. . . . Οὐ πρὸς τὴν οἰκείαν ἀξίαν ὁρῶν φθέγγεται· ἀλλὰ πρὸς τὴν ἀσθένειαν συγκαταβαίνων τὴν ἡμετέραν).

98. J. Chrys., *In Jn.* 42 (*PG* 59.240) "οὐ μάλιστα καὶ ἐντεῦθεν τὴν κηδεμονίαν ἔστι μαθεῖν, καὶ τὸ ταπεινὸν καὶ συγκαταβαστικὸν τὸ πρὸς ἐκείνους).

99. J. Chrys., *In Jn.* 64 (*PG* 59.356) (ἀνάξιον μὲν, εἴ τις πρὸς τὴν ἀξίαν ἐκείνην ἴδοι· ἄξιον δὲ, εἴ τις τὸν ἄφατον τῆς αὐτοῦ φιλανθρωπίας πλοῦτον λογίσαιτο). See also Rylaarsdam, *John Chrysostom*, 42–45.

100. *HA, Prob.* 9.9; *HA, Alex. Sev.* 20.1, 60.3; Diefenbach, "Zwischen Liturgie," 31–39; further developing Diefenbach, "Frömmigkeit," 51–52; Ch. Kelly, "Stooping." See also McLynn, *Ambrose*, 323–30; Tiersch, *Johannes Chrysostomus*, 277; Noreña, *Imperial Ideals*, 36–38; Wallace-Hadrill, "*Civilis Princeps*."

101. See chapter 1; *Pan. lat.* (2)12.20.4–6, (2)12.47.3; Eutr., *Brev.* 1.1, 8.4; Tac., *Ann.* 1.54.2, 2.23.3; Amm. Marc. 16–10.1–17, 22.7.1, 22.7.3, 25.4.18 (with critical remarks regarding Julian's excessive civility); Diefenbach, "Zwischen Liturgie," 33 ("Herabneigen"); Ch. Kelly, "Stooping," 227–28.

and others emulated—for the man "who can advance no further than the highest rank, the only way to go higher is to step down while secure of his greatness."[102] Emperors could afford to stoop (to the lowly level of a sick senator, say), Pliny added, because their position was so exalted that gestures of civil condescension were unlikely to be confused with humility.[103]

For all other members of the elites, Pliny suggested, humility was dangerous; even emperors had to be circumspect, lest their acts of civility be tainted by being too lowly. By the time of Pacatus's description of Theodosius's humble love of his friends, however, the nature of God had changed. The divine being whom Theodosius venerated had explicitly embraced the low, the humble. Thus, *this* emperor could risk a certain measure of humility, because his imperial fortune and magnitude, to use Pliny's terms, were so unassailable that occasional humble moments could not diminish them, and such moments evoked his God. Nevertheless, Gregory of Nyssa's association of miraculous humility with Flaccilla rather than with the emperor, and Ambrose's careful crafting of the living Theodosius as humble, a trait that became more pronounced once the emperor was deceased, indicate that these bishops were aware of the advantages and danger of expanding imperial *civilitas* to include this new lowness.

John Chrysostom made the changed ontological nature of the divine and that danger explicit when he emphasized the majesty of Christ. Though the humble and the humiliated were defined by the absence of dignity, this did not affect the condescending divine in the least. An emperor who stooped to the level of an abject person prostrate at the altar no more lost his imperial majesty than Christ's voluntary assumption of the most abject human form diminished God's omnipotence.[104] Moments of imperial humility, staged the right way, could become powerful instantiations—by analogy—of Christ's incarnation and offer glimpses into the emperor's humanity that were difficult to forget; though temporary, their impact was lasting. Chrysostom's homily in the presence of Eutropius created such moments for Arcadius and thus aligns with Gregory of Nyssa's and Ambrose's characterizations of members of the ruling family as humble. John too was a bishop, however, which makes it difficult to ascertain whether such humility language reflects episcopal moves, imperial intentions, or careful collaboration between both.

At any rate, John Chrysostom presented the most explicit staging of imperial humility while both the emperor and his consort were alive, shortly after his sermon for Eutropius. In a homily he preached in either 400, just after Eudoxia

---

102. Plin., *Pan.* 71.4 ("Nam cui nihil ad augendum fastigium superest, hic uno modo crescere potest, si se ipse summittat securus magnitudinis suae"), trans. Radice, with my modifications.

103. Plin., *Pan.* 71.5: "Neque enim ab ullo periculo fortuna principum longius abest quam humilitatis" (Because the fortune of princes is furthest removed from the danger of humility).

104. A fact that Pope Leo emphasized at the Council of Chalcedon: see *Coll. Nov.* 5.3 (Schwartz 2.2.1, p. 27.14); Brown, *Power and Persuasion*, 154–57.

became augusta, or 402, which later scribes titled "When the Empress Came to Church in the Middle of the Night," John offered an evocative description of one of the nighttime processions mentioned above.[105] The occasion was the transfer of relics from the Hagia Sophia to a new shrine in the suburb of Drypia, about nine miles distant. Preaching at dawn, John professed himself overcome by what he had witnessed, jumping with excitement and drunk with joy: Men and women of all ages, ethnic backgrounds, and social positions, from magistrates to the enslaved, had come together in that procession, forming a mass of humanity that lit the streets like a river of fire. Carried along in the middle, shining like the moon, was the empress Eudoxia. Her participation had brought forth everyone; like a new David, she united all to sing his psalms, in Latin, Syriac, the language of the barbarian, and Greek.[106] But what caused John's greatest jubilation was that Eudoxia had put aside her diadem and her imperial vestments. Dressed as she would be normally only in the presence of her eunuchs, the empress rivaled the apostles by walking nine miles behind the casket containing the relics "like a maidservant" or slave (*therapaine*), "quashing all vanity" and wearing in full public view "instead of the purple a robe of humility [*tapeinophrosyne*]."[107]

Like Gregory, John praised the astonishing imperial humility of a consort rather than that of the emperor. Eudoxia, according to John, had divided the obligations with her husband, so Arcadius remined at home for the nighttime celebration but would be present the following day. This showed good sense: had the emperor been there as well, his bodyguards and armed soldiers on horseback, added to her retinue, would have caused chaos instead of exuberance. It is difficult not to see in John's depiction a reflection of imperial intent. Eudoxia must have participated in this procession as he portrayed her for an audience of eyewitnesses. Like Gregory, John stressed the joint efforts of the imperial couple. Acting as partners in the *imperium* and in piety (in Gregory's expression, "koinonei tes basileias . . . tes eusebeias"), each assumed their part. Eudoxia, apostlelike in her

---

105. J. Chrys., *Hom.* 2.467–472 ("Cum imperatrix media nocte in magnam ecclesiam uenisset") (*PG* 63.467–472). Arcadius made Eudoxia augusta on January 9, 400. The episode has received a great deal of scholarly attention: see Ch. Kelly, "Stooping," 223–24, 231–32; Holum, *Theodosian Empresses*, 23–26, 56 for the date; van Nuffelen, "Playing the Ritual Game," 188, 197; S. Elm, "What the Bishop Wore," 165–67; Tiersch, *Johannes Chrysostomus*, 213–15; Groß-Albenhausen, *Imperator christianissimus*, 184–87.

106. J. Chrys., *Hom.* 2.468.7–469.5, 2.470.19–20, 2.470.50–51 2.472.8–15. See also Minets, *Slow Fall of Babel*, 290–95.

107. J. Chrys., *Hom.* 2.469.8–13, 2.470.60–62 (ἀλλ' ὥσπερ θεραπαινὶς παρηκολούθει τοῖς ἁγίοις, τῆς θήκης ἁπτομένη καὶ τῆς ὀθόνης τῆς ἐπικειμένης, καὶ πάντα τὸν ἀνθρώπινον καταπατοῦσα τῦφον, καὶ ἐν μέσῳ θεάτρῳ τοσούτῳ φαινομένη δήμῳ, ἣν οὐδὲ εὐνούχοις ἅπασι τοῖς ἐν ταῖς βασιλικαῖς στρεφομένοις αὐλαῖς θέμις ἰδεῖν . . . τὸν ἐντεῦθεν ἅπαντα τῦφον μετὰ πολλῆς ῥίψασα τῆς περιουσίας, ἐνδυσαμένη δὲ τὴν τῆς ταπεινοφροσύνης στολὴν ἀντὶ τῆς πορφυρίδος).

zeal, shared her piety with Arcadius, in the same way she shared his rule.[108] Given the gendered connotations of humility as more "female"—that is, associated with women, slaves, and the more humble (*humiliores*) as distinct from the more digni- fied (*honestiores*)—John's praise for the empress's magnificently staged lowliness offered the emperor choices. The bishop highlighted Eudoxia's action as modeling imperial humility, not least by granting her manliness through association with the apostles and David. By walking "like a maidservant," the empress had stooped much further than civility demanded. John emphasized that this reflected the imperial couple's will and shared obligations, but granted Eudoxia the agency to include Arcadius in her pious good works. Because the emperor was absent while his consort walked (like an apostle), his civility was never questioned, but thanks to their shared *imperium* he could claim as much or as little of Eudoxia's (manly) humility as he wished.[109]

When addressing the assembly on the day of Eutropius's fall, John Chrysos- tom offered the emperor similar room to maneuver. Here too John evoked Arca- dius while the latter was not present. Depending on how the audience wanted to characterize Eutropius, they could read Arcadius's imperial philanthropy and affectionate love as a sign of civility granted to a fallen *illustris vir* and consul or as imperial condescension all the way down to a truly humiliated eunuch. As the recipient of divine, imperial love and generosity, Eutropius as consul, but also as eunuch, became an adornment of the altar. Here John Chrysostom echoed Greg- ory of Nyssa's characterization of Aelia Flaccilla, the empress whose name, Aelia, and iconography, including the diadem and the paludamentum, Aelia Eudoxia had formally adopted.[110] About a decade prior, in the same church, Gregory had praised the deceased Aelia Flaccilla as Theodosius's equal in philanthropy, as an ornament of faith and adornment of the altar.[111] Calling Eutropius an adornment of the altar and recipient of love of (hu)mankind allowed John to speak for himself but also to evoke the imperial couple, at least in the minds of those who recalled Gregory's portrayal of Aelia Flaccilla and might now picture the current empress, rather than just the emperor, as an emblem of affectionate love. At the same time, such associations linked the fallen consul with the imperial consort, which could be risky.

---

108. J. Chrys., *Hom.* 2.472.20–30 (Ἐπεζήτει τῆς ἑορτῆς ταύτης ἡ εὐφροσύνη καὶ τὸν θεοφιλέστατον βασιλέα τὸν μετὰ σοῦ τὸ ἄροτρον τῆς εὐσεβείας ἕλκοντα. . . . Ὥσπερ γὰρ κοινωνεῖ τῆς βασιλείας αὐτῷ, οὕτω καὶ τῆς εὐσεβείας, καὶ οὐκ ἀφίησιν ἐν τοῖς κατορθώμασιν ἄμοιρον εἶναι, ἀλλὰ πανταχοῦ συμμεριστὴν λαμβάνει).

109. For different interpretations of the staging, e.g., as a sign of competition between bishop and emperor, see Diefenbach, "Zwischen Liturgie," 36–39; Ch. Kelly, "Stooping," 221–23, 228–32; van Nuffelen, "Playing the Ritual Game," 198–99; Tiersch, *Johannes Chrysostomus*, 213–18.

110. Busch, *Die Frauen*, 218–20.

111. Gr. Nyss., *Flac.* 480 = 4.20–25. See also chapter 5.

That risk paled, however, when compared to Chrysostom's insistence that the fallen consul represented fallen humanity, which included the emperor as a human being. As such, Arcadius too lay prostrate at the altar, and by embracing Eutropius with affectionate love, the emperor embraced himself. To the extent that Eutropius was Arcadius's "father" and, as consul, embodied him whenever the ruler was absent, such an embrace was well within the bounds of imperial friendship and civility. If, however, Eutropius fell as a eunuch, then Arcadius's affectionate love represented a startlingly steep condescension: The emperor became (at least emotionally) a humble eunuch himself.

EUTROPIUS THE EUNUCH?

Arcadius was evidently satisfied with the effects of John's homily. Rightly so: it was a bravura performance. John praised the manly Theodosian imperial virtues of victorious philanthropy, (civil war) clemency, and civility while expanding them to encompass motherly compassion, mercy, affectionate love, and moments of humility. The emperor as manly father and affectionate mother (the latter role enhanced by his shared rule with the empress), together with the motherly church, had won a victory over the fallen rich man by embracing him with divine forgiveness and love of humankind, which brought them all closer to the philanthropic God. Emperor, empress, and bishop shared the obligations of pious Christian rule. For those who were ready to hear it, John pushed the envelope even further. The emperor and the bishop, or the motherly church for whom the latter spoke, had acted in a truly philanthropic manner, because they had publicly and personally extended their affectionate love to someone who was now rather lowly: a formerly powerful *vir* and enslaved eunuch, whom they embraced as human being(s). John's *synkatabasis* was impeccable. Those in the audience who wanted to hear imperial civility could, and to those who were familiar with philanthropy as condescension as John had developed the concept in Antioch, the message was clear: Arcadius too shared the humility of fallen humanity, for which Eutropius was the icon at the altar, so that the emperor joined those begging the most philanthropic God for mercy.[112] But John never made this conclusion too explicit.

John's silence regarding Eutropius's physical condition was deliberate and granted him the broadest range in applying *synkatabasis* as appropriate rhetorical adaptation to his audience, which on that day included many who were not familiar with the innovative concepts he presented. For those who understood his *synkatabasis* as including the theological imperative to approximate Christ's divine condescension, Eutropius's condition as a eunuch enhanced that message immeasurably. To *become* a eunuch through philanthropy as affectionate love demanded

---

112. Already preached by Gregory of Nazianzus, in, e.g., *Or.* 14 (on which see Holman, *Hungry Are Dying*, 143–53).

more than emotional and physical closeness to someone often considered despicable. But how despicable was this particular eunuch at this moment? Were John Chrysostom and his audience, including the absent emperor, able to differentiate between eunuchs as powerful officeholders and those who were (expensive) household slaves? As mentioned above, modern scholars are unanimous in holding that John shamed and castigated Eutropius as a eunuch.[113] Indeed, elsewhere John expresses decidedly negative views regarding eunuchs, and this homily too offers much that echoes the traditional arsenal used to deride and denigrate them.[114] A prostitute stripped of her makeup and a person with chattering teeth and rattling bones in the grip of mortal terror, more wretched than a slave or a beggar, acting like a frog, hare, or tamed lion, the emblem of manliness deprived of its essential power—these images evoke "the eunuch."[115] Combined with Claudian's attacks and the condemnation of later historians, they easily explain the scholarly consensus. Nevertheless, the question remains: where on a sliding scale of opprobrium did John place this specific eunuch, a.k.a. Eutropius the consul?

As mentioned above, John's first, significant move was to denounce Eutropius as a rich man who had misused his wealth. The vitriol he elsewhere directed against the greedy extravagantly rich, who wasted their fortunes in frivolous abandon, was no less than what he exhibited here toward Eutropius. To John, such persons, surrounded by their swarms of eunuchs, prostitutes, and dogs, were despicable. He saw them as chained like slaves by their golden jewelry, made soft, feeble, and moist through extravagant feasting.[116] In keeping with traditional luxury critique, John considered the excessively wealthy less-than-manly and eunuchlike.[117] As a greedy rich man, therefore, Eutropius would have been marked as the equivalent of a eunuch even if he had not been one. That he was a eunuch made him only marginally more abhorrent, at least in John's eyes. Thus, the bishop's equation of the fallen consul with Mary Magdalene was meant to highlight Arcadius's miraculous imperial condescension in analogy with Christ's salvific force, though it slandered Eutropius: "The point is that she who was unclean didn't harm him who is

113. E.g., Sidéris, "Rise and Fall," 76; Roskam, "Emancipatory Preaching," 188–89, with further bibliography.

114. J. Chrys., *Subintr.* 10–11; see also Leyerle, *Theatrical Shows*, 75–99; Hartney, *John Chrysostom,* 87–94, 110–16, 193–94.

115. J. Chrys., *In Eutr.* 393.23–44, 395.1–3, 394.50–58. For tamed lions as a code for compromised manliness, see Leyerle, *Theatrical Shows*, 121–37; Leyerle, "Locating Animals," 286, 290–96 (for the shock John liked to deliver, e.g., when equating persons with dogs).

116. See, e.g., J. Chrys., *In 1 Cor.* 30.4–5, 32.4; for wealth as prostitute, *In Rom.* 17.4, 19.8 (*PG* 60. 569–570, 60.592–593); for golden chains dragging one down as much as fetters, *In Col.* 10 (*PG* 62.371); *In Eph.* 13, 21; *In Gen. hom.* 59.2; for "swarms of eunuchs," see, e.g., *In Eph.* 20.7. See also Leyerle, *Narrative Shape*, 65–68, 73–77; Roskam, "Emancipatory Preaching," 181–82; W. Mayer, "Poverty and Generosity"; Leyerle, "John Chrysostom on Almsgiving," 29–47; Hartney, *John Chrysostom,* 142–45, 159–63; in general, Brändle, *Matth.* 25, 31–46.

117. Cardman, "Poverty and Wealth as Theater," 159–75; De Wet, "Virtue."

pure. Instead, he who is pure and faultless rendered the accursed prostitute pure through the contact."[118]

In fact, John assigned a lower rank in his hierarchy of abominations to greedy rich men than to (ordinary) eunuchs.[119] One near-inescapable consequence of excessive wealth and its luxuries was that it rendered men less-than-manly, less restrained, and thus easily prone to "the frenzy for males."[120] John shared this assessment with others—evident, for example, in Dio Chrysostom's *Euboean Oration*, to which Synesius alluded, and certain strands of Stoic philosophy—so his words resonated even for those who were unaware of what he had said on the topic at Antioch.[121] He did not condone same-sex desire in any form, but in line with tradition he was particularly incensed by the desire of adult men for each other—the kind of desire, in short, that Flavius Nicomachus's law and the Lex Scantinia (ostensibly) censured.[122] John granted that this desire had a long history, but that did not make acting upon it acceptable. "In antiquity this matter even seems to have been a custom . . . allowing this privileged position for free men—or more accurately, this disgraceful one. . . . Many others of the philosophers' books . . . are full of this disease. But we do not say on account of this that the matter is to be esteemed. Instead, the ones who accepted this custom are pitiable and worthy of many tears."[123]

For John, adult men engaging in sexual acts with each other violated the divinely authorized order of nature—was contrary to nature, or nature falsified—and was thus a direct affront to God.[124] Such men "have become a woman, indeed have brought ruin to [their] existence as a man."[125] What incensed John the most was that some men had chosen same-sex encounters of their own volition and in clear knowledge that they invited scriptural censure by doing so.[126] Such willful defiance disrupted the social fabric. Indeed, these men were "enemies to themselves and to

118. J. Chrys., *In Eutr.* 394.22–25.

119. See, e.g., J. Chrys., *Virg.* 8.4–5.

120. J. Chrys., *In Rom.* 4.1 (*PG* 60.416.56–417.1) (ἡ κατὰ τῶν ἀρρένων μανία); 4.3, 4.4 (*PG* 60.420.41–42, 60.421.25): Πόθεν οὖν ταῦτα ἐτέχθη τὰ κακά; Ἀπὸ τρυφῆς, ἀπὸ τοῦ μὴ εἰδέναι Θεόν (From where are these evils brought forth? . . . From luxury, from not knowing God); wealth and indolence (*rathymia*) cause the "soul to get soft" (τὴν καταμαλακιζομένην ἐν τούτοις ψυχήν). See also J. Chrys., *Inan.* 16.239–256, on the feminizing of young boys through their fathers' love of luxury.

121. Especially in his commentaries on Romans 1:26–27. For Stoic condemnations of adult male same-sex erotic desire, see Anagnostou-Laoutides, "Sexual Ethics and Unnatural Vice," 273–82.

122. Dunning, "John Chrysostom and Same-Sex Eros," 658–59; Brooten, *Love Between Women*, 344–48; see chapter 1.

123. J. Chrys., *In Rom.* 4.16–18 (*PG* 60.418.61–419.13).

124. J. Chrys., *In Rom.* 4.18 (*PG* 60.419.13–16).

125. J. Chrys., *In Rom.* 4.22–23 (*PG* 60.419.45–47) (Οὐδὲ γὰρ τοῦτο λέγω μόνον, ὅτι γέγονας γυνὴ, ἀλλ' ὅτι ἀπώλεσας καὶ τὸ εἶναι ἀνήρ).

126. J. Chrys., *In Rom.* 3.15 (*PG* 60.413.10–11) ("Ever since the creation of the world his eternal power and divine nature . . . have been understood and seen through the things he has made. So they (who chose such wickedness) are without excuse"). For volition or reasoning power, see, e.g., *In Rom.* 3.29, 4.4 (*PG* 60.415.3–5, 60.417.23–26).

each other, causing a terrible kind of conflict . . . more lawless than any civil war."[127] Greedy rich men in the grip of sexual frenzy for one another made themselves far less than less-than-manly.

> I say not only that you have become a woman, but that you have also ceased to be a man, and have neither changed into that nature, nor kept that which you had, but you have become a traitor to both of them at once, and deserving to be driven out and stoned by both men and women, since you have betrayed the entire race [*genos*]. . . . For it is not the same thing to change into the nature of a woman as it is to continue being a man and yet to have become a woman; you are neither this nor that. But if you want to know the seriousness of the evil from other examples, ask for what reason the legislators punish those who make men eunuchs, and you will see that it is simply for no other reason than because they mutilate nature. And yet the injustice they perform is nothing compared to same-sex passion. For there have been those who were mutilated and were in many cases useful after their mutilation. But there can be nothing more useless than a man who has prostituted himself. For not only the soul but also the body of one who has suffered such things is disgraced and deserves to be driven out everywhere.[128]

In comparison to desiring (greedy rich adult) men like oneself and acting on that desire, being a eunuch was not particularly damning. Though not exactly exemplars of (manly) virtue, eunuchs usually had their physical condition forced upon them, often as infants.[129] Moreover, exceptional eunuchs such as Eutropius were and always had been undeniably useful, as anyone familiar with Xenophon's *Cyropaideia*, which included John's and Synesius's audiences, knew perfectly well.[130] Had Eutropius used his wealth and power as prescribed by John Chrysostom, for example by distributing alms instead of financing races or by promoting the

127. J. Chrys., *In Rom.* 4.2 (*PG* 60.418.19–22) (καὶ πολέμιοι ἑαυτῶν καὶ ἀλλήλων ἐγένοντο, χαλεπὴν τινα καὶ παντὸς ἐμφυλίου πολέμου παρανομωτέραν εἰσάγοντες μάχην).

128. J. Chrys., *In Rom.* 4.3 (*PG* 60.419.45–420.11):

Οὐδὲ γὰρ τοῦτο λέγω μόνον, ὅτι γέγονας γυνὴ, ἀλλ' ὅτι ἀπώλεσας καὶ τὸ εἶναι ἀνὴρ, καὶ οὔτε εἰς ταύτην μετέστης τὴν φύσιν, οὔτε ἣν εἶχες διετήρησας, ἀλλὰ κοινὸς ἑκατέρας ἐγένου προδότης, καὶ παρὰ ἀνδρῶν καὶ γυναικῶν ἄξιος ἐλαύνεσθαι καὶ καταλεύεσθαι, ἅτε ἑκάτερον ἀδικήσας τὸ γένος . . . οὐ γάρ ἐστιν ἴσον εἰς γυναικείαν μεταβαλεῖν φύσιν, καὶ μένοντα ἄνδρα γενέσθαι γυναῖκα, μᾶλλον δὲ μήτε τοῦτο μήτε ἐκεῖνο. Εἰ δὲ βούλει καὶ ἑτέρωθεν μαθεῖν τοῦ κακοῦ τὴν ὑπερβολὴν, ἐρώτησον τίνος ἕνεκεν τοὺς εὐνούχους ποιοῦντας κολάζουσιν οἱ νομοθέται, καὶ εἴσῃ, ὅτι δι' οὐδὲν ἕτερον, ἢ ὅτι τὴν φύσιν ἀκρωτηριάζουσι. Καίτοιγε οὐδὲν ἀδικοῦσιν ἐκεῖνοι τοσοῦτον. ἐγένοντο γὰρ καὶ μετὰ τὸν ἀκρωτηριασμὸν πολλαχοῦ χρήσιμοι οἱ ἀποτμηθέντες. ἀνθρώπου δὲ πεπορνευμένου οὐδὲν ἀχρηστότερον γένοιτ' ἄν. οὐδὲ γὰρ ἡ ψυχὴ μόνον, ἀλλὰ καὶ τὸ σῶμα τοῦ τὰ τοιαῦτα παθόντος ἄτιμον καὶ ἄξιον ἐλαύνεσθαι πανταχόθεν.

See also De Wet, "John Chrysostom on Homoeroticism," 204–5.

129. For the involuntary nature of castration, see J. Chrys., *In Rom.* 4.2 (*PG* 60.417.12–17); Hartney, "Manly Women," 41–48. Though I would not go as far as Sidéris, whose "Rise and Fall," 66–70, considers eunuchs under Theodosius to be chaste, his observations support my point.

130. See chapter 7.

bishop's church rather than hindering it through restrictive legislation, his condition as a eunuch would have been all but irrelevant. Those who allowed the indolence enabled by their excessive wealth to drive them to same-sex erotic relations, in contrast, were truly monstrous. They chose to make themselves hybrids of their own free will, both male and female or neither male nor female in the worst sense, because they chose to be sterile: they made themselves into eunuchs without being one.[131]

In sum, in his sermon on the occasion of Eutropius's asylum in the church, John did not attack Eutropius because he was a eunuch. He did not even attack him because he was wealthy. Neither was negative per se. Certainly, to be a eunuch was not wonderful, but it was a fate that Eutropius had not chosen. Moreover, Arcadius had loved Eutropius because the latter had done much for him—in John's characterization, even at the moment of his fall the emperor balanced Eutropius's negative characteristics against his positive ones, just as he would have done with anyone else close to him. It was true that power and influence had made Eutropius very wealthy. But wealth alone did not make a man less-than-manly. If a rich man embraced affectionate love and mercy and demonstrated both through ostentatious displays of charity, almsgiving, and personal interaction with and sponsorship of ascetics, monks, widows, and the abject, such as prostitutes, beggars, and lepers, he was virtuous and manly to the utmost.[132]

Everyone could act as the empress soon would and (temporarily) exchange less-than-manly displays of luxury—their gold chains, their sons' earrings, their bejeweled clothes and silver pisspots—for the simple, rustic garb of the manly (ascetic). Of course, a rich eunuch who used his wealth like that was a man, a truly illuminated *vir*, as capacious in his (Christian) manliness as the affectionately loving emperor and church as mother and father. Those who insisted on indulging in their excessive wealth, on the other hand, were less-than-manly, as less-than-manly as Eutropius at the altar. But those who chose to succumb to the frenzy for other men were the true eunuchs, because they had made themselves voluntarily sterile—and according to John, Eutropius had done nothing of the sort.

John's homily in quadruplicate presents a complex dramaturgy in which norms of manliness were expanded and reconstituted to set new boundaries. As Benjamin

---

131. J. Chrys., *In Rom.* 4.3 (PG 60.420.24–32): Καὶ γὰρ παράδοξος ἦν ὁ ὑετὸς ἐκεῖνος, ἐπειδὴ καὶ παρὰ φύσιν ἡ μίξις· καὶ κατέκλυσε τὴν γῆν, ἐπειδὴ καὶ τὰς ἐκείνων ψυχὰς ἡ ἐπιθυμία. Διὸ καὶ ἀπεναντίας ἦν ὁ ὑετὸς τῷ συνήθει· οὐ γὰρ μόνον οὐ διήγειρε τὴν γαστέρα τῆς γῆς πρὸς τὴν τῶν καρπῶν γένεσιν, ἀλλὰ καὶ πρὸς τὴν ὑποδοχὴν αὐτὴν τῶν σπερμάτων ἄχρηστον ἐποίει. Τοιαύτη γὰρ ἦν ἡ μίξις τῶν ἀνδρῶν τῆς γῆς Σοδόμων, τὸ τοιοῦτον σῶμα ἀχρηστότερον ἀποφαίνουσα (For that rain was paradoxical, since the sex was contrary to nature. And it deluged the land, since the lust flooded their souls. This is why the rain was also the opposite of the normal rain. Now not only did it fail to fertilize the womb of the earth for the production of fruit, but it even made it useless for receiving the seed. For this is also the nature of sex between men, making the body of this type of man more worthless than the land of Sodom).

132. S. Elm, "What the Bishop Wore"; Shepardson, *Controlling*, 131–38.

Dunning shows, "Organized along lines consonant with traditional Roman ideology [of manly virtues] . . . these conventions form a crucial part of the cultural backdrop Chrysostom *assumes* . . . as his homiletic rhetoric subtly transforms the function and meaning of the long-established tropes being mobilized."[133] To achieve his full didactic potential, John's Eutropius was first and foremost a consul, *patricius*, and *illustris vir*, whose loss of power transformed him in an instant into a less-than-manly person, a transition we have seen before. Imperial clemency, as we have also seen before, then restored his manliness: Eutropius became a new *illustris vir* through the divine philanthropy that the emperor showed him on the very day of his fall. According to John, however, this new Eutropius was an adornment of the altar as an icon of a new kind of imperial philanthropy. This philanthropy was a weapon that triumphed over excessive greed through merciful compassion and affectionate love, uniting the emperor and the abject Eutropius, the church and those assembled in it, because all were affected by the fragility of their shared humanity. As such, as human beings, all begged the philanthropic God for his loving mercy, and as such, they all became a model for the entire world.[134]

John thus made the fallen Eutropius into a universal symbol of a new, Christian understanding of imperial and divine philanthropy, even more expansive and copious with fatherly and motherly attributes combined into one. "Manly" philanthropy joined with "womanly" compassion, mercy, and affectionate love to achieve victories of generosity. In his dramatic performance, John expanded Theodosius's and Arcadius's concept of philanthropy as triumphant weapon into a visible symbol of divine condescension: the emperor embracing the most humble and the humiliated in imitation of Christ's incarnation. However, he did so in a way that allowed his audience and the absent emperor to "hear" as much of his new message as they were able to absorb—or deemed prudent.

Emperor and church were both as much mother and father as were the emperor and his consort, who shared governance and piety but represented aspects of each in different yet complementary ways. Arcadius shed tears for and embraced the fallen as consul, eunuch, or both without losing his imperial (manly) dignity. Eutropius, stripped of wealth and power, assumed, through the motherly and fatherly love of the emperor, the bishop, the assembly, and God, the true, simple manliness of the true Christian (ascetic). However, not unlike Theodosius through Nicomachus Flavianus's law, John indicated a limit to the expansive, copious manliness that he as bishop, Arcadius as emperor, and Eutropius as adornment of the altar embodied. Men must love each other, but they must not express that love in sexual ways. Theodosius had intended his condemnation of adult elite male same-sex intercourse as a warning to Rome's *viri* not to think about usurpation and civil war: He considered such unmanly acts an affront against his rule. For John

---

133. Dunning, "John Chrysostom and Same-Sex Eros," 658–59.

134. In 447, that model was powerfully adopted by Theodosius II: see Ch. Kelly, "Stooping," 221–24.

Chrysostom, though he alluded to but did not make this explicit in his sermon on Eutropius, those unmanly men were worse than physical eunuchs, because they were an affront against God. While setting these hard limits, however, Theodosius and John Chrysostom, the latter speaking to please Arcadius, vastly expanded the contours of elite Roman imperial manliness to make it soft, capacious, and all-encompassing.

So much for John's didactic theater, for the affective world in words he created while Eutropius listened silently at the altar. What his audience understood and how they reacted is an entirely different matter and must remain largely conjecture.[135] As far as the emperor's reception of this speech was concerned, we hear of no complaint. John had spoken on behalf of his church, but he was also Arcadius's bishop, chosen with Eutropius's support, and he had praised the imperial policies—or virtues—that he then expanded. Including (the absent yet present) Arcadius as a human being on a par with Eutropius in this didactic tableau was certainly consequential but not as risky as one might think, because *this* eunuch was first and foremost an *illustris vir*, *patricius*, and consul. That rank and office had also made it possible for Synesius to suggest that the emperor might share some of his most powerful adviser's eunuch(like) softness. Indeed, the earliest we hear about rifts between the bishop and the imperial couple is 401. According to Socrates, who wrote several decades later, John's speech in the presence of Eutropius was a success, though not entirely how the bishop had intended. According to Socrates, John's homily was controversial with some because it "rebuked those in office with immoderate vehemence"—for these listeners too, in short, Eutropius was first and foremost an *illustris vir* and consul. Moreover, the bishop had "not only denied mercy [*ouk eleei*] to the unfortunate, but added insult to cruelty" in their view, eliciting deep outrage by appearing to lack the very emotions he worked so hard to elicit—namely, the philanthropy, compassion, mercy, and affectionate love that the fallen consul and eunuch Eutropius so richly deserved.[136]

135. See Sandwell, "Preaching," 138–47, for how little we know about audience reaction.
136. Soc., *HE* 6.5.6; see also Soz., *HE* 8.7.4.

Conclusion

"I loved the empire . . ."[1]

Let us together enjoy your arms' glory. May your one shield [clipeus] *protect us, and your sole manly courage* [virtus] *sweat for both halves of our world.*[2]

On August 17, 399, the emperor Arcadius condemned Eutropius to exile with a law addressed to the newly installed praetorian prefect Aurelian, Synesius's patron, and dated with reference to the western consul Manlius Theodorus.[3] The "foul muck" of Eutropius's name had to be expunged from the year, so that neither those "who through their *vir*-ness [*virtus*] and wounds extend the Roman borders nor those who guard [them] by preserving through justice what is right, need not groan . . . that this excrement-covered prodigy [*lutulentum prodigium*] has defiled by its contagion the divine reward of the consulate."[4] All statues and images of the

1. Alexievich, *Secondhand Time*, 35.

2. Claud., *Eutr.* 2.600–602 ("Armorum liceat splendore tuorum / in commune frui; clipeus nos protegat idem / unaque pro gemio desudet cardine virtus"). *Virtus* (Stilicho's) is Claudian's last word against Eutropius: see Long, *Claudian's "In Eutropium,"* 254.

3. The law was probably Arcadius's response to a *suggestio*, issued, as customary, in the name of both emperors (aa): see Millar, *Greek Roman Empire*, 207–14.

4. CTh 9.40.17:

Idem aa. Aureliano praefecto praetorio. omnes res Eutropi, qui quondam praepositus sacri cubiculi fuit, aerarii nostri calculis adiunximus, erepto splendore eius et consulatu a taetra illuvie et a commemoratione nominis eius et caenosis sordibus vindicato, ut eiusdem universis actibus antiquatis omnia mutescant tempora nec eius enumeratione saeculi nostri labes appareat nec ingemiscant aut qui sua virtute ac vulneribus Romanos fines propagant vel qui eosdem servandi iuris aequitate custodiunt, quod divinum praemium consulatus lutulentum prodigium contagione foedavit. patriciatus etiam dignitate atque omnibus inferioribus spoliatum se esse cognoscat, quas morum polluit scaevitate. omnes statuas, omnia simulacra, tam ex aere quam ex marmore seu ex fucis quam ex quacumque materia quae apta est effingendis, ab omnibus civitatibus oppidis locisque privatis ac publicis praecipimus aboleri, ne tamquam nota nostri saeculi obtutus polluat intuentem . . . . dat. xvi kal. feb. Constantinopoli Theodoro v. c. cons. (All the possessions of Eutropius, who once was *praepositus sacri cubiculi*, we have annexed to

consul were likewise to be removed from public and private spaces, his honors and titles revoked, his legislative acts annulled, and his possessions confiscated by the imperial treasury. Eutropius himself was relegated to confinement (*vallatus*) on the island of Cyprus.[5] So much for philanthropy and affectionate love.

The language of this law recalls Claudian's invective. Eutropius the eunuch is back as a sordid, pestilential monster, whose mad, rabid ravings mixed up everything—and who finally got what he deserved.[6] However, Synesius's and John Chrysostom's carefully calibrated versions of "Eutropius" suggest additional interpretations. Admittedly, these authors wrote, respectively, while the consul was at the height of his influence and when he had just fallen. Still, although Synesius and John Chrysostom knew, of course, that Eutropius was a eunuch, they kept his condition in the background, since for them his office mattered most. Both considered him an *illustris vir, patricius,* and powerful consul, since as long as the emperor considered him such, that is what he was. His condemnation, at first reading, confirms the corollary: as soon as the emperor withdrew his grace, the ugly eunuch jumped to the fore. However, the law's very denigrations of less-than-manliness, less-than-Romanness, meant that Eutropius had to have *vir*-ness to lose. On closer reading, therefore, it corroborates Synesius's and John Chrysostom's understanding, because even less-than-*vir*-ness was a power language that confirmed elite membership when fortunes were reversed.

Eutropius, unable to become a father, could not have become an emperor. But the condemnation, which alludes to his condition only once, by referring to him as an ex–grand chamberlain (usually but not always a eunuch), would have

---

the accounts of our treasury. His splendor has been stripped off, and the consulate has been vindicated from the foul muck and from the need for remembrance of his name and its filthy squalor. This has been done so that, once every one of his acts has been revoked, silence may fall [on them] for all time and the stain on our age of his being listed [as consul] may not be made visible, and neither they who by their *vir*-ness and wounds extend the Roman borders nor those who guard [them] by preserving through their justice what is right, need groan at the fact that this excrement-covered prodigy has defiled by its contagion the divine reward of the consulate. Let him learn that he has been despoiled of the dignity of the patriciate and all lesser honors, which he has polluted by the perversity of his character. We direct that all statues, all images, be they of marble or bronze or painted or of whatever material they may be made of, be obliterated from all cities, towns, and public or private places, so that this blot on our age may not pollute the gazes of those who look upon [these images]).

Trans. adapted from Long, *Claudian's "In Eutropium,"* 260–61; Ch. Kelly, *Ruling,* 196. See also Seeck, "Studien zu Synesios," 456–58.

5. CTh 9.40.17: "Fidis custodibus ad Cyprum insulam perducatur, in qua tua sublimitas relegatum esse cognoscat, ut ibidem pervigili cura vallatus, nequeat suarum cogitationum rabie cuncta miscere" (Therefore, let him be conducted under the supervision of faithful guardians to the island of Cyprus, to which may Your Sublimity know he has been relegated, so that in that same place, walled in with vigilant care, he may be unable to mix together all things through the madness of his own devising). See Hillner, "Confined Exiles," 393–94.

6. Tiersch, *Johannes Chrysostomus,* 268–69, and n. 16; Sidéris, "Rise and Fall," 76.

sounded very similar had it purged a (fully equipped) man sufficiently close to imperial power to be tempted to seize it.[7] It evokes Claudian's Eutropius, but even more so Pacatus's Magnus Maximus. The same harsh language disparages the public enemy (*hostis publicus*) defeated in a civil war: "pestilential stain" (*labes*) and "polluting contagion" (*contaminatio*), "raging furor" (*rabies*), and "monstrous, filthy *prodigium*."[8] Exile and memory sanctions were elite punishments.[9] Statues could be removed only because they had been erected; ditto for laws and honors. *Relegatio in insulam* required the emperor's approval. It was reserved for the imperial family, senators, high-ranking officials, and members of the clergy.[10] In contrast to deportation, it both was temporary and preserved citizen status and portions of the seized property for the heirs.[11] It could also be reversed. Arcadius could easily have forgiven Eutropius and restored him to full *vir*-ness, to demonstrate the clement, affectionately merciful philanthropy that John Chrysostom had praised. The end of Eutropius's recall from Cyprus in execution was not a foregone conclusion.[12]

The law thus aligns with Synesius's and John's eastern Eutropius: powerful *vir* first, eunuch (distant) second. Moreover, it highlights Arcadius as arbiter of *vir*-ness, especially in the context of potential usurpation and civil war. All failed usurpers acted from a position of power, of full *vir*-ness, only to become, in the instant of loss, monstrous, most negligent little homegrown slaves, dependent (should they survive) on the emperor's transformative clemency to restore their virtues. Eutropius, "father to the augustus," then, may not have been the most important target of that law. It was ostentatious legislation reminding strong men and other members of New Rome's upper echelons of the possible consequences to their *virtus* of an ill-considered power grab while Arcadius was under pressure from marauding Gothic contingents. In that regard, it resembled the law that Nicomachus Flavianus had formulated nine years earlier on behalf of Theodosius to warn the male elite in the old Rome, through the sanctioning of "brothels of men," not to entertain rebellious ideas.[13]

The law, in short, confirms the obvious. At Rome's center stood, as always, the most sacred, divine emperor, here Arcadius, around whom everything else

7. Ch. Kelly, *Ruling*, 194–96.

8. Escribano Paño, "Social Exclusion," 39, 47–50, 59; Thome, "Crime and Punishment"; Jal, "*Hostis (publicus)*."

9. E. Elm, *Damnatio memoriae*, 159–88; Omissi, "*Damnatio memoriae*."

10. In contrast to *deportatio*, *relegatio* was not a capital penalty. The former included bodily markings and was reserved for low-status offenders, who were often condemned to the mines. See Hillner, "Confined Exiles," 394–99, 409–10; Hillner, *Prison*, 195–99; Barry, *Bishops in Flight*, 5–11.

11. Hillner, *Prison*, 196: as a rule, "late Roman emperors by far preferred the more severe *deportatio* to *relegatio*."

12. Soc., *HE* 6.5; Soz., *HE* 8.7.2–5; Philost., *HE* 11.6; Zos., *HN* 5.18.1–2; Hillner, *Prison*, 233–34, also 93–106 (Seneca on imperial clemency).

13. *Coll. Mos.* 5.3.1–2; see also chapter 1.

revolved. To be sure, like other late Roman emperors, Arcadius depended on his elites, especially his perfect servants—namely, the bureaucrats who bolstered and stabilized his regime.[14] Still, as Eutropius's rise and fall makes clear, the emperor's power was enormous. If he decided that a formerly enslaved person castrated at birth could embody the sacred augustus as consul, that person would. If he wished an infant to be emperor, that is what that infant became. If he wanted his augusta to share his *basileia* or *imperium*, she became an emperor while remaining a woman. Any time he wanted to show the extent of his clemency and philanthropy, for example by restoring former civil war opponents to their full Roman *vir*-ness, he could. Since being a *vir* implied being Roman, the emperor could make anyone thus, irrespective of their ethnic background.

As arbiter, the emperor was also in charge of his own *vir*-ness. He selected the virtues that best conveyed his message and influenced what features of manliness—rendered in images of bronze, marble, plaster, paint, or mosaic, on coins, and in words—would signal them. Here, the emperor's beauty was singularly important. Because the emperor was beautiful, he was loved and intensely desired—and the greater the beauty, the greater that love and desire (*dilexi / dilectio*). But the emperor also loved back. Clemency, benevolence, and love of man—indeed, humankind—or philanthropy were highly valued imperial virtues because they manifested the sovereign's love for all in his care. They lifted those thus loved and thereby lessened the immense gap that separated even his highest ranking subjects from the sacred, divine ruler.

The legitimate, good emperor had to be the most beautiful—whatever form that beauty took—because he was a god one can see. His beauty was divine, but what did the face, the body of God look like? The ways that the emperor chose to express his divinity—through what notions of *vir*-ness and *virtus*—made God visible. This was especially relevant in the last two decades of the fourth century, when Theodosius and then his sons tried to bring stability to a divine that was changing, its understanding constantly shifting.[15] The Christian God was One in Three, but how exactly should one understand that? Was God the Father essentially the same as his (infant) Son, or were they alike in their divinity (as many, especially in the East, thought)? Oughtn't the emperor's divine beauty express those shifts too?

When Theodosius, Arcadius, and Honorius were crafting imperial beauty as an increasingly youthful, capacious, and subtle or soft manliness, the nature of divine fatherhood was still being hotly contested. This fight pitched bishops, high-level members of the clergy, thinkers, ascetics, and monks against one another, all espousing different interpretations of whether and to what degree God the Father was of the same essence, being, or substance as his only begotten Son. Those in the Nicene camp argued for sameness, while the substantial number of Arians and

14. Ch. Kelly, *Ruling*, 186–92.

15. Bacci, *Many Faces*, 116–40 (Christ's polymorphic image, with conflicting hairstyles). See also Markschies, *Gottes Körper*, 247–34 (late antique theological discussions of Christ's body, including the anthropomorphite controversy of the 390s and early 400s).

Eunomians held that the Son was essentially subordinate, different from though like the Father. With *Cunctos populos*, Theodosius announced that he favored the interpretation of the bishops of Rome, Alexandria, and Thessalonica, professing a (Nicene) Trinity with one deity under equal majesty (*unam deitatem sub pari maiestate*).[16] Should the implications not be clear, Theodosius's newly chosen bishop of Constantinople, Gregory of Nazianzus, explained that this meant "to preserve God as in essence one and to profess three persons [*hypostases*], each with its own characteristic."[17] This was a three-tiered hierarchy in a unified oneness, in which the divine Father at the apex shared his divinity equally with his Son (and their agent, the divine breath or Holy Spirit): Each remained fully itself while also being fully the others.[18]

The same Gregory of Nazianzus had also claimed that he was father and mother to all those whom he, as philosopher, ascetic, and bishop, guided to salvation.[19] His friend and compatriot Gregory of Nyssa declared that, in Virginia Burrus's words, to achieve salvation "a man must make himself virginally female in order, as a woman, to restore humanity's created nature by making himself wholly male. . . . [Gregory] reimagines the body of a man as both penetrable and overflowing, alternately empty and full, hard and soft."[20] At the same time, he demanded that men maintain the necessary "austerity and intensity of virtue" to resist the "tyrant" who favors "the female form of life."[21] His assurance that "we are in some manner our own parents giving birth to ourselves by our own free choice in accordance with whatever we wish to be, whether male or female, molding ourselves to the teaching of virtue or vice," offers a capacious, expansive understanding of gender, of what being man, woman, father, mother, son, and daughter meant.[22] Exceptional Christian men and women, ascetics and monks, lived these notions, alone or in small groups, seeking to anticipate on earth the angels in heaven, who transcended gender, neither male nor female or both male and female.[23] These expansive forms of gender, of being father, son, and mother—each merging into the others while remaining fully itself—were particularly important for those divine beings

16. CTh 16.1.2.

17. Gr. Naz., *De vita sua* 1131–32; McLynn, "Moments of Truth"; S. Elm, *Sons of Hellenism*, 4, 479–87; Lyman, "Theology," pt. 3 (toward a Trinitarian theology).

18. MacDougall, "Theologies under Persecution," 80–90; Beeley, *Gregory of Nazianzus*, 30–39 (includes an [unfavorable] assessment of Theodosius at 30), 116–52, 201–34.

19. S. Elm, "Gregory's Women," 172–91.

20. Burrus, *Begotten, Not Made*, 131.

21. Gr. Nyss., *Vit. Mos.* 2.2. Who that tyrant might be is an interesting question. See also Burrus, *Begotten, Not Made*, 125; S. Elm, "Dressing Moses."

22. Gr. Nyss., *Vit. Mos.* 2.3.

23. As discussed in chapter 5, the scholarship on this topic is immense. See, e.g., Bodnaruk, "Historicizing Trans Saints"; Burrus, *Saving Shame*, 44–109; S. Elm, "Marking the Self"; Franco, "Byzantine Lives"; Krueger, "Between Monks"; Messis, *Les eunuques*, 75–85; Rapp, *Brother-Making*, 13–21, 40–47, 88–179; Tougher, *Eunuchs*, 68–79.

especially entrusted with guiding the souls in their care to salvation: the late Roman emperors.

Modern assessments of the *Christian* imperial rule that Theodosius I, his sons, and Theodosius II created and established rely to a significant degree on the writings of men like those just mentioned, Gregory of Nazianzus and Gregory of Nyssa, as well as those by John Chrysostom and Ambrose of Milan. These authors—bishops, other high-ranking members of the clergy, ascetics—insisted that the divine emperor must be subordinate to the One Supreme Divine Being, God. However, as I hope to have shown, this perspective is only one, though an important part, of the formulation of Christianity and of Christian imperial rule. Theodosius, Arcadius, and Honorius also had ideas about what it meant to be a most sacred, divine Christian imperator. The emperors remained critical drivers of the nature of the divine and the look of God. They designed the face and body of the divine; their beauty embodied the present god all could see. I am convinced that Theodosius, Honorius, and Arcadius, together with those at their courts in charge of the divine image, thought very carefully about how to make the present (incarnate, Nicene) imperial god visible: through their capacious, expansive, fluid, soft yet hard *vir*-ness, which layered and incorporated fathers and father figures, babies, boys and boys as young women, imperial consorts, and eunuchs to radiate the universal (*catholicos*) embrace of their love of (hu)man(kind) and affectionate compassion.

As indicated in the introduction, in this book I have foregrounded the political dimensions that made imperial gorgeousness so important. However, because these Christian emperors were divine, the multifaceted nature of their beauty always also involved what we now call the religious or the theological: there was no distinction.[24] In fact, Theodosius's, Honorius's, and Arcadius's legislation regarding heretics proves why imperial beauty was power: if the emperors' beauty embodied their concept of divinity—their own and that of the Christian God—then all deviations from the right way to characterize God had to be (and were) prosecuted by law, because they directly affected the emperor's divine *vir*-ness and not "just" the nature of God's Fatherhood and Christ's Sonship (that is, the Trinity).

The emperors did not explain their thinking with the eloquence of a John Chrysostom or an Ambrose, so I have had to zero in on their motives in roundabout ways. Theodosius, Honorius, and Arcadius chose to emphasize and propel youthful, smooth ways of being beautiful, and this book has sought to answer why. Attempting to make visible their understanding of the highest God, on whose behalf they acted, is one explanation. Expressing perhaps their most important function is another: to be a countercentrifugal force, drawing together in harmony or concord all the people in their realm through the unifying attraction of

---

24. Torp, *Rotonde palatine* 1:476–83, also suggests a theological message for Theodosius's Rotunda.

the imperial ensemble at the apex.[25] Here, child emperor rule offered a distinct—though counterintuitive—advantage, because it allowed for flexible, dynamic pairings of traditional hard, military forms of imperial beauty with variations of gorgeous youthfulness to increase the cohesive desirability of the whole.

The representational challenges posed by child emperor rule are evident—how can a toddler convince as a victorious augustus? But the model took off because it worked. It is difficult to discern what motivated Theodosius to resume Valentinian I's innovation. Nor is it obvious what propelled Valentinian I to make his eight-year-old son Gratian augustus in the first place, or why those in charge of the western court decided to raise the emperor's four-year-old son Valentinian II as his brother's coruler after their father's sudden death.[26] Succession interests certainly had something to do with all of these decisions. Yet earlier emperors had devised means to ensure dynastic continuity without elevating toddlers. When Valentinian I died, his adult brother Valens was the eastern augustus, and Gratian, then sixteen, could have ruled the west alone—so why make a four-year-old junior emperor? And why did Theodosius choose the same path? I think that the possibility of stability created or at least bolstered by representational composites of mature and young outweighed the risks.

As I have shown, the different configurations of mature and child emperors amplified imperial beauty and expanded the range of its erotic attractions. Gratian's youthful gorgeousness shows one way. Theodosius's use of the sensual powers of his close friend, general, and consul Saturninus to seduce diamond-hard Goths into sweetness shows another. By layering his own (Augustan and Republican) military excellence with that of the mature Saturninus, added to the youthfulness of Arcadius and Honorius and amplified by Aelia Flaccilla's manly *virtus* (the latter continued by Aelia Eudoxia),[27] Theodosius and his sons made visible the transformation of the imperial power language: victory reconfigured as divine clemency, and philanthropy, or love of mankind, indeed of humankind, as the most effective weapon, which the emperor alone could wield (while others could fight battles on his behalf).

The gradual move toward greater softness went hand in hand with expanded hardness, or maturity. Claudian, on behalf of Stilicho and Honorius, demonstrates the next steps. He created an imperial image in which subtle youth and the hope and renewal it represented took center stage, while each turn toward Honorius's youthfulness was accompanied by the expression of dynamic notions of fatherhood. This pairing allowed Claudian to portray the adolescent augustus as

25. That unity was also symbolized by, e.g., scepters with orbs or spheres such as those among Maxentius's insignia: see Panella, "Segni del potere," 47–76, and catalog nrr. 1–4. See also the *missorium* in chapter 4 (fig. 14).

26. Amm. Marc. 30.10.5; McEvoy, *Child Emperor Rule*, 52–55.

27. After John Chrysostom's fall, sources in his favor denounced Aelia Eudoxia as a bad emperor and monstrous tyrant: see Barry, *Bishops in Flight*, 108–17.

eager and prepared for battle, thanks first to Theodosius but then to Stilicho, who gradually took over as Honorius's father (figure). This combination had several advantages. It conveyed that expecting the young ruler to campaign was a mistake, because Stilicho (or another general) could carry the shield into battle, whereas the emperor alone could wield the weapon of love of mankind. As for the young Achilles in love, who was soft and subtle like the young women whose clothes he wore, Honorius's task was to master peacetime virtues. Stilicho's morphing into his father offered, at the same time, visions of a new stability. First, it expressed imperial concord in direct, dynastic terms: Stilicho would treat potential usurpers of Honorius's throne just as Theodosius had dealt with Magnus Maximus and Eugenius. Second, this father and son pairing expanded imperial beauty and the panorama of virtues even further. With Claudian's help, Stilicho made himself into Theodosius, while Honorius's subtleness increased, as modeled by the young Achilles—a combination that celebrated Rome's youthful renewal, fortified by martial tradition. Finally, marriage and fatherhood further cemented the bond and guaranteed Rome's eternal future. Stilicho was already a father. The mother of his children, Honorius's adopted sister Serena, now also became the emperor's mother with Honorius's marriage to their daughter, thoroughly amalgamating the (created) imperial family and promising future augusti and augustae who would prove the emperor's *vir*-ness beyond any doubt.

That, at least, was the idea, and its durability proves that the concept of layering (extreme) youth and maturity functioned. However, boys as emperors were a provocation. Every author I have discussed in this book—those seismographs of power—whether he wrote on behalf of the imperial court, on his own behalf, for the elite of which he formed a part, or for a combination of all three, grappled with toddlers as consuls and divine emperors. Because the beauty of these children could only be soft and smooth, it was easy to attack them through the well-known tropes denigrating less-than-*vir*-ness: a steep hurdle that representations of child emperors had to overcome. The *Historia Augusta*'s *Life of Heliogabalus* makes this point dramatically. Its author zeroes in on the model's potentially fatal weakness: the emperor's inability to transition from an adolescent and *puer* into a *vir* while beholden to a strong man who was not his father.[28] Dating the *Historia Augusta* is not an exact science, but the accepted late-fourth-to-early-fifth-century range is broad enough to suggest that the *Life of Heliogabalus* reflects the drawbacks of Stilicho and Honorius's *vir*-ness rather accurately—especially because the hoped-for offspring failed to arrive. The author's biting criticism confirms the changes to imperial manliness and stipulates conditions he and his peers considered nonnegotiable. If emperors were that young, they had to prove, through marriage, that they had transitioned from *puer* and adolescent to *vir* and were in

---

28. Nappa, *Making Men Ridiculous*, 180; Gunderson, *Staging Masculinity*, 216–18; Williams, *Roman Homosexuality*, 149–51 (the multivalence of *puer*).

no danger of being (or remaining) in thrall to strict fatherly supervision (by men who were not their fathers). Imperial softness as power discourse went only so far: it required, at any moment, demonstrations of stabilizing firmness delineating the limits that fluid elite *vir*-ness must not transgress.

Ostentatious legislation shows how these boundaries were drawn through the force of law. Theodosius and his court regulated same-sex encounters between free and unfree adult men as he celebrated victory in a civil war that had turned senators and other elites into less-than-manly supporters of an exceedingly ugly, defeated tyrant. The emperor restored the losers' Roman *vir*-ness while using this law to telegraph a warning against indulging the desire for strong men (other than the emperor) to the point of usurpation. Not only the regulation of bejeweled over-the-knee boots and tight trousers, both with (soft) Eastern connotations, but also Eutropius's exile, further enforced the thin line that separated the increasingly exuberant, capacious, fluid imperial manliness—made visible in part through the utterly illuminated, sparkling *viri*, all well worth looking at—from monstrosity. However, who was on what side of that thin line was a matter of perspective. Because the language of imperial softness negotiated power in agonistic contests, among peers but also in situations involving military conflicts and the threat of civil war, one side's divinely gorgeous beauty was the other side's monstrous ugliness.

Honorius and Stilicho (and the modern historian) are immensely fortunate that Claudian immortalized their perspective, that of the western court, with the indisputable power of his poetry. Arcadius's decision to make the castrated Eutropius a consul offered Claudian the perfect opportunity to show how far removed from that thin line Honorius, though not yet a father, and Stilicho, a strong man but certainly a man, were. To be sure, the defeat of Magnus Maximus, Eugenius, and Gildo and the continuing difficulties with Gothic contingents, exemplified by Alaric's refusal to behave, meant that the west, Milan and the Eternal City, had suffered a loss of prestige. However, as the western consul Manlius Theodorus's impeccable *vir*-ness proved, those missteps were nothing compared to the monstrous transgression that the eastern court had committed. Claudian made Eutropius into an icon of ugliness, into the abominable opposite of imperial beauty, with lasting results. His Eutropius dominates scholarship to this date. Eutropius's consulship was also proof to Claudian of why the resistance of parts of the (Christian and non-Christian) elites to Constantinople as the New Rome was entirely justified.[29] Granting a person of *alter sexus*, second or other sex, the power to represent Constantinople as its consul confirmed like little else that this capital could never be more than *altera Roma*, a secondhand Rome. This notion of the other, eastern, insufficiently manly, (negatively) queer Rome, so

---

29. August., *Ex. Urb.* 8.9 (Constantinople as more Christian than Rome); see also S. Elm, "Signs under the Skin," 68–73 (also on Job's ugliness); Benjamins, "Augustine's Romans," chapter 1 (debates regarding Rome's standing between Symmachus, Ambrose, Claudian, and Prudentius, which Augustine's *City of God* engaged). See also Chastagnol, "Constantinople en ombres chinoises," 85–93.

conveniently embodied by Claudian's western Eutropius, has also had a long afterlife,[30] not least as an example of orientalism *avant la lettre*.[31] Orientalism and its effects on Constantinople is not the topic of this book, but my demonstration of the importance of sparkling, capaciously fluid manliness to western Roman imperial power should help to dislodge such notions from the eastern perch on which they continue to be placed.

Claudian's western Eutropius, the ugly eunuch, has dominated the narrative because of the poet's brilliance, but also because Arcadius was not as lucky as Honorius. No Claudian or Themistius coordinated with him to sing his praises and explain how he wanted his choice of consul to be understood (or, to be precise, no panegyric offering unalloyed praise has been preserved). Nevertheless, Synesius and John Chrysostom, both also brilliant authors, offer sufficient evidence that they were keenly aware of the emperor's views, of his consul's usefulness, to force us to wonder how ugly Eutropius was in Arcadius's eyes. What degree of ugliness, of lowliness, might have been good for manly imperial beauty? When is divine ugliness beautiful?[32]

In Constantinople, Eutropius had been a father figure, so beloved by Arcadius that his fall moved the emperor to tears. Considered from that angle, he may have offered more than fatherliness to complement the emperor's youthful, subtle beauty. Roman jurists debated to what extent eunuchs were legally adult men with the right to marry, adopt, and bequeath their property, since they could not demonstrate beyond doubt, through children, that they had transitioned from *puer* to *vir*.[33] This might have made a highly accomplished fatherlike eunuch as *illustris vir* and *puer* a perfect counterpoint to the *princeps puer*: both soft yet capable, both *viri*, but only the emperor undeniably a father (who need not fear a strong man without testicles: see the *Life of Heliogabalus*). Moreover, the lingering ambivalence of Eutropius's gender might have suggested to Arcadius a means of making visible and integrating into the imperial image the complex, capacious ways of being human that Gregory

30. Betancourt, "Slash," 184, observes that the slash articulates ideas of Byzantium "that come to outplay the logic of the separation . . . that third-term that baffles and outplays their binary." See also Magdalino, *Roman Constantinople*; Ronchey, "La 'femme fatale,'" and Rapp, *Brother-Making*, 191–227; Krueger, "Between Monks."

31. Said, *Orientalism*, 3; Osterhammel, *Die Entzauberung*, 276; El Houkayem, "Orientalism"; Boone, *Homoerotics*, 23–43 (modern concepts). I address the topic elsewhere ("Eutropius the Cosmopolitan") in connection with the rediscovery of Theodora at the end of the nineteenth century: see Ronchey, "Teodora e i visionarii"; Boeck, "Archaeology of Decadence"; Carlà-Uhink, "Theodora A.P."

32. Bacci, *Many Faces*, 103–16 (was Christ handsome or ugly?). See also E. Burke, *A Philosophical Inquiry*, 43–78.

33. Gardner, "Sexing a Roman," 137; Kuefler, *Manly Eunuch*, 33–36; Messis, *Les eunuques*, 55. *Puer*, like the Greek *pais*, can also refer to an enslaved person: see, e.g., Gunderson, *Staging Masculinity*, 232n12. *Pais* and *puer* also denoted Christ and shaped his image: see, e.g., Bacci, *Many Faces*, 108–10. As a *puer*, Eutropius manifested what McEvoy has called infantilization (*Child Emperor Rule*, 324), albeit with a twist.

of Nyssa and his contemporaries formulated as a Christian ideal. Ascetics and monks strove to lead a life that allowed them to transcend gender, and eunuchs—or at least good eunuchs—represented just such a transformation.[34] Indeed, the late fourth century witnessed the emergence of eunuchs as saints.[35] Clad in shining white, selected for their youthful beauty, Theodosius's and Arcadius's eunuchs—including Eutropius—might well have been understood as representing the angels in heaven, accompanying the god one can see.[36]

Of course, Arcadius too may have considered Eutropius ugly; Synesius's and John Chrysostom's remarks imply as much (at least for many members of the elite, themselves included). If so, his ugliness might have complemented Arcadius's divine beauty in ways suggested by Gregory of Nyssa's evocation of Flaccilla's humility, later expanded by Eudoxia. Here, Martin of Tours's new ascetic and apostolic *vir*-ness offers an illustrative corroboration. According to his hagiographer Sulpicius Severus, Martin once witnessed the apparition of a being who was "sending before him a purple light in which (the better to deceive [Martin] with the glory of his assumed radiance) he was himself clad, robed in kingly raiment [*veste etiam regia indutus*], crowned with a diadem of gold and gems, his shoe smeared with gold, his countenance so calm, his face so joyful. . . . 'Martin, acknowledge', he said, 'whom you behold! I am Christ. About to descend on earth, I willed first to manifest myself to you.'"[37] Martin, stunned, hesitated but then understood. This emperor was not Christ but the devil. "'Not clothed in purple,' [Martin finally responded,] 'nor radiant with diadem did the Lord [*dominus*] Jesus say he would come. Unless he come in the fashion and form [*habitu formaque*] in which he suffered, unless he come bearing the marks of the Cross, I shall not believe that Christ has come.'"[38]

Christ's *forma, this* face of his divine beauty, was humble, scarred, humiliated, naked, and derided.[39] Perhaps through his beloved consul Eutropius, Arcadius consciously embraced humble ugliness, the lowliness of a mutilated former slave, as one facet of his own Christian imperial splendor, joined with but not the same as his own gorgeous beauty. Perhaps this allowed him to show that he was both a humble man and the most sacred, divine *imperator* (without stooping too low himself). This, after all, was John Chrysostom's message. Eutropius in all his humiliation—as a fallen rich man *and* as a eunuch—became the adornment of the altar because of his humility, a humility that he shared with every human being and with the one who had lowered himself for everyone's sake, the emperor

---

34. Kuefler, *Manly Eunuch*, 273–82 (eunuchs as monks).

35. In highly contested interpretations of Matthew 19:12: see Messis, *Les eunuques*, 62–68 (fourth-century Christian authors); Kuefler, *Manly Eunuch*, 256–64; Ringrose, *Perfect Servant*, 116–17.

36. Messis, *Les eunuques*, 75–82; Kuefler, *Manly Eunuch*, 238–42; Sidéris, "Eunuchs of Light," 161–76; Hatzaki, *Beauty*, 86–106 (eunuchs as angels and angels as eunuchs).

37. Sulp., *Vit. Mart.* 24.4.543–5.550.

38. Sulp., *Vit. Mart.* 24.7.553–56; see also Burton, *Sulpicius*, 125.

39. Bacci, *Many Faces*, 105–8.

included: Christ. This was the imperial humility that Arcadius's son, Theodosius II, made visible when he walked, on January 26, 447, sweating in the cold, with naked, bleeding feet, seven miles from his palace to the church of John the Baptist in the Hebdomon: the most sacred emperor partook in the lowliness that the humble Christ had redeemed.[40]

. . .

"Eutropius of all eunuchs was the first and the last to be consul."[41] These are the words that Marcellinus Comes chose to characterize the year 399 in the *Chronicle* that he composed in Constantinople between 518 and 519 and then updated through 534, to celebrate the emperor Justinian.[42] He was right, of course, but his terse characterization is not an explanation: Justinian abolished the consulate for anyone but the emperor because he did not like the competition, especially following the splendid triumph that his general and consul Belisarius celebrated in 535 after defeating the Vandals.[43] Justinian's other highly successful general was Narses, a eunuch: Xenophon's and Synesius's Cyrus would have approved. Eutropius, the last eunuch consul, did not spell the end of either identity but pointed toward the future careers of highly accomplished and commensurately highly rewarded eunuchs; meanwhile, the consulship was increasingly only for emperors, because of its costs and the (threatening) prestige it bestowed on the officeholder.

Roman emperors continued to sparkle in divine gorgeousness, as did their successors. For example, the Ostrogothic king Theoderic, who ruled as emperor between 493 and 526, claimed the titles, vestments, and *ornamenta* of the *princeps Romanus*—diadem, scepter, purple cloak, brooches, jewel-encrusted shoes—while acknowledging the superiority of his "brother," the emperor in the east, a custom that his successor Totila (or Baduila) maintained.[44] Imperial softness, capaciously gendered beautiful *vir*-ness, queerness at the center of power, also had a splendid afterlife in Byzantium. Indeed, Roland Betancourt considers Byzantium itself queer, because there "the center . . . worked more as an articulated hub in a broad network linked to various global and diverse centers . . . [allowing for] an immense degree of mobility and circulation across the Mediterranean and Middle Eastern worlds, as fluid and permeable as the gender and sexual identities that unfold across those spaces."[45]

40. Malalas, *Chron.* 14.22; Ch. Kelly, "Stooping," 221, 239; van Nuffelen, "Playing the Ritual Game," 186–87.

41. Marc., *Chron.* 2.66.

42. Croke, *Chronicle*, xix–xx.

43. No consuls are recorded after 541: see Cameron and Schauer, "Last Consul," 126–45; Croke, "Justinian's Constantinople," 77.

44. Arnold, *Theoderic*, 70–91, 94–108 (Theoderic dressed as emperor); Gr. Mag., *Dial.* 2.14 (Totila).

45. Betancourt, *Byzantine Intersectionality*, 206. See also Masterson, *Between Byzantine Men*, 67–145; Rapp, *Brother-Making*, 191–227; Krueger, "Between Monks."

Subsequent western sovereigns remained fully conscious of the power of transcendent *male* beauty, including its immense erotic, and homoerotic, attraction. For Renaissance princes, "the exhibition of noble bodies was as indispensable to lords' rule as were waging war, dispensing justice, acquiring territory, and collecting taxes. Brilliant bodies were the fundamental images and models through which signorial power was sustained."[46] In the homosocial masculine world of their courts, beautiful legs shown off in tight pants and ending in elaborately decorated shoes were "manifestations of specifically male courtliness and allure"—echoes of the boots and trousers laws.[47]

Hyacinthe Rigaud's famous 1701 portrait of Louis XIV in his coronation robes epitomizes such sparkling glitter, the "visible divinity" of the Sun King, who had acceded to the throne as a six-year-old.[48] When Rigaud portrayed him, Louis XIV was already sixty-three. But the painter draws the viewer's eye to the Sun King's youthful, strong legs, sheathed in shimmering white silk that matches his high-heeled shoes, further elongating the leg and guiding the eye upward.[49] Upward, but not as far as the mature face under a dark-haired wig. In Versailles, the picture was hung at the top of a staircase so that the eyes of those who ascended were first level with the shoes and then followed the legs up to rest on those parts that were, after all, for the monarch the most essential.[50]

Louis XIV and his court drew inspiration for their ceremonial grandeur from countless examples offered by the early Roman Empire and the Renaissance.[51] But they were also cognizant of the representational potential of the late Roman Empire. Thus, contemporaries compared the king favorably to Theodosius I.[52] And the king and his minister of finance sponsored "the founding father of Byzantine studies," Charles du Fresne, sieur du Cange, after an alliance with the Habsburgs against the Ottoman empire awaked their interest in the eastern Mediterranean.[53] In 1657, du Cange dedicated his *History of the City of Constantinople* to Louis as heir to the New Rome (and, of course, the old), and in 1680 he published his richly illustrated *Byzantine History*, with numerous images of statues, inscrip-

46. McCall, *Brilliant Bodies*, 10.

47. McCall, *Brilliant Bodies*, 81, and see 89–96.

48. Musée du Louvre, département des Peintures, inv. 7492. Quote in P. Burke, *Fabrication*, 41, and see 39–43. See also Vinken, *Angezogen*, 42–61; Tsikounas, "Gloire."

49. P. Burke, *Fabrication*, 113–15 (Louis's eternal youth on a medal celebrating his recovery after an operation in 1687), 188–98.

50. For Bouineau, "Réflexions politiques," 33, Rigaud's painting negates Louis's body in line with Christian rejection of the flesh (though at 15–17 he does note those legs).

51. Bouineau, "Réflexions politiques," 15–47 (including Louis as Apollo and Alexander the Great).

52. P. Burke, *Fabrication*, 102–5 (links the Edict of Nantes with *Cunctos populos*).

53. Shawcross, "Editing," 146. This alliance (173) prompted a French bishop to declare already in 1648 that Louis "could lay claim to the legacy of both the Western and Eastern Roman Empires, a privilege no ruler had had since Constantine the Great" (174–75).

FIGURE 20. Hyacinthe Rigaud, 1659–1743. Louis XIV at age sixty-three in grand royal costume, oil on canvas, 131 × 97 cm (post-restoration). MV3563 (another version located at the Louvre, INV7492). Chateaux de Versailles et de Trianon / Versailles / France. Photo: Christophe Fouin. © RMN-Grand Palais / Art Resource, NY.

tions, frescoes, coins, and mosaics, initiating what has been called the Byzantine du Louvre school.[54]

Louis XIV did not need Theodosius, Arcadius, or Honorius, nor later sparkling Milanese residents like the Renaissance signore Galeazzo Maria Sforza, to understand the importance of being gorgeous. All of these men and their elite contemporaries, at their courts and elsewhere in their domains, were highly attuned to the nuances of imperial, royal, noble beauty and its power. The ruler's beauty and its display included consorts and other elite women, but their splendor was subsumed into the combined sparkle at the center: the emperor's (or king's) body. However accentuated, revealed, or covered by the ruler's ornate vestments, enhanced by the insignia of sovereignty, the imperial and royal body stood for the health—and the future—of the realm, and therefore it was beautiful, hard, valorous, strong, subtle, youthful, and always immensely desirable. I have chosen a specific historically contingent moment, the last two decades of the fourth century and the rule of the early Theodosians, to illustrate how these emperors and their elites negotiated and implemented an exquisitely layered combination of *virtus*, of manliness, that was circumscribed yet expansive, stable, inclusive and flexible. This iteration of imperial beauty as Christian and the ways it mobilized the male same-sex erotic potential of the sovereign's body—that queerness at the center of power—responded to and shaped one imperial message: It showed what the Theodosian emperors wanted and how they set about getting it. Their success may go a long way toward explaining the durability of the *sacratissimus divinus imperator*, of the sovereign by the grace of God. But the importance of being gorgeous is not limited to specific periods of history, nor to the regions on which I focus. Beauty and desire, ugliness and repulsion are part of the body politic wherever that body may reside.

54. Shawcross, "Editing," 146 (date for *History of the City of Constantinople*), 156 (*Byzantine History*, Byzantine du Louvre), 177–78 (dedication to Louis). See also Shawcross, "Reinvention of Du Cange," 181–203; Ostrogorsky, *Byzantine State*, 3.

REFERENCES

PRIMARY SOURCES

Ambr.: Ambrose

    De fide. Ed. O. Faller in *CSEL* 78.

    De Noe. Ed. K. Schenkl in *CSEL* 32.1.

    De spiritu sancto. Ed. O. Faller in *CSEL* 79.

    De ob. Theod.: De obitu Theodosii. Ed. V. Zimmerl-Panagl in *CSEL* 106. Trans. J. H. W. G. Liebeschuetz. Liverpool, 2005.

    De ob. Val.: De obitu Valentiniani. Ed. V. Zimmerl-Panagl in *CSEL* 106. Trans. J. H. W. G. Liebeschuetz. Liverpool, 2005.

    Ep.: Epistulae. Ed. O. Faller and M. Zelzer in *CSEL* 82/1–3.

    Exp. ps.: Expositio Psalmi CXVIII. Ed. M. Petschenig in *CSEL* 62.

    Off.: De Officiis. Ed. M. Testard in *CCSL* 15.

Amm. Marc.: Ammianus Marcellinus, *Res Gestae*. Ed. and trans. J. C. Rolfe in *LCL* 331.

Anonym. *Olymp.: The Life of Olympias*. Ed. and French trans. A.-M. Malingrey in *SC* 13. Trans. E. Clark. New York, 1982.

Anonymus Valesianus. Ed. and trans. J. C. Rolfe in *LCL* 331.

Anth. Graec.: Anthologia Graeca. Ed. and trans. R. Paton and M. A. Tueller in *LCL* 67–8.

Anth. Pal.: Anthologia Palatina. Ed. and trans. F. Conca and M. Marzi. 2 vols. Turin, 2005.

Apul., *Met.: Apuleius, Metamorphoses*. Ed. J. A. Hanson in *LCL* 44, 453.

Arist.: Aristotle

    Eth. Nic.: Ethica Nicomachea. Ed. and trans. H. Rackham in *LCL* 73.

    Poet.: Poetica. Ed. and trans. W. Hamilton Fyfein and D. Russell in *LCL* 199.

    Pol.: Politica. Ed. and trans. H. Rackham in *LCL* 264.

August.: Augustine

    Ex. Urb.: Sermo de excidio Urbis Romae. Trans. E. M. Atkins and R. Dodaro. Cambridge, 2001. French trans. J. C. Fredouille. Paris, 2004.

De civ. D.: De civitate Dei. Ed. B. Dombart and A. Kalb in *CCSL* 47–8. Trans. R. W. Dyson. Cambridge 1998.

C. litt. Petil.: Contra litteras Petiliani. Ed. M. Petschenig in *CSEL* 52.

Conf.: Confessiones. Ed. L. Verheijen in *CCSL* 27.

Quaest. vet. et novi test.: Quaestiones veteris et novi testamenti. Ed. A. Souter in *CSEL* 50.

Serm.: Sermones. Ed. C. Lambot et al. in *CCSL* 41.

Aur. Vict., *Caes.:* Aurelius Victor, *De Caesaribus.* Trans. H. W. Bird. Liverpool 1994.

Aus.: Ausonius

Epigr.: Epigrammata. Trans. H. G. Evelyn White in *LCL* 115.

Grat. Act.: Gratiarum actio ad Gratianum. Ed. R. P. H. Green. Oxford 1991. Trans. H. G. Evelyn White in *LCL* 115.

Catul.: Catullus, *Poems.* Ed. and trans. F. W. Cornish in *LCL* 6.

Chron. Pasch.: Chronicon Paschale. Ed. and trans. M. Whitby and M. Whitby. Liverpool, 1989.

Chrysipp. Stoic.: Chrysippus Stoicus. Ed. von Armin. Leipzig, 1905–24. Ed. and French trans. R. Dufour. Paris, 2004.

Chrysipp. *Stoic.: Stoicorum veterum fragmenta,* vol. 3: *Chrysippi fragmenta moralia, fragmenta successorum Chrysipp.* Ed. H. v. Arnim. Reprint: Munich, 2004.

Cic.: Cicero

Fin.: De finibus. Ed. and trans. H. Rackham in *LCL* 40.

Har.: De haruspicum responsis. Ed. and trans. N. H. Watts in *LCL* 158.

Off.: De officiis. Ed. and trans. W. Miller in *LCL* 30.

Rep.: De re publica. Ed. and trans. C. W. Keyes in *LCL* 213.

Tusc.: Tusculanae disputationes. Ed. and trans. J. E. King in *LCL* 141.

Claud.: Claudius Claudianus

Bell. Gild.: De bello Gildonico. Ed. and trans. M. Platnauer in *LCL* 135.

carm. min.: carmina minora. Ed. J. B. Hall. Leipzig, 1985. Ed. and trans. M. Platnauer in *LCL* 136. Trans. N. Bernstein. New York, 2021. Ed. and French trans. J.-L. Charlet. Paris, 2018. German trans. Ph. Weiß and C. Wiener. Berlin, 2020.

Carm. Min. 10 = *Epithalamium de nuptiis Honorii Augusti.* Ed. J. B. Hall. Leipzig, 1985. Ed. and trans. M. Platnauer in *LCL* 135. Trans. N. W. Bernstein. London, 2023. German trans. Ph. Weiß and C. Wiener. Berlin, 2020.

III Cons. Hon.: Panegyricus de tertio consolatu Honorii Augusti. Ed. and French trans. J.-L. Charlet. Paris, 2000. German trans. Ph. Weiß and C. Wiener. Berlin, 2020. Ed. and trans. M. Platnauer in *LCL* 135. Trans. N. W. Bernstein. London, 2023.

IV Cons. Hon.: Panegyricus de quarto consolatu Honorii Augusti. Ed. and French trans. J.-L. Charlet. Paris, 2000. Ed. and trans. M. Platnauer in *LCL* 135; trans. N. W. Bernstein. London, 2023; ed. and trans. W. Barr. Liverpool, 1981.

VI Cons. Hon.: Panegyricus de sexto consolatu Honorii Augusti. Ed. M. Dewar. Oxford, 1996. German trans. Ph. Weiß and C. Wiener. Berlin, 2020. Ed. and trans. M. Platnauer in *LCL* 136.

Cons. Stil.: De consolatu Stilichonis. Ed. and French trans. J.-L. Charlet. Paris, 2017. German trans. Ph. Weiß and C. Wiener. Berlin, 2020. Ed. and trans. M. Platnauer in *LCL* 135–6. Trans. N. W. Bernstein. London, 2023.

Eutr.: In Eutropium. Ed. J. B. Hall. Leipzig, 1985. Ed. and trans. M. Platnauer in *LCL* 135. Trans. N. W. Bernstein. London, 2023. Ed. and French trans. J.-L. Charlet, *Claudien.* Paris, 2022. German trans. Ph. Weiß and C. Wiener. Berlin, 2020.

Laus Ser.: *Laus Serenae*. Ed. J. B. Hall. Leipzig, 1985. Ed. and trans. M. Platnauer in *LCL* 136. Trans. N. Bernstein. New York, 2021.

M. Theod.: *Claudiani panegyricus de consulatu Manlii Theodori*. Ed. and German trans. W. Simon. Berlin, 1975. Ed. and French trans. J.-L. Charlet. Paris, 2017. Trans. N. W. Bernstein. London, 2023. German trans. Ph. Weiß and C. Wiener. Berlin, 2020.

Prob.: *Panegyricus dictus Probino et Olybrio consulibus*. Ed. and trans. M. Platnauer in *LCL* 135. Trans. N. W. Bernstein. London, 2023. Ed. and German trans. W. Taegert. Munich, 1988.

Ruf.: *In Rufinum*. Ed. and trans. M. Platnauer in *LCL* 135. Trans. N. W. Bernstein. London, 2023. Ed. and French trans. J.-L. Charlet. Paris, 2000.

CJ: *Codex Iustinianus*. Ed. P. Krueger. Berlin, 1892. Reprint, 2014.

Clem. Alex., *Strom.*: Clement of Alexandria, *Stromata*. Trans. A. Roberts, J. Donaldson, and A. Cleveland Coxe. New York, 1885.

Coll. Av.: *Collectio Avellana*. Ed. O. Gühnter in *CSEL* 35.1–2.

Coll. Mos.: *Mosaicarum et Romanarum legum collatio*. Ed. and trans. R. M. Frakes. Oxford, 2011.

Coll. Nov.: *Collectio Novariensis de re Eutychis*. Ed. E. Schwartz. Berlin, 1933. Reprint, 1962. Trans. R. Price and M. Gaddis. Liverpool, 2005.

Cons. Const.: *Consularia Constantinopolitana*. Ed. R. W. Burgess. Oxford, 2017. Ed. and German trans. M. Becker et al. Leiden, 2016.

Coripp., *In laud. Iust.*: Corippus, *In laudem Iustini minoris*. Ed. and trans. A. Cameron. London. 2000.

CTh: *Theodosiani libri XVI cum Constitutionibus Sirmondianis*. Ed. T. Mommsen. Berlin, 1905. Trans. C. Pharr. Princeton, 1952. French trans. J. Rougé, R. Delmaire, and F. Richard in *SC* 497.

Dig.: *Digesta*. Ed. T. Mommsen. Berlin, 1893. Reprint, 2014.

Dio Cass.: Dio Cassius, *Roman History*. Trans. E. Cary in *LCL* 32, 37, 53, 66, 82–83, 175–77.

Dio. Chrys., *Or.*: Dio Chrysostom, *Orationes*. Ed. and trans. J. W. Cohoon and H. Lamar Crosby in *LCL* 257, 339, 358, 376, 385. For the Euboean Oration (*Or.* 7), ed. and German trans. G. A. Lehmann, D. Engster, and D. Gall. Tübingen, 2012.

Dion. Halicar., *Ant. Rom.*: Dionysius of Halicarnassus, *Roman Antiquities*. Ed. and trans. E. Cary in *LCL* 319, 347, 357, 364, 372, 378, 388.

Enn., *Ann*: *Ennius' Annals: Poetry and History*. Ed. C. Damon and J. Farrell. Cambridge, 2020.

Epit. de Caes.: *Epitome de Caesaribus*. Sextus Aurelius Victor and M. Festy. *Abrégé des Césars / Pseudo-Aurélius Victor*. Ed. and French trans. M. Festy. Paris, 1999. *Sexti Aurelii Victoris Liber de Caesaribus: praecedunt, Origo gentis romanae et Liber de viris illustribus urbis Romae, subsequitur Epitome de Caesaribus*. Ed. F. Pichlmayr. Leipzig, 1911.

Eunap., *Hist.*: Eunapius, *Historiae*. Ed. and trans. R. C. Blockley. Liverpool, 1983.

Eus., *Vit. Const.*: Eusebius, *De vita Constantini*. Ed. and trans. A. Cameron and S. Hall. Oxford, 1999.

Eutr., *Brev.*: Eutropius, *Breviarium ab urbe condita*. Trans. H. W. Bird. Liverpool, 1993.

Gell., *NA*: Gellius, *Noctes Atticae*. Ed. and trans. J. C. Rolfe in *LCL* 195, 200, 212.

Gr. Mag., *Dial.*: Gregory the Great, *Dialogues*. Ed. and French trans. A. de Vogüé. Paris, 1978.

Gr. Naz.: Gregory of Nazianzus

De vita sua. Ed. and French trans. A. Tuilier and G. Bady. Paris, 2004. Ed. and trans. C. White. Cambridge, 1996. Ed. and German trans. C. Jungck. Heidelberg, 1974.

Or.: Orationes. Ed. and French trans. J. Bernardi, M.-A.Calvet-Sébasti, and J. Mossay. Paris 1978–95. Ed. and Italian trans. C. Moreschini. Milan 2000.

Poem.: Poemata. Ed. and Italian trans. C. Moreschini, I. Costa, and C. Crimi. Rome, 1994–99.

Gr. Nyss.: Gregory of Nyssa

Eun.: Contra Eunomius. Ed. W. Jaeger. Leiden, 1960.

Flac.: Oratio funebris in Flaccillam imperatricem. Ed. A. Spira. Leiden, 1967. Ed. and French trans. P. Maraval in *SC* 606.

In Meletium. Ed. A. Spira. Leiden, 1967.

Vit. Mos.: Vita Mosis. Ed. and French trans. J. Danielou in *SC* 1. Trans. A. J. Malherbe and E. Ferguson. New York, 1978.

Hdt.: *Herodotus*. Trans. A. D. Godley in *LCL* 117–20.

Hieron., *Ep.*: Hieronymus, *Epistulae*. Ed. I. Hilberg in *CSEL* 54–6.

HA: Historia Augusta

Alex. Sev.: Life of Alexander Severus. Ed. and French trans. C. Bertrand-Dagenbach and A. Molinier-Arbo. Paris, 2014. Trans. D. Magie and D. Rohrbacher in *LCL* 140.

Gord.: Life of Gordian III. Ed. and French trans. F. Paschoud. Paris, 2023. Trans. D. Magie and D. Rohrbacher in *LCL* 140.

Hadr.: Life of Hadrian. Trans. D. Magie and D. Rohrbacher in *LCL* 139.

Heliogab.: Life of Heliogabalus. Ed. and French trans. R. Turcan. Paris, 1993. Trans. D. Magie and D. Rohrbacher in *LCL* 140.

Macr.: Life of Macrinus. Ed. and French trans. R. Turcan. Paris, 1993. Trans. D. Magie and D. Rohrbacher in *LCL* 140.

Max.: The Two Maximini. Trans. D. Magie and D. Rohrbacher in *LCL* 140.

Pert.: Life of Pertinax. Ed. and trans. D. Magie and D. Rohrbacher in *LCL* 139.

Prob.: Life of Probus. Ed. and French trans. F. Paschoud. Paris, 2001. Trans. D. Magie and D. Rohrbacher in *LCL* 263.

Tac.: Life of Tacitus. Ed. and French trans. F. Paschoud. Paris 1996. Trans. D. Magie and D. Rohrbacher in *LCL* 263.

Hom.: Homer

Il.: Iliad. Ed. and trans. A. T. Murray and W. F. Wyatt in *LCL* 170–1.

Od.: Odyssey. Ed. and trans. A. T. Murray and E. G. Dimock in *LCL* 104–5.

Hor., *Epod.*: Horace, *Epodes*. Ed. and trans. N. Rudd in *LCL* 33.

J. Antioch: John of Antioch. Ed. E. Roberto in *CCSG* 47.

J. Chrys.: John Chrysostom

Ad vid. iun.: Ad viduam iuniorem. Ed. in *PG* 48.599–610.

Compunct. Dem.: Ad Demetrium de compunctione. Ed. in *PG* 47.393–422.

C. lud. et theat.: Contra ludos et theatra (*nov. hom.* 7). Ed. in *PG* 56.263–70. Trans. W. Mayer and P. Allen. London, 2000.

De eleem.: De eleemosyna. Ed. in *PG* 60. 707–12.

De Hiero. Phoca: De s. Hieromartyre Phoca. Ed. in *PG* 50.699–706.

De Macc.: De Maccabeis homiliae. Trans. W. Mayer. Crestwood, 2006.

De perf. car.: Homilia de perfecta caritate. Ed. in *PG* 56.279–90.

De sanct. mart.: *De sanctis martyribus sermo*. Ed. in *PG* 50.661–6. Trans. W. Mayer and P. Allen. London, 2000.

De stat.: *De statuis homilia*. Ed. in *PG* 49.15–222.

Hom. 2: *Homilia secunda cum imperatrix media nocte*. Text in *PG* 63.467–72. Trans. W. Mayer and P. Allen. London 2000.

Hom. c. Anomoeos: *De incomprehensibili dei natura* (*Contra Anomoeos hom. 11*). Ed. in *PG* 48.701–48. Ed. and French trans. A.-M. Malingrey, J. Daniélou, and R. Flacelière in *SC* 28bis.

In Act.: *In Acta apostolorum homiliae*. Ed. in *PG* 60.13–582.

In Col.: *In ep. ad Colossenses homiliae*. Ed. in *PG* 62.299–390.

In 1 Cor.: *In ep. 1 ad Corinthios homiliae*. Ed. in *PG* 61.9–380.

In 2 Cor.: *In ep. 2 ad Corinthios homiliae*. Ed. in *PG* 61.381–610.

In Eph.: *In epistulam ad Ephesios homiliae*. Ed. in *PG* 62.9–176.

In Eutr.: *In Eutropium*. Ed. in *PG* 52. 391–396. Trans. W. Mayer and P. Allen. London, 2000. Italian trans. F. Conti Bizarro and R. Romano. Naples, 1987.

In Gen. hom.: *Homiliae 1–67 in Genesim*. Ed. in *PG* 53 and 54.383–530.

In Heb.: *In ep. ad Hebraeos homiliae*. Ed. in *PG* 63. 9–236.

In Jn.: *In Ioannem homiliae*. Ed. in *PG* 59.23–484.

In Matt.: *In Matthaeum homiliae*. Ed. in *PG* 57.21–472; 58.21–792.

In Phil.: *In ep. ad Philippenses homiliae*. Ed. in *PG* 62.177–298.

In Rom.: *In epistulam ad Romanos homiliae*. Ed. in *PG* 60.582–681. Trans. P. Papageorgiou. Brookline, 2013.

In 1 Tim.: *In epistulam 1 ad Timotheum homiliae*. Ed. in *PG* 62.391–466.

In 2 Thess.: *In epistulam 2 ad Thessalonicenses homiliae*. Ed. in *PG* 62.467–500.

In Tit.: *In epistulam ad Titum homiliae*. Ed. in *PG* 62.633–700.

Inan.: *De inani gloria et de educandis liberis*. Ed. and French trans. A.-M. Malingrey in *SC* 188.

Laz. et div.: *De Lazaro et divite homiliae*. Ed. in *PG* 48.963–1054.

Ne tim.: *In illud: Ne timueritis cum dives factus fuerit homo (Ps 48.17) homiliae*. Ed. in *PG* 55.519–28. Trans. R. C. Hill. Brookline, MA, 2003.

Theod.: *Ad Theodorum lapsum libri*. Ed. and French trans. J. Dumortier in *SC* 117.

Subintr.: *Contra eos qui subintroductae habent virgines*. Ed. and French trans. J. Dumortier. Paris, 1955.

Virg.: *De virginitate*. Ed. and French trans. H. Musurillo and B. Grillet in *SC* 125.

J. Lydus, *de mag.*: *De magistratibus*. Ed. and French trans. M. Dubuisson and J. Schamp. Paris, 2006.

Jul., *Or.*: Julian, *Orationes*. Ed. and trans. W. C. Wright in *LCL* 13, 29.

Juv.: Juvenal, *Satires. Juvenal and Persius*. Ed. and trans. S. Morton Braund in *LCL* 91.

Lib., *Or.*: Libanius, *Orationes*. Ed. R. Foerster. Leipzig, 1903–27. Reprint: Hildesheim, 1963–85.

Livy. *Ab Urbe Condita*. Ed. P.G. Walsh. Oxford 1999.

Lucian, *Syr. D.*: *De Syria Dea*. Ed. and trans. A.M. Harmon in *LCL* 162.

Malalas, *Chron.*: Malalas, *Chronicle*. Ed. and trans. E. Jeffreys, M. Jeffreys, and R. Scott. Leiden, 1986.

Marc., *Chron.*: Marcellinus, *Chronicle*. Trans. B. Croke. Sydney, 1995.

Marc. Diac.: Marc the Deacon, *Life of Porphyry*. Ed. and French trans. H Grégoire and M.-A. Kugener. Paris, 1930. Trans. C. Rapp. New York, 2001.

Mart., *Epigr.*: *Epigrams of Martial*. Ed. and trans. J. P. Sullivan and P. Whigham. Berkeley, 1987.

Mir. Th.: *Miracles of Thecla*. Ed. and French trans. G. Dagron. Brussels, 1978.

Notitia Dignitatum. Ed. O. Seeck. Berlin, 1876. Reprint: Cambridge, 2019.

Olympiodorus. Ed. and trans. R. C. Blockley. Liverpool, 1983.

Optatianus Porphyrius, *Carm.*: *Carmina*. Ed. G. I. Polara. Turin, 1973.

Orig., *c. Cels.*: *Origen: Contra Celsum*. Ed. and trans. M. Marcovich. Leiden, 2001.

Oros.: Orosius, *Historiarum Adversum Paganos Libri VII*. Ed. and French trans. M.-P. Arnaud-Lindet. Paris, 1990–91.

Ov.: Ovid

    Ars am.: *Ars amatoria*. Ed. and trans. J. H. Mozley in *LCL* 232.

    Met.: *Metamorphoseos*. Ed. and trans. F. J. Miller and G. P. Goold in *LCL* 42–3.

Pall.: Palladius

    Dial.: *Dialogue*. Ed. and French trans. A.-M. Malingrey in *SC* 341–2.

    Hist. Laus.: *Historia Lausiaca*. Ed. E. C. Butler. vol. 2. Cambridge, 1904. Reprint, 2014.

    Hist. mon.: *Historia monachorum in Aegypto*. Ed. E. C. Butler. vol. 1. Cambridge, 1904. Reprint, 2014.

Pan. lat.: *Panegyrici latini*. Ed. and trans. R. A. B. Mynors, C. E. V. Nixon, and B. Saylor Rodgers. Berkeley, 1994.

Paulin., *Vit. Amb.*: Paulinus, *Vita Ambrosii*. Ed. and French trans. É. Lamirande. Montreal, 1983.

Paulinus of Nola, *Ep.*: *Epistulae*. Ed. M. Skeb in *FC* 25.2.

Philost., *HE*: Philostorgius, *Historia ecclesiastica*. Ed. and German trans. B. Bleckmann and M. Stein. Paderborn, 2015. Trans. Ph. R. Amidon. Leiden, 2007.

Pind., *Ol.*: Pindar, *Olympian Odes*. Ed. and trans. W. H. Race in *LCL* 56.

Pl.: Plato

    Apol.: *Apologia*. Ed. J. Burnet. Oxford, 1902. Reprint, 1989.

    Hp. mai.: *Hippias maior*. Ed. J. Burnet. Oxford, 1902. Reprint, 1989.

    Leg.: *Leges*. Ed. J. Burnet. Oxford, 1902. Reprint, 1989.

    Phileb.: *Philebus*. Ed. J. Burnet. Oxford, 1902. Reprint, 1989.

    Rep.: *Republica*. Ed. J. Burnet. Oxford, 1902. Reprint, 1989.

    Symp.: *Symposium*. Ed. J. Burnet. Oxford, 1902. Reprint, 1989.

Plin., *NH*: Pliny the Elder, *Historia naturalis*. Ed. S. G. Owen. Oxford, 2015. Trans. H. Rackham in *LCL* 394.

Plin.: Pliny the Younger

    Pan.: *Panegyricus*. Ed. and trans. B. Radice in *LCL* 59.

    Ep.: Letters, 2 vols. Ed. and trans. B. Radice in *LCL* 55 and 59.

Plotinus, *Enn.*: Plotinus, *Enneads*. Ed. and trans. A. H. Armstrong in *LCL* 440–55, 468.

Plut.: Plutarch

    Alex.: *Life of Alexander*. Ed. and trans. B. Perrin in *LCL* 99.

    Mor.: *Moralia*. Ed. and trans. F. C. Babbitt et al. in *LCL* 197, 222, 245, 305–6, 321, 337, 405–6, 424–9, 470, 499.

Proba, *Cento*: Faltonia Betitia Proba, *Cento vergilianus*. Ed. C. M. Lucarini and A. Fassina. Berlin, 2015. Ed. and Italian trans. V. Sineri. Acireale, 2011.

Prud.: Prudentius
  Ham.: Hamartigenia. Ed. M. P. Cunningham in *CCSL* 126.
  Perist.: Peristephanon. Ed. M. P. Cunningham in *CCSL* 126.
  Contra Symm.: Contra Symmachum. Ed. M. P. Cunningham in *CCSL* 126.
Ps.-Clem., *Hom.*: Ps.-Clement, *Homiliae.* Ed. B. Rehm et al. in *GCS* 42.
Ps.-Hipp.: Ps.-Hippocrates, *Airs, Waters, Places.* Ed. and French trans. J. Jouanna. Paris, 1996.
Ps.-Martyrius: Ps.-Martyrius, *Epitaphios.* Trans. T. D. Barnes and G. Bevan. Liverpool, 2013.
RGDA: Res Gestae Divi Augusti. Ed. and trans. A. E. Cooley. Cambridge, 2009.
Ruf., *HE*: Rufinus, *Historia Ecclesiastica.* Trans. Ph. R. Amidon. Washington, DC, 2016.
Sall.: Sallust
  Cat.: The War with Catiline. Ed. and trans. J. C. Rolfe and J. T. Ramsey in *LCL* 116.
  Iug.: The War with Jugurtha. Ed. and trans. J. C. Rolfe and J. T. Ramsey in *LCL* 116.
Sen.: Seneca
  Clem.: De Clementia. Ed. and trans. S. Morton Braund. Oxford, 2009.
  Prov.: De Providentia. Ed. and trans. J. W. Basore in *LCL* 214.
Sid. Apoll., *Ep.: Epistulae.* Ed. and trans. W. B. Anderson in *LCL* 296, 420.
Soc., *HE*: Socrates, *Historia ecclesiastica.* Ed. and French trans. P. Maraval and P. Périchon in *SC* 477, 493, 505–6.
Soz., *HE*: Sozomen, *Historia ecclesiastica.* Ed. and French trans. A.-J. Festugière, B. Grillet, and G. Sabbah in *SC* 306, 418, 495, 516.
Stat.: Statius
  Achil.: Achilleides. Ed. and trans. D. R. Shackleton Bailey in *LCL* 498.
  Sil.: Silvae. Ed. and trans. D. R. Shackleton Bailey and Ch. A. Parrott in *LCL* 206.
  Theb.: Thebaid. Trans. A. D. Melville. Oxford, 1992.
Suet.: Suetonius
  Dom.: Life of Domitian. Trans. D. W. Hurley. Indianapolis, 2011.
  Nero: Life of Nero. Trans. D. W. Hurley. Indianapolis, 2011.
  Tit.: Life of Titus. Trans. D. W. Hurley. Indianapolis, 2011.
Sulp., *Vit. Mart.*: Sulpicius Severus, *Vitae Sancti Martini.* Ed. and trans. Ph. H. Burton. Oxford, 2017.
Symm.: Symmachus
  Ep.: Epistulae. Trans. M. R. Salzman and M. Roberts. Atlanta 2011.
  Or. 3: Oration 3 to Gratian. Trans. B. Saylor Rodgers 2015 (https://www.uvm.edu/~bsaylor/rome/Symmachus3.pdf).
  Rel.: Relationes. Trans. R. H. Barrow. Oxford, 1973.
Syn.: Synesius
  Ep.: Epistulae. Ed. and French trans. A. Garzya and D. Roques. Paris, 2000. Ed. and Italian trans. A. Garzya. Turin, 1989.
  De reg.: De regno. Ed. and French trans. Ch. Lacombrade. Paris, 1951. Ed. and Italian trans. A. Garzya. Naples, 1973. French trans. J. Lamoureux and N. Aujoulat. Paris, 2008. Italian trans. C. Amande and P. Graffigna. Palermo, 1999. Trans. A. Fitzgerald. London, 1930.
  De prov.: De providentia. Ed. and French trans. Ch. Lacombrade. Paris, 1951. Italian trans. S. Nicolosi. Padova, 1959.
  Dion. Ed. K. Treu. Berlin, 1958.
  Enc. Cal.: Encomium calvitiae. Ed. N. Terzaghi. Rome, 1944.
Tac., *Ann.*: Tacitus, *Annales.* Ed. F. R. D. Goodyear. Cambridge, 1972.

Tert., *De monog.*: Tertullian, *De Monogamia*. Ed. and French trans. P. Mattei in *SC* 343.

Them., *Or.*: *Themistii Orationes quae supersunt*. 3 vols. Ed. H. Schenkl, G. Downey, and A. F. Norman. Leipzig, 1965–74. *Orations* 1, 3–6, 14–17, 34. Trans. P. Heather and D. Moncur. Liverpool, 2001; *Orations* 6–13. Trans. S. Swain. Liverpool, 2021.

Theod.: Theodoret of Cyprus
   HE: *Historia ecclesiastica*. Ed. and French trans. J. Bouffartigue et al. in *SC* 501, 530.
   HR: *Historia religiosa*. Ed. in *PG* 82.1099–295.

Val. Max.: Valerius Maximus, *Memorable Doings and Sayings*. Ed. and trans. D. R. Shackleton Bailey in *LCL* 492–3.

Veg., *Mil.*: Vegetius, *De re militari*. Ed. M. D. Reeve. Oxford, 2004. Trans. N. P. Milner. Liverpool, 2001.

Virg., *Aen.*: Vergil, *Aeneid*. Trans. S. Bartsch. New York, 2021.

Xen.: Xenophon
   Ages.: *Agesilaus*. Ed. and trans. E. C. Marchant and G. W. Bowersock in *LCL* 183.
   Anab.: *Anabasis*. Ed. and trans. C. L. Brownson and J. Dillery in *LCL* 90.
   Cyr.: *Cyropaedia*. Ed. and French trans. M. Bizos and É. Delebecque. Paris 2003. Trans. W. Miller in *LCL* 51–2.

Zos., *HN*: Zosimus, *Historia nova*. Ed. and French trans. F. Paschoud. Paris, 1971–89.

SECONDARY SOURCES

Adams, J. N. "The Use and Meanings of Lat. *exoletus*." *Materiali e discussioni per l'analisi dei testi classici* 88 (2022): 143–81.

Albert, G. *Goten in Konstantinopel: Untersuchungen zur oströmischen Geschichte um das Jahr 400 n. Chr.* Paderborn, 1984.

Alexievich, S. *Secondhand Time: The Last of the Soviets*. Translated by B. Shayevich. New York, 2017.

Alföldi, A. *Die monarchische Repräsentation im römischen Kaiserreiche*. Darmstadt, 1980.

Alföldi-Rosenbaum, E. "Apicius, *De re coquinaria* and the *Vita Heliogabali*." In *Bonner Historia-August-Colloquium 1970*, edited by A. Alföldi and J. Straub, 5–10. Bonn, 1972.

Alvino, M. C. "Osservazioni sulla mimesi letteraria nel *De regno* di Sinesio." *Atti dell'Accademia Pontaniana* n.s. 62 (2013): 177–89.

Amande, C. "Il lexikon di Sinesio: Presentazione ed esemplificazioni dal *De regno*." In Seng and Hoffmann, *Synesios von Kyrene*, 66–72.

Anagnostou-Laoutides, E. "Sexual Ethics and Unnatural Vice: From Zeno and Musonius Rufus to Augustine and Aquinas." In Mayer and Elmer, *Men and Women in the Early Christian Centuries*, 271–92.

Ando, C. *Imperial Ideology and Provincial Loyalty in the Roman Empire*. Berkeley, 2000.

———. "The Palladium and the Pentateuch: Towards a Sacred Topography of the Later Roman Empire." *Phoenix* 55 (2001): 369–410.

Andrade, N. "The Processions of John Chrysostom and the Contested Spaces of Constantinople." *Journal of Early Christian Studies* 18 (2010): 161–89.

Angelova, D. N. "'By Divine Inspiration and the Greatness of His Mind:' Augustan and Christian Messaging on Constantine's Triumphal Arch." In Elm and Sessa, *War and Community*.

———. "The Ivories of Ariande and Ideas about Female Imperial Authority in Rome and Early Byzantium." *Gesta* 43 (2004): 1–15.

———. "Relics, Translation of." In *The Eerdmans Encyclopedia of Early Christian Art and Archaeology*, ed. P. Corby Finney, 407–9. Grand Rapids, 2017.

———. *Sacred Founders: Women, Men, and Gods in the Discourse of Imperial Founding, Rome Through Early Byzantium*. Berkeley, 2015.

Arce, J. "Dress Control in Late Antiquity: *Codex Theodosianus* 14.10.1–4." In *Kleidung und Repräsentation in Antike und Mittelalter*, edited by A. Köb and P. Riedel, 33–44. Munich, 2005.

Arnold, J. J. *Theoderic and the Roman Imperial Restoration*. Cambridge, 2014.

Aschenbrenner, N. and J. Ransohoff, eds. *The Invention of Byzantium in Early Modern Europe*. Washington, DC, 2021.

Avery, W. T. "The *Adoratio purpurae* and the Importance of the Imperial Purple in the Fourth Century." *Memoirs of the American Academy in Rome* 17 (1940): 60–80.

Ayres, L. *Nicaea and Its Legacy: An Approach to Fourth-Century Trinitarian Theology*. Oxford, 2004.

Azoulay, V. "Xénophon, le roi et les eunuques: Généalogie d'un monstre?" *Revue française d'histoire des idées politiques* 11 (2000): 3–26.

Bacci, M. *The Many Faces of Christ: Portraying the Holy in the East and West, 300 to 1300*. London, 2014.

Baglioni, I., ed. *Monstra: Costruzione e percezione delle entità ibride e mostruose nel Mediterraneo antico*. Rome, 2013.

Bagnall, R. S. et al., eds. *Consuls of the Later Roman Empire*. Oxford, 1987.

Bakirtzis, Ch., and E. Kourkoutidou-Nikolaidou. *Mosaics of Thessaloniki: 4th–11th Century*. Athens, 2012.

Bakirtzis, Ch., and P. Mastora. "Are the Mosaics in the Rotunda in Thessaloniki Linked to its Conversion to a Christian Church?" *Niš and Byzantium* 9 (2011): 33–45.

Baldus, H. R. "Theodosius der Große und die Revolte des Magnus Maximus—das Zeugnis der Münzen." *Chiron* 14 (1984): 175–92.

Ballabriga, A. "Les eunuques Scythes et leurs femmes." *Métis* 1 (1986): 121–38.

Balmaceda, C. *Virtus Romana: Politics and Morality in the Roman Historians*. Chapel Hill, 2017.

Bancaud, F. "L'esthétique du laid, de Hegel à Rosenkranz. Une 'esthétique de la résistance' ou de la résignation aux 'arts qui ne sont plus beaux'?" *Études Germaniques* 64 (2009): 899–917.

Bardill, J. "The Golden Gate in Constantinople: A Triumphal Arch of Theodosius I." *American Journal of Archaeology* 103 (1999): 671–96.

———. *Constantine: Divine Emperor of the Christian Golden Age*. Cambridge, 2012.

Barnes, T. D. "Leviticus, the Emperor Theodosius, and the Law of God: Three Prohibitions of Male Homosexuality." *Roman Legal Tradition* 8 (2012): 43–62.

———. "Oppressor, Persecutor, Usurper: The Meaning of *Tyrannus* in the Fourth Century." In *Historiae Augustae Colloquium Barcinonense*, edited by G. Bonamente and M. Mayer, 55–65. Bari, 1996.

———. "Synesius in Constantinople." *Greek, Roman and Byzantine Studies* 27 (1986): 93–112.

———. "*Ultimus Antoninorum*." In *Bonner Historia-Augusta-Colloquium 1970*, edited by A. Alföldi and J. Straub, 53–74. Bonn, 1972.

Barnes, T. D., and G. Bevan. *The Funerary Speech for John Chrysostom.* Liverpool, 2013.

Barry, J. *Bishops in Flight: Exile and Displacement in Late Antiquity.* Oakland, 2019.

Barthes, R. *The Fashion System.* Translated by M. Ward and R. Howard. Berkeley, 1990.

———. *The Language of Fashion.* Translated by A. Stafford. Edited by A. Stafford and M. Carter. London, 2005.

Barton, C. A. *The Sorrows of the Ancient Romans: The Gladiator and the Monster.* Princeton, 1993.

Bartsch, S. *Ideology in Cold Blood: A Reading of Lucan's "Civil War."* Cambridge, MA, 1997.

Bassett, S. "The Topography of Triumph in Late-Antique Constantinople." In *Der römische Triumph in Prinzipat und Spätantike: Probleme—Paradigmen—Perspektiven,* edited by F. Goldbeck and J. Wienand, 511–54. Berlin, 2017.

———. *The Urban Image of Late Antique Constantinople.* Cambridge, 2004.

Bastien, P. *Le buste monétaire des empereurs romains.* 3 vols. Wetteren, 1992–94.

Batty, R. *Rome and the Nomads: The Pontic-Danubian Realm in Antiquity.* Oxford, 2007.

Bauer, F. A. *Stadt, Platz und Denkmal in der Spätantike: Untersuchungen zur Austattung des öffentlichen Raums in den spätantiken Städten Rom, Konstantinopel und Ephesus.* Mainz, 1996.

———. "Urban Space and Ritual: Constantinople in Late Antiquity." *Acta ad archaeologiam et artium historiam pertinentia* 15 (2001): 27–61.

Baur, Ch. *Der heilige Johannes Chrysostomus und seine Zeit.* 2 vols. Munich, 1929–30.

Beard, M. "The Roman and the Foreign: The Cult of the 'Great Mother' in Imperial Rome." In *Shamanism, History, and the State,* edited by N. Thomas and C. Humphrey, 164–90. Ann Arbor, 1996.

———. *The Roman Triumph.* Cambridge, MA, 2007.

Becker, M. *Eunapios aus Sardes: Biographien über Philosophen und Sophisten: Einleitung, Übersetzung, Kommentar.* Stuttgart, 2013.

Beeley, Ch. A. *Gregory of Nazianzus on the Trinity and the Knowledge of God: In Your Light We Shall See Light.* Oxford, 2008.

Benjamins, J. C. "Augustine's Romans: Reshaping Masculinity, Empire, and Social Order After 410 AD." PhD diss., Berkeley, 2022.

Berger, A. *Konstantinopel: Geschichte, Topographie, Religion.* Stuttgart, 2011.

Bergjan, S.-P. "'Das hier ist kein Theater, und ihr sitzt nicht da, um Schauspieler zu betrachten und zu klatschen'—Theaterpolemik und Theatermetaphern bei Johannes Chrysostomus." *Journal of Ancient Christianity* 8 (2005): 567–92.

Bergjan, S.-P., and S. Elm, eds. *Antioch II: The Many Faces of Antioch: Intellectual Exchange and Religious Diversity in Antioch, CE 350–450.* Tübingen, 2018.

Berlincourt, V., L. Galli Milič, and D. Nelis, eds. *Lucan and Claudian: Context and Intertext.* Heidelberg, 2016.

Bertrand-Dagenbach, C. *Alexandre Sévère et 'l'Histoire Auguste.'* Brussels, 1990.

Berzon, T. S. *Classifying Christians: Ethnography, Heresiology, and the Limits of Knowledge in Late Antiquity.* Berkeley, 2016.

———. "Strategies of Containment." *Studies in Late Antiquity* 1 (2017): 124–49.

Betancourt, R. *Byzantine Intersectionality: Sexuality, Gender, and Race in the Middle Ages.* Princeton, 2020.

———. "The Slash as Method." In Betancourt and Taroutina, *Byzantium/Modernism,* 179–86.

———. "Why Sight Is Not Touch: Reconsidering the Tactility of Vision in Byzantium." *Dumbarton Oaks Papers* 70 (2016): 1–24.

Betancourt, R., and M. Taroutina, eds. *Byzantium/Modernism: The Byzantine as Method in Modernity.* Leiden 2015.

Biermann, M. *Die Leichenreden des Ambrosius von Mailand: Rhetorik, Predigt, Politik.* Stuttgart, 1995.

Bileta, V. "The *Venatio* in the Emperor's Presence? The *Consistorium* and the Military Men of the Late Roman Empire in the West." In *Gaining and Losing Imperial Favour in Late Antiquity,* edited by K. C. Choda, M. Sterk de Leeuw, and F. Schulz, 73–103. Leiden, 2020.

Bildhauer, B. *Medieval Things: Agency, Materiality, and Narratives of Objects in Medieval German Literature and Beyond.* Columbus, OH, 2020.

Bird, H. W. *"Liber de Caesaribus" of Sextus Aurelius Victor.* Liverpool, 1994.

Bleckmann, B. "Honorius und das Ende der römischen Herrschaft in Westeuropa." *Historische Zeitschrift* 265 (1997): 561–95.

Blockley, R. C. *The Fragmentary Classicising Historians of the Later Roman Empire: Eunapius, Olympiodorus, Priscus and Malchus.* Liverpool, 1981.

Blowers, P.M. "Pity, Empathy, and the Tragic Spectacle of Human Suffering: Exploring the Emotional Culture of Compassion in Late Antiquity." *Journal of Early Christian Studies* 18 (2010): 1–27.

Boatwright, M. T. *Imperial Women of Rome: Power, Gender, Context.* Oxford, 2021.

Bodnaruk, M. "Historicizing Trans Saints: Gender, Sexuality and Agency in the *Life of Pelagia*." In *Soul, Body, and Gender in Late Antiquity: Essays on Embodiment and Disembodiment,* edited by S. Panayotov et al., 276–99. London, 2024.

———. "The Politics of Memory and Visual Politics: Comparing the Self–Representations of Constantine and Augustus." *Annual of Medieval Studies at CEU* 19 (2013): 9–32.

Boeck, E. "Archaeology of Decadence: Uncovering Byzantium in Victorien Sardou's *Theodora*." In Betancourt and Taroutina, *Byzantium/Modernism,* 110–32.

Bönisch-Meyer, S. *Dialogangebote: Die Anrede des Kaisers jenseits der offiziellen Titulatur.* Leiden, 2021.

Börm, H., ed. *Antimonarchic Discourse in Antiquity.* Stuttgart, 2015.

———. "Antimonarchic Discourse in Antiquity: A Very Short Introduction." In Börm, *Antimonarchic Discourse in Antiquity,* 9–24.

———. "Barbaren als Tyrannen: Das Perserbild in der klassizistischen griechischen Historiographie." In *Das Weltreich der Perser: Rezeption—Aneignung—Verargumentierung,* edited by R. Rollinger, K. Ruffing, and L. Thomas, 3–30. Wiesbaden, 2019.

———. "Born to be Emperor: The Principle of Succession and the Roman Monarchy." In Wienand, *Contested Monarchy,* 239–64.

———. "The End of the Roman Empire: Civil Wars, the Imperial Monarchy, and the End of Antiquity." In *The End of Empires,* edited by Ph. Strobl, R. Rollinger, and M. Gehler, 191–212. Wiesbaden, 2022.

———. *Westrom: Von Honorius bis Justinian.* Stuttgart, 2018.

Bojcov, M. A. "Der heilige Kranz und der heilige Pferdezaum des Kaisers Konstantin und des Bischofs Ambrosius." *Frühmittelalterliche Studien* 42 (2008): 1–70.

Bonnell Freidin, A. "Gender in the Roman Empire." In *Companion to the Roman Empire,* edited by D. Potter. London, forthcoming.

Boone, J. A. *The Homoerotics of Orientalism.* New York, 2014.

Borg, B., and Ch. Witschel. "Veränderungen im Repräsentationsverhalten der römischen Eliten während des 3. Jhs. n. Chr." In *Inschriftliche Denkmäler als Medien der*

Selbstdarstellung in der römischen Welt, edited by G. Alföldy and S. Panciera, 47–120. Stuttgart, 2001.

Borri, G., C. La Rocca, and F. Veronese, eds. *Masculinities in Early Medieval Europe: Tradition and Innovation, 450–1050*. Turnhout, 2023.

Bouineau, J. "Réflexions politiques autour du portrait de Louis XIV par Hyacinthe Rigaud." In *Domination culturelle à l'antique et innutrition culturelle*, edited by J. Bounieau, 15–61. Paris, 2023.

Bowes, K. "Ivory Lists: Consular Diptychs, Christian Appropriation, and Polemics of Time." *Art History* 24 (2001): 338–57.

Bozinis, C. A. "The Natural Law in John Chrysostom." In de Wet and Mayer, *Revisioning John Chrysostom*, 493–524.

Brändle, R. *Matth. 25, 31–46 im Werk des Johannes Chrysostomos: Ein Beitrag zur Auslegungsgeschichte und zur Erforschung der Ethik der griechischen Kirche um die Wende vom 4. zum 5. Jahrhundert*. Tübingen, 1979.

———. "This Sweetest Passage: Matthew 25:31–46 and Assistance to the Poor in the Homilies of John Chrysostom." In Holman, *Wealth and Poverty*, 127–39.

Brändle, R. and H. Leppin. "Olympias 4." *Brill's Pauly* Online.

Brandt, H. "Die Rede περὶ βασιλείας des Synesios von Kyrene—ein ungewöhnlicher Fürstenspiegel." In *Consuetudinis amor: Fragments d'histoire romaine (IIe–VIe siècles) offerts à Jean-Pierre Callu*, edited by F. Chausson and É. Wolff, 57–70. Rome, 2013.

Breebaart, A. B. "Eunapius of Sardes and the Writing of History." *Mnemosyne* 32 (1979): 360–75.

Brenk, B. "The Mosaics of Thessaloniki: The State of Research." In Eastmond and Hatzaki, *The Mosaics*, 19–33.

Brenneke, H.-Ch. *Studien zur Geschichte der Homöer. Der Osten bis zum Ende der homöischen Reichskirche*. Tübingen, 1988.

Brilliant, R. "'Let the Trumpets Roar!': The Roman Triumph." In *The Art of Ancient Spectacle*, edited by B. Bergman and C. Kondoleon, 221–29. Washington, DC, 1999.

Brisson, L. *Sexual Ambivalence: Androgyny and Hermaphroditism in Graeco-Roman Antiquity*. Translated by J. Lloyd. Berkeley, 2002.

Brooten, B. J. *Love Between Women: Early Christian Responses to Female Homoeroticism*. Chicago, 1996.

Brown, P. R. L. *The Body and Society: Men, Women, and Sexual Renunciation in Early Christianity*. New York, 1988.

———. *Power and Persuasion in Late Antiquity: Towards a Christian Empire*. Madison, 1992.

———. *Through the Eye of a Needle: Wealth, the Fall of Rome, and the Making of Christianity in the West, 350–550 AD*. Princeton, 2012.

Buck, D. F. "Eunapius, Eutropius and the *Suda*." *Rheinisches Museum für Philologie* 135 (1992): 365–69.

Burger, G., and S. F. Kruger. "Introduction." In *Queering the Middle Ages*, edited by G. Burger and S. F. Kruger, xi–xxiv. Minneapolis, 2001.

Burgersdijk, D. P. W. "Creating the Enemy: Ammianus Marcellinus' Double Digression on the Huns and Alans (*Res Gestae* 31.2)." *Bulletin of the Institute of Classical Studies* 59 (2016): 111–32.

———. "Praise Through Letters: Panegyrical Strategies in Eusebius' *Life of Constantine* and the *Historia Augusta*." *Talanta* 45 (2013): 25–40.

———. "The Style and Structure of the *Historia Augusta*." PhD diss., University of Amsterdam, 2010.

Burgersdijk, D. P. W., and A. J. Ross, eds. *Imagining Emperors in the Later Roman Empire.* Leiden, 2018.

Burke, E. *A Philosophical Enquiry into the Origin of Our Ideas of the Sublime and the Beautiful.* Edited by P. Guyer. Oxford, 2015.

Burke, P. *The Fabrication of Louis XIV.* New Haven, 1992.

Burrell, E. "Claudian's *In Eutropium liber alter*: Fiction and History." *Latomus* 62 (2003): 110–38.

Burrus, V. *Begotten, Not Made: Conceiving Manhood in Late Antiquity.* Stanford, 2000.

———. "Mapping as Metamorphosis: Initial Reflections on Gender and Ancient Religious Discourses." In *Mapping Gender in Ancient Religious Discourses*, edited by T. C. Penner and C. Vander Stichele, 1–10. Leiden, 2007.

———. "Reading the Bride of Christ in Late Antiquity, and Now: Slippages and Subversions." In *Braut Christi: Familienformen in Europa im Spiegel der* sponsa, edited by S. Elm and B. Vinken, 53–64. Paderborn, 2016.

———. *Saving Shame: Martyrs, Saints, and Other Abject Subjects.* Philadelphia, 2008.

———. *The Sex Lives of Saints: An Erotics of Ancient Hagiography.* Philadelphia, 2004.

Burton, Ph. H., ed. *Sulpicius Severus' Vita Martini.* Oxford, 2017.

Busch, A. *Die Frauen der theodosianischen Dynastie: Macht und Repräsentation kaiserlicher Frauen im 5. Jahrhundert.* Stuttgart, 2015.

———. "Representatives and Co-Rulers: Imperial Women and the Court in Late Antiquity." In *The Roman Imperial Court in the Principate and Late Antiquity*, edited by C. Davenport and M. A. McEvoy, 203–17. Oxford, 2023.

Butler, J. "Kinship Beyond the Bloodline." In *Queer Kinship: Race, Sex, Belonging, Form*, edited by T. Bradway and E. Freeman, 25–47. Durham, NC, 2022.

Cameron, A. *Claudian: Poetry and Propaganda at the Court of Honorius.* Oxford, 1970.

———. "Claudian Revisited." In *Wandering Poets and Other Essays on Late Greek Literature and Philosophy*, 133–46. Oxford, 2016.

———. *The Last Pagans of Rome.* Oxford, 2011.

———. "A Misidentified Homily of Chrysostom." *Nottingham Medieval Studies* 32 (1988): 34–48.

———. "The Origin, Context, and Function of Consular Diptychs." *Journal of Roman Studies* 103 (2013): 174–207.

———. "The Status of Serena and the Stilicho Diptych." *Journal of Roman Archaeology* 29 (2016): 509–16.

———. "Wandering Poets: A Literary Movement in Byzantine Egypt." *Historia* 14 (1965): 470–509.

———. "Young Achilles in the Roman World." *Journal of Roman Studies* 99 (2009): 1–22.

Cameron, A., and J. Long. *Barbarians and Politics at the Court of Arcadius.* Berkeley, 1993.

Cameron, A., and D. Schauer. "The Last Consul: Basilius and his Diptych." *Journal of Roman Studies* 72 (1982): 126–45.

Campanile, D., F. Carlà-Uhink, and M. Facella, eds. *TransAntiquity: Cross-Dressing and Transgender Dynamics in the Ancient World.* London, 2017.

Caner, D. F. *The Rich and the Pure: Philanthropy and the Making of Christian Society in Early Byzantium.* Oakland, 2021.

Carlà-Uhink, F. "'Between the Human and the Divine': Cross-Dressing and Transgender Dynamics in the Graeco-Roman World." In Campanile, Carlà-Uhink, and Facella, *TransAntiquity*, 3–37.

———. "Teodora A.P. (After Procopius)/Theodora A.S. (After Sardou): Metamorphoses of an Empress." In *Orientalism and the Reception of Powerful Women from the Ancient World*, edited by F. Carlà-Uhink and A. Wieber, 166–83. London, 2021.

Cardman, F. "Poverty and Wealth as Theater: John Chrysostom's Homilies on Lazarus and the Rich Man." In Holman, *Wealth and Poverty*, 159–75.

Carlier, P. "L'idée de monarchie impériale dans la *Cyropédie* de Xénophon." *Ktèma* 3 (1978): 133–63.

Chambers, K. *Augustine on the Nature of Virtue and Sin*. Cambridge, 2023.

Charles, M. B., and E. Anagnostou-Laoutides. "Unmanning an Emperor: Otho in the Literary Tradition." *Classical Journal* 109 (2014): 199–222.

———. "Polemical Poetry in Late Antiquity: The Rise of a Eunuch–Consul in Book I of Claudian's *In Eutropium*." In *Polemic in Ancient Historiography, Literature, and Culture*, edited by T. Stevenson. *Acta Classica* Suppl. 11 (2022): 227–44.

Charlet, J.-L., ed. and trans. *Claudien: Œuvres*. 5 vols. Paris, 1991–2018.

———. "La romanité de Claudien, poète venu d'Alexandrie." In *Les Grecs héritiers des Romains: Huit exposés suivis de discussions*, edited by P. Schubert, P. Ducrey, and P. Derron, 321–50. Geneva, 2013.

———. "Lucain et Claudien: Une poésie politique entre épopée, histoire et panégyrique." In Berlincourt, Galli Miliç, and Nelis, *Lucan and Claudian*, 11–30.

Carrié, J.-M., and R. Lizzi Testa, eds. *Humana sapit: Études d'antiquité tardive offertes à Lellia Cracco Ruggini*. Turnhout, 2002.

Chastagnol, A. "Constantinople en ombres chinoises dans l'*Histoire Auguste*." In *Historiae Augustae Colloquium Bonnense*, edited by G. Bonamente and K. Rosen, 85–95. Bari, 1997.

———. *Histoire Auguste: Les empereurs romains des IIe et IIIe siècles*. Paris, 1994.

———. *Le Sénat romain à l'époque impériale: Recherches sur la composition de l'Assemblée et le statut de ses membres*. Paris, 1992.

———. "Trois études sur la *Vita Cari*." In *Bonner Historia-Augusta-Colloquium 1972/1974*, edited by G. Alföldi and J. Straub, 75–90. Bonn, 1976.

Chazan, B. *La rhétorique du blâme dans "l'Histoire Auguste"*. Paris, 2021.

Chenault, R. "Statues of Senators in the Forum of Trajan and the Roman Forum in Late Antiquity." *Journal of Roman Studies* 102 (2012): 103–32.

Chiasson, Ch. C. "Scythian Androgyny and Environmental Determinism in Herodotus and the Hippocratic περὶ ἀέρων ὑδάτων τόπων." *Syllecta classica* 12 (2001): 33–73.

Christiansen, P. G. "Claudian and the East." *Historia* 19 (1970): 113–20.

Clauss, M. *Kaiser und Gott: Herrscherkult im römischen Reich*. Stuttgart, 1999.

Cobb, L. S. *Dying to Be Men: Gender and Language in Early Christian Martyr Texts*. New York, 2008.

Colton, R. E. "Echoes of Juvenal in Claudian's *In Eutropium*." In *Studies in Latin Literature and Roman History* 15, 492–516. Brussels, 2010.

———. *Some Literary Influences on Sidonius Apollinaris*. Amsterdam, 2000.

Connell, R. W. *Masculinities*. Berkeley, 1995.

Connell, R. W., and J. W. Messerschmidt. "Hegemonic Masculinity: Rethinking the Concept." *Gender and Society* 19 (2005): 829–59.

Consolino, F. E. "La prosopopea di Roma e i primi due libri delle *Laudes Stiliconis*." In Carrié and Lizzi Testa, *Humana sapit*, 7–24.

————. "L'*optimus princeps* secondo s. Ambrogio: virtù imperatorie e virtù Cristiane nelle orazioni funebri per Valentiniano e Teodosio." *Rivista Storica Italiana* 96 (1984): 1025–45.

————. "Teodosio e il ruolo del principe cristiano dal *De obitu* di Ambrogio alle storie ecclesiastiche." *Cristianesimo nella storia* 15 (1994): 257–77.

Conway, C. M. "Masculinity Studies." In Dunning, *Oxford Handbook of Gender and Sexuality*, 77–93.

Cook, J. D. *Preaching and Popular Christianity: Reading the Sermons of John Chrysostom.* Oxford, 2019.

Coombe, C. *Claudian the Poet.* Cambridge, 2018.

————. "A Hero in Our Midst: Stilicho as a Literary Construct in the Poetry of Claudian." In *Literature and Society in the Fourth Century AD: Performing Paideia, Constructing the Present, Presenting the Self,* edited by L. van Hoof and P. van Nuffelen, 157–79. Leiden, 2014.

Corbeill, A. *Sexing the World: Grammatical Gender and Biological Sex in Ancient Rome.* Princeton, 2015.

Corcoran, S. *The Empire of the Tetrarchs: Imperial Pronouncements and Government, A.D. 284–324.* Oxford, 1996.

Cormack, R. "Exploring Thessaloniki—A Mismatch of Art History and Urban History." In *After the Text: Byzantine Enquiries in Honour of Margaret Mullett,* edited by L. James, O. Nicholson, and R. Scott, 317–27. London, 2021.

Coşkun, A. *Die gens Ausoniana an der Macht: Untersuchungen zu Decimius Magnus Ausonius und seiner Familie.* Oxford, 2002.

Cox Miller, P. *The Corporeal Imagination: Signifying the Holy in Late Ancient Christianity.* Philadelphia, 2009.

————. "Figuring Relics: A Poetics of Enshrinement." In *Saints and Sacred Matter: The Cult of Relics in Byzantium and Beyond,* edited by C. Hahn and H. A. Klein, 99–109. Washington, DC, 2015.

Cracco Ruggini, L. "Apoteosi e politica senatoria nel IV s. d.C.: Il dittico dei Symmachi al British Museum." *Rivista storica italiana* 89 (1977): 425–89.

Croke, B. "Arbogast and the Death of Valentinian II." *Historia* 25 (1976): 235–44.

————. "Ariadne Augusta: Shaping the Identity of the Early Byzantine Empress." In *Christians Shaping Identity from the Roman Empire to Byzantium: Studies Inspired by Pauline Allen,* edited by G. D. Dunn and W. Mayer, 293–319. Leiden, 2015.

————. "Dynasty and Aristocracy in the Fifth Century." In *The Cambridge Companion to the Age of Attila,* edited by M. Maas, 98–124. Cambridge, 2015.

————. "Justinian's Constantinople." In *The Cambridge Companion to the Age of Justinian,* edited by M. Maas, 60–86. Cambridge, 2005.

————. "Reinventing Constantinople: Theodosius I's Imprint on the Imperial City." In McGill, Sogno, and Watts, *From the Tetrarchs to the Theodosians,* 241–64.

Curran, J. *Pagan City and Christian Capital: Rome in the Fourth Century.* Oxford, 2000.

Dagron, G. *Naissance d'une capitale: Constantinople et ses institutions de 330 à 451.* Paris, 1974.

Dalla, D. *Ubi Venus mutatur: Omossessualità e diritto nel mondo romano.* Milan, 1987.

Damon, C. *The Mask of the Parasite: A Pathology of Roman Patronage.* Ann Arbor, 1997.

Danzig, G. "The Best of the Achaemenids: Benevolence, Self-Interest and the 'Ironic' Reading of *Cyropaedia*." In *Xenophon: Ethical Principles and Historical Enquiry,* edited by F. Hobden and Ch. Tuplin, 499–539. Leiden, 2012.

Daube, D. "The Self-Understood in Legal History." *Juridical Review* 18 (1973): 126–34.

Davis, W. *Queer Beauty: Sexuality and Aesthetics from Winckelmann to Freud and Beyond.* New York, 2010.

de Bonfils, G. "Considerazioni sui *quaestores* e la questura tardoantica: Un confronto con *The Law in the Crisis of Empire* di T. Honoré." *Studia et documenta historiae et iuris* 66 (2000): 289–314.

Delbrück, R. *Die Consulardiptychen und verwandte Denkmäler.* Berlin, 1929.

Delmaire, R. "Le vêtement dans les sources juridiques du Bas-Empire." *Antiquité tardive* 12 (2004): 195–202.

———. "Le vêtement, symbole de richesse et de pouvoir, d'après les textes patristiques et hagiographiques du Bas-Empire." In *Costume et société dans l'Antiquité et le haut Moyen Age,* edited by F. Chausson and H. Inglebert, 85–98. Paris, 2003.

Dench, E. *Romulus' Asylum: Roman Identities from the Age of Alexander to the Age of Hadrian.* Oxford, 2005.

den Hengst, D. "The Author's Literary Culture." In *Emperors and Historiography: Collected Essays on the Literature of the Roman Empire by Daniël den Hengst,* edited by D. P. W. Burgersdijk and J. A. van Waarden, 123–29. Leiden, 2009.

Dessau, H. "Über Zeit und Persönlichkeit der *Scriptores Historiae Augustae*." *Hermes* 24 (1889): 337–92.

Destephen, S., B. Dumézil, and H. Inglebert, eds. *Le prince chrétien de Constantin aux royautés barbares (IVe–VIIIe siècles).* Paris, 2018.

Dewar, M. *Claudian, Panegyricus de Sexto Consulatu Honorii Augusti.* Oxford, 1996.

———. "The Fall of Eutropius." *Classical Quarterly* 40 (1990): 582–84.

———. "Spinning the *Trabea*: Consular Robes and Propaganda in the Panegyrics of Claudian." In *Roman Dress and the Fabrics of Roman Culture,* edited by J. Edmonson and A. Keith, 217–37. Toronto, 2008.

de Wet, Ch. L. "John Chrysostom on Homoeroticism." *Neotestamentica* 48 (2014): 187–218.

———. "Virtue and the (Un-)Making of Men in the Thought of John Chrysostom." In Mayer and Elmer, *Men and Women in the Early Christian Centuries,* 227–50.

de Wet, Ch. L., and W. Mayer, eds. *Revisioning John Chrysostom: New Approaches, New Perspectives.* Leiden, 2019.

des Cars, L. "Jean-Paul Laurens et la peinture d'histoire sou la troisième République." In *Jean-Paul Laurens, 1838–1921: Peintre d'histoire,* edited by L. des Cars and A. Daguerre de Hureaux, 23–34. Paris, 1997.

Diefenbach, S. "Frömmigkeit und Kaiserakzeptanz im frühen Byzanz." *Saeculum* 47 (1996): 35–66.

———. *Römische Erinnerungsräume: Heiligenmemoria und kollektive Identitäten im Rom des 3. bis 5. Jahrhunderts n. Chr.* Berlin, 2007.

———. "Zwischen Liturgie und *Civilitas*: Konstantinopel im 5. Jahrhundert und die Etablierung eines städtischen Kaisertums." In *Bildlichkeit und Bildorte von Liturgie: Schauplätze in Spätantike, Byzanz und Mittelalter,* edited by R. Warland, 21–49. Wiesbaden, 2002.

Dillon, J. N. "The Inflation of Rank and Privilege: Regulating Precedence in the Fourth Century AD." In Wienand, *Contested Monarchy,* 42–66.

Dinshaw, C. *Getting Medieval: Sexualities and Communities, Pre- and Postmodern.* Durham, NC, 1999.

Döpp, S. *Zeitgeschichte in Dichtungen Claudians.* Wiesbaden, 1980.

Doerfler, M. E. "Coming Apart at the Seams: Cross–Dressing, Masculinity, and the Social Body in Late Antiquity." In *Dressing Judaeans and Christians in Antiquity*, edited by K. Upson-Saia, C. Daniel-Hughes, and A. J. Batten, 37–51. Farnham, 2014.

Dorfbauer, L. J. "Die *praefationes* von Claudian und von Prudentius." In *Text und Bild: Tagungsbeiträge*, edited by V. Zimmerl-Panagl and D. Weber, 195–222. Vienna, 2010.

Doyle, Ch. *Honorius: The Fight for the Roman West AD 395–423*. Abingdon, 2018.

Drake, H. A. "Constantine and Eusebius in Antioch." *Studies in Late Antiquity* 7 (2023): 106–36.

Drijvers, J. W. "Helena Augusta—the Cross and the Myth: Some New Reflections." *Millennium* 8 (2011): 125–74.

Ducloux, A. *Ad ecclesiam confugere: Naissance du droit d'asile dans les églises (IVe–milieu du Ve s.)*. Paris, 1994.

Dunning, B. H. "John Chrysostom and Same–Sex Eros in the History of Sexuality." In de Wet and Mayer, *Revisioning John Chrysostom*, 638–69.

———, ed. *The Oxford Handbook of Gender and Sexuality in the New Testament*. Oxford, 2019.

———. "Same-Sex Relations." In Dunning, *Oxford Handbook of Gender and Sexuality*, 573–91.

Duval, Y.-M. "Formes profanes et formes bibliques dans les oraisons funèbres de saint Ambroise." In *Christianisme et formes littéraires de l'Antiquité tardive en Occident*, edited by M. Fuhrmann, 235–301. Geneva, 1977.

Eastmond, A. "Consular Diptychs, Rhetoric and the Language of Art in Sixth–Century Constantinople." *Art History* 33 (2010): 742–65.

Eastmond, A., and M. Hatzaki, eds. *The Mosaics of Thessaloniki Revisited*. Athens, 2017.

Eberle, L. P. "Foreign Silk on Roman Bodies: Gender, Wealth and Empire in the Metropole." In *Gendering Roman Imperialism*, edited by H. Cornwell and G. Woolf, 203–22. Boston, 2022.

Eberle, M. *Im Spiegel der Geschichte: Realistische Historienmalerei in Westeuropa 1830–1900*. Munich 2017.

Eder, S. *How the Clinic Made Gender: The Medical History of a Transformative Idea*. Chicago, 2022.

Edwards, C. "Imaginaires de l'image de Rome ou comment (se) représenter Rome?" In *Images romaines: Actes de la table ronde organisée à l'Ecole normale supérieure, 24–26 octobre 1996*, edited by F. Dupont and C. Auvray-Assayas, 235–45. Paris, 1998.

———. *The Politics of Immorality in Ancient Rome*. Cambridge, 1993.

Edwards, C., and G. Woolf. "Cosmopolis: Rome as World City." In *Rome the Cosmopolis*, edited by C. Edwards and G. Woolf, 1–20. Cambridge, 2003.

Eigler, U. *Lectiones vetustatis: Römische Literatur und Geschichte in der lateinischen Literatur der Spätantike*. Munich, 2003.

El Houkayem, M. "Orientalism, Disorientation, and the 'Other Side of the World.'" *Studies in Late Antiquity* 7 (2023): 171–83.

Elia, F. "Sui '*privilegia urbis Constantinopolitanae*.'" In *Politica retorica e simbolismo del primato: Roma e Costantinopoli (secoli IV–VII): Atti del convegno internazionale, Catania, 4–7 ottobre 2001*, edited by F. Elia, 79–105. Catania, 2002.

Elm, E. "Die damnatio memoriae: Verordnetes Vergessen von der frühen römischen Republik bis in die christliche Spätantike." Habilitationsschrift Philipps-Universität Marburg 2010.

Elm, S. "The Dog That Did Not Bark: Doctrine and Patriarchal Authority in the Conflict Between Theophilus of Alexandria and John Chrysostom of Constantinople." In *Christian Origins: Theology, Rhetoric, and Community*, edited by L. Ayres and G. Jones, 68–93. London, 1998.

———. "Dressing Moses: Reading Gregory of Nyssa's *Life of Moses* Literally." In *Exploring Gregory of Nyssa: Philosophical, Theological, and Historical Studies*, edited by A. Marmadoro and N. B. McLynn, 49–73. Oxford, 2018.

———. "Emperor Julian on Statues (of Himself)." In *Classical Philology and Theology: Entanglement, Disavowal, and the Godlike Scholar*, edited by C. Conybeare and S. Goldhill, 126–48. Cambridge, 2021.

———. "Eutropius the Cosmopolitan." Forthcoming.

———. "Gregory's Women: Creating a Philosopher's Family." In *Gregory of Nazianzus: Images and Reflections*, edited by J. Børtnes and T. Hägg, 171–92. Copenhagen, 2006.

———. "Family Men: Masculinity and Philosophy in Late Antiquity." in *Transformations of Late Antiquity: Essays for Peter Brown*, edited by Ph. Rousseau and M. Papoutsakis, 279–301. Farnham, 2009.

———. "An Icon of Ugliness: Eutropius the Eunuch." In *From Living to Visual Images: Paradigms of Corporeal Iconicity in Late Antiquity*, edited by M. Bacci and V. Ivanovici. *RIHA Journal* 0222–0229 (2019), 0226.

———. "Isis' Loss: Gender, Dependence, and Ethnicity in Synesius' *De providentia* or *Egyptian Tale*." *Journal of Ancient Christianity* 1 (1997): 96–115.

———. "Late Roman Toleration, or How to Read an Imperial Edict: Theodosius to All the People on the Catholic *Religio*." In *Handbook on Religious Toleration in Comparative Perspective*, edited by K. Barkey and J. Laurence. Cham, forthcoming.

———. "The 'Law of War': Augustine on the Captured City (*Urbs capta*) and Sexual Violence Against Men and Women in the *City of God* (Book 1)." In Elm and Sessa, *War and Community*.

———. "Marking the Self in Late Antiquity: Inscriptions, Baptism and the Conversion of Mimes." In *Stigmata: Poetiken der Körperinschrift*, edited by B. Menke and B. Vinken, 47–68. Paderborn, 2004.

———. "Signs Under the Skin: Flogging Eternal Rome." In *Unter die Haut—Tätowierungen als Logo- und Piktogramme*, edited by I. Därmann and Th. Macho, 51–75. Paderborn, 2017.

———. *Sons of Hellenism, Fathers of the Church: Emperor Julian, Gregory of Nazianzus, and the Vision of Rome*. Berkeley, 2012.

———. "What the Bishop Wore to the Synod: John Chrysostom, Origenism, and the Politics of Fashion at Constantinople." *Adamantius* 19 (2013): 156–69.

Elm, S., and K. Sessa, eds. *War and Community in Late Antiquity*. Cambridge, 2025.

Elsner, J. "Visualising Women in Late Antique Rome: The Projecta Casket." In *Through a Glass Brightly: Studies in Byzantine and Medieval Art and Archaeology Presented to David Buckton*, edited by Ch. Entwistle, 22–36. Oxford, 2003.

Elton, H. *The Roman Empire in Late Antiquity: A Political and Military History*. Cambridge, 2018.

———. *Warfare in Roman Europe, AD 350–425*. Oxford, 1996.

Emion, M. "Des soldats de l'armée romaine tardive: Les protectores (IIIe–VIe siècles ap. J.-C.)." PhD diss., Université de Rouen Normandie, 2017.

———. "L'empereur chrétien et ses gardes du corps." In Destephen, Dumézil, and Inglebert, *Le prince chrétien*, 415–33.

Emmrich, Th. *Ästhetische Monsterpolitiken: Das Monströse als Figuration des eingeschlossenen Ausgeschlossenen*. Heidelberg, 2020.

Eppinger, A. "*Hercules Cinaedus*?: The Effeminate Hero in Christian Polemic." In Campanile, Carlà-Uhink, and Facella, *TransAntiquity*, 202–14.

Errington, R. M. "Church and State in the First Years of Theodosius I." *Chiron* 27 (1997): 21–72.

———. *Roman Imperial Policy from Julian to Theodosius*. Chapel Hill, 2006.

———. "Themistius and His Emperors." *Chiron* 30 (2000): 861–904.

———. "Theodosius and the Goths." *Chiron* 26 (1996): 1–27.

Escribano Paño, M. V. "Heretical Texts and *Maleficium* in the *Codex Theodosianus* (*CTh.* 16.5.34)." In *Magical Practice in the Latin West: Papers from the International Conference Held at the University of Zaragoza, 30 Sept.–1 Oct. 2005*, edited by R. L. Gordon and F. M. Simón, 105–40. Leiden, 2010.

———. "Maximus' Letters in the *Collectio Avellana*: A Comparative Study." In *The Collectio Avellana and Its Revivals*, edited by R. Lizzi Testa and G. Marconi, 50–85. Newcastle upon Tyne, 2019.

———. "The Social Exclusion of Heretics in *Codex Theodosianus XVI.*" In *Droit, religion et société dans le "Code Théodosien": Troisièmes journées d'Etude sur le "Code Théodosien" Neuchatel, 15–17 février 2007*, edited by J.-J. Aubert and Ph. Blanchard, 39–66. Geneva, 2009.

Falcasantos, R. S. *Constantinople: Ritual, Violence, and Memory in the Making of a Christian Imperial Capital*. Berkeley, 2020.

Fantuzzi, M. "Achilles at Scyros, and One of His Fans: The *Epithalamium of Achilles and Deidameia (Buc. Gr.* 157–158 GOW)." In *Brill's Companion to Greek and Latin Epyllion and Its Reception*, edited by M. Baumbach and S. Bär, 283–305. Leiden, 2012.

Fauconnier, G. *Mental Spaces: Aspects of Meaning Construction in Natural Language*. Cambridge, 1994.

Favro, D. "The IconiCITY of Ancient Rome." *Urban History* 33 (2006): 20–38.

Feldherr, A. "Viewing Myth and History on the Shield of Aeneas." *Classical Antiquity* 33 (2014): 281–318.

Felgentreu, F. *Claudians praefationes: Bedingungen, Beschreibungen und Wirkungen einer poetischen Kleinform*. Stuttgart, 1999.

Fitschen, K. "Der *Praefectus Praetorio* Flavius Rufinus: Ein hoher Reichsbeamter als Gestalt der Kirchengeschichte zur Zeit der Theodosianischen Wende." *Journal of Ancient Christianity* 5 (2001): 86–103.

Flaig, E. *Den Kaiser herausfordern: Die Usurpation im römischen Reich*. Frankfurt, 1992.

Fletcher, Ch., S. Brady, R. E. Moss, and L. Riall, eds. *The Palgrave Handbook of Masculinity and Political Culture in Europe*. London, 2018.

Flower, R. *Emperors and Bishops in Late Roman Invective*. Cambridge, 2013.

———. "*Tamquam figmentum hominis*: Ammianus, Constantius II and the Portrayal of Imperial Ritual." *Classical Quarterly* 65 (2015): 822–35.

Foucault, M. *Les anormaux: Cours au Collège de France (1974–1975)*. Paris, 1999.

Frakes, R. M. "Ammianus Marcellinus and His Intended Audience." In *Studies in Latin Literature and Roman History* 10, edited by C. Deroux, 392–442. Brussels, 2000.

———. *Compiling the Collatio Legum Mosaicarum et Romanarum in Late Antiquity.* Oxford, 2011.

Francis, J. A. "Verbal and Visual Representation: Art and Text, Culture and Power in Late Antiquity." In *A Companion to Late Antiquity*, edited by Ph. Rousseau, 285–305. Oxford, 2009.

Franco, L. "Byzantine Lives: Discussing Nonbinary Sexuality, Gender, and Race in Byzantium." *Harvard Theological Review* 114 (2021): 561–70.

Frank, G. "Macrina's Scar: Homeric Allusion and Heroic Identity in Gregory of Nyssa's 'Life of Macrina.'" *Journal of Early Christian Studies* 8 (2000): 511–30.

Fricke, B. "Tales from Stone, Travels through Time: Narrative and Vision in the Casket from the Vatican." *West 86th* 21 (2014): 230–50.

Fündling, J. *Kommentar zur Vita Hadriani der Historia Augusta.* 2 vols. Bonn, 2006.

Fuhrer, T. "Alter und Sexualität: Die Stimme der alternden Frau in der horazischen Lyrik." In *Alterstopoi: Das Wissen von den Lebensaltern in Literatur, Kunst und Theologie*, edited by D. Elm, Th. Fitzon, Thorsten, K. Liess, and S. Linden, 49–69. Berlin, 2009.

Gangloff, A. *Pouvoir impérial et vertus philosophiques: L'évolution de la figure du bon prince sous le Haut-Empire.* Leiden, 2019.

Garambois-Vasquez, F. "L'éloge de Stilicon dans la poésie de Claudien." In Berlincourt, Galli Miliç, and Nelis, *Lucan and Claudian*, 93–106.

———. *Les invectives de Claudien: Une poétique de la violence.* Brussels, 2007.

Garambois-Vasquez, F., ed. *Claudien: Mythe, histoire et science.* Saint Etienne, 2011.

García Ruiz, M. P., and A. J. Quiroga Puertas, eds. *Emperors and Emperorship in Late Antiquity: Images and Narratives.* Brill, 2021.

Gardner, J. F. "Sexing a Roman: Imperfect Men in Roman Law." In *When Men Were Men: Masculinity, Power and Identity in Classical Antiquity*, edited L. Foxhall and J. Salmon, 136–52. London, 1999.

Gavins, J. *Text World Theory: An Introduction.* Edinburgh, 2007.

Gazzarri, T., and J. Weiner, eds. *Searching for the Cinaedus in Ancient Rome.* Leiden, 2023.

Gehn, U. *Ehrenstatuen in der Spätantike: Chlamydati und Togati.* Wiesbaden, 2012.

Genette, G. *Palimpsests: Literature in the Second Degree.* Translated by Ch. Newman and C. Doubinsky. Lincoln, NE, 1997.

Gera, D. L. *Xenophon's "Cyropaideia": Style, Genre, and Literary Technique.* Oxford, 1993.

Gildenhard, I. *Creative Eloquence: The Construction of Reality in Cicero's Speeches.* Oxford, 2011.

Gilhuly, K. *The Feminine Matrix of Sex and Gender in Classical Athens.* Cambridge, 2009.

Gillett, A., *Envoys and Political Communication in the Late Antique West, 411–533.* Cambridge, 2003.

———. "Epic Panegyric and Political Communication in the Fifth-Century West." In Grig and Kelly, *Two Romes*, 265–90.

———, ed. *On Barbarian Identity: Critical Approaches to Ethnicity in the Early Middle Ages.* Turnhout, 2002.

———. "Rome, Ravenna and the Last Western Emperors." *Papers of the British School at Rome* 69 (2001): 131–67.

Gineste, M.-F. "Poésie, pouvoir et rhétorique à la fin du 4e siècle après J.C.: Les poèmes nuptiaux de Claudien." *Rhetorica* 22 (2004): 269–96.

Gleason, M. *Making Men: Sophists and Self-Presentation in Ancient Rome*. Princeton, 1995.

Gnilka, Ch. Review of Cameron, *Claudian*. *Gnomon* 49 (1977): 26–51.

Goffart, W. *Barbarian Tides: The Migration Age and the Later Roman Empire*. Philadelphia, 2006.

Gold, B. "Transgender Saints: Perpetua's Legacy." In *The Routledge Companion to the Reception of Ancient Greek and Roman Gender and Sexuality*, edited by K. R. Moore, 558–71. London, 2022.

Gowers, E. "Persius and the Decoction of Nero." In *Reflections of Nero: Culture, History, and Representation*, edited by J. Elsner and J. Masters, 131–50. Chapel Hill, 1994.

Gradenwitz, O. *Heidelberger Index zum Theodosianus mit Ergänzungsband*. Reprint: Hildesheim, 1999.

Gray, V. J. *Xenophon's Mirror of Princes: Reading the Reflections*. Oxford, 2011.

Greatrex, G. "The Background and Aftermath of the Partition of Armenia in AD 387." *Ancient History Bulletin* 14 (2000): 35–48.

Greatrex, G., and M. Greatrex. "The Hunnic Invasion of the East of 395 and the Fortress of Ziatha." *Byzantion* 69 (1999): 65–75.

Green, R. P. H., ed. *The Works of Ausonius*. Oxford, 1991.

Grig, L. "Competing Capitals, Competing Representations: Late Antique Cityscapes in Words and Pictures." In Grig and Kelly, *Two Romes*, 31–52.

Grig, L., and G. Kelly. "Introduction." In Grig and Kelly, *Two Romes*, 3–30.

Grig, L., and G. Kelly, eds. *Two Romes: Rome and Constantinople in Late Antiquity*. Oxford, 2012.

Gronow, J. *The Sociology of Taste*. London, 1997.

Groß-Albenhausen, K. *Imperator christianissimus: Der christliche Kaiser bei Ambrosius und Johannes Chrysostomus*. Frankfurt, 1999.

Gruen, E. S. *Rethinking the Other in Antiquity*. Princeton, 2011.

Grünewald, Th. *Constantinus Maximus Augustus: Herrschaftspropaganda in der zeitgenössischen Überlieferung*. Stuttgart, 1990.

Gualandri, I. *Aspetti della tecnica compositiva in Claudiano*. Milan, 1968.

———. "Claudian, from Easterner to Westerner." *Talanta* 45 (2013): 115–29.

———. "Sidonius' Intertextuality." In *The Edinburgh Companion to Sidonius Apollinaris*, edited by G. Kelly and J. van Waarden, 279–316. Edinburgh, 2020.

———. "Un 'generalissimo' semibarbaro suocero e genero di imperatori: Stilicone in Claudiano." *Acme* 63 (2010): 33–61.

Gualerzi, S. *Né uomo, né donna, né dio, né dea: Ruolo sessuale e ruolo religioso dell'imperatore Elagabalo*. Bologna, 2005.

Guggisberg, M. A. *Der spätrömische Silberschatz von Kaiseraugst: die neuen Funde: Silber im Spannungsfeld von Geschichte, Politik und Gesellschaft der Spätantike*. Augst, 2003.

Guidetti, F. "Between Expressionism and Classicism: Stylistic Choices as Means of Legitimisation in Fourth-Century Imperial Portraits." In García Ruiz and Quiroga Puertas, *Emperors and Emperorship*, 139–76.

———. "'First-Generation Diptychs' and the Reception of Theodosian Court Art." In *A Globalised Visual Culture? Towards a Geography of Late Antique Art*, edited by F. Guidetti and K. Meinecke, 211–40. Oxford, 2020.

———. "The Hero's White Hands: The Early History of the Myth of Achilles on Scyros." In Campanile, Carlà-Uhink, and Facella, *TransAntiquity*, 181–201.

Guipponi-Gineste, M.-F. *Claudien: Poète du monde à la cour d'Occident*. Paris, 2010.

———. "Pierres précieuses et pierres curieuses dans la poésie de Claudien." In Garambois-Vasquez, *Claudien*, 85–111.

Gunderson, E. *Staging Masculinity: The Rhetoric of Performance in the Roman World*. Ann Arbor, 2000.

Günther, O. *Epistulae imperatorum pontificium aliorum inde ab a. CCCLXVII ad a. DLIII datae Avellanae quae dicitur collectio*. 2 vols. Prague, 1895–98.

Guyot, P. *Eunuchen als Sklaven und Freigelassene in der griechisch-römischen Antike*. Stuttgart, 1980.

Haake, M. "'In Search of Good Emperors': Emperors, Caesars, and Usurpers in the Mirror of Antimonarchic Patterns in the *Historia Augusta*—Some Considerations." In Börm, *Antimonarchic Discourse*, 269–303.

Habinek, Th. "Satire as Aristocratic Play." In *The Cambridge Companion to Roman Satire*, edited by K. Freudenberg, 177–91. Cambridge, 2005.

Hagl, W. *Arcadius Apis Imperator: Synesios von Kyrene und sein Beitrag zum Herrscherideal in der Spätantike*. Stuttgart, 1997.

Hagner, M. "Monstrositäten haben eine Geschichte." In *Der falsche Körper: Beiträge zu einer Geschichte der Monstrositäten*, edited by M. Hagner, 7–20. Göttingen, 1995.

Hallett, J. P., and D. Lateiner. "Connotation and 'Com-motion': Putting the *Kinesis* into the Roman *Cinaedus*." In Gazzari and Weiner, *Searching for the Cinaedus*, 154–75.

Halsall, G. *Barbarian Migrations and the Roman West, 367–568*. Cambridge, 2007.

Harlow, M. "'Clothes Maketh the Man': Power, Dressing, and Elite Masculinity in the Later Roman World." In *Gender in the Early Medieval World: East and West, 300–900*, edited by L. Brubaker and J. Smith, 44–69. Cambridge, 2004.

———. "Female Dress, Third–Sixth Century: The Messages in the Media?" *Antiquité tardive* 12 (2004): 203–15.

Harman, E. "A Spectacle of Greekness: Panhellenism and the Visual in Xenophon's *Agesilaus*." In *Xenophon: Ethical Principles and Historical Enquiry*, edited by F. Hobden and Ch. Tuplin, 427–53. Leiden, 2012.

Harper, K. *From Shame to Sin: The Christian Transformation of Sexual Morality in Late Antiquity*. Cambridge, MA, 2013.

———. *Slavery in the Late Roman World, AD 275–425*. Cambridge, 2011.

Harrell, S. E. "Marvelous *Andreia*: Politics, Geography, and Ethnicity in Herodotus' *Histories*." In Rosen and Sluiter, *Andreia*, 77–94.

Harries, J. "The Empress's Tale: AD 300–360." In *Being Christian in Late Antiquity. A Festschrift for Gillian Clark*, edited by C. Harrison, 197–214. Oxford, 2014.

———. *Law and Empire in Late Antiquity*. Cambridge, 1999.

———. "The Roman Imperial *Quaestor* from Constantine to Theodosius II." *Journal of Roman Studies* 78 (1988): 148–72.

———. *Sidonius Apollinaris and the Fall of Rome, AD 407–485*. Oxford, 1994.

Harrison, C. *The Art of Listening in the Early Church*. Oxford, 2013.

Harrison, N. V. "Greek Patristic Perspective on the Origin of Social Injustice." In *Suffering and Evil in Early Christian Thought*, edited by N. V. Harrison and D. G. Hunter, 81–96. Grand Rapids, 2016.

Harrison, S. J. "The Survival and Supremacy of Rome: The Unity of the Shield of Aeneas." *Journal of Roman Studies* 87 (1997): 70–76.

Hartke, W. *Römische Kinderkaiser: Eine Strukturanalyse römischen Denkens und Daseins.* Berlin, 1951.

Hartney, A. M. *John Chrysostom and the Transformation of the City.* London, 2004.

———. "Manly Women and Womanly Men: The *Subintroductae* and John Chrysostom." In *Desire and Denial in Byzantium: Papers front the Thirty-First Spring Symposium of Byzantine Studies, Brighton, March 1997,* edited by L. James, 41–48. Farnham, 1999.

Hartog, F. *The Mirror of Herodotus: The Representation of the Other in the Writing of History.* Translated by J. Lloyd. Berkeley, 2009.

Hatzaki, M. *Beauty and the Male Body in Byzantium: Perceptions and Representations in Art and Text.* New York, 2009.

———. "Peacocks, Rainbows and Handsome Men: Perceiving Physical Beauty in Early Byzantine Mosaics in Thessaloniki." In Eastmond and Hatzaki, *The Mosaics,* 63–75.

Heather, P. J. "The Anti-Scythian Tirade of Synesius' *De Regno.*" *Phoenix* 42 (1988): 152–72.

———. *Empires and Barbarians.* Oxford, 2009.

———. *Goths and Romans, 332–489.* Oxford, 1991.

———. "The Huns and Barbarian Europe." In *The Cambridge Companion to the Age of Attila,* edited by M. Maas, 209–29. Cambridge, 2015.

———. "Liar in Winter: Themistius and Theodosius." In McGill, Sogno, and Watts, *From the Tetrarchs to the Theodosians,* 185–213.

———. "New Men for New Constantines? Creating an Imperial Elite in the Eastern Mediterranean." In *New Constantines: The Rhythm of Imperial Renewal in Byzantium, 4th–13th Centuries: Papers from the Twenty-Sixth Spring Symposium of Byzantine Studies, St Andrews, March 1992,* edited by P. Magdalino, 11–33. Aldershot, 1994.

Heather, P. J., and D. Moncur. *Politics, Philosophy, and Empire in the Fourth Century: Select Orations of Themistius.* Liverpool, 2001.

Hebblewhite, M. *Theodosius and the Limits of Empire.* London, 2020.

Hedrick, Ch. W. Jr. *History and Silence: Purge and Rehabilitation in of Memory in Late Antiquity.* Austin, 2000.

Hekster, O. *Caesar Rules: The Emperor in the Changing Roman World (c. 50 BC–AD 565).* Cambridge, 2023.

———. *Emperors and Ancestors: Roman Rulers and the Constraints of Tradition.* New York, 2015.

Henderson, G. E. *Ugliness: A Cultural History.* London, 2015.

Heslin, P. J. *Transvestite Achilles: Gender and Genre in Statius' "Achilleid."* Cambridge, 2005.

Hildebrandt, B. "Das Gewand des Honorius in der Dichtung Claudians." In *Weaving and Fabric in Antiquity: Materiality—Representation—Epistemology—Metapoetics,* edited by H. Harich-Schwarzbauer, 67–85. Oxford, 2016.

Hillner, J. "Confined Exiles: An Aspect of the Late Antique Prison System." *Millenium* 10 (2013): 385–433.

———. "Empresses, Queens, and Letters: Finding a 'Female Voice' in Late Antiquity?" *Gender & History* 31 (2019): 535–82.

———. *Helena Augusta: Mother of the Empire.* New York, 2022.

———. *Prison, Punishment and Penance in Late Antiquity.* Cambridge, 2015.

———. "A Woman's Place: Imperial Women in Late Antique Rome." *Antiquité tardive* 25 (2017): 75–94.

Hölscher, T. "The Transformation of Victory into Power: From Event to Structure." In *Representations of War in Ancient Rome*, edited by S. Dillon and K. E. Welch, 27–48. Cambridge, 2006.

Hoffmann, L. M. "Die Lebenswelt des Synesios von Kyrene—ein historischer Überblick." In Seng and Hoffmann, *Synesios von Kyrene*, 35–65.

Hollier, D. *Absent Without Leave: French Literature Under the Threat of War*. Translated by C. Porter. Cambridge, MA, 1997.

Holman, S. R. *The Hungry Are Dying: Beggars and Bishops in Roman Cappadocia*. Oxford, 2001.

———, ed. *Wealth and Poverty in Early Church and Society*. Grand Rapids, 2008.

Holum, K. G. *Theodosian Empresses: Women and Imperial Dominion in Late Antiquity*. Berkeley, 1982.

Holum, K., and G. Vikan, "The Trier Ivory, *Adventus* Ceremonial and the Relics of St. Stephen." *Dumbarton Oaks Papers* 33 (1979): 113–33.

Honoré, T. *Law in the Crisis of Empire, 379–455 A.D.: The Theodosian Dynasty and Its Quaestors*. New York, 1998.

Humfress, C. "Ordering Divine Knowledge in Late Roman Legal Discourse." *Collegium* 20 (2016): 160–76.

———. "'Cherchez la femme!': Heresy and Law in Late Antiquity." *Studies in Church History* 56 (2020): 36–59.

Humphries, M. "The Body Politic: Performing Character in Ammianus Marcellinus." In *Canistrum ficis plenum: Hommages à Bertrand Lançon*, edited by E. Amato, P. de Cicco, and T. Moreau, 187–205. *Revue des Études Tardo-antiques 7 Supplément 5*, 2018.

———. "Emperors, Usurpers, and the City of Rome: Performing Power from Diocletian to Theodosius." In Wienand, *Contested Monarchy*, 151–68.

Hunt, E. D. "Imperial Law or Councils of the Church? Theodosius I and the Imposition of Doctrinal Uniformity." *Studies in Church History* 43 (2007): 57–68.

Hurley, D. W., ed. and trans. *Gaius Suetonius Tranquillus: The Caesars*. Indianapolis, 2011.

Hutton, W. "The Importance of Dio's Travels." In *Travel, Tourism, and Identity*, edited by G. R. Ricci, 1–18. New Brunswick, 2015.

Icks, M. *The Crimes of Elagabalus: The Life and Legacy of Rome's Decadent Boy Emperor*. London, 2011.

———. "The Inadequate Heirs of Theodosius: Ancestry, Merit and Divine Blessing in the Representation of Arcadius and Honorius." *Millennium* 11 (2014): 69–99.

———. "Keeping Up Appearances: Evaluations of Imperial (In)Visibility in Late Antiquity." In Manders and Slootjes, *Leadership, Ideology and Crowds*, 163–79.

Icks, M., D. Jussen, and E. Manders. "Generaals in de groei: De militaire representatie van de kindkeizers Gratianus en Honorius op muntenen in lofdichten." *Tijdschrift voor Geschiedenis* 132 (2020): 541–88.

Iliadis, I. G. "The Natural Lighting of the Mosaics in the Rotunda at Thessaloniki." *Lighting Research and Technology* 33 (2001): 13–24.

Ingleheart, J. "Romosexuality: Rome, Homosexuality, and Reception." In *Ancient Rome and the Construction of Modern Homosexual Identities*, edited by J. Ingleheart, 1–36. Oxford, 2015.

Ivanovici, V. "Iconic Presences: Late Roman Consuls as Imperial Images." *Convivium* 6 (2019): 128–47.

Jacob, Ch. *Das geistige Theater: Ästhetik und Moral bei Johannes Chrysostomus*. Munich, 2010.

Jacobs, A. S. *Christ Circumcised: A Study in Early Christian History and Difference.* Philadelphia, 2012.

Jal, P. "*Hostis (publicus)* dans la littérature latine de la fin de la République." *Revue des études anciennes* 65 (1963): 53–79.

James, L. *Mosaics in the Medieval World: From Late Antiquity to the Fifteenth Century.* Cambridge, 2017.

Janssen, T. *Stilicho: Das weströmische Reich vom Tode des Theodosius bis zur Ermordung Stilichos (395–408).* Marburg, 2004.

Johne, K.-P. *Kaiserbiographie und Senatsaristokratie: Untersuchungen zur Datierung und sozialen Herkunft der Historia Augusta.* Berlin, 1976.

Johnson, W. A. *Readers and Reading Culture in the High Roman Empire: A Study of Elite Communities.* Oxford, 2012.

Jones, A. H. M. *The Later Roman Empire 284–602: A Social, Economic, and Administrative Survey.* 3 vols. Oxford, 1964.

Jussen, D. "The Collection and Its Collective: Pacatus and the *XII Panegyrici Latini*." *Classical Quarterly* 70 (2020): 871–83.

———. "Enduring the Dust of Mars: The Expectation of Military Leadership in Panegyric to the Child-Emperor Gratian." *Arethusa* 52 (2019): 253–73.

Kahlos, M. "The Emperor's New Images: How to Honour the Emperor in the Christian Roman Empire?" In *Emperors and the Divine: Rome and its Influence,* edited by M. Kahlos, 119–39. Helsinki, 2016.

Kamen, D., and S. Levin-Richardson. "Revisiting Roman Sexuality: Agency and the Conceptualization of Penetrated Males." In Masterson, Rabinowitz, and Robson, *Sex in Antiquity,* 449–60.

Kantorowicz, E. *The King's Two Bodies: A Study in Medieval Political Theology.* Princeton, 2016.

Kaster, R. A. *Emotion, Restraint, and Community in Ancient Rome.* Oxford, 2005.

Katos, D. S. *Palladius of Helenopolis: The Origenist Advocate.* New York, 2011.

Keegan, C. M. "Transgender Studies, or How to do Things with *Trans**." In *The Cambridge Companion of Queer Studies,* edited by S. B. Somerville, 66–87. Cambridge, 2022.

Kelly, Ch. M. "Bureaucracy and Government." In *The Cambridge Companion to the Age of Constantine,* edited by N. Lenski, 183–204. Cambridge, 2006.

———. "Emperors as Gods, Angels as Bureaucrats: The Representation of Imperial Power in Late Antiquity." *Antigüedad, Religiones y Sociedades* 1 (1998): 301–26.

———. "Pliny and Pacatus: Past and Present in Imperial Panegyric." In Wienand, *Contested Monarchy,* 215–38.

———. "Rethinking Theodosius." In *Theodosius II: Rethinking the Roman Empire in Late Antiquity,* edited by Ch. M. Kelly, 3–64. Cambridge, 2013.

———. *Ruling the Later Roman Empire.* Cambridge, MA, 2004.

———. "Stooping to Conquer: The Power of Imperial Humility." In *Theodosius II: Rethinking the Roman Empire in Late Antiquity,* edited by Ch. M. Kelly, 221–43. Cambridge, 2013.

Kelly, G. *Ammianus Marcellinus: The Allusive Historian.* Cambridge, 2008.

———. "Claudian and Constantinople." In Grig and Kelly, *Two Romes,* 241–64.

———. "Pliny and Symmachus." *Arethusa* 46 (2013): 261–87.

———. "The New Rome and the Old: Ammianus Marcellinus' Silences on Constantinople." *Classical Quarterly* 53 (2003): 588–607.

———. "Sidonius and Claudian." In van Waarden and Kelly, *New Approaches to Sidonius Apollinaris*, 171–91.

———. "The Political Crisis of AD 375–376." *Chiron* 43 (2013): 357–409.

———. "The Sphragis and Closure of the *Res Gestae*." In *Ammianus After Julian: The Reign of Valentinian and Valens in Books 26–31 of the Res Gestae*, edited by J. den Boeft, et al., 219–41. Leiden, 2007.

Kiilerich, B. "Color, Light and Luminosity in the Rotunda Mosaics." In Eastmond and Hatzaki, *The Mosaics*, 49–61.

———. *Late Fourth Century Classicism in the Plastic Arts*. Odense, 1993.

———. *The Obelisk Base in Constantinople: Court Art and Imperial Ideology*. Rome, 1998.

———. "Optical Colour Blending in the Rotunda Mosaics at Thessaloniki." *Mousiva and Sectilia* 8 (2011): 163–92.

———. "Picturing Ideal Beauty: The Saints in the Rotunda at Thessaloniki." *Antiquité tardive* 15 (2007): 321–36.

———. "Representing an Emperor: Style and Meaning on the *Missorium* of Theodosius I." In *El disco de Teodosio*, edited by M. Almagro-Gorbea et al., 273–80. Madrid, 2000.

Kiilerich, B., and H. Torp. *The Rotunda in Thessaloniki and Its Mosaics*. Athens, 2016.

King, H. *Hippocrates' Woman: Reading the Female Body in Ancient Greece*. London, 1998.

———. *The One-Sex Body on Trial: The Classical and Early Modern Evidence*. Farnham, 2013.

Klauser, Th. "*Aurum coronarium*." In *Gesammelte Arbeiten zur Liturgiegeschichte, Kirchengeschichte und christlichen Archäologie*, edited by E. Dassmann, 292–309. Münster, Westfalen, 1974.

Kliche, D. "Häßlich." In *Ästhetische Grundbegriffe: Historisches Wörterbuch in sieben Bänden* 3, edited by K. Barck et al., 25–66. Stuttgart, 2001.

Kolb, F. "Römische Mäntel: *paenula, lacerna*, μανδυη." *Römische Mitteilungen* 80 (1973): 69–167.

Konstan, D. *Beauty: The Fortunes of an Ancient Greek Ideal*. Oxford, 2014.

———. *Pity Transformed*. London, 2001.

———. "Themistius' *On Royal Beauty*." In *The Purpose of Rhetoric in Late Antiquity: From Performance to Exegesis*, edited by A. J. Quiroga Puertas, 179–88. Tübingen, 2013.

Koster, S. *Die Invektive in der griechischen und römischen Literatur*. Meisenheim am Glan, 1980.

Kovacs, M. *Kaiser, Senatoren und Gelehrte: Untersuchungen zum spätantiken männlichen Privatporträt*. Wiesbaden, 2014.

———. "*Praeclara in veste*: Kommunikation von Rang und sozialer Distinktion im spätantiken Amtsornat." In *Porträt und soziale Distinktion / Portrait et distinction sociale*, edited by D. Boschung and F. Queyrel, 373–430. Paderborn, 2020.

Krautheimer, E. *Three Christian Capitals: Topography and Politics*. Berkeley, 1983.

Kreikenbom, D. "Kyrene und die Ptolemaïs zur Zeit des Synesios." In Seng and Hoffmann, *Synesios von Kyrene*, 1–34.

Kristensen, T. M. "Embodied Images: Christian Response and Destruction in Late Antique Egypt." *Journal of Late Antiquity* 2 (2009): 224–50.

———. "Maxentius' Head and the Rituals of Civil War." In *Civil War in Ancient Greece and Rome: Contexts of Disintegration and Reintegration*, edited by H. Börm, M. Mattheis, and J. Wienand, 321–46. Stuttgart, 2015.

Krueger, D. "Between Monks: Tales of Monastic Companionship in Early Byzantium." *Journal of the History of Sexuality* 20 (2011): 28–61.

———. "Liturgical Time and Holy Land Reliquaries in Early Byzantium." In *Saints and Sacred Matter: The Cult of Relics in Byzantium and Beyond*, edited by C. Hahn and H. A. Klein, 111–31. Washington, DC, 2015.

Kuefler, M. "Between Bishops and Barbarians: The Rulers of the Later Roman Empire." In Fletcher, Brady, Moss, and Riall, *The Palgrave Handbook of Masculinity*, 37–62.

———. *The Manly Eunuch: Masculinity, Gender Ambiguity, and Christian Ideology in Late Antiquity*. Chicago, 2001.

Kuhoff, W. "Die Bedeutung der Ämter in Clarissimat und Spektabilität für die zivile senatorische Laufbahn im 4. Jahrhundert n. Chr." In *Atti del Colloquio internazionale AIEGL su epigrafia e ordine senatorio: Roma, 14–20 maggio 1981*, edited by S. Panciera, 271–88. Rome, 1982.

———. *Studien zur zivilen senatorischen Laufbahn im 4. Jahrhundert n. Chr.: Ämter und Amtsinhaber in Clarissimat und Spektabilität*. Frankfurt am Main, 1984.

Kulikowski, M. "Coded Polemic in Ammianus Book 31 and the Date and Place of Its Composition." *Journal of Roman Studies* 102 (2012): 79–102.

———. "The *Historia Augusta*: Minimalism and the Adequacy of Evidence." In *Late Antique Studies in Memory of Alan Cameron*, edited by W. V. Harris and A. Hunell Chen, 23–40. Leiden, 2021.

———. "Nation versus Army: A Necessary Contrast?" In Gillett, *On Barbarian Identity*, 69–84.

———. *Rome's Gothic Wars from the Third Century to Alaric*. Cambridge, 2007.

Lacombrade, Ch., ed. and trans. *Synésios de Cyrène. Opuscules* 2. Paris, 1951.

Laes, Ch. *Children in the Roman Empire: Outsiders Within*. Cambridge, 2011.

LaFleur, G., M. Raskolnikov, and A. Kłosowska. "Introduction: The Benefits of Being Trans Historical." In *Trans Historical: Gender Plurality Before the Modern*, edited by G. LaFleur, M. Raskolnikov, and A. Kłosowska, 1–24. Ithaca, NY, 2021.

LaFleur, G. "Epilogue: Against Consensus." In La Fleur, Raskolinkov and Kłosowska, *Trans Historical*, 366–78.

Laird, R. *Mindset, Moral Choice and Sin in the Anthropology of John Chrysostom*. Strathfield, 2012.

Lakoff, G., and M. Johnson. *Metaphors We Live By*. Chicago, 1980.

Lamoureux, J., and N. Aujoulat, ed. and trans. *Synésios de Cyrène. Opuscules* 2. Vol. 5. Paris, 2008.

Lange, C. H., and F. J. Vervaet. *The Historiography of Late Republican Civil War*. Leiden, 2019.

Laqueur, T. W. *Making Sex: Body and Gender from the Greeks to Freud*. Cambridge, MA, 1990.

La Rocca, C. "Masculinity and—Better Still—Masculinities in the Middle Ages." In Borri, La Rocca, and Veronese, *Masculinities in Early Medieval Europe*, 9–16.

Latham, J. "'Fabulous Clap-Trap': Roman Masculinity, the Cult of Magna Mater, and Literary Constructions of the *Galli* at Rome from Late Republic to Late Antiquity." *Journal of Religion* 92 (2012): 84–122.

Lecocq, F. "Le phénix chez Claudien: La fin d'un mythe: Pour une lecture politique du phénix: quelques arguments." In Garambois-Vasquez, *Claudien*, 113–57.

Lee, A. D. "Emperors and Generals in the Fourth Century." In Wienand, *Contested Monarchy*, 100–18.

———. *War in Late Antiquity: A Social History*. Oxford, 2007.

Lehmann, G. A., et al., eds. *Armut—Arbeit—Menschenwürde: Die Euböische Rede des Dion von Prusa*. Tübingen, 2012.

Lejdegård, H. *Honorius and the City of Rome: Authority and Legitimacy in Late Antiquity.* Uppsala, 2002.

Lemcke, L. *Bridging Center and Periphery: Administrative Communication from Constantine to Justinian.* Tübingen, 2020.

Lenski, N. "Constantine and the Tyche of Constantinople." In Wienand, *Contested Monarchy*, 330–52.

———. *Failure of Empire: Valens and the Roman State in the Fourth Century A.D.* Berkeley, 2002.

———. "*Initium mali Romano imperio*: Contemporary Reactions to the Battle of Adrianople." *Transactions of the American Philological Association* 127 (1997): 129–68.

Leppin, H. "Coping with the Tyrant's Faction: Civil-War Amnesties and Christian Discourses in the Fourth Century AD." In Wienand, *Contested Monarchy*, 198–214.

———. *Theodosius der Grosse.* Darmstadt 2003.

Lessing, G. E. *Laokoon: Oder über die Grenzen der Malerei und Poesie.* Reprint: Stuttgart, 2001.

Letteney, M. *The Christianization of Knowledge in Late Antiquity: Intellectual and Material Transformations.* Cambridge, 2023.

Leyerle, B. "Imagining Antioch, or The Fictional Space of Alleys and Markets." In Bergjan and Elm, *Antioch II*, 255–79.

———. "John Chrysostom on Almsgiving and the Use of Money." *Harvard Theological Review* 87 (1994): 29–47.

———. "Locating Animals in John Chrysostom's Thought." In de Wet and Mayer, *Revisioning John Chrysostom*, 276–99.

———. *The Narrative Shape of Emotion in the Preaching of John Chrysostom.* Berkeley, 2020.

———. *Theatrical Shows and Ascetic Lives: John Chrysostom's Attack on Spiritual Marriage.* Berkeley, 2001.

Lhuillier–Martinetti, D. *L'individu dans la famille à Rome au IVe siècle: D'après l'oeuvre d'Ambroise de Milan.* Rennes, 2008.

Li Causi, P. *Generare in commune: Teorie e rappresentazioni dell'ibrido nel sapere zoologico dei greci e dei romani.* Palermo, 2008.

———. "Mostri propriamente detti e creature *paradoxa*: Un tentativo di classificazione." In Baglioni, *Monstra*, 53–67.

Liebeschuetz, J. H. G. W. *Ambrose and John Chrysostom: Clerics Between Desert and Empire.* Oxford, 2011.

———. *Ambrose of Milan: Political Letters and Speeches.* Liverpool, 2005.

———. *Barbarians and Bishops: Army, Church, and State in the Age of Arcadius and Chrysostom.* Oxford, 1990.

———. "Friends and Enemies of John Chrysostom." In *Maistor: Classical, Byzantine and Renaissance Studies for Robert Browning*, edited by A. Moffatt, 85–111. Canberra, 1984.

———. "Letters of Ambrose of Milan (374–397), Books I–IX." In *Collecting Early Christian Letters: From the Apostle Paul to Late Antiquity*, edited by N. Bronwen and P. Allen, 97–112. Cambridge, 2015.

Lippold, A. "The Ideal of the Ruler and Attachment to Tradition in Pacatus' Panegyric." In *Latin Panegyric*, edited by R. Rees, 360–86. Oxford, 2012.

Liverani, P. "Roma tardoantica come spazio della rappresentazione trionfale." In *Der römische Triumph in Prinzipat und Spätantike*, edited by F. Goldbeck and J. Wienand, 487–510. Berlin, 2016.

Lizzi Testa, R. *Christian Emperors and Roman Elites in Late Antiquity.* New York, 2022.

———. "I vescovi, i barbari e l'impero di Roma." In *Potere e politica nell'età della famiglia teodosiana (395–455): I linguaggi dell'impero, le identità dei barbari,* edited by I. Baldini and S. Cosentino, 27–50. Bari, 2013.

———. "Martino vescovo santo: un modello di santità nell' Occidente tardoantico." *Cristianesimo nella storia* 29 (2008): 317–44.

———. "Memorie d'imperatori vivi, orazioni funebri e preghiere in suffragio per i principi defunti: Ambrogio di Milano e le sue innovazioni." *História (São Paulo)* 39 (2020): 1–21.

———. *Senatori, popolo, papi: Il governo di Roma al tempo dei valentiniani.* Bari, 2004.

———. "Significato filosofico e politico dell'antibarbarismo sinesiano: Il *De regno* e il *De providentia.*" *Rendiconti dell'Accademia di archeologia, lettere e belle arti di Napoli* 56 (1981): 49–62.

———. *Vescovi e strutture ecclesiastiche nella città tardoantica (l'Italia annonaria nel IV–V secolo d.C.).* Como, 1989.

Löhken, H. *Ordines dignitatum: Untersuchungen zur formalen Konstituierung der spätantiken Führungsschicht.* Cologne, 1982.

Lolli, M. "Ausonius: Die *Gratiarum actio ad Gratianum imperatorem* und 'De maiestatis laudibus': Lobrede auf den Herrscher oder auf den Lehrer?" *Latomus* 65 (2006): 707–26.

Long, J. "Claudian and the City: Poetry and Pride of Place." In *Aetas Claudianea: Eine Tagung an der Freien Universtität Berlin vom 28. bis 30. Juni 2002,* edited by W.-W. Ehlers and F. Felgentreu, 1–15. Munich, 2004.

———. *Claudian's "In Eutropium," or, How, When, and Why to Slander a Eunuch.* Chapel Hill, 1996.

L'Orange, H. P. *The Roman Empire: Art Forms and Civic Life.* New York, 1985.

Lowe, D. *Monsters and Monstrosity in Augustan Poetry.* Ann Arbor, 2015.

Lowrie, M. "The Egyptian Within: A Roman Figuration of Civil War." In *Translatio Babylonis: Unsere orientalische Moderne,* edited by B. Vinken, 13–28. Paderborn, 2015.

Lowrie, M., and B. Vinken. "Married to Civil War: A Roman Trope in Lucan's Poetics of History." In Lange and Vervaet, *The Historiography of Late Republican Civil War,* 263–91.

Lunn-Rockliffe, S. "Ambrose's Imperial Funeral Sermons." *Journal of Ecclesiastical History* 59 (2008): 191–207.

———. "Commemorating the Usurper Magnus Maximus: Ekphrasis, Poetry, and History in Pacatus' Panegyric of Theodosius." *Journal of Late Antiquity* 3 (2010): 316–36.

Lyman, R. "The Theology of the Council of Nicaea." In *St. Andrews Encyclopedia of Theology,* edited by B. N. Wolfe et al. St. Andrews, 2024.

Ma, J. "Public Speech and Community in the *Euboicus.*" In *Dio Chrysostom: Politics, Letters, and Philosophy,* edited by S. Swain, 108–24. Oxford, 2000.

Maas, M. "Barbarians: Problems and Approaches." In *The Oxford Handbook of Late Antiquity,* edited by S. F. Johnson, 60–91. Oxford, 2012.

———. *The Conqueror's Gift: Roman Ethnography and the End of Antiquity.* Princeton, 2025.

———. "Strabo and Procopius: Classical Geography for a Christian Empire." In *From Rome to Constantinople: Studies in Honour of Averil Cameron,* edited by H. Amirav and B. ter Haar Romeny, 67–84. Leuven, 2007.

MacCormack, S. G. *Art and Ceremony in Late Antiquity.* Berkeley, 1981.

MacCoull, L. S. B. "Gallienus the Genderbender." *Greek, Roman and Byzantine Studies* 40 (1999): 233–39.

MacDougall, B. "Theologies under Persecution: Gregory of Nazianzus and the *Syntagmation* of Aetius." In *Heirs of Roman Persecution: Studies on a Christian and Para-Christian Discourse in Late Antiquity*, edited by É. Fournier and W. Mayer, 79–94. Abingdon, 2020.

Machado, C. "Aristocratic Houses and the Making of Late Antique Rome and Constantinople." In Grig and Kelly, *Two Romes*, 136–58.

———. *Urban Space and Aristocratic Power in Late Antique Rome: AD 270–535*. Oxford, 2019.

MacMullen, R. "Some Pictures in Ammianus Marcellinus." *Art Bulletin* 46 (1964): 435–55.

Mac Sweeney, N. "Race and Ethnicity." In *A Cultural History of Race*, edited by D. McCoskey, 1:103–18. London, 2021.

Mader, G. "History as Carnival, or Method and Madness in the *Vita Heliogabali*." *Classical Antiquity* 24 (2005): 131–72.

Magdalino, P. *Roman Constantinople in Byzantine Perspective: The Memorial and Aesthetic Rediscovery of Constantine's Beautiful City, from Late Antiquity to the Renaissance*. Boston, 2024.

Maier, F. K. *Palastrevolution: Der Weg zum hauptstädtischen Kaisertum im Römischen Reich des vierten Jahrhunderts*. Paderborn, 2019.

Maiuri, A. "Il lessico latino del mostruoso." In Baglioni, *Monstra*, 165–77.

Malingrey, A. M., ed. and trans. *Palladios: Dialogue sur la vie de Jean Chrysostome*. 2 vols. Paris, 1988.

Malone, Ch. W. "Violence on Roman Imperial Coinage." *Journal of the Numismatic Association of Australia* 20 (2009): 58–72.

Manders, E. *Coining Images of Power: Patterns in the Representation of Roman Emperors on Imperial Coinage, A.D. 193–284*. Leiden, 2012.

Manders, E., and D. Slootjes, eds. *Leadership, Ideology and Crowds in the Roman Empire of the Fourth Century AD*. Stuttgart, 2020.

Marasco, G. "I vescovi e il problema della magia in epoca teodosiana." In *Vescovi e pastori in epoca teodosiana: XXV incontro di studiosi dell'antichità cristiana*, 225–47. Rome, 1997.

Marchal, J. A. *Appalling Bodies: Queer Figures Before and After Paul's Letters*. Oxford, 2020.

Marcone, A. "Stilicone *parens publicus*." *Zeitschrift für Papyrologie und Epigraphik* 70 (1987): 222–24.

Markschies, Ch. *Gottes Körper: Jüdische, christliche und pagane Gottesvorstellungen in der Antike*. Munich, 2016.

Martin, D. B. "*Arsenokoites* and *Malakos*: Meanings and Consequences." In *Biblical Ethics and Homosexuality: Listening to Scriptures*, edited by R. L. Brawley, 117–36. Louisville, 1996.

Masterson, M. *Between Byzantine Men: Desire, Homosociality, and Brotherhood in the Medieval Empire*. London, 2022.

———. "*Kinaidos*: The Afterlife of a Term in the Byzantine Empire." In Gazzari and Weiner, *Searching for the Cinaedus*, 274–98.

———. *Man to Man: Desire, Homosociality, and Authority in Late-Roman Manhood*. Columbus, OH, 2014.

Masterson, M., N. Sorkin Rabinowitz, and J. Robson, eds. *Sex in Antiquity: Exploring Gender and Sexuality in the Ancient World*. New York, 2014.

Mastora, P. "The Virtual Lighting of the Rotunda's Mosaics." In *Glass, Wax and Metal: Lighting Technologies in Late Antique, Byzantine and Medieval Times*, edited by I. Motsianos and K. S. Garnett, 217–24. Oxford, 2019.

Mathews, T. F. *The Clash of Gods: A Reinterpretation of Early Christian Art*. Princeton, 1993.

Mathiesen, R. "*Provinciales, Gentiles*, and Marriages Between Romans and Barbarians in the Late Roman Empire." *Journal of Roman Studies* 99 (2009): 140–55.

Matthews, John F. *Laying Down the Law: A Study of the Theodosian Code*. New Haven, 2000.

———. "The Roman Empire and the Proliferation of Elites." *Arethusa* 33 (2000): 429–46.

———. *The Roman Empire of Ammianus*. Baltimore, 1989.

———. *Western Aristocracies and Imperial Court AD 364–425*. Oxford, 1975. Reprint, 1990.

Mause, M. *Die Darstellung des Kaisers in der lateinischen Panegyrik*. Stuttgart, 1994.

Mayer, K. "The Schoolboys' Revenge: How the Golden Line Entered Classical Scholarship." *Classical Receptions Journal* 12 (2020): 248–78.

Mayer, W. "At Constantinople, How Often Did John Chrysostom Preach? Addressing Assumptions About the Workload of a Bishop." *Sacris erudiri* 40 (2001): 83–105.

———. "The Audience(s) for Patristic Social Teaching: A Case Study." In *Reading Patristic Texts in Social Ethics*, edited by J. Leemans, B. J. Matz, and J. Verstaeten, 85–99. Washington, DC, 2011.

———. "Doing Violence to the Image of an Empress: The Destruction of Eudoxia's Reputation." In *Violence in Late Antiquity: Perception and Practices*, edited by H. A. Drake, 205–13. Aldershot, 2006.

———. "John Chrysostom: Extraordinary Preacher, Ordinary Audience." In *Preacher and Audience: Studies in Early Christian and Byzantine Homiletics*, edited by M. B. Cunningham and P. Allen, 105–37. Leiden, 1998.

———. "John Chrysostom and Women Revisited." In Mayer and Elmer, *Men and Women in the Early Christian Centuries*, 211–25.

———. "John Chrysostom as Bishop: The View from Antioch." *Journal of Ecclesiastical History* 55 (2004): 455–66.

———. "John Chrysostom as Crisis-Manager: The Years in Constantinople." In *Ancient Jewish and Christian Texts as Crisis Management Literature: Thematic Studies from the Centre for Early Christian Studies*, edited by D. C. Sim and P. Allen, 128–43. London, 2012.

———. "Poverty and Generosity toward the Poor in the Time of John Chrysostom." In Holman, *Wealth and Poverty*, 140–58.

———. "A Son of Hellenism: Viewing John Chrysostom's Anti-Intellectualism through the Lens of Antiochene *Paideia*." In Bergjan and Elm, *Antioch II*, 361–82.

———. "Who Came to Hear John Chrysostom Preach? Recovering a Late Fourth-Century Preacher's Audience." *Ephemerides Theologicae Lovanienses* 76 (2000): 73–87.

Mayer, W., and I. J. Elmer, eds. *Men and Women in the Early Christian Centuries*. Strathfield, 2014.

Maxwell, J. L. *Christianization and Communication: John Chrysostom and His Congregation in Antioch*. Cambridge, 2006.

McCall, T. *Brilliant Bodies: Fashioning Courtly Men in Early Renaissance Italy*. University Park, 2022.

McCormick, M. *Eternal Victory: Triumphal Rulership in Late Antiquity, Byzantium, and the Early Medieval West*. Cambridge, 1986.

McDonnell, M. *Roman Manliness: Virtus and the Roman Republic*. Cambridge, 2006.

———. "Roman Men and Greek Virtue." In Rosen and Sluiter, *Andreia*, 235–61.

McEvoy, M. A. *Child Emperor Rule in the Late Roman West, AD 367–455*. Oxford, 2013.

———. "An Imperial Jellyfish? The Emperor Arcadius and Imperial Leadership in the Late Fourth Century." In Manders and Slootjes, *Leadership, Ideology and Crowds*, 181–97.

———. "Orations for the First Generation of Theodosian Imperial Women." *Journal of Late Antiquity* 14 (2021): 117–41.

———. "Rome and the Transformation of the Imperial Office in the Late Fourth–Mid-Fifth Centuries AD." *Papers of the British School at Rome* 78 (2010): 151–92.

McGill, S., C. Sogno, and E. Watts, eds. *From the Tetrarchs to the Theodosians: Later Roman History and Culture, 284–450 CE*. Cambridge, 2010.

McInerney, J. "Plutarch's Manly Women." In Rosen and Sluiter, *Andreia*, 319–44.

McLynn, N. B. *Ambrose of Milan: Church and Court in a Christian Capital*. Berkeley, 1994.

———. "'Genere Hispanus': Theodosius, Spain and Nicene Orthodoxy." In *Hispania in Late Antiquity: Current Perspectives*, edited and translated by K. Bowes and M. Kulikowski, 77–120. Leiden, 2005.

———. "Imperial Piety in Action: The Theodosians in Church." In Destephen, Dumézil, and Inglebert, *Le prince chrétien*, 315–39.

———. "Moments of Truth: Gregory of Nazianzus and Theodosius I." In McGill, Sogno, and Watts, *From the Tetrarchs to the Theodosians*, 215–39.

———. "The Transformation of Imperial Churchgoing in the Fourth Century." In *Approaching Late Antiquity: The Transformation from Early to Late Empire*, edited by S. Swain and M. Edwards, 235–70. Oxford, 2006.

———. "The Voice of Conscience: Gregory Nazianzen in Retirement." In *Vescovi e pastori in epoca teodosiana: XXV incontro di studiosi dell'antichità cristiana*, 299–308. Rome, 1997.

McNelis, Ch. "Bacchus, Hercules, and Literary History in Statius's *Achilleid*." *Classical Journal* 115 (2020): 442–55.

———. "Statius' *Achilleid* and the *Cypria*." In *The Greek Epic Cycle and Its Ancient Reception: A Companion*, edited by M. Fantuzzi and Ch. Tsagalis, 578–95. Cambridge, 2015.

Meister, J. B. *Der Körper des Princeps: Zur Problematik eines monarchischen Körpers ohne Monarchie*. Stuttgart, 2012.

Mellas, A. "Tears of Compunction in John Chrysostom's *On Eutropius*." *Studia Patristica* 83 (2017): 159–72.

Mentzos, A. "Reflections on the Interpretation and Dating of the Rotunda of Thessaloniki." Εγνατία 6 (2001/2002): 57–82.

Messis, C. *Les eunuques à Byzance, entre réalité et imaginaire*. Paris, 2014.

Meyer, E. A. *Legitimacy and Law in the Roman World: Tabulae in Roman Belief and Practice*. Cambridge, 2004.

Millar, F. *A Greek Roman Empire: Power and Belief under Theodosius II (408/450)*. Berkeley, 2006.

Miller, M. C. *Clothing the Clergy: Virtue and Power in Medieval Europe, c. 800–1200*. Ithaca, 2014.

———. "Introduction: Material Culture and Catholic History." *The Catholic Historical Review* 101 (2015): 1–17.

Minets, Y. *The Slow Fall of Babel: Languages and Identities in Late Antique Christianity*. Cambridge, 2021.

Mitchell, J. "The Eastern and Western Consulship in Late Antiquity." *Hiperboreea* 5 (2018): 5–16.

Mleczek, A. "Gratian as *Optimus Princeps*—the Literary Image of 'An Ideal Emperor' in *Gratiarum Actio Ad Gratianum Imperatorem* by D. M. Ausonius and the *Laudatio in Gratianum Augustum* of Q. A. Symmachus." *Classica Cracoviensia* 26 (2023): 357–405.

Molinier Arbo, A. "L'*optimus princeps* dans l'*Histoire Auguste*: Modèle politique ou figure utopique?" In *Utopia e utopie nel pensiero storico antico*, edited by C. Carsana and M. T. Schettino, 87–108. Rome, 2008.

Moore, S. D. "Queer Theory." In Dunning, *Oxford Handbook of Gender and Sexuality*, 95–116.

Moreau, T. "Le *De obitu Theodosii* d'Ambroise (395): Une refonte des genres littéraires dans le creuset du sermon politique." In *Shifting Genres in Late Antiquity*, edited by G. Greatrex and H. Elton with L. McMahon, 27–40. Farnham, 2015.

Morgan, F. Pennick. *Dress and Personal Appearance in Late Antiquity: The Clothing of the Middle and Lower Classes.* Leiden, 2018.

Morgan, T. *Roman Faith and Christian Faith: Pistis and Fides in the Early Roman Empire and Early Churches.* Oxford, 2015.

Muehlberger, E. "Wartime Effects: Synesius of Cyrene and the Sentiments of *On Kingship*." In Elm and Sessa, *War and Community*.

Müller, G. M. *Lectiones Claudianeae: Studien zu Poetik und Funktion der politisch-zeitgeschichtlichen Dichtungen Claudians.* Heidelberg, 2011.

Murgatroyd, P. *Mythical Monsters in Classical Literature.* London, 2007.

Näf, B. *Senatorisches Standesbewusstsein in spätrömischer Zeit.* Freiburg, 1995.

Nappa, C. *Making Men Ridiculous: Juvenal and the Anxieties of the Individual.* Ann Arbor, 2018.

Nardelli, J.-F., and S. Ratti. "*Historia Augusta contra christianos*: Recherches sur l'ambiance antichrétienne de l'*Histoire Auguste*." *Antiquité tardive* 22 (2014): 143–55.

Nardi, E. "La seta nella normativa imperiale Romana." *Atti della Accademia delle Scienze dell'Istituto di Bologna, classe di scienze morali, Rendiconti* 71 (1984): 75–105.

Nasrallah, L. "Empire and Apocalypse in Thessaloniki: Interpreting the Early Christian Rotunda." *Journal of Early Christian Studies* 13 (2005): 465–508.

Nathan, G. "The Ideal Male in Late Antiquity: Claudian's Example of Flavius Stilicho." *Gender & History* 27 (2015): 10–17.

Nauroy, G. "The Letter Collection of Ambrose of Milan." In *Late Antique Letter Collections*, edited by C. Sogno, B. K. Storin, and E. J. Watts, 146–60. Berkeley, 2016.

Nehamas, A. *Only a Promise of Happiness: The Place of Beauty in a World of Art.* Princeton, 2007.

Neri, V. "Considerazioni sul tema della *luxuria* nell'*Historia Augusta*." In *Historiae Augustae Colloquium Genevense*, edited by F. Paschoud, 217–40. Bari, 1999.

———. *La bellezza del corpo nella società tardoantica: Rappresentazioni visive e valutazioni estetiche tra cultura classica e cristianesimo.* Bologna, 2004.

———. "La dialettica politica fra l'imperatore e la sua corte nelle *Res gestae* di Ammiano Marcellino." *Koinonia* 40 (2016): 107–30.

———. "L'imperatore come *miles*: Tacito, Attalo e la datazione dell'*Historia Augusta*." In *Historiae Augustae Colloquium Perusinum*, edited by G. Bonamente and F. Paschoud, 373–96. Bari, 2002.

———. "L'usurpatore come tiranno nel lessico politico della tarda antichità." In *Usurpationen in der Spätantike: Akten des Kolloquiums "Staatsstreich und Staatlichkeit," 6.–10. März 1996*, edited by F. Paschoud and J. Szidat, 71–86. Stuttgart, 1997.

———. *Medius princeps: Storia e immagine di Costantino nella storiografia latina pagana.* Bologna, 1992.

Neville, L. *Byzantine Gender*. Leeds, 2019.

Niccolai, L. *Christianity, Philosophy, and Roman Power: Constantine, Julian, and the Bishops on Exegesis and Empire*. Cambridge, 2023.

Niquet, H. *Monumenta virtutum titulique: Senatorische Selbstdarstellung im spätantiken Rom im Spiegel der epigraphischen Denkmäler*. Stuttgart, 2000.

Noethlichs, K. L. "Hofbeamter." *Reallexikon für Antike und Christentum* 15 (1991): 1111–58.

———. "Strukturen und Funktionen des spätantiken Kaiserhofes." In Winterling, *Comitatus*, 13–49.

Noreña, C. F. "The Ethics of Autocracy in the Roman World." In *A Companion to Greek and Roman Political Thought*, edited by R. K. Balot, 266–79. Oxford, 2009.

———. "Hadrian's Chastity." *Phoenix* 61 (2007): 296–317.

———. *Imperial Ideals in the Roman West: Representation, Circulation, Power*. Cambridge, 2011.

———. "Self-Fashioning in the *Panegyricus*." In *Pliny's Praise: The Panegyricus in the Roman World*, edited by P. Roche, 29–44. Cambridge, 2011.

Norton, P. *Episcopal Elections 250-600: Hierarchy and Popular Will in Late Antiquity*. Oxford, 2007.

Nye, J. S. "Soft Power." *Foreign Policy* 80 (1990): 153–71.

———. "Soft Power: The Evolution of a Concept." *Journal of Political Power* 14 (2021): 196–208.

Oliensis, E. *Horace and the Rhetoric of Authority*. Cambridge, 1998.

Olovsdotter, C. *The Consular Image: An Iconological Study of the Consular Diptychs*. Oxford, 2005.

Olson, K. *Masculinity and Dress in Roman Antiquity*. Abingdon, 2017.

———. "Toga and Pallium: Status, Sexuality, Identity." In Masterson, Rabinowitz, and Robson, *Sex in Antiquity*, 422–48.

Omissi, A. "Civil War and the Late Roman Panegyrical Corpus." In Omissi and Ross, *Imperial Panegyric*, 211–31.

———. "*Damnatio memoriae* or *creatio memoriae*? Memory Sanctions as Creative Processes in the Fourth Century AD." *Cambridge Classical Journal* 62 (2016): 170–99.

———. *Emperors and Usurpers in the Later Roman Empire: Civil War, Panegyric, and the Construction of Legitimacy*. Oxford, 2018.

Omissi, A., and A. J. Ross. "Imperial Panegyric from Diocletian to Honorius." In Omissi and Ross, *Imperial Panegyric*, 1–22.

Omissi, A., and A. J. Ross, eds. *Imperial Panegyric from Diocletian to Honorius*. Liverpool, 2020.

Op de Coul, M. "Aspects of *Paideia* in Synesius' Dion." In Seng and Hoffmann, *Synesios von Kyrene*, 110–24.

Orlandi, S. "Altar of Stilicho." *Epigraphic Database Roma* = EDR111525, 2008.

Östenberg, I. *Staging the World: Spoils, Captives, and Representations in the Roman Triumphal Procession*. Oxford, 2009.

Osterhammel, J. *Die Entzauberung Asiens. Europa und die asiatischen Reiche im 18. Jahrhundert*. Munich, 1998. Reprint, 2010.

Ostrogorsky, G. *History of the Byzantine State*. New Brunswick, 1969.

Panella, C. "I segni del potere." In *I segni del potere: realtà e immaginario della sovranità nella Roma imperiale*, edited by C. Panella, 25–76. Bari, 2011.

Papadogiannakis, Y. "Homiletics and the History of Emotions: The Case of John Chrysostom." In de Wet and Mayer, *Revisioning John Chrysostom*, 300–33.

———. "Prescribing Emotions, Constructing Emotional Communities in John Chrysostom's Antioch." In Bergjan and Elm, *Antioch II*, 339–60.

Parkes, R. "Model Youths? Achilles and Parthenopaeus in Claudian's Panegyrics on the Third and Fourth Consulships of Honorius." *Illinois Classical Studies* 30 (2005): 67–82.

Paschoud, F., ed. and trans. *Histoire auguste*. Vol 4.1, *Vie des deux Maximins, des trois Gordiens, de Maxime et Balbin*. Paris, 2023.

———. "De *Historiae Romanae scriptores latini minores* à *Historia Augusta*: Évolution moderne du titre d'une collection de biographies impériales (1475–2009)." *Giornale Italiano di Filologia* 61 (2009): 197–204.

Pausch, D. "*Libellus non tam diserte quam fideliter scriptus?* Unreliable Narration in the *Historia Augusta*." *Ancient Narrative* 8 (2009): 115–35.

Pausch, M. *Die römische Tunika: Ein Beitrag zur Peregrinisierung der antiken Kleidung*. Augsburg, 2003.

Pazdernik, Ch. "Paying Attention to the Man Behind the Curtain: Disclosing and Withholding the Imperial Presence in Justinianic Constantinople." In *Bodies and Boundaries in Graeco-Roman Antiquity*, edited by Th. Fögen and M. M. Lee, 63–86. New York, 2009.

Pernot, L. "What Is a 'Panegyric'?" In Omissi and Ross, *Imperial Panegyric*, 25–39.

Petkas, A. "The King in Words: Performance and Fiction in Synesius' *De regno*." *American Journal of Philology* 139 (2018): 123–51.

Pfeilschifter, R. *Der Kaiser und Konstantinopel: Kommunikation und Konfliktaustrag in einer spätantiken Metropole*. Berlin, 2013.

Pichon, R. "The Origin of the *Panegyrici Latini* Collection." In *Latin Panegyric*, edited by R. Rees, 55–74. Oxford, 2012.

Pigott, J. M. "Capital Crimes: Deconstructing John's 'Unnecessary Severity' in Managing the Clergy at Constantinople." In de Wet and Mayer, *Revisioning John Chrysostom*, 733–77.

Pilipow, R. "The Jeweled Jurist: Late Roman Legal Aesthetics." *Studies in Late Antiquity* 4 (2020): 185–202.

Pope, M. *Lucretius and the End of Masculinity*. Cambridge, 2023.

Porter, J. I. *The Sublime in Antiquity*. Cambridge, 2016.

Quiroga Puertas, A. J. "Deconstructing Praise: Zosimus' Conception of the Emperor Theodosius' ἀνδρεία." *Mnemosyne* 68 (2015): 452–64.

———. *La rétorica de Libanio y de Juan Crisóstomo en la Revuelta de las Estatuas*. Salerno, 2007.

———. "Toying with Theodosius: The Manipulation of the Imperial Image in the Sources of the Riot of the Statues." In García Ruiz and Quiroga Puertas, *Emperors and Emperorship*, 199–217.

Racette-Campbell, M. *The Crisis of Masculinity in the Age of Augustus*. Madison, 2023.

Racette-Campbell, M., and A. McMaster. "Introduction: Toxic Masculinity and Classics." In *Toxic Masculinity in the Ancient World*, edited by M. Racette-Campbell and A. McMaster, 1–14. Edinburgh, 2024.

Rapp, C. *Brother-Making in Late Antiquity and Byzantium: Monks, Laymen, and Christian Ritual*. Oxford, 2016.

———. "Mark the Deacon, Life of St. Porphyry of Gaza." In *Medieval Hagiography: An Anthology*, edited by Th. Head, 53–76. New York, 2001.

Raspanti, G. "*Clementissimus imperator*: Power, Religion, and Philosophy in Ambrose's *De obitu Theodosii* and Seneca's *De clementia*." In *The Power of Religion in Late Antiquity*, edited by A. Cain and N. Lenski, 45–56. Aldershot, 2009.

Ratti, S. *Antiquus error: Les ultimes feux de la résistance païenne*. Turnhout, 2010.

———. *Polémiques entre païens et chrétiens*. Paris, 2012.

Rebenich, S. "Beobachtungen zum Sturz des Tatianus und des Proculus." *Zeitschrift für Papyrologie und Epigraphik* 76 (1989): 153–65.

Rees, R. D. "Authorising Freedom of Speech under Theodosius." In Burgersdijk and Ross, *Imagining Emperors*, 289–309.

———. "Bright Lights, Big City: Pacatus and the *Panegyrici Latini*." In Grig and Kelly, *Two Romes*, 203–22.

———. *A Commentary on Panegyrici Latini II(12): An Oration Delivered by Pacatus Drepanius Before the Emperor Theodosius I in the Senate at Rome, 389 CE*. Cambridge, 2023.

———. "From Alterity to Unity in Pacatus Drepanius' *Panegyric for Theodosius*." *Talanta* 45 (2013): 41–53.

———. *Layers of Loyalty in Latin Panegyric, AD 289–307*. Oxford, 2002.

———. "(Not) Making Faces: *Prosopopeia* in Late Antique Panegyric," In Omissi and Ross, *Imperial Panegyric*, 41–65.

———. "Pacatus the Poet Doing Plinian Prose." *Arethusa* 46 (2013): 241–59.

Retief, F. P., and L. Cilliers. "Causes of Death Among the Caesars (27BC–AD 476)." *Acta Theologica* 26, Suppl. 7 (2006): 89–106.

Richlin, A. "Invective against Women in Roman Satire." In Richlin, *Arguments with Silence: Writing the History of Roman Women*, 62–80. Ann Arbor, 2014.

———. "Not Before Homosexuality: The Materiality of the *Cinaedus* and the Roman Law Against Love Between Men." *Journal of the History of Sexuality* 3 (1993): 523–73.

Rimmel, V. "The Poor Man's Feast: Juvenal." In *The Cambridge Companion to Roman Satire*, edited by K. Freudenberg, 81–94. Cambridge, 2005.

Ringrose, K. M. "Eunuchs as Cultural Mediators." *Byzantinische Forschungen* 23 (1996): 75–93.

———. *The Perfect Servant: Eunuchs and the Social Construction of Gender in Byzantium*. Chicago, 2003.

Roberts, M. *The Jeweled Style: Poetry and Poetics in Late Antiquity*. Ithaca, NY, 1989.

———. "Light, Color, and Visual Illusion in the Poetry of Venantius Fortunatus." *Dumbarton Oaks Papers* 65/66 (2011/2012): 113–20.

———. "Rome Personified, Rome Epitomized: Representations of Rome in the Poetry of the Early Fifth Century." *American Journal of Philology* 122 (2001): 533–65.

Roche, P. "Lucan in Claudian's *In Eutropium*: Rhetoric, Paradox, and Exemplarity." In Berlincourt, Galli Miliç, and Nelis, *Lucan and Claudian*, 227–42.

———. "Staring at the Son: Strategies of Praise in Claudian's *Panegyric on the Third Consulship of Honorius*." *Journal of Late Antiquity* 14 (2021): 142–58.

Röckelein, H. "Die 'Hüllen der Heiligen': Zur Materialität des hagiographischen Mediums." In *Reliquiare im Mittelalter*, edited by B. Reudenbach and G. Toussaint, 75–88. Berlin, 2005.

Rodgers, B. S. "Divine Insinuation in the *Panegyrici Latini*." *Historia* 35 (1986): 69–104.

Rohrbacher, D. "Ammianus' Roman Digressions and the Audience of the *Res Gestae*." In *A Companion to Greek and Roman Historiography*, edited by J. Marincola, 468–73. Oxford, 2007.

———. *The Historians of Late Antiquity*. London, 2013.

———. "Physiognomics in Imperial Latin Biography." *Classical Antiquity* 29 (2010): 92–116.

———. *The Play of Allusion in the Historia Augusta*. Madison, 2016.

Rollason, N. K. *Gifts of Clothing in Late Antique Literature*. London, 2016.

Rollinger, Ch. "The Importance of Being Splendid: Competition, Ceremonial, and the Semiotics of Status at the Court of the Late Roman Emperors (4th–6th Centuries)." In *Gaining and Losing Imperial Favour in Late Antiquity*, edited by K. C. Choda, M. Sterk de Leeuw, and F. Schulz, 36–72. Leiden, 2020.

Romm, J. S. *The Edges of the Earth in Ancient Thought: Geography, Exploration, and Fiction*. Princeton, 1992.

Ronchey, S. "La 'femme fatale,' source d'une byzantinologie austere." In *Byzance en Europe: Actes du XXe Congrès international des études byzantines. Paris, 2001*, edited by Marie-France Auzépy, 153–57. Saint-Denis, 2003.

———. "Teodora e i visionarii." In Carrié and Lizzi Testa, *Humana Sapit*, 445–53.

Roques, D. "Synésios à Constantinople: 399–402." *Byzantion* 65 (1995): 405–39.

———. *Synésios de Cyrène et la Cyrénaïque du Bas-Émpire*. Paris, 1987.

Rosen, R. M., and I. Sluiter, eds. *Andreia: Studies in Manliness and Courage in Classical Antiquity*. Leiden, 2003.

Rosenkranz, K. *Ästhetik des Häßlichen*. Edited with an afterword by D. Kliche. Reprint: Leipzig, 1990.

Roskam, G. "Emancipatory Preaching: John Chrysostom's Homily *Peccata fratrum non evulganda* (CPG 4389)." In de Wet and Mayer, *Revisioning John Chrysostom*, 175–205.

Ross, A. J. "Ammianus, Traditions of Satire and the Eternity of Rome." *Classical Journal* 110 (2015): 356–73.

Roueché, Ch. "The Image of Victory: New Evidence from Ephesus." *Traveaux et Mémoires* 14 (2002): 527–46.

Rüpke, J. *Domi militiae: Die religiöse Konstruktion des Krieges in Rom*. Stuttgart, 1990.

Rylaarsdam, D. *John Chrysostom on Divine Pedagogy: The Coherence of His Theology and Preaching*. Oxford, 2014.

Sághy, M. "*Veste Regia Indutus*: Representations of the Emperor in the *Vita Martini*." *IKON* 5 (2012): 47–56.

Said, E. *Orientalism*. Reprint with a new preface: London, 2003.

Salway, B. "Roman Consuls, Imperial Politics, and Egyptian Papyri: The Consulates of 325 and 344 CE." *Journal of Late Antique Studies* 1 (2008): 278–310.

Salzman, M. R. "Ambrose and the Usurpation of Arbogastes and Eugenius: Reflections on Pagan–Christian Conflict Narratives." *Journal of Early Christian Studies* 18 (2010): 191–223.

———. *The Falls of Rome: Crises, Resilience, and Resurgence in Late Antiquity*. Cambridge, 2021.

———. "Symmachus and the 'Barbarian' Generals." *Historia* 55 (2006): 352–67.

Sánchez-Ostiz, Á. "Claudian's Stilicho at the *Urbs*: Roman Legitimacy for the Half-Barbarian Regent." In Burgersdijk and Ross, *Imagining Emperors*, 310–30.

Sánchez Vendramini, D. N. "The Audience of Ammianus Marcellinus and the Circulation of Books in the Late Roman World." *Journal of Ancient History* 6 (2018): 234–59.

Sandwell, I. "Preaching and Christianisation: Communication, Cognition, and Audience Reception." In de Wet and Mayer, *Revisioning John Chrysostom*, 137–74.

———. *Religious Identity in Late Antiquity: Greeks, Jews, and Christians in Antioch.* Cambridge, 2007.

Santini, F. "A Martyr of Civil Wars: Ambrose on the Death of Valentinian II." In Elm and Sessa, *War and Community.* Cambridge, 2025.

Santorius, N. *Zerrbilder des Göttlichen: Das Hässliche in der französischen Skulptur des 19. Jahrhunderts als Movens der Moderne.* Paderborn, 2012.

Sapsford, T. *Performing the Kinaidos: Unmanly Men in Ancient Mediterranean Cultures.* Oxford, 2022.

Şare Ağtürk, T. "A New Tetrarchic Relief from Nicomedia: Embracing Emperors." *American Journal of Archaeology* 122 (2018): 411–26.

———. *The Painted Tetrarchic Reliefs from Nicomedia: Uncovering the Colourful Life of Diocletian's Forgotten Capital.* Turnhout, 2021.

Savino, E. *Ricerche sull'Historia Augusta.* Naples, 2017.

Schade, K. "Die bildliche Repräsentation der römischen Kaiserin zwischen Prinzipat und Byzanz." in *Grenzen der Macht: Zur Rolle der römischen Kaiserfrauen*, 40–53. Stuttgart, 2000.

———. "The Female Body in Late Antiquity: Between Virtue, Taboo and Eroticism." In *Bodies and Boundaries in Graeco-Roman Antiquity*, edited by Th. Fögen and M. M. Lee, 215–36. Berlin, 2009.

———. "Women." In Smith and Ward-Perkins, *The Last Statues*, 249–58.

Scheithauer, A. *Kaiserbild und literarisches Programm: Untersuchungen zur Tendenz der Historia Augusta.* Frankfurt am Main, 1987.

Schindler, C. *Per carmina laudes: Untersuchungen zur spätantiken Verspanegyrik von Claudian bis Coripp.* Berlin, 2009.

Schlinkert, D. *Ordo senatorius und nobilitas: Die Konstitution des Senatsadels in der Spätantike.* Stuttgart, 1996.

Schmidt, P. L. *Politik und Dichtung in der Panegyrik Claudians.* Konstanz, 1976.

Schmidt-Hofner, S. "Ehrensachen: Ranggesetzgebung, Elitenkonkurrenz und die Funktionen des Rechts in der Spätantike." *Chiron* 40 (2010): 209–43.

———. "Epiphanien des Altertums: Ernst Kantorowicz und die Antike." In *Mythen, Körper, Bilder: Ernst Kantorowicz zwischen Historismus, Emigration und Erneuerung der Geisteswissenschaften*, edited by Lucas Burkart et al., 239–68. Göttingen, 2015.

———. "Ostentatious Legislation: Law and Dynastic Change, AD 364–365." In Wienand, *Contested Monarchy*, 67–99.

———. *Reagieren und Gestalten: Der Regierungsstil des spätrömischen Kaisers am Beispiel der Gesetzgebung Valentinians I.* Munich, 2008.

———. "Trajan und die symbolische Kommunikation bei kaiserlichen Rombesuchen in der Spätantike." In *Rom in der Spätantike: Historische Erinnerung im städtischen Raum*, edited by R. Behrwald and Ch. Witschel, 33–59. Stuttgart, 2012.

Schmitt, T. *Die Bekehrung des Synesios von Kyrene: Politik und Philosophie, Hof und Provinz als Handlungsräume eines Aristokraten bis zu seiner Wahl zum Metropoliten von Ptolemaïs.* Munich, 2001.

Scholten, H. *Der Eunuch in Kaisernähe: Zur politischen und sozialen Bedeutung des praepositus sacri cubiculi im 4. und 5. Jahrhundert n. Chr.* Frankfurt am Main, 1995.

———. "Der oberste Hofeunuch: Die politische Effizienz eines gesellschaftlich Diskriminierten." In Winterling, *Comitatus*, 51–73.

Schramm, M. "Neuplatonische politische Philosophie in der Rede *Peri basileias* des Synesios von Kyrene." *Elenchos* 38 (2017): 151–77.

Schweckendiek, H. *Claudians Invektive gegen Eutrop: Ein Kommentar.* Hildesheim, 1992.

Sedgwick, E. Kosofsky. *Between Men: English Literature and Male Homosocial Desires.* New York, 1985.

———. *Epistemology of the Closet.* Berkeley, 2008.

———. "Tales from the Avunculate: Queer Tutelage in *The Importance of Being Earnest.*" In *Tendencies*, 52–72.

———. *Tendencies.* Edited by M. Aina Barale, J. Goldberg, and M. Moon. Durham, NC, 1993.

Seeck, O. "Arkadius." *Realencyclopädie der classischen Altertumswissenschaft* 2 (1895): 1146.

———. *Geschichte des Untergangs der antiken Welt.* Vol. 5. Stuttgart, 1920.

———. "Politische Tendenzgeschichte im 5. Jahrhundert n. Chr." *Rheinisches Museum für Philologie* 67 (1912): 591–608.

———. *Regesten der Kaiser und Päpste für die Jahre 311 bis 476 n. Chr.: Vorarbeit zu einer Prosopographie der christlichen Kaiserzeit.* Stuttgart, 1919.

———. "Studien zu Synesius." *Philologus* 52 (1894): 442–83.

Segarra Crespo, D. "L'androgino biforme e la bella Cleopatra: Riflessioni sulla mostruosità a Roma." In Baglioni, *Monstra*, 191–204.

Seng, H. "An den Haaren herbeigezogen: Sophistische Argumentation im *Encomium calvitii.*" In Seng and Hoffmann, *Synesios von Kyrene*, 125–43.

———. "Die Kontroverse um Dion von Prusa und Synesios von Kyrene." *Hermes* 134 (2006): 102–16.

Seng, H., and L. M. Hoffmann, eds. *Synesios von Kyrene: Politik—Literatur—Philosophie.* Turnhout, 2012.

Sernagiotto, L. "The Importance of Being Lothar: The Power, Violence, Courage and Impiety of a Carolingian Emperor." In Borri, La Rocca, and Veronese, *Masculinities in Early Medieval Europe*, 127–59.

Severy, B. *Augustus and the Family at the Birth of the Roman Empire.* New York, 2003.

Shaw, B. D. "'Eaters of Flesh, Drinkers of Milk': The Ancient Mediterranean Ideology of the Pastoral Nomad." *Ancient Society* 13/14 (1982–83): 5–31.

Shawcross, T. "Editing, Lexicography, and History Under Louis XIV. Charles Du Cange and *La byzantine du Louvre.*" In Aschenbrenner and Ransohoff, *The Invention of Byzantium*, 143–80.

———. "The Eighteenth-Century Reinvention of Du Cagne as the French Nation's Historian." In Aschenbrenner and Ransohoff, *The Invention of Byzantium*, 181–204.

Shelton, K. J. "The Diptych of the Young Office Holder." *Jahrbuch für Antike und Christentum* 25 (1982): 132–71.

Shepardson, Ch. *Controlling Contested Places: Late Antique Antioch and the Spatial Politics of Religious Controversy.* Berkeley, 2014.

Sidéris, G. "'Eunuchs of Light': Power, Imperial Ceremonial and Positive Representation of Eunuchs in Byzantium (4th–12th Centuries)." In Tougher, *Eunuchs in Antiquity*, 161–76.

———. "The Rise and Fall of the High Chamberlain Eutropius: Eunuch Identity, the Third Sex and Power in Fourth-Century Byzantium." In Fletcher, Brady, Moss, and Riall, *The Palgrave Handbook of Masculinity*, 63–84.

Sinnigen, W. G. "The *Vicarius Urbis Romae* and the Urban Prefecture." *Historia* 8 (1959): 97–112.

Sivan, H. S. *Ausonius of Bordeaux: Genesis of a Gallic Aristocracy*. London, 1993.

———. "Was Theodosius I a Usurper?" *Klio* 78 (1996): 198–211.

Sguaitamatti, L. *Der spätantike Konsulat*. Fribourg, 2012.

Skinner, A. "The Birth of a 'Byzantine' Senatorial Perspective." *Arethusa* 33 (2000): 363–77.

———. "The Early Development of the Senate of Constantinople." *Byzantine and Modern Greek Studies* 32 (2008): 128–48.

Smith, R. R. R. "Late Antique Portraits in a Public Context: Honorific Statuary at Aphrodisias in Caria A.D. 300–600." *Journal of Roman Archaeology* 89 (1999): 155–89.

———. "The Public Image of Licinius: Portrait Sculpture and Imperial Ideology in the Early Fourth Century." *Journal of Roman Studies* 87 (1997): 170–202.

———. "Statue Practice in the Late Roman Empire: Numbers, Costumes, and Style." In Smith and Ward-Perkins, *The Last Statues of Antiquity*, 1–27.

Smith, R.R.R., and B. Ward-Perkins, eds. *The Last Statues of Antiquity*. Oxford, 2016.

Smith, R. "Measures of Difference: The Fourth-Century Transformation of the Roman Imperial Court." *American Journal of Philology* 132 (2011): 125–51.

Sogno, C. Q. *Aurelius Symmachus: A Political Biography*. Ann Arbor, 2006.

———. "Persius, Juvenal, and the Transformation of Satire in Late Antiquity." In *A Companion to Persius and Juvenal*, edited by S. Morton Braund and J. Osgood, 363–85. Oxford, 2012.

Späth, Th. *Männlichkeit und Weiblichkeit bei Tacitus: Zur Konstruktion der Geschlechter in der römischen Kaiserzeit*. Frankfurt, 1994.

Stancliffe, C. *Saint Martin and His Hagiographer*. Oxford, 1983.

Stanfill, J. P. "The Body of Christ's Barbarian Limb: John Chrysostom's Processions and the Embodied Performance of Nicene Christianity." In de Wet and Mayer, *Revisioning John Chrysostom*, 670–97.

Stefaniw, B. "Becoming Men, Staying Women: Gender Ambivalence in Christian Apocryphal Texts and Contexts." *Feminist Theology* 18 (2010): 341–55.

Steiner, D. T. *Images in Mind: Statues in Archaic and Classical Greek Literature and Thought*. Princeton, 2001.

Stenger, J. R. *Johannes Chrysostomos und die Christianisierung der Polis: "Damit die Städte Städte werden."* Tübingen, 2019.

———. "Text Worlds and Imagination in Chrysostom's Pedagogy." In de Wet and Mayer, *Revisioning John Chrysostom*, 206–46.

Stewart, M. E. *Masculinity, Identity, and Power Politics in the Age of Justinian: A Study of Procopius*. Amsterdam, 2020.

———. *The Soldier's Life: Martial Virtues and Manly Romanitas in the Early Byzantine Empire*. Leeds, 2016.

Stone, R. "Inviting the Enemy In: Assimilating Barbarians in Theodosian Panegyric." In Omissi and Ross, *Imperial Panegyric*, 233–54.

Strassfeld, M. K. *Trans Talmud: Androgynes and Eunuchs in Rabbinic Literature*. Berkeley, 2022.

Straub, J. *Heidnische Geschichtsapologetik in der christlichen Spätantike: Untersuchungen über Zeit und Tendenz der Historia Augusta*. Bonn, 1963.

———. "*Parens principum*: Stilichos Reichspolitik und das Testament des Kaisers Theodosius." *La nouvelle Clio* 4 (1952): 94–115.

Stroheker, K. F. "*Princeps clausus*: Zu einigen Berührungen der Literatur des fünften Jahrhunderts mit der *Historia Augusta*." In *Bonner Historia-Augusta-Colloqium 1968/69*, edited by G. Alföldy, T. D. Barnes, and A. R. Birley, 271–83. Bonn, 1970.

Stubblefield, S. "*Africa Catholica*: Augustine and the Conference of Carthage in 411." PhD diss., University of California at Berkeley, in progress.

Swain, S. *Themistius, Julian, and Greek Political Theory Under Rome: Texts, Translations, and Studies of Four Key Works*. Cambridge, 2013.

———. *Themistius and Valens*. Liverpool, 2021.

Syme, R. *Ammianus and the Historia Augusta*. Oxford, 1968.

———. *Emperors and Biography: Studies in the Historia Augusta*. Oxford, 1971.

Szidat, J. "Gaul and the Roman Emperors of the Fourth Century." In Wienand, *Contested Monarchy*, 119–34.

———. *Usurpator tanti nominis: Kaiser und Usupator in der Spätantike (337–476 n. Chr.)*. Stuttgart, 2010.

Tanaseanu–Döbler, I. *Konversion zur Philosophie in der Spätantike: Kaiser Julian und Synesios von Kyrene*. Stuttgart, 2005.

Tantillo, I. "Emperors and Tyrants in the Fourth Century: Outlining a New Portrait of the Ruler and His Role Through Images and Words." In García Ruiz and Quiroga Puertas, *Emperors and Emperorship*, 15–52.

———. "I cerimoniali di corte in età tardoromana (284–395 d.C.)." In *Le corti nell'alto medioevo: Spoleto, 24–29 aprile 2014*, 543–84. Spoleto, 2015.

———. "L'impero della luce: Riflessioni su Costantino e il sole." *Mélanges de l'École française de Rome. Antiquité* 115 (2003): 985–1048.

Taylor, R. "Two Pathic Subcultures in Ancient Rome." *Journal of the History of Sexuality* 7 (1997): 319–71.

Theocharidou, K. "The Rotunda at Thessaloniki: New Discoveries and Definitions After the Restoration Works." *Deltion tes Christianikes Archaiologikes Hetaireias* 4 (1991–92): 57–76.

Thome, G. "Crime and Punishment, Guilt and Expiation: Roman Thought and Vocabulary." *Acta Classica* 35 (1992): 73–98.

Thomson, M. *Studies in the "Historia Augusta."* Brussels, 2012.

Tiersch, C. *Johannes Chrysostomus in Konstantinopel (398–404): Weltsicht und Wirken eines Bischofs in der Hauptstadt des Oströmischen Reiches*. Tübingen, 2002.

———. "Wie christlich darf ein Bischof sein? Johannes Chrysostomus im Spiegel zweier Biographien." In *Biographie als religiöser und kultureller Text / Biography as a Religious and Cultural Text*, edited by A. Schüle, 125–52. Münster, 2002.

Tonias, D. E. "The Iconic Abraham as John Chrysostom's High Priest of Philanthropy." In de Wet and Mayer, *Revisioning John Chrysostom*, 563–86.

Torp, H. "*Christus Verus Sol—Christus Imperator*: Religious and Imperial Symbolism in the Mosaics of the Rotunda in Thessaloniki." In *Envisioning Worlds in Late Antique Art: New*

Perspectives on Abstraction and Symbolism in Late-Roman and Early-Byzantine Visual Culture (c. 300–600), edited by A. C. Olovsdotter, 178–98. Berlin, 2019.

———. "Considerations on the Chronology of the Rotunda Mosaics." In Eastmond and Hatzaki, *The Mosaics*, 34–47.

———. *La rotonde palatine à Thessalonique: Architecture et mosaïques*. 2 vols. Athens, 2018.

Tougher, S. "The Aesthetics of Castration: The Beauty of Roman Eunuchs." In *Castration and Culture in the Middle Ages*, edited by L. Tracy, 48–72. Cambridge, 2013.

———. *The Eunuch in Byzantine History and Society*. Abingdon, 2008.

———, ed. *Eunuchs in Antiquity and Beyond*. Swansea, 2002.

———. "Eunuchs in the East, Men in the West? Dis/unity, Gender and Orientalism in the Fourth Century." In *East and West in the Roman Empire of the Fourth Century: An End to Unity?*, edited by R. Dijkstra, S. van Poppel, and D. Slootjes, 147–63. Leiden, 2015.

———. "In or Out? Origins of Court Eunuchs." In Tougher, *Eunuchs in Antiquity*, 143–59.

———. *The Roman Castrati: Eunuchs in the Roman Empire*. London, 2021.

Tsikounas, M. "De la gloire à l'émotion: Louis XIV en costume de sacre par Hyacinthe Rigaud." *Sociétés & Représentations* 26 (2008): 57–70.

Turcan, R., ed. and trans. *Histoire Auguste*. Vol. 3:1, *Vies de Macrin, Diaduménien et Héliogabale*. Paris, 2002.

Turcan-Verkerk, A.-M. *Un poète latin chrétien redécouvert: Latinius Pacatus Drepanius, panégyriste de Théodose*. Brussels, 2003.

Upson–Saia, K. *Early Christian Dress: Gender, Virtue, and Authority*. New York, 2011.

Vaggione, R. P., ed. and trans. *Eunomius: The Extant Works*. Oxford, 1987.

———. *Eunomius of Cyzicus and the Nicene Revolution*. Oxford, 2000.

———. "Of Monks and Lounge Lizards: 'Arians,' Polemics and Asceticism in the Roman East." In *Arianism After Arius: Essays on the Development of the Fourth Century Trinitarian Conflicts*, edited by M. R. Barnes and D. H. Williams, 181–214. Edinburgh, 1993.

van de Paverd, F. *St. John Chrysostom, The Homilies on the Statues: An Introduction*. Rome, 1991.

Vanderspoel, J. *Themistius and the Imperial Court: Oratory, Civic Duty, and Paideia from Constantius to Theodosius*. Ann Arbor, 1995.

Vannesse, M. "La militarizzazione dell'impero: Il ruolo dei barbari (395–455 d.C.)." In *Potere e politica nell'età della famiglia teodosiana (395–455): I linguaggi dell'impero, le identità dei barbari*, edited by I. Baldini and S. Cosentino, 87–112. Bari, 2013.

van Nuffelen, P. "Episcopal Succession in Constantinople (381–450 C.E.): The Local Dynamics of Power." *Journal of Early Christian Studies* 3 (2010): 425–51.

———. "Palladius and the Johannite Schism." *Journal of Ecclesiastical History* 64 (2013): 1–19.

———. "Playing the Ritual Game in Constantinople (379–457)." In Grig and Kelly, *Two Romes*, 183–200.

van Waarden, J. A. "Sidonius in the 21st Century." In van Waarden and Kelly, *New Approaches to Sidonius Apollinaris*, 3–22.

van Waarden, J.A., and G. Kelly, eds. *New Approaches to Sidonius Apollinaris*. Leuven, 2013.

Varner, E. A. "Transcending Gender: Assimilation, Identity, and Roman Imperial Portraits." In *Role Models in the Roman World: Identity and Assimilation*, edited by S. Bell and I. L. Hansen, 185–205. Ann Arbor, 2007.

Vera, D. "I rapporti fra Magno Massimo, Teodosio e Valentiniano II nel 383–384." *Athenaeum* 63 (1975): 267–301.

Vinken, B. *Angezogen: Das Geheimnis der Mode.* Stuttgart, 2013.

Vitiello, M. "Emperor Theodosius' Liberty and the Roman Past." *Harvard Studies in Classical Philology* 108 (2015): 571–620.

———. "Theodosius, Virius Nicomachus Flavianus, and the Preservation of Rome's *Mores.*" *Journal of Late Antiquity* 11 (2018): 319–38.

Vössing, K. *Mensa regia: Das Bankett beim hellenistischen König und beim römischen Kaiser.* Munich, 2004.

Voicu, S. J. "La volontà e il caso: La tipologia dei primi spuri di Crisostomo." In *Giovanni Crisostomo: Oriente e Occidente tra IV e V secolo: XXXIII incontro di studiosi dell'antichità cristiana, Roma, 6–8 maggio 2004,* 101–18. Rome, 2005.

Volbach, W. F. *Elfenbeinarbeiten der Spätantike und des frühen Mittelalters.* Mainz am Rhein, 1976.

von Rummel, Ph. *Habitus barbarus: Kleidung und Repräsentation spätantiker Eliten im 4. und 5. Jahrhundert.* Berlin, 2007.

Vout, C. *Power and Eroticism in Imperial Rome.* Cambridge, 2007.

Waldner, K. *Geburt und Hochzeit des Kriegers: Geschlechterdifferenz und Initiation in Mythos und Ritual der griechischen Polis.* Berlin, 2000.

Wallace-Hadrill, A. "*Civilis Princeps*: Between Citizen and King." *Journal of Roman Studies* 72 (1982): 32–48.

Walters, J. "Invading the Roman Body: Manliness and Impenetrability in Roman Thought." In *Roman Sexualities,* edited by J. P. Hallett and M. B. Skinner, 29–43. Princeton, 1997.

Ward-Perkins, B. "Old and New Rome Compared: The Rise of Constantinople." In Grig and Kelly, *Two Romes,* 53–78.

Ware, C. "Claudian: The Epic Poet in the Prefaces." In *Latin Epic and Didactic Poetry: Genre, Tradition and Individuality,* ed. M. Gale, 181–201. Swansea, 2004.

———. *Claudian and the Roman Epic Tradition.* Cambridge, 2012.

———. "Eutropius, Lucan and the Ladies of Elegy." In Berlincourt, Galli Miliç, and Nelis, *Lucan and Claudian,* 257–69.

———. "Learning from Pliny: Claudian's Advice to the Emperor Honorius." *Arethusa* 46 (2013): 313–31.

Wasdin, K. "Honorius Triumphant: Poetry and Politics in Claudian's Wedding Poems." *Classical Philology* 109 (2014): 48–65.

Weber, C. *Queen of Fashion: What Marie Antoinette Wore to the Revolution.* New York, 2006.

Weisweiler, J. "Domesticating the Senatorial Elite: Universal Monarchy and Transregional Aristocracy in the Fourth Century AD." In Wienand, *Contested Monarchy,* 17–41.

———. "From Equality to Asymmetry: Honorific Statues, Imperial Power, and Senatorial Identity in Late-Antique Rome." *Journal of Roman Archaeology* 25 (2012): 319–50.

Welch, K. "Shields of Virtue(s)." In *The Alternative Augustan Age,* edited by K. Morrell, J. Osgood, and K. Welch, 282–304. Oxford, 2019.

Wessel, S. *Passion and Compassion in Early Christianity.* Cambridge, 2016.

West, S. "Herodotus and Scythia." In *The World of Herodotus: Proceedings of an International Conference, Nicosia, September 18–21,* edited by V. Karageorghis and I. Taifacos, 73–90. Nicosia, 2004.

———. "Scythians." In *Brill's Companion to Herodotus,* edited by E. J. Bakker, I. J. F. de Jong, and H. van Wees, 437–56. Leiden, 2002.

Wieber–Scariot, A. "Im Zentrum der Macht: Zur Rolle der Kaiserin an spätantiken Kaiser-höfen am Beispiel der Eusebia in den *Res gestae* des Ammianus Marcellinus." In Winter-ling, *Comitatus*, 103–31.

Wienand, J. "*O tandem felix civili, Roma, victoria!* Civil War Triumphs from Honorius to Constantine and Back." In Wienand, *Contested Monarchy*, 169–97.

Wienand, J, ed. *Contested Monarchy: Integrating the Roman Empire in the Fourth Century AD*. Oxford, 2015.

———. *Der Kaiser als Sieger: Metamorphosen triumphaler Herrschaft unter Constantin I*. Berlin, 2012.

Wijnendaele, J. W. P. "*Generalissimos* and Warlords in the Late Roman West." In *Warlords and Interstate Relations in the Ancient Mediterranean*, edited by T. Ñaco del Hoyo and F. López Sánchez, 427–45. Leiden, 2018.

———. "Sarus the Goth: From Imperial Commander to Gothic Warlord." *Journal of Early Medieval Europe* 27 (2019): 469–93.

Williams, C. A. "The Language of Gender: Lexical Semantics and the Latin Vocabulary of Unmanly Men." In Masterson, Rabinowitz, and Robson, *Sex in Antiquity*, 461–81.

———. Review of Hallett and Skinner, *Roman Sexualities*. *Bryn Mawr Classical Review*, October 16, 1998.

———. *Roman Homosexuality: Ideologies of Masculinity in Classical Antiquity*. Oxford, 1999. Reprint, 2010.

Williams, S., and J. G. P. Friell. *Theodosius: The Empire at Bay*. New Haven, 1995.

Winterling, A., ed. *Comitatus: Beiträge zur Erforschung des spätantiken Kaiserhofes*. Berlin, 1998.

Woolf, G. *Becoming Roman: The Origins of Provincial Civilization in Gaul*. Cambridge, 1998.

Zanker, P. *The Power of Images in the Age of Augustus*. Translated by A. Shapiro. Ann Arbor, 1988.

Zarini, V. "*Graiorum obscuras Romanis floribus artes/irradias*: Culture grecque et politique romaine dans les éloges de Claudien." In Garambois-Vasquez, *Claudien*, 27–43.

Zecchini, G. "S. Ambrogio e le origini del mito della vittoria incruenta." In *Ricerche di storiografia latina tardoantica* 2, edited by G. Zecchini, 109–20. Rome, 2011.

Ziche, H. "Barbarian Raiders and Barbarian Peasants: Models of Ideological and Economic Integration." In *Romans, Barbarians, and the Transformation of the Roman World: Cultural Interaction and the Creation of Identity in Late Antiquity*, edited by R. W. Mathisen and D. Shanzer, 199–219. Farnham, 2011.

Zimmerl-Panagl, V. "Zu Überlieferung und Textgeschichte von Ambrosius' *De obitu Theo-dosii* (und *Epistula extra collectionem* 1)." *Wiener Studien* 129 (2016): 299–330.

Zinsli, S. C. "Gute Kaiser, schlechte Kaiser: Die eusebische *Vita Constantini* als Referenztext für die *Vita Heliogabali*." *Wiener Studien* 118 (2005): 117–38.

———. *Kommentar zur Vita Heliogabali der Historia Augusta*. Bonn, 2014.

———. Review of D. Rohrbacher, *The Play of Allusion in the* Historia Augusta. *Bryn Mawr Classical Review* 2016.08.33.

abomination, 50, 178, 238

absurdity (*atopia*), 195

Achilles, 2; Arcadius as, 187, 198, 200–202; emperor as, 30, 198; Honorius as, 27, 96–97, 102–8, 116, 176; love for Patroclus, 105; playing with Deidameia, 104–5, 106*fig.*; Theodosius I as, 124, 126

Actium, battle of, 44

adolescens, 89–90

adoratio purpurae, 162

adornment (*kosmos*) of the altar, 30–31, 136, 138, 208–10, 221, 223, 225, 241, 253

Adrianople, battle of, 24, 72, 122, 197

adulthood, transition to, 11, 29, 69, 95–97, 99

adventus: of Aelia Flaccilla, 137, 140; Arcadius in Theodosius I's, 183; of Constantine I, 51; of Constantius II, 51; of Eutropius, 201; imperial, 141; of Theodosius I, 54, 66, 123, 141, 144

adviser: of the emperor, 30, 156, 184, 186, 189, 193; emperor truncated by his, 200, 205; how to choose, 125, 127, 187, 195–96; less-than-manly, 191; in possession of *andreia* (manliness), 200–201; too powerful, 206, 212, 242

Aelia Flaccilla, 30, 93, 102, 133, 134*fig.*, 139, 149, 177, 180; *adventus* of, 137, 140; as augusta, 128, 133, 135–36; as emblem of affectionate love, 235; Gregory of Nyssa's funerary oration for, 136–37, 149, 232–33, 235; humility of, 137–38, 145, 233, 253; manly *virtus* of, 249

Aeneas, 109, 119

Aeneid, 37

affection: language of motherly, 225, 227; reciprocal, 76–77

Africa, 38

Alans, 24, 59, 112, 122–23, 129

Alaric (Gothic leader), 30, 66, 102, 164–65, 185, 192–98, 200, 207, 251; eunuchlike, 193, 198; as *magister militum per Illyricum*, 165, 191, 206; "Scythian," 186, 193, 196, 201; as *vir illustris*, 165, 191

Alexander III (the Great), King, 2, 18

Alexander Severus, Emperor, *Life of*, 79–82

Alexandria, 26, 46, 94, 130–32, 211, 247

alienus, 35–36

almsgiving (*eleemosyne*), 230, 240

altar, 227; adornment of the, 30, 208–42; radiance of, 220

alter sexus, 177, 180, 251

ambition, 30

Ambrose of Milan (bishop), 28, 30, 56n105, 69, 76–77, 105, 107, 112, 119, 158, 248; as arbiter of Christian imperial manliness, 146, 148; funerary oration for Theodosius I, 1, 69–71, 144–51, 225, 232–33; funerary oration for Valentinian II, 73–74

amethyst, 99

Ammianus Marcellinus (historian), *Res gestae* of, 39–40, 55, 68, 73, 81, 108, 119, 135, 197

amplificatio (rhetorical technique), 82, 92, 174

Founded in 1893,
UNIVERSITY OF CALIFORNIA PRESS
publishes bold, progressive books and journals
on topics in the arts, humanities, social sciences,
and natural sciences—with a focus on social
justice issues—that inspire thought and action
among readers worldwide.

The UC PRESS FOUNDATION
raises funds to uphold the press's vital role
as an independent, nonprofit publisher, and
receives philanthropic support from a wide
range of individuals and institutions—and from
committed readers like you. To learn more, visit
ucpress.edu/supportus.